The Revelation of a Star's Endless Shine

A Young Woman's Autobiography of 20 - Year Victories over Victimization

Shirley Cheng

Foreword by New York Times Bestselling Author, Cynthia Brian

www.DanceWithYourHeart.com

Wappingers Falls, New York

Copyright © 2008 by Shirley Cheng
First copyrighted in 2003 by Shirley Cheng

ISBN: 978-0-6151-5044-4
Library of Congress Control Number: 2007904950

Dance with Your Heart! Publishing

www.DanceWithYourHeart.com
Wappingers Falls, New York, United States of America

Most names in this book have been changed to protect the individuals' privacy.

Credits:

Front cover: "Shirley Cheng Floating upon Cloud Nine"
Float on Cloud Nine, for life is happiness!
Design concept by Juliet and Shirley Cheng

Front cover background and spine rainbow:
© Corbis
Clouds:
© Photographer: Tomasz Dobrowolski | Agency: Dreamstime.com
Back cover background:
© Photographer: Elena Elisseeva | Agency: Dreamstime.com

All rights reserved by the author, Shirley Cheng. No part of this publication may be reproduced, stored in a retrieval system, or transmitted in any form or by any means, electronic, mechanical, photocopying, recording or otherwise, without the prior written permission of Shirley Cheng.

I dedicate this book to the most splendid person closest to my heart: my beloved mother Juliet Cheng, a beautiful woman in every sense of the word, who has conquered darkness and brought light into my life. This book is also to those of you who feel you have arrived at the end of a dark tunnel, thinking that there is not a way out…but there is.

Table of Contents

Foreword by Cynthia Brian 9

The Story Begins 11

Parental Rights in Children's Medical Care Advocacy 633

Give Parents the Right to Say No Petition 635

Spotlight Raves 637

About the Author 645

Acknowledgements

First and foremost, I would like to thank a very special person in my life. That person is my loving mother Juliet Cheng. Without her, this book would not exist. She provided me important and pertinent information about the early years of my life and the custody cases, bringing this book, which was once a dream, into reality, a tangible form for others to experience what we have gone through. Besides being a vital primary resource for the book, she has been giving me the sunshine of love, support, and encouragement from the first day I was in her womb.

She has said numerous times that we need to thank the bad guys in life; they had taught us lessons. So yes, I guess I will thank you: those of you who had made our lives dim of sunlight and put icicles upon our trees. But without darkness and coldness, this world would be an imperfect place. We have a balance of good and evil, though goodness always seems to be overwhelmed by the forces of evil. But in the end, the final battle between the two elements will always have a winner—the good.

Lastly, I thank every one of you who has been a part of my life, whether you were in it for a second or a once-stranger blossoming into years of treasured friendship. I thank you, my family, friends, teachers, doctors, and all the others who have woven into the fabric of my heart.

Foreword

By New York Times Best Seller, Cynthia Brian

It was just about a year ago in 2006 that the unstoppable Shirley Cheng asked me to write the foreword for her book, *Waking Spirit: Prose & Poems the Spirit Sings*, which has now won numerous awards. With great surprise and delight, I received another e-mail this year requesting that I pen the foreword for yet another book, this time her autobiography. In *The Revelation of a Star's Endless Shine*, you will marvel at the determination of a young woman to climb the highest peaks to see beyond, although she is blind and disabled from severe juvenile rheumatoid arthritis.

How, you might ask, can a young lady who is blind and disabled write award-winning books by the age of twenty? It's that one little word "survivor"! Shirley believes in surviving, striving, and thriving. Shirley is fond of saying that she is not disabled, she is ultra-abled. "Life took my eyesight away, I brought forth a new vision," is her powerful quotation on which she bases her life. She walks her talk and writes her rights.

Being a radio personality, I have the great privilege of interviewing amazing men and women who are truly pioneers on the planet. Shirley Cheng was a guest on my radio show, Starstyle—Be the Star You Are! a few years ago and ever since, I must admit to being her number one fan. Shirley is more than a survivor, Shirley is a force of empowerment. Blessed with an optimistic positive attitude despite the hardships in her life, she always, always, always, looks on the bright side of every situation. Whenever I have a conversation with Shirley, I am uplifted and rejuvenated. Talking with Shirley is like taking a mini-vacation.

I'd be remiss if I only extolled the virtues of Shirley without including the incredible bond of love and devotion that she shares with her devoted mother, Juliet Cheng. Like the stealth lioness she is, Juliet battled a corrupt, apathetic, uncaring medical system to save her beloved daughter from victimization. Although their journey was fraught with bumps, detours, and wrong turns, this immutable mother/daughter team kept their belief in God close to their hearts. They were victorious, never giving up hope for a happy, healthy life. What a true love story!

In this updated edition of her autobiography, you'll read about the triumph over tragedies as a child prodigy is born. You'll also be treated to photos and childhood drawings of this young lady with an endless shine. You'll learn how this juvenile with little formal education could score an exceptional 3280 on her GED test while doing all the math, calculations, chemistry, graphs and essays in her head without the use of Braille!

I agree that Shirley is ultra-abled and I want some of her prowess!

This is a big book written by a young lady with a big heart and big passions. Savor the message. Indulge in the innocence. Rejoice at the achievements. While reading about Shirley's challenges, you'll learn to be a proactive advocate for yourself. Let her be the beacon of light, love, energy, and hope that guides you to a safe harbor.

Shine on, Shirley! You are a bright beautiful STAR.

Cynthia Brian is a New York Times bestselling author, TV/radio personality, empowerment coach, and motivational speaker. She is the Founder and Executive Director of the charity, Be the Star You Are! She is available for personal growth, media, writing, acting, and presentation coaching. Contact www.star-style.com,, e-mail cynthia@star-style.com or 925-377-STAR.

Chapter One

The strong wind whirled, bringing dancing flakes in its invisible arms, equally distributing a thin layer of snow to other places of the frozen land. Small spheres of shimmering, crystalline flowers alighted upon the earth from their silvery home above, while the sun still slept peacefully below the horizon during this misty dawn. The sky jewels still twinkled ardently, as if calling news of most importance. Although the air was still and cold, it did not lack any emptiness. Faint songs of birds accented one another in counter harmony. Many creatures had packed their bags and sought shelter elsewhere, in a land of abundant warmth and merriment; some others snuggled cozily in their lairs for their long sleep.

Crisp laughter of children rang out loud and clear as these early birds played hide-and-seek in the snow, while honks from horns were audible on the streets. The roads were not filled with the usual volume of vehicles, for it was Sunday, and many people were still in bed after a long night of partying with friends and families; and more parties awaited them for the Super Bowl tonight. Yet, as these people slept, many lives were bustling about with energy and urgency. Ambulances rushed through the streets, and a few stopped outside a building.

The large building was filled with life. People dressed in white rushed to and fro to the assistance of others in need. The calling of nurses from the lips of the sickened patients traveled about in the building, mingled with coughs and sneezing. A telephone shrieked, and the tired receptionist answered, "Albany Medical Center." Above her hung a calendar set to the month of January in the year of 1983, with a scene of serenity of snow-covered trees and mountaintops. The countertop was accompanied by a desk calendar turned to the thirtieth in large, blue, bold numbers, with an inspirational quotation greeting the day: "Courage is the greatest of all the virtues. Because if you haven't courage, you may not have an opportunity to use any of the others." Underneath these words was the italicized name of Samuel Johnson. As the receptionist helped the caller with the unknown concern, the scene shifted to the stairs and to an upper level.

Voices came forth through an ajar door on the hallway. A nurse opened the door wide and walked in, closing it behind her.

In a bed, lay a gentle woman, who although in great physical pain, was filled with happiness of the most delicate nature. She was to contribute to the circle of life, secluded inside the thick medical walls, where a new era in her life would take place...

"Push, push," the voices urged her onward, but all she could hear was the beating of her own heart. She wondered how could one heart beat so loudly. Was it because it was two hearts—a tiny life inside her and her own—beating as one? The sheets were damp with the sweat that streamed down from her every pore. Her Oriental hair matted on her forehead. A new life would add to Earth's circle of life. That thought unconsciously swam in her mind, giving her the strength to do what the nurses had instructed: to push, push.

Her dark eyes focused on the ceiling above her as each contraction tore at her soul. Although it felt like a sharp knife was plunging deep into her, not a single cry of pain escaped her lips, nor did her eyes shed any tears. Instead, her heart danced with an immeasurable sense of exquisite joy. This was the most important day of her life, a day that would bring her forever happiness, so she gratefully took the bitterness to welcome the everlasting sweetness that was to follow. She and her child would spend the brightest and darkest days together, sharing all the surprises, both good and bad, that life would bestow upon them.

It was her first child, a gift given by the Heavenly

Father, and she would use her whole heart and soul to treasure the jewel. Awe and love filled every crevice of her soul once she learned of her pregnancy, and for the past nine months, she had been wondering what the baby would be like. Would dimples decorate its cheeks when it smiled? Would it laugh when she clicked her tongue? She did not know whether it was a girl or boy. She had gone to do the ultrasound, but it had been too early to detect the sex of the baby. It would simply have to be a surprise, a wonderful surprise.

So, on she pushed against the paralyzing pain. Sweat continued to pour out, adding to the small river that was collecting on the sheets underneath her. Her surrounding was a complete blur to her as her only focus was bringing out a new life. Yet what the doctor said next sharply cut through her concentration.

"The baby has to come soon, or we will have to perform a caesarean section,"

The doctor's gentle, but urgent words seemed to be amplified against her hammering body.

All of her energy had been drained a while ago, but the words charged her with new energy she never knew she could possess. Could she get her baby out in time, in time so—? She dared not finish that thought—she had no time to think. Her future—no, their future—now solely depended on her. Would she let both of them down? No, never. And after this victory of hers, she would climb to the highest peak and shout to the world she was a new mother.

Long seconds ticked by.

Time seemed to stand still. Seconds stretched on as minutes.

There was no time left. Not enough time left. She had no time to panic.

"Push, push," the chorus continued. Did they think that she would actually stop pushing if they ended the chant?

Then it happened, soundlessly.

No cry was audible, so one would have wondered if

anything had indeed occurred if it had not been for the next words, which seemed to have come from afar. They sounded musical to the expecting woman's ears.

"A beautiful girl, Mrs. Cheng!" the doctor announced with a big smile.

That smile was not even close in matching the one on the new mother's face. She had made it. Yes, she was now an honest-to-goodness mother, no more labels such as the expectant mother that she was impatient to alter. A girl! How her heart fluttered in her chest. She had thought it would be a boy, and had the name "Jordan" ready. The baby was twelve days late, so a boy was thought to be the reason. Well, she was pleasantly wrong. She knew she could dress her little girl up in the prettiest of dresses, with ribbons and laces...

The nurse by her bedside smiled and gently patted her shoulder. "You are so brave; you did not cry even once!" She returned the woman's smile with a smile that spoke a thousand words.

The doctor brought the baby over to Mrs. Cheng. The sight that met her eyes almost made her swoon with sheer delight, and vanquished any concerns she ever held. If the dictionary ever needed a definition for the perfect baby, she would describe her newborn. She was the most beautiful baby she had ever seen. She could not take her eyes off the child, from her head full of black hair down to her tiny feet. Her skin was as white and soft as the loveliest lily petals; not a single wrinkle was present, or any places of pinkness visible. In turn, the baby was returning the gaze with her large brown, penetrating eyes that were wide open, searching within her mother's soul.

They, at last, had found each other.

Mrs. Cheng held the baby lovingly in her arms. She carefully checked every part of the baby's delicate body, making sure all was fine. She touched the baby's small hands. She could not believe how miraculous it had been. She had a new life to be with her for the rest of her life, and it had taken only hours.

Then a knock sounded on the door, and in walked a man before he was even invited in. "Yi Ling?" he inquired. A nurse pointed in Yi's direction. Yi's eyes met those of the child's father. He was a man of few words, and he was seldom nonplussed; with today's special event not being an exception. With a cursory look at the baby, he walked away and out the door. Yi shook her head sadly, not for herself and the baby, but for the man. He was losing a great opportunity for happiness.

She had planned to drive herself to the hospital to have the baby, but he had arrived at her house, so he had brought her in last evening, and had waited outside in the waiting room. He never came in even once during the labor. She was a royal person who treated all with respect and honor. She had even cooked a bowl of noodles for him last evening just before he drove her to the hospital to have her first child. Thoughts of him quickly ceased as she turned her attention back to the baby girl.

Shortly afterward, tiredness overcame her being, so the nurse took away the baby. The mother closed her eyes to enter into her world of dreams that had just been added with the arrival of a new creature.

Chapter Two

Early the next morning, Yi's brown eyes fluttered open, and joy swept over her entire being once more when the thought of the birth rushed into her mind.

A nurse noticed she was awake, and brought her some paperwork that needed to be filled out. Yi quickly looked over the forms; it was the usual stuff. Her eyes fell upon her age: thirty-one. Many people who were unaware of her age would be dumbstruck with disbelief after reading that fact. She could be easily taken as in her early twenties. She was a gentle-hearted woman who bestowed kindness upon all with equality. Thus, the youth of her soul reflected outward in her appearance despite many years of hardship in her life. Not only was she youthful-looking, she was also a head-turner, and could be considered as a beauty, with large dreamy, dark, almond-shaped eyes that matched the beauty of the night sky; a captivating smile; and a curvaceous figure.

She came to this new country in December 1979, arriving at New York from Shanghai, China, after her mother Kwi Show Ling's arrival. Both of her siblings, who were all her seniors by a few years, were the last ones to immigrate. Her father, Dr. C.Y. Ling, a renowned urological surgeon, passed away when she was eighteen years old. She had lovingly taken care of him like a baby until his sad death. But she knew that he had to suffer no longer. Her soul was consoled at that thought.

After arriving at her new home in New York, Kwi Show married her deceased father's widowed elder brother, Dr. C.J. Ling, a psychiatrist and neurologist.

One day last year, Kwi Show was reading the Chinese newspaper as usual, when her eyes fell upon an ad. She called Yi over. It was an ad placed by a well-educated

Chinese man seeking companionship. "He seems nice," her mother concluded. There was no photograph accompanying the ad. Contact information was provided, so Yi decided to write a letter to the man. Some weeks later, she received his reply. She read the greatly written letter, with wonderment. Only a man of much intelligence could compose such a letter. She was mesmerized by it. She learned that he, Al Cheng, was a waiter, a computer programmer, and had received a bachelor's degree in mathematics from Hunter College in New York. Without having a second thought, she decided to meet this wonderful, mysterious gentleman.

She got a big surprise when they met and after she got to know him better; and it was not a surprise that could be cherished. He was a selfish, stingy man who had thoughts for only his business, besides those for himself. She was immensely disappointed. She was expecting to meet a kind person, and only found a man no better than a smart toad at the end of the path. His veins were filled with arrogance. He thought himself as the smartest person on the face of Earth. But he did not treat her with harshness, and never went out of his way to annoy her. In actuality, he was not a person who enjoyed doing much that would "waste" his time. Thence, being a nuisance was not amongst his busy agenda.

Again, Yi's thoughts quickly turned away from Al. There were not many thoughts of him. He was not someone who could add many pleasant memories to others' lives.

***

Downstairs in the hospital, a man wearing eyeglasses asked the front desk for information. "I'm Peter Ling, Yi's brother. Yes, Yi Ling." A nurse asked him to follow her, and directed him to the correct room.

"It is a girl," a nurse told him once he entered the room.

"Oh, really?" He walked toward the happy Yi and congratulated her. Then another nurse walked in, holding more papers in her hands; they were the baby's measurements. Yi scanned over the documents, and little gleeful shivers ran down her spine. The baby was twenty-one inches in length, weighing seven pounds and thirteen ounces. What a big, healthy baby!

Yi asked how the baby was doing. She received good news; the baby was doing absolutely fine, being an understatement.

"Her cries are the loudest in the entire room of newborns!" reported the nurse. "She can be easily found just by her loud cries."

Another nurse arrived in the room, carrying the baby girl in her arms. "The baby is hungry," she said, smiling. She handed the baby to Yi, who was eagerly waiting for this moment. The baby took the bottle readily into her small mouth with cherry-like lips. Immediately, she began to suck on it. They watched with astonishment as the baby hungrily took in the formula, with gusto matching that of an enthusiastic puppy. She quickly finished the whole bottle, without choking once. Amazement shone in Yi's eyes. Such a hearty appetite, and a skilled eater!

"You still need to name the baby," they informed her. Yi nodded. She had already thought of a few names long ago.

"How about Shirley?" suggested Peter, showing her an English-Chinese dictionary. Yi was surprised. It was one of the names she had picked among her favorites, including "Shelley" and "Juliet." But the name "Shirley" was her favorite of them all. So, since then, the baby girl was known as Shirley Cheng. In Chinese, the pronunciation of "Shirley" translates to "snow pear." Yes, Shirley would be the fruit for them all, giving love and fulfillment even during the harshest days. She would be a food for the soul; a blazing fire in winter. *Days shall be filled with much love and adventure*, Yi silently thought. Little did she know how right her predictions were.

Chapter Three

The new mother enjoyed every minute of the baby's existence. Days flew by so rapidly, like a hummingbird darting from flower to flower. She felt like there were millions of butterflies fluttering about inside her. For certain, it was not the same feeling before an exam, but a feeling of most unspeakable joy dancing within her. Seven restful days were spent in the hospital until it was time to go home. This time, she was introducing a new member to the family. How grand would their lives be! She had plans of bringing Shirley up well, spoiling her with every chance she could get. Many happy thoughts swam in her head. *She is my pearl, the brightest star in my life*, thought Yi. Then and there, Yi gave Shirley a Chinese name that means "star." Because the words "heart" and "star" are homonyms in the Chinese language, the name was just perfect for her dear baby who was both her heart and twinkling star.

She began to pack the few belongings she took with her to the hospital in the old bag from China. The bag was quite worn down, but was still sturdy enough for short trips. Kwi Show was a conservative woman, so most things were saved around the house. Some things were always useful for other occasions at later times.

Yi called a taxi to pick both her and the baby up. She meticulously bundled up Shirley with much care and gentleness, making sure that she was as snug as a baby could be. After she was done, little Shirley was a small ball of softness.

When the taxi arrived, she carried the nearly eight-pound bundle in her arms as a hospital staff member brought her bag over to the cab. The taxi driver, a man with tired lines engraved around the corners of his eyes, asked for Yi's destination. She told him the address of her parents' house.

On the road, many plans flooded her mind for her baby's future. She was so excited in the backseat that she could hardly sit still. She wished for Shirley to be happy, to enjoy what life had to offer, and to study in the best college. Of course, she thought, she would never force her to do things she did not wish to do. She would not be mad if she did not do well in school. She would be satisfied if Shirley only passed the classes with a mark of sixty-five. She asked no more of her daughter. Her only goal was to bring happiness to Shirley's life.

Her own parents were notably nice people, but were too busy to spend time with her during her childhood years. Her father, a 1942 graduate of Xiao He Yan (a medical school in Senyang of northern China that was founded and directed by British and Americans who also taught the classes), was always at the hospital performing surgeries that could last nearly the entire day. His hands were remarkably skilled with the work, not surprisingly since he was a highly intelligent and diligent individual who went straight to college, skipping high school after self-teaching himself all the material. Many lives depended upon his performances and patience. Never did he complain once, even though he had severe heart disease. For many years, he worked with British and American doctors, and he often commented how hardworking and responsible they were.

"They are just wonderful people, so kind and nice," he had said. Hearing this, Yi dreamed of going to America and being surrounded by these great people. Another reason for wanting to go to America was for her love of American music. She loved the top hits that came out in the 1950s and 1960s.

Kwi Show was also busy with work, being a librarian at one time, and a teacher at another. Yi's sister and brother were seven and five years older than Yi, respectively, so they thought her too young to play with. The days had been cold and lonely, and walking on the roads to school was not a memorable experience. Yi did not pay attention in elementary school; she always talked to other students in classes, so her grades reflected her lack of attention to the teachings. But when she started middle school, she made a silent vow to herself that she would listen in classes. And to her delight, it paid off. She became a straight A student in all subjects, ranking number one in the entire class, and was admired by many peers and teachers alike.

But crisis soon struck her when she was in middle school. She had badly injured herself one day as she was playing while she attended eighth grade. She crashed onto the cement floor, and could barely walk for a long time afterward; and her rib cage had hurt for more than ten years. Worse yet, her fall had badly damaged her waist; according to a doctor, it was the portion that regulated fluid circulation in the body, so her injury had permanently caused the inability of her body to regularly transport fluid between her lower and upper body. Ever since, she had been seriously ill, and painstakingly clung to life. She could not have any intake of salt, for it made her entire body swell with fluid. Thus, she began taking medicine that relieved her swelling, such as diuretics. Without the medicine, she would gain nearly ten pounds in just one day. After taking it, she was able to lose the excess fluid in her body, so her weight fluctuated dramatically in a single day.

At that time, it so happened to be a changing world in China. The Cultural Revolution struck. Education was forbidden; schools were closed, books burnt, and other practices were not permitted. Stylish, pointed shoes were cut on the spot if they were noticed. Everyone wore black, gray, blue, or any other dull, "acceptable" colors. Even if it had not been for the revolution, Yi would be unable to continue with schooling any longer. At first, she struggled, but her health could not permit her to go on. She loved to read and knew that she would miss it dearly. As for her siblings—they had all completed their studies, so they received showers of cheers. But there was nothing that Yi could do. She had done things to her best abilities: being a good girl, and taking care of her ill father till he passed away from heart failure. She also tried her utmost working to no avail. She was sent to a toy factory to assemble toy cars, but every time she worked for a mere hour, her hands would be so stiff to the point she could not separate her fingers. Each night, she slept for only one hour or two, for she would be up vomiting as effects of diuretics. Then she would drag herself to work. Not surprisingly, she could not go on working for very long. Despite her best efforts, her entire family and relatives constantly criticized and looked down upon her with disdain. Yet, Yi was at peace with herself and others; she knew herself the best: she was not a bag of lazy bones. She was trying her hardest just to cling on to the thread of life.

Then her family learned about the death of Dr. C.J. Ling's wife. Dr. Ling asked Yi's family to go to America to live with him there. Kwi Show would marry Dr. Ling since Yi's father had spoken highly of him. It all seemed like a fine plan: Dr. Ling, who was disabled due to a stroke, could have someone to care for him, and they would start a whole new life in a foreign country. The idea was accepted by the family, so everyone flew to America. Yi still remembered how she felt when she was on the plane flying to America. She felt so excited when she got her first sip of the juice in a pretty plastic cup from the airline.

Then her memory fast-forwarded to the following year. It was when she had received a special letter in the mailbox, telling her wonderful news—that she had passed the GED test and received the high school equivalency diploma. She had attended Albany Adult Learning Center for half a year, hoping to get the diploma. She knew only a few English words. But she was an eager learner, and was able to pass the test on her first try. She was thrilled. The diploma she held in her hands proved to the world her achievement.

Now, a new chapter of her life had begun with a small newborn life alongside her. She was a person with an innate loving nature for all others—she had been a good daughter, a good sister, and starting now, she would have the greatest opportunity to be a good mother. She, too, could be a good wife, she knew, but unfortunately, it was not the chance to be that just yet: Al was not her husband.

"Here we are, ma'am," the driver cut through her reverie. Yi, taking Shirley in her arms, got out of the cab. He carried out the bags for her and put them by her side. Rummaging through her purse, she gave him the money. He accepted the payment with a nod, and left the mother and daughter alone by the house at Sunset Drive in the town of Latham.

"Ah, Yi! Yi!" called a voice from inside the house. The storm window swung open, and out rushed Kwi Show as quickly as her body could allow. "Come in! You'll catch cold." Kwi Show was just about to pick up the baby from Yi's arms when Yi stopped her. She did not want to put strain upon her mother, who had been diagnosed with diabetes nine months ago.

"Carry the small bag," Yi told her. "I'll carry my baby." Reluctantly, Kwi Show took the bag, and together they went inside the warm house.

Small furry creatures of nature silently watched till the three figures disappeared inside. They exchanged glances of curiosity. None had ever seen the third tiny being before. They wondered what it could be. But in their little hearts, they knew that it was something good. Their souls waited till the day they could catch a glimpse of this little one again.

Chapter Four

"My, Yi, this is a beautiful one!" exclaimed the happy grandmother once she had gotten a good chance to see Shirley for the first time. "She is so adorable! Look how her eyes roam around the house. It seems she understands everything she takes in." Then she placed a few kisses on Shirley's rosy cheeks.

"Ma, sit down," Yi urged. "Don't tire yourself. Get some rest."

Dr. Ling, lying in his bed, called out to see the baby. Yi brought Shirley over to him. A smile swept across his features. He nodded with contentment. "Very beautiful."

Days passed by, each blossoming with cherished memories. They were quite a merry family. Each day was filled with surprises from the baby. Intelligence shone through her large brown eyes that seemed to be darker than the darkest night, yet appeared to be touched by moonlight as on a pond under the silvery rays.

One day while Yi was rocking Shirley in her arms, a loud, "Mama!" came forth from the baby's lips. Yi and Kwi Show exchanged astonished glances. They were taken aback. Shirley was never taught to call, "mama." Above all, she was only less than one month old! They were still speechless minutes later. None could believe their own ears. But after thinking back, they realized that they should not have been so dumbstruck. Shirley started smiling when she was only a few days old.

Not a single day was spent without the happy noises made by Shirley. The house was never absent of her loud, blissful sounds. She was known as the happiest and most active of all babies ever. Before her second month, Shirley was laughing with much enthusiasm by any little thing that tickled her senses—which was not much at all—maybe just a click of the tongue by Yi or simply a dancing hand before her eyes. In actuality, anything and everything amused the baby and made her laugh whole-heartedly, with the loudness that could surpass a whole room of babies.

***

After staying at her parents house for two months, Yi took Shirley to Al's place in Connecticut. She had moved into his apartment the previous year, and shortly afterward, she was pregnant with her first and last child, for she wished to have only one child. She saw the good qualities in Al: his intelligence and hardworking nature. He had recently become an owner of a Chinese restaurant. She sadly thought about the kind of man he was. The ad had stated he was a widower. But in actuality, he was married with four children; his wife was in China. Being an unemployed single-parent left Yi with no choice; she needed to stay with him for the time being. The man was her daughter's father after all. And she must admit: living with him was not bad; he gave her no pressure, and there was space to breathe freely. She needed to learn more and gain some knowledge to fit into the society. It was an alienating world for her. Her English was quite poor. But she would manage. She knew she could.

The days were left to the two of them in the little apartment; Al was seldom home. Yi felt blissful spending treasured moments with her little one, who was sent down by Him from His celestial throne.

Yi often thanked the Heavenly Father for such a blessing. Shirley was such a happy, delightful baby. She had the appetite of a grown person, gulping down bottle after bottle of baby formula. Yi avoided breast feeding Shirley, for she feared that her sickness would be given to her child. She did not want Shirley to drink her milk, which was probably contaminated with medicines and her illness.

Something that matched the abundance of Shirley's cheerfulness was the speed of her growth. Yi always encountered problems shopping for her. All clothes were too small for Shirley. Once, Yi bought a baby's outfit with the package that indicated it was for one-year-olds. She returned home and tried it on her three-month-old. It was one of the most difficult tasks she had to accomplish! At last, she got the baby's body inside the clothes. But the baby was too snug in it, so the next day, Yi returned it. "Guess I'll have to buy clothes that fit two-year-olds for Shirley!" she thought, giggles escaping her lips.

Two months later, she became ill, and discovered she was pregnant. Being overwhelmed with too much nausea to take care of Shirley, she decided to bring the chubby five-month-old to Dr. Ling's home for Agatha's care for a week. Agatha was a family member staying with Dr. Ling and Kwi Show.

"I'll take two hundred dollars to take care of her," stated Agatha, taking the baby from Yi's arms. Yi had informed them to take good care of Shirley. Having misgivings, she reluctantly left.

Yi then aborted the baby in her womb. She did not desire another child, so why bring an unloved child to this world?

During the week, Yi made calls to Kwi Show to inquire how her little darling was doing. "How's my pearl?"

"She's doing fine, she's doing fine," answered Kwi Show.

Yi sighed contentedly. She was sure that her child was being well-taken care of and that they would carry Shirley around. She had thought of bringing Shirley to a woman she knew, but she did not want to hand Shirley to a stranger. Then she thought of Agatha, who had always been bullying her since she was eighteen years old. Agatha constantly targeted Yi whenever she was around, as though Yi was a moving bullseye that could win her a million bucks. Every minute Yi was present, she would criticize her nonstop for no reason, always trying her hardest to find faults with her at every chance she got and blaming her on things she never did. For instance, once, before arriving in America when Yi, at that time twenty-eight, and Agatha went to row the boat with their family members, Agatha had criticized Yi the entire way to and from the trip home. When Yi, being in her usual tired state, graciously and truthfully offered to row the boat, Agatha told the others that Yi was only pretending and that they should not be fooled by her pretentious acts. She slandered Yi all the way home. Upon arriving home, one family member, unable to hold her curiosity any longer, questioned Agatha why she was always saying bad things about Yi. "I can't see anything wrong with Yi. I don't understand why you are always criticizing her," the relative had said.

Agatha's criticism never ended and it continued in America. Yi was the only one who could drive, so she brought Agatha and her husband Lloyd to English as Second Language class every day, and Agatha would fire bad false remarks about Yi during the entire way to and from class in the Adult Learning Center. Lloyd would simply listen in silence.

"Why don't you say anything to stop Agatha? I could get into an accident when she's continuously bickering with me," Yi had hissed at him. "You should tell her to stop it. Why don't you advise her?" A few months later, Agatha received her driver's license and was then able to drive to school on her own. Since then, Yi hitchhiked to and from school instead of being in the car with Agatha, so she was no longer forced to endure the criticisms.

During Yi's pregnancy, Agatha criticized her endlessly to the extent that Yi felt ill, feeling more ill than morning sickness.

When Yi had first learned of her pregnancy with Shirley, Kwi Show was just diagnosed with diabetes. Yi visited Kwi Show every day at the hospital to bring her a whole heavy bottle of hot water, never failing once, even when she was suffering from great spasms of nausea. When Yi returned home, she could not enter the house from the door that led her straight to her room because Agatha usually locked it. Dr. Ling's large house was actually his clinic, with the two outmost sides acting as homes. Thus, Yi had to travel to Agatha's side, which was quite far from her end, to enter the house from that door. Finally being in the house, the exhausted Yi would not have anything to eat. Agatha would stick only a bit of meat in her refrigerator and that was the only food for Yi.

"You are our family's most devilish, deceiving, and bad person with harmful intentions in your heart. The only reason why you are good to Mother is because you're after her money," Agatha had said at the time.

"Only we know in our hearts who is really, truly good to Mother," Yi had answered. She knew that Agatha was only jealous of her simple goodness. Not only was Yi good to her mother, but also to anyone who crossed paths with her, including Agatha.

Both times after Agatha gave birth to her sons, Yi took care of her during her sitting month, a period of usually one month for women to rest after childbirth in Chinese culture; yet, Agatha's sitting month each lasted more than six months. During this time, Yi cooked every meal for Agatha and washed every baby diaper. When Agatha's oldest son, Arney, was born, it was in the winter, so Yi endured bone-biting cold water while meticulously washing his diapers. Not only did Yi took care of Arney during infancy, she cared for him when he was five years old for half a year while Agatha was away. Yi cared for Arney as if he was her own son. After Agatha returned, not only did she failed to thank Yi but constantly asked Arney, "Arney, who are you most afraid of?" Being a child, he did not even know what she meant. Agatha would then say, "You are most afraid of Yi, are you not?"

Yi also cooked for Agatha outside of sitting month. Whenever Agatha was home, Yi cooked every meal for her daily. Agatha's favorite food was noodles, so Yi often cooked bowls of noodles for her, besides other dishes.

Yi cherished her family and held no grudges toward anyone. Despite Agatha's hostility, Yi continually treated her well.

But it was not the time to dwell on the past. Even though Agatha had been mistreating her all those years, and was still continuing, she thought Agatha would not mistreat Shirley. After all, they were family members. Moreover, she thought that Kwi Show could look over the baby as well.

When the week was up, Yi and Al went to Kwi Show's house to pick up Shirley. When they walked into the house, Agatha walked toward Yi with the baby in her arms. Once Agatha handed the infant to her, Agatha immediately walked away without uttering a single word.

Al gasped loudly when he saw Shirley. "She's so terribly thin!"

Yi's heart felt as though it had turned into a stone. She stood still, unable to believe what she beheld. Shirley had changed dramatically. She was nearly all skin and bones—she had lost nearly all of her body mass—and her face clearly showed that she had not slept for days. Shirley did not smile like usual; instead she just closed her eyes and rested her head on her mother's shoulder, not making a single sound.

Yi's spirit shattered with pain. She was furious at such a poor treatment Agatha had given Shirley. How could anyone be so cruel to a baby? She then remembered that Agatha had repeatedly said that she would put Shirley on a diet, but since she had not planned to have Agatha care for Shirley, she had not given much thought to it. She had been puzzled by what Agatha said and never imagined that Agatha would actually starve Shirley.

Yi had been so painstakingly caring for her child, bathing her daily, sterilizing her bottles by boiling them so that they could be as free of germs as possible. A blanket of sadness swept over her. Her dear pearl was withering. She vowed that she would try her hardest to bring Shirley back to as before, but she knew it would require much effort.

Ever since that day, Shirley's appetite plunged to the bottomless pit. Feeding Shirley became the most difficult task Yi had to face daily, spending hours on just feeding. Then Yi managed to feed Shirley up to the proper weight. But unfortunately, Shirley's gusto for food had vanished; most food never appealed to her without being coaxed into taking a bite.

One time, during Yi's conversation with Kwi Show, Kwi Show told her what that week had been like.

"Shirley cried until her voice became extremely hoarse." The descriptions of those seven days nearly made Yi faint with horror. She had trusted Agatha to care for her baby. She had never imagined such things could happen.

"And I tried to go care for Shirley, but Agatha wouldn't allow me," Kwi Show said further. "I asked her how come the child became so terribly hoarse, and Agatha replied only by repeatedly singing a song with the words 'don't blame anyone.' She did not say a single word in reply."

Yi could not bear to think that Shirley could have nearly died. Shirley had spent seven nights without being fed, and she had been in one room alone with the door closed. If it had been more than seven days... Cold chills ran down Yi's spine. Oh, so horrid! But even after the misfortune with Agatha, she did not feel any dudgeon toward her. She could not have any grudges with her family, people who she knew were the most vital part of someone's life. She was a pacifist, never wanting to argue or fight. All she wanted in life was to live peacefully and work with others in a harmonious rhythm. But if the mistreatment from anyone went on for an extensive period of time, she would fight back with reason and justice.

***

Day after day passed by. Yi worked feverishly to feed Shirley, spending hour after hour in doing so. Shirley simply turned her head when the bottle was offered. Before, she screamed for bottle after bottle of the delicious formula.

With all Yi's effort and unconditional love, Shirley grew to be a lively eight-month-old. While in the walker, Shirley often swung her little behind to the rhythm of the music from the radio. And she often had a happy smile upon her shiny face. Admiring eyes of Yi always enjoyed seeing Shirley dance to the music. It made Yi feel like dancing as well.

One afternoon when Yi and her baby were visiting Yi's parents' house, Kwi Show and Agatha suggested that Yi lay several items of all sorts in front of Shirley, who by now was nine months old. In Chinese tradition, the things that the baby chose would determine what the baby would be interested in life in the future. If babies picked yarns, they would turn out to be adults who work with clothes; if food, then a cook might be a possibility. Skeptically, Yi accepted their idea. Together, they laid many items of all colors, shapes, and sizes in front of Shirley. They ranged from colorful toys and yarns to food and pens.

Without a second of hesitation, Shirley crawled over to a piece of paper and a pen, picked them up, and held on to them tightly.

"My, looks like little Shirley will be a scholar of some sort!" analyzed Kwi Show. Yi was touched with much surprise, mingled with joy. How wonderful that would be— to have your child growing up being an intelligent one doing things with her brain. They each wondered if this tradition would be proven true in the years to come. Would Shirley be an artist? A writer? Exciting questions, such as these, rang in their heads. None could do much but wait till that day.

***

To maintain her baby's health, Yi routinely made trips to a local hospital in Waterbury, Connecticut, for medical checkups.

"Shirley has a very poor appetite. It is very hard for me to feed her," Yi told the pediatrician, Dr. Ballin. But he was unable to supply her with any help. He did not know what was wrong with the infant.

"I'll talk to Dr. Simmonds about your problem and see if he can do anything for you. He is the director of the hospital," said Dr. Ballin.

By and by, Yi got to talk to Dr. Simmonds, but he could not help her, either. At least, she thought, she knew another doctor. And Dr. Simmonds seemed to be a kind and caring person. Knowing kindhearted people was a plus in itself.

Chapter Five

Yi delightfully looked on as Shirley started to stand up with her chubby legs. She held her breath as the eleven-month-old infant took a step forward. Then another step. *Plop!* She fell down with a loud laugh. Tenaciously, Shirley got up and tried again. The memorable scene replayed. Yi laughed uncontrollably. She was touched with indescribable happiness that swept away her senses. Her baby was starting to walk. Shirley was able to walk for five steps before she fell. How much more wonderful could life be?

Then a ring of the telephone interrupted this picture-perfect moment. Yi walked over to the telephone and answered it, "Hello? Yes, speaking?" She listened as the caller from Dr. Ballin's office reminded her to take Shirley to get the tuberculin skin test done. The appointment for the test was scheduled for the next week at five in the evening.

Yi had the test done on herself when she was young, and had gotten quite sick as a result. She hoped that it would not sicken Shirley. But she thought that she should not worry too much. It was in the doctor's hands. *Doctors know best, right?*

That appointed day arrived with much swiftness. It was winter once again, so Yi dressed Shirley up in a pretty sweater that showed a teddy bear on a pink background. Not until Yi made certain that Shirley was warm enough did she bring her to the car. Yi buckled Shirley up in the baby's safety seat, double checking everything. Yi started the engine, and off they headed toward the hospital.

It seemed like a long drive from the apartment to their destination. But in fact, it was only a quarter of an hour away. At last, they arrived at the clinic. Yi brought Shirley to the front desk, and was told to wait till Shirley's name was called. Yi promptly sat down with the baby on her lap.

Shirley's eyes searched the entire waiting room. When something interesting caught her eye—which happened numerous times—she laughed with glee, while clapping her tiny hands.

"Shirley Cheng?" a voice announced. Following the nurse, Yi carried Shirley into an examining room. After the nurse performed the necessary routine tasks, she left them alone. Despite the gloomy atmosphere of the tiny room, Shirley still held on to her smile, which shone from her eyes. At last, the clock ticked to the time of the test.

"Hello, Mrs. Cheng," Dr. Ballin greeted Yi after walking into the room. "And are we ready, Shirley?" Shirley looked at him, knowing behind that smile, he was going to have needles waiting for her. He went to the sink to wash his hands. After he had everything ready, he posed the needle at Shirley's lower arm. Yi watched the thin needle pierce into Shirley's skin. In a few seconds, the test was done.

"Mrs. Cheng, we're done," the nurse told her. "You're ready to go." Yi took Shirley, now with a sensitive arm and a not-so-happy look on her face, and dressed her up again to set out for the journey home. What a day. It appeared as though it had only been spent on the road and the clinic. Not a fun time. She was glad it was over. Thank goodness she had a healthy baby who did not need to be brought to the hospital often.

After getting home, Yi plopped onto the bed with a sigh of tiredness. She was careful not to touch the sensitive area on the child's arm where the test had left its mark as she changed her back to something lighter to wear. It had just begun to snow. They were lucky that nature did not choose to snow when they were on the roads. It would have surely lengthened the travel.

When it was time for bed, Yi gently placed Shirley in her crib. Her own bed was next to it, so she would be available at all times. She never left Shirley alone longer than necessary. Shirley was always under the watchful eyes of Yi. She watched as the baby's eyes finally closed in a peaceful, deep slumber. Getting the baby to sleep was a lot of trouble. Shirley was much too active and playful to go to sleep. She never looked forward to bedtime. After waiting for the baby's sleep to enter into the deeper stage, Yi's tired eyes gratefully closed.

Snow fell heavily upon Earth. Trees began to sag under the accumulation of the weight. The misty night sky was not so bright as usual, for the stars seemed to be listless for some unknown reason.

Chapter Six

Yi's heart pounded loudly, so loud that the entire room was filled with its hammering. She read the number on the thermometer for the third time. "103.9 degrees!" Shirley had a fever that was undoubtedly quite high. She had taken the temperature after noticing the warmness of the baby's body. Shirley had been crying frequently that day—something that she did not normally do.

"What could be wrong?" Yi whispered. Shirley's wails drowned her words. Her mind raced, thinking of any possible causes.

Five days had passed when Shirley received the tuberculin skin test. She had not been out, and no one in the family had the cold or flu. Every day had been spent routinely. Nothing was new, besides the…

Could that be it? Yi shuddered when her thoughts returned to the tuberculin skin test. Could that be the cause? How could it? No one had given any kind of warning.

With a steady hand despite the terrifying moment, Yi dialed the hospital's number. She was asked to wait once her call was answered. She waited impatiently as the clock ticked on. After a couple of minutes into the wait, she was able to tell what was happening with her dear heart. She was told to bring Shirley in right away.

Yi dressed Shirley in another layer of clothes. The baby's loud cries shook the walls and devastated Yi's heart. Without losing a single precious minute, Yi drove her to the hospital, hoping it would be a bringer of good news. Little did she know that the news awaiting her was one of the most unbearable to the ears.

***

"Yes, she was crying all day." Yi quickly explained the situation to the nurse, once they arrived at the hospital.

The nurse took the baby's temperature, which was a number close to the earlier reading at home.

"The doctor shall be with you shortly." The nurse told her before exiting the room. Shortly? How short would it be? Five, ten, or fifteen minutes? Yi knew they all meant "shortly." Unlike last week, Shirley was not smiling. Something was most definitely wrong. She had never failed to smile. Yi silently prayed that nothing was the matter. After waiting for what seemed like an eternity, Dr. Ballin entered the room. He performed the routine medical checkup for Shirley.

"I will have a blood test done for her." And with that, he left. A nurse walked in, carrying the instruments that were necessary for the test. She stuck the needle in Shirley's arm and red fluid began to collect in the container. Yi concentrated on the blood, hoping that it would bring an answer even if it would be an undesirable one. An unwanted truth would always be more favorable than a happy blindness of falsehood.

"Okay, that's all, you can take Shirley home," the nurse told Yi. Someone would call her once they received the results. Yi thanked them and left. On the road, a million names of diseases pounded in her head. She thought of measles, small pox, and other serious diseases of which she dared not think twice.

Every day, Yi waited for the telephone to ring, hoping it would bring good news.

One afternoon in the following week, Yi answered the telephone to a lady from the hospital about the test results.

"We have the results in. You can bring Shirley over," the voice told her. Yi did as she was told.

Once she met the doctor, he told her the news, "The test results did not show anything wrong with Shirley. We can't find anything in the blood that would indicate a problem,"

Relief washed through Yi's being. But wait a minute. Not finding anything wrong did not necessarily mean that there was nothing wrong. Disquiet swept through Yi's soul once again.

Yi turned her eyes to Shirley when they got home. It was several days after Shirley had first developed the fever. But something more disturbing came into existence. Whenever Yi touched Shirley's left leg, Shirley would give a long wail of great pain. Yi could see that Shirley's left knee was swollen.

As days passed, Yi watched helplessly as the unknown illness spread throughout Shirley's body. Within a matter of a couple of weeks, Shirley's right knee was swollen. Both of Shirley's legs were hurting her tremendously.

"Certainly, there must be something the matter with my poor dear. If only I could find the right doctor to get the proper diagnosis," Yi thought out loud. "I *will* get the correct diagnosis."

Yi made another trip to see Dr. Ballin, hoping that there would be something he could do to lessen Shirley's pain; the travel was fruitless.

A few days later, Yi moved back to her parents home. She told her family of this elusive condition. Being a doctor in China and a current nurse, Peter told her about polio. "Maybe she has that." Yi was truly frightened now. She knew of the horrid illness, and she was too stunned to even think that Shirley could contract such a disease. She could not just sit here and do nothing to comfort Shirley.

She made a call to a doctor's office by her home and scheduled an appointment. She inwardly prayed that this time an answer would be found, along with a cure.

***

On the appointed day, Yi arrived at the doctor's office

with Shirley, bringing the test results. She showed the doctor the papers.

"Mrs. Cheng, your daughter has arthritis," Dr. Galvin arrived at the diagnosis right away, flipping through the files.

"Arthritis?" inquired Yi, a puzzled look painted on her countenance. She had never before heard that term. The doctor did his best to explain the disease, to no avail. Straight away, without a second thought, Shirley was admitted to Albany Medical Center in January. Everything was moving at a fast pace, swallowing them in a misty fog of terror.

***

"A...ar...arthritis," Yi muttered, her finger running down the English-Chinese dictionary. She read the definition of the disease. "Arthritis? It doesn't seem serious then. How could it be so? I know many people who have it." Yi said to herself.

She did not realize how harsh a life was awaiting them beyond their dusty roads.

At the hospital, Shirley underwent test after test until the certain diagnosis was achieved: Shirley had juvenile rheumatoid arthritis. They were shocked that a tuberculin skin test could cause the disease. Such an unfortunate, rare occurrence!

Once she was told of the disease, Yi got out the medical dictionary, which listed all the known diseases accompanied by photographs that were anything but pleasing to the eye. She read through the symptoms of this form of arthritis.

"It could cripple my child!" exclaimed Yi. For certain, it sounded like a dreadfully serious and painful disease. Above all, it had no cure. Yi's heart was torn. She ached with such pain that no words could describe. But with much conviction, she knew she would strongly stand by her daughter's side. She would try to make life the best experience for her. It would not matter if Shirley would be disabled for life. She would still give all her heart and soul, and love her more so. Shirley was so dear to her heart, and nothing could change the fact. Shirley could be deaf and dumb, and she would still love her no less. Yi's devotion to Shirley would never cease, not even if she turned into a vegetable. But she fervently hoped that it would not turn out to be so serious. Maybe it was a mild case of the disease. Shirley might still be able to walk, and her eyes and heart might not be affected by it.

But no amount of optimism could hide the fact: Shirley's days were spent in constant pain, making all chores, like dressing and bathing, highly difficult. Nights were spent with Yi rocking the suffering baby to sleep, often lasting long into the early morning. Yi became worn down and exhausted. Twenty-four hours and seven days a week were used up for the baby. Yi constantly stayed by Shirley's side. But despite the hours of pain that had spread to all her joints, Shirley still laughed between her tears whenever she saw a pretty fabric in the room. Her sharp, observant eyes were always in search of treats for the vision.

This was their fate. Yi accepted their Kismet and endured the hardship with no word of complaint. She would grit her teeth till the end and tenaciously move on. She would never give up for her daughter's sake. Shirley needed her more than ever now. Deep down inside, she knew they were watched over by Jehovah God Almighty. It was His plan, as unfathomable as it was, so it was futile to be angry, have vengeance upon her heart, and question God about their lives. She knew whatever He did was for a reason, so together with no one else by their sides, they persevered onward along their rugged path.

Chapter Seven

During the hospitalization, they gave children's aspirin to Shirley daily under the care of Dr. Packer, a doctor from the medical center. Later on into the hospitalization, Yi had to find someone to look after Shirley during the night hours because Shirley always cried, wanting to sleep with her mother as they had at home. Yi did not like the idea, but it was a Hobson's choice. She asked her mother's housemaid, Cassidy, to be the designated person to stay with Shirley. So, night after night, Cassidy came to the hospital, staying from ten at night to six in the morning. Each morning at 5:30, Yi visited Shirley. She noticed that Shirley was usually not wearing anything except a diaper. She told Cassidy to at least keep the baby covered. The woman only nodded, but never did as she was ordered. Yi also noticed that when Shirley was with Cassidy, she was more silent than usual. Yi had never felt comfortable choosing this lady to watch over Shirley, but she had no one else to take up the position.

Yi's uneasiness increased as days passed.

On the second to the last day of Shirley's stay in the hospital, Yi went earlier than usual to see Shirley, at five in the morning. Yi stepped into the room, and the scene that met her eyes froze her in place. Shirley was sitting by the open window without wearing any clothes besides the diaper. Cassidy was in a heavy coat, seated at a part of the room that was not touched by the wintry air. Upon seeing Yi, Cassidy stood up right away and closed the window. Yi immediately carried Shirley away from the window. She was touched by absolute speechlessness. No wonder Shirley appeared to be so quiet around Cassidy. Heaven knew how long this ill treatment had been afflicted upon the baby! Yi did not say a word; it was too late to do anything. Harm was already brought upon the child; it was useless to complain.

Ever since, Shirley developed a lot of sputum that often made her chest feel uncomfortable.

Shirley, who by now was twelve months old, left the hospital the next day after being admitted for three weeks. Not only had Shirley received no relief from the stay, the hospitalization had worsened Shirley's condition. Aspirin had made her extremely drowsy and weak. The lack of energy was so great that Shirley could not play during the daytime. She had always been able to spend part of the day playing in spite of her pain, but not this time under the medication. "Shirley has diarrhea, upset stomach, and she is drowsy and always nauseated," Yi told Dr. Galvin. "I'm planning to take Shirley to Shanghai to seek treatment," Yi further told him. He was not happy with the idea, but let them go, for he had no treatment for Shirley.

Before leaving for China, Yi called him up to find out if there might be any other treatment for Shirley besides aspirin.

"Continue with aspirin," he told her.

"But it is making Shirley's condition worse. She cannot take it anymore."

"She has to."

"No, I will not give it to her anymore. It is not making her any better. It is worsening her condition." They ended the call. Dr. Galvin, she thought, was upset.

Al bought a plane ticket to Shanghai. Peter had called Lang, a medical school classmate of his in China, who would be able to help them to get Shirley accepted in a hospital in Shanghai for treatment. Everything was arranged for the trip.

The day prior to departure, Yi scurried around the house to see if there were any other items that they would need on the trip. As she was sitting down to get some rest, her door received a few knocks. "Who could that be?" she wondered. She walked over to the door and opened it to a tall woman. Yi raised her head to meet the stranger's eyes with a questioning look. "Yes?" inquired Yi.

"This is the Department of Social Services," the

woman answered. Yi did not understand what it meant, but by the sound of it, it was nothing pleasant. The woman further continued that Yi was reported to be abusing Shirley. Yi was stunned that anyone could falsely accuse her of such a crime. How could she ever abuse Shirley? Yi had been lovingly taken care of Shirley and loved her since the day Shirley began to form in her womb. She could never abuse any living creature, not to mention her own child.

"We need to bring Shirley to the doctor for examination," ordered the social worker, "right now." They were told that Shirley had bruises from the "abuse." With not another word between them, they set forth to the emergency room, taking Shirley.

Once there and settled, the woman pointed at Shirley's leg after the baby was undressed. "This is a bruise," she said, her finger still pointing. Very carefully, the doctor checked Shirley's entire body.

"This is only a birthmark," he reported after he finished. "No bruises are present. There's no sign of child abuse. The baby's skin is clear and she seems to be well cared for." Therefore, the false charge was dropped. But it was an ordeal Yi could never forget. It was terrifying for them both. If the doctor had said that the birthmark was a sign of abuse, Yi would have lost custody of Shirley then and there. Yi knew that it was Dr. Galvin who had wrongly accused Yi of the alleged abuse. Yi was shocked by it. Just because Yi disagreed with his medical advice did not mean he should have the conscience or right to report a false accusation on such a loving mother.

Yi quickly left the country with Shirley in March. Al went with them in order to help them on the trip. But he would return to America once they were settled there.

Yi watched the scene outside the small, oblong window as the plane took off. The view of the landscape became wider as people shrank to tiny ants on the ground. Higher and higher it rose until only a green land was discernible under the large bird. It was the first visit to China for Shirley. They wondered if there would be hope waiting on the other side of the world. Perchance, Shirley might get better there, with a helping hand from God.

***

The group arrived at Hong Kong hours later. Al had read an article in a Chinese newspaper about a treatment regimen held at the practice office of Dr. Bo. His treatment involved the use of wooden sticks to exert pressure on the affected joints and surrounding acupuncture points. A mixture of alcohol and herbs would be applied to the wooden sticks. It was mid-March and several more of Shirley's joints were beginning to be affected by the disease. Her right wrist, ankles, and some small joints in her hands and feet all were notably swollen. Shirley now was like a statue, unable to sit or move. Thus seeing that the situation was getting out of her hands, Yi took a desperate measure. She had no way of treating Shirley's disease, so she hoped that the treatment with Dr. Bo would be of some help in relieving the pain.

After the first treatment, Shirley was crying more. Not only was the treatment ineffective, but had also brought more pain. Yi tried it on herself and found it was extremely painful. They had tried it again for Shirley, but the result was the same. Hence, they stopped the treatment and departed for Shanghai to seek another route.

The three arrived at Shanghai at Hong Qiao Airport one warm April day. Two of Yi's cousins, Rong and Da, picked them up. Prompt introductions were made.

"My, Yi, you haven't changed a bit since we had last seen you five years ago!" exclaimed Rong, studying her.

They drove Yi to her former home, which was on the first floor of a four-story building made of steel. On the road, Yi reminisced about those old times. The streets, she noted, had not changed, at least not to the point where it was noticeable. After Kwi Show and the children had left for America, they had left the house to Rong's family, which consisted of his wife and baby girl. They had agreed to leave the house if any of Kwi Show's family members ever returned. It was the most convenient place for Yi to care for Shirley. The comfortable house had running water, a kitchen, and a bathroom, all of which would be quite difficult to find in other places.

They stopped in front of the house Yi had spent all her years before moving to America. She felt quite lucky to be living in America, having the convenience and luxuries of life. She did not miss that house at all. She was glad of getting away from this place. Although many memorable years had been spent in China, life was difficult, and lacked much of the convenience found in America. Entertainment in China had been sparse. She found pleasure from walking on the streets at nights. The streets were quite peaceful, even during the late night hours. She had enjoyed reading foreign books that had been translated into Chinese, ranging from works by William Shakespeare to Honore de Balzac. Her family had always traveled either on foot or used public transportation to get to places. During the ten-year Cultural Revolution, listening to foreign music was forbidden, and books became a trouble to find. All in all, life there was simple and harsh.

After seeing that all was settled, Rong and his family left the house for them to stay. Yi began to unpack their bags. Tomorrow, she would take Shirley to start the treatment. Meanwhile, she put Shirley on the bed and sat down. They all were in dire need of the much-needed rest. It was quite cold in the small house, so she made sure Shirley was warm enough. It was in the afternoon, yet sleepiness overcame them. She got Shirley ready for bed. Together, they closed their eyes, with much effort on Yi's part to make the baby fall asleep. Al had long begun to snore before his head had even touched the pillows. He was such a sound sleeper. Yi knew that her night would be interrupted by the cries of the baby in pain. She had to try to get some sleep before the baby woke up. Yi entered into her dream world, her mind full of thoughts for the next waiting day.

Chapter Eight

The sunlight streamed in through the window, creating shimmering halos above their sleeping heads. Morning sounds were emitted from outside, not from nature's furry friends, but from the daily lives of Chinese folks. The streets were already filled with people bustling about with their business: some markets were being set up by the hardworking class, while children walked to school. Great gusts of wind hollered, bringing armful of dust in front of others' paths. Mothers carried their babies in large bundles as fathers set forth to work.

Yi's dark eyes opened to greet a new day. She groggily got up. She was awakened by the crying child numerous times last night, and each time, she had a hard time falling back to sleep. Al, oblivious to every happening, slept on like a log. Yi heard the loudness of Shirley's breathing during sleep. It sounded like her chest was stuffed with sputum. It saddened Yi. Those two weeks of "care" had caused serious problems which seemed as though they would be with Shirley forever. That one week with Agatha and the other week with Cassidy had done considerable damage to her health.

Once Shirley was awake, Yi tried to feed Shirley some milk. With much time spent, Yi managed to have Shirley drink the bottle. Contented that the baby's stomach was no longer empty, Yi started to get Shirley ready for the trip to the hospital. Then the snoring from Al ceased. A long yawn escaped from his lips.

"Going to the hospital?" he asked. Yi nodded. He got up and strolled over to get some bread. Yi still had not taken a bite of food for hours. But her mind was not on food now; she needed to get Shirley to the hospital and get the treatment started. Yi did everything tenderly and slowly for

Shirley, trying her best not to inflict more pain.

After Al finished eating, he told Yi that he would get a cab. Putting on his coat, he went out. Everything with him was done in silence as if they were in a silent movie of black and white. That was how dull the life with him was. But silence, she thought, was not bad. At least, there were no arguments.

***

Together, they went on their way to meet Lang. Lang brought them to see the doctor, and Shirley was taken in for examination. The doctor walked in after a moment's wait.

"I'm Dr. Wang," he introduced himself, shaking Yi's tiny, delicate hand. He began his examination as soon as he took a seat. Shirley wailed in pain every time he touched her. "Ah, too bad." He sadly shook his head. He was shocked to find such a sick baby. Compassion for this child shone in his eyes of many years. "This baby also has a very weak heart," reported the doctor after listening to Shirley's heart and taking her pulse. He ordered to have blood test done for Shirley.

"She has juvenile rheumatoid arthritis," Dr. Wang told them once the result was in a few days later. The disease was reconfirmed. "She also has severe anemia," continued the doctor. Shirley's lack of appetite had made it hard for her to obtain the required nutrients.

Shirley was to be admitted to the hospital the following day. Once again, a part of her young life was going to be spent under a microscope for study.

The next day, Shirley lay on the hospital bed, crying her little heart out. She was like a statue, being immobile from her stiffened joints. Yi sat by her daughter's side. The hospital gave 15 mg of prednisone. "This would help, and you won't have to worry about her appetite loss anymore, Yi; prednisone will fix it," the doctor told her. Yi knew that prednisone was a drug that could greatly increase one's appetite. Late into the night, Yi left the hospital and went home.

Early the next morning, Yi set forth to the hospital straight away. It became the daily ritual; it was the first thing she did on her schedule once she woke up. She wished that she could stay in the hospital, but they did not allow non-patients to live there. The travel to the hospital took an hour. But no matter how great the distance was, she continued to go. She rose early daily, for she had to prepare varieties of food for Shirley. She had bought a food grinder machine from Hong Kong. She used it to grind the best fish, vegetables, and other fine dishes. Shirley would not swallow solid food, thus it was the only way to feed Shirley.

With the usual container of food in hand, she set out to the hospital. She hoped the prednisone had worked.

She gave a stunned and happy gasp as soon as her eyes fell upon Shirley. The medication worked miracles; Shirley was sitting perfectly on the bed! No tears were visible on her face. Instead, a happy smile replaced the once-tear-streaked face. Yi's smile stretched on for a mile. Her elation overwhelmed her. This was for certain a wonder drug. But she knew prednisone had many severe side effects, and should be taken with much care. But it was a lifesaving drug at that crucial moment; it could at least temporarily relieve Shirley's excruciating pain.

When Al walked on the scene, he stopped in his tracks. "Shirley's sitting!"

Yi's smile widened. Then she told him of prednisone. Finally something excited this man.

"I will be leaving in a couple of days for America," he announced. Obviously, the excitement was short-lived.

Each day passed with improvements: more vigor filled Shirley and life shone from her eyes. But it was still hard to get Shirley to swallow. "I'm very surprised that the drug did not help to boost her appetite," remarked the doctor, shaking his head. "She truly has a big problem."

Many people in the hospital looked at the baby with

admiration gleaming in their eyes. Some nurses even fought over who could have the privilege to carry the little one in their arms. "Let me carry the Happy Baby!" one nurse chimed. "She's always so happy, this Happy Baby." All adulated this beautiful, adorable creature. Everyone sympathized with the pair. Such a horrid tragedy could strike such a loving, hardworking mother and a young life.

Four weeks flew by at the hospital. At long last, it was time for the discharge. Yi took the infant back to the house. Shirley's arthritis was much better now. Yi's hopes soared high within her, shimmering from her eyes in full bloom. She dared not think how Shirley would be if they had not gone to China to seek treatment. She knew that her baby would have died. How that would have utterly torn her heart and soul.

Yi took with her the prednisone the doctor had prescribed. He had advised her to use it carefully.

"Just taper off prednisone gradually. She is now at 10 mg," informed the doctor. "And here's another medication that may relieve the pain and swelling." He handed Yi a bottle of piroxicam before mother and daughter left. "But I'm very astounded that prednisone did not improve Shirley's appetite!" he had exclaimed again. "This child *really* has a big problem. Even prednisone cannot help!"

"Yes, I really wish there is some way to cure the problem," said Yi. "What could possibly be the problem?" The doctor shrugged.

Each day, Yi gave a dose of prednisone to Shirley. She always remembered to give the baby the pill. But one day it slipped her memory. As a result of this dangerous drug's side effects, Shirley instantaneously returned to her original condition before taking the medication, but with shattering force. Her cries shook the house. Yi watched in horror as Shirley's limbs constricted and contracted. Shirley was akin to a flipping fish holding on to dear life upon land. Yi had never before known of this. The medication was too frightful, and must be stopped. She had to get Shirley off it gradually. It was surely not a cure. A better treatment must be sought. She was concerned about giving Shirley piroxicam, not knowing how Shirley would feel on it. The doctor had made her aware of the adverse effects of the medication, so she did not administer it to Shirley. She thought that it would be the last resort if no other answers could be found.

***

One night at half-past midnight, as the two slept on, a loud noise woke Yi up. She instantly felt a tremor. The balcony door shook violently. At first, she thought there were burglars outside. Then her eyes widened in horror as the lights on the ceiling swung to and fro. Was she still dreaming? She briskly looked out the window. The streets were crowded with people of all ages. They ran out of their homes with their little ones held tightly in their arms. They simply stood in one place on the streets, not moving a muscle. Where was there to go? Ironically, Shirley, who was usually awakened by the tiniest sound, was sleeping soundly. Yi did not have the heart to wake her. Even if she took her out, they would only be staying in the cold. As thoughts raced in her mind, the earthquake abruptly stopped. The nightmare was over. No apparent damage was reported, and no innocent life was taken.

Chapter Nine

Being out of the hospital, Yi decided to take Shirley for some sightseeing around the city. Shirley's dark, curious eyes would surely lavish the various places, and she would appreciate everything she was to take in.

While bundled up in her mother's arms, Shirley's eyes traveled far and wide, capturing every scene before her. A blissful smile painted upon her little countenance. Yi brought her to a beautiful park in the area. It was already spring, yet the air still obstinately clung to the winter chills. The ground was starting to provide new life to the green grass and sprouts that were poking out their tiny heads to get their first breath of the new world. Sounds of songbirds were audible. A loud laugh escaped Shirley's lips as she saw birds hopping about on the earth in search of their sumptuous snacks. Yi walked along the sidewalks to show Shirley all the markets that were set up by the streets. Store windows held interests for Shirley. Little hands often pointed at the stores' openings. So, cheerfully, Yi took the little one to examine each store. Gadgets of all sorts amused the baby. Colorful pictures delighted her. The small things that raptured the baby would not even make others look twice.

Yi bought treats to munch on. Whenever Yi tried to feed some to Shirley, she only turned her little head away with a pout. Yi sighed. Shirley's enthusiasm for food had vanished. Only because of those seven days...

Not only was Shirley fascinated by simple objects and nature, but people amazed her as well. She was a remarkably friendly girl who smiled at everyone. All eyes were normally trapped in place by this dear one. Passersby marveled at the baby. Many went to their side, staring at Shirley. They had never seen any baby as wonderful as her, they often commented. Yi knew that Shirley looked just like a little angel, especially cupid. The more people present, the happier it made Shirley.

Days passed by in China, with Yi taking Shirley out to enjoy life. Yi also had visitors who dropped by at the house. An old friend of the family by the name of Zon was a frequent visitor. She had come to see if Yi and Shirley were fine during the earthquake. When she found them safe and sound she left. Yi was immensely grateful for her concern.

"This little one is so cute! Let me hold her," Zon often requested. Then the rest of the day was reserved for gossip between Yi and Zon.

"I will be taking Shirley back to America. It has been nearly two months here. And there is no treatment for this disease." Yi told Zon one day. All words were conversed in a foreign tongue to Shirley; it was a dialect of Shanghai. Al had bought a round trip ticket for them, so they were all set to go.

***

Yi boarded the plane with Shirley. Shirley was sustained on prednisone for the pain. Yi hoped to seek a better treatment in America. There was no more reason for them to stay in China. She closed her eyes in deep thoughts. The plane took off, entering into the June sky until all was in the abyss.

JFK Airport was crowded with the usual volume of people. Yi pushed Shirley in the stroller as she managed all the luggage. Then amidst the crowd, Yi spotted Al. He walked toward them.

"I missed you so much," he said, giving Yi a hug and a kiss. She returned his embrace. As passersby who looked on, they would think they had found themselves looking at a perfect, happy family.

Al drove them to Kwi Show's home. It was a long way from the airport to Latham. After about four hours on the road, they, at last, arrived at their destination. He helped

Yi with the luggage. Kwi Show quickly swung open the house door and invited them in. She went to get the bags, but as usual, Yi stopped her and told her to sit down.

"Ma, don't tire yourself."

"I won't," came the defiant answer.

"Sit down," Yi ordered. Kwi Show finally gave in. Yi knew that if Kwi Show got stressed, her blood sugar level would rise, along with her blood pressure.

Too tired to do anything else, Yi changed Shirley's clothes out of her travel attire, and they rested together. But she knew she could not rest long. She must feed Shirley again—a task that was harder than traveling between two countries. Therefore, after hours of finally getting enough food into Shirley's stomach, Yi was able to rest. But the rest could not last long; Yi had to unpack the bags and take out necessary items. Another few hours were spent on unpacking and sorting the many items, from the baby's medication to clothes. There were not many items that belonged to Yi. In actuality, most belongings were for Shirley's use.

One would think that Yi was finally able to get some real rest now. Not so; Yi had to get Shirley ready for bed, and make sure that the baby was asleep first. With a long sigh, Yi plopped onto the bed, praying that the baby would not wake up, and would sleep into the night. Al was long gone. He was probably snoring into his second hour. His restaurant business was not going well. He was no longer the owner.

Yi planned to stay at her parents' place for a while until another treatment was discovered. She wondered what the future had in store for them. She fell asleep after emitting a small sigh. The stars above in the celestial heavens twinkled long into the night.

Chapter Ten

Yi soon learned from Kwi Show that the lady from the Department of Social Services had come to the house several times after Yi and the child left for China. "She kept coming and coming," Kwi Show reported. "Then she asked when you're going to come back. Plus, she called several times."

Why could they not leave them alone? Were they blind? Could they not see how good a mother Yi was to Shirley? This was such a sad thing. Kwi Show and Yi shook their heads. In China, nothing such as this would ever happen. Patients always had the right to disagree with the doctors without problems, especially if the doctors themselves could not be certain that their treatment would be 100 percent effective. Patients already had enough worries upon their hearts. Anyone should be able to tell that Yi was a good mother after only a fraction of a moment. Shirley was always well-fed, well-dressed, and was kept clean at all times. Above all, Shirley's happy disposition reflected the tender treatment Yi unconditionally supplied Shirley.

Yi traveled back and forth between her parents' house and Al's apartment. But most of the time was spent with Kwi Show. Yi, knowing that Shirley could not stay on prednisone for the rest of her life, continued to seek a better answer. She had a friend who told her of a fine pediatrician in Schenectady.

"He's the third best pediatrician in the Albany area," he had said. Yi quickly called up the doctor, Dr. Sabeston, and scheduled an appointment.

When the appointed day arrived, Yi brought Shirley to Dr. Sabeston. "She's very well-taken care of. You have a very special situation here, so you need a very special doctor," he told Yi. "In your situation, it is important to have a very good doctor who not only knows the disease, but someone who is also very caring and compassionate. I'll recommend someone who I know will be understanding of your situation. His son passed away, so he can relate to you. His name is Dr. Robinson, who is a rheumatologist. You can go see him," suggested Dr. Sabeston.

Yi at once made an appointment to see Dr. Robinson. She was in high hopes of seeing the doctor. She was so thankful for knowing Dr. Sabeston, who appeared to be a remarkably kind person. Surely, Dr. Robinson would be good as well?

When the appointed day arrived in early August, Yi took Shirley to Dr. Robinson's private office. She felt wonderful when she laid eyes on the rheumatologist. Just as Dr. Sabeston had described, Dr. Robinson appeared to be a person full of compassion for others. He prescribed naproxen for Shirley.

The sixteen-month-old was on naproxen for two weeks. Between this period in August, Shirley was admitted to Albany Medical Center to receive corticosteroid injections in both of her knees to reduce the prednisone dosage from 5 mg down to 2 mg. Yi had managed to cut prednisone down to 5 mg before seeing the doctor. At the same time, Yi met Dr. Kaine, a doctor in the hospital, and asked him if he had any treatment for Shirley's loss of appetite. She had been telling all the doctors about her poor appetite, but no one had the correct diagnosis. Dr. Sabeston was aware of the eating problem as well.

"I'll examine Shirley," Dr. Kaine told her.

The next day, Dr. Sabeston called Yi. "There is a presence of a gastric bezoar," he informed Yi. "She needs surgery on her stomach, and it can be done tomorrow."

"What is a bezoar?" She looked it up in her dictionary, but still could not comprehend the meaning.

"A wad of hair is inside her stomach," he explained. "She needs surgery to have it taken out."

Yi gave a thought to the matter. She did not think that

any hair could be the long-term cause of Shirley's condition. Shirley already had a poor appetite, so she could not have swallowed any ball of hair in the first place. If she had the appetite of eating the hair, there would not be a reason for Yi to be here! She thought further that even if she, herself, had hair in her stomach, she would not lose her appetite.

"Can you give her another test?" And thus, a third upper gastrointestinal series was taken of Shirley's stomach.

Thirty-six hours after admission to the hospital, Shirley was discharged. A few days later, Yi received the results of the upper gastrointestinal test.

"There's no hair visible in her stomach," said Dr. Kaine. Yi was relieved. She knew that it would be the answer. Thence, she still did not have any diagnosis of Shirley's problem.

Being on naproxen, Shirley complained of having severe stomachache. Yi reported this to Dr. Robinson, who told her to stop the medication forthwith. Yi brought Shirley in to see Dr. Robinson again. He suggested, "Perhaps, injections of gold might help Shirley. But read this booklet, and you decide if you wish to go for it or not." He handed her a small booklet with explanations of gold injection treatments.

After reading through the booklet, Yi knew the treatment could not be given to Shirley. "It has too many side effects," she told Dr. Robinson.

"Yes, it does," he agreed. Seeing that there was no other medicine to sustain Shirley at the time, Yi decided to give her piroxicam. Meanwhile, she hoped that she could find another treatment quick.

At the beginning of October, a few days after Yi started piroxicam, Dr. Robinson recommended a pediatric rheumatologist located in Boston—Boston's Floating Hospital for Children at New England Medical Center.

"And there is another doctor from Columbia University in New York City," he further said. "But Dr. Schelling, the doctor in Boston, had written a book about arthritis."

"I think I will take her to see Dr. Schelling then," decided Yi. Before going there, Yi called up the hospital and told them of Shirley's situation. Then an appointment was made for the third of the month to see Dr. Schelling.

***

So as not to exert any pressure on Shirley's body to cause more pain, Yi carefully dressed her up appropriately. Yi strapped Shirley in the seat before Al started the car for the long drive to Boston from Latham. Yi and Shirley simultaneously let out a pair of yawns as Yi focused through the misty late morning.

"Finally here," Yi said under her breath when afternoon had arrived.

Al and Yi brought Shirley to the waiting room and sat down to wait. Moments later, they were called into a room, and a woman, wearing a white uniform, walked in. "Hi, I'm Dr. Persse," the woman introduced herself. Yi returned her greeting.

"Where is Dr. Schelling?" inquired Yi.

"Dr. Schelling will come to see Shirley later." The three seated themselves, Dr. Persse with her notepad in one hand, with the other poised above the clean sheet of paper.

Yi began to explain Shirley's history and her hopes for an effective treatment. "Shirley had been taking aspirin before, but she had very bad reactions on the medicine. Will you have other medicine?"

"Have her stay in the hospital and we'll see what we can do for Shirley," Dr. Persse answered.

"Shirley is currently on piroxicam, which is prescribed by the doctor in China," Yi said further. Dr. Persse scribbled all the information down, without saying more than a few words.

Accordingly, Shirley was admitted in the Boston's Floating Hospital for Children on the twenty-ninth of

October. Yi and Shirley lived in a room in the hospital they had provided for them. Yi had high hopes this time. She thought that it would bring promising results to help Shirley. She had stopped piroxicam after giving it to Shirley for a mere week when she did not find it improving Shirley any. Dr. Persse had explained that physical therapy would help. Yi waited to meet Dr. Schelling for the first time, wondering what the doctor might be like. Shirley did not see Dr. Schelling on the appointed day, so Yi had conversed with only Dr. Persse.

But a hopeful dream was shattered into pieces of sharp glass. It did not need to take long for Yi to learn that they had stumbled into a rose bush. It looked like such a perfect plan at first sniff, never aware of the thorns underneath.

On the very first day, the nurse administered a large dose of aspirin for Shirley. Yi was taken aback. She had informed the doctor that aspirin did not work from day one. But Yi had to give it another try; it was a Hobson's choice. If it did not work, she thought, they would stop and try something else. Let them find out for themselves.

Shirley's health became worse and worse on aspirin, with the same symptoms as the first time, but on a much more serious scale. The medication was given to Shirley on an empty stomach each time.

Even though the adversity was apparent, the hospital ignored it and simply continued administrating aspirin. Yi could not believe her eyes. How could they continue when the facts were clear?

Yi talked to them about it and requested that they give Shirley some other medication, but they only shook their heads.

"She has to continue to take it. It is the only way," they replied. They gave her the same response every time she asked them.

If aspirin is the only medicine they will give Shirley, how come I need to have Shirley hospitalized? Yi questioned herself. She could have given it to Shirley in the comfort of their own home.

By now, Shirley was running a high fever, and was in extreme pain day and night. But in spite of the ordeal, Shirley still laughed at any chance she got. She glowed when her eyes rested upon the animal pictures around the hospital.

Meanwhile, they gave Shirley physical therapy on a regular basis. Even when Shirley was constantly running a high fever of 104 and in great pain with red and swollen joints, physical therapy would still continue. Yi was outraged by their poor action. Yi asked them to discontinue with the therapies. It would bring only harm if done under such conditions. But they would not listen.

"I read an article in a medical book that states that under high fever and when the joints are in great pain, physical therapy should not be done," Yi told them.

Dr. Persse replied, "They provide wrong information in books sometimes."

Yi gave them a definite, "no" to the continuation of aspirin and physical therapy. Plus, the baby could not get any sleep in the hospital; whenever she fell asleep, they woke her up for physical therapy.

"If you do not cooperate with us, we will send you to court," they threatened. And true to their words, they sent over Louis Small, a hospital lawyer, who gave Yi the same message.

"Okay, I will wait and see how the treatment will turn out," Yi told them. Yi had no one to help her, and certainly she did not want to cause any problems. All she wanted was for Shirley to receive good care. Did they not understand that? Or did they just need reminding?

The second day, however, the torture of Shirley resumed. Yi, who could no longer bear the ill treatment, yelled to them next day, "Okay, I will see you in court!" She could not and would not stand there like a frightened, mistreated dog when she clearly saw that the hospital was making Shirley's condition worse. Like a mother lioness, she would rise and fight for her daughter's life till the utmost end, and only until victory would be achieved for Shirley.

Accordingly, a Care and Protection Order was obtained on November 5 from the Boston Juvenile Court. Before the court session, they asked if Yi would like to have an interpreter. And Yi nodded. "My English is not good."

Once the proceedings began, they immediately took away Yi's custody of Shirley. At the same time, the hospital increased the aspirin dosage from 75 mg to 120 mg a day for Shirley. They also enforced physical therapies twice daily and occupational therapy once daily.

Yi desperately needed to win, not for her own sake, but Shirley's. She knew that Shirley's health would deteriorate on a significant level under the rugged care.

"Mrs. Cheng gave Shirley medication without the supervision of a doctor," was the hospital's accusation they brought against Yi in court, not the real reason of the case: Yi's refusal of their medical care. They had known that Shirley had taken piroxicam from day one. Yi had told them of this when she explained Shirley's history before arriving in Boston. It was the reason why Yi had brought Shirley here; because none of the medications worked.

Despite this terrifying moment, Yi was calm and composed, and her eyes exhibited exuberant courage and stamina. Her interpreter was both a white student going for his doctoral degree in anthropology and a professor at Harvard University. He kindly translated what was said. Yi was grateful to him, as he was compassionate to her ordeal. Immediately, Yi was forbidden to stay with Shirley in the same room, but was allowed to visit Shirley.

"I will come to see Shirley whenever I get the chance," her interpreter, Samuel, told Yi. Yi was comforted a great deal by his kind offer.

That night after they returned from court, Samuel visited Shirley. "She is so adorable!" he exclaimed as soon as his eyes fell upon the baby. He gaped with much admiration. He could not take his eyes off such an amazing creature.

Since Yi could not sleep in the same room with Shirley, she went around the hospital on many nights, seeking a room to stay in for the night. They frequently changed rooms for her as if treating a vagabond. She sometimes waited till one or two in the wee hours of the morning to obtain a key to a room where she was to sleep. Still, on top of it all, Yi would remember to go to Shirley's room to feed Shirley a bottle of milk every morning at two, for it was the time when the hospital gave Shirley aspirin on an empty stomach. Yi was often startled by a sudden booming voice behind her, ordering, "Stop! Shirley is not allowed to drink at night." If it had not been for Yi, Shirley's stomach would suffer from severe bleeding. Yi would not let them stop her from caring for her own daughter, especially when she knew they were wrong in their actions.

"Mrs. Cheng, you're not allowed! I am going to write a report to the judge," they threatened.

"You go ahead," Yi fired back. Unflinching, Yi never stopped coming.

"You *still* did not go home Yi? You are exhausted!" commented Samuel one day when he was visiting Shirley. They had ran into each other several times when he and his wife were visiting Shirley. "You need to go home now." Yi only shook her head weakly.

Only for a few times, Yi, being overly exhausted in the hospital without any sleep, went home in Latham for one or two days. Shirley needed a strong mother to support her, so Yi needed to get some of her physical strength back to withstand the ordeal. Once, when Yi returned to the hospital, she could not find Shirley in her room. Frantic, Yi asked them where Shirley was. They told her that Shirley was quarantined because she had the common cold.

When Yi at last found Shirley, she was shocked to see the state Shirley was in. The sleepy Shirley sat alone on a bed; mucus from her nose ran into her mouth, her unchanged diaper was filled with her feces, and she was unclean from head to toe. Upon seeing this, Yi rushed over, picked up Shirley, and went to the washing room to bathe her.

"Mrs. Cheng, stop," they ordered. "You cannot give her a bath, she has a cold."

"That's why I must give her a bath. Shirley needs it. It can make her better," Yi fought them off and continued on her way.

The same picture was replayed and the same scene reenacted every time Yi returned from Latham. Each time, Yi only spent a mere day in Latham; and Yi had left only a few times during the whole span of the ordeal. How could she leave Shirley entirely under the hospital's supervision when they could not even properly care for Shirley for only one single day? Not only was it a physical torment, but also a calvary for both Yi and Shirley.

Chapter Eleven

Days slowly dragged on painfully, with each step more agonizing than the one before it, while they carried the crosses on their backs. Yi struggled to maintain her sangfroid to endure their harsh life. Each day ticked on with Yi always fighting to get the chance to feed Shirley at two in the morning in spite of the hospital's forbiddance. Yi saw that her daughter's condition was getting worse by the minute during the duration of the hospital stay. Because of Shirley's severe crippling disease, she would be prone to contracting uveitis. A split lamp examination of her eyes was performed under sedation and revealed no evidence of asymptomatic uveitis.

The most tortuous time for Shirley during the stay was receiving the therapies sessions. She was required to sit on the playroom's floor daily for at least three hours in the afternoon. When it was nap time for other children, the playroom supervisor would always carry Shirley to the playroom, many times waking her. Thus, the sleepy Shirley could not sleep, but had to sit alone on the cold, tile floor, sometimes with a few toys. The hospital said that Shirley needed to be active because of her arthritis. *So, this is called physical therapy, being on the cold floor to sit by herself for three hours a day?* thought Yi, incredulously.

Once, Shirley did not sleep the entire night because of her usual pain. At last, at six in the morning, her eyes closed. But instantly, she was awakened to drink two ounces of water, for they did not want to get her dehydrated since she was always lacking an appetite, so she could not receive enough nourishment.

"Can't you let her sleep? She didn't sleep the whole night," Yi pleaded. Her only answer was a definite shake of their heads. Yi argued with them. But it was too late to do anything; Shirley was already awake.

On top of everything, Yi had to attend court sessions and had to endure the false accusations made by the hospital. "Mrs. Cheng has a psychological disorder, high level of anxiety, and she force-feeds Shirley," they also accused. They asked that Yi be evaluated by a hospital psychiatrist. During all the court sessions, Yi could not speak for herself and tell them her side of the story—no one was providing any help to speak for her. Her court-appointed lawyer never spoke one word for her during any court session, for he did not know the full spectrum of the story. Once, the judge asked him some questions, and the lawyer only shrugged his shoulders and shook his head.

Samuel had spent an entire night, without any sleep, writing a long and detailed report on her case, hoping it would help. After writing the report overnight, he had given it to her the following noon right after he completed the detailed fourteen pages of typed report.

Unlike what Samuel and Yi had hoped, no one paid attention to the report. Yi was not sure who else had read it besides herself. She had read the report with trouble, for the English words were hard. But she was able to understand the content of the document. She read with a pounding heart and a shocked soul when she got to the part where Samuel had listed what the hospital psychologists had reported:

"Shirley was carried around by her parents and when approached by hospital staff, she would cry and hide her face. This behavior did not decrease with familiarity with staff."

"Shirley will at times display a great deal of anger during the therapy sessions, and refused to cooperate with the physical therapist. The behavior problem is exacerbated by the presence of her mother."

"Separation of parents and child during the course of this admission has been exceedingly difficult."

The statements made by the psychologists struck Yi with total disbelief. The spontaneous response of the twenty-two-month-old baby, in constant pain from the crippling disease, should not be taken as any signs of a dysfunctional family. Above all, Shirley had been separated from Yi by force. Should such reactions by an infant be taken as a family pathology?

Yi knew that she must win the battle. *There is no other way*, thought Yi. *This is the battle against evildoers.* She would permanently lose the custody to her own child if she lost. *Win, I must*, she thought with resolve. But how could their icy hearts listen to her reasons?

One day, Yi was called to the stand during a court session. At long last, the moment she had been waiting for finally arrived. She could now speak for herself. The judge asked Yi several questions. It was the moment she had been waiting for.

"Why did you give a prescription medication to Shirley without the supervision of a doctor?" asked the judge.

"The medication was prescribed by the doctor in China. So, I put Shirley on it. But she was on it for only one week. I did not know about the medical law of America. I will not give Shirley any medication without the doctor's supervision from now on," answered Yi.

The judge continued, "Why do you refuse to see this psychiatrist? If you give me a good reason, I will find a different psychiatrist for you."

"Everyone in the hospital says I have psychological disorders. This psychiatrist is from the same hospital, who already has bias toward me, so I think that she will naturally most likely say the same thing about me," Yi reasoned.

"Okay, very good, I'll make some phone calls right now," stated the judge. "Would you like a Chinese or an American psychiatrist?"

"I prefer a Chinese or an Oriental psychiatrist," answered Yi.

"There are no Chinese psychiatrists, but we have a Korean." He reported after he returned.

Yi nodded. "That is fine. Thank you, Your Honor."

"Okay, I appoint this psychiatrist for you." The people below listened on. At that moment, Yi knew that she was on the road to victory. It was the first and crucial step of the battle. She had scored a large point by having the judge appoint a different psychiatrist.

I didn't understand that in court, they would charge me with privately giving Shirley this medicine which I had brought back with me from China, thought Yi. *I find it strange that at the time when I openly conveyed this information to Dr. Persse, she didn't stop me, and later, used this honest admission as an accusation against me. I realized how accurate Samuel's report was regarding the case.* In it, he stated:

"Having taken hasty legal steps to secure custody, and continued to argue a hard line using problematic psychological concepts, the hospital had committed two levels of error..."

"...the pattern of multiple resort and individual initiative in providing medication is a very familiar one in China and indeed in all areas of the world where professional medicine has not achieved such total and absolute control over the pharmaceutical and medical markets."

"The first responsibility of the healer in the clinical encounter is sympathetically and fully to elicit the patient's background and explanatory model for the problem involved."

"Decision-making is a family process, complex disagreements may occur between family unit and physicians and nurses, before rushing off to court, and ruthlessly depriving the parents of their ancestral grounds for meaningful existence."

The judge's voice interrupted Yi's thoughts. "Don't worry, every afternoon at three I have a high level of anxiety myself," the judge comforted Yi with a smile toward the end of the session. Among the handful of audience listening to the session, most were doctors from the hospital. A few laughs rang throughout the courthouse. The psychiatric evaluation was scheduled to get underway.

"I would not speak as well in Chinese if I had stayed in China for only five years," the Massachusetts State social worker, Melinda, said to Yi when meeting her after the court session. "You did a really good job. You spoke very well, pointing out things very clearly."

"Thank you. I have the reason, the truth. The truth is on my side," said Yi.

"If you are found to have psychological disorders from the psychological evaluation, you'll permanently lose custody of Shirley and you won't be allowed to see her for twenty years."

***

Yi held Shirley in her arms outside her room. Yi gently rocked her to and fro, trying to sooth the crying child who was in pain. Yi lifted her head and noticed a figure coming their way. An Oriental lady with dark short hair came into Yi's view.

The woman walked toward Yi. "Are you Mrs. Cheng?"

"Yes. So, you are the psychiatrist."

"Yes," the doctor answered with a formal nod.

"Please come in," Yi showed her into the room. Yi gently placed Shirley into the stroller. Shirley continued to cry.

"Why don't you carry her?" asked the psychiatrist.

"Today's a bad day for you to come to examine us. My daughter is running a high fever of 103. She has been crying the whole day long. I don't know if I am allowed to carry her or not. They said I overprotect her, so I don't want to appear as though I am overprotective." Yi was unsure what to do. Should she carry Shirley, and look as if she was being overprotective? Or should she ignore Shirley? Would that look as if she was neglecting her?

"Go ahead," said the psychiatrist, "carry her," Grateful, Yi picked Shirley up and held Shirley in her arms for the remaining of the examination. Yi was expecting a Chinese interpreter to come that day, but she did not show up. The psychiatrist began to ask Yi questions that required only common sense, like questions that were asked on IQ Tests. The examination lasted for exactly an hour.

"I will tell you the result now," the doctor said, "not only don't you have any psychological disorders, but you are also very smart. Plus, you are a very good mother. And I'm going to write this in the report to the judge."

From that moment, Yi knew she would get Shirley back. No words could describe her happiness.

In such circumstances, when parents are found mentally incompetent, they will lose custody of their children. But if no disagreements between parents and doctors ever occur, mentally incompetent parents are still able to have children and maintain custody. People are not required to receive psychological evaluation to determine if they would be allowed to have children. But how come once parents disagree with doctors they will lose their parental rights if they are found to have psychological disorders?

Yi's thoughts rewound to the time before the custody case began. Dr. Robinson had recommended two doctors for Shirley: one from New England Medical Center in Boston, and the other one from Columbia University in New York City. He had told Yi the doctor in Boston had written a book about arthritis. Therefore, Yi had chosen Boston over New York. Then once Yi lost the custody, Yi was not allowed to bring Shirley to see Dr. Robinson, for he was not a pediatric rheumatologist. The judge had told Yi earlier that she was allowed to take Shirley to Columbia University. But Yi thought it would be too much for Shirley, and besides, they all had the same treatment. So, why have Shirley travel unnecessarily? Yi had also fervently believed that the hospital was still doing their hardest in Shirley's best interest. They would still help. Yi had even given Dr. Persse two scarves, never expecting that the doctor could so cruelly bring the fallacious charges against her. She had clung to that belief, and decided to stay in Boston. Yi sighed as she thought back. She had made a mistake. Only after she remained did the hospital accuse her of having psychological disorders.

Soon afterward, on December 20, Yi was allowed to take Shirley home at Latham following a Boston Juvenile Court appearance, but she still did not have full custody of Shirley. A full hearing was scheduled for a date several weeks later. Yi was ordered to bring Shirley to see the doctor at the Boston's Floating Hospital for Children on February 5 for a follow-up. Having her baby back was the best Christmas present she could ever wish for.

Yi, holding the bundle of treasure in her arms, left the hospital. Even after all the ordeal of the false accusations and the unnecessary physical and emotional torments, Yi did not hold any grudges toward anyone. It was futile to have vengeance and anguish upon her heart. She was grateful that she had won the case—she *knew* she had won the case even though she had not been told. It was God's help and the divine will of His plans.

At that time, Yi had learned that Dr. Persse had just had her first child and planned to depart for Canada. How could one woman bring such misery upon a whole family?

Chapter Twelve

"The full hearing is going to be in two months," Yi retold Kwi Show. "There, they will decide whether I can have full custody of Shirley." She and Shirley were back living with Kwi Show. Even in the comfort of their home, they were not let to live peacefully. They frequently had visits from the Department of Social Services to check how the two were "getting along."

One day, a dietitian visited them to survey the eating habits of Shirley. Yi had prepared all kinds of food in front of Shirley, and hoped that Shirley would pick up something and eat. As if understanding the urgency of the matter, Shirley started to eat from her tray. The dietitian wrote down the report, and she was to send it to the judge.

Before the full hearing, Yi brought Shirley to see Dr. Robinson in January. Shirley was still on prednisone. Yi had called him during the case, and he had no way to help.

"I can clearly see that Shirley's condition is worse! If I had known they would treat you like that, I would never have recommended the doctor, Dr. Schelling, to you," remarked the doctor, a few frown lines appearing on his forehead.

"But I have never seen her. Shirley has always been seeing another doctor, Dr. Persse." Yi told him. She had always inquired about Dr. Schelling, but Dr. Persse, the one who had exclusively been seeing Shirley, only told her that Dr. Schelling would see Shirley later. But she never did.

"*What?* You have never seen the doctor I recommended?" The surprise scintillated in his eyes. He gaped; his mouth was wide enough to hold an apple. He fell silent. Yi did not understand this sudden change. Why the silence? She did not question him.

"I am taking Shirley to North Carolina," Yi told him.

After the appointment with Dr. Robinson, another appointment soon followed: Yi's next stop was at Boston's Floating Hospital for Children, as ordered by the court. The appointment was scheduled at two in the afternoon on February 5.

"It is snowing so heavily!" exclaimed Yi on the appointed day. "This is definitely not a good day." She had no other choice but to go. She wanted her custody—the right to be her daughter's own parent—back, so she had to bow to their demands. Agatha, too, was going. Samuel was to meet them at the hospital. Yi had not been sleeping well for a long time.

The tired Yi started the Cadillac, Dr. C.J. Ling's car. "There are several inches of snow on the ground already." She wanted to get it over with, quick.

The falling snow had made the visibility extremely low. Yi gritted her teeth. She could not believe what torment the hospital had put on them.

At long last, after over four hours on the road, the car stopped at the hospital, the inferno. Yi dragged her tired body out of the car while carrying Shirley out. Samuel greeted them by their car. "Thank you, Samuel!" She was so very much grateful for his support. "It is absolutely freezing," commented Yi. It was a freezing hell.

They went inside the building and reported their arrival to the receptionist.

Yi plopped herself in a chair in the waiting room, the rest followed suit. She carried Shirley on her lap. She hoped that the wait would be short, so that they could head back home before the snow got too deep. She looked around the room. She could not spot any patients.

One hour had passed without any murmur from the hospital.

Two hours passed. "When are we going to see the doctor?" thought Yi aloud.

When the clock showed that nearly three hours had passed, a woman appeared before them. "There are no doctors available."

"No doctors?" repeated Yi, frowning with puzzlement and annoyance. The woman shook her head and left.

The group looked at one another. "So, should we go?" pondered Yi. She was still hesitant to leave. She did not want to miss any doctors. She did not want them to find any fault with her.

After several minutes, she decided it was time to go. They had waited long enough. Yi thanked Samuel several times before they departed.

The sky was black as ink. Flitters of white forms swirled in the atmosphere. Yi turned the car around and turned onto the road of the ghostly ambiance. She had to drive very slowly in this chaotic weather. "The roads are extremely slippery!" exclaimed Yi.

Being four hours on the road did not even take them half way home. "Slow" was a weak word to describe the traffic. The snow was falling nonstop. All in all, it was an agonizing experience. Yi could hardly keep her eyes open. She glanced at the clock and saw that it was after midnight.

The time slowly ticked on. It was two in the morning and Yi's hands were stiff from driving. "They forced me to the edge of the cliff. If they treat real criminals like this, the world will be a much better place to live! This is the worst day to drive. The roads are so dangerous and we could get into an accident. And this is especially horrible when an extremely sick child is in the car. How could they do this to us? They know that we're coming," hissed Yi. She was fuming. She felt a sudden rush of warm current sweeping over her. She was infuriated by the torture.

"Looks like we're home!" declared Agatha half an hour later, peering out the window through the thick snow while stifling a yawn.

"Yes, finally! It is three already. It is absolutely outrageous," steamed Yi. "We went. They can't have anything bad to say about that."

***

The full hearing at last arrived, and Samuel had offered to go and represent her. "You don't have to be there; there is no need to," he said to Yi. He only needed to stay and listen to what they would decide. Yi waited anxiously at home for their decision. It seemed like she was waiting for the court to order a life sentence upon her; actually, it was much worse than a life sentence. Shirley's life was thousandfold more important than hers. How could she go on living without Shirley? And how could Shirley live without her? They needed each other like plants needed sunlight. Shirley's life was depending wholly on their decision.

Sitting by the telephone, Yi held Shirley close to her heart. She hummed a soft tune in Shirley's ears in the quiet room.

Ring!

Yi's heart gave a leap. The ring of the telephone invaded the silence like a bomb.

"You got the full custody back; the judge said! You are free!" Samuel reported on the other line. He had called Yi as soon as he returned to his place from the hearing.

Tears of joy ran down Yi's cheeks. She was speechless from being overwhelmed with happiness. She managed to thank him between her tears.

"I have helped you, and at the same time, I have helped myself. I told the case to my students. It is a good lesson for everyone to learn," he said. "And…I was fired by the hospital," he further told Yi. Both of them burst out laughing. The hospital had fired him after he helped Yi in her case. Yi was sorry about the unfortunate happening. She was surprised by such a low action of the hospital.

"Thank you so very much for all your help," she graciously thanked him again. She was immensely grateful for Samuel's help. He was such a nice person who would go out of his way to bestow kindness upon a mere stranger, expecting no rewards in return. Yi knew God was helping her during the case; He sent a kind man to be her interpreter.

She sat down on the couch and leaned back. She let out a long sigh. Ah, this was the taste of true happiness! Neither fame nor money could make her happier. She hugged Shirley tightly. The baby's small mouth stretched into a wide smile; she knew it was a happy moment for them both.

The telephone suddenly rang again. Wondering who it could be, Yi answered it. It was Melinda.

"Mrs. Cheng, you would still be under monitor," she told Yi. Monitored? What did that mean? But deep inside, she had a feeling what it meant. After hanging up with the social worker, she dialed Samuel's number.

"No, you will not be under monitor," he assured her.

Why did Melinda report falsely? But what did it matter? What did anything matter now that she had won? Yi's heart rested completely now. She and Shirley would live their lives again, with no more court sessions, hearings… Life would be grand once again. And her journey of seeking a treatment for Shirley would resume. The living nightmare had ended; they had awoken after a long, terrifying sleep of darkness. The music to the macabre dance had ceased.

Chapter Thirteen

"I am going to bring Shirley to live in North Carolina where her father is," Yi had told both the New York State social worker and the Massachusetts State social worker after Yi's victory.

"Melinda said, 'We are all fooled by Yi. She's running away,'" the New York State social worker told Yi, chuckling. Yi joined in with laughter of her own.

Al had moved to North Carolina to open a Chinese restaurant, where he would be the owner. He had moved there while Yi was on her case. He was not present when they called his name during the full hearing.

"He shouldn't have missed this hearing," Samuel had remarked that day. It was pitiful that a father was not present at the most important time of his child's life.

Yi did not like going to North Carolina, but she would have a place to live there. She did not like to stay where she was, either, for she was concerned that she might encounter more problems with Melinda. Melinda had told her that she was going to be under monitor when, in truth, she was not. It was better to leave this place; better to be safe than sorry. And staying with Kwi Show was nearly impossible, for Agatha was a great disturbance. She frequently made raucous noise in the house and shouted across the hall to talk to Dr. Ling. Whenever Yi asked her to lower her voice, Agatha would start yelling at her, resulting in more noise. Shirley was often awakened by Agatha.

In March, a week after the full hearing, Al came to Latham and picked Yi and Shirley up. They began to live together in a peaceful rented house that needed only a ten-minute drive to his restaurant. But Shirley's condition was getting worse and worse. She cried in pain day and night, with the pain cutting through her like knives. She could not get a wink of sleep at nights. Yi brought Shirley to see a rheumatologist, but he could not help. Yi tried aspirin, but it provided no relief.

Yi constantly supplied Shirley with toys and other amusements. Shirley was kept occupied during the day to ease the pain. Yi also brought Shirley to the largest mall at Charlotte nearly every afternoon after a nap. Shirley never looked forward to the naps, for she did not want to stop playing. Somehow, Yi always managed to have Shirley close her brown eyes by rocking her in her arms.

In September, Yi took a test to become an American citizen, and she passed. They asked if she would like to change her name, to which Yi eagerly nodded. From that time on, she became Juliet Cheng. It had always been one of her favorite names. She had admired the name in the Shakespearean play, *Romeo and Juliet*. It was an elegant name, and she was happy she could finally be called by Juliet.

By and by, as days lazily passed, Shirley began to complain that her left eye was hurting her. Juliet brought her to an eye doctor right away.

"She has uveitis, which is caused by the arthritis," the doctor reported after the examination. He prescribed some eyedrops for her.

"Keep her on them for a month," he told Juliet. Juliet did as she was instructed. A month later, Shirley's eye was not bothering her anymore. But Shirley's right eye soon became a problem. Again, Shirley was required to be on the same eyedrops for the same duration. Once again, the eyedrops performed a miracle, and the right eye got well.

Meanwhile, during the visits to the eye doctor, Juliet made several contacts with a hospital in China. Shirley's suffering was too great. *She must be treated*, thought Juliet. *My pearl would die. She is at the edge of a high cliff already. I cannot let her fall.* Kwi Show had read an article in the newspaper about a doctor who had invented a new medicine to treat autoimmune diseases, such as rheumatoid arthritis and lupus. The article stated that the medicine, a Western medicine, was 98.5 percent efficacious.

"This sounds good." Kwi Show showed the article to Juliet, who began her contacts without any delay. Al had written to the doctor, Dr. Chung, asking him to send some medicine.

Soon, they received the doctor's reply. In it, he had written, "The medicine is shots, and therefore cannot be sent to you. But you are welcome to come for the treatment." Juliet called him up, and received his consent for Shirley to be admitted to the center.

Without any delay, they set out to their destination, a well-known rehabilitation center known as Tang Gang Zi, situated in the city of An Shan. It was an area that was often visited by people from far and wide, for it beheld breathtaking scenery. Before the trip, Juliet had shaved Shirley's head, so that her hair would not need to be cut if life ever got harsh. She did not know what the stay would turn out to be like and she wanted to be fully prepared for any difficulties that might arise. She brought some food on their way, including some soy sauce. She had heard that the northeastern province in China was extremely harsh, and could get quite cold during winter. It was December. She prepared for the tribulations that lay ahead for them.

They arrived at Beijing, with Shirley crying all the way. Juliet's energy was drawn out from her by the minute. As always, she spent hours feeding Shirley on the plane. At the capital, they boarded the train that was to take them to Tang Gang Zi.

Upon arrival at Tang Gang Zi, they had to pass by several fascinating features of the land to reach Dr. Chung. The scene that met Juliet's eyes nearly took her breath away. It was nothing she had ever prepared herself to see. Tang Gang Zi was one of the most beautiful areas upon which she had ever laid eyes. They followed a wide path in the spacious place, with views of majestic mountains and small glistening streams that ran under pagodas.

In a hall, they met a man dressed in a white uniform. The first impression he would give anyone was his well-groomed appearance, with a high prominent nose. He looked like a wealthy European, not a poor Chinese man. He was no doubt the doctor.

"Ah, so you have come," Dr. Chung exclaimed, realizing who the group was.

It was time to get the treatment started. They were sent to the sixth ward, where a large room was reserved for them by the center. Juliet grew more awestruck once they entered the rehabilitation center. The sixth ward was reserved for only people of high rank and status.

They entered Dr. Chung's office. A nurse then drew blood from Shirley's arm. Afterward, Dr. Chung examined Shirley. "You can go to your room now," said Dr. Chung after he was done. Juliet pushed Shirley to their room. A nurse came into their room two hours later. She carried a tray in her hands, and set it down on a table beside the bed. Shirley eyed the contents suspiciously. She knew it held nothing pleasant. The treatment was starting. The nurse gave Shirley a shot of a liquid with the color of tan. Juliet inwardly prayed that it would work. Even if just to give some relief. Shirley continued to cry. They had to wait till next day to see the effects of the medication. It was too soon to tell at the present time.

"She is so smart!" remarked the head nurse from the hospital when she saw Shirley later into the day.

"But she didn't even say much. How do you know she's smart?" inquired Juliet.

The lady shook her head in emphasis. "Yes, but what she says, well, most children cannot talk like her. She is very, very smart. I can see it. I am sure of it. She is just like Zhang Hai Di." She was referring to the well-known disabled woman of tremendous intelligence who had self-taught herself surgery. She was paralyzed from the waist down, and her only companion was the reflection in the mirror. But she had overcome all her hardships with cheerfulness and optimism. She had dissected any animals she could get her hands on, including frogs. By doing so, she had learned the organs of the animals. Soon, many people had traveled afar to seek her for treatment, and had been met with cures and relief. She was truly a wonder. But how could Shirley, barely a three-year-old, even come close in matching her intelligence?

Following the nurse's outburst of praise, a man, who was staying as a patient, exclaimed once he had laid eyes upon her, "Oh! Look at that child's head!"

"Her head?" repeated Juliet, wide-eyed.

"The shape, the size, the symmetry, clearly show that the child is highly intelligent. The shape of her head indicates an extreme intelligence. That is one remarkable head," he went on, not taking his eyes off Shirley's shaven cranium of high forehead, full head, and thick brows.

"This is very interesting," said Juliet. She had heard that a person's level of intelligence could be measured by the shape of one's head.

Juliet was still ruminating what everyone had commented about Shirley when she prepared Shirley for bed. *Such a precious child has to go through it all*, thought Juliet. She stroked Shirley to sleep. After much effort and several hours, Shirley finally fell asleep, her limbs painful and stiff.

The night slowly passed. Shirley had spent the entire night crying in great pain. She awoke right after she fell asleep. Juliet tried her best to comfort her. Whenever she saw Shirley cry, her heart would break piece by piece. Juliet did not get any sleep, and the next morning soon arrived.

Al left after spending a night there. Juliet fumed for his disregard and lack of concern, but she turned away to let him be on his way. He could not give any help if he stayed.

A nurse knocked on the door. Juliet opened the door, and the woman, dressed in white, walked in. It was time for Shirley to receive another shot. The nurse flashed Shirley smiles as she got everything ready. "Poor child," the nurse said to Juliet. "We all heard her crying during the whole night." Shirley gritted her teeth when the needle pierced her skin. "All set. You did well," said the nurse. Shirley smiled to the woman who went out of the room. Now, she had several hours without any shots before she was to get another in the afternoon.

"I'll go downstairs to buy some food," Juliet told Shirley. "I'll see if there is anything you might like. I certainly hope so."

It smelled delicious by the kitchen, and the food made Juliet's mouth water. "We will make any food especially for you; whatever you like," the kind cook told Juliet.

"My child's appetite is very poor," Juliet explained to them. "She is always nauseated when she eats something. I really don't know what is the matter with her. I've been feeding her all these years and my neck is really hurting me. You can imagine how painful my neck is after spending hours and hours of feeding daily. If I don't feed her, I know she'll die." They assured her that they would try to do their best in cooking some food that Shirley might like. Then they continued to converse for a while. Juliet told them about their situation, and they compassionately listened.

In the afternoon, Shirley received another shot. Shirley did not look forward to the shots. She cringed whenever she saw the needle. But she would get used to it, especially if it might help her.

Chapter Fourteen

Sunbeams crept in through the window the next morn. Shirley woke up without a single trace of a tear. She had peacefully slept straight through the entire night without any pain. Something magical was taking place in her body. Juliet was dumbstruck when Shirley was able to continually sit without even a whimper. Shirley's pain had disappeared into thin air as though a magician had just hidden it somewhere. Juliet was exultant.

When the nurse walked in to give Shirley the morning dose of shots, she was also taken aback. "Oh, she's not crying!" she exclaimed with a wide grin. A happy smile was still on her lips as she gave the shot to Shirley, whose fear by now had died down, especially when she knew it was beneficial to her.

It was for certain a miracle drug, for it had the effect of prednisone without any of its side effects. Anyone could be on these shots, ranging from young to old and the sick and healthy. The shots could be stopped without having to taper off gradually. But each shot cost three Chinese yuans. Many Chinese households had an annual income of only one thousand two hundred yuans. But Dr. Chung was not a wealthy man, for he could not receive much profit from it. He had tested the medicine for fifteen years before introducing it to the public; he had even tested it on himself. Many people had traveled from afar to seek his treatment; most were carried to his center, but left the place walking happily away.

Dr. Chung visited Shirley daily in her room. He had told them on the day of their arrival that the medication would surely work. Days passed with Shirley on the shots. She had no more high fevers, and stopped crying altogether. She could sleep into the night without awakening from the pain. The hospital days became more enjoyable for Shirley, for she could sit for hours with no trouble. She could even begin to crawl. Above all, the entire dosage of prednisone was stopped without any withdrawal symptoms.

The following week, a doctor began to come to massage Shirley on a daily basis. Days swiftly flew by with less worries upon the mother's heart.

During the stay, Juliet and Shirley made several friends and companions with the nurses and patients. They spent a few hours talking and laughing together each day. One day, a patient taught Shirley several Chinese words. Several days later, Shirley was asked to write them. Without forgetting a single word, Shirley quickly wrote down each. Shirley felt grand that she was writing words for the very first time. Many days passed, and Shirley still did not forget any word.

"This is astonishing! Shirley is so smart; she's a child prodigy," the lady marveled. "She is able to remember all the words I taught her just in a few minutes, and she will always remember them! Plus, her handwriting is so beautiful and neat!"

"Shirley is unbelievable!" Juliet echoed, with much pride for her child.

During the stay, Shirley received yet another admirer. Juliet had met an interesting person, who was one of the patients. "Wow, your child looks amazing," commented the man. "I really don't want to tell you this, but I'm a fortuneteller and I have some things to say about the child. To not say something that needs to be told would be a sin, so I think I should tell you, for I cannot resist it."

"You're a fortuneteller?" inquired Juliet, leaning forward in the bed.

"Yes; I have learned soothsaying, but no one knows I'm a fortuneteller; I'm just here for treatment," the man told her. "Your child looks exactly like a boy." He studied Shirley.

"But tell me, is my child a boy or a girl?"

"Even though she looks just like a boy, she is a girl," he said. "I can see that she is extremely smart." Juliet gave a cry of amazement. Everyone was saying how brilliant her little star was. She felt so happy for her child. Then the oracle turned his focus on Juliet. "You may be very modest, but inwardly, you think you are very smart." Juliet giggled. It was so true.

During the nights, exclamations would also be ejaculated, not because of Shirley's intelligence, but of her breathing, which could be heard from surrounding rooms. Some days, the sputum was a great discomfort to Shirley. They gave medication to ease the condition, but it could not be completely cured. Juliet had found a highly effective herbal medicine during Shirley's first visit to China, and it had greatly helped Shirley's bronchitis. But unfortunately, the quality of the medicine decreased. However, it had improved Shirley's lung condition on a grand scale even till the current time. Before that herbal medicine intake, Shirley's snores could be heard through a few walls.

***

In March, a new batch of the shots arrived. The patients continued on to the new shots. But the health of the patients deteriorated at once. The quality of the shots decreased to the point they were harmful, for they had put them on mass production because it was a way for a profit gain. Dr. Chung could not control their manufacturing. He was sorrowful that it happened. They did not care for the quality of the shots, only the quantity.

Shirley started crying again. She, along with all the other patients, had wholly depended upon these shots.

"I want to leave this center, for I am being treated poorly; no one listens to me anymore," Dr. Chung told Juliet. He was going elsewhere to work in another hospital, where he would be the director. He had received an invitation to go there by the hospital. "You can bring Shirley there next year."

"Thank you very much, Dr. Chung. I will bring Shirley to see you. Thank you again."

Sadly, Juliet had to bring Shirley back to America. Their dream was just about to come true: Shirley was starting to stand up on her own by holding on to something for support. Now, that moment had vanished; but hopefully, for just a little while. Shirley was unable to receive massage therapy any longer, for she was in too much pain.

Before returning to the United States, Juliet pushed Shirley out one last time for some sightseeing. As they passed some street markets, Shirley caught the eye of a cleaning woman, who immediately stopped sweeping the sidewalks and came forward to them with her broom in hand.

"Look at that child's brows!" exclaimed the woman, staring at Shirley, slack-jawed. "She is remarkable!"

"She is?" questioned Juliet. But she was not as surprised with the comments as before. She had heard so many remarks of Shirley's unique appearance and intelligence that she had gotten used to them, but would never get bored of them.

"Yes, she is surely remarkable! She is extremely intelligent. When she grows up, she will be a grand leader! Do you see that part of her face above her nose and between her thick brows?" She asked Shirley to frown. "She has a much thicker flesh there. Look, I don't have it; we don't have it. That indicates that she will be grand in the future." Both Shirley and Juliet listened with much awe. Shirley had always wanted to be a famous person, especially one who was a leader. The woman had to get back to her duties, so she took another look at Shirley and reluctantly returned to her place.

"Isn't that interesting?" asked Shirley.

"It sure is, and I have known from the bottom of my heart for a long time that you are very smart," replied Juliet. Then it was time for them to get back to their own place. Juliet needed to prepare for the trip home.

In May, Al picked them up to take them back to America. It was so close...

Juliet and Shirley stayed with Dr. Ling and Kwi Show for the rest of the year. Juliet patiently waited for the next year's arrival to seek treatment at Dr. Chung's new hospital, which was specialized in only autoimmune diseases.

One summer day, Al told Juliet of a radon mine in Montana. "Let's bring Shirley there. It will treat arthritis and other forms of diseases," he suggested. Many people had been there to seek treatment by staying in the mines that were miles deep into the earth.

With no other choice left, he picked them up from Latham and together, they took Shirley to Montana. On their way, they passed ten states, with scenery that changed from busy cities to total desolate wilderness of the west. They snapped shots as they went along; one of the places they relished was the breathtaking Niagara Falls. They stopped at their destination a week later.

On the second day after arriving, they rode down the mine on an elevator. They were to sit in the darkness with only a small light bulb providing the only illumination. They stayed there for the duration of a whole day, except for getting up for food. They used the mines' water to bathe Shirley, for they were told that it could help as well.

On the second day into the treatment, they met a gypsy who also was receiving the treatment. She took one look at Shirley, and said these words, "I will give a fortune reading for the baby for no charge. But for you," she turned to Juliet, "I will charge twenty-five dollars."

"Thank you. You can go ahead for the child," Juliet consented.

The oracle began with an air of mystery. "The child has just barely made it in life...she was almost unable to escape the slim chance. But the stars had allowed her to escape the danger. She has just made it through in the last second," said the gypsy. Juliet listened with much awe. The woman said that she would send her a diagram of Shirley's life which was reflected upon the stars. Juliet graciously thanked her.

Without any improvement, the family left the mine after staying there for a week. Juliet continued to live with her parents. Summer was leaving and autumn was slowly creeping in. Juliet knew it would soon be time for her to bring Shirley to China.

When a month had passed since they had met the gypsy at the mine, Juliet received the diagram, that the fortuneteller had promised, in the mail. It showed detailed and complex drawing of stars and their relations to one another. Juliet studied it, but she could not understand it. Thinking that she could study it in the future, she tucked it away with her other belongings.

Chapter Fifteen

The small family boarded the train in Beijing. The train would take them to Duen Hua, where the hospital resided. During the entire ride, Shirley cried in agony as her tiny body imploded with pain. Every small jolt of the train, every gentle touch from her mother caused explosive pain. Simply sitting on the seat was highly painful. She was unable to move and unable to be moved. The broken-hearted but hopeful Juliet could only watch helplessly. Deep inside, she hoped with all her heart, with all her soul, with all her might, that effective treatment was waiting for them when they arrived. How much longer could her pearl go on in such pain? If nothing else, the pain could end her life.

The train stopped at their destination at three in the morning. Stars scintillated above, amidst the September night. They stayed in a motel, and would set out for the hospital the next day.

Juliet dialed up Dr. Chung when daylight arrived. He was expecting them; Juliet had contacted him before they left. Dr. Chung personally came to pick Juliet and the child up. Another man, an official of the government, accompanied him. Once Juliet and Shirley got into the car, Al went away for America.

Once they arrived, Juliet was dismayed to find that there were no bathrooms in the hospital; people had to get out of the building in the courtyard for their bathroom needs.

Shirley received the treatment right away on the same but improved medication as before. The hospital manufactured the shots themselves, getting the necessary ingredients by hand. Dr. Chung gave the hospital the orders for the entire process of the production. To Juliet's unspeakable joy, Shirley had stopped crying that night after receiving her first shot. The improved shots were apparently better than the first. The shots needed to be administered only once a day, as opposed to twice daily as with the previous shots.

The following few days, Shirley began to receive massage therapies twice a day, each time lasting an hour and a half. The therapist was a blind man who patiently massaged Shirley, and entertained her with fabulous stories from his imagination as he went along.

Juliet could see that Shirley was improving on a noticeable level day by day. The now nearly four-year-old was absent of cries. Pain no longer bothered her. During the hospital stay, Shirley's intelligence spread throughout the place. A patient had taught Shirley a poem one day, and Shirley had memorized the verse in its entirety after only a few minutes. The patient asked Shirley to recite it a few days later, and Shirley had not forgotten a single word.

"She's so smart," they had commented numerous times.

Shirley's cheerfulness was widely known throughout the hospital. And Juliet's devotion and love as a mother had won her much admiration from everyone. "Such a good mother," and "I have never seen any mother like her," would come out of their lips.

But before, several people had been skeptical of Juliet's true actions. They had thought she was a spy who was spying on them for some reason, for they would not believe that anyone would be this loving to their children. Why would a woman come this far from America to such a dreary place in China just to seek treatment? But after a short time, all were convinced.

"No one could pretend this long with such truthfulness. I can't believe you're really not a spy. You are such a good mother." Dr. Chung had said one day with conviction.

Days sped by in the hospital room, and soon, Shirley's fourth birthday arrived. She fluttered her eyes open with happy thoughts. Her eyes focusing, she saw her mother by her side with a wide smile. "How do you feel, pearl?" inquired Juliet.

"Great! I'm four!"

"Yes, dear, you are. I love you so much!" The contented mother curved her lips into a smile.

"I love you, too!" Shirley's eyes traveled to Juliet's hands—or actually her arms, for her hands were hidden behind her back. Shirley's eyes grew wide. Juliet's smile grew wider. "Mom? What are you hiding?" Excitement was clearly audible in her voice. Slowly, Juliet held out her hands, in which a doll was held.

"I hope you like it. It took me some time to find it. They don't have much in the selection. I thought this was the best one—"

"I absolutely love it!" Shirley squealed, cutting Juliet off. Shirley hugged the doll close to her heart. The doll was dressed in a blue outfit with floral designs. It had eyes with long lashes that could open and close, depending on whether it was lying down. "I love it. I love you, Mom!" Shirley knew why she loved the doll so much—it was from her most beloved person: her mother. That fact had made it extra special. A doll, even bedecked with real gold and silver, would not mean half as much if given by someone else.

***

In March, as Dr. Chung and Juliet were conversing, something from the corner of his eye caught his attention. "Oh, Yi, look! Shirley's standing!" Juliet turned her head in Shirley's direction. He was right; Shirley was standing up on the bed while holding on to the bed stand! She could not believe the miracle she was witnessing before her! Shirley, on the other hand, was acting nonchalantly as if she could stand all along. They had built a bed stand at one side of her bed, hoping she would use it to stand. They were right in their predictions.

From that day on, Shirley initially stood on her own.

Soon, she did not need the support of the stand.

Exactly one year from receiving the treatment, Shirley was able to walk. One July day, the hospital had awakened Shirley to take a picture of her walking. Shirley was a bit touched by annoyance, but she enjoyed the feeling of being able to walk. It was her first official day of walking.

Being able to walk, Shirley became another source of worry for Juliet. Shirley would go around the entire building and into every room to make friends. Juliet always spent agonizing time searching for her. Shirley, meanwhile, would be engrossed in conversations with other patients. She became a greater hit since then. She enjoyed the times she spent talking with everyone.

People were not the only delight for Shirley; she loved all the living creatures she could find which happened to be mostly bugs of all sizes and colors. No bugs, neither spiders nor bees, scared her. She often studied them really carefully, sometimes catching them in her traps. Her life revolved around exploring all areas she could escape to. Juliet was always on a lookout for Shirley, but whenever she turned her back away for a mere second, Shirley would swiftly sneak away without making a sound. Thus, the task of finding Shirley would instantly appear on Juliet's agenda as a priority.

The shots had ended for Shirley. She was now receiving only massages, still twice daily. A shoe shop had made a pair of black leather shoes for Shirley for free. They were made to aid Shirley so she could walk with ease; one heel was higher than the other to accommodate her deformity since she could not put down her heels. The hospital told Juliet that they would consider performing surgery on Shirley in the future, but it would not be for a while until Shirley's arthritis was totally stable.

Meanwhile, Shirley was fine the way she was. She was able to skip, run, and dance with grace. Juliet often took pleasure in seeing the sight of Shirley dancing like a perfect dancer. Shirley laughed and sang with the patients, who enjoyed her company. Shirley only had to receive shots for two months yearly in order to maintain her health. But even still, Shirley's appetite remained poor. Dr. Chung's shots could improve one's appetite greatly, but they did not help Shirley any. His shots had improved other patients' appetite.

The days spent in China did not last long. In October, Dr. Chung brought Juliet and Shirley to Shanghai; it was time for them to get back to America since Shirley did not need to receive the shots again until next year. At that time, the quality of the shots decreased considerably, and the same thing happened as with the first time. With no other choice, Dr. Chung planned to go to another hospital to set up his treatment. The hospital was either going to be in Beijing or Si Cuan, where both had invited him.

From Shanghai, Juliet brought Shirley home alone. This time, Juliet did not have to push Shirley anymore. Shirley was able to board the plane by herself. What a magical feeling it was for both of them! It was the first time for Shirley to be nearly like all the other children, other than the fact that Shirley still had the disease, which would follow her for the rest of her life, and the lack of appetite, which appeared to be stuck with her as well. But the biggest mission was at last accomplished. Juliet could face any other challenge without any shudder. Her heart rested peacefully. The plane took off, with Shirley smiling to the outside world.

Chapter Sixteen

"Oh my, little Shirley is walking!" Kwi Show stared at Shirley, with her eyes wide open. Juliet had told her over the telephone that Shirley could walk. But seeing was believing; to satisfy the eyes, the heart would be convinced. Shirley skipped happily over to her grandmother. And together as a joyous family, they went inside their home sweet home.

Shirley spent time playing in and out of the house. She was an active girl with an abundance of energy for play. Her friendliness and gregariousness continued. Whenever there were guests coming to the house, she would instantaneously open the door for them, and then would politely order, "Follow me." She would then lead them to her grandfather's room, where he relaxed. The guests would get a few seconds of this delight whenever they visited the house.

Juliet bought ruffled dresses with laces for Shirley, who danced like a little fairy in the yard. It had taken so much and so long to get this far for Shirley. At last, Juliet was rewarded for her hard work and unconditional devotion. The award she received was the happiness Shirley shone from her eyes.

Besides having the ability to walk, Shirley was now able to do many things that she had never before been able to; she could dress, brush her teeth, and bathe herself with a bit of help from Juliet.

Juliet then decided to bring Shirley over to Dr. Robinson. "I am very impressed; I cannot believe my eyes! This is truly a miracle!" He looked at the walking Shirley before his eyes with his mouth wide open.

Another person who was taken aback was Dr. Ling's daughter, a pediatrician in Connecticut. It was a miracle that had happened before all eyes.

The winter passed with Shirley playing in the snow. Soon, trees were beginning to acquire a new set of green clothes; branches were in full bloom of foliage. New chicks hatched in nests amidst trees while parent birds rushed to and fro, searching for sumptuous delights for the babies. Shirley watched in awe as she took in the seasonal changes of nature. She ran about amidst the grass to catch butterflies and pick wildflowers. It was like a fairy tale with a happily-ever-after ending. The dog days of summer barked, sweeping through the valley, bringing an armful of warm current with it.

In August, Juliet noticed a change in Shirley. She did not walk that often, but instead had a look of strangeness upon her face. Then one day, the words that Juliet dreaded most were uttered from Shirley's lips.

"Mom, my legs hurt. I can't walk." She was unable to stand very well anymore, for her pain overwhelmed her. Juliet contacted Dr. Chung and scheduled for another treatment session. The time was up for Shirley to receive another two months of shots as planned. Dr. Chung had written to Juliet to let her know where he was going. Thus, Juliet bought the plane tickets and would set out to Beijing.

Juliet took Shirley alone this time, with no help from Al. Shirley, with much effort, dragged herself on the plane. Walking was causing much pain for Shirley, but she was still able to manage short distances.

In China, the climate was sweltering with crowded people on the streets. Once they arrived at the opposite side of the world, Shirley stayed in a hotel while going to the Chao Yang Men Hospital at the capital of China to receive a shot each day. Dr. Chung had reserved a batch of the shots from last year before the quality decreased. The shots cured Shirley's pain forthwith, and she was able to walk again.

The batch was quickly used up after one month, and the rest of the medication was of poor quality. The dream was shattered. No one and nowhere had the good shots. Shirley could no longer walk. Juliet prayed that she could pick up the broken pieces and do her best to reassemble them. She would turn in a new direction to search for another route. At the same time, she planned to find a treatment for Shirley's loss of appetite. She had been asking all around for a doctor who could help in lessening the condition. Then she heard of an esteemed pediatrician, known as Zhao Child, from Chang Chuen City located in Ji Lin Province. It was a long way from the hotel, therefore Juliet and Shirley needed to take a train to get there.

After hours on the train, they at last stopped at their destination. They stayed in a hotel by the hospital. They rested for the night and Juliet was to bring Shirley to see Zhao after daybreak.

"This child has anorexia," diagnosed Zhao after seeing the skinny Shirley. "Poor child, all skin and bones!" No matter how hard Juliet had tried to feed her, spending hours in a single day in the process, it was hard to get Shirley on the proper weight. Juliet was able to feed Shirley up when she was a baby by coaxing her into opening her mouth by providing distractions, such as toys and other fancies. But when Shirley grew up, it was made much harder in the task, for she would not open her mouth when toys were provided.

Juliet felt that Shirley had something else other than anorexia. Seeing there was no further help, she headed back to where she had started—the hotel in Beijing.

Back in the hotel, Shirley was given a pair of blue parakeets by a hotel staff member who was sympathetic of their situation. Shirley spent hours concentrating on and scrutinizing the parrots with much care and interest. And thus, the time in China quickly passed.

In the spring of 1989, protests broke out in the heart of Tiananmen Square. The pro-democracy demonstrations turned into acts of violence, and troops and tanks were sent to massacre the protestors. The hotel, where Juliet and Shirley were staying, was shutting down; they had no more running water. Juliet must take Shirley away from the frightful place. Acting swiftly, she scurried around the room, picking up articles of clothing and other personal items, and stuffed them in bags. The staff member, who had bought the parakeets for Shirley, would keep the birds after they left.

In two days, Yui, a friend of Dr. Chung, picked them up and drove them to a rural place in Beijing to a pharmaceutical factory. Yui was an engineer from another pharmaceutical factory, and he was well-acquainted with the factory to where they were heading. With his aid, Juliet and Shirley could be permitted to live there. Plus, it was a suburb, so Juliet did not know her way around the area if it had not been for his help.

On the way, gunshots were heard. The streets were filled with protestors, soldiers, and other Chinese citizens; and cars were unable to pass through. At last, they were out of the hands of danger. They arrived at the factory, where they stayed in a small hotel within.

Each day while occupying a room in the hotel, Shirley received massage therapy from a therapist who worked and resided in the factory. The therapist was recommended by Yui. But Shirley could not endure the massages for long because of the pain.

Juliet then discovered a medication, Red Ants, that could treat rheumatoid arthritis, and it did not have any side effects. She asked the factory if Shirley could take it, and they informed her that it was fine. Therefore, Shirley received her first capsule of the Red Ants.

"Mom, my vision is cloudy," announced Shirley two days later.

"What?" gasped Juliet. She scrambled to her feet and got in front of Shirley. Carefully, she looked at Shirley's eyes. "Oh, my goodness! Your left eye has white spots! It must be the Red Ants!" She immediately stopped the medication. "You need to see an eye doctor." Without hesitating, Juliet brought Shirley to a widely known hospital in Beijing, Xie He Hospital, the best hospital for ophthalmology.

"She has band keratopathy in her eyes, much more

severe in the left eye," reported the doctor. He prescribed a couple of eyedrops, and said, "There's no medicine to treat this disease." Shirley's left eye had permanently lost vision.

***

After the protest died down, they returned to the same hotel by the hospital.

One day, Juliet heard of a Chinese herbal medicine that treated arthritis. Shirley was being administered under the herb, Yi Sen Juan Pi Wan, and got well right away; her pain was eased considerably, so Juliet bought a whole batch of the herb. Knowing that there was nothing else to do in the country, Juliet brought Shirley back to America in autumn, taking the medication with her. It would at least sustain Shirley for a while until another answer would be sought.

Chapter Seventeen

Their eyes scanned the airport for the familiar face of Agatha, who was picking them up. Juliet pushed Shirley in the stroller, dragging the bags along, to a less crowded area for the wait. Soon, Shirley's eyes rested upon Agatha. Passing Agatha's black hair, her eyes met the sight of another figure next to her. It was a man with eyeglasses and a beard who carried a cane in one hand.

"Yi, the car is over there. We will get the bags for you," said Agatha. She got the bags and moved to the exit. The man followed suit. Shirley soon learned of his name, which was Ben, and was curious to learn more of him.

Juliet carried Shirley in the car before getting all the luggage in. Soon, the engine was started, and Ben drove off toward their home at Latham. On the road, conversation began. Juliet and Shirley soon found out that Ben was a coworker of Lloyd. Lloyd had found a new job and was spending hours on the road each day just to get to work at a place known as Poughkeepsie. It was where he worked as an engineer. Lloyd and Ben soon became friends while working together.

Sometimes during silent moments in the car, Juliet's thoughts drifted elsewhere to the usual subject: Shirley. *At least*, Juliet thought, *the last trip to China was not a waste; I have bought some good herbal medicine for my pearl.* It would give her a leeway before something else that was more effective would take its place.

In the early part of 1990, not wanting to spend most of the time on the road just for traveling to work, Lloyd's family moved to Poughkeepsie, where they would be only a few minutes away from work. Agatha, on the other hand, would have to search for a job around the area. Lloyd's family was not the only one moving; Dr. Ling and the rest followed. For the first time since coming to the United States, the families separated: Dr. Ling, Kwi Show, Juliet, and Shirley would make up one of the households; and Lloyd and Agatha, along with their children, would be the other. Juliet missed the beautiful area of her former home in Latham. But the new brick house was not bad, either. It had a large deck with a view toward the lawn of lush green grass. Kwi Show loved to plant flowers, so the lawn surroundings were perfect for flowerpots.

They were having a new start. Perchance, the area had some good doctors, and it was up to Juliet to pick them out among all that were available. She wished she could get some help in aiding her to find directions and get to places in this foreign area. Juliet had no more contact with Al. In actuality, the day he dropped them off in Latham after their trip from Montana was the last she had seen of him. His wife had arrived from China to America; they were together again, along with his children. It had been three years already. She did not have any feelings of missing him, nor did Shirley. He never had any influence on them, especially on Shirley, who knew she could not find a good person in him.

In spring, Juliet brought Shirley to a nearby doctor who saw both adults and children. As they waited in the waiting room, Juliet conversed with a woman, who was also waiting.

"Do you know any good pediatrician?" inquired Juliet.

"Yes; Dr. Frank, who is extremely nice. He is just wonderful."

"Oh, really?" Juliet got out her address book and wrote down the information. She was thanking the woman as Shirley's name was called.

"I know a rheumatologist in Newington Children's Hospital in Connecticut. Dr. Zammit is a very good doctor," the doctor recommended. Juliet was happy to receive the news. Shirley was starting to be in pain again when the medication she brought home was used up. She had just ordered more, but it would not be a few days till it arrived.

Juliet was not familiar with where the hospital was located. Ben, who was becoming a friend, offered to bring them there. Juliet was quite grateful for his offer of help. After scheduling an appointment, Juliet was ready to go seek treatment for her dear daughter.

They were seated in the back of Ben's car on the appointment day. It would take two hours to get there. Shirley did not look forward to the appointment. She knew it always meant that she was going to receive some kind of treatment that was uncomfortable. But she hoped that it could work this time, and that it could last a long, long time.

Both Juliet and Shirley were quite pleased when they saw the nice doctor who came to see Shirley.

"We will give Shirley physical therapy at the hospital," he told Juliet. She thought it was a good idea. She was really not familiar with American physical therapy. The experience in Boston was a nightmare, and she had a feeling that it would be a totally different situation at this hospital. Maybe it might be the answer for Shirley. Shirley was on the herbal medication again, thus her pain was temporarily controlled. Some massage might do some good for her. Juliet told him what had happened to them in Boston.

"Oh, yes, I know her," said Dr. Zammit after Juliet mentioned Dr. Persse.

"But can Shirley still be on these herbs? They are helping her."

"Yes, she can. And you are free to take her away from the hospital whenever you like." Hence, it was settled for Shirley to be admitted in the hospital. Shirley was not thrilled at all. She just about had enough of hospitals and shots. But what choice did she have? Besides, would it not be wonderful to stand up and play in the grass again? With these thoughts, Shirley felt better about staying in the hospital.

Before the hospital stay, Juliet took Shirley to the

hospital for an eye appointment. Examining Shirley's eyes was a difficult job, for she was highly photophobic and her eyes never failed to produce tears when light was flashed on her eyes. After the appointment, Juliet received the eye doctor's report, in where it stated that Shirley had band keratopathy, uveitis, esotropia, amblyopia, visual impairment in left eye, and photophobia. "Unfortunately, Shirley already has evidence of prior inflammation in the right eye with band keratopathy and it may be only a matter of time before the right eye also loses vision as the left eye has," the report also stated.

***

On the twenty-fourth of May, Shirley made a hospital her home once again, and Juliet rented an apartment that was twenty minutes away.

The hospital gave Shirley naproxen, but as before, it caused retrograde effects, including stomach ache. During the day, she had physical therapy, which was no better than naproxen. During the night, they strapped both of her legs to suspend them in the air, pulled tightly by weights of about ten or fifteen pounds on the other ends. This was done to stretch her legs as she slept. But she seldom slept, as it was the most uncomfortable position in which she had ever been, let alone for sleeping, a task that required utmost comfort.

Shirley was also on the herbal medication, which was the only thing that was helping. She also received psychological evaluation during her stay.

The hospitalization did not provide any health benefits, and yet it did not worsen her health, either. It was apparent to everyone that the hospitalization was not improving Shirley's condition any. Dr. Zammit had suggested surgery for Shirley on six of her joints: both ankles, both knees, and both hips, all in a single operation.

"But Shirley's health is not yet stable. She cannot be operated on under such conditions," reasoned Juliet.

"Okay, so Shirley can leave the hospital; it's not helping her," he stated. After only three weeks in the hospital, Shirley was discharged on June 12. When would all this end? Would an answer ever be found? Or would they continue on this search that appeared to take them from one dead end to another?

Seeing that physical therapy was not the answer for Shirley, Juliet decided to take Shirley back to China for the fifth time. Juliet saw that the massages that Shirley received in China had worked well. She planned to stabilize Shirley's condition under the herbs and massage therapies. And if everything seemed stable, Shirley could probably get operated on her legs. It might work. Juliet, therefore, cancelled the lease to the apartment. She would move back with Kwi Show, and buy the ticket for August.

One peaceful day of glorious sunshine, as Juliet had her hands in soapy dish water, the telephone rang. She quickly rinsed the soap from her hands and scrambled over to the telephone. "Hello?"

"It's Dr. Zammit. I just wanted to check how things are with Shirley."

"I'm bringing Shirley back to China to do some massage." She had told him of her plans earlier.

"How about coming again for a checkup before you go? She can also see the eye doctor," he suggested. Juliet thought it was a fine idea and scheduled an appointment. It was scheduled for July 13 at 9:30 in the morning. Juliet checked the calendar, and saw it was on a Friday. She shrugged her shoulders. It was just another of those silly superstitions.

On that Friday morning, Ben rode with them when Juliet drove them off to Newington. Shirley watched the scene outside the windows, but it was hard to keep her photophobic eyes open. Juvenile rheumatoid arthritis could cause so many problems. One would think that the autoimmune disease was more than enough to endure, but the disease itself obviously did not think so.

Juliet carried Shirley into the stroller with the help of Ben. It was certainly nice to receive some help once in a while. Shirley shielded her eyes with the back of her hand. She took a good look at the building. She knew in a little while, they would be away from the hospital. She did not wish to stay in there again.

Dr. Zammit told them to follow him after Juliet checked Shirley in. Both mother and daughter sensed something was amiss as they were led to a room on the first floor. A smile was absent on his face, which was normally all smiles.

He left them alone in the room, which held many officially dressed people whose expressionless faces turned to them. Minutes ticked by, yet none of the people moved or said a word. Their blank eyes burned into them.

The sickening feeling increased in Juliet. For the second time that day, the date flashed into her mind: Friday, July 13, a Friday the 13th. *But that is a silly superstition, right?* she thought again, wanting to dismiss it. But every time her eyes traveled back to the group of unmoving people, her disquietude grew.

The people continued to look at them attentively from their fixed places.

Shirley and her mother exchanged glances that seemed to spell out "What was going on?"

Dr. Zammit reappeared, still unsmiling. "Mrs. Cheng, do you want surgery for Shirley?" Juliet answered him as she had the first time. Taking a look at Juliet with his unsmiling eyes, he walked away, while the crowd, as if on cue in a suspense movie, closed in on them.

"What is going on? What are you doing? Did I lose custody again, just like what happened the first time?" questioned the stunned Juliet. From the looks on their faces, her fear was confirmed. Juliet stood there, disbelieving the situation before her.

Shirley's heart pounded, but her strong eyes did not shed a single tear, nor did they blink.

A lady immediately pushed Shirley away from her mother to an adjoining room. Was Shirley afraid? Yes, but the feeling of anger invaded her being, flooding most of the space, leaving not much room for fright. What could she do? She could not speak English, only understand some. Even if she could speak, they were not here for reasoning. Their ears were not open to logic, nor their hearts to compassion and understanding.

Knowing the situation all too well, Shirley kept calm and composed. She colored in the coloring books the lady, whose position was unknown to her, provided. She knew if she broke down, it would make the situation worse. What the child did would be of importance on how they would judge the parent.

"I can't believe this! I made an appointment to see both Dr. Zammit and the eye doctor, but you just stop us from going back home. We came here freely. If we didn't come here, you wouldn't have come to our home and held Shirley. This is a dishonest action, and it is supported by so many people, not just an action done by one doctor," steamed Juliet. *What a bad example! Dr. Zammit had committed a crime, cheating his patient. Is there any difference between this and the capture of the Jews during World War II?* Her body trembled with shock and fury. How low could they stoop?

Juliet knew she could win this case, just as she was victorious in the first, for she had grounds. She had the reasons, and because of this, she would regain custody—the right to be the parent of her own daughter. What she hated and feared the most was the fact that this involved Shirley. If she were just fighting for herself, she would not worry—it would simply be fighting. What would she lose besides her life, which was so much less important than Shirley's? Now, since her daughter's life was on the line, it was so much more than just fighting; to her, the world was at stake. It was all about winning.

Shirley knew within her soul that her mother would

defeat the battle between good and evil. She confidently looked at her mother as she was pushed away, down the hall and out of sight to the awaiting dungeon.

Chapter Eighteen

Juliet realized that it was a mistake to come to the appointment. She should have listened to the superstition. She was exhausted after talking for three hours with the social workers. She had wasted her breath talking to them. She might as well be conversing with stones from the apathetic reactions she received from them. They would not listen; they were here just doing their duties, separating families unreasonably.

As soon as Juliet got back to the apartment, she made several calls to her family, then to the local newspaper, the *Hartford Courant*. She told a journalist about her situation. After hanging up with the reporter, Juliet dialed the number to a legal aid service.

The next day, a journalist arrived at her apartment and wrote down all the information. After the young journalist left, Juliet drove to the lawyer's office to meet her new lawyer, Virginia. Virginia collected all the necessary documents and information for the case. With nothing else to supply the lawyer, Juliet left and headed to the hospital to see Shirley.

Juliet needed to feed Shirley the herbs daily, but she was allowed to visit Shirley for only ten minutes each day. It was not enough time to feed Shirley food and the herbs. She told the hospital this, but they were unrelenting; they did not even permit fifteen minutes. But at least she had the opportunity to administer the medication and give her cereal, which was the only food that could be eaten quicker than others.

One day, Juliet was giving Shirley Fruity Pebbles, but when it was time to drink down the milk in the bowl, Juliet needed to get a straw so that Shirley could drink the milk to swallow the herbal medicine without getting choked on the remaining cereal.

"No, Juliet, you don't have much time left," said the nurse who was monitoring them both as usual.

"But Shirley could choke on it," explained Juliet. No plea could give her permission to get a straw. Thus, Shirley had to drink the milk without a straw. Instantly, Shirley seriously choked on a piece of the cereal. It was a terrifying moment. Juliet watched helplessly as Shirley gasped for air. At last, her windpipe opened, and she was able to breathe. Juliet was furious at the hospital. They would not even give her an extra minute to get a straw for Shirley that could have prevented the accident from happening.

Shirley was often required to lie on her stomach upon a stretcher. They did not allow Shirley to sit up to take the herbs, so another serious choking incident occurred. The herbs, tiny small balls, were prone to cause choking if not taken in a proper position.

Juliet continued to make calls to seek help. One day, she received a call from a naturopath, Eileen. She had read the case in the newspaper, and had expressed an interest in helping.

"I can give Shirley some herbs, but not at this time when she's in the hospital. I will go there to see Shirley." And as she had said, she visited Shirley the following week.

A few weeks into the hospital stay, the hospital had increased Juliet's ten-minute visitation time limit to two hours.

The landlord of the apartment had found new tenants, so Juliet had to move out and find another place that was close by the hospital. She moved into the Maple Motel that was three minutes away from the hospital.

***

Soon, Dr. Zammit put Shirley on methotrexate, an anti-cancer drug, saying it was beneficial for rheumatoid arthritis. As a result, Shirley quickly experienced extreme difficulty in breathing.

"You must stop the drug," demanded Juliet. "Shirley is having problems breathing!" But he would not cease the administration of the medication. Juliet sought Eileen for help at once.

"I'm subscribed to the *Cancer Control Journal*, and I'm going to read you the drug's side effects. It has a lot of adverse effects, but here are the main ones: upset stomach, nausea, vomiting, loss of appetite, diarrhea, mouth sores, headaches, dizziness, skin rashes, hair loss, coughing, fatigue, shortness of breath, lung damage, liver damage." Eileen paused for a few seconds to scan the journal. Then she continued, "The doctor on here says that sometimes an antidote doesn't work and the patient dies. The article also mentions that it is strong enough to kill the patient as well, along with the cancer."

"The drug's side effects are worse than the cancer itself!" exclaimed Juliet, listening on as Eileen read one horrid description after another.

Outraged, Juliet talked to Dr. Zammit again, and demanded that he stop giving the drug to Shirley. She waved the article in front of his face, while pointing at it. "Look at this!" She showed him the side effects where shortness of breath was mentioned.

"Well, I never knew that," he said. After persistent convincing by Juliet, Dr. Zammit finally gave in.

Shortly afterward, Juliet heard more terrifying news from the lips of Dr. Zammit. "We will do a general anesthesia test on Shirley,"

"Why? You are not performing the surgery for Shirley, so why does Shirley need the anesthesia test?" asked Juliet in bewilderment.

"We want to see how far her legs can be straightened. The physical therapist asked to do this."

"No," Juliet was defiant. But Dr. Zammit would not listen.

After she arrived home, she called up her lawyer. She

had an idea that might just work.

"I would like you to help me do something. I would like you to come to the hospital to see Dr. Zammit. Please come to the hospital at one o'clock tomorrow. You tell him that Senator Dodd's office called you," Juliet told Virginia. "I can't have Shirley go through the unnecessary test." Dr. Zammit wanted to speak to Juliet that time, so she had asked for her lawyer to come then. It would be a nice scene. She inwardly smiled; he would not be braced for tomorrow.

Accordingly, right on time the next day, the lawyer went to the hospital to see Dr. Zammit. Juliet had arrived a few minutes earlier before her. A moment later, Dr. Zammit came into Shirley's room, where the two were waiting.

"I am from Connecticut legal aid service and Senator Dodd's office called me," the lawyer said to Dr. Zammit, as directed by Juliet.

"Oh," came from Dr. Zammit's lips.

Playing along, Juliet put a worried look upon her face. "Oh, she called me," said Juliet frantically, pointing at Virginia, "I don't know her! I don't want trouble! Why did she call me?" Juliet went on, pretending she did not know her own lawyer.

"Juliet said that you wanted to do the general anesthesia test on Shirley," continued Virginia.

"Yes," stated the doctor.

"You can't do it."

"We have to."

"Then if you want, go ahead. Have it your way..." The lawyer shrugged her shoulders nonchalantly. But by now, Dr. Zammit became less persistent. His eyes reflected doubt and hesitation. Juliet could see that he was falling for her trick.

"Okay, we won't do the test." He stated in the end. The parties split, with triumph in Juliet's heart. At least, she had successfully protected Shirley from this ordeal.

Within a two-week period after the nightmare had begun, Juliet attended the court session. Her lawyer was there, along with the social worker from the Department of Children and Youth Services. The intense moment would put much strain on any heart, making one cringe and run away. But Juliet stood tall and strong; her lips absent of any trace of a tremor.

Dr. Zammit went to the witness stand. "Shirley needs to have the surgery; it is best for her," he said. "The sooner she gets the surgery, the better it will be." There was no guarantee that Shirley would not be adversely affected by the operation. The surgery was not emergent, Juliet knew. It was not a life-threatening situation where Shirley had to have the surgery in order to live. The surgery could be done at a later time when she would be able to withstand both the surgery itself and the recovery that would follow. It was not just the surgery that she would have to endure; she would have to go through extensive rehabilitation and therapy afterward. Above all, how could Shirley have the surgery when the doctor did not even have any medicine to effectively control her current inflammation, not to mention the inevitable inflammation and complications that would follow the operation? This was not simply a life or death situation, Juliet knew; this was a paralyze or death situation, the latter would be easiest on Shirley. She knew that without effective medicine to control Shirley's inflammation before and after the surgery, she would end up kissing her star goodbye or worse. So receiving the surgery at that time was unquestionably the worst option for her, not the best, as the doctor had claimed.

After Dr. Zammit finished stating his reasons, someone from the door announced Dr. Sheridan's arrival to speak for Juliet. Dr. Sheridan was the homeopathic physician Eileen found for Juliet to be on her side. Juliet was extremely grateful to her; without Eileen, she would not have even known where to begin searching for the right doctor to help her in her case.

"No more witnesses," ordered the judge, not permitting Dr. Sheridan to come in.

Then the judge ordered immediate surgery for Shirley. "If the child dies as a result of the surgery, you cannot sue the doctor," she said, looking straight into Juliet's eyes, "you can sue me."

"Your Honor, may I speak for myself?" inquired Juliet after she saw that it was getting hopeless. No one was speaking for her; her lawyer was not helping any, either.

"You are not allowed. Juliet Cheng," boomed the judge, "you are a seven-year child abuser!"

When Juliet got out of the Hartford Juvenile Court, she spotted Dr. Sheridan, who was waiting for her. "I'm still here to help you," he assured her.

***

"The surgery will be next Tuesday," Dr. Zammit announced to Juliet a few days after the court session.

Her heart pounded wildly, but she did not show her panic. Her mind raced, thinking of another of her witty plans.

She immediately called up Dr. Simmonds. It had been a long time, she knew, but she hoped that the caring doctor might be able to lend a helping hand in this time of need. Was he still there? She fervently prayed that he would pick up the telephone. She glanced at the clock. It was late afternoon. "Please let him be there," Juliet whispered, her fingers quickly punching in the numbers. A woman answered the telephone. "May I speak to Dr. Simmonds?" asked Juliet. She was put on hold. Soon, the voice that she was hoping to hear spoke into the receiver. Without losing a single second, Juliet began her tale.

"What is the name of this doctor?" asked Dr. Simmonds after Juliet had explained the whole story to him.

"Dr. Zammit."

"I know him. Well, you have the right to a second opinion. I know a pediatric rheumatologist in Philadelphia." Juliet was immensely grateful for his recommendation. "I will contact Dr. Zammit." Feeling much better after the conversation, Juliet finally could relax some.

Soon, she received a call from the Department of Children and Youth Services, telling her the appointment date with the pediatric rheumatologist in Philadelphia. It was scheduled in the noontime on August 30, a month later. Upon hearing this, Juliet was instantly relieved. She was so thankful for Dr. Simmonds' help. If without him, the surgery would go underway right away and Juliet would have no way of stopping it. Now, they had another month. She felt that whenever it seemed as though they had arrived at a dead end, a savior would come their way.

There would be a whole month without many bad things happening to Shirley. Shirley was already suffering enough in the hospital. She had blood tests done every week, usually on Tuesdays. But Shirley did not inform her mother of this, for fear of causing her worry over something about which she could do nothing.

By now, Juliet was allowed to visit Shirley for a whole day, but must leave before eight at night. She usually cooked some food at the apartment and brought it to the hospital. Each time, Juliet worked hard to get food into Shirley's mouth. But she was not allowed to feed Shirley, being accused of force-feeding, and the hospital monitored them whenever they got the chance. Whenever a nurse came in as Juliet was feeding Shirley, the nurse would immediately move her eyes to Shirley's mouth to see if Juliet was feeding her. When that happened, Shirley would stop moving her mouth or quickly swallow the food.

Juliet also bathed Shirley. When the hospital gave Shirley baths, she often caught colds, for they gave her only a few inches of water with mostly bubbles in the tub; the not-so-warm water quickly got cold. All in all, the days passed uncomfortably for Shirley. Her most pleasant moments were when Juliet visited her, often with a present. She had also given Shirley a few photographs of themselves, and Shirley held on to them when sleeping. Indeed, it was a sad time for the little girl. She had to bear the weight of those harsh times when she was so young. But Shirley kept on smiling, and found little delights whenever she could regardless. The wall above her bed began to be crowded by her drawings. Amongst them was a picture of a dinosaur she had drawn. Juliet was surprised that she could draw so well and accurately, with quite a clarity.

Shirley never cried once in the hospital, not even when she was in pain. She enjoyed wheeling around the hospital, going past each room. She often sought other children to play with. But there was one particular girl who did not want to be with her. Shirley was quite puzzled at that, for Shirley had always been nice to her. But one day, when Shirley was dressed in a pretty dress that she had received as a present, the girl walked to her side and exclaimed with much astonishment, "You're a girl!" So that was it! The girl had thought Shirley was a boy, for her hair was short and she never wore dresses during hospitalization. Ever since that day, the girl gladly became her friend.

Besides roaming around and playing with others, Shirley received regular physical therapies at the swimming pool. Shirley liked the lady who was her regular therapist, for she was really nice to her. Shirley was able to walk while in the water. She often enjoyed the feeling of walking in the pool. But as Shirley was playing in the pool one day, her foot slipped and she went under. Reacting quickly, the therapist pulled her out of the surface. Shirley was gasping; it was such a close call. If she had been alone, she could have drowned. She became more careful while staying in the pool so not as to let the same thing happen again.

When Juliet came to visit Shirley, she often found Shirley waiting by the large door that separated one wing from another. But sometimes, the nurses closed the door when Shirley was waiting there. Thus, she could not have the view to the elevator, where her mother would appear. Often, when Juliet came, she brought a surprise or two for Shirley. One time, she bought a stuffed animal.

"Oh, a white dove!" exclaimed Shirley happily. She

looked at the tag and learned that the name of it was Lovydovy. From then on, she had brought it wherever she went. On the few occasions when she did not bring it, people would ask where her Lovydovy was. One person had called it a duck. Shirley inwardly giggled at that.

Once, Juliet had bought Shirley two dozen balloons. When Dr. Zammit saw all the balloons, he bought Shirley one.

Sometimes, while visiting Shirley, Juliet had chances to talk to Dr. Zammit. "Why didn't you take away the custody the first time?" Juliet asked him, raising her brows.

"Well, I saw that your life was too hard then, so I didn't," he answered. "If Shirley gets the surgery today, you can bring her home tomorrow and you can go to China next week."

"Since you say that surgery is so good, what happened to those kids? Why don't you perform surgeries on all those kids upstairs? They are all like statues!" She had been upstairs and had seen many patients, whose every limb was immobile. They seemed to be blind as well, for their eyes never moved when Juliet walked to their side. Her heart went out to all of them. They had to suffer so much. Shirley was in a much better condition compared to them. She was able to sit and move her limbs.

Dr. Zammit never replied to that question. He had plausibly performed heaven knew how many surgeries on them! It was apparent that none of the treatments ever worked for them.

On another occasion, Dr. Zammit had brought a magazine for Juliet to see. "Look, can you see that surgery can be successful and that the patient can walk as a result?" he asked, pointing at a pair of photographs; one showed a disabled body, and the second showed a body that was walking.

"Where are the heads? How do I know they are the same person?" demanded Juliet. Dr. Zammit never had an answer to that question, either.

Chapter Nineteen

She was running toward a glistening stream with fish of all colors flying out of the water. With laughter escaping her lips, she chased a white butterfly amidst the green field of wildflowers. Her black hair glowed with a halo of brightness, with sunrays dancing about her. The blue sky was accentuated by a shimmering rainbow, which was surrounded by white, puffy clouds. Her mother watched her little girl, dressed in white silk, skipping before her. But her joy quickly turned into worry, for the girl was running farther and farther away toward the other side of the field until her little figure was no longer discernible.

"Shirley!" yelled her mother. The girl was disappearing from her sight. "Shirley!"

"What?" The groggy voice came from Shirley's lips. Her sleepy eyelids slowly fluttered open.

"Wake up, Shirley." A fuzzy image of a nurse came into Shirley's view, towering over her by the bed. The nurse went to the closet and picked out a pair of blue overalls. Shirley was enjoying the dream, but she was snatched back to reality. It was the day of the appointment, but it would not be for another hour till it would be time to go. She was awakened up just to dress? The nurse put the much too small overalls on her, practically stuffing her in like stuffing cotton in a small sack. Shirley could hardly sit up when she had the overalls on her. It was too tight. She felt cold and sleepy.

Before leaving her room, the nurse carried Shirley into her stroller. As Shirley thought of the appointment, Juliet walked in.

"Oh, why did they wake you up so early? It's only 5:15, and we won't need to leave till six o'clock!" Juliet touched Shirley's hands. "Dear, you are cold! Why did they give you such small clothes to wear?" Juliet went to the closet and picked something else.

"No, you can't change her clothes," ordered the nurse when she walked back in.

"I know what I'm doing; I'm her mother. We need to change them!" Without paying any attention to the protesting nurse, Juliet changed Shirley into a comfortable outfit. Shirley was feeling much better after the change, having more breathing space and feeling warmer. The nurse walked away, leaving the two alone in the room. The only thing left to do was to wait for the social worker from DCYS; they were to go together.

***

Mother and daughter boarded the plane, escorted by two social workers. Juliet had brought with them a few of Shirley's necessities. Soon, they would arrive in Philadelphia.

Shirley watched the scene from her window, while the two social workers talked with each other. Juliet meditated in her seat, hoping that the doctor they were going to see would help her.

They had transportation waiting for them as soon as they got off the plane about an hour later. Juliet had carried Shirley on and off the plane, then into the car. They drove toward the hospital, Children's Seashore House (Children's Hospital of Philadelphia).

"I can't make the decision. The orthopedic surgeon needs to be here, so we can decide. You have to come here next time, and the orthopedic surgeon will be here," said Dr. Athorn after examining Shirley. Juliet felt comforted; at least he did not recommend surgery. The time was vital. Juliet must win as much time as she could.

***

"I know a lawyer who can help you." A man called

Juliet one day to supply the information. "He was a former mayor of Hartford." After writing down the contact information, Juliet called the lawyer up. She got all the directions to his office.

That afternoon, she set out to meet her new lawyer George Athanson, who was the former mayor for eleven "and a half years," as he had insisted. Juliet felt hope surging in through her. She knew that this case could be won only by name and power, not by intelligence. Virginia had told her to find another lawyer, for she could not help her.

"I'm Romeo!" was the jocose greeting that came from George, as they met for the first time. They exchanged warm handshakes.

"Nice to meet you," said Juliet. She followed him into his office. It was cluttered with piles of papers. She gingerly made her way to a chair across his desk, which was nearly hidden under more piles.

"You are very busy," commented Juliet, her eyes taking in all the files, folders, and paper.

He nodded. "Yes, and I don't get much help and money, either. I need money, money, money!"

Very patiently, he listened as Juliet narrated the story. The conversation was filled with jokes mingled with serious talk.

"Why do you cut your hair so short?" he asked, raising a brow.

"It's easy to manage," answered Juliet with a laugh, absent-mindedly raking a hand through her black hair.

She handed him all the documents, but George had already saved all the newspaper clippings on her case. He handed her several business cards. "Tell them, 'This is my lawyer.'" He winked. Juliet accepted them graciously.

"I will pay you." After all was said, and several jokes told, they parted with another handshake. Feeling quite good inside, she got into her car. She knew for certain that she could win the case, and save Shirley from their grasp.

On the second day, Juliet gave George's business

cards to the social workers, the doctor, and anyone else who was involved in the case. They read the name on the card with surprise and respect. She could see the immediate change they had with her now.

A week later, Juliet was scheduled for another court session in the Hartford Juvenile Court. Before that day, George had told her that he met the judge the other day, and told the judge he had just accepted a new case that she was also involved in.

"Oh? Then which case is it?" the judge had asked.

"Cheng." Upon hearing this, the judge was startled and astonished. "How about a little help?" suggested George.

"No, absolutely not! Not with *this* one."

The day of the court session swiftly arrived, with Juliet bringing her new lawyer with her. All eyes turned in their direction, and they were surprised at the sight of Juliet with the former mayor.

"I have received the report from Dr. Athorn from Philadelphia. He recommended immediate surgery for Shirley," announced the judge. Juliet was immensely dismayed, but was not taken aback. She knew it was going to be this way. But still, she was not without hope.

The audience filed out of the court, including Eileen, who had taken her time to attend the session. She felt sorry that Juliet had to go through all this, and was disheartened by what the judge said.

"Shirley will have the surgery on Tuesday," Dr. Zammit told Juliet afterward.

It felt like deja vu. It was Friday, so she had to work fast. Frantically, she called George at his office at five. They scheduled to meet in a restaurant later that evening. At eight, he, with one of his assistants, met Juliet at a table.

"You must do something to stop the surgery!" Juliet threw a check on the table in front of him.

"I'll try my best."

On Sunday, George called ten judges, but some were unavailable at the time.

Juliet anxiously waited at home. She could not let herself come to the realization that the surgery would be in only two days.

Chapter Twenty

What would happen tomorrow? It seemed that they had finally come to an impasse. Would they have a way out of it? The boat was filling with water, and sinking fast. If only they could have a way to patch up the large hole.

Shirley spent the day trying not to think about the next day. But no matter how hard she tried, her thoughts would always return to the surgery. She watched the clock tick on and on. Wheeling around the hospital, she passed a nurse. "I will have surgery tomorrow?" she managed to ask. She was picking up some English quickly, and was able to converse in English with extremely easy words.

"No, I don't think so," answered the nurse, and went away. Shirley hoped what the nurse said was true. Oh, how she had hoped with all her might!

"There must be a way, there must," Juliet was saying to herself at the motel. She would pay the lawyer everything she had, but all knew it would be fruitless. With her heart aching, she went to the hospital to visit Shirley. Her face reflecting no worries, she came to see her beloved daughter, the one person who was so dear to her heart and soul. Shirley was the sunshine in her life. Shirley must live! She must be well!

"There will be surgery tomorrow, right?" asked Shirley, her eyes wide.

"No, there won't. We're trying." Juliet hoped she could keep her promise. She asked a nurse about the surgery when it was approaching six in the evening.

"I don't know anything about it," came the cursory answer from the nurse.

After hugging Shirley for a long time, not bearing to part, Juliet left with a heavy heart. She would go home and think some more. But before returning home, she drove to her lawyer's office. She had been calling him numerous times, but he would not answer the telephone.

"You must stop the surgery, you have to," pleaded Juliet once she got inside, towering over his desk.

"I just can't. I tried!" he barked.

Without waiting to hear what else he had to say, she drew more money out of her pocket.

"Here." She put down one thousand dollars. "Stop the surgery."

Wordlessly, he buried his head in his hands. He could not stop the surgery even with all the money in the world. He was frustrated by it all. They needed to wait for a miracle to happen. Juliet was drained. She knew that George was, too. He had been working on her case exclusively, putting all other cases aside. He and his assistants often stayed up in the office late at night, putting their heads together to get Shirley out of the confines.

While the two were in the office, Shirley was on her hospital bed pondering about the surgery. It was the second time that she had heard of the surgery being on a Tuesday. She had prepared for the surgery last time, but to her unspeakable relief, it did not happen. She wondered if her luck would still be with her this time. The hour hand on the clock moved rapidly, making its way toward the ninth mark that evening. Shirley tried to go to sleep, but wanted to savor the moment. It might be her last night. She wanted the time to last long before tomorrow would arrive with its deadly deed. Dwelling upon the frightful event would not do her any good. She closed her eyes and thought of happy things as she drifted off to sleep, hugging the photographs and Lovydovy close to her heart.

Disheartened, Juliet left George's office and went home. Seeing that nothing was moving in the direction of victory for her, she sadly accepted the horrid fact. She had to know what time in the morning that they would perform the surgery for Shirley—the time they would plunge the chisel inside. She dialed up the number where she would be connected with Dr. Zammit, the man who had awfully wronged them. She left a message on the answering machine. She was fully prepared for the surgery. She sat by the telephone in full concentration. It was the biggest nightmare she had ever lived through.

Her heart gave a start when the telephone shrieked in the empty room. Dr. Zammit was on the other line.

"What time's the surgery?"

"There's no surgery," Dr. Zammit replied.

"No surgery?" Juliet repeated. Did she hear him correctly?

"Your lawyer cancelled the surgery. Didn't he tell you?"

"No." Juliet's soul lifted high until it touched the clouds. Her spirit was filled to the brink with exquisite elation, yet she did not let her voice show it. A mountain of fears and doubts had been taken off her shoulders. After hanging up, she called George. "The surgery is cancelled!" she happily announced into the mouthpiece. She could not stop laughing. It was the happiest moment of her life after a terrifying ordeal. They had escaped from a part of the nightmare. But she knew the nightmare had not ended, and it would be a while till it would. They still had a long, rugged road ahead of them.

"The surgery, *cancelled*? That's great!" He was taken by surprise. At least one of the judges he had called must have helped. They were so thankful for the decision. Shirley was saved once again! Juliet wished she could tell Shirley the wonderful news, so she could sleep in peace, but it was too late. With a triumphant and contented sigh escaping her smiling lips, she lay down on the bed. The past few days were a frightful experience that she would never forget. One man could bring forth such misery upon the whole family! But Juliet still did not have any hatred toward him. She only felt sorry for him. He could have chosen to do so much good for his patients, but had blindly chosen this path instead.

It had been some time since she had a good night's

rest. Tonight, she knew, would be a fine one. She shut her eyes, her muscles relaxing. The September wind blew gently outside her windows. Trees whistled a tune of triumph and rejoicing. The caliginous sky held millions of twinkling eyes that winked to one another, knowing it was He who had helped.

Chapter Twenty-One

Early the next morning, Shirley was immensely delighted when she heard about the cancellation of the surgery. Her hope had helped. She looked in the mirror and smiled at her reflection. Yes, she was still here, alive and well.

But how much longer could they keep this up? The surgery had been blocked twice, as well as a full-body anesthesia test. Juliet must win the custody case in order to save her pearl from a fate worse than death. There was no if's.

***

"I will bring the case to the federal court," stated George while Juliet was on one of her routine visits to his office. They needed to bring the case up to a higher level. It was not going anywhere at the Hartford Juvenile Court.

George leaned against his chair and shook his head. His eyes flashed with admiration when he commented on her invincible spirit. "You are just like Mao Zedong and Zhou Enlai. If you could, you would have fought with them for justice."

Once informed of the case, the federal court—the supreme court in Connecticut—asked for the court transcript from the juvenile court judge, but only received a rejection from the judge.

At the same time, a reporter from *The New York Times* called Juliet, asking if she could go to the hospital to take a few photographs of them. "It would be impossible for you to come to the hospital since you're from the newspaper," said Juliet. "But since you have the dog, you can bring it when you come to see Shirley. Just tell them you're bringing the dog for Shirley to see, and they would not expect that you are from the newspaper."

Early on the morning before meeting the reporter at the hospital, Juliet went to Eileen's home for her daily dose of energy treatment. Ever since she met her, Juliet had been going every morning, where Eileen would make her fresh carrot and beet juices and give her several kinds of herbal medicines. After taking them, Juliet felt almost instant relief and energy, and she would lose several pounds, as they acted like diuretics. For many years, she had not been able to take any diuretics. Without going for the treatment, she would not have had enough strength to continue fighting for Shirley's life, appearing in courts and meeting her lawyer. Before stepping inside Eileen's home every morning, she would be bloated and weak; then she would step out a changed person. This particular morning, she went especially early, at five. Looking ill in the newspaper photograph would not help her case, she knew. Thus, she was immensely grateful to Eileen for helping her case in so many ways.

The reporter arrived at the hospital dressed casually in a T-shirt, with her dog. As Juliet had predicted, she was able to visit Shirley in her room without raising any suspicion. Once inside, the reporter took out her camera and snapped shots of Juliet and Shirley. When she was done, she quickly left with a whole roll of shots.

"What's going on? What is this?" demanded a hospital staff member, showing an article to Juliet a couple of days later. It was the article and their photograph in *The New York Times* entitled *Can Choosing Form of Care Become Neglect?* by James Feron. Around then, an article of the case also appeared on the *Newsweek* magazine entitled *Does Doctor Know Best? Overriding the Family* by Geoffrey Cowley with Lauren Picker.

"Go ask *yourself* what's going on!" Juliet fired back. Ever since that day, Shirley was not allowed to have any visitors to the hospital, except family members.

Meanwhile, upon reviewing the court documents

(after a long while, the judge from the juvenile court finally relented and sent the transcript over), the supreme court decided to take up the case, which had not been fairly administered. The judge from the juvenile court had not allowed Dr. Sheridan, who was representing Juliet, to speak for her. It was only a one-sided trial of the hospital. It was an unjust case. Juliet knew that the juvenile court judge had made a big mistake in not letting Dr. Sheridan into the courtroom. The mistake became Juliet's victory, she knew from deep inside.

The supreme court then appointed a legal guardian for Shirley. Juliet won a reprieve when the supreme court judge ordered Juliet and DCYS to have an agreement: In a two-month period, Juliet was to find a doctor to treat Shirley, following the treatment of her choice; the doctor must be a licensed medical practitioner (M.D.), and the medical facility at which Shirley received treatment could be at any northeastern location, including Newington Children's Hospital. At the same time, Shirley's legal guardian should find two doctors: one an orthopedic surgeon, the other a pediatric rheumatologist. These three doctors in turn would determine whether Shirley needed the surgery. If two doctors stated that Shirley did not need surgery, there would not be any surgery for her. Otherwise, if two decided upon surgery, there would be one. After the two-month period, the court would arrive at a decision on the statements made by the three doctors. The term would end on December 10, 1990.

Juliet decided to have Shirley remain in the hospital to receive the treatment from Dr. Sheridan.

Therefore, Dr. Sheridan promptly put Shirley on his homeopathic medication, and all the other medications she was taking, including naproxen, the herb, and all laxatives, were dropped. The laxatives, glycerin suppositories and fiber tablets, had been administered to Shirley numerous times by the hospital because of her chronic constipation, but they had never been successful in relieving the condition, and instead had made her extremely uncomfortable. She normally ate small amounts of food, so each time after receiving the glycerin suppositories, the only thing that could come out was the suppository.

Dr. Zammit and the nurses said that Shirley's condition appeared to be worse. But Shirley was not well from the beginning, and it was too soon to judge the medication's effectiveness. Dr. Sheridan also let Shirley receive treatment from Regional physical Therapy in Hartford, so Juliet brought Shirley there three times a week.

Juliet continued to come to the hospital to bathe Shirley daily. Before, she was not allowed, but now the hospital had actually begun to depend upon Juliet for the bathing needs. Once, Juliet was too tired to bathe Shirley, for she had been traveling all day going to the lawyer's office and the court.

"No, you have to," ordered the nurse. Thus, Juliet had to bathe Shirley. Even though she was permitted to give Shirley baths, she was still not allowed to feed Shirley.

One evening, Shirley was running a fever, and wanted some ice cream. Juliet knew it was nearly time for her to leave, for the clock was ticking toward the eighth mark. She went to the hospital's freezer and brought over some ice cream. But Shirley needed help to eat it.

"Juliet, you have to leave. It's eight already," said a nurse, standing by the door.

"Wait, give me a minute, I have only half of this ice cream left to feed Shirley. Just give me another minute and I'll be done," said Juliet, holding out the half-empty four-ounce container of ice cream.

"No, you have to leave now. I will call the security man if you don't."

"Okay, you go ahead, go and call the security man." Juliet would not budge, and stood there vehemently, spooning the ice cream into Shirley's mouth. Shirley was quite frantic by now.

"Mom, you have to leave. The police will come." Juliet shook her head obstinately. She needed to tend to her own child. She would leave as soon as she finished feeding. There were only a few more spoonfuls to go.

Shortly, Shirley finished the ice cream. Meanwhile, the security man from the hospital, who, in fact, had been showing compassion for the two, had told Juliet to follow him downstairs. The nurse had just then threatened to call the police. Grateful for his offer, Juliet stayed behind him as they went down to the lobby. He escorted her to her car. Juliet hurriedly started the engine as police cars parked in front of the hospital. Breathing a sigh of relief, she drove away from the hospital grounds, safe and sound. All this had happened during a few minutes; the hospital clocks pointed to six minutes after eight.

***

One day, George received a call from CBS, asking if he and Juliet would go to their studio to be aired on *This Morning* show with host Paula Zahn, to which both consented. George and Juliet were picked up and drove to a large prodigious Hotel in New York City.

The next morning at eight, they were aired on the show. Paula started the five-minute live interview by asking, "Hi, Juliet, why do you not agree to have your daughter Shirley receive the surgery?"

"Because," started Juliet, "with rheumatoid arthritis, the inflammation is inside of the joints; the surgery will only fix the outside of the joints. If you don't have the powerful medication to control the inflammation inside, a successful surgery would still fail. The joints will go back to their original state, and would be even worse."

***

"CBS just called and said that one hundred doctors had called them, telling them that Juliet had well explained the reason for not wanting the surgery. And they wanted to help Juliet in the case," a paralegal of George, had reported after they returned from the city. "They had never received so many calls after any show." The secretary of Taiwan's former first lady Soong May-ling was one of the callers who had expressed an interest in helping Juliet. Apart from the calls received at the television studio, Juliet had been receiving calls from various places and well-known people. Connie Chung left a message for her at her motel when she was out one time.

"Katharine Hepburn had written to me," Dr. Sheridan had told Juliet, "and she wishes to help you." But Juliet never saw the letter and did not know how the actress would like to help her. Her case had been broadcast internationally, reaching China, Hong Kong, Canada, along with other countries. Once, Juliet had declined the invitation to New Jersey by NBC, for she had no time to go.

Meanwhile, under the treatment of Dr. Sheridan, the hospital still had blood tests done for Shirley weekly, as well as performing numerous x-rays on her. They knew that Shirley was staying there to receive treatment from Dr. Sheridan, and that they were not allowed to treat Shirley. Therefore, they were violating the agreement by doing blood tests and taking x-rays. Above all, drawing blood weekly was unnecessary.

One day, the nurse drew Shirley's blood without any success. After sticking the needle in Shirley's bony arm, not a single drop of blood could be drawn out. Taking the needle out, the nurse stuck it in again in a different spot, but with the same result. With a last try, the needle was stuck in a third spot. This time, only a tiny amount of blood was collected. Soon after, when the nurse left with Shirley's last drop of blood, dark blue spots began to appear on the arm, quickly spreading throughout her body. Shirley was frightened when she saw this happening.

When Juliet visited Shirley that day, Shirley was hiding herself under blankets and clothes.

"What's wrong?" inquired the concerned Juliet. Ever

so slowly, Shirley took out her arm. "This is horrible!" Juliet was puzzled. *What could have caused this?*

"They have blood tests done on me every week. And today, the nurse couldn't get any blood out of me. Then this happened to me," explained Shirley in a low voice. Juliet was stunned. She had never imagined that this could have ever happened to Shirley. Why were they drawing so much blood from her so frequently? Were they vampires?

"Why didn't you tell me this earlier?"

"I'm scared. You can't help." Arguing with the hospital, they both knew, was useless. But Juliet silently vowed to herself that she would stop them from doing blood tests on Shirley whenever she could get the chance. No one had ever communicated to her regarding any tests, so she had to catch them red-handed. But whenever Juliet was with Shirley, no one would order any test or x-ray. Therefore, Juliet usually did not see them doing this until she had caught them in the act.

"No, you can't give blood tests for Shirley," demanded Juliet when Dr. Zammit called her one day after she had refused to let them draw blood from Shirley.

"But we have to do the blood tests for the doctors to see. They are coming…" he explained.

"No," she insisted.

"Okay, so we won't do it." Dr. Zammit gave in. "But we need to do an x-ray."

Juliet sighed, "Okay, go ahead." Therefore, an x-ray was done on Shirley's whole body.

Not only had Dr. Zammit ordered blood tests and x-rays for Shirley without Juliet's knowledge, but also had the hospital perform a tuberculin skin test on Shirley. The appalled Juliet steamed when she found out and told Dr. Sheridan, who expressed great dismay. But fortunately, Shirley's health did not worsen after the test.

Mother and daughter, hand in hand, still continued on their rough road, with each helping the other. Their strong bond of love had kept them going, never giving up for a minute. They were like a pair of binary stars, ever revolving around each other, and always emitting warmth. They would continue to strive to defeat the injustice. Justice shall always prevail in the battle against evil in the end. Inequity may use force and have weapons, but good has reasons and the powers of virtue.

***

"Why have you been scratching your elbows?" inquired Juliet after noticing that Shirley had been scratching her elbows and knees for a couple of days.

"I'm itchy," said Shirley, in a low voice. Juliet carefully examined Shirley's body and found bilaterally symmetrical rashes on both of her elbows and knees. If the rash appeared on her inner right arm, her inner left arm would bear the same rash.

"What could be the cause of this?" Juliet was growing quite concerned. The skin felt rough and scaly where the rashes were. Some rashes looked like burn-marks while the newer ones were small red bumps. She was perplexed.

The hospital applied some cream on the brownish rashes, but it did not help in curing the condition, only lessening the itchiness somewhat.

"You will have to go soon," noted Shirley, gazing at the clock. "It's almost nine." The hospital had extended Juliet's visitation time by an hour.

Juliet nodded and sighed. "Yes, it is time."

"Mom, I love you! I'll see you tomorrow."

"I love you, too, dear." Juliet gave a lingering wave. Then she went out the door.

Chapter Twenty-Two

On December 8, Dr. Thomas J. A. Lehman—a pediatric rheumatologist from the Hospital for Special Surgery in New York City and a professor of Clinical Pediatrics of Weill Medical College of Cornell University—came to check Shirley. He was one of the doctors the legal guardian had found.

"Would you like me to talk to you first or your mother first?" Dr. Lehman asked Shirley.

"My mom first," answered Shirley, smiling at the doctor, whose aura shone with nobility. His kind countenance tightly wrapped Shirley and Juliet in comfort.

Juliet followed Dr. Lehman out of the room and into the next, which was vacant.

"Why don't you want to do the surgery?" inquired Dr. Lehman.

"Because the doctor had told me that without surgery, Shirley would never be able to walk. But when Shirley was four and a half years old, she was able to walk for a year without surgery in China." Juliet took out the photographs, which depicted the event, and showed them to him.

"How beautiful that Shirley was able to walk!" he exclaimed, looking over each photograph.

"The medications that the doctors gave are not effective for the arthritis; they could not control the inflammation," Juliet continued, "They can't even control the inflammation, so how could they do the surgery? Surgery is just fixing the outside. We need to fix the inside while fixing the outside; not just fix the outside."

After the questioning and explaining were completed, Dr. Lehman examined Shirley.

Following Dr. Lehman, an orthopedic surgeon, Dr. Goldstein from the Boston New England Medical Center, was the next to examine Shirley on the tenth of the month. After completing, he left without directing a single question toward Juliet.

***

"Juliet, the reports are in," George told Juliet over the telephone four days later. The judgment day had at last arrived. Shirley's legal guardian had received all the doctors' reports, which held the key to either total destruction or the happiness that could be elicited only by the Garden of Eden.

Juliet headed toward George's office to wait for the sentence. Once there, she managed to pass all the reporters who were crowding outside the lawyer's office. She stepped into the tiny office, where George and two of his assistants, who were lawyers themselves, were found. Their faces exhibited high alertness. They each had the same thought: whether Juliet had won the case. Would Shirley be in Juliet's arms once again, or would she forever be out of the reach of her loving mother? They would exert so much force to break the steel bond of the inseparable pair.

Suddenly, the door to the office opened, and in walked a very tired legal guardian. "Gosh!" he exclaimed, shaking his head. He had a hard time getting away from the mob outside. The reporters nearly ran him down. He looked at the four people before him. They searched for an answer in his eyes, but could not read anything from them. They held their breath.

"Well," he said, clearing his throat to add to the suspense, "would you want to know the whole story or the bottom line?"

"The bottom line!" all cried in unison.

The legal guardian walked toward Juliet, put out his hand, and patted her right shoulder. "You won, you won, Juliet."

Juliet nodded, her lips spreading into the widest smile her face had ever owned. Was she surprised? No. She always had faith that she would win. Her confidence had grown more so during the past two months of the trial. She had been praying, seeking support and guidance from the Almighty One. Yes, He had answered her prayers.

"But even if you did not win the case," the legal guardian continued, "no surgeon from any of the hospitals throughout Hartford, including this one, is willing to do the surgery for Shirley." The internationally reported case had become the talk of everyone. The hospitals would not dare perform the surgery on Shirley even if Juliet lost the case. Juliet had many supporters, and it would have caused much trouble if they laid a single hand on Shirley when it was so strongly disagreed with.

One of the assistants, Steve, who always doubted her strong confidence of winning, went over to Juliet. "I believe you now," he said, shaking his head. Indeed, miracles do happen.

Juliet gave George a hug and a peck on the cheek.

"Hey, what about me?" asked Steve. Juliet gave him a hug and a peck, too.

Although the room was small, its happiness was radiating larger than the whole world. The celebration was not a loud one, but the expression on each face was more than any boisterous rejoicing could ever replace.

"So, do you have a back door?" inquired the legal guardian after handing George the three reports. Chuckling, George led him to the back door, where he could leave peacefully without getting trampled on by the reporters.

It was getting late, and Juliet was physically exhausted, yet her spirit had the energy she never before possessed; her soul floated on Cloud Nine. She could be with Shirley again! It had been five, long months. She had won the case, but only with His support, just as with the first. Before leaving the office, Juliet received copies of the reports from her lawyer. Closing the door, she thanked him once more.

The lobby was filled with reporters, each snapping

shots around the place, while others held out microphones, hoping to catch something nice to air.

Into one microphone, Juliet simply said, "It's God's will."

Without waiting another minute, Juliet went straight to the hospital to give Shirley the grand news. On the road, she could not help but smile uncontrollably in her car. After she parked in front of the hospital building, she nearly jumped out of her car.

She flew into Shirley's room. "We won!" She did not need to say anything else, for those two words were clear in meaning.

Shirley was speechless from the elation. She joined her mother on Cloud Nine. The pair shared a huge embrace.

Suddenly, Shirley vomited on her pillow; she had vomited a large amount of blood. A nurse entered her room that moment and gasped loudly when she saw the blood.

Shirley was getting remarkably ill as days passed. They had been giving naproxen to Shirley on an empty stomach. They usually gave her only one spoonful of baby sauce with crushed medication. When Shirley asked for more baby sauce, they refused nearly every time. And thus, the burning sensation of the medication remained in her mouth, throat, and down to her stomach. At such times like this, she collected saliva in her mouth to wash it down.

Very soon, her stomach was bleeding, and vomiting began. Whenever Juliet had asked if Shirley had some food with the medication, they would only answer, "She had some JELL-O." Juliet had spoken to Dr. Zammit concerning the matter, and he had replied that he would speak to the nurses about it. And that was that.

Even though intense happiness filled Shirley, her illness would not permit her to celebrate it with much enthusiasm.

"You can bring her home now," a nurse informed Juliet from the doorway. The joyous news came as a surprise to Juliet. She did not expect that she could bring Shirley home so soon. It was already dark outside, but Shirley was excited at the thought of leaving the horrid place, even if it was midnight.

As Juliet was about to prepare for the return, Dr. Zammit walked in, a camera held in his hands. Shirley looked at him quizzically. A camera?

But before she could ascertain why he had brought it, the nurse turned to him and pointed at the bloody pillow. "Shirley just vomited." The doctor froze in his tracks.

Once he tore his gaze away from the pillow—and after the nurse left the room—he said with a smile, "I would like to take pictures of you." He held up his camera.

"But why?" asked Juliet.

"I want to remember you forever."

Is he crazy? thought Shirley. She shrank away when he got to her bed side.

"No, I don't want to take the picture," said Juliet, waving her hands, backing up. Dr. Zammit persisted, holding out the camera. Juliet waved her hands and shook her head again. She stepped back a few more paces.

"Well, can I take Shirley's?" He walked toward Shirley. Shirley wanted to scream no. She did not want him to take her photograph. Juliet reluctantly nodded her head. He snapped a shot of an unsmiling Shirley. With that, he walked off.

"He is so crazy!" commented Juliet.

"I didn't want him to take a picture of me," said Shirley, shaking her head with utmost distaste. He wanted to remember them forever? She knew with certainty that *she* would never forget him. She would never forget what misery he had brought upon them.

Dismissing the odd happening, Juliet began to prepare for the trip. She must work fast to get Shirley home before it got too late. Moving to the closet, she began to take out all Shirley's belongings. With as many bags as she could manage to find, Juliet stuffed all the clothes in until there was no room left for even an ant. She went in and out of the building to take the bags into her car, cramping them as best as she could.

Panting, Juliet dragged herself back into Shirley's room. It was, at last, time to bring her loved one home! She carried her daughter into the wheelchair. Shirley felt like a bag of bones in her arms. The child had suffered so much during the duration of the hospitalization. From being a girl with rosy cheeks and a healthy weight to sheer skin and bones.

With one last look at the hospital (and not a lingering one, either), they went inside the elevator that would take them away and close the door from the five months of living hell. Was this the feeling of the slaves after being manumitted?

Chapter Twenty-Three

It felt grand for both Juliet and Shirley to be finally together. Five horrid months had passed, separating them from each other. But the hospital had only managed to separate them physically, for they could and never would be spiritually separated. But the experience had left them with fear. Shirley knew that she would be fearful whenever she was to see a doctor. A third custody case could happen any time without any warning. How could she ever feel safe being with a doctor? They could do anything they wanted. Juliet could not speak out. She could not refuse any medical advice. Doctors, Juliet thought, should be friends of every patient. But how could they ever trust another doctor? Yet they had met some really wonderful doctors, such as Dr. Sabeston, Dr. Simmonds, and Dr. Robinson. They knew that they could not judge all doctors based on two negative incidents.

Shirley immediately felt her body recovering when they reached the rented house. Juliet had rented the house a month earlier, for she had planned to have Shirley start school when she got discharged from the hospital. It was December 14, and for the second time, it was right before Christmas Day. Was their reunion always going to be the present of the holiday season?

It was time to put the past behind them.

Juliet brought Shirley inside the house, their home for the time being. Seeing the cozy room, Shirley was rejuvenated.

"I would like to play on the floor," requested Shirley with glowing eyes. Juliet carried her onto the floor, and began to tidy up the place.

Ring! The telephone demanded attention. Juliet was hesitant to answer it, for fear of nagging reporters. But not wanting to miss any urgent calls, she decided to pick it up. Her suspicion was confirmed; it was a journalist. After hanging up, the telephone rang again. One call was followed by another; and all were from reporters from different newspapers and news channels. When the ringing telephone finally came to a stop, Juliet knew there were no more local newspapers left. But when Juliet was about to resume her cleanup, the doorbell rang. She knew all too well who was behind the door.

The reporters, along with their video cameras and notepads, swarmed in like hungry bees feasting on honey. She did not welcome them, but what choice did she have? Shirley was moving about on the floor as they took shots of her. She shyly smiled into all the hungry cameras. They asked her how it felt to be home, and she replied that it was good, wishing that she knew better words to describe how she really felt. Juliet did not know who was who, but she knew the *Hartford Courant* and The Associated Press were there.

"Your news will be aired tonight at eleven," said a man with a video camera hoisted upon his shoulder. Shirley was excited. She wished to see the news, but she was quite sleepy and could not stay up that long.

Juliet breathed a sigh of relief when the reporters left, satisfied with the information they had gathered. Juliet tucked Shirley into bed, and continued with her work.

Once snuggled under her cover, Shirley's eyes soon closed; she would surely have a fine night for the first time in a long while. She could sleep in peace, and would not wake up to the dreary life of the hospital.

In the living room, Juliet finally got everything tidy. She plopped on a chair before the television. It had been an exhausting time for her, but it was all worth her effort; she had won the case, and that was the biggest reward that any mother could ask for. "This case is ridiculous. It was beyond belief," she said to herself, repeating what she had been telling reporters. She thought about the news articles and shook her head. No article mentioned the fact that Shirley had actually walked for a whole year in China and that she was cured using Western medicine, not Eastern. She had given a photograph to *Hartford Courant* that showed Shirley walking, but the newspaper had printed the photograph with only Shirley's head showing.

The clock was ticking toward eleven, so Juliet turned the television on, and waited for the news to begin. "Oh!" A small cry escaped her lips when she saw her daughter on the set. Shirley looked beautiful with large, smiling eyes and shining shoulder-length black hair. Juliet did not catch much of what was said, for she was captivated by the images.

Afterward, Juliet got out the doctors' reports. What magical words lay inside that had such powers over her God-given parental rights? But again, it was the past, no matter how frightening it was. During her case, she saw both ends of the good-and-evil spectrum. For one, the particular two doctors, whose reports she held, were saviors of her child. She would be immeasurably grateful to both Dr. Sheridan and Dr. Lehman for as long as her soul was in existence. Their wise judgments had returned Shirley back into her arms. It was a gift too great to be thanked enough. Of course, she was also incalculably thankful to George, who had put all his heart and soul into fighting for her. How could she possibly have the ability to thank them enough? How many thanks would suffice?

After reading through the reports, she saw that each doctor, including Dr. Goldstein, had made fine points. But why did Dr. Goldstein recommended immediate surgery when the statements in his report clearly indicated that the surgery was highly risky? From the reports, she also arrived at the conclusion that the psychologists had made false accusations about Shirley's personality and behavior. She felt more stunned than anguish at first, but the feeling slowly turned to anger. Shirley was never once depressed during the duration of the custody case, though she was naturally apprehensive for her future health status. Would anyone not exhibit the same feeling if they were in her situation? But she was not the least bit apprehensive when Dr. Goldstein examined her, unlike what his report implied.

The readers can now take part in examining a few excerpts from the three doctors' reports below:

Dr. Sheridan
December 6, 1990

"...Shirley came to the hospital in a very frightened state (this last according to the nursing staff). When I met Shirley, however, she was alert, bright, and not at all frightened or shy."

"There has been a great concern expressed by all parties (Mrs. Cheng, the staff at Newington Children's Hospital, and myself) regarding Shirley's eating habits."

"In working with the nursing staff and with Mrs. Cheng in the last two months, I believe that more time was spent on this than any one other issue in Shirley's case. It became apparent to me that the fundamental issue could be Shirley's loss of appetite (rather than the mother's force-feeding), and that if the appetite could be corrected all the behavioral issues could be resolved."

"To understand Shirley's present condition and responses to treatment, it is important to go back to her early childhood. Her health was quite good until the age of approximately three months. At that time, owing to her mother's hospitalization for one week, Shirley stayed with (Agatha), whose child-rearing practices were different in two significant ways: 1) (Agatha) believed that children should sleep by themselves (Shirley had always slept with her mother), and 2) (Agatha) did not believe in feeding an infant at night if they cried (Shirley's mother always fed her milk in a bottle at night.) When her mother returned home, Shirley did not have her formal appetite, and was "sad." This change in appetite did not resolve, but continued. Shirley, who had been "chubby," became thin, and lost most of her interest in food, which forced her mother to invent ways of distracting her in order to feed her."

"In addition, should surgery be forced upon Shirley, without her mother's consent, I believe that the involved stress would severely compromise any good that the surgery might do."

Dr. Lehman
December 8, 1990

"Psychological evaluation has shown that Shirley has several deficits and indeed psychology shows that she is depressed and exhibits marked oppositional behaviors throughout her hospital stay.

"On examination by me today, Shirley is an awake, alert, oriented, but anxious and somewhat tearful Chinese female in no acute distress."

"In regard to the specific questions asked today, I do not feel that emergent or immediate surgery is necessary for Shirley's ultimate benefit. The complexity of her illness, the poor yield in long-term management with surgical releases and the confounding factor of both Shirley's mother and Shirley's personal disbelief in American medicine and the benefits of the procedures to Shirley, mean that her recovery will be marred by poor effort and perhaps even overt opposition on the part of both Shirley and her mother. This opposition is likely to outweigh all potential benefits of the surgery since the recovery from the surgery will be marred substantially if there is not intensive effort to overcome the associated pain at the time of physical and occupational therapy. Shirley's ultimate well-being requires that she not only undergo appropriate medical care from a strictly scientific point of view but in order to recover from the pain with the procedure and do well, she must have a significant level of belief in the benefits of the therapy and significant effort must be invested on her part to recover appropriately."

"Absent the belief and willingness to invest

significant effort to overcome pain and limitation secondary to surgical procedures, such a procedure has low potential yield for recovery of true ambulation."

Dr. Goldstein
December 10, 1990

"A detailed psychological evaluation revealed an eating disorder, a dependant personality, and comprehensive skill deficits."

"She is a thin female with a chronic illness, friendly, but somewhat apprehensive."

"If the goal is walking, it is my opinion that medication, and physical therapy modalities will not be sufficient, an orthopedic surgery will be needed. If one looks at only the bones and joints, it is apparent from her x-rays and from the contracture on physical examinations, that there are clear and straight forward indications for surgery on both feet, both knees, and both hips. However, if we look at this child there are other issues that might override or even preclude a decision to operate. This includes family investment in the process, the cultural and psychological factors, the risks of complications, the risks of reoccurrence, and the natural history of JRA. If one is to measure the "episode of illness" and therefore the duration of treatment, it goes well beyond act of surgery. Without commitment, without assurance of long term compliance, the likelihood of surgical failure and of reoccurring deformity is great."

***

Juliet had already enrolled Shirley in the first grade at a local elementary school, but Shirley could not go, for she was in pain every day. She continued to vomit blood as an aftermath of naproxen. It had caused severe bleeding in her stomach, and it would take some time for Shirley to recuperate. So Juliet stopped giving it to her.

A social worker from a nearby school had stopped by a few times, always requesting Shirley to start school. Although the pain was apparent before her eyes, she could not be convinced. No pursuit could change the fact that Shirley was physically unable to attend school. Shirley yearned to go, but her health did not permit her to do so.

Between her moments of pain, Shirley was occupied with coloring books, which Ben had bought for her. There were also visitors from the hospital and the kind upstairs neighbor who had bought several story cassettes for Shirley. The cassette tapes also came along with coloring books. Shirley ravished over the books and colored the pages between her tears of pain. But the joint pain was not the only thing she had to suffer. Her nausea was worse than ever. She often sat up in bed and tried to vomit into a small bowl, but nothing would come out. Juliet felt awful when seeing Shirley amidst her sufferings.

"Mom, I'm itching," Shirley said one afternoon, pointing at her behind.

With a worried look, Juliet turned Shirley around, so she could examine her. She gave a gasp. She saw a whole family of tiny worms in her anus. She nearly gave a jump. She had never expected to see such a sight! "Oh my! You have pinworms!"

"I do?" Shirley was as shocked. Juliet got a tissue and wiped them away. Some were even out of the anus.

"Yes, you have it. I can't believe it. Is it… Is this the reason that you have such a poor appetite and that you're always so nauseated?" wondered Juliet out loud. She scurried to her medical books and flipped through the pages until she found the topic of parasites. She read each worm's description and the findings confirmed her suspicion. The symptoms of pinworm infestation matched those of Shirley: loss of appetite, difficulty in sleeping, bilaterally symmetrical rashes, nausea, and constipation. Yes, Shirley had pinworms. There was no doubt about it. But what could have caused it? She knew she had kept all of Shirley's belongings and eating utensils extremely clean and maintained good hygiene at all times.

Juliet asked Dr. Sheridan to prescribe a medication to treat the pinworm infestation. He gave her one tablet. Juliet gave the tablet to Shirley right away.

When Shirley went to the bathroom after the dose intake, Juliet gave a gasp louder than the one she emitted upon the discovery of pinworms. Shirley's feces were entirely the color of white. "Your stool is covered in pinworms!" Shirley took a look and shrank from the sight. She was disgusted. She had never before seen white feces. She saw a few worms floating on top of the water in the commode. "Poor dear! You have so many of them inside of you. How can we get rid of them all?" Surely, one tablet would not be enough.

Days passed with the pain, nausea, and itchiness. Shirley still continued to be occupied with her coloring books and audio tapes regardless. Then they soon received visitors. Three teachers from the hospital came to see her, bringing presents for her eighth birthday. She happily and graciously took the boxes of gifts, ranging from Barbie dolls to the dolls' fancy outfits. Juliet and Shirley gave their thanks.

"You're very welcome, Shirley," they answered. They helped Shirley to open the packages. Shirley's large eyes gleamed as she admired the pretty apparel, while the teachers and Juliet conversed.

"Shirley is such a smart girl," one teacher said to Juliet. Juliet smiled widely. She had heard this comment from them each and every time she ran into them in the hospital.

"Happy birthday to you. Happy birthday to you." Their happy song rang loud and clear in the house, the melody traveling far and wide. "Happy birthday, dear Shirley!"

***

A Chinese doctor, introduced to Juliet by a friend, visited them to see if he could do anything to ease the condition of Shirley, whose pain was no better.

"Here's some herbs for her. I hope these will work." He handed a bag of herbs to Juliet.

Sadly, after being on the herbs for some time, Shirley's pain did not lessen. Juliet, knowing there was no reason to stay at the house any longer, decided to bring Shirley back to live with Kwi Show. Juliet had really wanted Shirley to attend school, but Shirley was simply too sick. The school social worker still continued to visit unannounced. It would be nice not to have those uninvited visitors for a change.

Chapter Twenty-Four

Days for Shirley were filled with many amusements and delights at the cozy brick house. Shirley's pain became manageable after she got back on naproxen. Juliet had decided to put her on it again, knowing she had no other choice. Shirley was able to sit for long hours in the daytime with not much discomfort. It was at night when she suffered from great pain. Yet, she spent the days happily. She passed the time by sitting on the deck, shaded by a large umbrella. She loved to enjoy nature's bliss; colorful butterflies sometimes alighted upon her grandmother's planted flowers, and birds hopped about before her. Once in a while, Shirley was lucky to observe a hummingbird darting from flower to flower. But it would swiftly fly away before Shirley could get a closer look. It was the loveliest sight that she had ever seen. The brilliant glow of blue and green of the bird simply made Shirley awe-struck with fascination.

When evenings approached, a large black cat often passed the house. Shirley was captivated by the sight of such a sleek creature. She never had been fortunate to be with an animal before. Soon, she called out to the cat. To the delight of Shirley, the black cat learned to stay at one place under the deck, so that the two could study each other with much scrutiny and concentration. One night when the stars were out, scintillating with full force, the cat sprang onto the deck without any warning. The much-startled Shirley gave a short scream. Abruptly, the cat jumped off.

After that night, Shirley yearned for the cat to be on the deck again. She began to coax the cat onto the deck. To her dismay, the cat never came on the deck; he simply stayed on the grass below. And together, the day flew by with much speed.

Although it appeared to be a pain-free life, it needed

much endurance on both Juliet and Shirley's part. Shirley continued to vomit blood and she had frequent nose bleeds. Naproxen was sustaining her arthritis, but it had already done too much damage. Each time, Juliet made sure that Shirley had enough food in her before taking the medication. But it was too late. Only time could heal the wound. None of the doctors could help with the problem. Above all, the pinworms were causing so much discomfort to Shirley. Juliet continued to seek a treatment for the condition. Shirley's feces were often covered entirely with pinworms.

"I wish there's a good doctor that Shirley could see," sighed Juliet during Agatha's visit one day.

"Actually, my son sees a really nice pediatrician. His name is Dr. Madison. You can go see him," suggested Agatha, supplying the name of the medical group.

"I know where that is. I know that place is good. Wonderful; I'll take her to see Dr. Madison."

An appointment was scheduled with the pediatrician. On the appointment day, Juliet brought Shirley in and they were both pleasantly surprised when they saw the kind countenance of the doctor, who had offered to carry Shirley onto the examining table. He was one of the nicest doctors Shirley had known.

Dr. Madison agreed to take a test of her stool sample, so Juliet brought a sample of Shirley's stool on the following appointment.

"Oh!" he exclaimed once he saw that the stool was entirely white. He knew that even though it was apparent that Shirley had a pinworm infestation, the test result might not show it. As he had expected, the test results came back negative. But he knew what Shirley had—the evidence was clear enough. He prescribed some medication to treat the parasitic infestation, but the medication did not cure Shirley's condition.

"It seems as though I will never get rid of the pinworms," analyzed Shirley. Juliet was driving her home after another appointment.

"Yes, it appears to be so, poor dear. But at least you have a kind doctor. That is one very important, fortunate thing. You can see him from now on for any matters."

Back at the brick house, Shirley went straight to the deck. She continued to admire the black cat. It stopped by only during the late hours in the day, sometimes staying long into the night. Soon, Shirley saw a handful of other wildcats in the area. Before, they had never come close to the house, but after seeing Shirley always welcoming any animals, they readily came. One by one, the family of cats steadily added to the deck.

Thus began Shirley's life with her furry friends. She named each of the cats, and learned which cat belonged to which family.

One day, Shirley had a sudden urge to pick up a pen and draw. She picked up a black marker with a thin head and a small notepad, and began to draw. Shortly, a black cat appeared on the paper.

"Mom," Shirley called out excitedly, "look, I drew this," Juliet came into the room, walking over to where she was sitting. Her eyes grew as round as a full moon.

"This is wonderful! I can't believe it! It looks exactly like the black cat; looks life-like." Juliet, taking the notepad in her hand, made her way to the kitchen to show the drawing to others.

Dr. Ling chuckled. "It looks real," he commented. "She will be famous one day."

Kwi Show shook her head in amazement, her silvery hair swinging to and fro. "This child is amazing. Yes, she'll be famous." The black cat on the paper looked as if it could jump out of the notepad any moment.

Shirley's love for cats grew as she began to depict them in her artwork. She was able to draw cats in all actions and styles. She drew each of the wildcats with utmost clarity. There were dancing cats in ball gowns, mother cats pushing their little ones in grocery carts, and beautiful cats mirroring mermaids with large glistening fish fins.

Cats were not the only companions she had in the backyard. Small inhabitants of the sky were also her little friends. She often patiently waited for butterflies, moths, and dragonflies to alight upon places in her reach. Sometimes, she was lucky enough to catch a Monarch butterfly in a jar. After a closer look, she would set it free. She had also caught crickets, and she took care of them for weeks. She fed them daily, changed their green bedding, and supplied water. Once, Shirley had filled the jar with more than enough water for the cricket, and consequently, it drowned. Shirley's heart quickened its pace. Thinking of any way to bring the small insect to life, she picked up a straw. Without another second of hesitation, she began to blow gently into one end of the straw as the other end covered the head of the unmoving cricket. To her delight, the cricket began to move. She dried up the cricket. Soon, the cricket was back and well. She was intrigued that she was able to resuscitate an insect with such an unusual method. As Shirley was engrossed with her thoughts, mulling was also going on elsewhere.

"The pinworm infestation—what could have caused it?" Juliet asked herself over and over again. She had been cogitating the probable cause of the parasitic infestation.

Eileen had taken a test of Shirley's saliva. She had sent the cotton swab to the lab and the results showed that Shirley had small worms.

"I did not pay much attention to it back then." How she wished that she could rewind time!

Then she thought back to that one week with Agatha. She knew that Shirley had lost appetite ever since that week. "I really wonder how Shirley got in all the pinworms. There are a number of possibilities: Agatha must not have washed the baby bottle, probably not even once—I saw Shirley had the bottle all over on the bed and she would just suck on it; the bottle got contaminated on the cutting board; Agatha fed Shirley leftover formula—formula that stayed in the bottle from the previous days… Since Shirley was under six months old, she had no protection." She had read that infants not breast-fed would be prone to have a weak immune system. She sighed. Agatha had given the pinworms to Shirley. It *must* have been her. Who else could have given it to Shirley? She, herself, could not have, for she had been excessively clean while caring for Shirley. Now she understood why the then-five-month-old refused to eat anything after that one week.

Shirley's skin rashes had traveled to her lower legs. She itched badly. The cream did not help since Shirley's problem was caused by pinworms. The worst rashes looked like burn-marks with thick skin.

Juliet leaned against the chair on which she sat. "No wonder she doesn't want to eat anything." Shirley did not eat when they went out to restaurants, on airplanes, during family gatherings. She often felt ill. She could not eat even when she was hungry because she felt so nauseated.

***

Several months had passed in the recovery of Shirley. She was in a better health, and her joints did not hurt as much. The frequency of her nose bleeds was less, and her stomach was stronger.

Every day she spent her time on the deck, soaking up the glorious sunlight, and having memorable times with the wildcats. One cat, she noticed, had given birth to a litter of kittens. She often caught the mother cat stealing food to give to her young ones, leaving only scraps for herself. "She is a wonderful mother," Shirley often commented.

From the family of cats, many lessons could be learned, from pride to prejudice. There was one particular kitten that had a messy coat, and it received poor treatment from fellow cats. Thus, it became an unloved, frightened cat, one that scrambled away as soon as others neared. Shirley also was aware that cats with sleek furs and beautiful poses were greatly admired by other cats.

Shirley was grateful for the time spent with the cats.

Not only did she find them fun, but discovered that they seemed nearly human, possessing human-like characteristics.

Kwi Show was not very fond of cats. One particular reason being that every cat loved to recline on her patio chair. She often found several balls of furs curling lazily upon the chair. No matter how many times she hushed them away, they never failed once to get back on as soon as Kwi Show turned her back. One clever cat, with large black cow spots on his white fur, had chewed the screws of the chair off and thrown them away.

"Look, he takes off the screw, and then he brings it over to the stairs and chews it until it breaks," said Shirley one day, pointing at the devious act of the cat.

"Amazing, he is quite mad with your grandma for not letting him sleep on the chair," declared Juliet, laughing.

"How about a game of checkers?" asked Kwi Show after lunch.

"Of course!" Shirley could hardly wait for another round of checkers. They had been playing it every day after lunch. Shirley had been the one who had it going; she had taught the game to her grandparents. And ever since, they had been enjoying rounds and rounds.

"I think I will be a good player soon," laughed Kwi Show. They all knew that Shirley usually won any game over whomever she challenged. After Kwi Show and Shirley finished the game, Dr. Ling was next to challenge Kwi Show.

After the games, the family relaxed, with small talk. "I don't like to sue anyone; it is not a good thing to do," Juliet was saying. "Let us leave it all to God; He will ultimately judge everyone and everything." After the custody case ended, she had received many calls from people telling her that she should sue the hospital. "Suing someone does not mean you will receive justice."

***

"I have to take her to China. She is still not well. There must be a treatment for her arthritis and pinworm infestation." Juliet pondered. She knew it was time again to head back to mainland China. The quest began once more.

And the travel day swiftly arrived. Juliet carried Shirley, who was now eight years and eight months old, into the seat in the plane. Heaving a sigh, she struggled with the bags she brought. It would be another long sleepless flight. She never got to sleep a wink during trips, for she had to help Shirley fall asleep on planes. As usual, she brought food along, knowing that several rounds of feeding were ahead. She had wrapped all the containers tightly to keep them from leaking. She ardently hoped that this time was the right time.

Chapter Twenty-Five

"Over here, over here!" Pan, a friend of Juliet, called out. He was waiting for their arrival at the Beijing Airport. She had known him for four years, from the time Shirley was able to walk.

"Thank you for your help, Pan," said Juliet. They headed off to pick up their luggage.

"My, so much stuff!" exclaimed Pan with wide eyes. "Why so much luggage?"

"Shirley's stuff—a lot of important things she needs for her daily necessities."

"You're such a hardworking mother," he said, shaking his head. He gathered up all the luggage.

With much sweat, Pan managed to get all the bags, then Shirley into a cab. "What place would you like to go to?" asked the driver.

"We're going to Beijing Zong Yi Yan Qiu Yuan," supplied Juliet.

After arriving at the hospital in Beijing, Pan carried Shirley out, putting her into the stroller. Juliet pushed Shirley in the building, with Pan trailing behind with the bags. Dr. Liu, another friend of Juliet, had already reserved a room in the hospital for them. There were no rooms for patients, for the hospital was the place for medical checkups and research. The room was on the second floor and the building did not have elevators. Juliet held on to the stroller as Pan carried Shirley up the flight of stairs. Juliet placed the stroller down and Pan placed Shirley in.

"Ah, here we are at last!" exclaimed Juliet with an exhausted look. It was late at night, and they desperately needed some sleep, especially herself. Pan handed the room's keys to her. He had everything taken care of before they arrived. Seeing the two beds in the room, Shirley yawned.

"Thank you, Pan. You have a good night," said Juliet before closing the door. He was to stay in another room and would leave when things settled. He had come from a city far away just to assist them.

Juliet made Shirley comfortable in the bed. Then she took out a few things that Shirley needed and put them on the table that was between the beds. With tired sighs, mother and daughter closed their eyes.

***

Hundreds of demons dressed in armor-like costumes streamed into the dusty streets. It was a murky day, but Shirley could clearly make out what they were doing. She saw they were taking her mother away. Shirley noticed that the demon warriors held heavy clubs with sharp spikes and large chains. A small form of a demon was discernible among the crowd. For an unexplained sense, she knew it was a good demon. "Please," Shirley pleaded to the small devil, "could you do something? Please save my mom!"

"I don't know how!" said the devil, helplessly. Then the scene shifted, and Shirley found herself before a small square building made of only steel. Her mother, dressed in a long lavender dress of silk, was chained to a wall by her arms. She had her head hung to one side, with closed eyes. The sitting figure was still, and was unaware of her surroundings. Shirley knew everything was hopeless.

Suddenly, a face most hideousness, with red, glowing eyes and long, white fangs sprang in front of Shirley. Her heart gave a grand leap.

Shirley woke up.

Her heart thumped within her. It was such a frightening dream. At that instant, Juliet woke up. "You're awake?" asked Juliet.

"Yes, I had a nightmare."

"So did I!" exclaimed Juliet. "It was horrendous!"

Shirley began to tell her the dream. In the middle of

her storytelling, Juliet gasped. "Oh my, I had the same dream!" They stared at each other in the dimly lit room with sheer astonishment painted on their faces.

"I can't believe it! We dreamt of the same thing, and woke up the same time," stated Shirley. They talked for a while before going back to sleep. What did the dream mean? It was amazing that two people would dream the same dream at the same time. Surely, it must have meant something.

***

A knock sounded on the door. Juliet opened the door to Dr. Liu. "How's everything?" he asked. "Everything ready?" It was time to visit Dr. Zhang, a well-known doctor who was the chief editor of Eastern Medicine magazine, to treat Shirley's pinworm infestation. After a few words were exchanged, he carried Shirley down the stairs, with Juliet following behind, the stroller in hand.

With much hope in her heart, Juliet accepted his escort graciously. They arrived at the doctor's clinic.

"I have the herbs to treat her," reported Dr. Zhang. Shirley winced at the thought of herbs. All the herbs she had to drink tasted bitter, though she never made a fuss or gave anyone many problems during her years of treatment. She knew the herbs were good for her health.

The doctor wrote down the prescription and handed the note to Dr. Liu, who retrieved the herbs shortly.

Juliet brewed the herbs as soon as she got them in her hands. Shirley held her breath and gulped down the bowl of brown liquid. It tasted anything but pleasant. Juliet had tasted the herbs before Shirley drank them.

"I really hope it will cure the pinworm infestation," breathed Juliet.

Juliet was met with happiness when, two days later, Shirley expressed an interest in food.

"I feel that my appetite is much better. I am actually hungry!" declared Shirley, clapping her hands together.

Juliet nearly jumped off the floor with elation.

"The herbs have made you hungry. The pinworms are losing! What would you like to eat?"

"Noodles!"

"Wow, noodles!" Juliet knew Shirley disliked noodles, which nauseated her. "I'll cook some spaghetti for you. I have a can of tomato sauce."

"This is good," commented Shirley, a mouthful of noodles in her mouth. The positive change did not end there. Within a short time, the rashes on Shirley's arms began to dissipate. "Look at my elbows—the skin is coming off with the rash and I don't feel so itchy anymore," observed Shirley, a wide grin clearly visible.

"So it is! I can see the skin flaking off! This is truly a wonder medication. Thank God. I believe that you will be cured with the herbs. This is absolutely so grand! But we are running out of it. It is only for a week's supply."

Juliet immediately asked Dr. Liu to get more from the pharmacy. "The prescription is all torn," was the bad news he told her. "I ran all over the place getting the herbs, and I kept the prescription in my hand, so it was scrunched up. I will have to get the doctor to rewrite the prescription." Therefore, he went by himself to Dr. Zhang's office.

The happiness ended there. The new prescription did not bring the same, promising results as with the first. "The herbs taste different than the first," reported Shirley. Juliet, feeling a mountain was weighing down upon her heart, asked Dr. Liu about it.

"Dr. Zhang said that the new prescription has the same ingredients," Dr. Liu told her.

"But the taste is different. I tasted it also. I can see that the color is not the same, either!" remarked Juliet.

Hence, there was not a happily-ever-after ending. Discouraged, knowing that there was no reason to stay at the hotel, Juliet decided to live in Dr. Qi's vacant house. Dr. Qi, a surgeon, was one of her cousins. Shirley was receiving massages daily, and the therapist was to go there to continue the therapy sessions. Each day was spent uncomfortably in the small room. Their daily tasks were made difficult because of the lack of space. Juliet called Dr. Qi, and the next day, he picked them up.

"Here we are," he announced when the cab parked in front of the compound. Their rooms were on the fourth floor of the building. There was an elevator, but people were not allowed to take it up to any floor level that was below the fifth floor.

"Why such a strange rule?" asked Shirley. Juliet shrugged.

As Dr. Qi was going to pick up Shirley to take her up the stairs, they were stopped by a lady standing beside the elevator. "Wait, you can ride the elevator; you don't have to carry her," she kindly told them. She stepped inside the elevator to give them room. She was the operator of the elevator. Juliet was quite grateful for the lady's kindness.

"I'm Yi, and my daughter has juvenile rheumatoid arthritis," Juliet told her. This news was received with a sympathetic look from the woman.

"You're such a hard worker. If you ever need help, just ask me," offered the lady.

Dr. Qi showed them the room. Shirley thought the place was quite spacious, compared to the places they had been staying. There was also a television in the room. Dr. Qi put Shirley on the bed. After seeing all was settled, he left.

As usual, Juliet began to unpack the bags, along with the herbs. She would brew a bowl for Shirley later.

Days slowly glided by with daily visits from the massage therapist. At the same time, Juliet had bought some of Dr. Chung's shots, and found a nurse to administer them to Shirley. Although Shirley was not in a hospital, it certainly felt like it. But at least, they had a television. There were two particular movies that Shirley and Juliet got hooked on. Shirley watched them while receiving the therapies.

"It is not working for her. I think it can be stopped," the nurse said one day after giving a shot to Shirley. Juliet sadly nodded. Apparently, no matter how hopeful she was, the medication was not like the first.

Meanwhile, they had visitors to their place. A coworker of Dr. Qi came by several times to check on them, providing any help she might be able to offer. Dr. Liu was another visitor who had bought two parakeets for Shirley as a surprise. Shirley's heart danced with glee once she saw the colorful birds of blue plumage, just like the ones she had when she was six years old. Juliet gave Shirley a pair of chopsticks, for which she had asked. With them, Shirley would train the birds to stand on them. Juliet was glad to see her so happy playing with the parrots. Shirley loved animals so much.

Juliet had found a math tutor for Shirley. But she was in pain often, and was unable to learn with her. After a few days without succeeding in tutoring Shirley anything, the tutor had to stop the sessions. She was simply in so much discomfort that nothing could be taught.

But during their stay, Juliet had managed to take Shirley out of the building for strolls. She also brought along some paper and pens to occupy Shirley. She ate in the restaurants as Shirley sat beside her, engrossed in her drawings since she never ate.

"Wow! Look at that child's drawing!" came the exclamation from a customer at a table next to theirs. "She is amazing!" Then he got up from his seat and walked over to Shirley. "May I take this and show others?" he requested. Shirley nodded. He quickly went around the restaurant and showed the restaurant workers. Everyone stared at the drawings of different cats and girls with pretty dresses and straw hats.

"How about you draw and let others see you do it?" suggested Juliet.

"Sure!" Shirley immediately drew several images on a piece of paper in a matter of seconds.

"My goodness; she is fast!" commented one woman. In simply a few minutes, a crowd was surrounding the table where Juliet and Shirley were seated. Shirley looked around her with amazement.

"You're being surrounded," chuckled Juliet.

The restaurant happening was merely one of numerous, similar incidents. Thus, wherever Juliet took Shirley, she never failed to bring papers and pens. Each time Shirley drew, people instinctively moved forward, surrounding them like a hungry swarm of bees. Sometimes, a block of street was filled with spectators adulating Shirley's performance. Many times, small talk started. People often asked what illness Shirley had. Upon learning the name of the disease, they gave sympathetic words and encouraging support.

"She may appear to be free of illness, but the truth is that she is never free of pain," Juliet told them.

"This is such a shame," they usually replied. Shirley felt loved among the throng. She had never received such attention in America. In actuality, Americans seldom gave her much praise for her artwork.

***

With her mind racing, thinking of what to do, Juliet took a pen and some paper to a table and began to write to Dr. Chung. "My pearl cannot last long in her condition. She must need relief for her sufferings," she murmured. In the letter, she inquired about the shots—whether he had some shots of good quality. "I hope that he might be able to send in some good ones." Everything seemed to be at a standstill for Shirley. Now, she just had to wait for the reply. He was staying at a military hospital located in Si Pin.

Several days later, Juliet received his prompt reply. "I can come to bring you over," said the letter. "We have new shots, number three." Upon reading the news, Juliet grew more hopeful. She believed that the new shots would help Shirley.

Chapter Twenty-Six

The train station was full of people going about, finding their trains and meeting new arrivals. It felt like an anthill with tiny ants bustling hither and thither, with twigs on their backs in a small space. Juliet pushed Shirley, following Dr. Chung to board the train. Juliet stopped under the train's stairs, and Dr. Chung carried Shirley onto the train and down the aisle, with a final stop at her seat. Together, Juliet and Dr. Chung managed the bags, putting a few of the smaller ones under the beds. She had also brought a few oranges along the way and put them inside the baskets on the wall.

Shirley peered out the window with tiny ruffled curtains. She loved looking out, watching passersby going to and fro, carrying luggage in their hands. Most were dressed in overcoats, for the wind was getting chilly in the month of November. Shirley turned her attention to the people on their train. She wondered how many of them were going to Si Pin as well. She rested her head against the wall where she sat. It was another one of those trips, she thought. She did not look forward to getting the shots.

Juliet sat down on her seat across Shirley. Shirley noticed her tired look. "That's all," she breathed. "That's everything. Are you hungry? Do you want something to eat?" inquired Juliet, holding a carton of food under Shirley's nose. Shirley shook her head. Juliet always asked the same question when they went on trips; and the answers received were always a shake of Shirley's head.

"What time is it?" asked Shirley. She could feel the train was getting ready to start on its journey. She saw many people resting in their places. One man went around to check on everyone. Juliet took a glance at her watch and told Shirley the time.

Shirley wondered how long the train ride was going to last. She enjoyed being on trains, but not as much as being on planes. Planes, she thought, were her favorite way to travel. But it was also the most difficult form of transportation for them. The most frightful experience with flights was going on the escalator. Juliet would have Shirley in the stroller, while holding on to it. Together they would ride the escalator. She still shuddered when she thought back to those times. Juliet always traveled alone, except for the times Al took them to China.

There was another issue that would make a flight an unpleasant experience. Since Shirley had limited mobility, she could not easily reach her ears to get her earwax out, so both of her ears were stuffed. Consequently, when the planes descended, she often felt extreme pain in her ears, to the point that she felt her ears were going to explode. Juliet had dripped fluid, earwax remover, inside of her ears, but it did not help. Rather, it had only made the matter worse.

Then the train's rattling sound brought Shirley to the present world. Dr. Chung was staying in the next compartment, but went over to where they stayed. "May I have one of these?" he asked, pointing at the oranges. Juliet nodded. Shirley wrinkled her nose at the thought of oranges.

"Are you hungry?" Juliet asked Shirley again.

"No, I'm not. Thank you." She simply wanted to get the treatment over with. She concentrated on the rhythmic clanking of the train. Shirley lay down on the bed. The compartment, she noticed, was getting darker. She peered out the window and saw that the sun was nowhere to be seen. It was apparently hiding elsewhere, perhaps behind the train.

"I think we'll be there soon," announced the doctor. He was correct; the train soon slowed. Shirley held on as the train came to a halt. The level of volume on the train grew louder as passengers got up from their seats and rose up from their beds to pack up.

Juliet got the stroller ready as Dr. Chung carried Shirley off the train. They went out of the station and stopped by the sidewalk. "I'm getting a cab," said Dr. Chung.

***

Shirley's eyes roamed around the room. It, she thought, was just another of their temporary places to stay. But the room had a bathroom adjoining it, therefore it was a comforting thought. The sun was nearly completely under the horizon, other than a tiny rutilant head poking out. She admired the exquisite beauty of nature, with its sky painted in streaks of violet and pink. How wonderful would it be to walk underneath the enchanting sky. She knew it would take a lot to get there. She fervently hoped with all her might that someday her dream would come true.

Chapter Twenty-Seven

Tears involuntarily stung her eyes as the needle was stuck in. Shirley gritted her teeth. The pain was great. She had to go through this during her entire treatment? How long would this last? *This just has to work*, she thought. It was the first day of the treatment, and it was already going painfully. The nurse walked away, leaving a sore spot for Shirley. She managed to sit up.

"Are you in much pain??" inquired Juliet, seeing the wince upon Shirley's thick brows.

"A lot," Shirley replied with a nod, rubbing her sore behind. Juliet was saddened that her daughter had to go through all the treatments. Her disease was already more than enough for anyone to bear, and she had to endure the therapies and shots as well.

Being an adventurous and outgoing person, Shirley asked to be taken out of the room to look down the halls, hopefully to make new friends. Juliet did as Shirley had desired. Shirley took a good look at the halls. There were doors on one side and a staircase at the end of the hallway on the right side. There was a desk by the stairs. A man was seated behind the desk. She knew that everyone, or close to it, was associated with the military. Ill military officers and some of their family members occupied the patients' rooms. She inched closer to the desk. She was able to go about places by leaning forward and back, consequently moving the stroller forward. She was also able to move it in other directions. She enjoyed how easy it could be for her to move around in it.

When she got close enough, Shirley gave a shy smile to the person at the desk. He returned her smile. At least, the place would not lack companions, people to lessen the pain and help to pass the time. She planned to come out every day and meet everyone.

The days passed with painful shots in the beginning and Shirley's sightseeing afterward. The groups of soldiers, perhaps around their early twenties, often laughed and joked around with one another. Sometimes, they played cards and Shirley sat by engrossing in the games even though she did not understand them. Once in a while, she asked them for a pad on which to draw. Ever since she had begun to draw cats, her innate artistic love grew. Soon, the pad was filled with pictures of turtles, porcupines, crabs, and of course, cats. One who looked upon her now would not have the faintest idea of what hardship she was going through. Her joints were quite painful, and worse yet was that the shots did not help an ounce in lessening the pain. It had been a week and no apparent relief was felt.

At the end of the two-week period, Juliet sought Dr. Chung. "The shots are not working. And they are very painful themselves. It's no use; just stop it."

"Yes, we'll stop," he sighed. Juliet was highly disappointed. Oh, how she had wished that the shots could have been as good as the first! Those batches were bundles of miracle.

"We're leaving here," Juliet told Shirley a moment later. "There's no reason to stay." Shirley clapped her hands joyfully. How grand it would be to get away from those shots!

The bags were packed up the following day. Dr. Chung was to bring them back to Dr. Qi's house. *Back there we go again*, Shirley thought. Juliet bundled up Shirley in a thick coat, a scarf, and a pair of wool pants.

***

"Oh, he is adorable!" exclaimed Shirley, feeling the yellow chick's feather gently. Juliet had bought one chick for her when she passed a man who was selling a whole clutch of chicks by a sidewalk. She knew Shirley would love to have one again. Shirley had one when she was six, but it sadly died. Chicks, she thought, were quite difficult to care for; maintaining their health was nearly impossible in cold weather. Nevertheless, she paid the man and bought the chirping chick home to Dr. Qi's house. Shirley clapped her hands gleefully once she heard the chirps even before seeing it. Before going to Si Pin, they had given the parakeets to Dr. Liu. Shirley wondered how they were doing. She lovingly petted the chick.

"I hope this one won't die," said Shirley.

"Yes, but it is very cold, and it might not survive the winter," replied Juliet. True enough, the chick sadly met its death in a few days. They had tried their hardest to care for it, providing food and water, to no avail. It perhaps missed its family greatly and that had been partly the cause of its passing.

"Poor chick," whispered Shirley. Her eyes followed her mother's figure as she went out to dispose of the body. It was merely its fate, something that no being could ever change. Shirley reluctantly turned her attention from the loss and focused on the visitors whom they were expecting. Juliet's cousin, Li, and her daughter were coming over. Just as Shirley was thinking of them, a few knocks sounded on their door.

Li and her daughter walked in, giving quick greetings to Juliet before going over to Shirley's side. Shirley knew she was going to hear more praise from Li. Sure enough, Li began to say how smart and special Shirley was. Shirley, smiling, could never get tired of hearing compliments. She was getting used to them.

"I know a place where Shirley can go for treatment. It's at a suburban area in Beijing," Li told Juliet when the subject changed to Shirley's treatment.

"Oh? How do I get there?"

"I can take you two there."

"Thank you, but that would be too much trouble for you."

Li shook her head. "No, I will have time next week. I can do it; that's no problem."

Shirley wondered what the treatment would bring this time. For some reason, Shirley's health was better. Her joints were not bothering her much and she was able to sleep well. It seemed that she simply got well by herself. Half a year had passed by since they had stayed at Si Pin. Perhaps, the time had arrived for Shirley to be well. Maybe her life would make a turn for the better. Everything was in God's hands. They simply had to follow His guidance.

Chapter Twenty-Eight

Shirley held tightly on to her mother, sitting upon her mother's lap, as her mother sat on a stool while the small wagon moved onward on the bumpy road. It was not a pleasant moment for either of them. They were heading to the doctor's office Li recommended. Li was the driver of the wagon. Shirley hoped the ride would end soon.

Without any warning, the half end of the wagon crashed to the ground, sending both Juliet and Shirley down. Juliet's back hit the ground with a loud thud. Shirley tumbled on top of her. It all happened in the duration of a wink and they did not know what had befallen them. Shirley was not hurt for she had been held on by Juliet, who on the other hand, got hurt quite badly.

"Everything okay?" inquired Li, rushing over to them.

"I'm okay," answered Shirley weakly. Juliet echoed the reply. Li set up the wagon and they boarded again. Juliet held on to Shirley more tightly. Juliet heaved a sigh. She did not feel comfortable coming on this trip in the first place, but Li had insisted. Li also said that they could stay with her for a few days. Juliet hesitantly agreed to the idea. The fall from the wagon was a bad omen.

Juliet, her back hurting, pushed Shirley inside the office where the doctor was seated.

"I don't know how to treat her disease," said the doctor after examining Shirley for merely a few minutes. "I don't treat juvenile rheumatoid arthritis." Juliet was not surprised at the news. They had come all this way for nothing; everything was wasted. And now they had to live at Li's place for a while.

***

"Finally back home," said Shirley with a tired yawn. The whole visit was a wild goose chase. She was glad to be home—at least, Dr. Qi's place had been her home for some time now. She missed her home in America. She wished to go back there and then. What Shirley disliked most about China was its food. She longed to have a bowl of cereal. In China, getting a bottle of milk was a highly difficult task. Juliet bought bottles of milk from a small grocery store across the street, but the milk often changed in texture, sometimes thick, other times thin and watery. Shirley rarely could enjoy a cup of milk. Above all, there was no cereal—at least, not like the ones in America. Because of this, Juliet had asked Kwi Show to send them a box of Cheerios.

When the package arrived, Shirley nearly gave a leap. Her mouth had never been so watery. Never did she expect that she would be so eager to eat cereal. But she could not deny her appetite. She spooned in the cereal into her mouth with much gusto.

"Oh, this is delicious!" Shirley finished every last bite, down to the very last piece of the donut-shaped cereal that was floating above the surface of the milk just a second ago.

With a loud, contented sigh, Shirley rummaged the package, wondering if the box held more goodies. In fact, it did—several sheets of animal stickers. She yelped with joy. She always cherished stickers of all kinds, especially animal ones. And some of these were with sparkles. How her eyes relished each sheet. Kwi Show had also sent cans of Spaghetti O, which was one of the few food Shirley could eat because of her nausea. Sour-flavored food helped calm her nausea temporarily.

A knock on their door made Shirley turn her attention away from the stickers in her hands. Shirley had an idea of who might be standing behind the door.

"Hello, Li," greeted Juliet after opening the door. Li answered her welcome and crossed the room to reach

Shirley's side.

"How are you doing, Shirley?" Shirley saw that Li's daughter came also. "It's a nice sunny day. You should come out. We can take you for a walk."

Shirley looked at Juliet for approbation. "I would love to," said Shirley after receiving Juliet's consent. Li carried Shirley into the stroller. Juliet normally stayed by Shirley wherever she was to go, but she did not this time; she trusted them—they were family members.

Shirley watched fellow passersby on their daily duties as she got out of the building and onto the streets. "What would you like to see?" Li asked her. Shirley shrugged. They passed several street markets and tiny shops. Shirley pointed at a store overhead, and Li pushed her in that direction. Shirley's keen eyes never failed her; she was brought to a shop filled with delightful, small fancies, ranging from toys to decorative objects. Her eyes instinctively rested upon an aisle that held several cans of Play-Doh.

"I would like to see those," said Shirley, pointing at the colorful cans of Play-Doh. Accompanying them were machines that could produce spaghetti and other shapes, ranging from flowers to stars.

"You like them?" inquired Li. Shirley gave a definite nod of her head. After a moment, Li said, "Then I'll buy them for you. Which ones do you like?" Shirley pointed at two boxes.

They went to the counter. After receiving the money, the lady handed Shirley a bag full of Play-Doh, along with a machine. Shirley was elated.

"Oh!" exclaimed Juliet after looking inside the bag when they returned. "That must have cost you a lot. How much? Let me pay you back."

"It's my present to her," insisted Li.

Right away, Shirley happily played with the cans of Play-Doh. Soon, a whole bunch of blue spaghetti appeared before her eyes. Then she added a few yellow flowers on top.

Summer slowly left the busy land, taking its warmth with it. The mugginess was replaced by billowing winds that brought dust along in its powerful arms. Many people shielded their eyes while going about on the streets. Shirley's favorite month had arrived, but it did not bring red and orange leaves to the area, for there were no deciduous trees. She would be home soon—her real home in America. Juliet had received several letters from Ben, who announced that he wished to visit them. The building where they lived did not have access to mailboxes, therefore Dr. Liu was their personal dispatcher, bringing her mail over every time she had new mail.

"So, I will pick Ben up at the airport," stated Dr. Liu. All was ready for his arrival. *Why not go back to America since he's coming here anyway? He could take us back*, Juliet had thought.

Chapter Twenty-Nine

"Oh, hello, Juliet and Shirley!" greeted Ben, giving them both a large hug. He felt good and strange at the same time visiting China for the first time. He had checked into a hotel by the house. Dr. Liu did not have any problem recognizing Ben; it was a task of most simplicity. Ben was one of the few Caucasian men at the airport, and his prominent beard was highly distinguishable.

Ben took the two to his hotel. "I have a present for you, Shirley."

"Thank you!" Shirley was unable to communicate with him well, for English was still a foreign language to her. She commonly replied, "I don't know English." She peered over the bed, guessing what he could possibly have for her. Her eyes grew round at the sight that met them. Ben held a long box with an electronic keyboard in it.

"Wow!" exclaimed Shirley, "Thank you so much!"

"You're very welcome," said Ben. He got the keyboard out of the box. He hit several keys and yellow buttons. She listened in awe at all the different sounds it could make. It also could play several popular songs, such as *Jingle Bells* and *Happy Birthday*. Taking the keyboard onto her lap, Shirley began to play it. She never learned how to play piano, but Juliet had shown her the keys to a few easy songs. Shirley still remembered how they went, and started to produce the melody to *Twinkle, Twinkle Little Star*. "This is really nice. I like it a lot," remarked Shirley.

"How about we go to a restaurant?" suggested Juliet a moment later. It would be a treat for Ben.

"That sounds wonderful," he gushed. Shirley was happy about the decision as well, not because she wanted to eat, but because she merely wished to go out and watch others in the restaurant.

Juliet pushed Shirley along a sidewalk, searching for a good restaurant. On the way, small talk was made.

"Yes, we fell down from the wagon. Actually, it just went down suddenly," Juliet was saying.

"That's horrible!" declared Ben.

Juliet nodded. "And when I looked in the mirror, my back had bruises."

"How is it now?"

"Oh, it is much better now. Thank goodness nothing worse happened. Mostly, Shirley didn't get hurt." Juliet hastened the pace. "Let's go here," she pointed, "This looks nice."

Once settled down at a round table, the conversation resumed. Shirley folded the napkin on her lap carefully, smoothing out the lines.

"Well, anyway, I bought the tickets for you," said Ben, holding out the tickets. Shirley's lips spread into a wide smile. At last, she could have some real milk! Was the trip this time to China necessary? It seemed that nothing had been accomplished, and yet, Shirley's condition was remarkably better. Perhaps, the reason could never be sought.

As the conversation continued, Shirley began to draw on a napkin. "This is beautiful," commented Ben, tilting his head in scrutiny. "She is a child prodigy and will be famous someday."

***

"It is so wonderful to have you two back again!" Kwi Show welcomed Juliet and Shirley, opening the door to them. "Thank you, Ben," Kwi Show said, turning to him.

"No problem," he replied.

"I'm so tired," sighed Juliet. "I'm bringing Shirley into the bedroom. She is very tired also." Juliet got her on the bed, changed her clothes, and plopped on the bed beside her. "Rest now. It has been a long trip."

"Yes, but Finland is beautiful!" exclaimed Shirley. Around two weeks had passed since Ben had gone to China. After they bought some souvenirs from various shops, bags got packed, and off they went for America. Ben's tickets included a stop in Finland for a night. There, they stayed at a large hotel with room service. Shirley could still remember that first sip of the milk from a sparkling plastic cup. Oh, and the pitcher was lovely!

"I wish I could go back there again; to simply have that milk once more," Juliet echoed Shirley's thoughts.

"Same here; I was just thinking of that," stated Shirley.

"You know I told you about that hotel—that I had dreamt of it a long time ago?" asked Juliet. Shirley nodded. "That's how it looked in my dreams. It looks exactly like it. So strange, and yet lovely at the same time."

"I dream of fancy buildings like it, with wide halls that are dimly lit."

Juliet rose from the bed. "I'm off to get things unpacked. Do you want anything to eat?"

"No, thanks." Shirley swung her legs to and fro and thought of the past trip. Would she ever stop going to China about every two years or so? She turned her head toward the window, trying to catch any cats that might be around the yard. She was unable to see outside, so she inched closer. There were no cats present anywhere. Shirley knew that her grandmother did not welcome the cats, thus they had probably found another house to stay.

"Well, they'll come back as soon as I get out there and call to them," Shirley said to herself. Taking a pen and a piece of paper, she began to draw dancing and playing cats. "I wonder if they would still remember me?" It had been two years since she had last seen them. The female cats perhaps had a litter of kittens. She could hardly wait to see the whole family. She started to bounce on the bed. It got others annoyed sometimes, for she did it for hours at times. She felt remarkably better, but she was not completely painless.

Juliet walked back into the room with the usual tired expression. Shirley could see that she was pondering a matter in her mind. She had a feeling of what the thought was: Shirley's treatment.

***

The next day, Shirley rose with a wide grin. She would see her cats again! "Mom, I would like to go out."

"Sure. It is getting cold. Let me get your small coat." She went to the closet and took it out. After She properly dressed up Shirley, she pushed her onto the deck.

"Meow, meow, meow!" called Shirley, her loud, high-pitched, nightingale-like voice traveled to all sides of the yard, penetrating the tiny woods beyond the deck. Not a cat was discernible. Shirley was not discouraged; she repeated her call.

Then a movement from the corner of her eye caught her attention. "Tommy!" Shirley was absolutely delighted. It was the gray cat with stripes, the one she loved dearly. He jumped onto the deck and meowed while looking at both her and Juliet.

"They'll all come soon!" declared Juliet.

"Yes, I'm sure they will." It was another fresh start for them. In a few months, Shirley would turn ten. She had spent her childhood years in constant pain, confined to a wheelchair. Hopefully, this year would be a turning point in her life. Yes, she would get well, she thought as she greeted a few more furry guests to the deck.

Chapter Thirty

"Happy birthday to you!" sang Juliet on a snowy day. She gave Shirley an embrace of much warmth. "And here you are," said Juliet, handing the ten-year-old a present. It was a Barbie doll in blue silk dress with the words, "Happy Birthday" written on it.

"It's so beautiful!" Shirley's eyes took in all the details of the doll, from the delicious-looking birthday cake it held in his tiny hands to the sparkling party dress with floral designs upon it. The blue dress accentuated the doll's blue eyes. As Shirley was playing with it, combing its golden hair, she noticed that it was not the only present from her mother. Juliet handed her several small animals, ranging from a turtle, a dog to a lamb. "Wow! I love them. The duckling is so cute." Juliet was blissful in seeing her dear daughter of precious pearl so happy. That was all she could ever ask for in life—not fame or wealth, but happiness within a family.

By and by, Shirley grew stronger. Her body was at last making a combat. Sadly, her appetite was still poor. She had taste for only a few certain foods, from cheese to chocolate. Juliet still had to take hours to prepare food, and she had managed to feed most to Shirley.

In April, Juliet made an appointment with Dr. Lehman at the Hospital for Special Surgery. She wished to thank him for the part he took in the case, resulting in her victory over injustice. She had been keeping in contact with him, being grateful for his wise decision.

Dr. Lehman did a general checkup of Shirley's health status on the appointed day.

"The next time you come, other physicians will come to check Shirley," said the doctor. Thus, another appointment was scheduled for the following month.

In the meantime, Juliet and Shirley were expecting a visit from Linda and Kathy, who had been in close contact with Juliet after reading the court case in 1990. Both of the ladies were Roman Catholics, thereupon, they had always been speaking about the Word of God during their many telephone conversations.

"We wish to come to visit you two," Linda had said.

"We would love to meet you. You are very nice people," stated Juliet. Soon, a day was scheduled for the visit. It was going to be on Juliet's birthday. She was also waiting for her new car, a Ford Escort, to arrive, perhaps on her birthday.

***

"Oh, here's the car!" Kwi Show called out when she saw the blue car, which was driven in front of the house, with a final stop outside the garage. Juliet excitedly went out of the house. It was like a birthday present, though no one had planned it; it just so happened to be delivered on that day. Juliet never celebrated her birthdays—she found no reason to. "It's just like any other day," she often commented.

"No; this is not the color I picked out that day!" Juliet was disappointed. "The color I picked out was much prettier. Oh well. But this is nice, too."

Shirley watched the scene from the living room's large window. *It is a nice car*, she thought. The day was bright and warm, so she had to shield her eyes from the glaring sun. Even if the days were cloudy, she still would have to shield her eyes; her eyes were that sensitive.

Juliet came back in the house after studying her new car. She planned to go for a test drive later. But in the meantime, the time of the visit was approaching.

"Oh, how wonderful it is to see you!" exclaimed Linda. She gave each one a hug when they arrived. Then Kathy followed suit.

"We have presents for you," said Kathy, handing Shirley two gift-wrapped presents. With her countenance shining with mirth, Shirley gently tore the wrappings off the gifts.

"I love bunnies. This is beautiful," said Shirley, holding the music box to show to Juliet. Noting the next present, Shirley's eyes grew larger. It was a coloring machine with a roll of coloring pictures. Shirley turned the knobs on it and a new picture came into focus. "I love this, too!" She thanked them several times. Shirley was picking up some simple English from the cartoons on television. She opened the small container that held the crayons of basic colors. She began to color in the first picture.

"We brought a bottle of the green drink," Linda was saying as Shirley colored. "This is really good." She handed the glass bottle to Juliet, who began to read the small print on the label. Linda further told Juliet of many other products she had in the store owned by her father. His health store sold numerous herbal foods, which they were known as.

"I'm going to buy some of the medicine," stated Juliet.

"This is not medicine. All these are foods," explained Kathy.

Food? We certainly cannot eat them as real food, thought Juliet.

***

"There are two options. One is to have Shirley receive physical therapy first, then have surgery; or perform the surgery first," suggested Dr. Lehman on the day of the appointment. Shirley did not like any of the choices she was hearing, but she would choose the first one. "She can stay in Blythedale Children's Hospital," he continued.

"Okay, she can stay in the hospital first, and see how she will be after the therapy," decided Juliet.

Shirley received the decision with an inner sigh. But

she knew it was her life, and she should make the best of it. No complaints were uttered through her lips. She simply readily smiled at the decision. Many doctors had examined her a moment ago. She readily held out her arms when each doctor approached her for examination. Each doctor took a few minutes, checking each of her limbs. When her legs were checked, she held up her skirt with blue flowers printed upon fuchsia background. It was a matching outfit with the top, a full skirt, and pants all in the same design.

Despite the circumstances of all the studies under the eyes of doctors, she still felt happy and pleased for some reason only she knew. Her countenance was never absent of smiles. Even if Shirley was not physically smiling, her soul would be filled with smiles. By the look of Shirley, one would surely know that Juliet was a grand mother. One should know that Juliet had played the most important role in maintaining Shirley's happiness. Although their lives were harsh, each held on to the other for emotional support, thus making their lives much less stressful. Wherever Shirley went, Juliet always dressed her up in the prettiest of dresses, sometimes accompanied with a fancy hat. Shirley often felt like a little princess. Surely, only princesses could receive such a lavish treatment.

"Shirley, we have a drawing contest. Would you like to enter?" inquired a social worker.

"Sure! I would love to!" Shirley chirped, so the social worker went out of the room and reappeared a minute later, holding a large piece of paper and some colored markers. Shirley quickly received the materials with a huge smile. Without missing out a single moment, she began to draw. Dr. Lehman exchanged glances with Juliet. Juliet watched with pride as the picture rapidly formed on the paper.

"I'm done!" announced the much-excited Shirley. The picture of a cat doctor holding the stethoscope upon a cat patient's heart appeared on the blank piece of paper after a couple of minutes.

"It's lovely. Thank you!" said the social worker,

putting it on a table to get ready for the contest submission. "This is very nice," she continued, scrutinizing the drawing with interest. The winning entry of the art contest would be displayed at the hospital for the fifteenth anniversary celebration of children's and hospitals week of March 20, 1994.

"It's fine for Shirley to be on those herbs," reconfirmed Dr. Lehman after agreeing with Juliet, who had brought the bottles with them to show to him. "These are fine." Juliet had ordered the herbs soon after the visit from the two ladies. Juliet could see that they were highly efficacious for Shirley, whose once pale cheeks became rosy. And one day, Shirley had said that her eyes were less sensitive to sunlight now. Oh, at long last, some good news!

"Thank you again for the lovely picture," said Dr. Lehman before Juliet was to take Shirley home.

"You're welcome!" answered Shirley perkily. Shirley knew that she was going to see Dr. Lehman many more times. She was going to stay in a hospital once again. She would spend more lonely nights on her hospital bed. But she did not dread the prospect of being hospitalized again. She was looking on the bright side: perhaps, they would have good treatments waiting, she would make new friends with her hospital mates, and learn more English by interacting with English-speaking people. But she did hope that the coming hospital stay would not turn out like previous experiences. The custody cases were living nightmares. She trusted Dr. Lehman. She did not think that a person who had saved you from closing jaws would swallow you himself. At least, that was a strong hope. Dr. Lehman had always been kind and understanding with them. Surely, she could trust him.

Chapter Thirty-One

"Follow me," instructed a nurse. Juliet pushed Shirley down a white hallway with doors on one side. Each door had a glass window on the top portion. "This is her room," the nurse directed, moving toward an empty bed, "and this is her bed."

So, this is my new home for now, in Valhalla, New York, thought Shirley. She noted there to be three other beds in the room. Shirley saw a Mexican girl across her bed and a Caucasian girl to the left of her. The bed in front of the Caucasian girl was empty. She wondered who occupied that bed. She turned her head to the nurse, not that she was not listening to her attentively in the first place; her ears never stopped picking up the speaker's words.

The nurse went away for a minute and came back the next with the usual hospital equipment. Shirley received her temperature and blood pressure readings; they were all fine. After the lady with the white uniform left, Juliet began to make the hospital Shirley's home as best as she could. She would go back home and bring more things over if necessary. She put the few belongings in the cabinet beside Shirley's bed. Shirley looked at the two girls and gave them shy smiles.

"Hi, what's your name?" asked the girl next to her.
"Shirley, and what's yours?"
"Brook."
"How old are you?"
"Twelve," answered Brook matter-of-factly.
"Oh, I'm ten." Shirley turned her head toward the Hispanic girl. She learned she was also twelve, and that her name was Alexandra.
"She is Japanese and I think she's ten, too," Alexandra told Shirley about the mysterious roommate that

Shirley had not met, yet.

"Mom, can you please give me my stickers?" asked Shirley. Rummaging through the bags, Juliet found the pink bag with pink designs of a darker shade upon it, and handed it to her. Shirley quickly opened the bag, took out some stickers, and showed them to Brook. "Here are my stickers." She had been collecting stickers quite recently. Kwi Show sometimes received *Highlights* magazine, to which some stickers would be attached. Juliet had also ordered several sheets of stickers for her. Shirley had first known about stickers one day when Juliet was pushing Shirley down a street in China where sheets of stickers in a street market had caught her eye. Hence, ever since that day, stickers became a passion for Shirley, who barely used any; instead, she simply collected them and admired them each day.

"Wow," exclaimed Brook, "this is cool!"

Shirley nodded her agreement. "Do you want some?"

"Sure, if you like." Shirley asked for a pair of scissors from her mother. She cut out a few stickers and stretched her arm out to give them to Brook. "Thanks!" exclaimed the girl.

"You're welcome!" The corners of Shirley's mouth curved upward. It was going quite well. It seemed that she had already made new friends.

Later in the day, Shirley wheeled around the floor, seeing if she could find anything interesting to study. She moved around a large desk where a few nurses were stationed. She passed several rooms and noticed that there was a room with toys and other fancies. She could see that it was the recreation room. She could hardly wait to go there when it was time. A lady in the room smiled at Shirley before walking over to her. Shirley introduced herself.

"How old are you?" inquired the woman.

"I'm ten."

"When's your birthday?"

Shirley thought for a moment before forming an answer. "I don't know what it is called, but it is the first month, And the day is thirty," Shirley answered as best as she could.

"So, it's January 30?"

Shirley nodded. She repeated the word in her head. So she had learned her birthday, and she was quite happy about it.

Their conversation ended and Shirley wheeled over to the desk again. Her eyes caught a few plates on it. The plates held several sandwiches. She asked for a piece. *This is delicious*, she thought, taking bites with gusto. Juliet happened to walk in on the moment. Her eyes widened. Shirley was actually eating something on her own! She saw that the sandwich had a slice of cheese and a piece of salami with plenty of mayonnaise. It was not healthy, but at least, Shirley was enjoying it. Then, Shirley's face paled. She felt the sudden nausea. It was the cheese. She took out the slice of cheese and gave it to her mother. Most kinds of cheese nauseated her.

Together, they headed back to Shirley's room, with Shirley finishing the sandwich along the way. It was getting quite late. Juliet had gone back to pick up a few things. She had rented a bungalow near the hospital.

"You had a blood test?" inquired Juliet after noticing the bandage on her left arm.

Shirley nodded. "I hope they won't do it every week."

"I doubt it," said Juliet. "He won't do anything like that," she continued. "He is a very wonderful doctor who won't harm his patients. He cares for all. He even agreed for me to take you to see Dr. Atkins. Linda has contacted him for us, so everything is ready for us to go." Shirley saw Dr. Robert Atkins once, before arriving at Blythedale. Dr. Atkins, famous for his low carbohydrate diet and nutritional supplements, had kindly offered to give Shirley free treatment. Shirley had received some of his medications, but they did not work for her. Hence, Shirley would go see him again to try other medications.

"Really? So, I'll see him during my stay here?"

"Yes, I'll probably take you there. It is very kind of Dr. Lehman to give me the permission to take you there. I don't think that many doctors would allow that." Shirley agreed with a nod. "So, how's everything with you?"

"It is good so far," reported Shirley. Juliet stayed with Shirley until the night was darker than ink. At length, it was time to go. They reluctantly hugged goodbye. She would come back the next morning.

Shirley lay down and closed her eyes. It had been a reasonably good day. She had met the Japanese patient. She had burn-marks on her arms, which had stumps at both ends where hands were supposed to be. She was also unable to talk. *It must have been a horrible experience for her*, Shirley thought, her heart going out to her. Some people just had to go through so much in life, while others had not a single worry in the world, but who still were not satisfied with their lives.

Her mother was on her mind before she fell asleep.

***

A bright light suddenly glared into Shirley's eyes. She squeezed her eyes. The light was not going away. Slowly, she managed to open her eyes wide enough to see what was happening. Was it daybreak already? The lights in her room were turned on. She saw a nurse moving about in the room, picking up stuff from the floor, placing miscellaneous items into the cabinets, and doing other tasks that seemed so unnecessary at such a time of the hour. Shirley saw that the wall clock read one in the morning. Was the nurse always going to come nightly for the cleanup? She was fully awakened. The nurse did not see that Shirley was awake, for Shirley did not make a single sound. She wished that the nurse would finish up soon. Several minutes later, she left, leaving Shirley wide awake. Shirley tried going back to sleep, but it was a most difficult task! After an hour, she drifted into a light sleep.

A few hours later, Shirley opened her eyes to a busy world. She heard scurrying nurses outside the room. Her roommates were still in bed. Her eyelids felt heavy, for her night had not been a good one since the disturbance from the late-night cleanup. It was still quite early for Juliet to come. Shirley needed to go to the bathroom. But she thought she should wait for another few minutes until Juliet came. After several minutes, she felt that her bladder would burst. She had not gone to the bathroom the entire night. She glanced to her right and found the device that would bring a nurse to her. She pushed the red button and a reddish light by the desk blinked right away. She was able to see it, for the desk was right across her room. A minute later, a nurse walked in. Shirley knew that she was the head nurse.

"What is it?"

"I need to go to the bathroom." The nurse took a bedpan and put it underneath Shirley. "But I can't go like this. Please, I need to sit."

"No, just go like this." Without hearing another word from Shirley, she left. Shirley was devastated. Her behind was situated uncomfortably upon the bedpan. With much effort, she managed to empty her bladder. She pushed the button again.

"Hold on," the head nurse brusquely said outside the door. Shirley tightly pressed her legs down on the pan as hard as she could, hoping it would not spill. She became quite weak a minute later. She pushed the button for a second time. Sullenly, the nurse walked in. She took the bedpan out from under the now exhausted Shirley.

"Please," requested Shirley, pointing at her behind, while gesturing her hand in a wiping motion. The nurse cursorily wiped Shirley. After pulling Shirley's pants back up, she left silently. Shirley thought of her roommates who could walk and therefore did not have to wait for others to help with bathroom needs.

Several minutes later, Juliet walked in. Shirley sighed; her mother had just missed it. Shirley did not tell her of what had happened. She knew that it would not resolve anything. They had plenty of bad experiences to support Shirley's doubt.

"Please come every morning to help me pee," Shirley requested. Juliet was glad to do so.

Ever since, Juliet came every morning for Shirley's bathroom needs. There were a few times that Juliet did not come early enough, and Shirley had to experience the unfortunate difficulty with the nurses. But no other nurse was worse than the head nurse. As a result, Shirley never urinated during the entire duration of every night. She had to hold her urine till the morning. Sometimes, she felt that she would burst any minute. Above all, she was awakened nightly, sometimes at midnight, other times at one. Shirley had mentioned this to Juliet, who had noticed that Shirley looked tired. There was no way for her to change the hospital's schedule. She felt awful that Shirley had to go through this. But it was not just Shirley; other children might be affected as well. But Shirley was a light sleeper, so she could get awakened much more easily.

Since Juliet came every morning, she noted what the morning schedule was like. She was highly dismayed, but not surprised, when she saw the routines. The first thing that the nurses did for patients was to wipe each of them with a wet cloth with a small amount of soap. The lukewarm water would quickly turn cold, thus it was quite chilly for the patients. Shirley always shivered after the wipes, and her body often felt sticky, as the nurses never wiped off the soap using clear water. Following the wipes was the time to brush teeth.

"This still has toothpaste on it!" exclaimed Juliet several times when Shirley was just about to brush her teeth with the toothbrush. "They never wash it out completely. And the next morning, they will just squeeze on some toothpaste on top of the leftover paste. Then you will brush your teeth with a dirty toothbrush!" Juliet was furious. She could no longer stand this, and began to assist Shirley with the brushing ever since then.

Nights were spent without much sleep. And days were filled with coldness in the mornings and heavy eyelids throughout the entire day. Blythedale was where they would have her stay after surgery. How could she possibly get the rest and proper care in this hospital after an event as critical as an operation?

The most agonizing moment was when Shirley had to hold in her urine. All the basic necessities of living creatures, that should have been the easiest tasks to perform, became the hardest and most uncomfortable ordeals Shirley had to endure each and every day. Oh, the life of a disabled was so harsh and difficult! Depending upon others for bathroom needs was the most horrifying thing there was. Healthy people never thought of such difficulties that disabled people would go through; they simply look at the surface, seeing that their only problem was the inability to walk—not seeing the dreadful outcomes of such disabilities.

***

"Dr. Atkins is very nice," remarked Juliet after Shirley had seen him. Shirley nodded, eagerly agreeing with her mother's comment. "Now, you can try another of his medicines."

It was a week into the hospitalization at Blythedale. Shirley looked out the car window as Juliet turned onto the lane that would bring them back. Shirley nodded, enjoying the view from the window, while Juliet talked. "I hope this time, they would work for you."

But after being on the new medications, Shirley had not benefited. She was scheduled for another appointment to see him.

Chapter Thirty-Two

It was July and a month had gone by in the hospital. Shirley felt the days were passing slowly. But despite the hardships, Shirley still held on to her smile obstinately. She did not utter a word of complaint or shed a single tear. She managed to find fun moments at the hospital during recreation times, talking with fellow patients, and roaming the halls.

The time in the hospital was not too vapid. There were times for physical therapy, times spent with a psychologist by the name of Dena, and the weekends. Ah, the weekends were special, for all the patients who had homes were allowed to go back! The hospital had special vans to pick them up on Friday evenings and bring them back to the hospital Sunday nights. Shirley always looked forward to going back.

Each time she got into Juliet's car, she fell asleep right away. From this, Juliet could see that Shirley did not sleep well in the hospital. She was utterly heartbroken by this. She felt helpless. She could not change it. Seeing Shirley sleeping, Juliet often made several unnecessary turns in order to go the long way home, for she wanted Shirley to sleep longer.

"Mom, it's okay; don't do that," Shirley had said after noticing Juliet's tactics. But Juliet never listened. She needed to get Shirley some much-needed sleep back.

Whenever Sunday afternoons arrived, Shirley knew she was going back for another week of hospital stay. She had mixed feelings of going back. She did enjoy interacting with other children. She was also able to attend the hospital school. She loved the short classes, which were taken up by coloring and drawing for the most part. The teacher, Nora, was a kind person. "Shirley is very bright," she had commented to Juliet several times. "She is a fast learner." They had reading moments, where they learned simple words from picture books. Shirley could not understand any words, except extremely simple words. But she was able to recognize the same word the next time she came to it. Unfortunately, they did not have reading moments often enough for Shirley to learn to read. Most of the time was spent doing other activities. Once, the children were provided with glitters. After drawing a girl in a fancy gown, Shirley squeezed some glue on the picture where she wanted to apply the glitters. She then sprinkled some glitters on the picture. The entire content of the small bottle was poured out.

"You don't know how to use glitters!" a girl remarked, glaring at Shirley.

"Yes, I do." Shirley made sure all the glue was touched with the glitters. Then she put the rest of the unused colorful glitters into the container. They could easily see that Shirley in fact did not use much of the glitters.

"She knows how to use it," corrected Nora. "It's very nice," she told Shirley, who thanked her promptly. Along with the creative times in the class, Shirley also drew during recreation. One day, a lady, who was in charge of art, told the children to draw a picture.

"It's a contest. The picture that wins will be made into greeting cards for the coming holiday season," said the lady. Shirley knew what she was going to draw. Only a few minutes later, a happy winter scene of a snowman in the middle with a squirrel and birds appeared on the paper. She began to color in the picture.

"Color the clouds gray," instructed the lady. Reluctantly, Shirley did as she was told. She did not intend the clouds to be gray, but she should do as requested. The time was almost up, and they were asked to clean up. Seeing the picture was not finished being colored in, the woman told Shirley that she would complete it for her. Shirley wished to finish it herself, but she knew it was not possible.

Besides those activities, Shirley also enjoyed her time with Dena, who always had a variety of tasks for her to complete, ranging from answering some questions after listening to Dena reading some passages from booklets to rearranging puzzle blocks to form the exact picture from a diagram. Shirley had no problem with the puzzles; she was fast in copying the diagrams. She highly enjoyed all the tasks.

"Well, my English is not good, but I will try my best," said Shirley before Dena was to ask her some questions.

"That's fine," said Dena. With her best effort, Shirley completed the questionnaires.

"So, Shirley, tell me your three wishes. What would you wish for?" Dena further continued with the exams.

"My first wish is for me to be able to walk. Then I hope my mom will get better," answered Shirley. She saw that Juliet was never feeling well. She could only watch on helplessly. She did like to help her mother. "My last wish is to have my own cat." Shirley thought of her cats from her grandmother's house. She missed them dearly. It would be so nice to have her very own cat. Dena recorded Shirley's replies on her notepad. Then she got a few coins out of her pants pocket. She showed one of each kind to Shirley.

"So, Shirley, what is this?" asked Dena, holding up a quarter. Shirley did not know what the coin was called. She could only shake her head. "How about this?" the psychologist was holding a penny. Again, Shirley only shook her head. She did not know the names to any of the coins. Shirley thought that Dena should not be surprised. Dena would be unable to name the money in China if she went there without knowing any Chinese.

"That's all for now. I'll see you soon."

"Thank you, Dena." Shirley wheeled herself out of the room and down the hall to her room. She knew her next stop was the physical therapy room. She did not look forward to it. They were starting a new therapy for her: wax therapy. She would be required to put her hands into hot, melted wax. She stayed in her room for a while until the therapists came to seek her. She followed them to the room.

"Put your hands in," instructed one therapist, Karen. Shirley did as she was told, but with a finger first. It felt like fire. How was she going to put both of her hands in? Were they expecting to cook her alive? With a deep breath, she put one hand in. She quickly took it out. It was burning.

"Now, Shirley, keep it in," insisted the other therapist. Gritting her teeth, Shirley did. "Put the other hand in." Shirley could not understand why the treatment would be beneficial for her. Her hands were not the major problems she had. Her legs were the reason why she was here in the first place.

"I'll give you this sticker if you keep your hands in," coaxed Karen. Even if it had not been for the stickers, Shirley would still do it since she had no choice. It was plain torture, she thought.

Juliet was outraged. She knew it was utterly senseless to have Shirley continue with this therapy. She demanded that they stop. Seeing that the treatment indeed did not help Shirley after several sessions, the therapists stopped upon their own decision. Shirley was greatly relieved. They should have known it was not the right treatment for her. They should treat each patient according to his or her unique needs, not following the same kind of treatment for every patient.

Shirley continued to receive other physical therapies, such as rolling on large balls and swimming in the pool. Shirley was required to lie face down on top of a large plastic ball to stretch her body. She felt highly uncomfortable in the position, for it sometimes hindered her ability to breathe. But what caused the most difficulty in breathing was being in the pool. Shirley had heart disease because of the arthritis, therefore, swimming in the pool made it difficult for her to breathe. What made matters worse was the water's temperature, which on many days could get quite chilly. She often came out from the water with goose bumps on her arms. Shirley made the best of it, splashing water gently so as not to get it on others. Juliet had bought her a fuchsia bathing suit for this pool activity. Shirley loved the suit; it was pretty and comfortable.

***

Since Shirley's appetite was still poor, Juliet often came to the hospital, bringing her own cooked food for her to eat, for the hospital meals did not appeal to Shirley. But as days went on, a dietitian from the hospital began to pay visits to Shirley during lunchtime. Her name was Elma and she stayed with Shirley during the entire lunchtime, trying to assist her eating needs. Shirley preferred to get her own tray, balancing it upon her lap as she wheeled herself slowly and watchfully to her table. At the same time, Elma brought over several plastic cups of juice, grape juice being the juice that was offered most often. Upon settling at the table, Shirley started eating from her tray. "Take a sip," said Elma, so Shirley took a sip of the grape juice. After having another bite of her food, Shirley was asked to take another sip. Hence, for every bite, Shirley had to take a sip. In no time, Shirley got full from all the sweetened juice, which made her feel sick. Juliet saw that the function of the dietitian's procedure, that was supposed to help Shirley, was causing discomfort.

"This is ridiculous!" exclaimed Juliet. "Please don't come here anymore," she requested Elma. "She can't eat like this." Shirley had finished nearly six cups of the fruit juice before she barely had enough bites. Sometimes, Shirley had drunk an entire cup after taking one bite. Elma insisted that she should continue on her plan, but Juliet ordered her to leave. Accordingly, Elma left, her feathers ruffled.

"What a relief. Her plan was quite senseless and rubbish," remarked Shirley, taking a bite without a sip. She had enough of the juice!

Days turned cooler as October approached. Her daily routine in the hospital continued, never missing a beat. She had regular sessions of physical therapy and psychological evaluation, along with other hospital practices. She often looked forward to the times she could roam freely in the hallways and visit other patients.

"Mom, I won the contest!" announced Shirley one day after seeing her winter picture had been made into greeting cards. But she was dismayed at the sight of the colors. The lady had painted the sky dark blue, and it did not turn out well; it had an uneven texture and quality. She wrinkled her nose at the gray clouds; white would look much nicer. "Oh well," she sighed. Juliet echoed her dismay. The greeting cards were for a donation, for what Shirley did not know. Many people had bought a box of cards. Shirley soon learned that Dr. Lehman had also bought her cards when she visited him for a checkup at the Blythedale clinic.

A dermatologist from the clinic, whom Shirley had seen, had prescribed cream for Shirley's rashes, which were getting worse, spreading to her upper arms. But the cream, as always, did not cure the condition.

Back in her room after the checkup, Shirley got out her pink nail polish and began to polish her nails. She had often been complimented on what an excellent job she did. Everyone had thought she had them professionally done by a manicurist.

"I wish I could polish like you," gushed Brook.

"I can polish your nails if you like."

"Sure!" Shirley wheeled over to Brook, who was holding out her hand. Shirley gently and steadily applied the polish on her nails. "Oh, you got it on my finger!" exclaimed Brook.

"It can be washed out with hot water or alcohol," stated Shirley. She got it on her fingers, too, and was able to wash it out without any problem.

"Well, be careful next time," said Brook. There was never a next time. Shirley did not offer anymore and Brook never asked again.

As the time passed, Shirley had visited Dr. Atkins two more times. Each time, Shirley had tried a new medication, but none worked for her, so it was decided that there was no more reason to go. At least, they had tried. There was no regret at going. Dr. Atkins was a wonderful person. Shirley was well-liked at his office. She had drawn many pictures for him and they had hung all her artwork in his office and by the desk. Everyone loved her drawings and in turn, she enjoyed drawing for them even more.

***

Dr. Lehman asked for Shirley to have both of her legs in casts to keep her legs in the straightest position, thus Shirley soon had the casts put on, and physical therapy ended.

"You can take the wheels off," explained Karen a few days later. Juliet did not know how to take the wheels off Shirley's wheelchair. It would help if the wheelchair was ever needed to be placed in a tight place for travel. "Just do this," said Karen, showing Juliet how to remove the wheels. Then she put them back on. Now, Juliet knew the trick. But she did not need to know it just yet, for she still used the stroller to take Shirley to places.

That day was a Friday, so they would go home that evening. Juliet would go back to the apartment to get ready for the trip.

After the therapy session, Juliet and Shirley went to her room. "I'm coming back later to pick you up," said Juliet before she left.

Shirley went out of the room to roam around. She saw drivers of the van getting ready for the trip as well, as they came in and out the elevator. She made several rounds on the floor. The floor was designed so that people could make a complete circle, passing many rooms in one trip without having to turn into another hallway. She was able to go quite fast with the wheelchair.

Without any warning, she fell. A loud thud sounded as her head hit the floor hard. Her cries rang loud, echoing off the walls. Through her tears, she saw legs running her way. Two of the van drivers picked her up, along with the wheelchair. The wheel had fallen off; Karen had not locked it in securely. Fortunately, her legs were in casts, therefore they did not receive any damage from the fall.

The men set the tearful Shirley down on her bed. Her head was in so much pain. She could feel it throbbing. At that instant, Juliet walked in. She gave a loud gasp when she saw Shirley's state.

"Oh my, what happened?"

Through her tears, Shirley told her. Juliet was horrified. She examined Shirley's head and found a large bump. A nurse came in to administer two tablets of Tylenol for Shirley. "I'll give them to her," offered Juliet. The nurse agreed and left with that. "I will not give it to you. I read that people should not take this type of medicine within two hours after an injury, as it is very harmful."

"Really? I never knew that."

"Yes. I am going back to the apartment to fetch some Chinese medicine." Without wasting a single minute, she headed off.

In just several minutes, Juliet was back. She applied the powder, mixed with some alcohol, on Shirley's bump. She also give the capsules to Shirley. She knew the medication was a miracle; it could treat any injury, whether it be internal or external.

"My head does not hurt anymore," announced Shirley, smiling.

Juliet examined her head again. "I told you this works like a miracle!" said Juliet, smiling back. "The bump is much smaller now. Good thing I have the medicine."

"I'm glad, too. I'm much better now."

Juliet was grateful that the injury was not great. Shirley could have easily gotten hurt a lot more badly, and the bump on her head could have been a lot worse.

Juliet was fuming. "It is Karen's responsibility to make sure that the wheels are properly put back in place." As the woman was in her thoughts, she saw Karen walking past the room, not coming in to check how Shirley was doing, let alone to apologize.

"Good thing I have the casts on; my legs did not get hurt at all." Shirley patted the casts, which had several of her drawings and people's signatures and good wishes.

A moment later, Alexandra went over to Shirley and showed her own sticker collection and a coloring book. She also brought over some crayons. Alexandra was going to stay for the weekend.

"It's time to leave," reminded Juliet.

"Mom, I don't want to go."

"But why?" Juliet was disheartened. Shirley wished to stay and play with Alexandra. Without any hope, Juliet reluctantly relented. Juliet was to return home alone. But no doubt she would soon be back.

Juliet dragged herself to the elevator. Before the doors closed, a great waterfall of tears streamed down her face.

"What's wrong?" inquired a concerned lady.

Juliet could not answer. Her soft sobs were overwhelming. She missed her daughter already!

She painfully moved toward her car, got in, and started the engine. All the actions seemed to have controlled by an outside source; it did not feel that her body was doing all this. She glanced at the empty seat next to her and more tears fell. Her eyes blurry, Juliet entered the streets. An hour later, the still-sobbing Juliet went inside the house. Kwi Show had no idea what had happened.

"The wheelchair fell down and Shirley received a large bump," said Juliet. "And...she won't come home." After only a few minutes, Juliet stood up from the sofa, marched over to the main door, and announced that she was heading back.

"But you just merely arrived!" Kwi Show watched Juliet close the door behind her.

Meanwhile, in the hospital, Shirley lay in her bed. She wished she had gone home. She had a feeling that her mother would come back. True enough, Shirley saw her figure outside the window an hour later.

"Mom, I would like to go home."

"Yes, I'm bringing you home!" Without uttering another word, Juliet brought Shirley straight to her car. It was quite late, passing ten. As usual, once Shirley got in the seat and Juliet drove off, Shirley fell fast asleep.

Chapter Thirty-Three

"You're leaving for good?" asked Alexandra. Shirley nodded a confirmation. She had been discharged from the hospital after Dr. Lehman had noticed that the stay did not help Shirley at all.

Shirley was not sad about leaving. She was glad to leave this place. It had been four tiring months. No one mentioned the word "surgery" for Shirley. Dr. Lehman decided that there was no treatment available for her. But her health was quite stable from taking the herbal foods.

It was thus time to bid everyone farewell. Shirley said her goodbyes to all the patients she knew.

Shirley visited Dr. Lehman after the discharge from the hospital. Then Juliet took Shirley around the hospital to bid some people goodbye. They went to Dena's office; Dena had a present waiting for Shirley. It was a stuffed ballerina hippopotamus dressed in pink ribbons and laces. Shirley hugged the stuffed animal close to her heart, and thanked her. She really enjoyed the times spent with the nice person. Dena was always kind and good to her.

The last stop was at the hospital classroom on the second floor.

"She has been such a pleasure in the class!" exclaimed Nora. "We're going to miss her very much."

"You've been so nice to her," Juliet thanked her. Before they left, a teacher handed Juliet a packet of papers, saying that they needed to be given to Shirley's school. With one last wave, Juliet and Shirley went away.

"We're all ready to leave," confirmed Juliet. Shirley nodded. Shirley was glad, but yet felt somewhat sad to be leaving some of her friends. She had fun in the recreation room. She recollected the carnival the hospital had some time ago. She was an extremely good player at all the games she played, including throwing hoops and hitting objects at targets. As a result, she had won three stuffed animals. She had noticed that the number of prizes she won surpassed the majority of players. She also had photographs taken and they were made into buttons that could be pinned onto clothes.

Shirley held on to her small notepad tightly as they went down the elevator. It was a telephone book Shirley used as an autograph book. She had everyone she knew sign it. Unfortunately, she could not read most of the words. The signers had read her the entries, but it would be much nicer to be able to read it over and over again on her own.

"We're home!" Shirley eyed the brick house gleefully. Kwi Show came out and helped them inside. Home sweet home; no place in the whole world could replace a warm home.

After all was settled, Juliet took out the packet the teacher gave. She scanned the documents. Her eyes rested upon the psychologists' report, which was dated August 1993.

Her blood froze when her eyes took in its content. Her mind felt numb and yet, at the same time, felt like a burning furnace. She could not believe what she beheld. She read these horrible words of slander and sheer lies:

"Upon introduction, Shirley was very fearful of working together despite familiarity with this evaluator."

"Although all aspects of testing were previously discussed, Shirley was tearful until she was shown the testing environment and sample tasks."

"She demonstrated little confidence in her abilities as well as a very low frustration tolerance. Throughout all testing sessions, her initial response was that she was unable to complete specific items, and required reassurance and encouragement to tackle such tasks. This was seen on both verbal and manipulative activities. During testing, Shirley was immediately stressed by such tasks and required constant reassurance that these unfamiliar tasks were not beyond her capabilities."

"On projective testing, Shirley expressed childlike fantasies as well as fear regarding her functioning, familiar relationships and illness. Her pictures displayed figures whose limbs were withered and ineffective; yet despite their "bent" stature, they remained vital objects. Her three wishes were to walk, that her mother could feel better, and to have her own cat. Such worries were reflected in her infantile behaviors, lack of self-confidence, as well as tremendous anxiety with new experiences and challenging activities."

Juliet was steaming by now. She continued reading.

"It is recommended that Shirley be placed in a small structured classroom environment. Shorter tasker assignments should be given so Shirley will not become overwhelmed and frightened."

What shocking, truly outrageous statements. It was a gross distortion of the whole situation. It contorted Shirley's image, brought a slander upon her! Juliet's blood boiled. She was definitely not showing this to the school. She was going to seek justice. No one should ever do this to anyone. Every single word typed on these papers was an untruth. How could Dena have done such a blind thing? Juliet had thought so well of Dena. She knew now that it was a mask she had been seeing all the time.

"I shouldn't have told Dena about my custody case of 1990," Juliet said to herself. "I saw that she had been so nice, so I told her." The report stated the name of another psychologist who had written it besides Dena.

Juliet was still distraught some moments later. Shirley inquired about it once she saw her. Juliet told her of the report. Shirley was stunned. Never had she thought that anyone could write such an untrue report. She thought back to those days with Dena. She was never tearful or frightened. In fact, she had looked forward to each task. She never groaned, but only smiled. Dena knew that; she had seen her smiles during the tests. Needed reassurance? That was not true. She never needed reassurance from anyone. She did not prefer reassurance from others, for it was no use for her from the start. She had always been confident with everything she did or was going to do. She had only expressed concerns about her poor English. Shirley had said nothing negative. And the attacks on her drawings and three wishes went overboard. It was monstrous! What reason had Dena had for writing such lies?

"Mom, don't worry. We can't do anything about it." She furrowed her brow as a thought struck her. "But I never saw the other psychologist. I remember just seeing Dena."

Juliet sighed. "I can't believe that there can be some people out there who could do this." She shook her head. "This will never happen in China. Just imagine—even a mother like me is accused of being abusive to her child, and they even say that I'm crazy! I travel the world seeking care and compassion. Everyone admired us in China." She turned her attention to other things. "I think you can start school now. I have tried everything for you here, and have done my best. Nothing works for you here. I think the school will be a great environment in which to be. We're moving to an apartment and I'm finding a school in that area." It was time to move out for Shirley's education.

This was definitely new news for Shirley. She wondered what school would be like. She had often dreamt of riding on the yellow buses. How grand it would be! She could finally learn how to read English.

The next month in November, Juliet set out to search for a place to live. Finding an apartment in a good location with handicap accessibility was not an easy job. At last, she found a nice apartment with brick construction. After renting the apartment, she set forth on the hunt for a school. She made several calls for information. She obtained a few numbers to the local schools. She called a few schools and finally found the right school. She was connected to the school psychologist, Mr. Jeffs. An appointment was scheduled with him for the following week. Juliet went home to tell Shirley the good news.

***

Juliet parked her car in front of the elementary school. She headed straight to the front desk where she asked to see Mr. Jeffs. "I have an appointment with him." After hearing the directions, she made her way to his office.

"Nice to meet you," said Mr. Jeffs, giving Juliet a handshake. Once they seated in the chairs, Juliet started telling him of Shirley's situation.

"She can't read or write English. She didn't receive any form of education, except activity times in the hospitals."

"We are very excited to have Shirley here," stated Mr. Jeffs. "I had never heard anything like this—someone starting school at age eleven! It's certainly a very unique case." It would be an interesting experience for both Shirley and the school.

He told her about special education. She had never heard of such classes. He explained they were for students with special needs. Hence, Juliet registered Shirley in a special education class.

"Her teacher will be Mr. Crisfield."

"So, we're going to meet him first?"

"Yes, you can have that scheduled."

"Thank you, Mr. Jeffs."

"We look forward to seeing Shirley."

Juliet left the school grounds with many thoughts. Would the teacher be nice? Would Shirley have fun? She did not expect Shirley to learn much; her main objectives were to let Shirley have fun and interact with children her age. It was going to be a whole new life for Shirley. A life, Juliet hoped, that Shirley would enjoy. It was time to focus on other things other than treatment. That one year when Shirley was four years old was rewarding. But Juliet knew it would be remarkably hard for them to get to that point again. They would continue to try later. But now it was time for some fun.

Chapter Thirty-Four

The misty sky appeared as though wrapped in a thin aluminum foil. The songs of birds became absent as days flew by. A sphere of crystalline flower would alight upon the cold ground soon. All the trees were naked of their green clothes, while the ground was barren of lush grass. Stores were getting up the decorations for the coming holiday season. It would be a relaxing Christmas for Juliet and Shirley.

"Okay, I'm warm enough!" Shirley exclaimed under a warm, fuzzy hat, wrapped in a thick scarf.

"I need to make sure," reiterated Juliet for the third time. "We have everything ready," she said, while checking the bag that hung behind the stroller.

"*The Cat in the Hat* is in there?" asked Shirley, referring to the blue story book by Dr. Seuss. Juliet nodded. Everything was all set for the departure.

Juliet and Shirley went on their way to visit the man who was to be Shirley's very first teacher. On the road, many thoughts floated into Shirley's mind. The prospect of starting school for the first time excited her on a grand scale. She had often wished to read a book or even just a single sentence. She had many books at home, mostly filled with colorful drawings. She often held a book in her hands and pretended to read it. She frequently asked her mother to read it, but Juliet was either too busy or tired to do so for long. Therefore, Shirley could only enjoy the pictures. She fervently hoped she could read. And she could not believe that the time had finally arrived; a chance for her to learn not just English, but all things of life. Although her mother was always trying her hardest to keep Shirley busy, Shirley's life was simple and bare. True, she could draw. But it could get boring after some time. She watched cartoons and *I Love*

Lucy comedy show on television, but had a hard time fully understanding what the characters said. She did, however, manage to understand the content of the shows. She was excited about meeting her teacher.

Juliet met the teacher a few days ago and came back home, with her eyes shining with mirth. "He is a very kind person," Juliet had reported. Now it was Shirley's turn to meet him.

"Is this the school?" Shirley inquired when Juliet stopped by the building. Juliet nodded. She got out the stroller from the trunk, set it up by the door, and carried Shirley out with much effort. Shirley was getting quite big for the stroller now, but still managed to sit in without discomfort. She was not a tall girl; her growth had ceased at five feet. Shirley's eyes flashed with excitement. She could hardly sit still. Juliet pushed her to the main office, where a few ladies were busy typing and answering phones behind the desk.

"We're here to see Mr. Crisfield," Juliet told a lady who was standing up to assist them.

"Okay, great, Mrs. Cheng." A smile was prominent on her face. "Hi, Shirley, I'm Mrs. Tompkins," she kindly greeted the pair. Then she told Juliet his classroom number in case she had forgotten.

They passed many closed doors to classrooms full of students who were listening—or pretending to listen—to their teachers. They soon arrived at the appointed room. The door was ajar. Juliet gave a few knocks. Footsteps sounded, and the door swung open to admit them in.

The eyes that Shirley saw soothed her soul and vanquished all worries she ever had. Mr. Crisfield's kind eyes greeted them with a smile.

"Good to see you, Mrs. Cheng and Shirley!" He asked them to follow him into the room. Shirley saw a circle of students in the center. There were around eight or nine kids who were all her age. They looked at her with curiosity, but with no trace of hostility or prejudice.

"So, can you read?" The teacher asked Shirley in order to better understand her situation. Shirley could not read a single word, other than extremely simple words such as "cat" and "boy." Dena had reported that she knew only six cited words. Shirley turned to the first page of *The Cat in the Hat*. With her finger under the words, she began to read. In actuality, she had listened to the cassette tape of the story so many times that she had memorized the entire story. If anyone asked her to read any random word in the book, she would be unable to accomplish the request.

After a few minutes into the interview, they agreed upon the date Shirley was to start in his class. They were all excited about this special event in her life. She was to start on December 6, right before the new year of 1994 when Shirley would turn eleven. It would be an unquestionably promising year for her.

Juliet was concerned that Shirley would be too tired, and suggested that she arrive at school later in the morning rather than arriving at the regular time.

Shirley would use the wheelchair the hospital had given her to get around the class. The frame of the wheelchair was in the color of bright hot pink as Shirley requested.

Then a few knocks sounded on the door before it was swung open to admit Mr. Jeffs in. He came to meet Shirley, followed by an occupational therapist, who introduced herself as Dyan. Shirley cheerfully greeted all of them, flashing a winning smile.

"It is so good to have you start school," said Mr. Jeffs.

"I am very excited about it," chirped Shirley.

As she spoke those words, another woman walked into the room, her warm countenance shone with smiles.

"Hi, Shirley, I'm the school nurse, Mrs. James," she introduced herself, holding out a hand, which Shirley readily shook.

Everyone appears to be so nice, thought Shirley,

feeling heavenly.

Their conversation continued for another few minutes until it was time to get going.

"I am looking forward to it," Mr. Crisfield told Shirley as they were leaving.

"Me, too, Mr. Crisfield."

They left the room, with Shirley holding the blue book. She knew she would be reading much more advanced books than this book.

"So, what do you think of him? He seems like a really nice person, doesn't he?" Juliet remarked when they got into her blue Ford Escort.

"Yes, he does. I think I will be very happy there." Shirley declared with a wide smile; her eyes sparkled.

***

Shirley listened as Mr. Crisfield read the book in his hands. Her eyes roamed around the room, taking it all in. The kids, she thought, seemed quite nice. She concentrated hard on what the teacher was reading, but could not understand the content of the story. The English was hard to grasp. She noticed a shelf full of books at the right corner of the room. They were neatly stacked in place. She wondered what adventure each of the books held between its pages. She yearned to pick one and start reading it fluently. It was December 6 and she had awoken that morning with a happy cry. It was her first day in a school and no words could replace the fulgent light that emitted from her eyes.

Shortly, it was dismissal time. Before Shirley left for the day, Mr. Crisfield walked to his bookcase and fingered through the titles. His hand then rested upon a thin yellow book, and took it out. He brought it over to Shirley. "You can take this home and start reading it."

Shirley flipped through the picture book; drawings of all kinds of vegetables decorated its pages. She could not even read its title. Did he expect her to know every word for tomorrow? She had to work fast then.

Shirley thanked the teacher before she left. It was a day she would never forget, a day that would be engraved in her mind forever. She could hardly come to the realization of the fact that she had finally attended her first day of school, and moreover, that the day had been spent so happily.

She boarded the yellow school bus. Everything was so new to her, and she welcomed each change enthusiastically.

Juliet was waiting by the window. When Shirley's small bus arrived, Juliet got out of the apartment and went out to take her in.

"How was school?" Juliet asked Shirley as soon as she saw her in the bus.

"It's wonderful!" Shirley answered with an excited nod of her head. "I also brought a book home," she reported, holding out the yellow book, which her teacher put in a plastic ziplock bag. It also contained a folder to record her reading progress; every student had it. After each book was read, a parent or guardian was to sign the paper alongside the title and author's name. Another item in the transparent bag was a note to Juliet from the teacher. She wondered what it said. Surely, it was the progress of Shirley's first day.

Once Juliet wheeled Shirley inside, Shirley handed the book to Juliet. "I cannot understand any word in it." Juliet looked over the book. It was quite an easy book with simple words below the pictures of a boy planting his own garden.

Juliet pointed at a random word, "This reads carrot." She told Shirley the meaning in Chinese.

Shirley repeated the word aloud accurately. After she learned "carrot," she moved on to "pineapple." Consequently, she learned each word this way.

After several minutes, Shirley was able to read a complete sentence on her own with Juliet's assistance.

Soon, Juliet had to do some chores, so had to leave Shirley to figure out the rest of the book on her own.

A couple of hours later, Juliet checked on Shirley to see how she was doing. She opened the door to their room, and she was greeted with a huge grin on Shirley's face.

"I can read most of the book!" She announced happily. At long last, she read a book all by herself. She could hardly believe that she could finally read. They were nevertheless *words*, even if they were simple words. She truly enjoyed the new feeling. It was her first official academic achievement. Much more awaited her in the years to come.

"I read the note from your teacher and it's really nice," Juliet told Shirley. "I'll read the note to you." She cleared her throat before beginning. "Mrs. Cheng: Shirley's first day went fabulously. She worked hard, seemed to be enjoying what she was doing, and was welcomed by the other students. I have sent home a book that may be too easy, but I'd like to give it a try. If it is too hard, then she should try it and practice and we'll check it tomorrow. Thank you."

Upon hearing it, Shirley felt quite pleased. "The book is definitely not too easy for me, but I learned how to read it!"

Chapter Thirty-Five

"I love you!" mother and daughter each called to the other the following day. They waved goodbye as Shirley boarded the bus.

Shirley looked out the bus' windows, and thought of the good news she was going to tell her teacher. He would certainly be pleased with her.

As she had expected, he was glad, mingled with surprise. He knew that he had got a fast learner in his class.

Shirley brought the same book home on the second day. She wanted to be certain that she was able to read every word before starting a new book. Soon afterward, each and every day, Shirley brought a new book home.

On December 10, Shirley brought home another letter from the teacher. Elation filled Juliet as she read each word. Then she read the note to Shirley, who listened to it with a wide smile. "I'm glad that Shirley has responded with such a positive attitude toward school. She really is a joy to have in our class."

"I enjoy being in his class so much! The days are wonderful. I feel so happy when I am able to read simple words now," said Shirley. Juliet felt like crying with joy. After a week, Juliet no longer helped with Shirley's reading, for Shirley could learn all the new words entirely by herself.

Before a two-week period, Shirley began to write poems on any notebook she happened to find at the time. One day, she wrote a whole notebook of poems.

"Mom, here's another letter from Mr. Crisfield!" announced Shirley on the afternoon of January 13 after she came home from school. Juliet pushed her in the apartment. "I'll read it to you," said Juliet. "Mrs. Cheng: This is a quick note to let you know how well Shirley is doing. Her writing, her reading, her math are just great! Everyone enjoys her being in class and she seems to enjoy being here." Juliet paused, for further down the letter, he had requested to meet her. "He would like to meet me to discuss your progress and to let me know what he has planned for the rest of the year."

Accordingly, Juliet scheduled an appointment with him, and it was scheduled toward the end of the month.

"Shirley is brilliant! She is very fast with all of her studies," he told her once the appointed day arrived.

Juliet beamed with happiness. She felt herself the luckiest mother ever. "But you are a wonderful teacher. Shirley likes being in your class so much. She comes home with a big smile each day," she said.

Following the meeting, Shirley brought two boxes of cupcakes to class to celebrate her eleventh birthday. Her birthday was on a Sunday, so she celebrated with the class on Monday. Everyone cheered and smiled with a cupcake or two in hand. There was soon no more left.

Shirley returned home that day, humming the birthday song. "How was the day?" questioned her mother, wheeling her inside the apartment.

"It is great, as usual. But quick—I need to use the bedpan!"

Juliet rapidly got Shirley on the bed. Shirley received immediate relief. Juliet shook her head, emitting a sigh. "This is nonsense!" There was one barrier that hindered Shirley from achieving a complete state of happiness in school. Juliet was forbidden to go to school to take her to the bathroom. And there was no one else who could take her. As a result, she could not use the bathroom for the entire school day. She had to hold in her urine for hours. She relieved herself when she came home every day. It was her first priority once returning home; homework was her second. Juliet had contacted Taconic Resource, seeking their help. But they could not offer any solution. Shirley had to continue to spend entire days without going to the bathroom.

In spite of the situation, she never complained. She kept on smiling. It did not stop her from enjoying each day, though she needed to be highly careful not to wet herself. Sometimes, it was extremely hard for her to hold it in, especially when she had to do physical therapies.

The physical therapist gave her therapy every day while she received occupational therapies with Dyan once a week. As a result of physical therapies, Shirley often missed classes. She was in disfavor with it, but she had no choice. She was required to receive both therapy sessions, even though none was improving her health.

"I know."

"They can't let you go on like this. Your days in school could be much more enjoyable without this hindrance."

Shirley shrugged. She was clueless as to what to do. She did not understand their rules, either. "Well, let me do my homework now."

"You need to rest a bit."

"No, I don't want to. I want to do it. I also brought a few books home to read."

"More books? You are unbelievable! You just brought home a few books yesterday."

"I finished them."

"You are too fast."

"My English is getting so much better. I love it. I love the feeling of being able to read!"

"I remember you always wanting me to read to you, and I never could. My throat hurts me a lot."

"Yes. But now I can do it all on my own now." Shirley's smile widened.

"You know, it had just been a few months since Dena wrote those lies! Now, she has definitely been proven wrong. How can a person become so smart in such a short time, especially how she had put it? The report states that it was written when you were ten years and six months old."

Shirley laughed and rolled her eyes. "There are simply people like her out there. You know that I'm not like the way she described; I know as well. She knows, too, and that's all that matters."

***

The school had P.A.R.P., a reading program to encourage the students to read with the participation of parents. In March, each student was asked to create a creature they would like to have as their reading buddy. The school would pick the best picture to be on a cover of the P.A.R.P. booklet.

Shirley was highly excited about the project. She always welcomed each drawing assignment with much enthusiasm. A furry creature swiftly formed in her head. She quickly drew down the little friendly monster on a piece of paper. The creature had two round parts, one for its head and the other for the body. It had two antennas sticking out of its furry head. She had drawn a cute smile upon its features.

At the same time, she had made greeting cards for St. Patrick's Day and distributed it to all she knew.

"Thank you so much, Shirley! It's a beautiful picture!" commented the principal of the school. "You'll be famous one day."

Days later, the school chose the picture for P.A.R.P. Shirley's eyes widened when she heard that she had been picked. She soon received a certificate for her picture.

The year approached the spring month of April, during which Shirley learned she had won another competition. She received a certificate in the mail for her winning art entry for the contest to celebrate Children and Hospitals Week. The drawing was displayed at the Hospital for Special Surgery. She wished that she could see the display of her drawing, but because she was starting to visit Dr. Lehman at the Blythedale clinic, for it was much closer than traveling to the city, she would not be able to see it. Shortly, she received another piece of mail. It was a letter from a social worker from the hospital, thanking her for her artwork.

By May, Shirley was reading fourth-grade-level books. All the picture books became too easy for her. She could easily whiz through two hundred pages daily. Juliet got tired signing all the paper. Shirley was reading too much. Juliet, herself, could not keep up with the English.

At that time one day, Mr. Crisfield told Shirley she could go to the fourth grade class instead. "She will do fine there," he said to Juliet. Juliet was skeptical, but Mr. Crisfield was confident. Shirley would do great in a regular class. Hence, Shirley went to the fourth grade class, and was allowed to go back to the special education class if she ever wished. She liked the new class, and the teacher was a nice person, but she missed her old class and their schedule. Shirley understood the fourth grade's content, but she found it dull. She decided to return to the special education class. After all, she had attended school for only a remarkably short time, and needed to stay in special education for a while longer until she could fully grasp everything.

Each day, Shirley looked forward to boarding the bus to school. Not only did she love learning, but she loved her teacher and classmates as well. Her first impression of them was correct; they were all kind people who held no discrimination toward her. But then, she was always admired and treated well by most children. Not a single child had ever made fun of her disabilities. She was surprised at that, for she had heard many unfortunate stories of kids being teased because of their differences.

Shirley had befriended all her classmates. But her best friend was a girl by the name of Laura. They often joked around in the class and sat together at all times. Yet Mr. Crisfield was the biggest joker in the class. He often teased students in a friendly way and made silly faces until the whole class was filled with laughter that traveled down the hall.

Whenever it was time for the students to pair up to read to each other, Mr. Crisfield often warned the class of Shirley's loud voice. With a sheepish grin, Shirley would then lower her voice. She often lost herself in the story and enjoyed each reading session so much, it made her read with much gusto.

They were starting to learn to write in cursive. Each student was handed a practice book for the lessons. They would copy the words in the book. They also had worksheets to practice their handwriting. Shirley was a fast writer and was able to finish each worksheet in only a few minutes.

"Here's the worksheet. I'm done with it," said Shirley, handing it back to Mr. Crisfield so he could check it over.

"Shirley, you have to do it. Copy the sentence."

"But I did. This is what I wrote."

"You mean that you wrote this?" asked the astounded teacher. He had thought that what Shirley had written was the printed text on the worksheet. He was fooled by her handwriting because of its neatness and accuracy. Despite her severe arthritis and painful fingers, she wrote beautifully.

***

Winter came and went, followed by spring. Soon afterward, it was summer's turn to poke out its rosy head. Summer arrived with pink blossoms upon the full foliage of green trees, and new chicks in the nests that rested upon the branches. It was a happy time for everybody, except one. And that person was Shirley. She never wanted to miss a day of school. She winced each time the radio announced a snow day. And now that the summer was here, it meant that Shirley could not go to school for nearly ninety days.

Before the school year ended, the class had put on a play, where Shirley played the role of a rabbit. Because of her good memory, she had memorized her entire part in a matter of minutes. She had a wonderful time during the play, which was repeated a few times, so that many classes in the school could come to enjoy it.

Shirley had to sadly bade goodbye to everyone on the last day. Then a happy thought replaced her sadness: she could now enjoy all the books the world had to offer. She was able to read books that were at fourth and fifth grade levels with ease. No longer would she wait for others to read to her. She could read as much as she wanted. Thereupon, she completed three books each day.

Therefore, the summer was spent with books surrounding Shirley's life. She also kept a journal and put down her daily happenings and thoughts in it.

It, she knew, was a year worth remembering for years to come. She would always cherish that first moment when she could read a book by herself. She loved her teacher and classmates tremendously. After being in school, she had brought home a wealth of knowledge, high grades, and much praise that could be treasured for years, including this comment made by Mr. Crisfield: "Shirley is an enthusiastic, brilliant, and highly motivated student. She is well-liked and always approaches her work with enthusiasm. She always wants to do well and takes pride in doing a good job. Her happy, friendly disposition, and eagerness to learn has made her a real joy."

***

One day out of the blue, the telephone rang, interrupting the quiet moment. Juliet answered it. "Hello?"

"Yi? This is Al."

"Al?" she did not disguise the shock in her voice. It had been a few years since they had last spoken. What had brought him to make a call? It must be a big event for him to waste his precious time.

"I wanted to see how everything is," he was saying.

He did? Juliet was skeptical. "Everything is fine," she answered. Then she told him of Shirley's successes during her first year of school. "She attended only a total of ninety days or so of class, and she can read really well now. Her teacher had even asked her to attend a fourth grade class just this past spring."

"Good," came the laconic response. "I think I should take her back to China and seek treatment for her, and you can stay here. I will take care of her." After all these years, never spending over a minute with Shirley, he wanted to take care of Shirley all by himself? Something was not right. "Shirley needs to go for treatments," he continued.

"I need to go. I will not have you go alone with her. You don't know her. All these years it has been I who has been caring for her."

"Fine," he reluctantly agreed.

Days later, Al went to their apartment to urge Juliet further. After some careful thinking, Juliet agreed. Thus, Shirley was to go back to China for the sixth time.

Shirley was horrified at the thought. She immediately thought of school. She just started school, and now she was going to leave. She was saddened by the plan for many days.

Chapter Thirty-Six

The dreaded day knocked on their door. All the bags were packed, which were quite a few. Al picked up the pair, and together they drove to the airport. It was September, and leaves were about to begin to turn into all shades of colors. Autumn was Shirley's favorite season. She loved the beautiful, mystical scene of autumn, and the falling leaves as they alighted upon earth one by one. Above all, she loved the season because it was time for a new school year. Shirley thought of all her friends who had started school just a few days earlier.

She sighed as she boarded the plane, carried by Al, who placed her on her seat by the window. She always sat by the window; it was her favorite place to be. She must admit, she loved being on planes. But too bad she did not find the Chinese airline food tempting. It was only on Western flights where she had enjoyed the menu. The fruit salad in small, blue bowls were mighty mouth watering. As she thought back, most foods did not hold her interest. She knew what ill fortune had befallen her when she was five months old. And it was the cause of the pinworms, thus a loss of appetite was a result. The only foods she liked were chocolate, some certain cheese, and pickles, which she had been eating for years and they had helped her with her nausea. Pizza and french fries were also fine. But they were not good for her. Plus, even if she could eat them in abundance, she would be unable to physically endure the tremendous nausea that often overwhelmed her when she had oily dishes. She understood it all too well. She often joked that she always liked the food that was not healthy. She tried eating those food labeled as "good for the body," but each time she got it down, nausea invaded her body. She was always filled with nausea. "Just like a pregnant woman," her mother often commented. Many people could not understand what she had to go through each and every day; only Juliet knew. Yes, Juliet knew with all her heart, and had been working hard to feed Shirley daily.

It would be an extremely long trip, for the tickets Al brought were nonstop, without any rests in between. Consequently, they would have to be on the plane for over thirty hours straight.

"Al, why did you buy such tickets?" demanded Juliet.

"They are perfectly fine."

"You don't care for Shirley's well-being at all. You have bought the cheapest tickets!"

Al turned away and ignored her.

The flight attendants went to each passenger, asking which meal they would like. After receiving the trays, Juliet opened the lid of the bottle that held the fruit juice on Shirley's tray. Each passenger received one bottle, and there would not be more given.

"Yummy, this is good," said Shirley. Juliet smiled. She did not touch the bottle on her own tray, saving it for Shirley. She gave Shirley her own juice after Shirley was done drinking from her own cup. Juliet glanced at Al. He picked up his own cup and drank the juice down to the last drop. She knew he would not save anything for Shirley. Juliet cut the meat in Shirley's tray into small pieces. Shirley wrinkled her nose. "Just have some of this. Try it. If you don't like it, I'll give you the food I brought," said Juliet, handing Shirley the fork.

Using her left hand, Shirley took a small piece of the meat into her mouth. She was nearly ambidextrous, so if her right hand got tired, she could use her left. She could do almost everything with her left hand, except writing. But her left-handed writing was not bad at all; it was better than many right-handed handwritings she saw. She tried drawing with her left, and it was the same as with her writing; not bad but not as good as her right-handed work. She was also able to draw with both hands at the same time. She had a riot doing that.

The tired Juliet helped Shirley fall asleep after Shirley managed to get a few bites down in her stomach, but they were obviously not enough fuel for her. She had refused to eat anything else. When would the flight end? Juliet was too drained. She could hardly wait to get to a hotel after the ride ended. Little did she know that many hardships were in store for her and Shirley.

***

The flight finally ended at an airport in Shanghai. The plane's descent was an awful experience for Shirley, whose ears were hurting tremendously. Before the trip, Juliet took Shirley to the emergency room to get her earwax removed for the upcoming flights, but the doctor was unable to remove it. Dr. Madison was not at the office at the time, so Juliet had brought Shirley to Dr. Frank.

At the appointed day, the day before the departure to China, Shirley offered to draw a picture for Dr. Frank. "Here are some sheets of paper and a pen," Juliet said, supplying Shirley with the equipment that she had brought with them. She always had sheets and pens with them.

In simply a matter of minutes, a picture of a beautiful girl in a flowery dress appeared on the paper. "Wow," gushed Dr. Frank," his eyes widening. "It's wonderful!" Appreciation and admiration shone in his kind eyes. He gave his thanks.

"You're welcome!" chirped Shirley. Both Shirley and Juliet could see that Dr. Frank had a gentle countenance, a confirmation of what the woman had said. But the appointment did not bring relief to Shirley. The earwax was still in both of her ears. She had to board the plane with her ears stuffed with it.

Juliet, with dark circles around her eyes, got off the plane, and pushed Shirley among the throng. She did not sleep a wink, but had made certain that Shirley got some. Al, on the other hand, had snored like a pig beside her. It was approaching noontime.

Without stopping for any rest, Al led the two to board a huge bus.

"Can't we ride in a cab?" demanded Juliet.

Al only shook his head. He obstinately moved forward toward the bus. It was the cheapest transportation. He had saved the money for the worst transportation possible.

Juliet was furious. "We need some rest! We've been on the plane for thirty-two hours!" No words could persuade him. Disheartened, she could only follow him.

It was a high bus in the color of blue. Juliet had a hard time climbing onto it. It felt like climbing a mountain.

Al carried Shirley onto Juliet's lap on the front seat right by the steep stairs. Juliet held on to Shirley tightly. Al made his way to the back for a comfortable seat. Shirley's heart pounded so hard that it seemed as though it would jump out of her throat at any minute. With her eyes reflecting terror, she eyed the stairs underneath her dangling feet.

Without any warning, the bus started with a jerk. Shirley nearly screamed, but restrained herself. She held on to her mother with all her might. Her knuckles turned white from the force. She tried to close her eyes, but they would not obey and instead continue to stare at the black hole before her. The bus drove on, weaving into the crowded streets, which were filled with people on bicycles, buses, and cabs. She gasped whenever the bus got very close to the people in front of it. She hoped that there would not be any accident. The streets were too crowded. Each time the driver stepped on the brakes, the bus jerked, thus shaking Shirley. She had never been so frightened in her life. The bus ride to Shi Liou Pu Pier seemed like an eternity. It would last two hours.

Before the trip, Juliet had contacted Dr. Lion, the doctor who had invented Yi Sen Juan Pi Wan. He had promised that they would brew some herbs for Shirley.

Therefore, Juliet thought it was a fine plan.

After the bus came to a halt, Al carried the much-weakened Shirley off and placed her into the stroller. She had no more strength left in her. Her heart still pounded.

Shirley was horrified when a few men, including Al, started carrying her stroller with her in it onto the boat. Her eyes glued to the rippling waters below. The boat rocked as the men inched their way toward it with the stroller in hand. This was unbelievable. How long would the ordeal last? She would not be surprised if they were to send her on the rockets next. The men heaved and shoved. Shirley clung tight to the stroller. She did not want to fall. Juliet watched on helplessly.

Shaking, Shirley let out a long sigh. They had gotten her on the rocking boat. She was safe and sound, sitting next to her mother.

"This is outrageous! How could you do this to us? What is this?" Juliet hissed at Al, who was nonchalant about it all. He did not care for them. He got his rest. Plus, he had saved plenty of money with the bus and the cheapest plane tickets.

Shirley, with heavy eyelids, tried to go to sleep. But it was hard to do so. She did not feel so well on the undulating Huang Pu River. The boat would take them to Nan Tong City in about five hours.

Juliet put her hand underneath Shirley's head to support her as Shirley started to drift off in a restless sleep. Juliet maintained her hold during the entire time. "Al, could you please support her head? My hand is really getting cramped," whispered Juliet an hour later. Her hand was starting to feel like a block of cement. He simply shook his head. Juliet, therefore, continued to support Shirley's head. She wanted Shirley to sleep. Juliet felt as though a ton of mass was weighing on her eyelids, but she could not sleep; she still kept supporting Shirley's head, which by now felt like one hundred pounds rather than just eight.

About four hours later, Shirley woke up to scurrying

feet and rustling clothes and luggage. "We're there?"

"Yes," answered Juliet, slowly taking back her stiffened hand. She tried to rub the soreness away. She glared at Al. How could he be so heartless?

Shirley's heart started to pound as she was carried off the boat, which was rocking to and fro, with much difficulty. She glanced at the dark water, kissed by faint moonlight. The stroller's four wheels finally touched the ground, and Shirley let out a sigh.

Wan, Dr. Lion's daughter, was waiting for them and was going to take them to a hotel. The hotel seemed heavenly to Juliet. She was exhausted. She had not slept for forty hours. They had nearly covered all types of transportation.

"Get some rest," said Wan. She left them at the hotel a few minutes later. Juliet flung herself on the bed. She had never been so grateful for a bed. She then got back on her feet. "You need to get some sleep now," she told Shirley, tucking her comfortably in bed.

"I wish I could have some milk," said Shirley, wistfully.

"Al, could you please go buy some milk for her?" Juliet implored. Al was settling down in bed. He gave a shake of his head. "Then I'll have to go find some milk." Juliet slowly raised her tired body from the bed. It was late and the stores might be closed. She had no idea if she could have any luck in finding the precious fluid.

"Mom!" Shirley gasped. "Don't go—you are too tired!"

"No, I will be back shortly. You need to drink some milk." She did not wait to listen to Shirley's protest and left. She started at the nearest store, working her way further down the streets. Each time, she came out empty-handed. There was no milk anywhere. But she continued on tenaciously. It was past eleven at night and very few people were on the streets. Her eyes scanned the dark environment, feeling her way along the sidewalks. The air was heavy with eeriness. She asked all the few open stores if they sold any milk.

"Sorry, we don't," were the repeated answers. Her search was in vain. She painfully dragged herself back to the hotel two hours later. She was physically and psychologically drained of energy. She told Shirley she could not find any milk.

That horrid night slowly passed, bringing sunlight through the windows the next morning. Juliet still had plenty of the tiredness left from the trip, or rather, torture, as she called it. She regretted that she ever had decided to come with this terrible man. What had she gotten Shirley and herself into? What else lay ahead?

"I'm taking Shirley to the library," declared Al.

"What?" Juliet was shocked. "But she is too tired!"

"What's tiring about it? She is not tired." He turned to Shirley. From the shallow sleep she got last night, she felt better. And she did like to go out, to look around...

"You shouldn't go, dear, you'll get sick," warned Juliet.

But Shirley's mind was made up. Juliet was too drained to follow them. She let them go. What was there to do?

Al pushed Shirley down the street, passing markets by the sidewalk. Shirley pointed at one of the stores that caught her eye. Following her finger, he pushed her there.

Once inside, Shirley's eyes immediately rested upon stacks of paper sheets with designs of houses, animals, flowers, and many other pictures. She remembered she had those before when she was in China the last time. The designs could be cut out and made into three-dimensional figures by folding at the dotted lines and gluing in the flaps.

"I want these." She held out the sheets. He went to the counter and paid for them.

After a few more minutes roaming the streets, Al brought Shirley back to the hotel. He did not mention any library.

"How are you feeling?" Juliet asked Shirley once they were inside.

"I'm fine." Shirley showed her the goodies.

Juliet only nodded. She still did not feel comfortable about the whole situation. "You need to have something to eat." She turned to Al, "Could you go out and buy a chicken for Shirley? Please don't buy the cheap ones."

"Fine, I'll go now." And with that, he was out.

Shirley was getting hungry. Both of them, especially Juliet, had not eaten for forty hours. Shirley loved the kind of chicken they had—those ones with herbs and special seasoning that were not present in American dishes. Her mouth was starting to water.

"Can you give me a pair of scissors?" asked Shirley, getting excited about the fun time ahead with the craft. Juliet handed one to Shirley. Soon, several shapes of colorful pictures laid before her. They had no glue to stick the flaps together. But she had some other way to glue them in place. Chinese folks—at least, her family—used cooked rice in the place of glue. Rice could be quite sticky when mashed between papers. They had no rice at the moment, so it needed to wait.

Some time later, Al walked in, holding a styrofoam container. Juliet got up from the bed and opened the box without sitting down.

"Just wings?" shouted Juliet. She fingered the skinny chicken wings. "I said to buy her a whole chicken! How could she be full with these? You know she doesn't like these things; things with tendons and cartilage."

Not a single word came from his lips. He opened the door and walked out, closing it behind him.

Juliet examined the wings and began to tear off strips of meat, which was scarce. She barely collected a handful of stringy meat. She fed them to Shirley. After only a few mouthfuls, there was no more left.

"Mom, I don't feel well."

"How do you feel?" Juliet searched Shirley's face for

any sign of the unknown discomfort.

"I can't breathe well!"

It happened all of a sudden. Juliet grew frantic. Her sickening feeling was correct.

Shirley's lips turned pale. She gasped for air. She had been too tired and had not eaten anything for so long. Certainly, Juliet had expected, Shirley would get sick. It was why Juliet had to consistently feed Shirley. No one could understand their situation. "If you don't feed her, she'll eventually get hungry and will eat on her own," many had commented. No, that statement never applied to Shirley, who seldom felt hungry. Even if she did, she could not eat enough on her own because of her nausea.

Juliet rushed out of the room to seek the hotel staff's help. "My daughter can't breathe! Please help."

One staff member immediately went out to get a cab, while two others brought out Shirley.

"Poor child. How old is she?" inquired one man, with a frown.

"Eleven. She has juvenile rheumatoid arthritis. She has been too tired and had not eaten for so long, so that's why this happened," Juliet quickly explained.

A cab drove to where they stood and parked. It was a hotel cab. Juliet thanked God that there happened to be a hotel cab available; otherwise, they would have encountered great difficulty in finding a cab from the streets.

A man carried Shirley onto the backseat. Her lips were turning into a shade of blue. The second after all the cab doors were closed, the car sped off. It would be difficult to get to the hospital fast in such crowded streets, but the driver nimbly maneuvered around all the pedestrians as best as he could.

Once arriving inside the hospital, Juliet pushed Shirley to the doctors rapidly. "She can't breathe!"

"We're going to give her some oxygen. Bring her here," directed a nurse. Oxygen tubes were inserted into Shirley's nose.

"Tilt the stroller like this," Juliet showed them by leaning the stroller backward, making the front wheels dangle in midair. "It is better for her." Her motherly instinct told her that Shirley would be most comfortable in this position. The two men from the hotel staff, who came with them, did as they were instructed.

A moment later, the color slowly returned to Shirley's face. Her chest was not heaving so heavily.

"I can breathe better now," came the feeble words. "After you tilted the stroller, it made me feel better."

"What happened?" asked the busy doctor, who just walked in on the scene. Juliet repeated the story.

Meanwhile, a patient, lying upon a bed, had passed away. Family members rushed in with sad wails. Their tears spattered onto the lifeless body. Then the sheets were drawn over his face.

One life was spared and one life was taken away. Juliet and Shirley left the hospital with cries still audible in the distance.

Chapter Thirty-Seven

"Here's a chicken for her," one of the kind hotel staff members, who had helped in saving Shirley's life, handed the container to Juliet. He had gone out and bought it after Juliet had told them of the chicken incident.

"I really don't know how to thank you," said Juliet with much appreciation shining from her eyes.

"Don't mention it," they replied.

Shirley graciously had some of the chicken. Her cheeks were better in color.

"I told you that you're going to be sick," scolded Juliet. "You never listen to what I say!"

At that instant, Al walked in. Juliet looked at him with pity. "Shirley went to the emergency room because she was unable to breathe. I told you not to take her out after such a long trip. What were you trying to do?" she demanded, confronting him nose-to-nose. She glared into a pair of apathetic brown eyes a few inches above hers.

"Oh, she couldn't breathe?" Was that all he could say?

"Those kind people saved her. Give them some money!" ordered Juliet.

"No."

"No? What are you? You are too cheap!" He refused still. Juliet had not much money with her. If she gave them, she would not have any for Shirley and herself. Steaming, Juliet turned away to attend to Shirley.

"You have to eat something, if you don't, you won't be able to breathe again," said Juliet.

"But I don't know what to eat."

Juliet knew Shirley despised most of the Chinese food. She had never had a good eating habit in this country. Juliet fed more chicken to Shirley, it was not doing much to help her recover. Her once-rosy cheeks were still somewhat pale.

Juliet went out and brought back more Chinese food. Shirley tried to swallow them, but since she did not like them, they did not do her much good.

"I want milk," mumbled Shirley. Juliet knew that was nearly impossible. Where was she to get it? She had searched far and wide around the whole area.

Juliet was looking forward to receiving the herbs from Dr. Lion like he had promised her, but he was unwilling to come. Al suggested that he would go to him and ask him to come. Some time later, he came back and told Juliet that he had given the doctor some money.

That night, Shirley had a light sleep. Juliet hoped that she would get well soon. How she wished they were in America now. Shirley had never had this happened to her ever. It was only with Al that it happened. He was a bad omen, she knew. He was never with them during the day. Juliet had no idea where he went to every day.

And so, Al was not in the room with them the next day. But they preferred this way anyhow. He was no help to have around. Again, Shirley tried to eat something. Juliet clearly saw that Shirley was getting worse. She grew weak and tired.

Dr. Lion arrived at their hotel room that afternoon. He examined Shirley's joints. He did not say much. After he was done, he left without staying for another moment. Juliet was disheartened. Where was the herbs? Was the entire trip wasted?

Al came back that night. They did not exchange any words worthy of mention. He simply sat himself down on the bed with an apple in hand.

"Oh…I can't breathe," gasped Shirley all of a sudden.

Juliet's body tensed. She stood up and carried her into the stroller. "She needs to go to the emergency room again."

They made their way out of the empty hotel, absent of the kind staff, for it was very late at night. Al called a cab.

Shirley was admitted to the hospital. Oxygen did not help her this time. Juliet was emotionally beaten. She had no help for her. "If you could only eat something that you like! Then you will be able to breathe!" Juliet said those words more to herself than to Shirley. Although Shirley often made every effort to eat something, she would nearly vomit anything she ate because of the nausea.

At that moment, a woman walked into the room. "I'm Wang, Wan's friend. She told me about you, so I thought I would come to check on you." She then inquired what was wrong with Shirley. Juliet explained the problem to her.

"She just wants some milk. I believe she will get well after she drinks some milk."

"Oh, hold on. I ordered a bag of milk to be delivered every day to my house. Let me go home and get a bag for her. I'll be right back." Juliet was grateful to Dr. Wang, who was a doctor in a factory. She had self-taught her way in earning a college degree.

Minutes passed with Shirley's lungs struggling to obtain some air. "Here's the milk," announced Dr. Wang when she returned. Juliet got a cup and poured the content in. She held it out to the pale lips. Shirley took several sips.

The milk was like a God-sent medication, for after only a small amount of milk was taken in, Shirley immediately could breathe! Juliet was not surprised.

"I am so grateful for your help! You are most kind." Juliet thanked Dr. Wang.

"It's really nothing." Juliet felt so lucky to have received the assistance of wonderful people during this ordeal. Once again, Shirley's life was saved. And this time, there was extended hope for Shirley. Dr. Wang was to give the bags of milk for Shirley daily to recover. One would be surprised, or even skeptical, that merely an ounce of milk would save a person's life.

Shirley fell asleep the very next moment after the milk intake.

Juliet sat beside Shirley, watching her peacefully

sleep. It was the first time during and after the trip that Shirley was really sleeping. She had not gotten real sleep for all these days. Juliet knew that Shirley would not have become so ill if she had received good rest.

Al was nowhere to be seen. She had requested for both of them to stay in the hospital with Shirley, so that she, herself, could get some sleep when he watched over Shirley, for she did not have much sleep since the journey had begun. He had argued with her and stormed off. *He must be snoring at the hotel now*, she thought with distaste. Juliet lay down in another bed that was next to Shirley's. The room was otherwise vacant besides the two. A sigh escaped her lips. Her eyes closed, but she did not enter into her world of dreams until a period of time had passed.

Chapter Thirty-Eight

Days dragged on in the hospital. The nurse had suggested that she give IV for Shirley, but Juliet had dismissed it. "It won't help her," said Juliet. "That's not the problem. The only way we can help her recover is to give her things she likes to eat, which is now the milk."

"Yes, you're absolutely right," agreed Dr. Wang. "IV won't help in her case." Shirley needed only milk and bedrest.

They decided to stay in the hospital for some time. It was a sanctuary for them after the horrifying incidents. It was a quiet hospital with few patients. Their room remained unoccupied by any other patient. Al seldom came to visit them. When he did come, he stayed for only a few minutes. He never brought any food with him. Shirley did not care whether he came. She had no feelings for him. She did not even like to call him "father." Without his presence, she called him by name. Although they were blood-related, their spirits were like oil and water. Juliet and Al were like compelling magnets, like fire and water.

Days were not so lonely. Dr. Wang often visited them, bringing Shirley a bag of her own milk. They were highly grateful to her for her caring heart. They also had visits from nurses, who struck up conversations with them. One of the nurses, Huang, was especially friendly.

"There is a well-known psychic named Wu in the area. Many people had their fortunes told by her. Her readings are extremely accurate," she said one day.

"Really? Where can we find her?" inquired Juliet, raising her brows.

"She's very busy and plus, she is in her eighties and blind since birth, so it will be hard for her to travel here. But I will find her and bring her here for readings." She also told them that the psychic spoke a different dialect, one that Juliet and Shirley did not understand. "I know a bit of the dialect and I will try my best to translate what she says." Shirley listened with much interest. "I have to go for now." The nurse got to her feet, bade goodbye, and walked out the door.

"I wonder what the psychic would say about us." Shirley pondered.

"She will say that we have a very hard life." Their conversation was interrupted by an excited Huang.

"Guess what? As I went out the building, Wu was just passing by!"

Such a coincidence, thought Shirley.

"I'll bring her in; she's waiting outside the door." Seconds later, the blind lady was led in. She seated on a chair beside Shirley's bed. Juliet was sitting in another chair across the psychic. Shirley did not say a word as Wu began her reading, starting with Juliet.

"Ever since your childhood, you have been through tremendous tribulations and encountered many hardships. There's always someone who attempts to harm you. You are very smart and you have a lot of clever ideas, but no one ever listens to them. You have to be on your own to handle everything by yourself. You have no one in your family to help you. You have to go on trips alone and even pack your own bags. This is your eldest child and she's a girl. And she has you in her heart, always thinking of you."

Shirley grew quite excited. She had not uttered a word, so it was not by her voice on how Wu would have known of her gender. She wished that she could understand the words that the soothsayer directly spoke without having a translator who could not interpret everything.

"You have a very good fortune, a nine-word fortune," Wu continued. A nine-word fortune for women was considered to be nearly the best fortune. Was it paradoxical? Juliet's life was filled with overwhelming obstacles, and yet, she had a nine-word fortune.

The oracle began Shirley's reading with a question.

"Is it correct that if it had not been for you, she would have died a long time ago?"

"Yes!" answered the wide-eyed Juliet.

"She is very weak and feeble. Wind can easily blow her down," Wu continued. "She must need a Rabbit to be her mother." Juliet was amazed. She was a Rabbit, born in 1951. "If you were not a Rabbit, she would have to go find a Rabbit to be her mother. She is very stubborn." Every word that came from Wu was true; it could not get more accurate than this. "She likes to drink cold drinks. But it is harmful for her menstrual cycle. She is extremely, exceptionally intelligent. She has a fortune of an emperor." How ironic was it all! An emperor's fortune was the highest and best fortune that one could ever have. True, she was extremely well-taken care of by her mother. And as for her intelligence—well, none of the soothsayers had ever left out that piece of information.

The next statement that came out of Wu's mouth took them aback. "She will still need the care from her mother when she's in her twenties, but between thirty and sixty-two, she will not have a single health problem. She will be completely healthy."

Huang tried hardest with the translation, but was unable to translate much of what Wu had said, for some words were slang. Shirley remained silent throughout the reading. She was mesmerized by each and every word.

After the session had ended around half an hour or so later, Juliet handed her some money. Wu felt the paper money in her hands. Then she departed with Huang.

"That was amazing!" exclaimed Juliet.

"What she said was the exact truth," remarked Shirley. The fortuneteller could not have gotten any information from anyone, not even from Huang, who had not known any of the information Wu said.

"And between thirty and sixty-two, you will be totally healthy! Thirty-two years! So, you can walk." Juliet could not control her happiness.

"But I wonder what will happen after I turn sixty-three." pondered Shirley aloud.

"Now you see, even the devil knows every little detail about our lives. Nothing we do can escape from God's eyes. Obviously, God knows a lot more than the devil. When this point is realized, I will no longer seek any fortunetellers."

"The devil is nothing; fortunetelling is nothing," added Shirley. "The reason why people believe in fortunetellers is that they can give you an accurate reading of your past. Being told of your past is useless."

"Exactly. That's the devil's tactics to fool our hearts, to make us believe in him. That's why God tells us not to believe in fortunetellers. I feel much better now; we can live our lives in peace without any care upon our shoulders since He knows each and every one of us, and He watches over us."

Al then sauntered in. He was doing his usual checkup to see how they were doing. Then his stingy nature noticed some money was missing.

"Where did some of the money go?" he asked quizzically, looking in Juliet's direction.

"I don't know." Juliet shrugged her shoulders.

He frowned. "Someone took it," he muttered in disgust.

Then Juliet told him of the psychic's visit.

"How much did you give her?"

"Just five," lied Juliet, who gave twice as much, and that was all she had.

***

A few days later, Shirley was discharged, and they went back to the hotel.

"I'm going to leave my home for you to stay," said Dr. Wang. "I'm going to move my stuff out and I will live somewhere else." Such a kindhearted woman! She would have to transfer all of her medical and study books from her own place to a temporary home.

A week later, the family moved into Dr. Wang's house. Al would stay at the outmost room, while the two would stay in the inner room.

"We're so fortunate to know Dr. Wang," said Juliet.

Days were peaceful with no visits, except from Dr. Wang. As always, Juliet and Shirley seldom saw Al. Shirley occupied herself by drawing. Juliet had bought her crayons and paints. Dr. Wang had given her a box of watercolor pencils. Once, she drew portraits for each one. With the one for Al, she had written "Most Wanted" above his head. Juliet burst out laughing.

"It looks so much like him!" Wang joined in the laughter once she saw it. Shirley had clearly depicted Al's scrupulous looks like that of a criminal. Juliet and Shirley had commented that he looked like a bad person, from his unkind eyes to thick lips of canniness.

"I'll find an art teacher to come teach Shirley watercolor," announced Al one day. Shirley was thrilled. Shortly several days later, Juliet opened the door to an art teacher from an art college.

"I'll draw one picture, and then you copy it," he said to Shirley. With much concentration, Shirley watched his quick, artistic strokes. A colorful watercolor painting magically appeared on the paper in a matter of minutes. He certainly drew beautifully. "Okay, now you copy that."

Shirley picked up the brush, dabbed it on the paint, and began the strokes.

"Amazing! That is such an exact copy!" exclaimed the teacher.

Shirley soon quickly copied several more drawings, from mother hens to panda bears. "She even draws better than my students and I!" he told Juliet.

Unfortunately, the lessons could not go on for long. After only a few days, it had to end, for Shirley was in discomfort from her arthritis. It was odd that Shirley was in pain when arriving in China this time. On her previous trips, her joints did not worsen. Once again, the trip was a misfortune.

Following the art tutor came another tutor a doctor recommended. She, a retired teacher, was to teach Shirley how to read and write Chinese. Even though Chinese was Shirley's primary language, she received no education in the area. But as with the art lessons, it could not last long. On the last day, the tutor exclaimed, "Shirley has learned two hundred words in just nine days! That's equivalent to one whole year's study! She is remarkable. She is so smart! She is a child prodigy! Her handwriting is fantastic!" Shirley truly enjoyed the short lessons; most lessons could not last more than fifteen minutes due to Shirley's great pain.

One day, Shirley heard loud chirps from behind the door. Her heart gave a summersault when Al came in, holding a cage with two parakeets in it. Shirley gave a happy cry.

"It's one blue and one green," chirped Shirley gleefully. Juliet loved seeing her daughter so happy. Shirley asked for a pair of chopsticks. "I'll train them," announced Shirley.

"How about writing a letter to Mr. Crisfield?" suggested Juliet moments later.

"Sure!" With a pen in hand, Shirley began the letter on the thin letter paper. Each sheet was nearly transparent, thus words on one side could be made out from the other side. Many times, the head of the pen left scratches on the paper. Shirley wrote as gently as possible. But the ink of the pen would not come out easily. Chinese pens and paper were of poor quality. Juliet checked over the letter once Shirley finished. It was written neatly in cursive.

"You write very well. And you haven't written in a while," commented Juliet.

"Yes, I had a bit of a problem remembering a few words in the beginning, but they came back to me as I was writing," stated Shirley. It felt like a long time since she had last spoken English. Since they always exchanged Chinese words and that everyone in China spoke Chinese, remembering a foreign language that was just learned would need a good memory, of which Shirley had plenty.

Chapter Thirty-Nine

Life was bleak and quite boring at the house. Juliet wished to go back to America, but Al did not abide by her wish. A month had gone by and Al told them about Fujian. He had mentioned the place several times. "It is wonderful there, with lots of seafood. I will have a tutor teach Shirley everything." From his descriptions of his homeland, the place really sounded like a fine area for them to live.

Juliet thought of the life in America. Shirley's school life was harsh. Since the school did not allow Juliet to go to school for Shirley's bathroom needs and no one could help Shirley, Shirley had to hold in her urine for the entire school day. Juliet did not want Shirley to go through the misery. It was ridiculous that she was not allowed to go to the school to help Shirley. She thought that life in Fujian would be much better. Al had promised to find a good tutor and doctors for Shirley.

Accordingly, the decision was made. Bags were packed and they were ready to set off. Juliet thanked Dr. Wang again for her hospitality and kind acts. The pair of parakeets were left with Dr. Wang. And so, the family left the house that had been their home for the past month.

Shirley was horrified when they arrived at the pier. She had to be carried to the boat again! This was definitely not her dream vacation. Her eyes glued to the rippling waters underneath her and the rocking boat as they steadily carried her. One man had almost lost his grip on the stroller. She could not bear to think what could have happened. Worse yet, it was a windy day, making the ordeal more dreadful. It felt all so unreal to her. She sighed a sigh of relief as soon as she got on the boat.

***

Shirley's eyes traveled around the dilapidated hotel they were to stay in Shanghai. From there, they would set out to Fujian by plane. Al was to buy the tickets the following day.

"This is such an exhausting trip," remarked Juliet.

"It sure is," agreed Shirley. "How long have we been here?" She had lost track of time, for she did not have good access to any calendars. It seemed a year had passed, but she knew it was much less than that.

"Only less than two months. Maybe like seven weeks," calculated Juliet.

It was approaching nighttime and the exhausted party got ready for sleep. Shirley longed to be in New York then, playing with her furry friends. And she missed being in school dearly. She fell asleep thinking about her teacher and classmates.

***

"I'm hungry. Let's go to the eating area," suggested Al the following noontime. There was an area by the hotel where lodgers could eat in. Juliet dressed up Shirley again before setting out. It was only a short distance, but a mere second in the cold would suffice to make Shirley ill. Under her mother's intensive care, Shirley had never caught a cold during the entire span of her life, not even when in contact with many people. But then, the cold cases in China were much less compared to America. Shirley often saw Americans with colds. In China, people bundle up a great deal. Shirley was taught in school that being in cold weather did not cause colds—viruses did. But being in the cold was one way viruses could get into the body. Hence, it was an indirect cause of cold, making the body more vulnerable and susceptible to infections. There was another difference she had noticed on how the two countries view cold weather. Chinese people would especially bundle up more in arthritic conditions, and if they saw that others were bundled up for the winter, would understand the reason and necessity for the care. But in America, Shirley was often made fun of for being bundled up in cool temperatures. And grown ups were the ones who had made the insensitive comments. They did not understand her situation at all. One friend of the family had said the same thing—that people looked at her oddly when she simply wore gloves to protect her arthritic hands from the chills. Shirley frowned upon the ignorance and the inability for others to respect, if not understand, unique, or otherwise a normal situation in the eyes of Chinese.

They seated at a round table. Shirley grimaced, taking in the uncleanliness of the place. Flies flew about at every corner. How can people eat in an environment like this? But anywhere that people can eat was a blessing in itself. There were millions of famished and homeless people who would think this restaurant was paradise. A few dishes were ordered, but Shirley did not want to eat anything as usual.

"This does not taste good at all," winced Juliet after having a mouthful of heaven knew what.

"I must agree," confirmed Al. They tried every dish on the table—none was good. As they managed to get the food down, Shirley's eyes followed the flies around the room. Many were buzzing above fellow restaurant diners.

"Try to eat some of these," Juliet said to Shirley. "You can't go on without eating anything." Shirley had tried a few things, and she reflected their opinions. Her mouth would not open again.

"Would you like me to save this for your husband?" asked a waitress after they finished. The dish of seaweed, which was hard like ropes, was left over.

"Yes, thank you." *Here are lots of flies and...* thought Juliet, secretly smiling a devilish smile.

They returned to their small room with full, but not so satisfied, stomachs.

"I'm going to buy the tickets now," said Al, closing

the door behind him. Juliet got out the coloring books for Shirley to look at. She had brought many of them on the trip. They were things to keep Shirley occupied. Shirley had colored in only one of the books, for she simply enjoyed looking at the pictures. She loved artwork and really cherished each picture she saw.

Time quickly flew by. Footsteps were heard in the hallway before Al's body appeared in the doorway. He would have to go back a few days later to retrieve the plane tickets.

"I'm going to the restaurant to get the seaweed," he decided. Shirley's ears followed his wobbly footsteps until they were no longer audible. He had not a pretty walking gait. He resembled a large duck that was confused about which way to go. Juliet, on the other hand, walked like a model. Actually, better than a model, for it was natural and free. And Shirley's walk was quick and nimble. "You walked in a way that is extremely cute," Juliet had commented several times. Oh, how they wished that they could return to that time again!

"I've come to pick up the seaweed," Al told a waiter.

"Oh, yes, it's right here." The man went into the kitchen and reappeared with the dish. Al took it without saying thanks. When it came to people he found unworthy, Al was absent of manners. Juliet had scolded him for his impoliteness, but he got infuriated. He finished the seaweed alone and gave the dish back. Happy that he did not waste any money, he traced his steps back to the room.

***

Juliet went to Al's side. His face was distorted in great pain. His hands were upon his stomach as he lay silently on the bed. It was the next day following the consumption of the seaweed, which must have been contaminated by all the flies. The seaweed dish was simply placed on the countertop, making it accessible to all the germs that the flying bugs carried.

"I'm going to the doctor," he managed to say. Wherever he felt something was amiss with his body, the first place he would stop at was at the doctor's office. The pain had started a few hours after eating the seaweed. He had spent the whole night in great pain.

Still in pain, he came back later into the day, with medication in hand. He gulped down some water, hoping the medication would work. He had a terrible stomachache during the first trip to China with Shirley. The cause then was not the flies, but with snails. He had ordered a plate of large snails with shells intact at a restaurant in Hong Kong. Juliet, disgusted and feeling uncomfortable, had refused to eat it, thinking it might not be a wise idea. Plus, she was somewhat allergic to such foods, including crabs and lobsters. Soon, great spasms of pain had invaded his body as a result.

Chapter Forty

The cab drove down the streets, bringing them closer and closer to a restaurant in Fujian. Al had rented a house, but he was going to leave them at the restaurant, for he wished to do something first; he did not make his plans clear to Juliet. The flight from Shanghai to Fujian had taken about an hour. Juliet and Shirley waited in anticipation for the new world to where they were heading. Would their eyes meet a heavenly paradise as described by Al? Only they would know the answer. And they soon found out.

"Do I stop here?" asked the driver.

"Yes, just at that spot." Al pointed to the right. Juliet's heart sank at once when she took in the scene before her. Shirley was speechless. Once they got out, Juliet and Shirley exchanged doubtful glances.

"Okay, you wait here. I will pick you up later." Al's figure was soon out of sight.

"Oh, what a terrible place!" exclaimed Juliet with terror in her voice. "It is the worst place I have ever seen." The whole street, as far as the eye could see, was lined with tiny restaurants that were one hundred times dirtier than the last restaurant they were at by the hotel.

"The people here are different, it seems." noted Shirley.

"Unsmiling," finished Juliet. "It looks like we're trapped here."

"It will be very hard to get away from this place."

"He tricked us."

"This is nothing like he had described." Shirley was already feeling physically uncomfortable, for the climate was humid.

"I shouldn't have listened to him," Juliet said. "It is very humid and muggy here. Your joints are going to get worse. Let's check out this place further." She stood up from the cracked chair and started to push Shirley down the sidewalk. But it was a difficult task, for the grounds were dented and filled with litter.

"I'm furious," declared Juliet. Shirley could not see her, but she knew her eyes must be glowing with fury like a devastating hurricane. Yet, they were the ones who were devastated. Wearily, Juliet returned to her seat. It was useless; no amount of walking would bring them to a decent place. It felt quite strange to not have people smile or even look at them, especially at Shirley. Wherever they went in any parts of China, people had instinctively looked at Shirley with sympathetic light reflecting from their eyes. Many had often gone up to Juliet and inquired about Shirley's condition. Not here; no one paid any attention to them. Juliet felt defeated. Surely, he would not let them get out of the place. They would be trapped in this place for perhaps a long, agonizing time. Shirley dared not think of the word "forever."

"Here he comes," announced Juliet while looking over Shirley's shoulders.

"Okay, we can go now," he said.

"What do you think you're doing? What is this place? What are you doing?" demanded Juliet loudly. Without any words from him, they got into the cab.

Juliet hoped that the house would be nicer than where they had been staying. But she had a sinking feeling that it was a slim chance. The cab brought them closer and closer to the house of unknown status. Would it be a dungeon?

The car parked at a curb. Shirley saw only a path before them, with trees on each side. The driver drove off, leaving them in this doom. They followed the path that led them to the house. Shirley felt chills running down her spine as she examined the trees. Describing them in a book was quite uneasy, for one needed to personally take a look at them to understand the eerie feelings. The trees were like palm trees, but yet possessed an uncanny quality as if witches had cast a spell upon them, making them frightful-looking. Their large head of foliage swayed in the wind, sending flying shadows upon the three. They reminded Shirley of giant tarantulas.

At the end of the path, the house became visible. Al fingered for the keys in his pockets. He opened the door and the two went in. The room, which Shirley guessed to be a living room, was nearly empty, other than a few chairs and a small dining table. To the right was a green door that was shut. It was the door to a tiny kitchen.

Juliet then let out a loud gasp. With a shaking voice, she called out to Al.

"There's a giant spider in that corner!"

"Where, where?" asked the frightened Shirley. She was arachnophobic. This was definitely not a good sign.

"Behind you," answered Juliet.

"I want to see it, turn me around." Shirley wanted to know where it was hiding. Knowing was better than getting an unpleasant surprise. Juliet turned the stroller around. Shirley's blood froze. She was sure her face had lost its color. Right before her eyes, at the upper right corner of the door, was a giant black spider the size of her hand. It was the most peculiar-looking spider that she had ever seen. Unlike other spiders, this one's thick eight legs were spread flat out on the wall, not curving upward at the joints.

"Kill it," Juliet said to Al. He went to another corner and picked up the broom. "What are you doing? Are you crazy? How are you going to kill it with that?" She was horrified when she saw him pointing at the spider from the handle end of the broom.

"It is probably dead," he said, "I'll just bring it down." He moved closer to the spider with the end of the broom inching closer to its black body. He poked at the spider. It immediately ran down the wall and under the kitchen door. Shirley was too scared to let out any sound.

"See? How can you do such a thing? You knew that would happen!" Juliet was outraged.

"I'll just buy a spray. I'll spray the whole kitchen. It will die." He nonchalantly opened another door to let them in the bedroom. The spider still invaded Shirley's mind. She could not get it off her mind. It was the most frightening creature upon which she had ever set her eyes.

Two queen-sized beds set in the room, covered in hard, plastic wrappings. They were pushed together to form a large bed. It would be large enough for both Juliet and Shirley. Shirley needed a lot of pillows and sheets to support her legs and arms when she slept. Al was to sleep in another room. There was a wardrobe and a whole unit of dressers across the beds. The room did not lack any furniture; a large television set was present. Juliet and Shirley had nearly forgotten that they were tired until they saw the beds.

"Take off the plastic. We need to get some rest," Juliet said, turning to Al.

"Why? You can sleep on the plastic."

"Sleep on the plastic?" Juliet fumed. "No, you're taking it off!"

"The beds are going to get dirty."

Reluctantly, she gave in. She would have to take it off herself. Still flaring, Juliet got Shirley as comfortable as possible on the bed. Then she lay herself down. "This is a very hard bed," stated Juliet. This must be the cheapest bed that he could find.

Things apparently turned from bad to worse as time passed. Juliet soon learned that the kitchen was filled with buzzing mosquitoes. Al left them alone to buy the bug spray.

"I can't believe this," said both the marooned mother and daughter.

"No, we cannot sleep on hard, cold plastic! We are not rocks like him!" Ergo, she tore off the plastic.

Moments later, Juliet found another of the strange spiders. It was the size of a peach pit, so she managed to kill it. She had never been scared of spiders. Now she knew how it felt.

I just have to make the best of it, thought Juliet. But

no amount of imagination and optimism could make things any better. Juliet had to protect Shirley from all the mosquitoes. She did not need to worry about cold weather, for the climate at Fujian was warm.

Some time had passed when the main door swung open. Al opened the spray and began to spray the kitchen. "This should do it." Finished with the work, he went to the bedroom. "You took off the plastic?" he asked, a disappointed look painted on his features.

"Of course," hissed Juliet.

The first day and night slowly passed. When morning arrived, Shirley smiled, looking at the bright side: she had passed the night even though her joints felt that they had been smashed in a grinder. She could get through it, however long it might last. She glanced around their room and her eyes rested on the television. What shows did they have? "How do you use the remote control?" Shirley asked Al as he walked in several moments later.

He shrugged. He picked up the remote control and studied it. He turned on the television. He hit a few buttons. "Don't know," he answered, shaking his head. "I'd have to read the instructions."

"Here, let me see that," offered Shirley. "I do this all the time." She was one who always figured out how to use a new gadget whenever the household brought something home. She stretched out a hand and winced as pain bolted down from her shoulder. She was becoming like a robot. Once she received the remote control, she studied it carefully. "So many buttons!" She pressed a few buttons, recording down what function each performed in her mind's notebook.

Minutes later, Shirley was using the remote control like a pro. "I figured it all out," she called to Al.

"I knew it," remarked Juliet, smiling.

"It's a piece of cake; a delicious one, too, if I may add." Shirley giggled.

Chapter Forty-One

More difficulties came their way. Juliet learned that Fujian's food was bland. She did not like all the food she tried, thus there was no question whether Shirley liked them. But Juliet had a good appetite, so she had no problem getting them down. The problem was with Shirley as usual.

Shirley soon lost her energy and her joints became sore because of the severe humidity. Not receiving nutrients also made Shirley's health fail quickly. Most days, she could not even sit up in bed. Her pain and stiffness were so great that she could not raise a pinky. On top of it, her difficulty in breathing started again. She was often short of breath.

Juliet was in deep pain seeing the extent of Shirley's suffering. Al appeared to be blind from it all. He paid no attention to them. He never spent time with his daughter.

But one day, he walked over to Shirley when Juliet was in the kitchen and sat down beside her on the bed.

"You know, Shirley, I have been sending you money every month, but your grandmother takes it away, never telling you," he said.

"No, my grandmother would never do that," answered Shirley. Al was required to pay child support, but he never did. It was the only time that Al had really spoken to her. Without saying another word, he got up and left the room. Shirley shook her head in pity. Did he actually think that she would fall for what he had said? Was she stupid?

Al had stayed with them for a couple of days until he announced he was going back to America. He had a life there. He would return some other day. He planned that the house would be their permanent place to live for the rest of their lives.

"How could you be so heartless? Can you see Shirley's awfully sick? Look at her! Just look at her. Don't you see her complexion?" pleaded Juliet. Shirley had acquired a waxy complexion. "She looks like someone who is about to die. She had never looked like this in her entire life, not even when she was in extreme pain." But he would not take a single glance at Shirley. "Take us back!"

To her horror, Shirley watched the scene grow heavy. The two began to shout at each other. Juliet pulled at Al as he was walking away. He pushed her to the bed, nearly crashing into Shirley. Then he began to hit her with his fists. She fought back with all her might. Using her feet, she kicked him as hard as she could.

With all the hatred boiling inside, Shirley used every ounce of her strength to leap toward Al, scratching his arm with her long nails. In a flash, she also took the black address book he always had in his shirt pocket. Shirley could see that she had hurt him.

With a piece of skin gone from his arm, he left. So Al was gone after staying a week. He had left them to be on their own in a horrid world, where there was no one they could seek for help.

Shirley felt her fingernail and saw there was a piece of his skin. "I took this," Shirley handed the little black book to Juliet. Juliet flipped through it while Shirley peered from beside her. They saw there were many names of banks and his social security number. From the looks of it, he was a wealthy man.

The tutor he had promised for Shirley was a false promise. He had given them nothing but despair. There must be a way out of this place. But by what means could the task be accomplished? Where could she get help?

Agonizingly, the days continued. Juliet tried to ease their hardship by taking Shirley out for strolls in the daytime. If anything caught Shirley's eye, she would buy it. Close by the house, they had a street market that sold plastic pots and pans and other pretty cookware for children to play house. Shirley took a fancy to them, thus Juliet bought the whole pack. Soon, her toys added up as Juliet bought more of the plastic shapes, from tiny furniture to little people. Shirley returned home with a wide grin. Then she played with them for hours on end. Juliet was glad to see Shirley so happy despite the severe pain she had to endure daily. At least, it was something to keep her from the harshness. But they could never escape from reality.

Juliet tried her hardest to have Shirley eat something. She searched in all the stores for something that Shirley might like. She got lucky one day. She found a place that sold tasty egg rolls. Thereupon, she often bought some for Shirley.

"Why did you bring the child here?" asked an elderly woman at a street market. "This place has very humid weather, and it is the worst place for arthritic people!"

"I didn't know about this," answered Juliet. Then a sudden thought sank into her. She had just remembered, a long time ago, that Al had said that he would someday take them to California because the climate there was dry, which was best for arthritic people. His joints were painful when he returned to Fujian every time, for it had highly humid climate. "Tricked again," Juliet said to herself, steam rising. She made her way back to the small prison, where Shirley was waiting for the egg rolls.

Going out was quite difficult for Juliet. She noticed that once the door was locked, it was tricky to get it open again. Once in her frantic state, she had thought that she had locked herself out. She went for help. A man, whom she found by the sidewalk, was able to open the door; the lock was merely jammed. Very much relieved, she came to Shirley's side and gave her a long, tight hug.

There were never visitors, except a nephew of Al. "Can you buy a comfortable bed for us?" asked Juliet one day.

"Sure. He had bought you very poor beds." Consequently, both Juliet and Shirley finally had a soft bed on which to sleep. He then bought two ducklings for Shirley.

"Oh, thank you! I love them!" Shirley's chirp was

met by the ducklings' quacks.

Juliet kept the ducklings in a large red washing bowl. It was light, so it could be carried wherever she pleased. Several days later, the ducklings began to jump out of the bowl every night. Then Juliet had to get up from the bed and put them back in. But they would jump out again. And therefore, Juliet had to pick them up and place them in over and over again.

The two ducklings were always together, never parting from each other. If one duckling had wandered off, the second would go look for it. If the two could not find each other, they would start to quack loudly until they could unite.

"They are inseparable. I wish humans could be as close as they are," said Juliet. "We are like them."

The ducklings also tried to squeeze into Shirley's armpits when she held them. Sometimes she laughed when it became too ticklish. "They like the warmth and protection," stated Shirley.

In no time, two more new members were added to the family. The nephew bought Shirley two tortoises. How gleeful she was! Juliet kept the tortoises in another plastic bowl, yellow in color, with an inch of water. She changed the water daily so it would not build up with their wastes.

Shirley tried to get the small tortoise, the size of a spoon, to eat to no avail. The tortoise was worse than Shirley; it would not open its mouth to any food. On the other hand, the larger tortoise, which was about five inches in length, loved chicken.

With the colorful blocks that Juliet had bought, Shirley built houses with great walls and placed the small tortoise inside. It crawled around, trying to find an opening to get out. Sometimes, it tried to climb over the walls and had successfully knocked off a few small blocks. Shirley felt herself seeing a mirrored image of herself and her mother: trapped.

***

Juliet called Zhang one day for help. Perhaps, she could get them out of the place.

"Al came over here and told me all the bad things you have said about me, so I'm not picking you up," she told Juliet. Juliet could not believe her ears. From the airport at Shanghai, Al had to travel an hour to get to Zhang's house. He had to go through all the trouble to close one door on Juliet. Well, he certainly had succeeded.

Next, she called Pan and Dr. Qi, but both could not come. Her mind raced fast. She thought of other contacts she knew.

"Just stay there," Kwi Show had said to Juliet when Juliet called her.

Juliet sighed. How were they able to get out? Then Agatha called a friend of hers, Xiu, who was in China, to help bring them back to America. Juliet could finally rest her heart. They were going to be saved!

She had thought that Al's nephew could bring them to Shanghai, but she could not find him anymore. He and his father had left the area.

Juliet began to get ready for the move. Shirley's happiness was on a grand scale. She was unable to endure the humidity. Her joints were more painful than she could bear. Her fingers on her right hand were starting to bend. She tried to keep them straight by holding out the fingers. She did not want the fingers to be like the ones on her left. She was unable to do many things because of the bent fingers. The only straight fingers she had on her left hand were the index and thumb. But soon, she noticed that the index finger was beginning to swell, therefore making it difficult to bend. So she had to remember to bend it several times during the day. It was such a harsh life. But thank goodness that it would not last forever. There was hope, and the flame grew brighter and brighter as it became discernible at the end of the dark tunnel.

Chapter Forty-Two

Juliet opened the knocking door to Xiu. They greeted each other formally, lacking no courtesy. They did not know each other that well; they had known each other through Agatha. She was going to stay with them for some time until she could get the plane tickets to Shanghai. Getting the tickets was not an easy task; it required some time and effort.

The long-awaited day finally arrived; it was the day for departure. All the bags were packed. They were bringing the tortoises with them in a red bucket. The ducklings were given away to the neighbors.

"Mom, I need to go to the bathroom!" Shirley announced after waking up. She had taken some medication to ease constipation last night. Her stomach hurt a great deal. She struggled to keep it in.

Juliet was frantic. She had disassembled the commode which they had brought here from America, and the pieces were already packed in the luggage. But it was the only way Shirley could go. Juliet moved with the swiftness of an arrow and reassembled the parts. Juliet had never before assembled the commode, yet she successfully did it.

Shirley, moaning, held her stomach with two hands.

With no time for even a sigh, Juliet carried Shirley onto the commode, who received immediate relief. Two sighs were let out simultaneously.

"I did pretty good!" Juliet laughed. After cleaning Shirley carefully, she disassembled the commode. Now, it was time to leave.

It was a rainy day, so the travel was made inconvenient. Juliet pushed the smiling Shirley out of the house, an inferno they planned to stay away from forever. Shirley did not give it another glance as they moved away. She looked at the spider-like trees one last time. They had fallen into the trap, but had managed to sneak out. She could never forget what Al had done to them. How could her own father have done something like this? Juliet was so grateful to Xiu. She was their savior!

The heavens continued to pour down the rain with full force. It was dangerous for Shirley to be carried onto the plane outside in the rain, but there was no choice if they wanted to get back. A man carefully carried her up step by step while she clung to him tightly. Panting, he set her down on her seat. Juliet, with rain soaking her, managed to get the stroller and bags in. Mother Nature had to choose this day to cry.

Juliet took off Shirley's wet coat. "Are you cold?" she asked, feeling Shirley's hands.

"No, I'm fine, thanks."

They were thirsty and waited for the flight attendants to serve the juices. They would arrive in Shanghai soon. Shirley looked out the window, hoping the rain would be replaced by sunshine. Maybe it was not raining in Shanghai.

The plane soon stopped at a bright Shanghai. "We're here!" announced Shirley. Shirley was carried down the plane. Then all went inside the airport to gather up their luggage.

Shirley felt like a bouncing ball, always being flung to and fro in various directions. This time, she was brought to another hotel. She had seen enough of hotels. She wondered when she could finally go back. She looked at the tortoises inside the bucket. Did they know where they were? Would she be able to bring them to America? She hoped so.

Their room was on the second floor, so Xiu's brother came especially to carry Shirley up the flight of stairs. The room was quite small with a single bed. It was the hotel in which Dr. Wang had helped them to be accepted. If it had not been for her, they would have to pay a lot, for they were Americans. Juliet did not have enough money in her pocket, so this would have to do.

It was near freezing in the hotel without any heat.

Juliet had brought one blanket on the trip, but it was not enough to keep Shirley warm. She asked the hotel for another blanket. She disliked the temperature in Shanghai; in summer the weather could be so sweltering, that raw eggs could be cooked on the pavements, and in the wintertime, it would be too cold to even snow.

Meanwhile, Juliet was going to shop around to buy some medicine to bring to America. There were numerous good medicines that America lacked—those with no side effects, only with quick and fine results. She also hoped to purchase some cotton pants for Shirley, who needed them to sleep in. The pants had to be large so that Shirley could easily turn positions in bed. But buying such pants was hard, for most of them were small in size, therefore they were uncomfortable for Shirley to sleep in. At the same time, she was to get the plane tickets.

"I found a good place to live for the time being instead of here. It has one room and it is very big, too," said Xiu a week later. Therefore, things were packed again, along with the tortoises, and a cab was called. It was late in the evening and the sky was with the absence of sunlight.

"Okay, this is the place," said Xiu when the cab stopped in front of a square house. It had a hard time squeezing in through the narrow path that led to the house. The car had just made it through in the tiny space, which had walls on both sides.

The house looked tiny, with one door and one window. *What kind of place is this?* thought Shirley. It looked like an outhouse rather than a place to live. Juliet had misgivings about the situation simply by looking at the house from outside.

Xiu opened the door and let them in.

"It is freezing," Juliet shivered. Once she saw the interior, her heart sank down to the bottomless pit. The one-room "house" had only a small hard bed and a tiny table. Juliet was utterly speechless. She did not know what to say or do, to cry or laugh.

Xiu brought in their bags. Juliet had brought everything they had, making the room appear even smaller. "We can't live here," stated Juliet, shaking her head, "we have to leave here right away tomorrow."

"Okay, I'll come to take you away tomorrow," Xiu said with an air of nonchalance. Juliet and Shirley exchanged the same look as the one when they were left alone at the Fujian restaurant.

"What is this?" Juliet felt as though the nightmare would never end. "There's no heat and there are so many mosquitoes! How are we going to pass the night?" There was only a source of cold water. It was no better than a prison cell, for even jails have access to toilets, which the room had none. "I've been tricked again." She believed in others too much and too easily. She needed to learn not to trust people and depend on them wholly. It was simply her nature. She had an idealistic outlook on everything, and saw everything in rose-colored glasses. But she had to stop worrying and help get the night over with. Worrying could not lend a helping hand.

Juliet gave Shirley all the blankets she had, leaving herself with cold stabbing into her bones.

The bed was the most uncomfortable bed on which Shirley had ever lain. They snuggled close to each other, trying to keep warm and for support. But they had no choice, either—the bed was too small.

"I'll find a way out of here," promised Juliet. Remarkably, the two fell asleep, but with no lack of difficulty.

The wind hollered with rage as day dawned upon the frozen land. Juliet stiffly got out of bed. It was an awful night, but they managed it.

Juliet worried that the hotel might be full now. She hoped that their room was not taken. She had to contact them right away. "I'm going to make a call," Juliet told Shirley. She made certain that Shirley was fine before closing the door.

She walked down the streets and checked all the stores for any access to a telephone. She came to a tiny grocery store where miscellaneous items were sold. She picked up the telephone and quickly dialed the number to the hotel.

"Yes, this is Yi. Is the room still vacant?" she asked into the mouthpiece.

"Yes, it is."

"Oh good! We're coming back today."

"Okay, we'll save it for you." Juliet heaved a sigh of relief. She graciously thanked the woman and hung up.

She rapidly returned to the cell, where Shirley patiently waited. White mists, that were formed from her breaths, whirled before her as the freezing woman opened the door.

"How was it?" asked Shirley.

"I called the hotel and we can go back. The room is still vacant."

The only thing left to do now was to wait for Xiu to pick them up. There was not a way for communication between them, for people seldom had phones in their homes.

Chapter Forty-Three

Shirley daydreamed about America, swinging her legs to and fro at the edge of the bed. She planned to buy more books to read. She had not read any book for what seemed so long. She could hardly wait. She would buy some of those books that had picture buttons that could be pushed to make various sounds to go with the story. She had seen some and she had quickly taken an interest in them. She wished she could get her hands on them now. The time would come soon. Meanwhile, she occupied herself with electronic candles that Juliet had bought for her. The candles played *Happy Birthday* when lit. Shirley was in awe when she saw such a magnificent invention. Juliet had also bought musical cards with all kinds of drawings, from flowers to a wedding couple, with the bride dressed in layers of white silk and laces and the man in black tuxedo. She truly loved them all. China had so many wonderful things, most of them held exquisite beauty and delicateness. Those things were not found in America, especially the delicate colorful paper cutouts. Shirley studied the cutouts as if they were the most precious gems. She gently held each to her eyes, wherein each cutout's beauty coruscated. They were cut with great care and details that it would seemed nearly impossible to achieve, and yet they were cut by hand. There were cutouts of butterflies, flowers, birds, and ancient Chinese beauties with flowing gowns and long sleeves.

The hotel days were not as lonesome as Shirley had expected. They had two visitors from the hotel who often came to converse. But the two possessed a quality that was elusive. One lady was the believer of some spiritual belief, while the other woman was her follower of some sort. Many other people from the hotel had warned the latter of the believer's deceptions. "She is a fake, not someone you should believe in," they often warned. But the woman would not listen.

One day, the spiritual woman began telling Juliet and Shirley of a place. "You can live there. It is a wonderful place." Juliet had thought it a fine idea. She thought of the life that awaited them in America, so thought it a better plan. Although life in China lacked the convenience found in America, it held no pressure for her. She did not have to deal with any school and hospital staff. America simply had too many rules and regulations that were laid out with no exceptions to unique circumstances. No doctor in China would ever take away a mother's custody when she simply disagreed with medically recommended treatment. In fact, she was stunned that such a system ever existed in the first place. She was shocked when Americans took her child away from her twice. In China, no such things would ever happen. No one would even thought of doing it. And it was not much better in school. Parents were not allowed to be in American schools for any other reason other than those stated by the schools. They would feel odd when seeing parents inside the building. What was wrong with that? She could not comprehend it. In China, parents could freely go to the school while the classes were in session.

After talking it over with Shirley, Juliet realized what the woman had been saying sounded too good to be true. Therefore, it could not be true. She would not get tricked again this time. She had nearly fallen into the trap, but had caught herself. Everything needed time to be thought out; decisions could not be made from first hearing of the news. Juliet knew it was a wise decision. To America they would go.

And so, that day of farewell arrived. Juliet packed everything and they would leave in the morning. Their numerous bags made it look as though that ten people were going on the trip, not just two. They were even bringing the plastic toys and a few stuffed animals home. One stuffed animal was a large gray rabbit, the size of a two-year-old, that resembled Thumper in *Bambi*. But the tortoises were not going with them. Shirley had not seen the reptiles after they came back to the hotel the second time. She was clueless to where they had gone, and missed them already.

Shirley was in a high jubilant state. The happiness was reflecting outward from every inch of her soul. From her joy, her health had become remarkably well.

"Your joints are not hurting you, right?" asked Juliet. She could see that Shirley's cheeks had their rosiness back.

"Yes, I feel so much better. Look, I can bounce around!" Shirley began to bounce on the bed gleefully. Juliet was amazed. Happiness did do a lot to ease someone's health. They said that laughter is the best medication—what a true statement!

"All set?" asked Xiu's brother. Both of them were going to bring the two to the airport and make sure they would get on the plane safely.

Everyone from the hotel said goodbye to the group before the cab drove away.

The wide smile was still upon Shirley's features as they waited for the time to board the plane. An hour later, the time had arrived. Juliet hugged Xiu and her brother. She was grateful to Xiu for getting them out of Fujian and into the hands of freedom, despite the place to where she had brought them.

"Take care," Xiu and her brother said. Shirley took one last glance at her surroundings before she went inside the plane. This magical machine was going to bring her home.

Chapter Forty-Four

The airport was overcrowded with holiday travelers. It was an evening before Christmas, and many looked forward to the time they could celebrate the special event with friends and family members. Some only had the chance to see their family once each year, and thus this time of the year would be memorable. Amidst the crowd was the exhausted Juliet, struggling to push Shirley while handling luggage after luggage. Many spectators looked on with sympathy as the woman managed over seven bags full of clothes and heaven knew what else. The gray rabbit was taking the whole space of a bag. It was too much for anyone to handle alone.

"Yi! Yi!" Called a familiar voice amongst the crowd. Juliet looked around and saw Peter, who was picking her up to bring her home.

After meeting them in the building, he left them outside the airport to fetch his car. What should have been only a few minutes of wait turned out to be hours. Mother and daughter, their bodies shivering from the biting cold, felt they could last no longer when his car finally pulled up in front of them.

"I couldn't find my way back!" he exclaimed. "I went all over looking for where I left you."

The dark blanket of night had nearly lifted from the land as he drove them home. The car was cramped with all the bags, but they managed to squeeze in. This was the most exhausting trip on which Juliet and Shirley had ever gone. None of the previous five trips to China even got close in matching this one. It was a horrible experience for both of them, especially for Shirley, whose health was damaged. Before, her fingers on her right hand were all straight, but after the painful ordeal, the fourth finger was bent a bit. And she was unable to lift her fingers up the way she used to. Her right hand was quite flexible before; now it was no longer. Also, her left index finger could never bend again. Consequently, she looked as though she always pointed at somewhere mysterious. Not only was the trip not beneficial, but it had brought harm to them. It was an experience that none could ever erase from their memories. It had lasted only three months, but it seemed as if it exceeded an entire lifetime.

Juliet shuddered at the thought of how she had managed all the way. It was hard for her to carry Shirley, especially on planes and tight spots. Between stops, she had asked people to help. She was ignored several times, but she received help from kind men in the nick of time. Their plane seats were in the front row, so they had a large space in front of them. It made it possible for Juliet to take care of Shirley's bathroom needs. Using the bathroom on planes was impossible now that Shirley had grown. Therefore, Juliet had carried her to the floor and used the bedpan. Shirley was highly reluctant to do such a private business in front of others, but she had no choice. But before the plane was making its final landing at JFK Airport, Juliet had asked if Shirley needed to relieve herself. Shirley denied her urge to go. She decided to hold in until they got home. "It's a long drive. You need to go now," Juliet had insisted. Being the headstrong person she was, Shirley refused.

On the ride to Kwi Show's home, Shirley's bladder felt as though it would burst open any minute to release its yellow burden. She was unable to move, afraid that she would let it out. "I told you to go on the plane. You just won't listen," scolded Juliet.

"I can hold it in." Shirley did not want to urinate in front of fellow passengers. It was a humiliating experience, one that she never wished to go through again. How she wished that the car would sprout wings and fly them home!

Juliet was hoping for a speedy return as well, for her entire body had turned into ice. Peter had his window half open. The chilly fingers of winter sought out every crevice and corner of her body. She was defenseless, for she had given her coat to Shirley, leaving only a thin sweater to protect her, not that it protected her in the least. "I can't breathe well, so I have to have the window open," Peter had told her.

It was almost eight in the morning when the car stopped outside their destination. The lights in the brick house were faintly discernible from behind the curtains. As soon as she saw them, Kwi Show rushed out in assistance.

"Mother, get inside, you'll get cold!" yelled Juliet, trying to push her into the house. Reluctantly, Kwi Show retreated inside. Peter carried Shirley into the stroller and Juliet pushed her inside right away. Kwi Show gave Shirley a kiss on her cheek. Shirley felt so good to be home. The lovely feeling was exquisite, like the first time hearing a nightingale sing a haunting melody of enchantment.

After all bags were taken in, Juliet sank down onto the sofa. Every ounce of energy had been sucked out from her soul. "Oh, so horrible," muttered Juliet. Kwi Show was sure to hear all about their experience.

Juliet brought Shirley into the room, where they would temporarily stay until Juliet found an apartment, so they could move out. She would contact the school to get Shirley started with the schooling once more.

"I'll never forget this trip," said Shirley, thinking back to the past three months.

"We never will."

"You know, we had been there for only a little over three months?"

"Three months?" It was hard to believe, but Juliet knew it was true. "It seemed like at least a year."

"It felt like three years."

"Al is such a bad person. He left us there. He knew you were going to die if we would stay there for long. Did you notice that he wouldn't even look at you? You looked like a ghost." During their recollection, Juliet got Shirley something to eat.

"Yes, I know. And look at my finger," Shirley showed her left index finger. "It won't bend."

Juliet was horrified. She had known it earlier, but had not expected that it would permanently remain this way.

"You had suffered so much. I shouldn't have gone with him. I am so stupid. After all, I thought he is your dad, and so I didn't think he would treat you this way…" Juliet's words trailed off. She sighed. "Let's go to sleep.."

With Juliet's hand holding hers, Shirley's eyes closed. It was time to put the past behind them. They could not undo the harm the trip had caused, but they could move forward. Hopefully, Shirley's index finger would return to normal. If not, she simply had to accept it. It would make work extra more difficult to do than before. She squeezed her mother's hand. Then she saw the wildcats in her dream.

Chapter Forty-Five

Shirley was to start school once again in just several days in the same classroom. It would be in January after New Year's Day of 1995. She was in high spirits for that special day; a day she would resume her studies and see her old friends and make new ones.

She had not much strength to wheel herself after coming back from the last visit to China; it had drawn out her energy. But she would manage. If she could not, she would receive help in class.

Learning and going to school was a passion in her life. She loved it when they were to take tests and quizzes. Everyone was surprised at that, for none even got close in liking exams. Shirley loved facing challenges and overcoming difficulties. She had overcome overwhelming hardships in her lifetime, and achieving academic goals was a thrill for her.

In school and anywhere else, making friends was a breeze for Shirley. They would all come over for a greeting even if Shirley was too shy at first. Shirley was a quiet student in class, never interrupting a lesson, and she always concentrated hard on the teacher. Never once did she speak in classes. Some of her classmates thought of her being overly good in school. She was a teacher's pet—doing well in school, working hard, having distinguished manners, and being a contributor to the community.

Juliet had moved into the same apartment complex, but in a different building. It was the only place she could find that suited them.

***

"Welcome back!" Greeted Mr. Crisfield when

Shirley managed to wheel herself in. Shirley returned the welcome with a big smile. Shirley noticed most of the students were new, but her best friend, Laura, was there. On the wall next to the door, Shirley saw that they had posted the letter she had written to Mr. Crisfield while in China. She felt quite honored that she was so well-liked. Shirley continued reading the books on the bookshelves. Her choices of books got thicker as her reading level reached sixth grade. Soon, she had almost finished all the books on the shelf. Juliet bought many books for Shirley, and Shirley soon finished them all. She was reading an average of four hundred pages a day. Hence, she was known as a bookworm.

In the classroom one day, Mr. Crisfield told the class of an idea he had thought up. For each book they read, they would write the title, author's name, date, and their own names, on a piece of construction paper cut in a circle. They would stick each circle on the wall as a border, so after many books were read, the circles would make a complete circle around the room. Each student was assigned a different color. Since Shirley's favorite color was hot pink, she chose a construction paper that was closest to the color: fuchsia.

After several circles were cut out, Shirley turned to her teacher. "I'll bring some cupcakes tomorrow." It was going to be her twelfth birthday and she was planning to celebrate it with the class just as last year. She could not believe that one year had already passed. The second year was going more smoothly than the first, for one, Juliet was allowed to come to the school daily to take her to the bathroom, and she no longer received physical therapy because the school found it unnecessary. However, she continued the occupational therapies with Dyan.

"That sounds great," said Mr. Crisfield, with a smile. Shirley smiled back. She had two boxes of cupcakes stored in the refrigerator at home. One box had pink icing and the other had white icing; both had red sprinkles on them.

Therefore, laughter filled the classroom as the party began the following day. Shirley had a cupcake with pink icing. She felt grand listening to them all; they sang the birthday song to her.

***

One spring morning, when Shirley woke up for a new school day, she felt itchy on her face. Soon, her face was flushed. Juliet was horrified when she saw Shirley. Her face had several rashes. Juliet checked her body, and discovered the same rashes covering her body. But Shirley stubbornly persisted that she would go to school anyway.

"I want to go to school! I can't miss one day."

Juliet went away and came back with a mirror. She showed Shirley her face. Shirley gave in. She had to admit that she was sick, and could not give it to people in school. Shirley was so much saddened. She had not missed any days of school, even during days she felt quite sick, except once back in January.

She soon developed pimple-like rashes all over her body and face. She restrained herself from scratching them, knowing that it was an unwise action. Juliet called the school and reported that Shirley had chicken pox, and it would be some time till she could get better and return. Shirley was devastated. How long would that be? It was at the end of April, and school would end in two months. Would she get well by then? Juliet had brought Shirley to see a pediatrician, and he confirmed the illness.

Being stuck at home with the pox, Shirley started a new journal. Each day, Shirley wrote a few pages, recording down her daily happenings and thoughts. Her first entry was dated April 28, and a part of it stated:

"Hi! My name is Shirley Cheng. I'm 12 years old and I'm on the wheelchair. I love my mother, I love to draw, write, read, sing, tests, and help people.

"Next September, I'm going to junior high school. This is my first time at school. I only went to school 166 days in all my life!"

April went and May came. Shirley became well as each day passed. Recovery for her was slow, because of her autoimmune disease. She could not receive any shots. That tuberculin skin test had already done permanent damage to her body, and another test could risk everything.

As Shirley was writing in her journal one afternoon, Juliet received a surprise phone call. "Al!"

"How are you doing?" came the canny voice.

"What do you think? You left Shirley to die there!"

"I think we should go back there. I will take you there," he suggested, nonchalant to the silence that followed his request.

Is he crazy? Does he think that I am really that stupid? thought Juliet, frowning with disgust. "How could you even think that?" she demanded.

"Can I talk to Shirley?" Shirley heard the question. She vigorously shook her head.

"No," supplied Juliet, wanting to end the nonsense. She had not to worry for long; Al quickly ended the call. "He is crazy!" Juliet declared to the room.

"That was such a surprise to hear from him. He really wanted us to go back there again?"

"He sure did." She rose from the bed where Shirley was sitting. "I'm going to get some chores done—take out the garbage, get the mail, and many other things."

"Okay. I'll just do some reading," supplied Shirley, whose eyes were already moving on the words in a book.

An hour later, Juliet came in the bedroom and handed her a thick brown envelope. "This is for you, dear!" Juliet smiled.

"Oh, my greeting cards!" Her teacher had told her over the telephone that the class had made her greeting cards.

Juliet carefully tore it open. "My, they are beautiful cards!" Together, their eyes feverishly looked over all the colorful cards. Each and every one of them was hand-made from her classmates. Messages of encouragement and get well wishes were written on them.

"How very kind of them!" exclaimed Shirley, touched by their concern and thoughtfulness.

***

By mid-May, Shirley was finally able to attend school. She had a few scars left from where the rashes had been, but the disease would be no longer contagious, and a relapse was not probable. Shirley was elated to be going back.

"Shirley, great to have you back. We miss you." The whole class welcomed her.

"It's great to be back! I miss it so much and thanks a lot for all the great cards you made for me!" said Shirley, her eyes moving across everyone's face. They were all such lovely people. She was glad to be so fortunate to have Mr. Crisfield as her first teacher and to be in his wonderful classroom.

Mr. Crisfield bought a few more books and had arranged them neatly on the shelves. Shirley became their first reader. Before they knew it, the entire round of circles of construction paper was completed. All colors of the rainbow were present on the border, but most of the circles were in the color of bright fuchsia. Shirley had speeded the task up and completed it in no time.

As with last year, the class was busy with the preparation of a play. Each student was to be a color of the rainbow, and they were required to only dress in that color as props.

Shirley had picked to be the color green, not because she liked the color, but she had read the script and found out that it was the major role in the play. She wanted to have a big part in the play. She loved acting. But before she could perform, she needed to get a green dress first, so Juliet took her out shopping.

"Shopping for a green dress is so hard! I had never thought that it could be so difficult," said Shirley after going through aisle after aisle of dresses in all colors but green. There was a green shirt, but she wanted a dress. She had rarely gone out without wearing either a dress or a skirt. She liked to dress this way. Pants, she thought, were for boys. She finally found a green dress. Juliet tried it on her and it fit. "This will have to do," said Shirley, satisfied that she had found what she was looking for.

When the big day arrived, Shirley repeated her lines in her head. She had a fine line for the closing of the play, where all the colors would join together to form a rainbow. She had made a rainbow for the play with a friend of hers.

"Okay, so is everyone ready?" asked Mr. Crisfield. All answered with nods, with Shirley nodding the most enthusiastically.

The performance went smoothly. The entire day was filled with the event. The play was repeated twice.

***

Sadly, Shirley realized that summer had arrived, and vacation was going to start in two days. Earlier, Mr. Crisfield had met with Juliet to discuss future educational plans for Shirley. He told her that Shirley should start sixth grade in a regular, mainstream class in the fall. Shirley was certainly ready for sixth grade. She would do wonderfully there. Shirley no longer belonged in his class. Shirley had spent only about 180 days in school in her whole lifetime, and had miraculously achieved grade level in all subjects.

Shirley felt glad about going to middle school in sixth grade, but she knew it would be much harder for her. The subjects would be more intense and difficult. But in her heart, Shirley knew she would be able to do it. She waited for that day to arrive with much excitement.

On the second to the last day of school, Shirley said goodbyes to Mr. Crisfield, thanking him for a memorable school year; to all her friends, and many staff members. Tomorrow would be the last day, but Shirley was not planning to go. The school bus driver was not kind to Shirley, and had the radio on at highest volume. They had repeatedly told him to keep it lower, but he never listened to them. There would not be any lessons that day, so she would not miss anything.

"I can't believe that my driver turned out to be like this," sighed Shirley. "He was so good to me in the beginning."

"I know! Seeing him always so good to you, I cooked Chinese food for him as a token of our gratitude," recalled Juliet. "But steadily, we noticed the change in him. The more I cooked for him, the worse he became." Juliet had made the driver dumplings and Lo-mein several times. "I worked so hard to cook for him and I gave him plenty."

"You gave him a bag-full each time!"

"When we give people presents, they'll wonder why and get suspicious of our intention. It seems that we can't give other people things to show our appreciation in this country."

"Too bad that I will have to stay home on the last day of school. I really want to go." Both Shirley and Juliet knew they were to give out awards in school. Juliet was certain that Shirley was going to receive one. And sure enough, a few days later, Shirley received a letter in the mail, enclosed was the award. She had received an award for "Outstanding Academic Achievements in All Areas." Thrilled was not the word to describe how Shirley was feeling then. No words could describe the sense of happiness and achievement that swept through her entire being, flooding every crevice of her soul.

Chapter Forty-Six

Besides reading and keeping a journal, Shirley also planted a few seeds of marigolds and dandelions in a small flowerpot. She drew a chart in her diary to keep a record of the growth of each plant. She was touched by awe and great wonderment when the seeds began to sprout. *Life certainly offers much magic and miracles!* thought Shirley.

She completed her second diary over the summer in August. But she did not have any time to start another, for school was going to open shortly. Before the opening, Juliet had brought Shirley in to meet her sixth grade teacher and her aide. Shirley had drawn a large picture of a white cat sitting upon a cloud with a rainbow in the background. She was going to give it to her new teacher. Shirley often brought pictures she drew to present to others. Other people gave apples to teachers; Shirley gave her priceless artwork.

Juliet pushed Shirley down the hall after asking for the directions. Shirley could no longer wheel herself. During school, she would need a one-on-one aide to push her between classes, get her necessary materials, and help her with any other physical work she needed assistance.

A tall woman with dirty blonde hair opened the door to them. She let them in. "Nice to meet you," she welcomed them. Shirley returned her greeting. Shirley's heart sank once she saw her teacher. She was disappointed that she did not detect any warmth in the woman's eyes. But she thought that she could not depend wholly on looks; maybe the teacher was a kindhearted person. She fervently hoped so.

Shirley handed the teacher her picture. "This is for you, Mrs. Hackett. I drew it for you." Thanking Shirley for the beautiful drawing, Mrs. Hackett put it aside. Shirley then turned her attention to the woman who was soon to be her aide, Mrs. Cartney. She seemed nice, she thought.

"And Shirley, I can relate to your problems. I have arthritis myself, but of course not as bad as yours." Mrs. Hackett showed Shirley her hands, which had fingers touched by the disease. "As for the homework—don't work too hard on them. If you can't finish them, don't worry about it."

The teacher rose from her seat and showed Shirley the place where she was to be seated during class. Shirley saw the special desk they had ordered for her. Each desk had a name tag of the student who was assigned to sit there. A boy's name was on a tag next to Shirley's. Shirley's desk was larger than all the others, with an inward curve to allow her wheelchair to be better positioned. She tried the desk; it felt comfortable with the right size and height.

After all was said, they thanked the teacher and left the room. "What do you think of Mrs. Hackett?" asked Juliet once they got inside her car.

Shirley shook her head in dismay. "She doesn't seem that nice."

"That's what I thought, too."

"But maybe she will turn out to be a nice person," Shirley pointed out hopefully. They would just have to wait and see. Only time would tell. Time was always the judge in all matters. "But Mrs. Cartney appears to be a good person."

Juliet nodded her agreement.

***

On the morning of a day in early September in 1995, Shirley was in high spirits as she rose from her bed. It was her first day of school in sixth grade. She quickly ate her breakfast, took her herbal medication, and got dressed.

"Hi, Greg!" Shirley cordially greeted her driver. Loud music filled every crevice of the bus; the noise boomed in Shirley's head.

She relished the view as he drove. He was driving Shirley to the middle school where she was to attend her sixth grade class. She was touched by sheer excitement. It was not a long drive to the school; it took only a few minutes. When they arrived at the back entrance, Shirley saw her aide waiting by the door.

    Shirley greeted Mrs. Cartney right away. The aide returned her smile and wheeled her into the building and took off her jacket. Shirley usually wore a jacket, for she had poor circulation and could get cold easily. Mrs. Cartney put away her stuff in her locker, and pushed her down the hall in the direction of the classroom. Shirley noticed that the students were all seated. Mrs. Hackett opened the door to Shirley with a smile. Then she continued with the instructions. All eyes turned to Shirley. Shirley was pushed to her desk. She saw that instead of a boy sitting next to her, it was a girl with pretty wavy brown hair, who was unsmiling. That was not going to let Shirley down. In all likelihood, the girl was too shy. Shirley would have to get to know her later. She noted the girl's name was Erin. She also noticed Mrs. Hackett had hung her picture up at the back of the room, at the top, touching the ceiling. It was the least noticeable of places. Some students were still looking at Shirley. One girl who sat in front of Shirley gave her a tiny smile. Shirley readily returned the smile.

    The teacher introduced the schedule of the class to the students. She explained that there would be a reading time before the first period, followed by the English period. Later, math, science, history, and other subjects would be taught. Then a recess period followed lunch. Shirley thought it sounded nice. There was another grown up in the class to assist students in their study. She, Mrs. Wilson, was to help Shirley on anything she needed. Mrs. Cartney was there for physical needs only, and was not to help her academically. Shirley seldom asked for help anyway. She always figured how to do things by herself. Only after trying for several minutes would she give in and ask for assistance. She was an independent person who liked to do things on her own.

    Some moments later, each student was to complete

some math sheets on a timer. They were simple addition, subtraction, multiplication, and division, all of which were regularly done in the special education class. Shirley was almost always the first one who finished each worksheet, and would make it several seconds before the timer went off. The timer was set to sixty seconds for each math worksheet.

Mrs. Hackett handed the students the worksheets. Shirley whizzed through them. "My, Shirley, you're fast!" Mrs. Wilson remarked each time Shirley asked for the next sheet. Shirley felt these problems were too easy. When would they get to the hard stuff? She thought it might be a warm-up.

Later, Shirley concentrated as Mrs. Hackett taught the class history. Shirley did not find social studies interesting, but she understood mostly what was being said. Shirley had loved the geography worksheets in Mr. Crisfield's class, and she scored one hundred on most. She had learned about mountains, deserts, and tributaries. Those things fascinated her.

Soon afterward, lunch period came. Shirley was wheeled out toward the cafeteria. On the way, a boy with dark hair and eyes said a greeting to Mrs. Cartney. Mrs. Cartney introduced the boy to Shirley. "Adam, this is Shirley." The two greeted each other with wide smiles. Adam, a seventh grader, seemed like a really outgoing person. Shirley felt that she already made a new friend in Adam. Little did Shirley know that this first day of meeting would blossom into a friendship for many years to come.

At the cafeteria, Shirley did not order anything to eat. Shirley normally had something to eat after she got home from school to take the herbs and vitamins. She scanned the crowded cafeteria. The students were all in her grade. Each grade level had their own lunch period in school. Mrs. Cartney left for her own lunch, so Shirley sat alone at a round table. Soon, several girls went over and sat at the table. They each smiled, and some small talk began. Shirley listened on without interrupting. Then a few questions were directed her way, and Shirley courteously answered each.

***

Back in the classroom during recess, Shirley tried to seek out anyone to strike up a conversation, but all the students were going out to the school yard. Shirley had to wait till the next day to try to seek conversation.

After all lessons were taught, the dismissal bell rang, signaling the end of the day. All students rushed out of the room. Mrs. Hackett and Mrs. Wilson inquired how the day had been for Shirley.

"It was great, I really like it here," she enthusiastically answered them.

"That's good. Well, see you tomorrow."

"Yes, Mrs. Hackett," Shirley waved goodbye. She was eager to start the next day. The first day had gone by smoothly. Perchance the teacher was not a bad person after all.

"So, how did it go?" inquired Juliet after seeing Shirley in the bus.

"It went well!"

"I'm so happy to hear that! Are you tired?"

"No, I'm fine."

"See you tomorrow, Shirley!" Greg called as Juliet was pushing Shirley inside.

"Yes, see you! Thank you," said Shirley.

Chapter Forty-Seven

"You have to eat something during lunch. It is not good for you to always skip lunch at school!" Juliet was repeating her insistence several times until Shirley finally gave in.

"But I am really not hungry."

"How about some soup? I can heat some soup and put it in a container for you to take to school."

"Okay. That's fine." Shirley had soup at home often. She liked the Campbell's vegetable and noodle soups. Juliet shopped for a thermal lunch bag to keep the soup warm. She found a purple one with black straps.

"This is perfect. I'll just put the soup in the plastic container. I hope it won't get spoiled, though." She counted her fingers. "It's about five hours till lunchtime."

Shirley brought soup to school daily. Her aide stored it in her locker until lunchtime came.

During lunch, Shirley remained silent, listening to the conversations around her. She noticed that several girls wore makeup. Shirley decided to wear lipstick to school since many others were doing so. She liked lipstick, for it enhanced her large eyes and made her appear as if she wore other makeup.

And thus, she applied her lipstick, in a shade of fuchsia, on her full lips and set out to school. It was not to gain popularity or attract people, but simply for fun. She caught a few people taking sneak peeks at her. At lunch that day, she went to her usual table with the group of girls.

"You're wearing lipstick," noticed the tallest girl. Shirley nodded in reply. "But why?" Shirley thought that it was a strange question to ask.

"Other people wear it." Shirley shrugged, giving them a why-not-me look. The girl said nothing else.

Shirley continued wearing the lipstick for a few more days, but stopped when her lips were starting to chap. "How are they able to wear all that makeup every day?" Shirley asked herself. "It is so uncomfortable!" She noticed that quite a few girls wore plenty of makeup in school.

Juliet agreed. "I start to itch if the makeup stays on longer than just a few hours." The only kinds of makeup she wore were eyeshadow and lipstick, both of which she slightly applied. "Anyway, do you need help on your homework?"

"No, I can do it." They had a large assignment on *The Golden Goblet*, and it would be due next week. But Shirley had completed it in just a few days. Homework began to increase in size as days slowly passed by. Shirley began to stay up late in the night to complete all the work. The large gap between elementary and middle school was felt more easily, as the work she received included difficult materials—at least, it was much harder than that of the special education class.

The class was starting to read *The Golden Goblet* by Eloise Jarvis McGraw, a book which Shirley found somewhat difficult. But she never gave up and only tried harder as the work load increased.

Juliet had spoken to Mrs. Hackett about its reading level. "It is hard for Shirley."

"It is not a hard book," said Mrs. Hackett. Of course, it would not be hard for people who had already gone to school for six years. Shirley, in her unique case, had skipped an entire worth of elementary school studies.

Work hours quickly spanned long into the night, leaving Shirley nearly sleepless for school the next morning. She never failed to continue completing her work, even if it meant that she would barely get any sleep.

Once, however, she was unable to complete one piece of her homework, which was a reading assignment of *The Golden Goblet*. She hoped that Mrs. Hackett would not mind, who knew Shirley's persistence from the beginning.

She had never before missed any homework ever since she first started schooling at age eleven.

When the reading period was announced by the ringing bell, Mrs. Hackett checked to see if all students did the assignment.

"Shirley, you did not do your work," she said in front of all the students. Many glances directed Shirley's way. Shirley, lost for words, did not say anything in defense. She was disappointed and hurt that the teacher was not understanding of her circumstances. Did she forget that she had told her from the start not to tire herself if work was too much to handle?

Later that day, the teacher added, "Don't wait to do your work at the last minute."

Shirley was stunned that those untruthful words would come from the teacher's lips. All knew that Shirley was a diligent student, who never procrastinated with any work.

Consequently, ever since that day, Shirley would be extremely concerned if she could not complete any work.

After completing an assignment one day, Shirley gave the packet of the assignment to Juliet for safekeeping until it was time to hand it in. "This needs to be handed in next week. Please don't lose it," said Shirley.

"I won't. I'll put it right here," assured Juliet, going over to a shelf. "You work too hard for your own good. It is not good for your health. You can't go on like this forever."

"No, I have to," insisted Shirley, obstinately. "You know what will happen if I don't complete a work." She was not mainly concerned about any negative comments made by her teacher; she was a person who never dawdled or missed anything in life. She started on her work as soon as she got home every day. She never wasted a single second. Juliet always urged her to rest for a moment, but Shirley refused each time, except at times when she was unable to keep her head up from exhaustion and lack of sleep from the previous night. Many times, Juliet had offered help, but Shirley had refused most of the time. But when Shirley wrote essays, Juliet copied what Shirley wrote into one piece, decreasing the length of time Shirley had to write. Even with Juliet's help, Shirley's right arm hurt badly, to the point the joint was unable to bend. As a result of a long writing project, Shirley's right arm became immobile, making her unable to straighten or bend it (though both of her arms were never able to be straightened more than ninety degrees).

Chapter Forty-Eight

"I don't think that Shirley should take the test. She has been in school for merely a few months in her lifetime," insisted Juliet.

"Don't worry. The IQ test is not going to affect her grade. We just need to do it," said Mr. Jeffs, the former elementary school psychologist who had been transferred to the present school.

"Then, go ahead," Juliet agreed reluctantly.

For several days, Shirley stayed in his office to do the test. It involved plenty of the English language, thus she had to make guesses. But she knew she did well on the visual parts.

"Do you need some rest?" the psychologist asked Shirley.

"No, I am fine. I am enjoying it."

"You are?"

"It is fun!"

"You are too enthusiastic for me," he laughed.

Shirley soon received her score: ninety-five. She was not sure what it meant, but had a feeling it was not high. She simply still did not know enough English to successfully take it.

***

At the back entrance of the middle school, two buttons, each with a white wheelchair symbol against blue background, were beside the double glass doors, one outside and the other inside. If they were pushed, the doors would automatically swing open. They were devices implemented recently to aid handicapped people, but Shirley was the only disabled student in the building other than another girl who was able to walk when a wheelchair was not in use. Mrs. Cartney pushed the button every morning to enter the building, then pushed Shirley in. But one morning, Mrs. Cartney decided to do otherwise. "Shirley, push that button."

"But I don't have enough energy to do it."

"Try it," insisted her aide. She had known of Shirley's condition well, and had been advised of the severity of her arthritis. So Shirley stretched out her left hand while leaning forward from her wheelchair to reach the button. She gave a push, but the exertion was not enough to push it down. Plus, three of her fingers could not be straightened, thus making the task more difficult.

Seeing that it was an unsuccessful attempt, Mrs. Cartney put her hand on top of Shirley's and pushed it, hurting Shirley's hand as a result. Shirley was still in some pain a minute later. The scene was reenacted the next morning.

"But my hand hurts," said Shirley. But Mrs. Cartney simply took Shirley's hand in hers, moved onto the blue button, and pushed it down.

After arriving home, Shirley told her mother of the blue-button incidents.

"She knows you have severe arthritis," said Juliet. "She shouldn't be doing something like this! I'll have to talk to them about it and ask her to stop."

At the same time, other problems had sprung into existence, adding to the issue of the buttons. For each problem, Juliet made calls to the school but received no result. The problems began to mount as days passed.

In classroom, Shirley was always attentive to every lesson and to every word that the teacher said. She never missed a single word and often had her eyes glued to Mrs. Hackett. But sometimes, she turned her eyes somewhere else for a few seconds. It was a natural action done by anyone. But whenever Shirley looked away for mere seconds, Mrs. Cartney would use the ends of pencils to poke at Shirley's arm. "Pay attention, Shirley," she had ordered while poking her.

"I am paying attention," replied Shirley, trying to ignore the pain that the pokes had caused. Shirley knew she had looked away for only ten seconds. It was repeated several times afterward. Therefore, Shirley always feared of turning her eyes away from Mrs. Hackett. Her eyes and neck followed her every move. Lesson time therefore became a tense moment.

Since Shirley, as all humans, needed to use the bathroom daily, she had to sit on a black hard pad, that was used to lift her up while hooked onto a lift in the restroom, throughout the school day. The seating hurt Shirley when she sat on it for long hours, especially since the schooldays lasted till three in the afternoon; her behind usually got sore. But she had no choice. The sling would be hard to put underneath her once she was already in the wheelchair. After finishing the bathroom duty, the sling would not be taken away, for the school saw it unnecessary, even though it would be very easy. Such little effort would not be used to make her comfortable.

Shirley had a bathroom especially for her, one that was always locked. A narrow bed was set against the wall on the left side of the room. She wanted to use the bedpan, for it was the most comfortable way for her, but Shauna, a lady in charge of helping disabled people, did not think it was necessary to do so. "Shirley can just be lifted onto the toilet and go from there," she had said. And the pad would not be taken away from under her as she went. Hence, she had to be careful so not as to get the pad dirty. The hard seat of the toilet hurt her immensely because of her arthritis. But Shauna *would* not understand.

During bathroom time, Mrs. Cartney had banged Shirley's feet against the lift and walls several times. She had been asked to be highly watchful of Shirley's painful feet, but still managed to do things swiftly and carelessly in the small restroom. Shirley had gotten hurt as a result.

When it was time to go home, Mrs. Cartney needed

to dress Shirley in a coat and other warm articles of clothing as days grew colder. She had been told to be extra careful of Shirley's arms and legs while dressing her, but still hurt her tremendously during the process.

In spite of the hard life of being with the aide, Shirley still smiled on all occasions, special or not. And if the day was a holiday, Shirley would make greeting cards for each and every one in her class. Her favorite holiday was Easter; she adored drawing bunnies holding Easter baskets, little chicks with ribbons tied around their necks, and colorful Easter eggs of all designs, on her Easter greeting cards. In each card, she wrote the personalized message in cursive, wishing the card recipient a very happy holiday.

Special days not only included holidays but quiz and test days as well. She looked forward to each exam, making others look at her with questioning spirits shining from their eyes.

With the problems stacking up till it was no longer bearable, Juliet wrote a letter to the school, listing all the issues. She had spoken to Dr. Black, the Special Education Chairperson of Pupil Personnel Services, numerous times, asking for a change in aide, but only received rejection after rejection.

Then Juliet asked to have a meeting to discuss the problems, and it was scheduled.

She went to the meeting, bringing the letter she had written. Mrs. Hackett; Dr. Black; and the principal, Mr. Patricks, were the attendants at the meeting. Shirley, to her extreme dismay, was also present.

Juliet began by reading the letter, which Shirley had helped to write. "Shirley has severe arthritis, and to push the button is extremely painful for Shirley. But Mrs. Cartney even put her hand on top of Shirley's to push the button."

"She needs to be independent," replied Dr. Black to the situation. Mrs. Hackett agreed.

"Independent! Her hands hurt. She has arthritis." Juliet explained, her voice rising. How many times were they needed to be reminded of the fact? "Mrs. Cartney bumped her feet against the bathroom walls and the lift," Juliet continued.

"I'll contact Mrs. Cartney, and after I speak to her, I'll call you," said Dr. Black. And thus, the meeting had ended, with no apparent results at the time.

Not to the surprise of Juliet, Dr. Black stated a few days later that she would not change the aide. Juliet would not give in. The issue with the blue button was resolved, but other more serious problems still existed.

Not withstanding the poor treatment that Shirley was receiving, Juliet dialed Mrs. Cartney's number. "I need to talk to you about some problems." She repeated the issues.

After hearing everything, Mrs. Cartney did not want to continue with the work. She had quit on her own initiative. Thus, after what seemed like a long, grueling time, Shirley received a new aide.

Shirley, therefore, greeted her new aide, a woman named Connie. As the first day went by, Shirley felt that everything was going to work out well. Connie was a person who dressed her with care and did not hurt her in the bathroom. All in all, she was a capable person to care for Shirley.

Each day after arriving home, Shirley told Juliet how the days were going. "Connie is a very good aide."

"I'm glad that Mrs. Cartney quit on her own," said Juliet. "Now you can enjoy school more."

The first week with the new aide quickly sped by. Although Connie was fine with her work in most areas, pushing Shirley in the halls was often dangerous. The halls were crowded with students, some running and turning back abruptly. Some people often bumped into Shirley, hurting her feet as a result. Even though she had footrests, it still hurt her tremendously when they were bumped against people; any vibration hurt her legs and feet. But footrests could not protect her from direct impact all the time; when people were hit from behind, some would topple over a bit, hitting her legs.

Thinking of anything that might prevent bumps, Shirley figured that she could say "Excuse me" when coming near behind others. Thus, down the halls every day, a high voice was heard saying those words many times. Shirley had found it to be working and was happy to having finally found a solution, though it was harsh on her voice.

Chapter Forty-Nine

Shirley listened as Mrs. Hackett told the class about the next writing assignment. Each student was to write a poem and start each line with the letter of the alphabet. "The highest grade will be an A, but if it rhymes, it will receive an A+."

Not wasting any time, the first thing Shirley did after returning home that day was working on her poem. With a pen in hand, she quickly wrote down each line. If one saw her writing the poem, one would think she had memorized the entire poem, for the speed of the words appearing on the paper was much swift. In no time, all twenty-six lines of the poem were completed.

She checked over the poem and saw it did not need to be corrected—at least, she was unable to catch any mistakes. Before tucking it away in her folder, she showed it to her mother. "Here's my *Funny Animal Poem*."

Juliet read each word with relish.

"A is the adder that is slithering up a ladder
B is the baboon that is looking at a moon
C is the crane that got a good brain
D is the dingo that sings Jingle Bells
E is the earwig that is wearing a wig
F is the fish that is making a wish
G is the goat that is eating a coat
H is the horse that is in a chorus
I is the ichthyosaur that is a friend to dinosaurs
J is the jelly fish that is washing the dish
K is the kangaroo that is making a rule
L is the llama that cries for her mama
M is the mink that writes with ink
N is the nightingale that is afraid of the hail
O is the ostrich that is very rich

P is a puppy that likes to sniff poppy
Q is the quail that is fishing for whale
R is the rabbit that jumps as a habit
S is the skunk that is eating some junk
T is the turtle that is very little
U is the unicorn that eats lots of corn
V is the vulture that eats dead creatures
W is the walrus that got a lot of virus
X is the animal that does not exist
Y is the yellow jack that hijacks
Z is the zebra that is my friend Barbara."

Juliet smiled. "This is a great poem! I really don't know how you are able to write this. Where did you learn these words? I don't know many of these animals myself, such as the adder."

"It's nothing. I don't know how I know them; I just do."

"Maybe it's because you read so much."

"Yes, and I hope that my teacher would feel the same way about it. It rhymes, so I will get extra credit."

"She should like it," said Juliet.

"But there are so many shoulds in life that never got to become reality."

Next school day arrived and Juliet said her goodbye to Shirley as the ramp doors on the bus were closed. Shirley was excited to show the poem to Mrs. Hackett. The poem would not be due till another day later.

But she did not get a chance to show it to her right away, for the morning hours were cramped with work, leaving little time to do other things. The time to show it to her, Shirley decided, would be during recess. Thereupon, she waited patiently for the clock to tick to that time.

"Mrs. Hackett, I finished the poem. Here it is," Shirley took out the sheet of paper and handed it to Mrs. Hackett, who began to read it. She quickly finished it.

"Shirley, why would a yellow jack hijack?" asked Mrs. Hackett.

Shirley did not prepare herself for that sort of questions. Mrs. Hackett had startled her with the inquiry. Thinking of something fast, she simply answered, "It is just something made up from my imagination." Mrs. Hackett asked nothing else and never commented on the poem that day. Soon, Shirley had found out that she had done the assignment incorrectly. The poem should be about school items, not other topics, so she wrote another poem and handed it in on the due date.

"Shirley wrote a good poem, but it was not on the correct subject," Mrs. Hackett told Mrs. Wilson. Shirley was surprised that the teacher had thought it good, for she had never told her personally.

***

One day in class, the students were required to take a New York State Social Studies Test, consisting of multiple-choice questions and an essay. Mrs. Hackett told the class not to worry, for it would not affect their own grades; it was just something for the state to see as a statistic.

Shirley read through each question carefully, but no matter how hard she thought, she did not know the answer. All the questions were on US history, which was not part of the materials Shirley had ever learned. She could only make educated guesses by eliminating the choices that seemed improbable.

After she finished answering the multiple-choice questions, she turned to the essay. Students were to choose one of the two topics about which to write. The first essay subject was about a well-known person. Shirley never heard of the person before, so she had to pick the second. The second topic, she thought, was a lot easier. She knew which kinds of inventions she could write about, and how they had changed the lives of many people. She quickly finished the essay. It needed to be done in ink, but the only pen she had with her that day was one with green ink.

Writing was an easy thing for Shirley; it was actually one of the easiest things she knew. And she frequently received compliments for her beautiful handwriting; people commented that it was extremely neat with a classical style.

She neatly stacked her test and put it at the corner of her desk. She was a person who was organized at all times; every item must be put neatly away and work should be done to perfection. Yes, Shirley was also a perfectionist.

During recess that day, Mrs. Hackett walked to the side of the building when she was outside, and spoke to Shirley by the window. "We read your essay, it was very good."

"Really?" Shirley was delighted.

"Yes, you did a great job." That comment made Shirley happy for a long time, long into the week. But she knew she had done well with the essay even if no one confirmed it. She was confident that she wrote a well-written piece, though she knew there were probably many grammatical errors.

***

Halloween was approaching as the end of October was drawing nearer. Shirley, her hands folded in front of her on the desk, listened with much concentration to what the teacher was saying. "No dangerous objects can be brought to the school," Mrs. Hackett informed them, referring to Halloween costumes and accessories. Shirley had never dressed up for Halloween before, thus she was eager to dress up for the first time. Juliet had bought a witch costume for her, along with a black hat and a small broom.

Shirley's hand shot up.

"Yes, Shirley?" said Mrs. Hackett, pointing in her direction.

"Can I bring in a broom?" asked Shirley, gesturing to show its approximate size. The class burst out laughing, joined in by the teacher.

"Of course, unless you decide to swing at others with it."

Erin giggled beside Shirley, who was starting to blush. She smiled back at Erin. They had become friends after a short class project. Mrs. Hackett had asked students to have partners for the assignment. Erin already had a partner with a girl named Anne, who appeared to be a good friend of hers. Seeing that Shirley did not have a partner, Mrs. Hackett suggested that they work together. Shortly, the three were laughing with one another. Ever since that day, they had been good friends, sharing jokes and secrets with one another. It had taken some time, but it was worth the wait.

Halloween arrived with monsters, doctors, and skeletons flooding the school grounds. With the broom in hand and a pointy black hat upon her head, Shirley arrived at the school with a wide smile and excited eyes. She held the broom wherever she went, and set it at the corners of the desks in classes.

When the time for lunch neared, students were anxious to pack up their writing utensils, notebooks, and textbooks, to get ready to leave their classes. Shirley looked forward to the time when she could talk with her friends. Lunch period was nearly the only opportunity she had to spend time with them. She had changed her lunch table to sit with Erin and her friends.

The bell rang and immediately, loud students poured into the halls. As her aide was pushing her toward the cafeteria, Dr. Black came up to them and asked that Shirley be pushed to the main office. Shirley had a sinking feeling. She knew that the news awaiting her was not good. Nothing was pleasant with Dr. Black, who seemed to be the boss in the school. Even the principal was uncomfortable speaking out around her.

Dr. Black, all six feet of her, sat down on an office chair in front of Shirley. Mr. Patricks and Connie were also present. Dr. Black folded her hands on her lap and began the meeting.

"Don't say 'Excuse me' in the halls. It is getting very annoying. You are a big girl now and you need to be a good girl." Shirley listened on silently to those words. She had nothing to say to this woman. She might as well talk to stones. "It is rude to say it all the time." But it was the only way Shirley could prevent her aide from bumping her feet into others in front. She shook her head; no matter how much Shirley explained, they would not understand. Her feet were hurting immensely when the aide slammed them into others.

Dr. Black continued with lecture after lecture on how Shirley should behave and be a good girl. What did Shirley do wrong? Nothing, Shirley knew. They did not know how to appreciate a good student when they saw one in front of their eyes. But nothing could ever get in her way of achieving her dreams and aspirations. She would continue to reach for the stars, no matter how high they were or how difficult a task it was. She knew many rough trials lay ahead for both her and Juliet. But like the team that they had always been, they would overcome all fierce dragons and conquer daring quests in achieving the impossible.

Chapter Fifty

The first quarter was about to end in a few days. Mrs. Hackett had recorded down all the grades and averages of each student. She would send in the reports to parents and guardians while the school would send out the official report cards. Shirley's eyes followed Mrs. Hackett's figure as she went around the class, showing the students how they did. "The grades with circles around them are tests and quizzes," she informed the class. Shirley wondered how her grades were.

Shirley prepared herself as Mrs. Hackett came toward her. With the paper in hand, she pointed the grades to Shirley. "Shirley, you are doing very well!" She saw a couple of seventies, while all the others were mostly mid and high eighties. Shirley was quite pleased with her progress. Mrs. Wilson repeated Mrs. Hackett's statement.

Coming home that day, Shirley told Juliet her grades. Juliet was elated. She was surprised, not by her grades, but because she had never expected that Shirley would really take everything so seriously and actually learn in the classes. Her main objective for having Shirley attend school was to have her play and have fun with other children her age since she could not when staying home. They were just the opposites from most other families. Other parents asked their children to do well in school and work hard, and if they did not do well, they would be grounded. But in the case with Juliet and Shirley, it was the contrary: Juliet asked Shirley to relax and enjoy the fun of it all, while Shirley refused to play and continued working hard with every single assignment. She had great confidence that Shirley would do remarkably well in a regular classroom, even after only a short time of schooling, and she had been right.

***

The long wait ended—it was time to return the New York State Social Studies Test. Shirley patiently waited till she received her copy. She saw there were two scores in a box; one was a 10, and the other a 59. She wondered what the numbers meant. She noticed that many of her classmates had 9 and 8 in place of her 10, so hers was higher than everyone's she saw so far.

After all tests were returned, Mrs. Hackett walked to the front of the class. From the looks of it, Shirley knew she was going to announce something important. Shirley could often guess what someone was about to do just by looking at their expressions.

"The 10 is the perfect score for the essays. And Shirley received a 10 on it." She told the class. All eyes turned to hers, some with admiration. "She had only some schooling, so she did not know the answer to the multiple choice questions. But she did very well with her essay."

Shirley was smiling ear to ear. She found out someone else in the class also received a 10 on the essay, so there were at least two people who got a 10. But she knew that there would not be more than three.

"Amazing!" exclaimed Juliet after Shirley shared with her the good news that afternoon.

"But it was very easy."

"But you are a good writer, that's why you think it is easy!"

"No, it is easy. Others didn't have a hard time with it."

"You think everyone can write well. I sure can't." Juliet laughed. Shirley joined in. Stating the facts of an issue was not a problem for Juliet; but she cringed at creative writing.

***

"It's time for computer class," said Shirley gleefully. She loved going to computer class. It was her first time using a computer. It was also a time to relax and not to be under the cold gaze of Mrs. Hackett. But the downside of going to another class was the chance of getting hurt. She had stopped saying "Excuse me," for she had received a scolding from Mrs. Hackett as well. "How many times did you get hit?" Mrs. Hackett had asked.

"Two times," answered Shirley. She had gotten hurt badly both times.

"That's not many times. Don't say, 'Excuse me.'" Thus, what else could Shirley do? She had to stop.

Therefore, Shirley tucked in her feet under her wheelchair as Connie pushed her to the computer room. But she was careful not to have the wheels hit her. When Shirley was settled down in front of her computer, she asked Connie to hand her the book that was needed for the class.

"The book isn't in your bag," said Connie after rummaging through her bag. Shirley had thought it was in it.

"Connie, could you please go back and bring the book? I didn't know that I didn't bring it. Sorry."

"Okay, I'm going now." Shirley felt bad at having her travel back, but it was the first time that it had happened. Since she could not stand, she was unable to see what she had in her bags. Therefore, she could know the contents of her bag only when she needed a certain material.

***

As Shirley was working on a worksheet in French class a few days later, Connie interrupted her, and pushed her out of the classroom. Shirley did not have any idea why she was being brought back to her sixth grade classroom. Mrs. Hackett sat down behind her desk across Shirley. Shirley was locked in place. She felt she was waiting for a sentence to be brought upon her. Connie sat to her left.

"Mrs. Hackett, I'm missing French," Shirley said,

looking into her teacher's eyes.

"Shirley, I am missing *my* own lunchtime." Came the answer. She pointed at the Reese's peanut butter cups that Connie had given Shirley. "Do you know why Mrs. Bresnahan gave you these?" Shirley did not answer. Mrs. Hackett continued, "Why do you make greeting cards for everyone on holidays?"

"Because I like making cards. And I like my classmates."

"Mrs. Bresnahan gave you the candy because she likes you."

Shirley nodded in agreement. She was brought here to only listen to this reason?

Mrs. Hackett went on, "Shirley, you are not Mrs. Bresnahan's boss, and she's not your servant."

Shirley was speechless. She had never treated Connie like a servant. How could Mrs. Hackett say something like that?

"You should not ask Mrs. Bresnahan to fetch a book you forgot to bring to class." Shirley had asked Connie twice to go back to the classroom and bring back a book that she did not bring to the computer class. Shirley certainly did not do it on purpose. It did not mean that Shirley was bossing Connie around.

"Also, you should not call Mrs. Bresnahan by her first name. You should call her Mrs. Bresnahan. It is disrespectful."

"She had difficulty pronouncing my last name, so I told her she can call me Connie," supplied Connie.

"Well, okay," said the teacher.

The next question Mrs. Hackett asked Shirley came as a surprise to Shirley's ears, "Will you still come to school if kids make fun of you?"

"Yes, I will still come to school," Shirley answered her, her voice unwavering and her gaze steady.

"If kids make fun of me, I will never come to school."

Shirley did not know how to remark to the comments. She was shocked that such words were emitted from a teacher's lips; such a discouraging, hurtful thing to say to anyone, let alone a disabled student who was such a bright and hardworking person.

When Mrs. Hackett ended the meeting, Shirley noticed that it was time for the next class; she had missed an entire period of French class. She would just have to get whatever notes she had missed and hopefully figure out any new work.

As Shirley was engrossed with math class, Juliet had stopped her car in front of a house. a sign indicating a garage sale had caught her eye as she was on the road heading back home. She had always wanted to buy some furniture for the apartment. She loved to make their home nice and comfortable. The apartment at the current time had no living room sets, and Juliet wanted to buy a set of sofas and a coffee table. She stepped out of her car and headed toward the house. She spoke to the homeowners and discovered that they were selling a set of blue sofas. Juliet found the set pretty. She handed the sellers some cash. The two sofas would be delivered to them that afternoon. Happy with the purchase, Juliet left, knowing that the apartment would not look so vacant now. *It will make Shirley happy as well*, thought Juliet. She grimaced about what the school days were like for her.

The days with Mrs. Hackett became more unbearable. But Shirley went every day, never missing a single day, not even when she was sick. Despite the harsh treatment, Shirley soared in the class. Her grades of mid and high eighties became mostly nineties.

That afternoon, as promised, the sofas were delivered to the apartment as Shirley was arriving home from school. Shirley bade the homeowner, who had delivered the purchase, a "hello," with a smile.

"What do you think of the sofas?" asked Juliet.

"They look very pretty," answered Shirley.

"But since they are old sofas, I'm going to clean them." Juliet planned to go over to the garage sale again to see if she would find anything else that might be useful. She planned to buy the cleaning products at the same time.

"My husband came back and kept on telling me how beautiful your daughter is!" the woman told Juliet when she arrived at their house. "He told me she is so beautiful and that she has beautiful hair!"

Juliet smiled and replied, "Thank you." She had always thought Shirley beautiful with her large almond-shaped eyes, that were similar to her own, and long, shiny black hair that was down to her waist. Her hair had always been short before, but she desired long hair, so she started to grow it out when she was ten after the hospitalization. Everyone was surprised when they had found out that it had taken her only two years to grow her hair down to her waist. *But too bad the rashes are starting to affect her face*, thought Juliet with a frown. The rashes were moving upward and Shirley's face was starting to get itchy. But others would not notice, for they were still not really noticeable.

Seeing that there was nothing else that she needed from the garage sale, she left. She headed to the markets for the cleaning product. She came out with a LYSOL spray.

The next day while Shirley was attending school, Juliet sprayed the entire set of sofas. She planned to bring Kwi Show over for a visit. Kwi Show wished to take a look at the set.

Juliet glanced at the clock. It was almost time for Shirley to be home. *Time sure flies by quick*, she thought. She stood by the sliding door in the living room to wait for the yellow bus to come. She glanced at the clock again. Four minutes had passed the time that Shirley was supposed to come home. She could feel herself growing worried.

Another five minutes passed.

She was always concerned for Shirley's safety. She went to the telephone and rested a hand upon the receiver. She was deciding to call the school when she heard the screeching of the bus' tires. She let out a breath. She quickly went out the door and arrived at the side of the bus.

"What happened?"

"Sorry, the bus was late getting to my school," explained Shirley. "Don't worry about me. I'm fine."

***

The three were in the living room conversing the following afternoon. "I heard you're doing extremely good in school," said Kwi Show.

"Yes," chirped Shirley, gleefully. "I like going to school but…"

"But too bad you're having so many problems with the aides and teacher," finished Juliet, rubbing her eyes. Shirley noticed that her grandmother was squeezing her eyes. Now that she thought of it, her own nose, too, was bothering her.

"I think you sprayed too much of the stuff," said Kwi Show, turning to Juliet. "My eyes are getting irritated."

"Mine are, too," remarked Juliet. "It has already been a day. I guess it takes time for it to wear off. The sofas are really too old and dirty."

After a period of time, it was time to take Kwi Show home. As Juliet went to get her keys, Shirley let out a loud sneeze. "Did you get a cold?" Juliet inquired with a look of concern.

Shirley shook her head. "My nose doesn't feel comfortable; it is irritated by the spray, too."

***

As days quietly flew by in the apartment, Shirley's nose was still irritated. Juliet watched on in sheer disbelief. Shirley was sneezing often and she needed to carry a box of tissue wherever she went. "I feel awful!" exclaimed Juliet. "I can't believe that you will get so irritated by the spray. Look at you, you're sneezing the entire day!"

Shirley looked at her through watery eyes. "I didn't know—" A sneeze interrupted her. "I didn't know this would happen, either!" She sneezed again. "But I think that I should stop sneezing later on." Little did she know how wrong she was.

Juliet got rid of the sofas and bought a set of new ones, but Shirley continued to sneeze. The damage had been done. There was no way to rewind time.

Chapter Fifty-One

"What time is it?" Shirley asked groggily, her voice scratchy from sleep. Her eyes sleepily fluttered open to the streaming sunlight. Her heart gave a leap. "What time is it?" she repeated with a horrified expression.

"Don't worry, we have time," replied Juliet with assurance.

"Mom, I told you not to do this!"

"But I don't have the heart to wake you."

"Please wake me up sooner! I don't like to rush." Shirley was getting quite irked. Juliet never liked to wake up Shirley in the mornings for school, especially when Shirley had just fallen asleep not a couple of hours ago, as on this day. Juliet would wait until they had only a few minutes left before deciding to wake her up. Then Juliet would do things extra fast than before in preparation. On days like this, Shirley could sometimes skip her morning dose of the green drink and herbs.

"Do I have everything? How about last night's homework?"

"Yes, I have all your work in the bags," assured Juliet.

"Oh, I need the box of tissue, I almost forgot."

Juliet handed her the tissue box with a sigh. "You're still sneezing!"

"Yes. Let's go, the bus is here!"

"I love you!"

"I love you, too, Mom!"

Juliet's eyes followed her daughter's bus as it drove down the block. She hoped it would be a good day for Shirley, one with less or no problems from her aide and teacher. She walked inside and entered the kitchen for something to eat.

"Oh!" she gasped when her eyes rested upon the container of soup that was supposed to be in Shirley's bag. "I'll bring it in before lunch." She knew Shirley's schedule by heart. Shirley had told her the time of every class, along with the lunch period. She looked at her watch. She was going to Kwi Show's home to pick her up to take her to the bank in just a few minutes. She hoped she would be back in time before lunchtime started at the school. Grabbing her keys and putting on her coat, Juliet rushed out of the apartment.

Meanwhile, Shirley was mulling over what she had just learned. It was December and the school had put up a program for all students to enter in. It was the National Reflections Program, and areas in literature, visual arts, photography, and a few other categories were available in which students could express their creativity. Those who entered the contest would be judged on the school level, state level, then on a national level. Shirley went to the main office to get a packet for visual arts right away. She could hardly wait till she could start on it.

Then students got ready for lunch period. Shirley had found out that her mother had forgotten to pack the soup in her bag. She did not mind. She could do without ever having anything to eat for lunch. Little did she know that a blue Ford Escort was rushing toward the middle school, with the container of tomato soup beside the driver.

Juliet glanced at her watch again. *I am just in time*, she thought. Lunch would not start for another seven minutes. She had gone straight home after coming back from Kwi Show's place, then headed out to go to Shirley's school. She did not want Shirley to miss a single time of having something for lunch.

She walked in through the main entrance. The lobby was crowded with people after the bell rang. She knew Shirley would soon be coming. She was standing by the cafeteria when Mrs. Hackett walked over.

"What are you doing here?"

"I forgot to give the soup to Shirley this morning,"

explained Juliet, lifting the bag in emphasis, "so I brought it now."

"I'll give it to her. You have to leave."

"Can't I see Shirley for a minute?"

Mrs. Hackett shook her head. "No, Mrs. Cheng, you have to leave right now." Defeated, Juliet handed over the soup and walked away after thanking the teacher.

All this was unbeknownst to Shirley while her aide pushed her toward the cafeteria. The aide locked her wheelchair before she was to leave Shirley by the table. Then Shirley saw her teacher approaching.

"Shirley, your mom brought you this."

"Oh, when did she come?"

"Just some time ago." Shirley thanked her and asked her aide to open the container. After all was settled, the aide left.

I just missed her, thought Shirley, disappointed, wishing that she was able to see her mother.

***

The first thing Shirley did that day after getting home was to get started with her artwork. She had already thought of the image in her mind while riding on the bus; it was a winter scene with a smiling snowman at the center, with children surrounding it. Furry and feathered friends of nature were also among the merry scene.

After Shirley was done drawing and coloring the picture on a medium-sized poster, she added glitters of all colors to it, accentuating the beauty. Juliet mounted the poster on a cardboard, for the contest rules had asked for it. Now, it was ready for submission, and Shirley would bring it in the next day. It was soon time for vacation, for Christmas was about to knock on their door. Shirley could not believe that another year had passed by. She wondered what adventure and challenges the new year would bring. A new year also meant her birthday. She already planned a party for that special day, and would soon hand out the invitations. She would be a teenager. She felt quite excited. She knew she was the oldest in the class. She planned to tell her friends about her background once they were to arrive at her apartment for the party.

"I'm going to write a letter to Connie," Juliet interrupted Shirley's concentration on her plans for the party. "I've been telling her to dress you up well for winter." On the past several days, Shirley had been coming home with her red coat improperly buttoned. The coat, like with most other coats, had buttons in the front and two strings at the waist for shrinkage purposes. Juliet tied the strings to make the coat fit more snuggly, thus preventing more cold air coming into contact with Shirley. But Connie simply tied the strings without buttoning up the coat. Juliet was more than annoyed when it happened over and over again after informing Connie many times. Hence, her next resort was to write the letter.

"I'm going to put this in your bag," she said after completing the letter, pointing at Shirley's small plastic bag which she kept with her at all times during school. It contained not only pens and pencils, but also a mini stapler, a tape, a small pair of pink scissors, a six-inch purple ruler, several erasers, and a glue stick. Shirley learned their usefulness whenever the time called for a stapler or a ruler. Juliet added the letter to all the other contents after reading it to Shirley. "She was so good to you before Mrs. Hackett said those words! She tried to sabotage your relationship with the aide, and she has succeeded!" Juliet fumed.

"I know," sighed Shirley. "It was so good in the beginning. I'll give the letter to her tomorrow." She finished the sentence with a loud sneeze.

She handed the note to Connie as soon as she was inside the building after getting off the bus the following morning.

Everyone was in a cheerful mood as the vacation drew near. All the invitations for her birthday party were distributed—twenty-four cards in all. Shirley knew there would not be many people coming, for it would be on Super Bowl.

Before vacation, Shirley received a new aide. Connie had been taking Shirley out in the cold to wait for the bus. She had replied to Juliet's letter concerning the coat, saying that she had always been dressing her up properly. She simply blindly insisted. Juliet's voice was not being paid attention to. But as life had laid everything down, Connie had to leave on her own accord, for she had to change her job, no longer working with the home care agency that the school used. Following her, Leigh became Shirley's new aide.

Shirley found out that Leigh was not someone who would hurt her. Shirley was happy with her, but her happiness could not last long. Leigh was a heavy drinker and often fell asleep during classes.

"Wake up," said Mrs. Hackett, shaking Leigh's shoulders. She was asleep beside Shirley. Shirley needed to go to another class, but was unable to wake her up. Groggily, Leigh blinked her eyes. "She needs to go to her next class," the teacher told Leigh.

"Oh, I'm sorry." The sleepy Leigh then slowly rose from her seat and began to put Shirley's books back into her bag. Although the scene often repeated, Shirley was not quite unhappy. She was not being mistreated. But it became the concern of Juliet.

"What if something happens? What if there's an accident? She can't take you to the bathroom when she's so drunk!" exclaimed Juliet. She called up Dr. Black and left a message with the special education secretary, Lois, who often received Juliet's calls. Juliet waited for the chairperson to return her call, but she never did. "She rarely returns any of my calls! I really hope that Leigh would not fall down in her drunken state and hurt you."

But Juliet did not need to worry for long, for the school had fired Leigh shortly afterward. The cause of firing

Leigh was not her drinking situation, but her letter. She had written a letter to one of the male teachers, asking him out for a date.

"Ha!" Shirley burst out laughing when she found out. The idea of her aide writing the letter amused her. But she was somewhat saddened by the event. Leigh had always been nice to her. It was the first time that Shirley was happy with an aide. "If only she did not drink and write that letter."

After Leigh, came Samara, a smoker. "First a drinker, then a smoker," commented Shirley, shaking her head. She soon discovered that the smoker was worse, much worse, than the drinker. Samara often left Shirley alone in the classroom to go out of the building to smoke. She had even left her alone during recess. Mrs. Hackett was well-aware of the situation, yet permitted the aide to continue.

"Thank goodness vacation starts tomorrow," said Shirley, with relief visible in her countenance. "I'll just continue with the horrid days with her when the new year arrives. It is really getting inconvenient. I have no one to take out any necessary items for me. I had to raise my hand in the middle of lessons to ask Mrs. Hackett to get the things," Shirley muttered to herself. "But I guess it could be worse."

Chapter Fifty-Two

The vacation was filled with books for Shirley. She had bought over a dozen of books at a book sale her school had some time back.

"You have to rest your eyes, dear. It is not good for you to read the whole day. Plus, you're holding the book too close to your eyes," said Juliet.

"No, I'm really fine," replied Shirley.

"You have to rest for a few minutes."

"Just let me finish this book, I'm almost done," answered Shirley absent-mindedly, absorbed in her book. Shortly, she finished it.

Putting down the book on the table in front of her, Shirley reached out for another, but decided otherwise. She asked for some paper and some markers instead.

"Here is a pad for you to draw. You always draw on scrap paper, and all of your drawings are so great, so I want to save them in a good drawing pad," said Juliet, handing her the pad. She had been saving all of Shirley's drawings as best as she could. Her drawings covered the walls of the living room; they ranged from ballerina cats to parakeets and cockatiels.

They owned four parrots in two cages. There were two yellow parakeets named Tommy and Shirley, while the two white cockatiels were known as Whitey and Franky. For many hours other than reading, Shirley watched the birds with much interest and care. She, along with Juliet, could learn a great deal from them. They, as the wild cats, possessed human-like characteristics. Shirley, the talker among them, was always seeking affection from Tommy, who always returned her love with a mean peck. He never wanted to be bothered by her. In fact, he frequently chased her around the cage, hopping from one perch to another, trying to grab at her tail that was getting longer and longer from him constantly pulling on it.

"Not a very good pair!" joked Juliet.

"Yes, I made a bad pick!" They both laughed.

Shirley let the parakeets out daily. They flew freely in the living room. But Shirley was not an organized flyer, and often bumped into things and landed with not much grace. Tommy, on the other hand, ventured to every corner and crevice, landing nimbly on shelves and chairs and once, on Shirley's head. Juliet had taken a photograph of that scene with Tommy on the smiling Shirley.

They rarely let Franky out of the cage, for she (whom Shirley had named by mistake) did not know how to go back inside the cage and it was hard for Juliet to get her back.

But Whitey was the most impossible of them all. From the very first day he came to the household, he had been scared to death of everything in sight. That first day, he was restless in his cage, constantly hissing and going about wildly.

"He appears as though he had received an awful scare before. He probably suffered a trauma, like abuse," analyzed Juliet.

Shirley nodded in agreement. "Poor bird."

Once, they let Whitey out, but they soon learned it was a horrid mistake. He simply held on to the same spot where he landed on after getting out. He hissed whenever Juliet neared. Never been badly bitten by birds, Juliet gently got a hold on him. Immediately, his hooked bill plunged into her fingers. Blood oozed out. She tried to free her hand, but his hold on her would not loosen. With all her might, she finally got him inside the cage and was able to get her hand free. From that day on, they dared not let him out. He had accidentally gotten out one day, and the same thing happened.

Juliet had bought two gray cockatiels before she purchased Whitey, but had to return them, for the first nearly camouflaged against the dark cage, and the second was simply too lazy, doing nearly nothing the entire day. When Juliet returned to the pet store for the third time, she decided to buy the white cockatiel, for he seemed the most active in the flock. And thus, Whitey came to live with them, followed by Franky, Tommy, and Shirley.

Not knowing the genders of the birds, Shirley simply named them without accordance, except with the parakeets, for which she had faint ideas. She had heard that the part of the bill that surrounded the nostrils of parakeets could help to indicate their genders: males were blue, while pink for females. Because of the uncertainty of the cockatiels' genders, Shirley received a big surprise when she found Whitey and Franky mating one day. Since then, she discovered that Franky was actually a female.

It would soon be time to return to school. Days quickly flew by, and the crystal ball dropped at Times Square, marking the start of the New Year 1996.

Chapter Fifty-Three

After every student gloomily returned to class, the daily routine was quickly reinforced. The teacher announced that there would be a New York State Reading Comprehension Test, but a practice test was given first. Shirley took the test eagerly, and began right away when they were told to. At the beginning of the exam, the questions were easy, but as she got further into the test, the questions became harder. Shirley made educated guesses on only a few questions. She thought most of the questions were easy.

Although Shirley continued to enjoy being in school, she was full of frowns having Samara. Samara was the most incapable person to be her aide. She did not know how to do her work, and frequently forgot to put her books back in her bag.

"I need to go to school and teach Samara how to do her job," Juliet muttered to herself. She picked up the telephone and called the school. She explained to Dr. Black about the problems that Shirley was experiencing with Samara.

"Mrs. Duggan said that she can teach her. She said that Samara is doing a good job with the work," said Dr. Black.

"How does she know? She doesn't check on Shirley." Juliet was sizzling. She knew that the school nurse never saw how Samara was really doing her work. It was likely that she had merely taken a few glimpses. That meant nothing, let alone being counted as teaching.

Juliet insisted that she must come to see Samara, but Dr. Black refused. Defeated, Juliet hung up. Her shoulders were not sagging. She was not giving up. There should be a way to either get Samara to do her work properly, or get her switched.

But as days passed, Juliet did not know what to do. Samara continued going out to smoke. She continued to forget to put Shirley's belongings in her bag. But above all, Samara was beginning to call in absent. Without Samara, Shirley could not go to school, so the school had to supply her with a substitute. But as Samara's absences became frequent, often missing days and days, the school had to change her to someone else.

"It is so hard for me to switch an aide, but they can do it all the time," mumbled Shirley.

"Good riddance!" declared Juliet. "I do hope you'll get a good person next."

"I'll keep on hoping for someone to be good to me, but all my wishes were in vain. I kept wishing that I'll get someone nice as my next aide, but it never came true," said Shirley. "No one listens to my problems. They never see my aides treat me badly. Everything is done undercover, without the notice of anyone. My aides are with me nearly the whole day, and most of what goes between us is always done in privacy. No one comes to check how they are treating me during bathroom times, while they are dressing me, and pushing me... They just see the surface. They see that all aides were smiling, and they think they were nice. But when they do see hints of poor treatment, they do not a thing, just like, for instance, with the smoking habit. They don't know how aides are treating me, and they won't listen when I complain. No one is willing to listen to me; no one asks me how my aide is treating me, or checks on me."

Shirley soon received Mrs. Penney as her fifth aide. Mrs. Penney was a woman with smiles and friendliness toward others, immediately receiving their approval. But Shirley knew that they did not know what was inside of her.

But before the readers could see what Shirley knew of Mrs. Penney true nature, let us focus on the next happenings.

The students got the practice New York State

Reading Comprehension Test back. Shirley's eyes quickly rested upon her test score. Next to her score, the cursive word "fantastic" was written. There were a total of seventy-seven questions, and she got fifty-four of them correct. Mrs. Hackett told her that it was notably good. Shirley knew that her mother would be so happy to hear that. Therefore, the first thing she said to Juliet when she arrived home that day was her score.

"You did that well on an English test?" asked Juliet, her eyes wide.

"Yes, Mrs. Hackett said that if you get to that level, you can read newspapers!"

Ring! The telephone interrupted the moment of celebration.

Juliet answered it. "Sure, hold on please," she said to the caller. "It is for you; it is Erin," she handed it over to Shirley, who gladly took it. She had been talking to Erin nearly every day after school; some conversations lasted well over three hours.

"Are you ready for the party?" inquired Shirley.

"Yes. Who else is coming?"

Shirley sighed, "I had given so many invitations, but I'm now expecting just six or seven people."

"It is on the Super Bowl."

"I know. Oh well. But it will be so much fun. I can't wait!" Shirley squealed into the telephone.

Juliet left her side to wash the dishes. She was happy that Shirley could have fun with her classmates.

Three hours later, Shirley hung up with Erin. She tapped on the table, thinking what to do next. She had already finished all of her work. She thought of her days in school and all the classes. Then she thought of Greg. He had told her that it was his last year, and shortly, Shirley was to have a new driver, whom she had met, a lady named Diana, who seemed quite nice. Shirley did not wish to be on the bus again with the deafening noise. She was looking forward to having Diana as her new driver next year.

Lastly, her thoughts turned to her books. She decided that she could start on a new book. A smile played and lingered about her lips as she began to read.

***

The living room, decorated with colorful streamers and balloons, was filled with laughter as Shirley's party was underway. As she predicted, only seven people came, and all were girls. Her best friend from special education class also came. Of a certainty, it was a happy moment for her. She had never had a party before, and it was a time to forget all her pains and obstacles. She was finally no longer in need of hospitalization; her health was stable on herbal treatment.

"Wow, you're thirteen!" noted one friend, counting the glowing candles on the chocolate cake.

"Yes," and with that, she vanquished the fire with one blow.

"Did you make a wish?" asked another girl. Shirley nodded. She had wished for the ability to walk someday. It had been her most fervent wish for as long as she could remember.

"She had never been to school until eleven years old," Juliet began to share her background with the girls.

"Then she must be really smart," commented one with short brown hair after Juliet finished the story.

"She *is very* smart," reconfirmed Juliet.

The party continued with laughter ringing loud and clear throughout the apartment, with many jokes shared and dares accomplished. Shirley's face was never absent of a smile for a single second. But it could not last forever. Her friends left at eight in the evening. But Erin stayed till nine, adding more to the joy-filled memory.

***

"The next thing we're going to do is to write. Just

write what has been happening in your life or anything else you would like," Mrs. Hackett told the class.

Shirley knew right away about what she was going to write. With pen in hand, she began the assignment. "My friends came to celebrate my birthday," she wrote. Mrs. Hackett nodded her head with approval when she walked past her desk.

"To celebrate your birthday?" asked Mrs. Penney. "I think you should put, '…to celebrate the day of my birth.'"

"But I like to write what I have written," replied Shirley. It was her work; she had the right to write what she liked. "Mrs. Hackett, is what I have written okay?"

Mrs. Hackett listened on as Mrs. Penney said that what she had suggested was better.

"Either way is fine," decided the teacher.

Shirley therefore did not change what she had written. Mrs. Penney silently leaned back.

Soon, the dismissal bell rang and all the students rushed out of the building. Shirley inwardly sighed as she was pushed to her locker. She gritted her teeth as Mrs. Penney swiftly dressed Shirley in her coat. Shirley rubbed her hurting arm on the way out into the cold to get on the bus.

"Hi, Greg, how are you today?" Mrs. Penney asked her bus driver.

"I'm fine, and how are you?"

"Fine. I hope that spring would be here soon."

"I hope so, too. No one likes wintertime."

Shirley waited for the conversation to end, so that Greg could get her into the bus. But Mrs. Penney continued to chatter on, unmindful of Shirley. Shirley was freezing. She wiggled her toes in her slippers, and noted that they were numb from the cold. She pulled her sleeves out to cover her hands to keep them warm. She waited some more. Mrs. Penney had been holding up the time by talking to the bus driver for several days now. At long last, Mrs. Penney bade the driver goodbye, ending the conversation. Greg strapped her wheelchair in and then he closed the bus doors. But Shirley was still freezing.

"Why are you always so cold now?" asked Juliet once she got Shirley in the apartment. "Is Mrs. Penney still using up time to talk to Greg in the cold?"

Shirley, her body shaking, managed to nod. "Yes, she's still doing it. And she's still hurting me when she dresses me."

"I have been talking to Lois, and her only answer is that Mrs. Duggan is watching over you."

"That's a lie. Mrs. Duggan never came to check on Mrs. Penney. But even if she comes to the class for one minute, that will not help. Nobody's seeing how Mrs. Penney is really treating me," said Shirley. "When would all this end?"

***

The time for the actual New York State Reading Comprehension Test swiftly arrived. Again, Mrs. Hackett told the class that it would not affect their grades. As with the first, Shirley took the test with much enjoyment. She waited for the result with high hopes. She knew she did quite well on it.

Sure enough, when the results came in, she saw she got sixty-nine questions correct out of a total of seventy-seven questions, tying with one of the smartest students in the class.

Shirley was rising toward the stars; and she would touch one soon. She would shine with them; perhaps shine even brighter.

Then her thoughts traveled to something else that was adding to her happiness. A few days before spring had arrived, the school had announced the winners to the National Reflections Program; Shirley was included. Upon hearing the news, Shirley's eyes shone brighter than the glitters on her winning entry. They were scheduled for an award assembly several nights later. It was an event not to be missed.

Therefore, on that night, Juliet and Shirley happily prepared for the event.

"I'll wear that dress with the straps," Shirley decided with rapidness, pointing at the dress in the closet.

"This one?" Juliet fingered the tan and white dress. "This is a pretty dress."

"I wonder how many people won."

An hour later, Juliet parked by the curb at the school. She took the wheelchair, instead of the stroller. The assembly would not start for another five minutes. She wheeled Shirley inside the building, down the halls, and stopped in the front row.

Everyone listened attentively as the winners were announced and awards presented.

Shirley's name was called.

Juliet was unlocking her brakes as the announcer went over to them and handed the award to Shirley, not giving them a chance to go up to receive it in front of everyone.

Shirley turned her award around in her hands and studied it. She received a gold key chain for winning third place. Her name was engraved on it.

"She should have waited for us to go up there so you can get your award yourself," fumed Juliet.

"It's okay, Mom, it's okay," assured Shirley. She was disappointed as well. But what choice did they have?

The *Poughkeepsie Journal* was there, and took a picture of Shirley and all the other winners. "That's such a beautiful picture with so much details!" remarked a reporter, marveling at the artwork. "You should have won first place."

"Thank you." Shirley smiled a big smile.

After all the necessary photographs were taken, it was time to leave.

The very next day, on March 27, the news was published in *Southern Dutchess News*, and the event was captured in three photographs. Shirley was in two of the photographs; the largest photograph was taken up exclusively by Shirley and Juliet. She felt honored to be in the newspaper for her achievement. Sure, she was on many large presses before, but they were nothing about her accomplishments, only of the ordeals they had to go through.

Shirley's ordeals could never cease, it seemed. The problems Mrs. Penney gave Shirley were mounting day by day.

The next school day, as Mrs. Penney got up from her chair to push Shirley to the cafeteria, Shirley inwardly shuddered when Mrs. Penney's large hand bag hit Shirley's hand. Mrs. Penney always carried a large bag wherever she went with Shirley. Shirley never saw her without the brown bag.

Shirley lifted her feet as she was pushed out of the classroom and down the hall. "Could you please go slower?" she implored. Mrs. Penney ignored her request and continued to push the wheelchair swiftly. She nearly bumped her feet into the students in front of them. Shirley tucked her feet in even more, but her legs were in danger as well. She wished that Mrs. Penney could go slower, but she knew it was not possible. All she could do was to pray that she could get to her table soon.

Chapter Fifty-Four

When all the birds had returned to the valley, some bringing a newfound love, adding to their wholesome families, the school suggested that Shirley might benefit from a laptop; it could ease her writing load. Shirley had been writing so much to the extent that her joints became stiff and painful. Shirley had never used a computer to do her work, except during computer class. The school therefore scheduled an evaluation from the Assistive Technology Team at Westchester Institute for Human Development.

On the appointed morning at the start of May, Juliet attended the meeting to discuss the best way for Shirley to use a laptop. Juliet, always bringing important files of Shirley's accomplishments at every meeting, did not fail to bring them for the evaluation.

Juliet met the two evaluators. Dr. Black was late in arriving, thus Juliet took the advantage by introducing Shirley's situation while showing some of the work Shirley had done, as well as her report cards and the letters from Mr. Crisfield.

"This is the book Shirley wrote for a project," Juliet said, holding out a hardcover book. The book was covered entirely in gold glitters as a background, with blue glitters used for the title, *Fancella*. Mrs. Hackett had told each student to make up a myth and write the story inside the blank hardcover books and draw pictures to accompany the tale. She had given them time to get started on the project in class. She had gone around the room, checking how everyone was doing. When she had arrived at Shirley's desk several minutes later, she saw that Shirley had already thought up the name of her main character, Fancella, the goddess of fire, and had completed two paragraphs. Shortly, she had finished writing the entire story and was the first to complete the book, except the section about the author, which she had taken a long time to write so as to make it as perfect as possible.

Dr. Seymour, one of the evaluators, with kind eyes, scribbled several things down as she examined each paper, no doubt adding them to her report she was going to write for the evaluation.

Just as they finished seeing what Juliet had brought, Dr. Black walked into the room. "Shirley's still in class, but she is coming out soon for the evaluation," she told the evaluators. She did not stop there. "Shirley's an immature girl who always goes home and complains to her mother."

"She never got anyone to listen when she complained to the school," retorted Juliet. She challenged her to continue. The doctor became silent.

A few minutes later, the bell rang and Shirley soon appeared at the doorway. Without having any time to speak to her mother, Shirley was brought to another room for the evaluation. After introductions, the ladies set a laptop in front of her, opened the top, and pushed the power button.

"This is a laptop and it works like those regular computers," said one of the ladies. Shirley had never seen one before and she was with much awe as the laptop finished booting. It was so small and yet so powerful.

"Does it have a mouse?" asked Shirley after studying it.

"Actually, this is used as the mouse," answered Dr. Seymour, pointing at a red button-like feature on the keyboard. She showed her how it worked. "It probably would be hard for you to do. Here, try it." So Shirley did. It was not easy on her fingers, but it was not the major problem she faced.

"The screen is dark. I can't see the words well," reported Shirley.

"Let's see if I can change the contrast." Shirley watched the woman's fingers fly about on the keyboard. "Okay, this is the brightest I can get it. See if this is better for you."

"It is still hard for me to see."

A moment later, it was apparent to them that the laptop was unfortunately not an option for Shirley. She was unable to see the words on the programs menu because of its small text against the dark background.

"Thank you Shirley. I'm sorry that you can't use the laptop," said Dr. Seymour.

"Thank you. Yes, I know. It is just too dark for me to make out the text well." Being done with the evaluation, Shirley went away to attend her next class.

All the sixth graders and teachers were busy preparing for an upcoming event. It was going to be a Medieval fair, where everyone was to dress in Medieval costumes and present the Medieval way of life, and various forms of entertainment would be the highlight of the event. Mrs. Hackett instructed that each person would need to do some research on a Medieval topic and present it to others during the fair. Other people from other grades would be the guests, learning and watching all the activities that would be scheduled for the big day.

Shirley wondered what topic she could research. Would a project on castles be nice? Or perhaps on kings, knights, or priests? The classroom was provided with a shelf of books on Medieval life from the school library.

"So, what subject would you like to do?" asked Mrs. Penney.

"Let me see," said Shirley, scanning the titles. "Oh, yes, I will research Medieval food," decided Shirley, quite pleased with her decision. Her aide handed the books to her. She began her research right away. She read over the table of contents and the index to find what might be helpful.

"I think this dress is very pretty," Mrs. Penney said, beside her, looking at the fashion magazines, which she often brought. "Do you think it is pretty?" she asked, pointing at the picture. Shirley absent-mindedly nodded. She was trying to concentrate on her work, but did not want to ignore Mrs.

Penney, thinking it would be rude. "I'd better lose some weight," her aide continued.

"You look fine," murmured Shirley, writing down what utensils the Medieval people used.

"So, Shirley, are your mother's breasts bigger or mine?" asked Mrs. Penney, startling Shirley out of her concentration. Shirley did not know how to answer such questions, so she pretended that she did not hear it, and continued writing.

The students had plenty of time to do their research at school, but were able to borrow the books and take them home for a short time. Shirley brought back a few books with her. It was impossible to get her work done in school. Mrs. Penney had been a great disturbance in her class, interrupting her whenever she had to do a writing assignment.

Without having another thought on her aide, she continued her work at home. She noticed that she had not gotten much done in class.

Researching, Shirley knew, was not enough. That was not the only task she needed to complete. She had to think of where she could obtain the proper apparel. But she soon found the dress that could do.

The following day, Mrs. Penney had told her of a dress she had. "I think I have just the right dress. I'll bring it tomorrow." As she promised, she brought the dress the following day.

"Oh, it's very nice," remarked Shirley, feeling the sparkling sequins of blue, gold, and shades of cream, between her fingers.

"It is very heavy," stated Erin.

"Yes, it is," said Mrs. Penney.

"Can I try it on?" asked Erin.

"Sure, go ahead." Erin was not the only one who was excited about trying it on; Anne was as well.

A moment later after the two girls had tried it on, they came back. "It doesn't look too good on me," said Erin.

"Me, either," echoed Anne.

Mrs. Penney decided to try the bejeweled dress on Shirley. She put it on top of the dress that Shirley was wearing.

"It looks good on you," they commented in unison.

"Thank you for the dress! I now have something to wear. But I also need a headpiece like one of those fancy hats." Shirley flipped through the books, studying the style of the hats from that era. She pointed at a picture and said, "I'll have to make something like this." It seemed like it was an easy hat to make. Shirley was a good student in Home and Career class, so sewing would not be a problem for her, though her arthritis might get in the way. But she believed she could do it with some help when heavy work was required, such as stuffing.

Days quickly shot by like an arrow and before anyone realized it, it was time for the fair. That morning, Juliet dressed Shirley in the sparkling dress, making her look like a little princess. Lastly, Juliet put the hat on Shirley.

"The hat is too heavy. Will you be okay?" asked the concerned mother.

"I'll manage. It's only for one day."

"But it will be an entire day. Maybe you ought not to wear it for so long. Let Mrs. Penney take it off when you don't need to."

"No, really, I'll be fine," insisted Shirley, balancing the heavy stuffed hat on her head. It would be tricky to keep it on. She was unable to turn her head freely. She hoped it would not hurt her arthritic neck. It *was* awfully heavy.

"It will be so much fun," Shirley squealed. "I have memorized my entire presentation."

"Don't get cold."

"It's not going to be cold. It will be quite warm in this dress!" Juliet was comforted by that thought, knowing that Shirley was right.

Juliet pushed her little princess out to the waiting bus. Shirley could hardly sit still in the bus as it went on its way, getting closer to the school.

Once the bus arrived, Shirley saw that all the sixth graders, along with their teachers, were dressed in Medieval style. She felt she had traveled back in time. Mrs. Penney took her in and waited for the instructions so that she could take her out to the designated spot. They had areas with tents and special places reserved for entertainment at the school yard.

Shirley was pushed under one of the tents, where she and her two friends were to present to others. Soon, people streamed around the yard to be enlightened and entertained.

With smiles between her speeches, Shirley told others how the Medieval people used to eat. "Their utensils included forks, spoons, and fingers," stated Shirley, holding out a finger to emphasize the fact. Many people had laughed at this part, finding it quite amusing.

As the day progressed toward a young afternoon, a man came to share with the spectators the topics of falconry, explaining how falcons were used in the hunts. Shirley watched his demonstrations with much awe and fascination. The gliding falcons and hawks captivated her with amazement and wonderment. She stayed by the man during the entire presentation. He was dressed as a falconer from the thirteenth century.

"Shirley, it's time for the feast. People are going to their seats," said Mrs. Penney.

"Where am I supposed to sit. I won't be sitting with the princesses, for my role is not one," thought Shirley aloud. Mrs. Penney asked one of the sixth grade teachers to where she was supposed to push Shirley. The teacher pointed her to an empty spot at a long table. Soon, Shirley was situated at the proper place.

All kinds of food were served, from breads to chicken. Shirley did not prefer to eat anything, but everyone received a plate. She studied the chicken before her eyes and decided to try it. She found it not bad, but she was not hungry, so the dish was mostly left untouched.

Chapter Fifty-Five

"Mrs. Duggan said that she has been watching over Mrs. Penney and said that there's nothing wrong with her," said Lois when Juliet was on the telephone with her, reporting more problems with Shirley's aides. Disgusted, she ended the conversation, knowing her insistence would not get her anywhere. Without setting down the receiver, she dialed the home care agency. The agency's nurse, Della, picked up the telephone.

"I really can't help you with the problems with the aide," said Della.

"But this is abuse! Shirley is suffering with her and no one listens to me. The aide needs to be changed."

"You can call the health department and see if they can help you."

"I will. Thank you." After hanging up, Juliet searched for the telephone number of the health department. Repeating the number to herself, she quickly pushed the seven digits. When a woman answered the telephone, Juliet began explaining the reason for her call. "The treatments being afflicted upon Shirley are harmful to her health, her well-being. I need to change the aide."

"I'm sorry, but we can't do anything about it. It's between you and her school. You just have to talk to her school about it."

"But we've been talking to them ever since the problems started. She had so many problems with all her aides." Juliet sighed. She raked her short black hair with her fingers. It was hopeless. She thanked the woman and hung up.

She glanced into the mirror in front of her. The image of a woman with circles around her eyes glanced back at her. She studied herself closer. She had spent countless, sleepless nights ever since Shirley had first experienced problems at the start of the school year. In spite of her hardship and weeks of worrying about Shirley, her youth and beauty still bloomed with fullness. With someone who was as tired and drained as her, she surely did not look it. Many people in China had often commented how young she looked despite the trials and tribulations in her life ever since childhood years. She looked away and rested her eyes on Shirley's drawings. She knew what was the main cause of her youth and happiness for many years. It was her pearl.

"Although I may be the most tired person in the world, I am the happiest," she said to herself. "She is such a wonderful creature. She is the reason for my existence. I live for her. But she has to go through it all...and being treated so poorly." Mrs. Penney was not the only cause of her pain. She was also restless with the issues concerning Mrs. Hackett.

Juliet was immensely shocked at what the teacher had said to Shirley about "kids making fun" of Shirley. No such words should be spoken by anyone, let alone someone in her profession.

With all of her other concerns about the teacher mounting, she decided to write a letter to the Superintendent of the school district, Dr. Murphy.

Soon, a meeting was scheduled to discuss the concerns. The exhausted Juliet, who did not sleep the entire night, sat down at the long table, smiling to each one, including Mr. Patricks; Mr. Jeffs; Mrs. Duggan; Dr. Black; and Shirley's OT, Dyan.

With the paper of the listed problems in hand, Juliet started the meeting. "First of all, please let me thank all of you, especially Dr. Murphy, for your time to attend this meeting. And thank you, Dr. Murphy, for your immediate response to my telephone call." She paused, scanning the list. She knew each problem by heart, but she had to read it to get her English correct.

She started listing the issues with Mrs. Hackett. "You said to Shirley that she did not do her homework in front of the whole class, putting Shirley to shame. You know she works hard. You also said that she does her work at the last minute, which is not true. When Shirley asked Connie to get her book because she forgot it, you pulled her out of her French class and you said, 'Shirley, you're not her boss and she's not your slave.' Shirley had to miss an entire class that day," said Juliet, looking at Mrs. Hackett. "It is an inflammatory speech!"

"I did not say 'slave'; I said 'servant.'"

"Okay, 'servant.' You tried to sabotage the relationship between Shirley and the aide who was very nice to her in the beginning before you said those words. I learned the word 'sabotage' from Shirley's vocabularies," said Juliet with a smile. "And you said, 'If kids make fun of you, will you still come to school?' When Shirley said that she will, you said, 'If kids make fun of me, I will never come to school.' No one should say something like this!" Even thinking about it made Juliet flush with distaste.

Mrs. Hackett did not have a reply. She remained silent.

Juliet continued listing the problems. "You don't allow Shirley to say 'Excuse me' in the halls. You had even asked her that how many kids did she hit. Saying 'Excuse me' was the only weapon she had to prevent her feet from being bumped into others. That conversation had caused Shirley to miss another entire period of class. Since she has started school not so long ago, each day is precious to her. She doesn't want to miss a single day of class. She came to school even when she was very ill." She paused again.

Not much was said by anyone else in the meeting. They simply listened, including the cause of the meeting.

"Mrs. Wilson had said to Shirley that she should not come home and tell me all the problems she had in school," said Juliet. What kind of request was that? "You do not allow Shirley to leave the class a few minutes early before everyone else, so that she could get to her next class safely. Either have her leave early, or push her carefully. She never feels safe and secure in the halls. You don't allow her aide to get in front of the line when she gets Shirley's lunch when she wanted to eat something. Thus, she barely has enough time to eat. Also, I know that parents are allowed to visit their children during lunch periods. But you kicked me out when I only brought a soup for her. From how you treat me, I can imagine how you treat Shirley!" Juliet looked around the table; no one spoke. "When one of Shirley's aides smoked, you did not care. You simply let the aide go out of the classroom, leaving Shirley unattended. She had no one to get her books out for her. I am always so worried for her." She rubbed her forehead, emitting a sigh.

"Don't worry, Juliet," comforted Dyan.

"Why would we ask for problems?" asked Juliet, taking out Shirley's drawings and awards, "Shirley works so hard on everything. She had only six months in the special education class before she came here. She is always so happy."

"Shirley is doing extremely well. She is in the top ten in the class," informed Mrs. Hackett.

Afterward, at the end of the meeting, Dr. Murphy spoke up. "Shirley is amazing. If everyone were like you and Shirley, there would never be any problem in this world." Juliet and Shirley were an ideal pair of people working hard in life, never wanting to cause a single problem.

Mrs. Hackett, smiling, walked toward Juliet and held out her hand, which Juliet kindly shook. Juliet did not hold any vengeance in her heart. She wished all to work together harmoniously. *Perchance the teacher would change her ways and that everything would be better*, thought Juliet with high hopes.

***

"The picture that wins the contest will be created as a design on the T-shirts," Mrs. Hackett said, explaining the details of a project to the class. They were going on a trip to

Washington, DC, before the school year ended in June. Shirley would not go, for it was difficult for her to go on any trips. She had been urged to go, but declined the invitation. She had wished to be on the trip, but her health could not permit her to do so. How would she use the bathroom? The nature's necessities were tasks of most simplicity for most, but they were sheer difficulties for Shirley.

Each student was to draw a picture that symbolized Washington, DC, and the country. Each class would vote for a winning design in their own class, then everyone would choose a winner from all the finalists from all the classes.

Shirley grew quite excited. Art was a breeze for her. She loved to draw, and could draw anything that was assigned to be drawn. She immediately started working on it. The students were given a large square paper with shiny surface on which to draw their pictures. After merely a few minutes, Shirley finished the project. Her drawing showed a dove carrying a ribbon in its beak, with a raised American flag to the left. Bells and stars were also present as a decorative border. All in all, it was a picture that showed peace and patriotism.

There were only two others in her class who participated in the project, for it was not mandatory.

When it was time to vote for the best picture in the class days later, Mrs. Hackett hung the three drawings on the chalkboard facing everyone. She labeled them A, B, and C.

"This is Mike's, this is Tim's, and this is Shirley's," she indicated, pointing at each picture, her finger resting on letter C when Shirley's name was mentioned. "So, please put your heads down on your desk, and raise your hand when you want to vote for the called letter." All did as directed.

"A," called Mrs. Hackett. Shirley raised her hand. She could not raise it high because of her arthritis, but she raised as high as she could.

"B," Mrs. Hackett announced. Last but not least, the letter corresponding to Shirley's picture was called.

"Okay, you can open your eyes now. Tim is the

winner, with one more vote than Shirley's."

Shirley's heart sank. She forgot to vote for herself. But she was also surprised, for the picture of Tim showed nothing but a rock. Her friends were also surprised. Shirley shrugged her shoulders.

Later that day while the pictures still hung on the board, their Health teacher, Mr. Joice, walked past the room, pushing a television stand, but stopped and decided to drop in for a minute. His kind eyes always greeted Shirley with a smile and often stopped on his way to greet her.

"That is a wonderful picture, Shirley," he exclaimed. "Surprised you did not win." Not knowing what to say, Shirley shrugged again in answer.

Juliet was unpleasantly amazed when she found out how the contest was conducted. "She shouldn't have told others which picture belonged to whom. All contests should be held anonymously."

But soon the contest was all forgotten. All were in a great state of excitement in the prospect for the upcoming trip. The weather was getting quite warm now and the days became longer. Shirley's coat changed to a thin jacket. She was glad that she could abandon her winter attire. She felt like a stuffed turkey in all those clothing and scarf.

Chapter Fifty-Six

The end of the school year was just a step away as summer approached the valley. Everyone had returned from the trip to Washington, DC, with stories, memories, and video tapes that captured the moments. The tapes were shown to the class, making some burst out laughing during comical scenes. Shirley wished she could be one of the smiling people in the tapes, but she knew it was not possible—the tapes had clearly confirmed it. The class had picnics out in the grass under the blazing sun. They also had a few dips in the waters. The class relaxed while they watched the tapes. There was not much work left, for only several more days were left till the year drew to a close, concluding the yearbooks for each and every student. Shirley was glad to be moving forward and excitedly waited for seventh grade to start. She felt relieved that she would not have Mrs. Hackett as her teacher anymore. She would be attending different classrooms for each subject. She wondered what the schedule would be like and who her teachers would be.

On the last day of school, there will be a drawing of the Good Time Tickets to pick the lucky winners who would receive gift certificates from Barnes and Noble, one of her all-time favorite places to be. She loved spending hours in the store, going from shelf to shelf to simply read each title. She had a strong feeling that she would be one of the winners of the drawing. Good Time Tickets were given to any student who had done well on a particular task and who used the vocabularies they had learned in English class with accuracy. She had been using the vocabularies on any chance she got. Her writings were peppered with them, and her daily conversations were not absent of them, either. Back on May 10, Mrs. Hackett clearly confirmed Shirley's vocabulary usage in a note she wrote to Juliet: "Shirley's work continues to be outstanding. Her effort in vocabulary is superb. Shirley is a rare student, a teacher's dream." Thus, Shirley's collection of the tickets steadily grew. She had been keeping them in a small maroon bag, counting them every so often.

***

On the last day of school, students spent the day talking with their friends and relaxing. Later in the day after recess, Mrs. Hackett had one of her important looks on her face. Shirley felt a shiver going down her spine. She knew there would be good news.

Mrs. Hackett told the class she had an award for everyone. They were fun ones, nothing serious. Shirley got one for having the most Good Time Tickets, which they later learned were ninety-two in all. After all awards were given out, a more serious look replaced Mrs. Hackett's face.

"I have a Student of the Year Award. I have given it much thought, and I know a few of you would be eligible for it. But there is someone who deserves the award," she paused for some effect. Everyone waited in anticipation. Who would it be?

"The Student of the Year is Shirley!" the teacher announced as she handed the award to the much-surprised Shirley. Erin gave Shirley a big smile. The class applauded. Then Mrs. Hackett explained Shirley's situation to the class. "And she had never missed a single day of school, except that one day when she had to move." Yes, Shirley was always present. She had even gone to school during the many times she had colds, most of them had lasted into the third week. She never was lazy and ungrateful for the school days. Juliet's heart broke whenever she saw Shirley go on the bus when she was ill. She had often told her to stay home, but Shirley refused each time. Yet Shirley had to take a day off from school when they moved to a different building in the complex, hoping to have more space, but it turned out that the first building was actually better.

"I knew it would be you," Anne later told Shirley. "I had seen Mrs. Hackett writing the award."

Then it was time to go out for the drawing. As everyone had expected, Shirley won a certificate.

"I am surprised that Shirley was picked out only once," Mrs. Hackett later remarked.

Finally, it was time for farewells and sad partings till next year. Shirley said goodbyes to her good friends. "Call me," Shirley said to Erin.

"You call me too," they both agreed. They knew it was a promise that could not be easily broken. They often spent hours on the telephone every day after school. From strangers to best friends; it was surely a grand feeling.

Going through her memories, Shirley thought of the entire year. She fully enjoyed sixth grade and the rewards it brought forth. She had fun with her friends, and had learned a good deal, not only academically, but she had learned the facts of life as well. She learned that there were just some people out there who were unkind. It was an unfortunate thing. But happy thoughts filled up her mind. Nothing could easily get Shirley down no matter how hard they tried. Shirley never gave up on her life and her dreams. There were several unhappy times that year with her aides, but they did not hinder her from enjoying her school days. If only she had a nice aide—that would make her experience in school a perfect one. From the beginning before Shirley started school, Juliet had thought highly of school. She thought it would be a heavenly place with no worries and difficulties. Shirley would at last be free of the pain and misery of her past years. But she had been hit in the face from all the hardships they had encountered.

A sigh of contentment came from Shirley's lips when she got off the bus. It was a year well-worth remembering for a very, very long time to come. As Shirley waved goodbye to her bus driver, she knew she had succeeded in life again.

Chapter Fifty-Seven

The hazy summer days quickly wound down until it was nearly time to go back to school. Juliet thought that the time had passed by too rapidly. She knew that there would be more problems for the upcoming school year. First, Shirley was in dire need of getting Mrs. Penney changed. She had composed a long list of the problems concerning the aide. There were twenty-six issues in all. She was stunned; it was the most problems Shirley had ever encountered with just one aide. Juliet had to think of a way. She asked the school to schedule a meeting to discuss the problems. She hoped that it would be a successful step.

As appointed, the meeting was underway on a humid day of August 30. One of Juliet's friends, Wally, was also present. He had told her about a home care agency he knew: Bountiful Care. He suggested that Shirley use it.

Shirley sat beside her mother, with the list in front of them. Grimacing inwardly, they both read each of the problems, hoping that someone from the meeting would be moved. But Shirley saw it was not possible as she looked around her.

"I have been watching Mrs. Penney and she seems to be doing fine," remarked Mrs. Duggan, turning her face with heavy makeup to Shirley.

Shirley felt she was telling her problems to a ventriloquist's dummy. She looked into Mrs. Duggan's eyes and shook her head. "No, Mrs. Penney has been hurting me. She bumped me into people. She kept on pushing even when the students were backing up—nearly backing into me."

Feeling helpless, Juliet and Shirley left the school. They had not gotten any matters resolved. It appeared that Shirley was stuck with Mrs. Penney for seventh grade.

"School will start in September," sighed Shirley, who

for the first time, was saddened. Only a few more days left before she was to fall back into the hands of her aide. She hoped that the school year would be a quick one. But it would be impossible. It would just drag on slowly.

That was when the telephone rang. Juliet found the home care agency's nurse on the other end of the line. "I just wanted to let you know that Shirley will be getting a new aide when she goes back to school." Shirley's ears perked up as soon as she heard the muffled words.

"Oh, they changed the aide?" asked Juliet, making doubly sure.

"Yes."

With a smile, Juliet hung up and turned to the gleeful Shirley.

"The meeting worked?" asked Shirley.

"I really don't know. I don't know why they changed their minds."

"I guess it will always be an enigma." Shirley was thrilled! She was at last free of Mrs. Penney's torments.

***

Once again, green leaves slowly changed into apparel of red and orange before leaving their homes amongst trees. Branches steadily lost their clothes as days flew by while Shirley attended seventh grade. Seventh grade was more enjoyable, for most of her teachers were nice, and she did not have to stay in one classroom for all subjects. But it also meant that she had to be pushed more often, therefore her chances of getting her feet hurt raised considerably.

Unfortunately, as with the previous years, Shirley's bad luck with the aides did not change. She was still being mistreated. Changing aides was still a task of most difficulty. The school did not allow her to change the aides when she complained to them, even when she was suffering on a grand scale. All the problems experienced this year were the repetition of last. But it did not stop Shirley from continually obtaining an education and soaking up knowledge.

But let us start from the beginning. Shall we?

A meeting was held on the first day of school, the same day that Mrs. Jasper was to be Shirley's new aide. As with all the previous meetings, Dr. Black was present, promising to provide a scolding to Shirley.

"Shirley, do you know how many aides we have changed for you?" scolded Dr. Black.

"That's because she always had problems with the aides. Why would we want to go through the problems to just change aides without good reasons?" reasoned Juliet. Did they actually think that Shirley enjoyed switching aides? They had only managed to switch two of her aides since the rest had either left on their own initiatives, or had been fired by the school. "We don't want trouble. Shirley doesn't like to change any of her aides, but she was forced each time." Dr. Black said nothing else after Juliet finished with her statement.

"Don't ask Shirley personal questions. She won't like it," Dr. Black told Mrs. Jasper. What kind of warning was that? It made Shirley appear as though she did not like going beyond the relationship to a friendship level between her aide and herself.

The meeting ended and everyone left the room.

"I'm going to teach Mrs. Jasper how to dress Shirley," said Juliet.

"No, you must leave now," ordered Dr. Black.

"I just want to show her how to dress Shirley!"

"No, Mrs. Cheng."

Feeling utterly disgusted, Juliet exited the building.

In spite of it all, it was the first time in a long while that Shirley felt happy with an aide. Mrs. Jasper had done a good job in caring for her, dressing her with care and did not bump her against walls and other people. *At last*, she thought, *I will not have to worry about aides and can solely focus on my studies*. She shared the good news with Juliet, whose soul was immediately washed with relief.

"Finally, a capable person to take care of you."

"I hope she'll be my permanent aide."

But it could not be so. Shirley soon received an unpleasant surprise. She noticed something was troubling Mrs. Jasper. She became sulky. Not to Shirley's knowledge, Mrs. Jasper had visited Mr. Jeffs for a concern of hers. Thus one day, Shirley was informed of the situation. She was called in to see Mr. Jeffs at his office.

"So, Shirley, how's everything going?" asked Mr. Jeffs.

"Everything is great."

"How do you like Mrs. Jasper?"

"She is really nice. She doesn't hurt me. I like her."

"Well," he cleared his throat, "she said that you don't talk to her."

With a puzzled look, Shirley answered, "But I do talk to her." She always talked to every single one of her aides. She never ignored anyone, not even when they mistreated her.

"She said that you don't talk to her during lunchtime."

"I talk to her most of the time during the day. She is with me every moment, so I get to talk to her often, a lot more often than I get to talk with anyone else. But during lunchtime, I mostly talk to my friends, because that is the only time I can talk to them. So, I cannot talk to Mrs. Jasper so much. But I do manage to talk to her for a bit during lunches. You see? I am not ignoring anyone."

Mr. Jeffs nodded in understanding. "But she doesn't understand it."

The short meeting did not bring a solution to the issue. Mrs. Jasper became more unhappy and soon announced that she was going on a vacation, not informing anyone when she planned to return. Shirley was disheartened. She could not comprehend it. She tried to involve Mrs. Jasper in the conversations with her friends, but it was rather obvious that it did not work.

Juliet asked Dr. Black and others when Mrs. Jasper might return, but no one had any idea. "I think she doesn't want to come anymore," guessed Juliet.

"That might be it," said Lois.

"So, Shirley needs another aide."

"We are planning not to use the current home care agency that we have been using. We're going to switch to another agency."

"Can you use Bountiful Care?" inquired Juliet.

"No, we're not going to use them."

Juliet was not surprised. All she could ever get from them was a negative answer.

While the school was still using the same agency, they sent out a new aide to Shirley, a woman known as Selma. From the very first day, the experience was an unpleasant one. The only word that could describe Selma was "mean." Not only was she mean to Shirley, but also to everyone else. She never saw Selma smiling or greeting anyone. Being dressed by Selma was naturally painful.

Although Selma seemed like a person who could turn a sunny day into hails and storms, Shirley was still smiling in school. Her mind was focused on a much more important matter.

The school had a special program: each month, a student was chosen to be the Student of the Month. The student must be a diligent person who not only kept good grades, but a role model to others, setting high personal values and emitting merit. She had not known of the existence of the Student of the Month in sixth grade. It came to her as a surprise when they had announced the award to one of her friends in September. Therefore, she waited excitedly for next month.

In October, to her sheer delight, Shirley was chosen to be the Student of the Month, and got a free cookie as an award. Any student who made the honor roll also received a free cookie. But as always with the cookies, she gave it to a friend, for it was a pleasure to see a smile alight upon a friend's eyes. Her grades were mostly in the nineties, thus honor rolls always had her name. She had missed the honor roll only once by one point for the first quarter in sixth grade with an eighty-four.

She wished that she could share her happiness with Selma, but it was impossible. She wished that she could have someone else. She knew, switching her would require much work on both her and Juliet's part. But she would soon see that Selma would be changed quite soon without them having to waste a single ounce of strength.

One day, while being in her usual offensive mood, Selma was more than upset by a comment made by one of Shirley's classmates. Shirley knew that he was simply joking. But Selma had taken it too seriously. "What did you say, young man?" demanded Selma.

"What?" questioned the student in puzzlement. Shirley, her heart pounding, watched the scene grow heavy. Selma had turned something that was simply a comment into an argument. The readers could be spared with the details and the words being flung back and forth between the two. It appeared as though a fight would break out at any moment when a teacher broke them apart in the nick of time.

Instantly, the school fired Selma, much to Shirley's relief.

"Man, Shirley, she was mean!" a classmate of Shirley had exclaimed.

"Yes, she was." For the first time, someone other than just Shirley had experienced the nature of an aide, though it was merely a small fraction of what Selma was really like.

"So, I get a new aide," came the tired voice of Shirley when she arrived at school, where a stranger waited for her by the door. "I've seen so many faces and I'll lose track of who was who!" She greeted her aide, "Hi, Trixie!" She fervently hoped with all her might that she was welcoming a permanent aide.

By and by, taking little effort on her part, Shirley

learned that it was going to be temporary.

Shirley looked at her wrinkled notebooks, some with a few pages ripped and torn off. *Trixie*, Shirley thought with sadness, *is a very lousy aide*. She had stuffed Shirley's work into her bag with as little care as she could manage. Even people stuffed turkeys with much more care than that. "Fortunately, my assignment book is not messed up," sighed Shirley, making a note of the date.

High spirits of festivity quickly swept through the valley; Halloween approached. Juliet had gone to Party City, where she had bought the witch costume, and found a beautiful angel costume. She knew that her daughter would look splendid in it. Above all, it was an easy costume to put on Shirley, for the sleeves were wide and the fabric was soft. Without waiting for another minute, she tried it on Shirley as soon as they came home from the weekend shopping.

"I should take a picture of you now. You look absolutely beautiful!" She was getting her camera when she remembered something. "I just remembered; I don't have any empty films. I need to get some. So, you'll wear this tomorrow. I'll put it here, along with the halo, wings, and the wand," said Juliet, laying them out on a chair. "You don't even have to dress up as an angel! You look exactly like one already, dear. You especially look like cupid." Shirley was excited about dressing up again. She had truly enjoyed the first time, though it was nearly spoiled by Dr. Black. Well, she did not succeed.

"I can't wait for all my friends and teachers and Diana to see it," chirped Shirley.

"At last, you have a good bus driver now!"

"I am so happy about it." Shirley could see Diana was nice from the way she took care of her on the bus. Her attitude was friendly and kind. They hit it off straight away on the first day, talking on the entire way to school.

***

"Ah, a perfect angel!" remarked Shirley's French teacher once Shirley, dressed in her angel costume, was wheeled into the room for the lesson. Shirley received a few smiles from her classmates as the result of the comments; they all agreed. Shirley thought French class was relaxing. It was an easy class for her and all the grades she had been receiving were in the high nineties. Being the best student in the class meant that she was a second teacher in the class. During the times when students were to work on their worksheets, Shirley often had lines of students seeking help from her. She had willingly helped them, though sometimes it had gotten overwhelming, leaving barely enough time to complete her own work. But she was a fast writer with a good memory, therefore she was able to finish every one of her own worksheets while assisting others.

It was as much relaxing in English class as it was with French. In actuality, English class was the easiest class, where students were merely required to read and write on their own, with seldom an assigned work from the teacher. The teacher had handed everyone a sheet, stating how much was required from each one for the quarters. Shirley saw that the more reading and writing that one did, the higher the grade would be. *I could easily get one hundred for each quarter*, she thought, with smiles in her heart. Juliet had bought more books for her, enough to last for the whole school calendar.

On the first few days of school, each student was given a red assignment book to keep track of daily homework assignments and record important dates and numbers. It was also a fine resource, providing measurements and symbols for mathematics. Shirley had decided to utilize the book to its full potential. She recorded down all her grades ever since the first day so as to have an idea of how her quarterly report cards would turn out. She did not have to ask what her averages might be; she had a close idea now. Her science grades, she noted, were mostly in the high nineties. But she got a surprise when the first report cards were distributed in November. All the report cards were given to the students for them to bring home, and places for parents' signatures were provided on the envelopes. Hoping that her report card would not get damaged, she handed it to Trixie to have her tuck into her bag. She had read each grade carefully. She saw her science average was only eighty-eight. She was dumbstruck. *Perhaps it is a mistake*, she consoled herself. But to obtain the reason was the right way to go.

During recess the following day, Shirley asked her science teacher about it.

"It is the correct grade," answered the science teacher.

Shirley looked at her incredulously. "Really? But I had gotten mostly high nineties." From her own records, the average came out to be a ninety-seven.

"This is the way it is," the teacher finished.

Not being satisfied with the answer, but having no other choice, Shirley simply turned away. What was Shirley to do? *It is probably just this time; the grade will be accurate next time*, thought Shirley. Then the thought of her other averages brought several smiles upon her countenance. She had received a ninety-six in English class and ninety-seven in French class, which, according to her French teacher, was one of the two highest grades in that quarter. When math class entered into her thoughts, she frowned. She had gotten in the mid eighties. The work in the class was easy for her, but she was not actually being taught at times. Although the math teacher was a kind person, who treated her well, he had often asked the students to teach one another, therefore, Shirley was unable to learn properly. She sighed when she thought of the class level. The math class she was put in was a seventh grade math level. But she was eligible to attend an eighth grade math class, for her grades were mostly nineties in sixth grade. Mrs. Hackett did not approve for Shirley to be in a higher level class. Shirley could not understand the reason. She knew she would be able to do fine in a higher level. She had no chance now. She could never rise to a higher level just because of the decision made by Mrs. Hackett.

Chapter Fifty-Eight

Several days later, Trixie called in sick, so Shirley received a substitute aide. She wondered if the new aide, Hailda, would be better than Trixie. Unfortunately, she was a great deal worse.

Hailda was not good from the very first day. She did not do things as asked by Shirley. But worse yet, was the fact that the woman was really ill with a cold.

"You are very sick," said the concerned Shirley.

The aide nodded. "I probably have pneumonia."

"Oh! Then you shouldn't have come here," said Shirley, frightened for her own health. The woman was aware of her condition and still came in school ill. It was most important for Shirley's aide to be healthy, with no colds or flu, for she was with Shirley at all times and in close contact. Shirley's health was frail and she had a weak immunity. Catching any disease was extremely easy for her.

The woman continued to come, each day worse in health than the day before. She coughed constantly when taking care of Shirley. Soon, Shirley developed a sore throat. When the woman was too sick, she stopped coming. But the damage had been done. Shirley immediately fell ill, with the worst cold she had ever had. It promised much more serious conditions in the future as the reader will soon find out.

As days progressed, the cold worsened. Shirley was horrified that a cold could bring such misery to her.

Suddenly, she was unable to breathe well. She tried to ignore it, but the longer she did, the worse it got. Not trying to run away from the painful fact, she told her mother. "My chest feels tight and it is getting hard to breathe."

Alarmed, Juliet called her pediatrician, Dr. Madison, to schedule an emergency appointment. Juliet saw that Dr. Madison was always kind, so she did not think that there was a need to switch him to Dr. Frank. "May I bring her in now?" The receptionist said that she could. But Dr. Madison was not in that day, so Shirley had to see someone else. It was a weekend, so Shirley was not missing any school. But even if the day was on a school day, Shirley, for the first time, would not argue with Juliet about canceling one school day. She was feeling too sick.

Juliet got Shirley into the doctor's office right away. With Shirley gasping for breath made it harder for Juliet to carry Shirley in and out the car. But quickly as she could, Juliet got Shirley to the doctor. But they still needed to wait in the waiting room. Juliet hoped it would not be for long.

"It is getting...really...tight," gasped Shirley, her face turning pale.

"Oh, poor dear," managed Juliet, holding on to Shirley's hands.

Finally, Shirley's name was called and Juliet pushed her to the small examining room. But it did not mean that she would see the doctor right then. She still had some waiting to do. But it was much quicker compared to emergency-room visits.

The doctor walked in, carrying a chart. "And what's the matter today?"

"She cannot breathe. I think she has pneumonia," said Juliet, who had read her medical book and had concluded from all the symptoms that Shirley had pneumonia.

"I don't think so. Her lungs don't sound like she has it. It's just a cold."

"No, I really think she has it."

"I'll have her take an x-ray of her lungs." And with that, he left.

A moment later, Shirley was brought to a dimly lit room. It was the x-ray room, where she had been a few times previously.

"Take a deep breath," instructed the nurse. Shirley did as best as she could, but she was unable to heave her chest fully. She struggled each time that she was asked to do so.

Juliet's heart ached. She knew from the medical book and motherly instinct that Shirley had pneumonia for the very first time. She knew that the sick aide had given the disease to her. She was furious that no one ever checked on them to see how the aides were doing when they were assigned to Shirley. No one ever queried Shirley how everything was with any of her aides. How could they be so irresponsible? It was their duty to make sure that each student, particularly the disabled, was well cared for. Each aide should be screened for any contagious health problems and harmful habits and behavior.

"How are you feeling now?" asked Juliet, hoping that somehow, Shirley was better.

"It is…still very tight. I…feel awful," the weak words came from her pale lips.

"The doctor is unhappy that I suggested it to be pneumonia." Juliet shook her head.

Just then, the doctor appeared in the doorway. He brusquely sat down. "I looked at the films and she has pneumonia," he said, not meeting Juliet's eyes.

The doctor rapidly scribbled something on the prescription pad and tore out the paper. "Here's the medication." Then he left.

"He's really upset! But there's no time to waste. I knew he was going to be upset when I said that you have pneumonia. I didn't want your illness to be delayed."

Juliet wasted no time. She dropped off the prescription at the pharmacy as she passed it on the way home. She hoped that Shirley could hold on. She saw Shirley was extremely weak now. "How are you feeling?"

Shirley did not answer. Heart pounding, she questioned again. This time, she was replied by a whisper.

"I'm nauseated."

"Oh, you need to vomit?" Juliet hurriedly got her out of the car and pushed her inside the apartment. Frantic, Juliet searched for a container where she could vomit.

"I'll try to hold in. But get me a bowl in case." Juliet got the plastic washing bowl Shirley used to wash her hands and face, and held it under her mouth. Juliet sat down beside her and put her free arm around her.

"It's ready if you need to."

Shirley shook her head and pushed it away. She was going to hold it in.

Juliet picked up the medication as soon as it was in. As swiftly as a flying arrow, Juliet made it back home and administered the medication to Shirley, but only after she got some food inside of Shirley's stomach. She knew Shirley needed some food to withstand the medication. She prayed that it would work as Shirley swallowed the first dose. Shirley needed to take ALEVE later with food as well. Juliet had started giving Shirley ALEVE to relieve her arthritic pain. It appeared to be working during times of severe pain, but it was not the long-term solution. Shirley had been seeing Dr. Lehman for regular checkups. They were extremely grateful to be under the care of a loving doctor who truly wanted the best for his patients.

"You can't go to school tomorrow like this," said Juliet, firmly. Shirley did not protest. "I'll call you in sick tomorrow. You need time to recover!"

To their unspeakable joy, Shirley was showing recovery after a few doses. The medication was working. Shirley did not have to gasp so often. Her chest was getting less tight as time passed with each dose. When Shirley was just recovering, she wanted to go to school, but Juliet stood firmly. Therefore, Shirley had a couple of days more at home. But Shirley was soon protesting more, so Juliet had to let her go.

"Don't catch another cold. I'm afraid the same thing will happen. Don't get cold. Ask your aide to bundle you up."

"The aides never listen to me. You know that. And Trixie is so sloppy, she never does anything right. But I'll have to go back to her tomorrow. At least, *she* called in absent! I wished that Trixie had never gotten sick. I would not have gotten ill from Hailda."

***

Trixie unlocked the bathroom door, pushed Shirley in, and closed the door. She situated Shirley's wheelchair next to the small bed and pushed the lift in front of Shirley. Then she took the four ends of her sling out, where the hooks were located. After hooking Shirley to the lift, she cranked the handle of the lift, and Shirley was raised up. After getting her high enough, Trixie moved the lift closer to the bed, so that the sling was over the bed. She cranked the handle backward and the sling went down. The process so far had taken around seven minutes. Then another ten or fifteen minutes would be used up before Shirley could get to the cafeteria.

Trixie held the bedpan down as Shirley went. She wiped her after she was finished. Shirley really hated the whole process. Not only was it time-consuming, but also tiring; it often used up a lot of her energy, leaving her tired afterward. She was glad that she could have about twenty minutes of rest during lunch.

"Ouch!" exclaimed Shirley. Trixie had hurt her badly as she unhooked the seat from the lift. The hard edge of the sling had jammed into her waist, hurting her tremendously.

***

"Trixie doesn't want to come anymore," Juliet reported to Shirley, who was recovering from the injury. Mrs. Duggan had checked her back and did not find any bruises. And so, she had thought the injury was not serious. "Not everything will have bruises!" exclaimed Juliet, shaking her head in disgust. "How are you feeling? Are you still hurting?"

"No, I'm okay now. I was hurting for a while after the accident, but hours had passed and I'm okay now. So, Trixie quit?"

"Yes, I think she's scared that she had hurt you. But now the thing is that you can't go to school tomorrow."

"But I must! I must."

"Mrs. Duggan said that you can't, because they don't have any aides for you tomorrow. They are not going to use their home care agency and yet refused to use the one Wally told me. I'm going to call Dr. Black."

"I can't miss school. They can't do this."

Juliet made calls to Dr. Black, but only ended up talking to Lois, as usual.

"Please let her call me back," implored Juliet.

"I'll give the message to her," said Lois.

An hour had passed on this Wednesday afternoon and the telephone finally rang at 4:30.

"Shirley can't go to school this week, and she probably can't go to school next week as well. We're finding another agency. I will send a tutor over for Shirley," Dr. Black told Juliet.

"But can't you just use Bountiful Care?"

"No, we won't."

As the conversation went on, Shirley was boiling. She started to scream, loud enough for Dr. Black to hear. "No, I will not miss school! I need to go to school. I will not stay home!"

Hearing her screams, Dr. Black paused, obviously having second thoughts. "Okay, we'll use Bountiful Care temporarily and Shirley can go to school tomorrow." Shirley glared at the telephone, satisfied that the chairperson had relented to her wishes.

Chapter Fifty-Nine

After Shirley returned to school, she received a new aide for a trial. If the aide was good to her, she could have her as a permanent aide.

With much hope flooding her heart, Shirley began her days with Valerie. She crossed her fingers that Valerie would be a nice person, so that she did not have to switch her to someone else. Much to her joy, the first few hours of the first day went smoothly. *Maybe, she's the right aide for me*, thought Shirley, her hopes soaring. But she knew she should not judge the quality of the woman based on merely one day. She knew that Valerie would have to go through several tests, one of which was coming up. The dismissal bell rang.

Valerie slowly pushed Shirley to her locker, without bumping her feet. "Shirley, which arm hurts you the most? I don't want to hurt you, so I'll dress it first," said Valerie before putting on her coat. It was approaching winter and the winds were already quite chilly for Shirley.

"My left arm is not good," answered Shirley, thinking it was considerate of Valerie to be concerned. The new aide had scored another point. Valerie gently dressed Shirley, not hurting her an ounce.

After boarding the bus, Shirley happily waved to Valerie. "I'll see you tomorrow!" She could not wait to get home and tell her mother the grand news.

Once the bus stopped in front of the apartment and when Shirley was able to see Juliet after the driver opened the doors, her smiling lips began telling Juliet the news. "Mom, my new aide, Valerie, is so nice. She even asked me which arm to dress first and did not hurt me at all." She continued with the tale once inside her home.

"That's wonderful news! But let's wait another day to call Dr. Black to ask her to keep Valerie," said Juliet.

Shirley nodded, blowing her nose with a tissue. "I had aides who treated me well for the first few days, then the treatment went downhill afterward. So, we ought to wait. But I do hope Valerie would stay like this!"

"Is your *nose* going to stay like this forever?"

"It seems so. It is an enigma!"

Ergo, Valerie underwent another day of test. The same caring acts were repeated for the second day. Shirley could hardly contain herself. Could Valerie be the perfect aide? Was she the one? Perhaps, her luck was finally changing. She had been through so much. It was time to receive someone who was gentle to her. Shirley arrived home with the same joyous news. She did not hesitate any longer. "You can let Dr. Black know that I would like to keep Valerie as my aide." Juliet happily made the call and gave the message to Dr. Black.

"Finally, after all this time, after all the hardships, after all the misery, you have a caring person to help you in school! You can enjoy your school life so much more now," sighed Juliet in contentment. She had not sighed such sighs for a long time already, except only when Shirley told her of her accomplishments. Shirley echoed her sigh.

***

"Well, the bus is not here, but we'll go out and wait for it," stated Valerie.

"But it is cold," said Shirley, "I would like to wear my coat, please."

"No, it's not cold." Without another word, Valerie pushed her toward the exit, but was hindered by a chair that was in the way. She simply used Shirley's wheelchair footrests to push the chair aside, so that she could get through. Shirley did not prepare herself before the chair had tilted a footrest, and then slammed into her feet. She did not expect Valerie would do such a thing. She did not know what to say. She was speechless. Was this the same woman who had dressed her so gently just yesterday? It was the fourth day with Valerie and she seemed changed. Shirley quickly dismissed her thoughts. Perhaps, it was just this once.

The air was chilling her bones as they waited for her bus. She prayed that it would arrive soon.

When Shirley came home, Juliet saw that Shirley was not wearing her coat. "What happened? Why aren't you wearing your coat? Why isn't it on you?" Juliet sent barrages of questions her way.

"She said that it wasn't cold. And I had to wait for the bus."

"What?" gasped Juliet. "Tell her you want your coat! And you should wait for the bus inside the building."

Next day quickly arrived, with Shirley hoping for the best. But she found another unpleasant surprise as soon as she was being undressed by Valerie. Using just one hand, she unbuttoned Shirley's coat and the hood. Unbuttoning the buttons under the hood became a painful experience for Shirley, who got slapped by the tugging motion of the hood. Instead of carefully taking off her coat, Valerie roughly took it off from behind, hurting Shirley's arms. There and then, Shirley knew she was entering into the horrid hell. The first three days had been a rest for her, to prepare her for the harsh days that lay ahead.

It did not take Shirley long to know that Valerie was manyfold worse than any of her other aides. In actuality, Valerie was the worst aide she had so far. She learned the hard way that winter time was the most important time of the year to have a good aide.

Valerie often pushed Shirley out of the building to wait for the bus without putting the coat on Shirley. It was toward mid-December and the clouds held the potential to snow any moment. "I'm cold," Shirley often reported to no avail. Waiting for the bus sometimes took a few minutes, but even one second could turn Shirley's whole body icy. Sometimes, they did not have to wait for the bus and Shirley just needed to go out to board it. But she still needed to wear her coat. Boarding the bus took several minutes itself: getting on the lift, being lifted into the bus, getting strapped in place, and at last, closing the door, all took considerable time, lasting well over seven minutes. But seven minutes was not the only time Shirley was in coldness. Since she was always sitting the entire day, she had poor circulation. Getting warm would nearly take an hour. Shirley was all blue when Juliet came out the apartment to take her back.

"This is outrageous!" fumed Juliet. "Shirley, you have to demand that she should not take you out! And it is raining. Why isn't your umbrella open?"

"She doesn't want to open it. She doesn't listen. I have no control. I am being pushed."

"I know," agreed Juliet wistfully. They must change Valerie, who had everyone under her spell. The school liked her, for she was polite to the teachers. She also sang hymns often and carried a Bible with her at all times. Everyone saw the surface, but not the wolf under the sheep's clothing.

Shirley quickly got extremely ill again. And it was the same symptoms as the previous illness. Shirley was brought to see her usual doctor, but he was not in again. She had to see someone else.

"She doesn't have a fever," said the doctor after a quick examination.

"She *does* have a fever," declared Juliet, touching Shirley's warm forehead with her hand. "I know she has pneumonia."

"No, she doesn't."

"Can't you do an x-ray for her?"

"No," the doctor persisted while shaking his head.

"But she can't breathe! It was like this the last time. She needs the medication!"

"I'm not going to prescribe anything for her. Thank you." Before Juliet could utter another plea, the doctor walked away, closing the door behind him. Devastated, Juliet had nowhere to go, so she took Shirley home.

As Juliet was in the kitchen for a moment, Shirley vomited as she sat on her bed. Juliet, hearing the noise, rushed over to her. Her eyes grew wide as she saw what happened.

"Mom, it's all mucus," said Shirley. Juliet saw it was true. She bent down and wiped the thick pile of mucus from the carpet. *Why does anyone want carpet? It is so unclean and hard to keep clean*, thought Juliet.

"My chest is feeling a bit better after I vomited the mucus. It is less tight, but I still can't breathe well." Juliet wished she had some medication left for her.

Shirley was getting worse the following morning. Juliet called up the medical group and found out that Dr. Madison was in. Immediately, an appointment was made for the afternoon. It was a vital appointment, for the doctor agreed to prescribe some medication for Shirley's pneumonia. Once more, she was saved.

"Shirley doesn't only have pneumonia, she has asthma, too," stated Dr. Madison.

"Asthma?" asked Juliet, skeptically. How could Shirley have asthma? She was perplexed. Shirley had never had such breathing problems, except that time in China, but even then, it had not been asthma.

"You can take the nebulizer machine home for a while," he continued. The machine was used for asthmatic patients to ease their breathing difficulty. Soon, Shirley was also diagnosed with chronic bronchitis.

Because of the weak condition she was in, Shirley needed to stay home for a little while. The school sent a tutor for her to bring her any missed work. The still much-weakened Shirley greeted the tutor. To her delight, she was a woman she knew to be a kind and caring person. She had always been friendly to Shirley whenever she substituted for a class.

"Actually, there's not much work. The class is watching a movie, and this is the tape," she announced, taking the video tape out of her bag. "Can we watch it?"

Juliet handed the remote control to Shirley, who ejected a video tape from the VCR. Juliet then inserted the school's video tape.

After the movie finished playing, the tutor left. "That's just a waste of time," muttered Juliet. "But it's so good that the tutor is a nice person." Then her thoughts turned to Shirley's aide. "This is outrageous, terrible! Valerie must be changed!" declared Juliet, smoke rising out of her nostrils.

"But the school will not listen. They're always making everything so difficult. Mrs. Duggan insisted that she has been carefully watching Valerie, but I barely see her!"

"It is best to leave the school and attend another school."

"But I like it here."

"How could you say that when you're suffering so much here? I know you are thinking of your friends, but you'll make a lot more in the new school. Plus, the kids here are so…" Juliet wrinkled her nose in distaste.

"So arrogant," Shirley finished for her. Although no children had ever made fun of her or were mean to her, Shirley could see that many were jealous of her. She also saw that bullying was certainly not absent in classrooms and hallways as some students were picked on by the class bullies. It was an unfortunate thing. She did not like seeing anyone getting mistreated. But surprisingly, none of the bullies had ever picked on her. On the contrary, they had treated her with respect and often said "Thank you," when Shirley provided them with an item, such as a pen.

"You're going back there tomorrow?" Shirley nodded in response to her mother's question. She had already missed several days of school because of her pneumonia she had twice. She knew other students had gotten many more days off from school when they had only the common cold. Having the common cold could never be a reason for Shirley to be absent from school.

It was time to go back. She hoped that she could

make up all the work on time. Having the tutor was not enough to keep her from missing any material. She needed to be in classes in order to learn the material completely.

***

That year around the same time as last year, Shirley entered the National Reflections Program. The theme of the contest was "anything could happen." Thus, her artwork showed a dark-haired girl getting up from a wheelchair. It had always been a fervent dream of Shirley to rise from her wheelchair. She would relish the feeling of walking by the ocean, to feel the gentle breezes kissing her face. She would do so much in life!

Soon afterward, it was time for vacation, which meant that she could escape from her aide for a while. She gave a sigh of relief and disappointment at the same time. Every time they had a vacation, Shirley was saddened at the thought of leaving her friends and not learning. But when she thought of leaving her aides, her whole body relaxed, as relaxed as the cats that snuggled close to one another on Kwi Show's patio chair. She thought of the happy times in school. Her other pleasure in school, other than receiving an education, was with her friends. She did not have many times during the day to converse with them, so she looked forward to lunches and in between periods where they switched classes.

She often passed Adam in the halls. They often greeted each other with a few quick words. Those few words between classes were not enough. Thinking of an idea, she had begun a letter to him, asking if he would like to be pen pals. Soon afterward, to her delight, he agreed in his letter, and they began to exchange letters every week. Shirley loved writing letters, so she appreciated a good pen pal. Following the letters, telephone numbers were exchanged, resulting in conversations that mostly lasted for an hour with each call.

Shirley thought of her other friends and a smile lit up

her countenance.

She was going to have a party for her fourteenth birthday, and she had made sure it would not fall on the last Sunday of the month so as to avoid it being on Super Bowl. Juliet was already starting to decorate the apartment with the accessories she had bought from Party City.

Shirley's eyes swept through the living room, taking in all the colors. Streamers and cutouts hung on the ceiling. There were even decorations for Valentine's Day and Easter, and there were also tropical designs. All in all, it was a wondrous sight for any eyes to take in! But Juliet did not stop there. She was adding more items to the galore, from dazzling table centerpieces to colorful balloons

Shirley had already distributed the invitation cards, each showed a white merry-go-around horse against pink background. Juliet bought other party items that matched the cards in design, including paper plates, table cloth, and napkins.

Then Shirley's eyes traveled to the bookshelves, where her treasures were kept, including a book on which Tommy had chewed.

Picking up a book, Shirley began to enter into a different world, a world that she could escape to from her surroundings. After the first quarter, she had begun to increase her reading and writing volume. She read three books a day, averaging five to six hundred pages. She was going for a one hundred average on her next report card for English. But she was not just doing it for the grades. She truly enjoyed reading. She could never put down a book once she had started on it. Her English teacher had told the class a few times about what an ideal student Shirley was. She never saw Shirley attending a single class without a book in hand. She was also her homeroom teacher, thus she saw Shirley read from the early morn.

But one day, the English teacher's comments had annoyed one of the students. In front of everyone else, she fired back with hurtful words. "That's good that Shirley can read. It's the only thing she could do. So, let her read!" Words were boiling up in Shirley's soul, but she uttered none, knowing it would only make the matter worse. She had never gotten along with the girl, who always ignored Shirley in classes and used her tissue without permission. But Shirley never minded. She did, however, think the comment made by her was rude. *If I am like one of you, I would be much better off than you*, thought Shirley. The English teacher asked the student to apologize to no avail. Shirley did not care for an apology. Her comment was unimportant. What was important for her was to continue reaching outward in achieving her goals.

On top of reading three books a day, her portfolio for her English class was nearly an inch thick. Whenever someone was asked to fetch her hot pink folder, that had her drawing of two parakeets in green and blue, for her, the person would give a gush of sheer surprise at the thickness of it. Shirley was famous for her reading and writing. She was always seen with her nose buried in a book. A few students got away with calling her a nerd. But she did not mind. In actuality, she would be inwardly smiling. She knew only exceedingly smart people had the privilege of being known as a nerd.

The doorbell cut through her reverie. "Janice is here," said Juliet. She welcomed the Jehovah's Witness missionary after she opened the door. Juliet had been starting to have Bible studies with the woman not too long ago. Juliet always wished to have Bible studies, but she could not find any time to attend churches. So, when she had learned about the organization, she readily began the lessons. They came to people's homes for the studies and it was just what she needed. Above all, Juliet had found Janice to be an excellent teacher, who explained everything clearly to Juliet, knowing that her English was not very good, though Juliet seldom needed any explaining of the Bible passages. She had a wealth of common sense and her own personal values, thus she utilized them to understand the Bible. She was able to answer any questions that were put to her, without needing to find the answers or hints from the Holy Scriptures. Her English had been improving as time passed. She had been influenced by Shirley and the interaction with English-speaking people. Many people had commented that her English was quite good.

On top of learning the Bible, Juliet had been telling Janice of their situation.

"Shirley has pinworms, that's why she has such a poor appetite," Juliet told Janice.

Shirley tried to concentrate on what she was reading with all the noises going on; the parrots' chirps were adding to the conversation.

"I actually have a medicine that treats parasites. I've been taking it. I'll bring you a bottle next time when I come."

Chapter Sixty

"I saw your picture. It's really good. You sure are a good artist," commented Adam, passing Shirley in the halls when Shirley was heading to the cafeteria. It was after vacation and all the submissions for the National Reflections Program were stacked in the main office.

"Thank you, I hope I will win!" Shirley did not have a chance to say anything else. Valerie pushed her in the direction of her next class, nearly bumping into someone in front of them. The mistreatment still continued; Valerie still took Shirley out in the cold without dressing her up. On top of it, she had been hurting Shirley a great deal when taking off Shirley's coat in the mornings. She always stood in one place, usually on Shirley's right side, to take off the coat, thus twisting Shirley's left arm in the process. Valerie never bothered to move to the left side to undress the left side of Shirley. Once, she had twisted Shirley's left shoulder badly, resulting in pain that lasted for a few days. Juliet had been reporting the numerous problems to the school. But as always, her complaints were ignored. Mrs. Duggan kept repeating the same words—that she had been watching Valerie. There was no help from Mr. Patricks, either. "Shirley is no different than other people. We treat every student the same way," he had told Juliet once. "Don't put me on the spot," he had said on another occasion.

Shirley had reminded Valerie several times to be extra careful with her feet when she helped her in the bathroom, but the aide simply ignored her.

Valerie also did not hold down the bedpan when Shirley relieved herself, so It was quite hard for Shirley to make sure that it would not spill. "She doesn't need to hold down the bedpan," Mrs. Duggan had said.

Valerie said one thing and did something else. She

promised Shirley that she would be careful with her feet, but never kept her promise. Other than the problems that the readers were told of, Valerie had also been bumping Shirley into people. She did not stop when the people in front of them stopped. Once, a student had toppled over Shirley's wheelchair and nearly sat upon her lap, but managed to get away limping. Shirley was always under constant pressure in the hallways. She was tense and constantly nervous. There was no feeling of protection when she was being pushed. She had no idea what would happen next and had to brace herself for the worst.

Also, Valerie always piled all of Shirley's books on her desk, leaving barely enough room for her to write. "Valerie doesn't need to make unnecessary trips to the locker," Mrs. Duggan had said. But Valerie did not need to go to the locker. She simply needed to put the unused books away in Shirley's bag, so Shirley's desks would not be cluttered with books that had been used for the previous subjects.

Juliet kept calling everyone, seeking help. She called Bountiful Care, and got connected with the agency's nurse, Kelilah.

"I'll come over and we can discuss the problems with Valerie," Kelilah told her. Thus, an appointment was made.

The first impression that Juliet received of her was not pleasant. Kelilah was two hours late arriving at the apartment. Juliet told her of the issues with Valerie, asking for a switch. Kelilah refused to change Valerie, saying that the aide was a capable person to care for Shirley. Knowing that she had no luck with this woman, Juliet wrote a letter to Mr. Patricks, pleading with him for a switch. She also called Dr. Murphy to no avail. No amount of begging would move their hearts.

But Shirley could forget the painful times for at least several hours, for her birthday party was coming up. Juliet had continued to decorate the living room, making a colorful jungle out of it.

"Mom, this looks wild. It's like a kaleidoscope!"

"Oh, I have more!"

"More?" Shirley had to laugh. Some of the wall hangings were even blocking the chandelier.

It would be a fun time. The party was on a Saturday, and she was expecting around the same number of people, perhaps one or two more than last year.

"Oh, another thing—Janice brought over the bottle of the medicine to treat the parasitic infestation this morning when you were in school. I'll give you the medicine now." Juliet gave two capsules of the medicine to Shirley, who was reluctant to take them. But she had taken so much medicine before, and she rarely had major problems with any. Then she received a second dose the next day after school.

While Shirley was on her bed reading, she suddenly felt her vision changing. She looked up from her book, blinked a few times, and the vision change would not go away. It was a hazy sight. Soon, before her mind registered what was happening, black spots appeared before her. They looked like tiny insects flying hither and thither in front of her. When she moved her eyes to follow them, they quickly darted away. As she continued to observe the spots, a few thin strands began to appear. Now she had flying insects and strands of hair.

She called out to Juliet. "Mom, don't worry about what I'm going to tell you," she began, crossing her fingers. But there was already a worried expression on Juliet's features. "Black spots and thin lines have suddenly appeared in my eyes," she finished, her voice low.

"What?" gasped Juliet. "What do you mean?"

"Something is wrong with my eyes."

"But how?" Juliet thought what could have caused the problem. "Could it be the medicine Janice gave?"

"It seems so. I had never before experienced this problem. But after taking four capsules of it, this happens…" Shirley's voice drifted off.

"Yes, otherwise, what else could have caused it? It's

the only new thing you have taken. I really believe it may be the cause." Juliet scrambled over to the bottle and reread the ingredients. They seemed harmless. She had looked up the few ingredients she was unfamiliar to—lipase, amylase, and protease—in her dictionary before giving it to Shirley, and found out they were simply digestive enzymes. All the other ingredients were present in Shirley's herbs. The enzymes must be the culprit. She jotted down the ingredients in her address book. "I'm going to bring you to the eye doctor. I'll give Janice a call, too."

Juliet spoke to Janice about the matter. "I've been taking it for half a year without any problem," Janice said. Juliet had also called Janice's doctor, and he told her that the medicine was used to treat parasitic infestation. Juliet was puzzled. How could enzymes treat parasitic infestation?

But oh so sadly, Shirley's vision deteriorated from that day. Even though she had received helpful eyedrops from the eye doctor which had cured the black spots and threads, her vision was not as good as before. The medication had caused the development of cataract. She was unable to see the projectors and chalkboards in class. She encountered many more problems as a result. She needed to borrow notes from teachers and classmates for each and every class.

She was more than devastated. There was no word in any language that could possibly describe how she was feeling then. But her loss was not affecting her eupeptic personality, and all others did not know that anything had happened to her. She smiled on. Her teachers were sympathetic of her vision deterioration, but they did not question her, so she was not obligated to answer any inquiries. Of a certainty, her days in school were made more difficult. But luckily, her near-sight was not affected on a noticeable level. She was still able to read and write.

She quickly turned her thoughts to happier ones. Her birthday was nearing.

On the morning of the big day, Juliet brought home a

bunch of balloons. "Wow, this is spectacular!" Shirley's eyes sparkled, taking in all the colors. The balloons had accented the blissful ambiance, adding to the festive feeling.

"There are lots more prettier balloons, but they are for Sweet Sixteen. I'll get you those when you turn that age," promised Juliet, who was always doing her best in making Shirley's heart desires come true.

"I think Erin is here," announced Juliet, looking out the sliding door. Erin was one of the few most prompt people Shirley knew. That was one important quality, thought Shirley, who was always prompt herself.

Soon, all her friends streamed into the room, making it as loud as a small cafeteria.

"You sure have a lot of Disney books," said Anne, eyeing the last level of the bookshelf, which was full of Disney hardcovers.

"Yes, I collect books."

Shirley then decided to let the parakeets out of their cage. The room was filled with more laughter and a few screams as the birds glided by their heads. Shirley had a total of three parakeets now. She had recently bought another yellow parakeet, which she had named Lily. Ever since Lily was added to the family, Shirley, the parakeet, had been so much happier, having a companion that would let her be preened. Above all, Lily was a bird that did not like bullying. She pecked Tommy back whenever he dared. Thus, Tommy stopped pecking at Shirley and Lily. As an aftermath, noticed both Shirley and Juliet, Tommy had loss energy and interest in coming out of the cage.

"I guess some people just can't live without bullying others—they will get sick if they don't," remarked Juliet once.

"That is true—just like my aides." Shirley giggled.

But Valerie was not on Shirley's mind as the party continued and the birthday cake was brought out. Again, Shirley made the same usual wish before blowing out the candles with one breath.

As with last year, Erin stayed longer than the rest of the group. "So, what did you get for second quarter?" asked Erin.

"Oh, mostly nineties, except for science." answered Shirley. The same thing had happened as with the first quarter. She had calculated her science average to be in the mid nineties, but received ninety instead. She did not bring up this matter anymore; it would be futile, and she would simply receive the same answer as the first. She knew she had calculated all the grades carefully. The other subjects' grades showed on the report cards were all as she had calculated. She had also thought she was going to receive one hundred for English, for she had easily exceeded the reading and writing volume for achieving one hundred, but instead had gotten a ninety-eight. The reason the teacher gave was that Shirley did not participate much in class. But her participation level was the same as with the first, so her participation grade, ninety-eight, for the first quarter should have remained the same for the second quarter, and it would not have lowered her English average to a ninety-eight since all of her other grades for English were one hundred each. Yet the best reward she received was reading in itself. English was no longer any problem for her. She was able to read anything she happened to pick up, which was anything and everything. She should be thankful for that. And she was, more so than anyone could ever imagine, except Juliet, who knew how important books were for her.

Chapter Sixty-One

Juliet had been calling the school over and over again to try to switch an aide for Shirley. Soon enough, the school would get tired from hearing from her, she felt.

After her birthday, Shirley became extremely ill again. She had to stay home. She had another case of pneumonia as a result of a cold because Valerie failed to dress her up. Juliet watched, heartbroken, as Shirley vomited. She had a high fever and her chest was tight and hurt whenever she coughed. She tried to constrain each cough, so that her chest would not hurt so much. Juliet hugged Shirley close to her after she vomited some of the sputum.

Shirley felt so sad. Why could they not open their hearts to their pleas? She was suffering too much.

Her health was still not well the following week. Her chest was still tight and she felt that she had finished one hundred miles of swim. She continued bedrest for another week. Was the school satisfied? It would be a task of most simplicity for them to change an aide for her. It needed merely the same amount of energy as raising a little pinky. Instead, they had turned the easiest project into something as hard as moving a mountain.

The school sent out a tutor for Shirley, but she could not learn anything; the tutor did not know how to teach her any of the materials.

As Shirley rested at home, Valerie had no job. She was put on another assignment, therefore automatically switching an aide for Shirley. How pitiful was it all!

When Shirley was somewhat better, she demanded to return to school. "I can't miss so much work. Otherwise, I would have to work very hard to get them finished. I really don't like it," said Shirley.

Juliet had to relent and send Shirley off to school, where her new aide was waiting.

The new aide was a much better person than Valerie, for which Shirley was highly grateful. The aide, Bianca, dressed Shirley with care and made sure she had her clothes on before going out. At last, Shirley was smiling because of a good aide.

Shirley was soon met with another piece of good news. She had learned that her artwork entry for the National Reflections Program was awarded first place, but it was not sent to the state level. Juliet and Shirley made inquiries, but no one supplied answers.

"They just won't send off your picture up a level!" fumed Juliet. "This isn't right. Then it shouldn't be called '*national*.'"

"We can't do anything about it. At least, I won first place," Shirley pointed out, holding the prize in her hands. It was a transparent paperweight with her name, grade level, and prize level, engraved on it with white lettering. They did not have any assembling this time, so the awards were simply handed out in school.

In the meantime, Shirley was getting a custom-made power wheelchair, so it would make traveling for her so much easier and enjoyable. She could drive herself, rather than relying on people to push her, thus, above all and most important, one of the biggest problems would be omitted. But she would not get it until the end of the school year. She would start using it for next year. She had already tried out one of the power wheelchairs and was able to drive it with the skills akin to that of someone who had driven it for years; she did not bump into anything and was able to make turns in tight places.

April arrived with a new computer for Shirley. A friend of Juliet had helped her buy a computer, along with a color printer and a Tweety Bird mouse pad. Shirley was nearly speechless with happiness when she came home from school to find a computer on her desk. She no longer had to spend hours writing her essays and stories by hand. She immensely enjoyed typing in school, and now she would be able to do it in the comfort of her own home.

She had taken computer class in sixth grade and a quarter during the present year. Since she was a fast learner and an eager student, she quickly established the computer skills the teacher taught. She was able to type using only her two index fingers because of her arthritis. But in spite of her limited function, she could type thirty-six words per minute, faster than most people she knew.

Not only did she love typing, but she also loved drawing on the computer using the paint program; it was heavenly for her. She was able to draw nearly as well on the computer as with a pen and paper. Once, after she had completed a drawing assignment for the computer class, the teacher was astounded by the accuracy of her drawing.

"Did you copy that and increase its size?" the teacher asked, pointing at one smaller fish she had drawn. Shirley shook her head. "Wow, this is really good." He gave her a ninety-eight on the assignment.

***

Days quickly flew by in school. Shirley's writing soon exceeded two inches in thickness, and students were beginning to look at her with awe mingled with jealousy for some. She received plenty of compliments from her English teacher, who enjoyed reading her short stories and essays. "Where do you get your ideas for your stories?" many had often asked, to which Shirley always answered with a mysterious smile and said that she simply thought of them from her vivid imagination. Writing, she knew, was a form of art, and since she was a creative person, she loved to express her feelings and thoughts with words. She relished the feeling when others read her work. She liked reading her stories to her friends. "You should be an author when you grow up," some of her friends suggested. Shirley shook her head at that idea. She loved writing, but she did not want to write as a career. She was passionate about the visual arts and science, so writing would be a "side dish," a hobby. Of course, good writing skills would come handy in any situation.

Sometimes, she enjoyed taking exams more than writing. She wanted to challenge her mind, testing herself to see just how much she remembered from the daily lessons. When Shirley told some that she enjoyed taking tests and quizzes, she received more odd looks than ever before. "You're mentally ill," one student had said.

"I'm not. I just like tests, that's all. Everyone's different," stated Shirley. But Shirley did not mind. She knew why she said it. She was the only one who had ever said that about Shirley. At least, none of the students had ever made fun of her disabilities.

On an afternoon in May, as the school day was drawing to a close, all the students were asked to go to their homerooms. What was scheduled for them? Shirley knew it must be some news of most importance. Her thought was confirmed when she saw the serious look on her English teacher's face. As all students were in their seats, the teacher began with a melancholy tone.

"Today Mr. Joice was not in school for class, as you all have noticed," she began. "He passed away this morning because of a heart attack."

The room fell silent.

Shirley's eyes flew wide open. Her heart stopped in her rib cage. "Oh my God," whispered Shirley, in shock.

The teacher stood up and distributed a letter to each student. Shirley quickly and carefully read the letter, but she soon was unable to finish it through the blurriness. Ever so steadily, but swiftly like a running stream, tears trickled down her face like tributaries of a river. She choked on her sobs. The teacher handed Shirley some tissue. Shirley's sobs grew louder. Then Bianca pushed her out of the room.

Shirley's tears never stopped flowing as the bus took

her back home.

"Oh my, what's wrong? What happened?" asked the much-startled Juliet after seeing Shirley crying. "Tell me, what happened! Did the aide mistreat you?" She repeated her questions over and over again, but no words came forth from Shirley's lips. She simply held out the letter to Juliet. Juliet scanned the letter, but still could not comprehend the situation.

"Her Health teacher has passed away," supplied Diana wistfully.

"What?" Juliet's ears were not taking in the information. Her brain was not registering the words.

"Mr. Joice...he...died," managed Shirley between sobs.

"What?" was the only word that Juliet was able to utter. Shirley did not forget to say her goodbye to Diana before she was pushed in.

"Bye Shirley, feel better soon," said Diana. Shirley sighed and nodded.

"He really died?" asked the disbelieving Juliet.

"Yes, from a heart attack and he was only fifty-four, choked Shirley.

"That's such a shame! Good people always have to leave early. You told me that the kids often gave him a hard time?"

"Yes. Many kids would not listen to him and always misbehave in classes. Sometimes, I wished I could wipe away their disrespectfulness." Shirley's sobs subsided as anguish invaded her heart, recollecting how the students had given him trouble. She noticed that students never mistreated mean or strict teachers. It was always the patient and kind people who received poor attitudes.

Shirley's eyes were still misty the next day. "You're *still* crying?" inquired Anne after noticing Shirley's watery eyes.

"Not really. I just feel sad. It's a great loss." She knew that every creature on the face of the earth would someday arrive at that point. It was merely the process of life. Yet, with many plans for the funeral that had been planned for a few days later, Shirley glowed with a sense of rest and serenity for her teacher's passing. She knew he no longer needed to keep the students in their seats and had no more lawns to mow. A person's life could end so suddenly without any warning! She had just seen him a day before his death and he was smiling. No one could ever expect that The lawn mowing at his house would cause his heart attack.

She had written a poem entitled *Elegy for Mr. Joice: My Teacher Died of a Heart Attack*. Juliet had ordered a bouquet of flowers of all varieties to be sent on his funeral day. Both Juliet and Shirley would attend his funeral.

When his funeral arrived, Juliet picked Shirley up from school. Shirley was dressed in a black top with white floral designs. Bianca was going with them as well. Juliet carried Shirley into the car and folded the stroller. She put the stroller inside. Bianca sat in the back.

The drive to the funeral home took several minutes. There were many cars parked there. Juliet drove around to find an empty parking lot that was handicap accessible. At last, she arrived to one.

"Do you have an elevator?" Juliet asked one of the funeral directors.

"Yes, over here." He led them to a tiny white elevator. Shirley and Juliet took the elevator while Bianca used the stairs. They rode up to the second floor—or was it the third? Shirley could not tell, for she could not fully see the structure of the building.

Shirley sat solemnly at the front of the funeral home. She had never before been to a funeral home. She scanned the room with intrigue. Everything seemed spotless to the eye. She saw flowers of all shades, shapes, and colors. Then she spotted the bouquet of flowers she and her mother bought for her teacher.

Her eyes glued to the teacher's casket during the whole service. A few tears trickled down her face, but her sadness diminished when she thought that he was resting in peace. She noticed that the same girl who was the most disrespectful student in his class was crying the most. *Maybe she feels sorry for her actions*, thought Shirley. *Oh well; everyone makes mistakes in life*. It was not for her to judge.

Soon, a few days after the funeral, an assembly was put in the school's gym and many classes gathered on the floor. One of Shirley's good friends read her elegy to the audience, for Shirley did not feel like doing so. A few other students also had written a poem for the occasion. *If only they showed him this kindness when he was alive*, thought Shirley.

Then Mr. Joice's family gathered in front of everyone and presented awards to those students who had contributed to the sad event. Shirley was one student who received an award. It was the first time Shirley's features were without smiles when presented with an award.

"Thank you," said one of Mrs. Joice's family members, handing the blue award to Shirley.

"I'm so sorry," whispered Shirley.

Afterward, those students, including Shirley, who were in chorus sang a song they had learned that year. It was one of the songs she and her class sang for the chorus evening a while back earlier in the year. She had missed the first chorus event, for Juliet was unable to carry Shirley into her car. But Shirley's chorus teacher had insisted that she should go to the second one because it was required for the class. The school had arranged for a bus to pick her up. She was glad she went. She enjoyed singing at the top of her lungs. "You look good in the tape," Erin had commented after the video tape, which had captured the event, was shown to the class.

Shirley soon found something to laugh about when a fly started to buzz around her head as she sang. She waved her hands to no avail. It had made up its mind to fly around her and to be her companion, bringing a little joy during this dismal time. Shirley saw that a few students in front of her in the audience laughing at the comical scene before their eyes. Shirley's lips formed into a grin. Perhaps, Mr. Joice was smiling down also...

Chapter Sixty-Two

Toward the end of the school year, Juliet had been a few months into her search of a new place in which to live. The situation with the current school was too harsh, and Shirley had been suffering too much with the aides. Although Debbie, a woman who became Shirley's new aide after Bianca had to leave for another job, was a wonderful person, the problems might continue into future years in the school district. There was not a single percentage of guarantee that the following years would be free of problems. The main issue was with Dr. Black, who was always making things difficult for Shirley, so it was a good idea to have her attend a different school. Plus, Shirley was in dire need of a really good aide since her vision was not as good as before. The medicine had caused permanent damage.

What was most singular about the case was that whenever Shirley had her menstruation, her eyes would become cloudy, just like seeing through wax paper, sometimes to the point that it was difficult for her to get around. Along with the cloudiness, her eyes felt thick and dry. But one week after the menstrual cycle, her vision would return to as before as if nothing had ever happened. Odd, it certainly was. Doctors did not comprehend her condition when she explained it to them. They simply said that she had cataracts. "But why does it fluctuate like that?" she had been asking. There was no answer. Deep inside her soul, she strongly believed it was caused by the medicine.

Juliet found a condominium in a school district that seemed promising. She had heard many good comments about this district. Juliet thought it was a good choice. Meanwhile, words of Shirley's move spread throughout her grade. Her friends told her they would miss her a great deal.

Shirley's feelings were reciprocated. But she knew it was a right move. Perhaps, she thought with a glimmer of hope in her, her luck with the school officials and aides might be better in a new school district.

On the last day of school, Shirley was dressed for the occasion, in a flowery tank top matched with her full white skirt.

"I have something for you," said Debbie, handing her a gift-wrapped present.

"Oh, you shouldn't have!" exclaimed Shirley, touched by Debbie's kindness.

"Well, open it."

"Oh, I know what it is," said Erin.

"I know, too." Shirley giggled. She carefully tore the wrapping off. "A photo album. I love it! I love Tweety Bird. Oh, thank you so much." The two exchanged warm hugs. Shirley would miss Debbie, who was the best aide she had ever had so far. She shuddered when she thought of her previous aides. Then she thought of her past teachers. Most of her teachers were gentle people. The only problem she had this year was with the science class. The report cards she received for every quarter on science did not reflect Shirley's true grades which she had earned by her hard work, except for one quarter.

Her academic rewards were great. She had received an award in her French class for achieving straight A's for the entire year. She was more so an avid reader that year, completing 210 books; meaning 210 signatures of Juliet were present in her files.

"I also brought a camera," announced Debbie. She took it out of her bag and began snapping shots of Shirley with everyone. All the students gathered in the gym to exchange last-day greetings, so Shirley had a chance to take photographs with each of her teachers. But oddly, she did not see more than a few friends of hers. She wished she could see them then, but apparently, it could not be so. Soon, the camera began to wind.

"Oh, that's the last of it," said Debbie. After the camera stopped winding, she took out the film and handed it to Shirley.

Then it was time for Shirley and her friends to say a tearful goodbye.

"We'll keep in touch," said Shirley. She knew it would not be the last time to see her good friends, Erin, Annie, and Adam, though it might be the last time she could see her driver, Diana.

"Take care of yourself," Debbie hugged Shirley once more. Ah, saying farewells was certainly hard!

Debbie pushed her out of the school building. Shirley glanced at the school as the yellow bus drove away.

Tears were present in Diana as they shared a hug. "Here, let me take a few shots of you two," said Juliet, posing in front of them with a camera around her neck. Diana and Shirley smiled into the camera. "You've been so good to Shirley," Juliet thanked her.

"It's nothing. Shirley is a wonderful girl."

Juliet and Shirley sadly waved goodbye to her. Shirley's eyes watched the yellow bus leave the parking lot until it was a speck in the far off distance. Their eyes were misty as Juliet pushed Shirley inside.

Chapter Sixty-Three

At the end of July, the twenty-eighth to be exact, Juliet carried bag after bag out of the apartment and into the car. It was moving day once again. Shirley hoped she could stay in the new location for a long time this time. She had enough of moving. Juliet felt the same way. On top of it all, Shirley had a cold. For once, it was not caused by an aide. She sneezed into a tissue as her watery eyes followed the movers.

"Don't forget Mickey!" Shirley reminded her mother.

"Of course not. He's coming with us in the car," answered Juliet. Shirley looked at the small Dwarf Hamster inside his glass cage. Juliet had bought the hamster two days ago. Shirley had first seen it when visiting a local pet shop, and had quickly gotten attached to the hamsters. After returning home, she still could not get the hamsters out of her mind. Thus, she asked for one. She brought home a hamster that was half the size of a golf ball a few days later. Thinking of Mickey Mouse, one of her favorite Disney characters, she named the hamster Mickey.

Juliet had given the five parrots to the same pet shop. The store owner refused to pay her any money for the birds, including the cages and feeding. But a kind worker had given her twenty dollars. Juliet was getting too tired to care for the parrots on top of all the household chores, not to mention what she had to do for Shirley daily. Shirley felt sad that she had to part with her feathered friends, with whom she had spent happy years.

Before Shirley bought Mickey, she had a cat, which she had named Tommy, for three weeks. Tommy was given by a friend of Juliet, but Juliet could not care for him any longer, so she had to return the cat back to his original owner. Both Juliet and Shirley missed the orange tomcat dearly. He was an extremely friendly cat, always following Juliet wherever she went just like a royal puppy. The following-around was constant and it grew dangerous when Juliet was not aware of his presence under her feet. He often jumped onto the kitchen counter top and stole the leftovers. He frequently meowed at nights, asking to go out. Then, in the middle of the night, he scratched the screen on the sliding door, wanting to come in. Therefore, Juliet had to wake up to let him in.

All the furniture was moved out of the apartment, and it was time to drive to the condo some fifteen minutes away. Juliet got Shirley into her blue car, followed by Mickey. Letting out a big sigh, she started the car. She felt so tired from all the work. She had been making trips to and fro from the condo and apartment, each time bringing some items over to the condo.

Once they arrived at the new place, the exhausted Juliet scurried around the condo, moving everything to its proper place.

After several hours on her feet, Juliet lay on the bed, but only after she got Shirley on it first.

"This is not a good day. You have a cold and I barely have time to attend to you. You must be hungry now." Juliet had not eaten for the whole day, either.

"No, I'm not hungry. But I don't feel so well with this cold."

"You should eat something."

"I just want to eat the canned fruit." It was already approaching nighttime, though the sun was still half present at the horizon.

"I'm afraid I don't have the kind you want. I just have the other one—the one you said is too sour."

"I'll have it," said Shirley, who was getting weaker by the minute. Juliet poured the contents of the can into a bowl and handed her a spoon. Shirley ate some of it with winces.

Suddenly, Shirley's face lost its color. She pointed at her tightly closed mouth. Juliet gasped. Shirley needed to vomit! Rushing over to the plastic bowl, Juliet picked it up and held it under Shirley, who immediately vomited in it.

"Oh, what's the matter?" inquired Juliet, frantically.

"Sudden nausea... Get me to bed," whispered Shirley. Juliet made Shirley comfortable on the bed, putting two pillows under Shirley's legs to support them and one pillow under each of her arms. After the pillows, came the bed sheets, which Juliet put and fluffed under Shirley's elbows and hands as supports. Lastly, she covered her with two of the toddler blankets that she had bought for her a few years back. Shirley was unable to use comforters and other regular-sized blankets, for they were too heavy for her. The pillows and bed sheets were required to support both her arms and legs, which were bent at a ninety-degree angle. After a quarter of an hour had been used up to make Shirley comfortable, Juliet was free to leave the room for more unpacking, but she hesitated.

"Dear, I think I need to stay with you," said Juliet.

"You don't need to. Mom, I love you."

"I love you very, very much. Call me as soon as you need anything. I'll come to check on you in a bit." Reluctantly, Juliet got up from the bed and walked out.

Juliet felt uneasy in the living room, so she came back to check on Shirley after merely half an hour later. She sat down on her side of the bed and asked how Shirley was doing. Shirley feebly nodded that she was okay, but Juliet could see that Shirley was struggling to hang in.

The night passed with much worry upon Juliet's heart. She prayed that tomorrow, the sun would bring light upon Shirley's health.

***

Juliet, her heart quickening its pace, could see that something was awfully wrong with Shirley. It was the following evening before Shirley was to go to bed.

"Mom, I can't breathe!" Shirley gasped for air. Juliet

was alarmed onto her feet. "I need to…go to the…hospital."

"Okay, I'll take you there!" Juliet quickly carried Shirley onto her stroller and into the car. Juliet was gasping too, for she had to use much energy to carry Shirley. She had bought a van that had a handicap conversion, but it would not arrive till later. Shirley's chest heaved in a great struggle as Juliet rushed to St. Francis Hospital to the emergency room.

Once they arrived inside the building, Juliet quickly made her way to the desk. "My daughter, Shirley Cheng, can't breathe," she told the lady. She promptly received some paper to sign in return.

"Are you okay? Can you breathe now?" asked Juliet, getting to Shirley's side, who continued to gasp. She shook her head in answer. "I hope they won't let us wait long. Hold on."

They waited and waited and waited some more. The clock showed that two hours had passed in the waiting room. Juliet scanned the room, noticing that most of the patients appeared as though they had nothing bothering them. She wished that there was a real emergency room for real emergency cases that needed immediate action, not a place for everyone with small problems to see the doctor forthwith. Therefore, it would not deprive those cases from the immediate attention that they required.

At last, Shirley's name was called! Juliet glanced at the clock; the hour hand had moved three more hours.

A nurse snapped a machine on Shirley's finger, causing much pain. It was the machine that would tell them of her oxygen count. Several minutes later, the reading was taken, which turned out to be lower than average. Simultaneously, an oxygen tube was stuck into Shirley's nose. Shirley quickly took in the precious gas. But to her horror, it did not lessen the tightness of her chest. But she was, however, able to get a few breaths in.

"Can you prescribe penicillin for her?" requested Juliet.

"Yes, I will. Next time, you should bring her to Vassar Brothers Medical Center, because they deal more with children, and therefore, will be more familiar with her," suggested the doctor. Juliet thanked her and took Shirley home. There was no reason to stay further. Juliet had the medication now and she hoped that it would cure the illness.

But sadly, it did not, at least not for the first day. Shirley requested to go to the emergency room again the following dawn. "I'll call an ambulance for you this time, okay?" It was hard on both of them when Juliet had to carry Shirley in and out of her car. Shirley nodded in agreement. It was five when Juliet dialed for an ambulance. "My daughter can't breathe and she needs to go to the hospital."

Soon, the ambulance arrived. The paramedics rushed into the room.

"Is she conscious?" asked one paramedic.

"Yes, she just can't breathe well."

"We're going to give her IV."

"No, there's no need for it."

"You are uncooperative."

"Just don't do it," insisted Juliet. She already had enough experience with the medical system. She knew too well that no matter what caused the emergency, the paramedics would automatically stick a needle in the patient's arm. The unhappy paramedics relented to Juliet's order.

They carried Shirley onto the stretcher and lifted her into the ambulance. It was the first time that she had ever been in one. She weakly looked at her surroundings, but quickly closed her eyes. The energy needed to move her eyes was leaving her no more energy to keep them open. The shallow breathing and tightening of her chest had enervated her soul, leaving barely enough energy to lift a finger.

Juliet followed the ambulance close behind as it rushed to Vassar Brothers Medical Center. On the road, the paramedics checked Shirley's blood pressure and pulse. They put an oxygen mask on Shirley's face. They did not turn on the siren, for which Shirley was glad. She would be unable to stand the loud sound. She needed as little noise and disturbance as possible.

They lifted Shirley out of the ambulance and into the emergency room. She squeezed her eyes when the lights invaded her field of view.

The hospital staff came to tend to Shirley without having her to wait. Coming in from an ambulance was much faster and received more promptness than coming in by other means.

Shirley continued on the oxygen for a while, then they switched her on a nebulizer machine. There was no information passed between the hospital and the patient. During all the years of Shirley's hospitalization and doctor visits in America, the hospital seldom shared with her information concerning her examination readings. Everything was kept as a secret. Thus, her oxygen count was not told to her, either. But she knew it was low from the looks on their faces.

The nebulizer machine provided slim help; Shirley's chest was still tight.

"She can go home now," announced the doctor. They had nothing else that could ease Shirley's suffering. Juliet was numb from the whole ordeal. She would find another route after bringing Shirley home.

Juliet noticed that the staff had just changed shifts. A new doctor traded places with the doctor who had attended to Shirley earlier.

"Who is her pediatrician?" asked the doctor on the new shift.

"Dr. Madison," replied Juliet.

"Let me make a call." With that, he turned and left.

Juliet sat back down in the chair by Shirley's bed. Shirley wanted to go home right then. She needed to lie down and go to sleep. She did not sleep well at all last night.

Moments later, another doctor appeared. To her dismay, Juliet saw that he was the same doctor to whom she had first suggested that Shirley had pneumonia.

"She needs to be admitted to the hospital," he said.

"No, I need to take her home. She can't stay here," answered Juliet, firmly.

"If you don't have her stay in the hospital, I'll call the Child Protective Services," he threatened. "She's too sick to go home."

"You go ahead! Call them! Call them!" Juliet was furious. She had enough of it all. Every time they had treated them as puppets on strings, and if they would not listen to their preemptory command, Child Protective Services would be called in. Juliet knew that Shirley was extremely sick, but she also knew that the hospital would not be able to offer any help. At home, she could think of some way.

"Mom, don't say that! What if you'll lose custody again?" said Shirley in a low voice.

"Don't worry. They can't do that to us." But they both knew that they could do anything to them.

More energy was drained from Shirley as a result of the fright. She would not be able to stand another custody case! She just could not!

"Don't worry," repeated Juliet.

Shirley's keen ears quickly caught the sound of a set of distinguished footsteps. A smartly dressed woman came into view and walked over to them.

"Hi, I'm Mary, and I'm a social worker from the hospital," she introduced herself, handing Juliet a business card.

Shirley forgot she even had a breathing problem. All her thoughts turned to the woman before her, waiting for the life sentence.

Mary took a chair and sat down facing Juliet, who began to tell her the situation. Mary listened patiently with nods between Juliet's words.

"You can take her home," said Mary when Juliet finished.

"What?" asked Juliet in disbelief. "I can take her

home?"

"Yes."

"I can't believe it!" *Even at such a life and death situation, I can still take her home*, thought Juliet. *Why did they not allow us to leave in Newington? We were just going there to see the doctor, just like this time except that this is an emergency visit rather than an outpatient one.* It truly flummoxed her.

Then Juliet explained her reason for wanting to take Shirley home. "Shirley has been here for two hours and I haven't seen any improvement. If I take her home, I may have slight hope to have different treatment for her. In here, Shirley will be disturbed. They will do unnecessary testings for her. I can't tend to her. She can't eat or drink whenever she likes. Everything will be hard to do. If she's at home, I can get her to sleep, give her a sip of a drink… I can really take care of her at home." She clearly knew that if Shirley died when she took her home, she would be charged with murder. But for the tremendous love for her daughter, she would risk it.

"Yes, that's true," agreed Mary, nodding her head. "I see your reason. You can take her home now."

"Thank you so much! Shirley will have a much better chance of living. Thank you!" Mary shook Juliet's hand before leaving.

"Thank goodness for her," said Juliet, immediately carrying Shirley into the stroller.

Shirley was extremely nauseated at the time and felt highly uncomfortable, but she had managed to smile and look well at Mary's presence. She felt like vomiting any moment. She was trying her hardest not to do so. She needed to get back home as soon as possible, so she could vomit. She had never felt as ill as she was now.

On the road, Shirley vomited all over herself. "I had been holding it in all this time," said Shirley.

"Poor dear. I'll get you home soon."

"I feel a bit better after I vomited." Shirley did not

look down at herself, fearing that it would nauseate her further. She was certain that it was all mucus just as previous times. Her lungs were filled with sputum. She wanted to get all of it out of her lungs.

Chapter Sixty-Four

Juliet massaged Shirley's head as she slept. Shirley's breathing was rapid and shallow. Whenever she had pneumonia, she did not snore. A plumber was working in the adjoining bathroom of the master bedroom. Juliet had scheduled this appointment a long time ago. He was to take away the toilet and construct a shower place for Shirley. But today, he would not start on the construction, for it would make a lot of noise. It was pivotal not to disturb and wake her up. Thus, he could take away only the toilet. After his work was done, he quietly left the condo as instructed by Juliet, who had informed him of the situation.

Juliet knew that Shirley would continue to live. She could not bear it if Shirley left the world. She would miss her so much. She was her entire life—she depended upon her entirely.

After some time had passed, Juliet quietly got up from the bed. Shirley was such a light sleeper; the tiniest sound could wake her up. There was still so much left to do for Juliet. All the visits to the emergency room had resulted in everything else unattended.

Her movements were quiet, and yet quick, as she moved about in the rooms. Still, the floors cracked under her feet. *It is not a very good construction*, thought Juliet. She had wanted to move to another complex, one that was much better, but the school district was not as good, so she chose this place over the other one. Then she thought there was another reason of picking this place over the other one: the driveway access was poor unlike the condo, where it was convenient; Juliet could park her car right in front of the condo.

She sighed when her thoughts turned back to Shirley. When would pneumonia invade her body again? "Is it going to turn into pneumonia whenever she catches a cold?" Juliet asked herself. It appeared to be so. And what was most frightening, more frightful than pneumonia itself, was asthma. She was stunned when she had learned that Shirley had asthma. It seemed as if it would be stuck with her for the rest of her life. It was the most frightening disease that Shirley had encountered so far. She knew that asthma was serious—she had heard awful stories of it.

Then, she thought she heard Shirley calling her. She quickly stopped what she was doing and went into the bedroom.

"Pearl, did you call me?" asked Juliet.

Shirley had her eyes opened somewhat and was looking at somewhere unknown. "No, but I was just about to call you."

"Then, I just came right on time!" Juliet smiled. It was not rare for such an occurrence. Sometimes, Juliet would think she had heard Shirley calling her, and she would come to find that Shirley was just thinking of calling her. It seemed as though they sometimes communicated through telepathy.

"What do you need? How do you feel now? Better?"

"I do feel a little better." She took a deep breath. "My chest doesn't feel as tight. I would like to sit in the living room."

"I'm so happy to hear that!" She was so much relieved. It had been so close. "Sure, let me get your wheelchair." After getting the wheelchair beside the bed, Juliet carried Shirley onto it. She pushed her down the short hallway and into the living room. Shirley had not gotten a chance of a good look at the place.

But they did not have the quiet moment to themselves for long, for the door sounded with a few quick knocks. "Who could that be?" pondered Juliet out loud, rising from the couch. Deep inside, she had a sinking feeling who could be behind the door.

"Is this Juliet Cheng?" asked the woman. From her official outfit, Shirley knew it was not a visit of which they would be glad.

"Yes."

"I'm from Child Protective Services. I am just checking on how things are."

"Oh, please come in." Juliet stepped back, opened the door wide, and invited her in.

After they seated at the sofa and Shirley situated herself in front of them, Juliet started telling her the situation. The woman listened without interrupting. "She is better now after a nap," finished Juliet. Shirley gave her a wide smile as a confirmation.

"Yes, she does look nice," the social worker smiled back. "Well, that's all I wanted to know. Glad she's doing better. I'll check on her later." She stood up, bade a temporary goodbye to the two, and went out the door Juliet held open for her.

Two simultaneous sighs were released following the closing of the door.

"She startled me," said Shirley.

"Don't worry. I was expecting such a visit," stated Juliet, shaking her head. "At least, they are nice people. We are fortunate this time." Shirley nodded in agreement. "Or else, they would give us trouble." Shirley nodded again.

***

"Mom, I need to go to the hospital again," announced Shirley.

Juliet gasped. "But not back there again," she said, referring to Vassar Brothers Medical Center. "Oh, but where can I take you?" thought Juliet, frantically. *There are only two hospitals in this whole area*, thought Juliet. *Where can I take her?*

Then and there, Juliet knelt by the foot of the bed and prayed to God, asking for a place to take Shirley, who was starting to gasp for breath.

Suddenly, a name formed in Juliet's mind.

"Medicus!" She felt a surge of abundant energy sweeping over her entire being like a lightning bolt.

"Medicus? What is that?" asked the puzzled Shirley.

"It's like an emergency room. But I am not sure how to get there. I think there is one by your grandmother's house, but I don't know the directions!" Quickly, Juliet thought of the realtor, who had helped her in buying the condo and dialed up her number.

"Hi, Lauren? Yes, it's Juliet. Fine, thank you. Yes. Oh, it has been terrible. My daughter is really sick. Do you know how to get to Medicus? Oh, really? There's one here close by? That's wonderful! How do I get there?" Juliet listened anxiously as the realtor told her the directions. "Thank you so very much! Yes, I'll take her there now." She quickly hung up and glanced at the clock. "I hope it's not too late. I need to give them a call. I hope they don't close too early on Saturdays!" It was well past five in the afternoon on the same day they escaped Vassar Brothers Medical Center. She needed to act fast. She called information and obtained the number to Medicus. She called them up.

"What time do you close today? At eight? Okay, thank you."

Juliet knew she needed physical strength to go through the trial that lay ahead. She quickly wolfed down a slice of wheat bread which Shirley liked and she despised. Then she took some vitamins, and off they went.

It was six when they got on the road. Juliet glanced at Shirley beside her several times on the road, clearly seeing that she was suffering on a grand scale. It had been worse than before. Shirley's lips were turning blue and her eyes glassy. She prayed that Medicus would be the holder of good news.

"Here we are," announced Juliet, parking in front of the primary health-care center. "There are only a few cars here. Good—it will be faster."

Juliet pushed Shirley to the door and opened it,

noticing it was quite heavy, but it would not remain open. It quickly swung shut. Someone then came to their assistance. "I'll hold it for you," offered a kind, elderly woman.

"Oh, thank you so much!" Shirley whispered her thanks as well.

"My daughter is here to see the doctor. She can't breathe."

"It's an asthma attack!" exclaimed a nurse as soon as she saw Shirley. They asked for her to be pushed into an examining room immediately. Juliet turned her around, so that it was a better position for examination.

Shirley looked like a gasping waxed doll, sitting limply in the stroller. The nurse held out a machine to Shirley and asked her to put it in her mouth. "Blow into the mouthpiece," she instructed. Shirley blew as hard as she could, but she merely forced out a tiny amount of air just enough to blow a feather from a table.

The doctor came in then and quickly went to work on her case. Together, the two brought over a machine and gently inserted the mouthpiece into Shirley's mouth. Shirley took quick breaths.

As if by magic, Shirley felt her chest loosening by the second. And after merely a minute's use of the wondrous machine, she could breathe freely on her own.

"Look, she can breathe, and she looks better now!" exclaimed Juliet, completely taken aback from the miraculous happening.

"Yes, she looks *much* better," agreed the nurse, her lips curling into a big smile.

"I feel so much better now. I can breathe again!" said Shirley, a happy smile touching her lips, which were regaining their color. Shirley had never before recovered so swiftly and so completely. She felt like a whole new person.

"It's amazing! How were you able to do it?" inquired Juliet, amazement engulfed her voice.

"We use oxygen combined with the medication. This way, it will open the lungs, so the medicine can get into the lungs fast, unlike the usual way that other people do it—that will not open the lungs and therefore, the medication could not get into the lungs," explained the nurse, supported by the doctor, who repeated the same words.

"This is a miracle!" exclaimed Juliet. "This is wonderful." She laughed, joy radiating throughout her entire being. "Why don't others do the same thing?"

The doctor and nurse shrugged. Everyone should know such a golden secret to treat the horrid condition!

The joy-filled pair left only after thanking the two saviors profusely. Medicus had saved Shirley's life. Juliet would never forget them. She felt at ease at last as she drove home.

Chapter Sixty-Five

Shirley speeded around the new condo in her power wheelchair that they had custom-made for her a few months before. She went in and out all the rooms, curved around the halls, and entered the living room where she had started, all done with a wide smile.

"It is very nice here," Shirley chirped. "More space and room here."

Shirley even had an office of her own in the second bedroom. It had all her school materials, along with her desk with the computer and printer, on it. A bookshelf full of books was situated to the right. The condo was not a big place, but it was enough for the two of them. And it was quite convenient with two bathrooms, one of which was in the master bedroom. Juliet had the toilet there taken out and the construction of a shower place for Shirley was going underway.

But nothing could ever be perfect: the condo had one faulty feature. At the doorway, where it led to the parking lot, there was a step that was a few inches higher than the ground, thus it would be hard for Shirley to go in and out of the building. Shirley's power wheelchair was powerful, but the sudden jerks resulted from going down the step hurt her joints. Juliet had to think of a way to level it.

It was the first time Shirley had an opportunity to see their new home. She was still weak from the illness, but after a couple of days had passed from the visit to Medicus, recovery began. "It is nice here," repeated Shirley, trying to get Juliet's attention, who was mulling over something.

Juliet had been calling Medicus to ask about their secret remedy since a couple of days ago, but only received angry replies in return. What was even more disturbing was the fact that the two people who had saved Shirley denied ever saying about the "oxygen combination" to "open the lungs."

"You kept calling and calling here! We never said that. I have no idea what you are talking about," the doctor had said, his voice rising.

Juliet was stunned. It seemed as though the doctor and nurse had been abducted by aliens and then brainwashed.

Juliet dialed the telephone again and asked to speak to the doctor.

"Sorry, ma'am, but he doesn't work here anymore," said the receptionist.

Numbly, Juliet hung up. So, with their secrets, they had vanished into thin air. At least, Shirley had been saved and that they had learned the magic cure. From now on, she knew what to request from doctors.

"They said that they never said anything like that, about combining oxygen with the medication," said Juliet.

"That's so strange."

"Yes, I know I wasn't imagining it—you heard it, too."

"Yes, I did."

"How do you feel now?"

"My chest is much better, but sometimes I have a hard time getting a deep breath." Shirley's eyes wandered to the sliding doors. "It's a nice day out," she noticed.

"Would you like to go for a stroll?" Shirley nodded. "It's not windy out today. I'll bring your jacket just in case." Seeing that all was set, she opened the door and together, they went out.

They nearly bumped into a woman who was just coming in the main entrance of the building. Mother and daughter simultaneously recognized the woman. She was the social worker from Child Protective Services who had been there not long ago. Juliet promptly led her in, with Shirley following behind.

Like the first visit, the second was short. The social

worker was simply checking to see how Shirley was doing. Shirley hoped it was the last visit from any social workers as the woman stepped out.

***

"My chest is tight again," reported Shirley weakly. Juliet took Shirley to the hospital, but they had no help. Shirley had stopped seeing Dr. Madison, for there was no good relationship between the medical group and Juliet. One doctor had called Child Protective Services, so it would not be a wise decision to continue going there. Shirley would see Dr. Frank instead.

"I'll take you back to Medicus," said Juliet. She asked the new doctor about the secret trick once Shirley was called in the examining room.

"I never heard of it, though I will try my best to do so. I'll just bring the oxygen tank and put the medication in the compartment of the mouthpiece," said the kindly-looking doctor.

A nurse did as he was instructed. Shirley received quick relief, but it was not as immediate and potent as with the last time.

"It helps her a lot," stated Juliet.

Juliet and Shirley thanked the doctor before leaving.

"It's so strange that the former doctor had denied the oxygen treatment," said Shirley. "This time it helped, too, but it was not as quick."

Juliet nodded. "I really can't believe that you suddenly have asthma after you got pneumonia. You have suffered too much in that school. It's a good thing you left."

"I do hope that the new school will be good."

"We'll meet the special education chairperson next week."

Shirley was excited to be going to a new school in three weeks. She was to go to a middle school that was farther than the one she was supposed to go to, for the closest school did not have wheelchair accessibility. Shirley had heard of the school district many times, especially during snow days, for it commonly was the first district being announced on the list of closings and delays on the radio.

The vacation was almost over, and Juliet scheduled an appointment with the school's principal to meet him before school started. They had come back from the district office, which was located across the street from their complex, where they had met with the Director of Special Education, Mrs. Costin, a chairperson of the Committee on Special Education (CSE).

"She is so much nicer than Dr. Black," commented Shirley, relief flooding throughout her being. Juliet happily agreed.

"The principal sounds very nice over the telephone," Juliet told her. "We will meet him next Monday."

"Hopefully, my aide will be good, too!"

Another duty was going to be added for her aide: copying down notes from the chalkboards and projectors, for Shirley could not continue on with borrowing other students' notes.

"We will also meet her as well. Mrs. Costin will bring her there."

Shirley was in a grand state of excitement at the thought of seeing her new school for the first time. She also could hardly wait to drive her power wheelchair in the hallways. She drove at the fastest speed, with agility.

***

The tall man opened the door as Shirley drove to the ramp at the back of the school. The man held out his hand, introducing himself as the principal. Shirley and Juliet readily took his warm hand in a handshake. "Nice to meet you."

"Nice to meet you, too, Mr. Caufield," answered Shirley. Beside him, Mrs. Costin, Shirley's new aide, the district OT, and the school nurse, were present.

Shirley smiled at her aide but no smile was returned. Prompt introductions were made before Mr. Caufield began the tour of the building for Shirley.

The school had two floors, but it had no elevators.

"All your classes will be on the first floor," said Mr. Caufield. "And here's the homeroom where you will come first," he informed. He pointed at the room, walking in its direction. All her other classrooms were showed to her.

Shirley's eyes took in the cleanliness of the halls. Not a speck of dust was seen. Surely, he had watched over his school with much care.

On the way, a woman went over to them, holding out a hand. "Hi, Shirley, I'm Mrs. Nelson, your guidance counselor." Shirley returned her smile. "I'll see you later to discuss your schedule, Shirley." Then she walked away, heading to perhaps her office.

Mr. Caufield continued the tour. He kindly showed Shirley's desks to her, "Is this desk right for you?" Shirley tried it.

"It is a little high for me." She showed him that her arms were uncomfortable.

"Let's see." He bent down and examined the legs. "I think this will do," he stated after lowering it to the lowest possible level.

"This is perfect," said Shirley, with appreciation in her voice. Shirley and Juliet both thanked him profusely for his caring actions.

"Now, let's see how things can be worked out in the bathroom," said Fran, the OT. She led Juliet and Shirley to the bathroom. Shirley saw there was a portion of the bathroom that could be used for her. The OT brought in the lift and the seating. They were a different lift and seating than the ones Shirley had used previously in her last school.

Juliet pushed Shirley in the correct position. Fran situated the lift in front of Shirley and got the seating under her. Shirley leaned and shifted to each side to get it under her. She nearly had to start panting from all the exertion she used. Fran cranked the lift, lifting her out of the chair.

"Oh, wait. The seat is hurting me," said Shirley.

"Where is it hurting you?" asked Fran.

"At the sides." Shirley said, pointing. The two sides of the seat squeezed Shirley's legs.

"Other people can use it fine," said Fran.

"But Shirley can't use it," stated Juliet.

"She will just have to use it. That can't be helped. There's no other way to do it. This is the only way that it can be done. So, she will just have to use it."

Gritting her teeth, Shirley was completely lifted from the chair and then placed on the commode for the demonstration.

"And you'll have to take off her pants, wait outside, and when she's done, just wipe, pull them back up and lift her off," Fran instructed the aide.

After the practice, Juliet tried to get the aide's attention, so she could let her know how to dress Shirley without hurting her. But the aide would not talk to her and ignored her examples of dressing Shirley. Juliet, in frustration, gave up. She knew it would not work out with the aide who acted as though she had no work to do for Shirley. How could she take care of Shirley?

Fran, knowing that her duty was done, left with the aide. Then it was time to go to the guidance office to discuss Shirley's schedule for the year.

Juliet sat down at the office table with Shirley beside her. Mrs. Nelson handed them a sheet of paper. "This is what you'll take." Shirley's eyes looked through the schedule, noting that she had two study hall periods.

"May I take a higher level of math?" asked Shirley.

"No, you can't, because you had completed seventh grade math so you will have to take the eighth grade math class," replied the counselor.

"But Shirley could do it. She had nineties for math in sixth grade, but the teacher won't let her take a higher math level for seventh grade," explained Juliet.

"Well, that's too bad," said Mrs. Nelson. "She can't skip a math level now."

"But I have a higher level of science class, right? It is Earth science," noticed Shirley. In her previous middle school, students could take Earth science if their grades were high, rather than an eighth grade science class.

"No, that's not."

"That's not?" repeated Juliet, questioningly. It flummoxed Shirley. Perhaps, the new school's system was different.

"Is this schedule okay?" asked Mrs. Nelson. Shirley nodded, a tint of disappointment shining in her eyes. "I know you want to take those advanced classes," she commented.

"I can't wait to start school here," said Shirley.

"We look forward to it as well."

Coming out of the guidance office, Juliet pushed Shirley in the direction of the main office. "Mr. Caufield?"

"Yes, Mrs. Cheng?"

"I really don't like the aide. She doesn't talk to me and doesn't listen to what I tell her," reported Juliet.

"If you don't like her, you can change her!" replied Mr. Caufield.

"Do you really mean it?" asked Juliet with astonishment. She feared that she did not hear him correctly. It could not be so simple in changing an aide, could it?

"Yes, you can change her. You can change her when you don't like her."

"Before, changing an aide was so difficult!" gushed Juliet. "But it is so simple now! We really need to."

Thus, it was settled: Shirley would receive a new aide. Shirley was also amazed by the principal's understanding. He had made the once most difficult thing the easiest! She was glad to have her aide replaced. The aide ignored her as well. How could the aide be able to work with her like that?

"Thank you so much, Mr. Caufield," repeated Juliet

for the third time.

"You're very welcome."

"I can't wait till the school starts," said Shirley.

After all was said, it was time to leave. Saying another round of thanks for everyone who had come to meet them, Juliet and Shirley went out.

"Do you need any help?" called out the principal at the doorway.

"No, thank you!" said Juliet. "I appreciate it."

Starting the engine, Juliet asked, "What do you think of the school?"

"This is a nice place and the principal is very caring. He is so nice. He even fixed the desk so it won't be too high for me!" Commented Shirley, watching cars pass by on the road through her window.

"He seems very nice. He seems that he cares for your well-being." Juliet reiterated. They both agreed that this year looked promising. A good principal was vital to each student's experience in school, especially to those students who needed special attention, such as Shirley. A good person would make so much importance to others. People's happiness depended upon those who led people in societies, setting good examples and establishing trust with others.

Chapter Sixty-Six

"The bus still has not come," Juliet said into the receiver. They had been waiting for Shirley's school bus on the first day of school. They began waiting by the door half an hour ago.

Shirley looked at her schedule, noting it was already second period. Shirley had typed up her schedule and printed several copies of it. She was to give one to her aide, one to put in her binder, and one to hold in her hands. She was fully prepared. Her bag that hung at the back of her wheelchair had several folders, notebooks, and other school supplies. As usual, Shirley held a small bag that contained pens, white out, erasers, a mini stapler, and anything else that would be helpful in times of need. Many students in school had borrowed her stuff. Whenever they needed something, they always knew they would find it in Shirley's bag. But the borrowing had gotten out of hand. People began to use her tissue without asking. All in all, some became rude and ungrateful. But not a single word of complaint escaped her lips. She graciously lent anything to her fellow classmates. She knew if without a pencil, someone could not take a test. She did not like seeing anyone unable to complete something just because they did not have the necessary material.

"I wish I have the van now, but we won't have to wait long. It should be delivered soon," said Juliet.

"The bus is here!" Shirley called to Juliet, who was just going to make another call to the bus station in school.

"Finally!" hissed Juliet, opening the door for Shirley.

Since the threshold on the main door was raised, Shirley had to drive over it carefully. But she had to face another bump at the driveway, where a level of a few inches was present. Fortunately, there was a space where the wheelchair could go down at a small slope.

"Why are you so late?" Juliet asked the bus driver.

"I had to get another student to another school," he answered.

The ramp unfolded itself and slowly made its way to the ground. Shirley drove herself onto the ramp and it lifted her upward. She was to sit at the back of the bus, where straps for the wheelchair were located.

After Shirley was strapped in and before the doors were closed, mother and daughter waved. But they were not waving goodbye. Juliet was going to follow the bus to school, so she could meet Shirley's new aide. She was grateful for having a nice principal; it was because of his kind nature, she knew, that she could go to school and meet the aide. The engine started, and Shirley was off to school.

Shirley suddenly nearly jumped off her seat. Although her wheelchair was leveled with the ground, her heart was doing summersaults. Then the rear end of the bus jumped again, sending her heart off a few beats. She knew what was causing the sudden jumps. It was the speed bumps. Getting in and out the condo, they had to pass three speed bumps on each way. And the driver went by the bumps quickly. Each time, Shirley's joints got hurt from the great vibration. The rear of the bus was jumpier than the front, thus it would be better if she sat in the front. But the straps were located only at the back.

Shirley was still shaking as the bus pulled up to the back entrance, where the principal was waiting. The bus ride had been an atrocious experience. The bumping continued even without going over the speed bumps. It was simply too jumpy at the back.

Greeting Mr. Caufield, Shirley got off the bus. He opened the door for her. "How are you this morning?" asked Mr. Caufield.

"I'm fine, thanks," replied Shirley, "and you? The bus was very late."

Juliet came out from her car and together, they went inside the building. They first went to the main office where

Shirley's aide was waiting.

"This is Lorna," the principal introduced the woman to Shirley, who quickly flashed her aide a smile, but it was not returned. "Ready for class?" inquired Mr. Caufield.

"I sure am."

Seeing that all was fine, Juliet thanked Mr. Caufield and left.

Shirley turned to Lorna. "This is a copy of my schedule," Shirley told her, handing a sheet to her.

"Oh, I got a copy already, but this is much better!" The schedule that Shirley typed out was in a larger and clearer print than the original copy, which had print in the size of ants.

"It is already third period," said Shirley.

"Well, let's find the room then."

As she passed her first period class, her teacher waved to her from inside with a smile. "See you tomorrow, Ms. Cheng," he said. Shirley nodded happily.

Looking at the room number, Shirley found her third period class. Her math teacher greeted her with a friendly smile, opening the door. Shirley instantly liked the teacher. As always, Shirley was greeted with thirty or so pairs of eyes when she entered the classroom.

She made her way to her desk at the front. The aide situated her in, and took out a notebook labeled for math. Shirley had labeled all her notebooks and folders for each class several days ago.

The first day was like any other first day. The entire day was spent listening to teachers' instructions. Shirley collected a pile of rules and regulations for each class. She read each paper over carefully. "Do not talk in classes, arrive here before the final bell rings," and so forth. It was all the same for each class.

With sighs of relief escaping from students lips, they rushed out of the school as the dismissal bell rang in the afternoon. Shirley drove down the hall to meet her bus. On the way, she was stopped by the principal. "How was the day?"

"I love it here!" Shirley told him. "Thank you very much!" Assured that everything went well with Shirley, Mr. Caufield left. Shirley boarded the bus and set out. Juliet would surely be glad to hear of how well Shirley's day went. She prepared for the bumpy ride home.

Juliet, with an anxious look upon her face, inquired, "How did the day go?" She was soon relieved to hear that it went well. The two went in, where they continued their conversation.

"But the driver drives quite fast over the bumps," finished Shirley.

"I'll talk to him about it tomorrow morning."

The bus was still late the next morning, but not as late as the first time. "Hi, Bob," greeted Shirley.

"Could you please go slower over the bumps? It is too bumpy for Shirley and it really hurts her joints. She has severe arthritis," requested Juliet.

"I didn't go too fast."

"But will you go slower?"

Bob grew agitated at her request. He shook his head, getting Juliet irritated. She continued persistently until he held up his hands.

"I'll go slower, but I was going slow already."

But Shirley soon found out that it was just as bumpy as the day before.

Juliet would not let it continue further. She called the bus station and asked them to talk to Bob about it since she was unsuccessful. After doing so, the rides became less bumpy and Shirley got less hurt.

"Now, I have to do something about the bump at the driveway," Juliet said to herself after Shirley had gone to school one day. She called the building manager, but they would not level it out by putting a small amount of cement. She next spoke to Bernice, her neighbor, a board member of the complex, but she was told that they would not have it leveled because the water would easily get inside the building. Juliet thought it was all gibberish. "I just need it to be leveled only a tiny bit—put a bit of cement so that my daughter can get up and down easier." But no amount of begging could help her. She would continue to search for a solution. She wished that she could get some help from anyone.

Chapter Sixty-Seven

"How do I look?" inquired Juliet on one early October morning, standing before Shirley, who was dressed for another school day.

"Wow, Mom, you look beautiful!" gushed Shirley. "That dress is lovely; it's my favorite." Shirley admired the angelic lady before her. She felt special for having a woman who was beautiful both inside and out as her mother. Juliet looked in the mirror for the fifth time that morning. The floral-designed dress had stylish sleeves, making them appear as almost puffed at the top, and the style of the dress showed off her curves.

Juliet giggled, "Thanks." She glanced at her watch. "Bob should be here in a bit. And when you get on the bus, it will be time for me to head off also."

"How do *I* look?"

"You look beautiful as always, pearl!"

"Let me know how it goes at the meeting. It's at the district's office, right?"

"I will. Yes. I hate meetings, but I have to do what I must do."

"Let's go now; Bob has just arrived," announced Shirley. They made their way out the door and Shirley drove slowly down the raised driveway.

"I must get the step leveled out," declared Juliet. "But they won't listen to me. Have a nice day." They waved goodbye to each other and the bus drove away a few minutes later. Juliet knew the time was almost up for her to go. She got the car keys out of her jacket's left pocket, inserted a key in the lock, and swung the car door open.

Less than five minutes later, Juliet arrived at the entrance of the office. She went inside the building and announced her arrival. In the lobby, she waited for the meeting to start. She saw Mr. Caufield coming out of a room. He walked toward her. "Mr. Caufield, I really appreciate that you came here for the meeting." At school a week ago, she had asked him if he had heard of the meeting. He had not known about it. He had asked if she would like him to attend, to which she had nodded.

"Don't worry; I'm here. I brought along my people: Mrs. Nelson and Mrs. Trish," he stated.

Juliet went inside the meeting room. Several people were already seated at the table. She shook everyone's hand.

Within a few minutes, the meeting started. A variety of topics was discussed regarding Shirley's schooling. "For anything in the future concerning Shirley, the first person you should talk to is Mrs. Cheng," Mr. Caufield said to Mrs. Costin. Juliet was grateful for having someone on her side. It was the first time that it had ever happened. She knew that with a good person like Mr. Caufield as the principal, there would not be a single problem with other officials they had to deal with. And if any problems rose, she knew it would be resolved easily and simply by a single command made by him.

After a span of thirty minutes, the meeting drew to a close. The only thing, it seemed to Juliet, that the meeting had helped was that everyone had learned that Mr. Caufield was standing on Juliet's side, so no one would treat Juliet and Shirley as poorly as before.

Juliet left the building feeling good. Even though the meeting was mostly unimportant, it would change the attitude of everyone.

Juliet spent the rest of the day doing chores and paying bills until it would almost be time for Shirley to get home. Humming a tune to an oldies song, she swept the kitchen floor. With that done, she moved over to where the radio sat and turned it on. Music of the 1950s floated throughout the room. She and Shirley both loved oldies; they had the same taste in nearly everything in life, ranging from music and television shows to furniture and art. Juliet had introduced Shirley to many esteemed world literatures, ranging from Stendhal's *The Red and the Black* to tales from *Arabian Nights*. During the old days in China, Juliet cherished the moments when she could relax with a book in hand. She missed those days where she had time to read. She simply had no time anymore after she had Shirley. It was work for twenty-four hours a day, seven days a week. But she did not mind. Her daughter was the biggest gift that had ever been bestowed upon her. Just thinking about Shirley brought a smile upon her features as she dusted the computer.

The current school year was refreshing, without any difficulties. And if any rose, Juliet had someone to resolve it. Shirley changed her schedule, so she would not be too tired to stay in school for an entire day. She dropped two periods, one of which was the study hall. Now, she started school on third period.

As her thoughts were on Shirley, Shirley's concentration was on what her English teacher was announcing to the class. The teacher, Ms. McCaffrey, told the class of a Halloween short story contest put by the *Poughkeepsie Journal*. Upon hearing it, Shirley's eyes lit up with anticipation. She was for certain going to enter.

"And whoever wins will receive five bonus points on the test," Ms. McCaffrey said further. They were going to have a unit test on the book they recently finished. Shirley would have no problem with the test. She was confident like always; sometimes overconfident.

Shirley left the classroom with an air of excitement. She was in deep cogitation, no doubt thinking about the contest, going by the expression painted on her face. She told her mother the news as soon as she returned to the condo.

That night, lying in bed, trying to go to sleep, the story for the contest rapidly entered her mind with full force. She knew what she was going to write, and she did not spend any time brainstorming; it simply came like a lightning bolt in a storm.

The first thing she typed on her computer the next day was the story. Only after less than ten minutes, the story was complete before her eyes. She excitedly printed it out and showed it to her mother. Then Shirley returned to her office to begin other things. Her homework had been completed. She had signed onto America Online since she had first gotten the computer. She loved writing e-mails to her friends from school. But most of her friends were people she met over the Internet. She was unable to add more buddies to her Buddy List, for it had reached its maximum number: one hundred.

Soon afterward, Juliet rushed into Shirley's office with a look of sheer amazement painted on her countenance.

"I can't believe it. Your story is wonderful!" exclaimed Juliet. Shirley was touched by happiness that moment. "You will definitely win the contest. It is beautiful. I was on the edge of my seat when I was getting to the end. I truly love it!" Juliet showered Shirley with more compliments before she went away to finish her uncompleted mission.

Juliet was still trying to get the driveway leveled. She had contacted Taconic Resource several times, but they could not help, either. They had sent a man over to the condo to check out the problem. He had written a letter to the building manager. And that was the end. They could not help further. The letter did not bring any resolution.

Other than the driveway, she had noticed something odd about the condo. Ever since they had moved in, she noticed the ceiling above the shower place was sagging. She was puzzled, but did not ask anyone about it.

The next day, as Juliet was at home doing chores, Shirley was asking Ms. McCaffrey to correct any grammar errors that she might have made on her story. After the editing, with a few corrections, the entry was submitted to the contest. Now the waiting period had begun.

At the same time, Juliet spoke to Mr. Caufield about the situation at the bathroom. "Shirley's really hurting with the lift. Can you have them carry her instead?"

"I'll look into that. I think they can carry her," he answered.

Shortly, a nurse began to come to school each day so she could do a two-man lift of Shirley with Lorna. Shirley was greatly benefited. She had to suffer no longer with the painful process of lifting and it had cut down the time by more than half.

Juliet's job did not stop just there. She had contacted a company that installed electronic wall lifts and she requested a lift be installed at the condo. She would continue to carry Shirley, but it would be available in case she ever needed to use it. Jerry, the installer from the company, went to the condo for an evaluation to see how he could install the lift. He had also tried different seats for Shirley to see which one was the most comfortable. After trying about half a dozen of the seats, Shirley at last had found a comfortable one that did not hurt her legs and hips. A lift therefore was installed in the bedroom.

Following the installation, Juliet informed the school of the seating. She soon received a call from Shauna, asking to take a look to see how the lift worked. Hence, an appointment was made and Shauna arrived at the condo on the appointed day.

"This is really neat," commented Shauna once she saw how it worked. Juliet pushed a button and the lift rose. Then she pushed the second button, lowering the lift. "And this seating is fine for you?"

"Yes, it is the best for me," answered Shirley. They could clearly tell that the seating was perfect to use at the school in conjunction with the lift. Both of the lifts had the same design of hooks, so the seating would be able to be hooked properly on the school's lift.

***

Halloween arrived in the valley. Shirley had planned

to dress up, but the students were not allowed to. Shirley had thought of the story contest. "It should be in the newspaper soon, if not today," she said to herself. But no one mentioned it. "It might be tomorrow."

On the bus going home, Shirley asked to see the newspaper that the driver was reading.

"Did I win the contest?" Shirley asked after she had seen glimpses of the short stories.

"I did not see your name," the driver answered. The driver, Katrina, had become Shirley's new driver when Bob had to change a bus to drive. Now, she had two women, instead: Katrina was to drive the bus, while the other, Prunella, was to strap her wheelchair in.

Katrina handed the newspaper to Shirley. Shirley flipped through the pages until she got to her grade level. "Oh my, I won!" Shirley announced. Her eyes read through her winning entry. It, *Mary Miller, the elusive lady*, was awarded Honorable Mention. She wrinkled her nose as she read the first-place story. She did not like it, but she was not to judge. Her eyes found the judge's comments. She was perplexed once she finished reading the comments: "Shirley Cheng's lyrical and evocative 'Mary Miller, the elusive lady' probably has more literary values than Harry's piece, but it doesn't have cheeseburgers. It's not too early for Ms. Cheng to learn that if you want to be a classy artist, you can't expect to fare as well in the market place." What did that mean? Was it saying that fine, lyrical works could not get top in the societies? It appeared to be so.

The next day, Lorna remarked that Shirley should have been the first-place winner; her story was much better. "I am going to write to the judge," she lastly stated. Ms. McCaffrey also agreed with Shirley's aide. They all loved her story.

Earlier that day, her Earth science teacher had read it to the entire class before the day's lesson. Shirley received loud claps from her peers. And during lunch, her social studies teacher had asked for her autograph.

"Sign here." He pointed at a spot on the newspaper. Shirley felt famous already, and it was definitely lasting more than just fifteen minutes. And two days later, her English teacher read her story on the loudspeaker, so the entire school heard it.

Sadly, Shirley's problem-free days in school ended when Lorna was fired. She had come to a school dance uninvited, bringing her daughter and her daughter's cousin. As a result, she had broken the school rules. With Lorna gone, the privilege of being carried in the bathroom had also ended. But Shirley was not too much dismayed. She was going to use the comfortable seating that she had at home.

Shirley soon received an aide from another home care agency other than Bountiful Care. But it did not work out with the aide. She did not listen to what Shirley had asked her to do.

"The woman won't do many things for Shirley that were all necessities," Juliet told Mr. Caufield. "Shirley really can't work with her."

"Well, then you can change her!" he said.

Shirley received another aide, but the woman was a living mess. She always dressed in a black mini skirt under a T-shirt. She carried her lunch tray to the main office, eating the entire way, causing not a pleasant sight. "Her handwriting is atrocious," said Shirley whenever she read the notes that her aide had copied.

But worse yet, she had given her cold to Shirley. During that time, it happened to be the day before Shirley's birthday.

"So, what's new with you, Shirley?" asked a friend of hers, Sarah.

"Actually, tomorrow is my birthday."

"Tomorrow is your birthday and you didn't tell me earlier? How old will you be?"

"I'll turn fifteen."

"Wow, you'll be a big girl!"

Shirley nodded. She was excited about coming to

school on her birthday. She knew what she was going to wear.

Her fairy-tale dream vanished the following morning on her big day. "I'm very nauseated," whispered Shirley weakly, pressing her lips together firmly. She felt like vomiting.

"You shouldn't go to school today. How can you go like this? Are you crazy?" scolded the much-worried Juliet.

"I have to go. I don't want to miss school. I can make it."

Defeated, Juliet dressed her up in her floral dress and put a pink ribbon in her hair. As she pushed Shirley out of the bedroom door, Shirley nearly vomited. "Be sensible! You can't go like this. Do you want to end up in the emergency room again? Your cold is developing into pneumonia."

Feeling utterly hopeless, Shirley faintly nodded. She did not have enough energy to whisper a reply.

"The driver is here. I'll let her know you can't go." Juliet went out the door, but the driver was just coming in, with balloons and a present in hand. "I'm so sorry, Kelly, but Shirley is very sick. She is all dressed up, but she knows she can't go at the last minute." Then she showed Kelly in the condo to see Shirley.

Kelly's eyes shone with sympathy. "I'm very sorry about it, Shirley. I bought these. I hope you have a nice birthday. Get some rest."

Shirley, with a small smile, nodded in reply. She really liked Kelly, who became her new driver recently. "Thank you," she managed to whisper.

After Kelly left, Juliet carried Shirley back to bed and changed her into her nighttime attire.

"You need to sleep. You need a lot of bedrest with pneumonia."

Shirley felt saddened by the whole situation. She had been looking forward to going to school on her fifteenth birthday. But she knew she was too ill. She drifted off into a feverish sleep.

When she awoke, she felt better. Her nausea had subsided, but she still felt sick in her stomach. "I'd like to sit in the living room," requested Shirley.

"I see that you're feeling better." Juliet got her into the living room. Then with a secret smile, she stood in front of her.

"Mom, what is it?" Her mother was hiding something from her.

"I have something for you!"

"What? What?"

Juliet slowly took out her right hand. Shirley's eyes flew wide open at the sight her eyes beheld. Juliet's hand held a beautifully wrapped gift box with floral designs on an indigo background. On the top of the box was an artificial rose in Shirley's favorite color combination for flowers: pink trim on yellow petals. Juliet giggled. She was glad Shirley liked the box.

"It is my favorite colors on flowers! How did you know?"

"It is? I didn't know. It is perfect then. Open it."

Shirley, ever so gently, but excitedly, tore off the wrapping. She found a velvet jewelry box. Shirley grew more excited. She slowly opened the lid of the case. There, upon the blue velvet, held a beautiful ring. "Oh my! This is my favorite design of all!" The ring was in the shape of a flower, with the sparkling white petals of diamonds surrounding the heart of the flower, a rich sapphire.

"I'm so happy you like it!"

"I *love* it! I love sapphires!"

"The saleswoman told me that everything's genuine, including the gold. She said that Princess Diana has one just like it but a bit larger. I think I have seen it, too."

***

Since Shirley's birthday was on a Friday, she had the

weekend for rest. She returned to school on Monday. Her fortune was with her this time. Luck finally met her when Shirley was assigned a new aide by the name of Marilyn. At first, Shirley was concerned of how Marilyn would treat her. She, as with Lorna, did not return Shirley's smile on the first day. And Shirley felt that Marilyn's eyes were not kind. Dismissing her thoughts, she hoped for the best.

As days passed, she learned that Marilyn did her job for Shirley with care and diligence. She dressed Shirley with gentleness, copied down the class notes with accuracy, and got her stuff routinely without being reminded. Shirley, for one, was thrilled with her aide.

"Let's go," said Shirley, glancing at the wall clock in her social studies class. She gave a low sigh. *Too bad the schedule is not perfect*, thought Shirley. Each day, Shirley had to use half of her social studies class time to go to the bathroom, thus she had to miss half of the lesson. Because of the unfortunate situation, Shirley's grades in social studies were quite low compared to her other classes. She had received a seventy-four for the first marking period, thus she was not eligible to be listed on the honor roll for that period since it required a grade no lower than an eighty for each class. But Shirley tried her hardest at bringing up her grades. She had borrowed the missed notes from classmates, but the job was often made difficult, with some students giving Shirley problems in the process; they either refused, or let Shirley wait and follow them around during lunchtime. With her effort, she had managed to bring her social studies grades up to eighties, then later nineties. Seeing her name on the honor roll always lit up her eyes for each marking period. She was not a person who was easily let down and was one who would never give up.

Chapter Sixty-Eight

"Dress up as a Hawaiian tomorrow and you'll get an extra point on the test," Shirley's social studies teacher, Mr. Mellis, told the class the previous day before April Fool's Day. He was a person who always managed to have fun in classes. Some days, Shirley could not help but roll her eyes when he was simply being ridiculous with his jokes and teasing. But above all, he was a great target for a trick on April Fool's Day.

Shirley's eyes gleamed. She already had her trick planned out. But she was somewhat hesitant about going for it, for she did not wish to get into trouble. *They should understand*, thought Shirley, *it is the only chance I got*.

With an innocent, angelic look upon her face, a halo above her head, and a devilish plan in her head, she greeted Mr. Mellis before the class started the next day. She had worn a colorful lei, that she had made, along with a bracelet with the same fabric and design. "So, Shirley, you got the point," he said. Shirley nodded and smiled in reply.

Halfway into the class, it was time for Shirley to go to the ladies room. After she finished, she came out of the bathroom and saw him. He was passing the main office. Mustering a serious look, she went up to him.

"Mr. Mellis, I just passed Mr. Caufield and he wants to see you."

Without even a glance toward her, he quickly went into the main office with a worried look.

Nearly giggling aloud, Shirley quickly escaped the crime scene and drove to the cafeteria and to her table. But the fun would not end there. She had another victim.

With the same serious look on her face, she tapped on the shoulder of her friend, Phil. "Phil, Mr. Caufield wants to see you."

"Why?" he asked, incredulously. "What for?"

"I really don't know," she replied, frowning. As she opened her mouth to add to those words, Mr. Mellis went over to her table, a serious look on his face.

"Shirley, Mr. Caufield wants to see you for what you just did. He wants to see you now."

"Uh-oh," said Phil, glancing at Shirley. Shirley glanced back.

"Let's go," she told her friend. Together, they headed to the main office. On her way, she hoped that she did not get into trouble. She knew that it might be a trick, but she prepared herself for the punishment in case.

"Wait a minute," said Phil when they were getting closer to the main office, "is this a trick?"

Darn, thought Shirley, wincing. "Well, please don't get upset. It is!"

Phil laughed, "Ha, that is a good one. I really fell for it."

But you were quick in coming to the realization that it was a trick, thought Shirley.

They went into the main office.

"Mr. Caufield wishes to see me?" asked Shirley.

"Yes, he'll be with you in just a bit," answered the secretary, who had always been courteous to her and Juliet.

A few minutes later, a smiling principal walked out of his office and posed himself by the desk. "That was a fine trick you played on Mr. Mellis, Shirley!"

"So, I'm not in trouble?" asked Shirley, smiling.

"No."

It was a trick. She had somewhat fallen for it. But she had fun that time.

When they returned, Shirley was greeted with a laughing social studies teacher. "Got you! Ha, Mr. Caufield wants to see you!"

"No, you copied me," said Shirley with a shake of her head.

"You should have seen the look on your face!" he

continued. Shirley rolled her eyes. She knew that he would tell the class of what had happened. Sure enough, he told them of the tricks on both sides.

"You should've seen the look on your face," said Shirley, giggling.

But it was soon time to be serious as the lessons were started. She smiled to herself. She was having a blast in school this year. Changing an aide was an extremely easy task; it required only one word from her and Juliet. Mr. Caufield, she thought, was such an understanding and caring person. She wished that all people were like him. He was easy to talk to, and he was a good listener. He truly cared for his students. He was a leader that all communities should have.

***

Later into the school year in spring, students were required to take a New York State essay test, along with writing a business letter. The English teachers had prepared all the students for the exams. Shirley took the test in the guidance office, and finished it up in the cafeteria when it was vacant. Mr. Caufield had turned on the heat in the cafeteria; he wanted to make sure that the large room was warm enough for Shirley.

"Is this your handwriting?" The principal inquired when he saw her essay.

"Yes."

"Amazing. It is beautiful!" He was with so much awe. "*I* can't write like this!"

"Thank you very much!" She grinned gleefully. She had received numerous compliments for her handwriting; she got used to them.

Around the same time, she had taken another New York State Reading Comprehension Test. She found it quite easy. Her English, she was certain, had improved a great deal in the past two years.

Before the end of the school year, the students were to meet their guidance counselor to set up their schedules for next year when they would enter high school. All students were excited at the thought of being freshmen. Shirley was more so, with her happiness shining in her eyes. Juliet and Shirley went to see her counselor as appointed.

"You can take Intro to Physical Science," her counselor said.

"But how about biology?" Shirley pointed out. She was eligible to take biology class. It was for anyone who did well in science in eighth grade. Not only were Shirley's grades in Earth science fine, but also were the highest in her class. The counselor finally consented.

"I want to take Honors English," Shirley told her. She was also a straight A student in English. But Shirley would take Regents global studies, for her average in social studies was in the eighties.

"How about Math Course II, instead of Course I?" Shirley inquired. The counselor shook her head. She could not skip one grade of math.

"And I have your scores on your tests," announced Mrs. Nelson, fingering through some files. She handed Shirley a sheet to look over. "You received one hundred on the essay test." Shirley simply nodded; she was not that surprised for scoring another one hundred on a state essay test. She read another score that was screaming for her attention.

"I got seventy-one questions correct out of seventy-seven questions on the Reading Comprehension Test!" exclaimed Shirley to herself. She was with a smile when she waved goodbye to the counselor.

"So, I'll see you later then when you get home," said Juliet, giving Shirley a kiss on her cheek. When her mother left the building, Shirley turned to Marilyn to get ready for her next class. Her eyes lit up as another blissful thought entered her mind.

"I know what you're thinking of," said Marilyn,

reading her mind.

Shirley dramatically clasped her hands in her happiness. "Yes!" she squealed.

"You sound like a little bird," laughed Marilyn. Shirley rolled her eyes. "So, you got the dress ready?"

"Yes!" Shirley had carefully prepared for the big day: the semi-formal dance for eighth graders.

The highlight of the school arrived after a long wait for Shirley. She had been looking forward to it since the first day she had heard of the dance. Juliet already had her dress ready: a navy-blue dress with several layers.

"I'll see you at the dance!" Shirley declared to her friends before she left lunch that day on the special occasion. She was looking forward to it. It would be her second dance that she had ever attended. The first one was in seventh grade, but it was too boring to be memorable. What she could remember and thought of it as eventful was that her friends, Erin and Adam had spent the time with her. She did not dance that night; she only watched others dance. And she believed that she was not going to dance this time, either. Her good friends, Lynn and Phil, were going there. The thought excited her more.

Juliet asked Brian, the son of her mother's current housekeeper, to come to put Shirley's power wheelchair in Juliet's trunk so Shirley could use the chair at the dance instead of a manual wheelchair. Brian had been the one who had helped Juliet move several times, so he was known for his strength. Lifting the power wheelchair required great energy, for it weighed a few hundred pounds. The sweating Brian finally got the chair inside the trunk after he had taken out the batteries, for they were the things that added most weight. Thus, they were ready to go.

Shirley's face glowed brighter than her shiny dress.

When they arrived at the school, Brian took out the wheelchair and put the batteries back in. Juliet turned on the wheelchair to see if everything worked fine. To their utmost dismay, especially Shirley's, the wheelchair did not move.

Brian checked the batteries and said that he had put them in correctly. The principal, who was always there when one needed his help, came out and provided a manual wheelchair from the nurse's office. It was better than nothing. But all the energy was wasted. And how would they get the wheelchair fixed? The problem was soon forgotten when Shirley saw her friends.

Phil became the chauffeur for the night, wheeling Shirley everywhere on the dance floor and to where they were taking the pictures. Not only was he a good aide, but also a fine dancer. Shirley was so glad she decided to come to the dance. It was one of the happiest moments in her life when she danced to the rhythm of the music.

But like all moments, it could not last forever. The dance ended, and Shirley returned home. The power wheelchair was not working. And it still did not work several days later.

"Mom, I really think that Brian had put the batteries in incorrectly," said Shirley.

"But he said he did put them in correctly," replied Juliet. She called up a technician from the place where they got the wheelchair. Following the call, a technician showed up.

"The batteries are not put in right," supplied the man.

"I was correct!" Shirley giggled, relieved that it was not a major problem.

***

"I have made an appointment for you to see an allergies doctor," said Juliet one day. "Your sneezing is growing out of hand. You have been so uncomfortable with it."

"Allergies? I can't believe that one incident could cause a lifetime of sneezing for me! I sneeze all year round. I can't believe that I can have allergies; I never ever had them before."

"I know. But I have nowhere to take you. This is very strange—that the spray could cause such a horrible condition for you. And you've been sneezing nonstop all these years. I hope that the doctor can do something for you."

When the day for the appointment arrived, Juliet brought Shirley to see the doctor. He performed a skin test on her to find out to which allergen she was allergic.

"She is allergic to dust mites and tree pollen," he announced after the test result came out.

"Tree pollen? And dust mites?" So she truly did have allergies! He prescribed some medication to treat the condition.

After taking a few doses of the medication, Claritin, Shirley was experiencing problems breathing, so she had to stop taking it. Besides, it was not providing any help. She still continued to sneeze.

Trying to think of anything to lessen her sneezing problem, Juliet bought a Kirby vacuum cleaner. A man from the company had come over and demonstrated how to use it and explained it would suck in all the dust mites. After showing it to her, he gave the same vacuum cleaner to her. When he left, Juliet saw it was an old one. It broke the following day and she had to call the company to fix it.

Besides getting the Kirby, Juliet bought pillow cases and bed sheets to prevent dust mites. Despite all her effort, Shirley's sneezing was still not cured.

Juliet gave a loud sigh. It appeared as though Shirley would be known as Sneezy for a long time to come. She looked at her daughter sadly. Another thing that was making her sad other than Shirley's sneezing problem was her rashes. Shirley's face was being invaded with more of the rashes, resulting in itchiness. Worse of all, Shirley's once-fair skin now had the ugly rashes, but Shirley was still beautiful. But she could be so much more beautiful without the rashes. The pinworms would not stop attacking her skin. Once in a while, a few pinworms would be visible on Shirley's feces. The pinworms simply clung to existence stubbornly in her body. Juliet put cream on her face to ease the redness. But she soon learned that the cream could cause wrinkles, so she had to stop administering it on her face. But fortunately, there were "good days" when the rashes would not be visible.

"So, you bought some boxes of tissue?" asked Shirley.

"Yes, you'll have a new box to take to school tomorrow." Shirley had already used up dozens upon dozens of boxes of tissue. Some days, she had used up over an entire box of tissue in a single day. Not only was the condition a great discomfort, but also an inconvenience. Bringing a box of tissue to anywhere she went was a nuisance. Above all, she often encountered the problem of having nowhere to discard her dirty tissue.

So, with a new box of tissue in the color of blue, Shirley left for school. She soon learned of an upcoming event. They announced that an Honors Assembly would be held in early June. Shirley inquired, "What is the assembly for?"

"Some students will receive awards for achieving high grades," supplied her Earth science teacher. The Honors Assembly was scheduled in the morning right after school started. It was coming up in a couple of weeks. Marilyn was convinced that Shirley would receive at least one award. Her only answer was always a roll of eyes from Shirley.

"I am positive you're going to get an award."

"I'll bet that I am not going to get an award," Shirley declared. "We'll bet one penny," Shirley burst out laughing. Marilyn joined in.

"We're on," agreed Marilyn.

"I'm going to wear the same dress I wore to the dance." She had everything planned out. She was going to arrive to school at the regular hour, not the usual time she came to school. Everything had been taken care of by Mr. Caufield.

***

Shirley, her hands folded on her lap, sat attentively in the front row as the students played the instruments. It was the morning of the Honors Assembly, and they were starting the assembly with students playing instruments. At length, the time that Shirley was waiting for had arrived—the announcement of the students who would receive awards for their outstanding academic performance. Awards for English, foreign languages, and math were called out. Students received loud applause as they received their awards.

Then it was time to hand out the Earth science award. The principal announced the name, "and the person with the highest grade in General Earth Science is Shirley Cheng!"

Shirley's eyes flew wide open. She was cheered on as she drove herself to receive her framed award. She was too happy for words. Marilyn gave one of her I-told-you-so looks. Shirley had lost the bet.

After the Honors Assembly, the yearbooks were handed out to the students. With her yearbook in hand, she went around and asked her teachers and friends to sign it. Her Earth science teacher had written words of congratulations for receiving the award. She knew that he had played an important part in her achievement. He was an excellent teacher, who had taught his class remarkably well in spite of the fact that it was his very first year of teaching after graduating from college.

The next day, Shirley handed Marilyn a penny.

"I'm going to hang it up and frame it," stated Marilyn. Again, she was answered with laughter from Shirley. They always had so much fun together. Shirley felt really good this year, not just because of her academic successes, but of finally having a good aide to be with her and help her.

"Well, it's the end of the day again," Shirley said to herself, driving to the back entrance to wait for the school bus. She winced as she thought of her bus driver, Katrina. She no longer had Kelly for some unknown reason. They simply kept changing the drivers. Pamelia no longer worked for the bus station, so Katrina had to strap her in. She never strapped in her wheelchair properly and tight enough, thus her wheelchair shook from side to side when the bus made turns. Sometimes, Shirley's wheelchair had moved toward the aisle four or five inches, causing a scare for her. She had called out, but her cries were only answered with silence. Hence, each day, Shirley was apprehensive before boarding the bus, bracing herself for another amusement ride, though it was anything but amusing. "Here's my bus," Shirley muttered. Marilyn held the door open as Shirley wheeled out of the building and into the jaws of the yellow beast.

Chapter Sixty-Nine

To everyone's delight but to Shirley's utmost dismay, the school year was drawing to a close. A warm blanket of summer covered the land with its fulgent light. Shirley would keep in touch with her close friends via e-mail and telephone. She had collected everyone's e-mail addresses and telephone numbers. But it would mean that she was going to leave her teachers, whom she truly felt lucky for having.

At the last day of school, she gave all her teachers cards she had made; each had words of "goodbye" with tears running down each letter "O."

Meanwhile, Juliet was contacting the high school to arrange the necessary desks and rooms for Shirley. She made an appointment for the day they would meet Shirley's new principal and guidance counselor before another new school year.

During summer, those students who were enrolled into the Honors Program for English class were required to read two books from the list given by the school and write term papers about the books. The assignment would take considerable time, but it took Shirley less than a week to finish.

At the end of August, the day of the meeting arrived, and Juliet drove Shirley to the high school in her van. The high school was once the north campus of the two high schools in the district. Instead, the south campus became an elementary school, and a new section was added to the north campus. The high school would be having over 2,500 students that year. They were still constructing the new section as they arrived at the school. Shirley drove herself in, with Juliet following close behind. They went into the main office and told the lady of their appointment.

The principal, Mr. Broderick, a tall man with

eyeglasses, greeted them soon afterward. The meeting went underway in a room inside the main office. The guidance counselor, Mrs. Milton, smiled several times throughout the meeting. Shirley felt she again had good luck on her side. The school year appeared as though it would be a nice, promising experience. Shirley would still have Marilyn as her aide. She was happier with that thought in mind. She looked forward to the first day, especially when she was to start biology. She wondered if the teachers were as nice as the ones of previous year. She had been met with good luck, for throughout her entire schooling, most of her teachers were nice and caring.

The red circle marked on the calendar would receive an X as the school day inched closer. Juliet would bring her to school since she had unfortunate experiences with Katrina. Shirley would begin the school days on second period, for she would be unable to stand a long day. She was to take six classes, including French.

Just as in other years, Shirley received paper after paper of rules for each class on the first day of opening. Her first period was Honors English. The teacher seemed quite helpful; he provided a waste basket by Shirley's side since she frequently sneezed. And he had also taken the stumps off her table legs, so the table would be the correct height for her. She had graciously thanked him for each considerate act. Every teacher, Shirley noted, was nice.

One teacher stood out from them all: her biology teacher by the name of Mrs. Lalli. The first impression Shirley had of the teacher was that she was organized and an excellent teacher. Shirley had thought Mrs. Lalli looked like a college professor. And true to her thoughts, Mrs. Lalli turned out to be the nicest and best teacher Shirley had ever had. She taught the classes with utmost clarity with excellent examples, while cracking a few jokes along the way. All students liked her, thus making the class more enjoyable. But Shirley soon learned that both Ms. Zanker, her global studies teacher and Mrs. Jennings, her math teacher, were superb as well. Ms. Zanker had photocopied class notes for Shirley on her own initiative, so that Marilyn did not have to copy down any notes for the class. Mrs. Jennings was friendly, caring, and joked with everyone.

Days sped by, and Shirley grew tired because of the long day in school. Juliet thought that Shirley could drop one class for the year. Thus Shirley had French dropped after seeking consultation from her guidance counselor. She was to take French next year, and she would still receive a Regents diploma. Shirley was extremely relieved when she learned of it. Regents diploma required three credits of a foreign language.

"But it won't matter," Mrs. Milton had explained, "no one will know if you get a Regents diploma or not. Many colleges won't know. It is exactly as a regular diploma."

Shirley did not want to drop French, but her health would not permit her to take it. But she knew that it was not the most important thing. What was crucial was to do well in school and succeed in her academic goals.

In the high school, two honorable lists were posted on the walls; one was the principal's list for those students who had achieved an average of at least a ninety-five with no grades lower than an eighty-five, and the second was the honor roll for averages of at least an eighty-five. Being a person who always went for the top, Shirley's goal was to get on the principal's list. And it appeared that she was going to be on it, for her grades she had been receiving so far were mostly high nineties. She had received a ninety-seven for the Honors Summer Reading Program. She did her work well and quick. Because of her swiftness, she had completed an English research paper quicker than most of her classmates.

Using her spare time while others were doing their research, Shirley decided to show Juliet around the school building. "This is my math class and here is the east elevator." Shirley pointed at a small elevator. The school had two elevators, one in the west wing, which was the new section of the building, and one in the old part. Then Shirley brought Juliet back to where they had started—by the library.

"Shirley, we've been looking for you. Where have you been?" asked the security man, Mr. Martin.

"I was just showing my mother around, so that she knows where I am during the day if she ever needs to find me."

"You are not allowed to go around the school. You should stay with your class."

"I'm sorry." Shirley did not mean to cause any problem. It had taken her only a few minutes. While the conversation went on, her English teacher was present with a frown.

But the incident was soon forgotten. Shirley learned of a poetry contest that she could enter. She knew right away what she was going to write. As with all her writings, the poem, *The Colors of the Rainbow*, was completed in no time.

***

All appeared to be going smoothly for Shirley at the high school. But underneath the surface, she was starting to encounter problems. One issue was concerning the fire drills. Every time the fire drill sounded, everyone had to go out of the building, and that also meant Shirley. Fire drills were planned even when the weather was cold. Shirley froze when she got out without any warning beforehand. Shirley kept a jacket in her bag at all times, but it was not enough to keep her warm. She had no problems with the fire drill in eighth grade, for Mr. Caufield had given Shirley the permission to stay inside the building, but just to move to a location near an exit. She faced the same problem in sixth and seventh grade, and now she was facing it again. But it was much more serious than any other year, for when Shirley was upstairs when the alarms were sounded, no one was allowed to use the elevator, thus putting Shirley in difficult circumstances. The high school had told Shirley and Juliet that they would carry Shirley down the flight of stairs during the drills. And they would start with a practice.

But after all the time and energy had been spent on the matter, the school decided not to go forward with their plan after all, even though Juliet had reluctantly relented to it. Afterward, with much insistence from Juliet, Shirley was allowed to stay inside the building during the drills. The drills also had caused another problem as Shirley found out one day in October.

Shirley was driving herself to her next class while Marilyn walked beside her. Shirley was going at a leisurely pace, for she was not in a hurry to get to her class. She had extra minutes in hand. As the two were passing the main office, the heavy iron doors suddenly swung inward. Shirley gave a gasp. She quickly moved out of the closing doors' path just in time before she was made into a human sandwich. The fire drill had sounded. Whenever the alarm went off, all the iron doors in the building would automatically shut. Consequently, Shirley was in the middle of a pair of the doors when the alarm went off.

"That was such a close one! I almost got squashed!" exclaimed Shirley. Shirley could see that Marilyn, too, was greatly startled. Ever since, Shirley had been alert going through the doors.

Another problem that was rising in school was with Mrs. Milton, her guidance counselor. She never supplied Shirley with any information on her own initiative. Only after Shirley questioned her about something did she provide the information. Shirley had to find out everything on her own. Together, Juliet and Shirley wrote letters to the school, requesting a change in guidance counselor, but only received rejections from the principal.

"We don't change guidance counselors," he had told them.

The third problem Shirley was starting to face was with the English class. The first quarter ended and report cards were sent out. Shirley looked it over and was touched with dismay; all her grades were between ninety-five and ninety-nine, inclusive, except for her English class with a B. She was puzzled why her English teacher had been giving her seventies and low eighties on assignments on which Shirley knew that she had done well. She was dumfounded; she could not understand the reason for the low marks on her essays. She knew most of her essays were well-written. Above all, all the other essays she wrote for her global studies class received mostly nineties. The ninety-seven she got on her Summer's Reading Program assignment was one of the few assignments that earned above a ninety for her. She thought back to the earlier days. He had been correctly giving her the grades she had earned. But he had begun giving her low grades ever since that day Shirley was scolded for going around the building during her free time.

Shirley still did not get on the principal's list the second quarter, with the same grades as last time. Her biology was one hundred, along with her math average. She was doing so well in math because she was able to see what the teacher was writing on the chalkboard, as opposed to reading the notes after class, trying to figure out things by herself. Before, she had a different math classroom that had a green chalkboard. After noticing there was a black chalkboard in the next room, the entire math class was moved to the next room. "White chalk on black background is the best color contrast, therefore, I can see it," explained Shirley. Her eye doctor had agreed with her.

"But green boards are good for the eyes, so that's why we mostly have green chalkboards in classrooms, rather than black ones," said the principal. But he had ordered that her math class be switched to another room that had the black chalkboard after receiving a note from Shirley's eye doctor, stating that Shirley would greatly benefit from black chalkboards because of the high contrast.

"Oh, this is so much better. Now I can see what the teacher is writing and learn the material at the same time," said Shirley, "rather than figuring out what the equations mean after class ends."

One problem was solved and one problem sprang up. Shirley was experiencing problems with Marilyn, who had changed into a totally different person to the extent that Shirley could no longer recognize her. Marilyn did not do what she was told and began to hurt her while dressing. Sadly, Shirley had to change another aide, but the process might take some time.

In the meantime, once again, Shirley had entered the National Reflections Program in visual arts. She wondered if she would win for the third time in a row.

Another happy moment was blooming when Shirley celebrated her Sweet Sixteen with a few friends. It was a nice and more subdued party than the previous ones, for only three people came. She did not mind. She needed the peace and quiet. Her life had been filled with unfavorable moments. She wholeheartedly welcomed the peaceful moment with open arms.

Soon after her birthday, Shirley had a new aide. The woman, Meredith, treated her perfectly for the first three days, but the treatment became poor afterward. Meredith often missed copying down sections of class notes in classes because she read novels in class. Shirley then had to tap on her arm to get her attention. But since Shirley could not see the board, she often did not know where Meredith had missed the notes.

But Shirley had received a diversion from her current problems when she received her poetry contest award in the mail. Shirley received a merit certificate and her poem would be published in the anthology, *Celebrate! New York's Young Poets Speak Out*. Juliet proudly added the award to Shirley's collection of awards.

"I'll add this to your portfolio as well," declared Juliet on an afternoon when Shirley handed her yet another certificate of achievement. It was from the National Reflections Program. She had also received a blue T-shirt. They had no assembly this year, so Shirley simply fetched her awards from the guidance office. She could hardly wait till the next National Reflections Program. She loved entering into contests, and the idea of competing with others thrilled her.

Chapter Seventy

Shirley had pneumonia for another time during the second quarter when she was with Marilyn and subsequently had missed school for a few days. She insisted on going back to school after one day of rest. "You shouldn't return, yet. You'll relapse!" Juliet had insisted, but only wasted her breath in turn. Shirley, as always, was headstrong and refused to remain at home. She went to school while still on the medication. It was clear to everyone that Shirley never wished to miss a single day of school. It was made even clearer when one day, she had a horrid case of diarrhea. Juliet was distressed, and yet not surprised, when Shirley insisted on attending school.

"I have a test in math class today. I don't want to miss it. And no, I'll not make it up. I'm going. I can manage," said Shirley through spasms of pain that were spreading down to her two cold feet.

"If you need to go to the bathroom, don't be afraid of going. Let Meredith take you there. You can't hold it in." Juliet had many worries as she parked her van at the school. "Call me if you need anything."

"I will and don't worry about me. I can do it." Shirley's hands were sweating from the pain, but she ignored it as she greeted Meredith. Juliet informed Meredith of the situation.

"She shouldn't have come," said the aide.

"I know! But she won't listen."

Meredith, her head shaking, followed Shirley inside the school building. "What if you have an accident? You'll get embarrassed."

"I won't, Meredith." Shirley gritted her teeth.

The day slowly dragged on. Each hour seemed it had been added another one hundred minutes. Shirley yearned for the day to be over. She had made it through half of the day without any problem, except she was still in great pain. She held it all in. She did not even go when she urinated.

At last, it was lunch period, meaning she could rest for a period.

"You look like you're going to kill someone," remarked Meredith.

Shirley was hurt. Not only did Meredith not comfort her, but instead said those words. She did not reply to her comment. She simply sat there and began her homework for that night. She had only one more period left: math class. She glanced at her golden watch on her right wrist.

"Let's go up there now," suggested Shirley. It was a bit earlier than usual. She thought she might be able to finish the test before the class started. Her math teacher had a study hall that period.

"I don't feel well today. May I take the test now?" Shirley asked her kind math teacher after she rode the elevator up to get to her class. Shirley was going over to her desk when Meredith stopped her.

"You're just going to take the test and stay for a bit, so you don't need your desk. Here," Meredith said, pointing at a small desk next to Shirley, "you can use this."

Without a word, Shirley obediently twisted her body to the left and used the corner of the desk to do her test. It was a highly uncomfortable position, especially when her body was invaded with the abdominal pain. Shirley's hand wrote swiftly, but made not a single mistake with the math calculations. She had been receiving a perfect score on all of her work at the current quarter.

Just when the bell rang, indicating that the period had ended and that the last period of the day was to start in a few minutes, Shirley handed her teacher the completed test. She was free to go at last!

She flew from the classroom, into the elevator, then out the building in a flash. She would head straight to the bathroom once she got home. She had made it!

Chapter Seventy-One

In April, it was time for students to run for student government. Upon hearing the news, Shirley drove to the main office and got herself a packet of the rules for student government. Students were able to run for either a class government, meaning for their own grade levels or for student body, which meant for the entire school. Shirley was interested in running for a position in the student body. She carefully read over the entire packets several times. She chose to run for student body vice president. She wanted to be the president, but it stated that the student must have previous experience in student government, which she did not.

"I would have run for student government early this year if I had known about it!" she muttered to herself. "But that's not a problem; I can make up for the lost time. How much I would enjoy all the duties, my responsibilities! I could do so much. I will try my best."

She set out her plans right away. During her lunch period, she used only a few minutes to write the platform statement required for all candidates. She needed many signatures for her petition. Therefore, without another minute's delay, Shirley went all over her cafeteria, around tables and chairs, asking students to sign it. After she finished going through her cafeteria, she went to the adjoining one. Soon, she drove herself to the other side of the school toward the two larger cafeterias. She was unable to get to the center, so she stayed at the borders.

At that time, she had shared her decision with Mr. Martin, who had quickly become her friend earlier in the year. She found him to be a highly kindhearted person. She had also made friends with another biology teacher, who was happy for the good news and wished her well.

In biology the next day, she also got most of the students to sign the petition. Before the end of the day, Shirley had extra signatures. She was too excited for words. Even if she did not win the election, she would cherish the moment of campaigning as a vice president candidate of the student body. Without another minute's delay, she headed to the main office. Mentally kissing her application, platform statement, and petition for good luck, she dropped them into the box that was set on the countertop in the office. The next step was to wait for approval, and she would know if she received it only if she saw her name on a list that would be posted for all to see.

Every second felt like a minute as she waited, yet the wait was not long, for the list was posted within a few days. Upon noticing the list secured to the window outside the main office, she headed straight to it, with her eyes for only the list. Once there, she raised her head, leaned forward, and stretched her upper body. Was that her name? The list was situated too high above her. She asked her aide to make sure. "Yes!" was what she inwardly shouted when she received the desirable answer. She had made it. Her campaign had officially begun.

At home, she immediately got to work. She designed a flyer that she planned to distribute throughout the school. With the flyer in hand, she started her campaign. Meredith had made many copies of the flyers. During lunch period, Shirley went around all the four cafeterias until only a few flyers were left by her side.

"Everyone, vote for her!" Called a boy when he received a copy of the flyer. "She will make a difference to our school!" Many people wished Shirley well with the election. She already had many people on her side.

"This is good—it will give you a chance to be independent," commented Meredith.

Is independence all that matters? thought Shirley, bitterly. Was she not independent enough already? Someone had commented once that if Shirley was like others who had started school regularly, who knew where Shirley would end up—perhaps as the "president of the United States" or already a "graduate of Harvard University!" She was already being independent as best as she could. What more could they expect from her?

On the same day, the student government also had a meeting after school for all the candidates. Right on time, Shirley arrived at the designated room, smiling widely. Juliet waited outside as the meeting went on.

"Your daughter is so amazing; she is never without that smile of hers," a teacher commented to Juliet.

"Thank you. Yes, she's always happy."

"Mom, the meeting is over," Shirley told her, getting out of the room. "There will be an assembly a few days later," Shirley excitedly reported, "and an election afterward."

"That's wonderful." Juliet was gleeful alongside Shirley. "You're simply amazing."

The important moment was interrupted by a bomb threat one day when Shirley was in math class. Everyone got up with a start. They were all in a state of confusion, for the alarm went off unplanned. They knew it was not a practice fire drill, for the drills had been over since winter. Shirley rushed out the classroom. What was she to do?

Meredith and Shirley went out to the hallways, seeing if anyone was coming up to look for her. The school had said that during any emergencies, the security men and other officials would look for them. But no one was to be seen. Then they decided to get downstairs.

Moments later, Shirley found out that it was a bomb threat. "It's just someone copying what happened at Columbine High School," Shirley heard one say. The recent tragedy at Columbine High School had shattered many souls, those of the school and strangers alike. A shooting had broken out in a high school located in Littleton, Colorado. Fourteen students, including the two shooters, ages seventeen and eighteen, and one teacher were killed, while twenty-three others were wounded by bullets in the school shooting. The shooters turned their guns on themselves at the end of the rampage. *It was such an unfortunate thing that should have never happened. There should not be any access to guns in the world. Anyone could legally purchase guns for their own use. And guns could easily get in the hands of minors*, thought Shirley. *Well, I will try to make the school environment a safer place, if not change the systems.* She was just one girl out of the entire population of six billion people, but this girl wished to make a difference to the world.

***

The morning of the assembly arrived. Shirley had been waiting quite impatiently for the day. She dressed in her sparkling black dress for the event. Her eyes glowed brighter than her dress. Shirley had not realized the caliber of the assembly until that day arrived.

The entire freshman class was present in the auditorium. Shirley scanned the entire room. She sat upon the stage with her fellow candidates. The assembly was for ninth graders only, but Shirley was the only one who was running for a position in the student body government. Her opponent, a sophomore, was also there, seated to her right. Her opponent was the only candidate on the stage who was not a ninth grader. He had to be present because he was running against Shirley. Shirley was the second to last to speak, being her opponent the last. With her platform statement in hand, she waited till it was her turn.

When her turn arrived, she got in front of the stage with a microphone in her left hand. Shirley struggled to hold the heavy microphone, but she did not give in. "Good morning, my fellow students! How is everyone?" She happily began. Loud shouts of "great" came in reply mingled with cheers and claps.

With that, she continued, "My name is Shirley

Cheng, and I am running for vice president of the student body." She began reading from her paper. "I want to run for vice president of the student government because I have always been interested in helping guide people to making the right decisions, leading to the best directions in life. Of course, I make my share of mistakes, but I'm always striving to be my best and to do my best and to help others the same way. It just feels great to help out others and to be in a friendly, caring environment.

"I believe that the number one priority for our wonderful high school is to make it a safe place for the students, the teachers, and the staff. Schools should be one of the safest places to be. The tragedy at Littleton, Colorado should never have happened. We need to work together to prevent any kind of violence from happening in our school, or any school for that matter. We need to teach kids how to understand and express their anger in a proper way, instead of hurting others verbally or physically by getting violent." She glanced at the people below between each sentence.

"My second goal is for the school to be a fun and caring place. Fun is one of the major factors in education. And courtesy toward teachers and peers is extremely important. Students would participate more and be more aware of their environment. School is not only about education, but about meeting new friends and helping others. We have very good clubs and activities in our school, such as SHADES and Youth Against Racism that teach about people's cultures, customs, and beliefs, and how we can live in harmony with other people no matter what their backgrounds or beliefs might be."

Loud applause from the audience interrupted her. A smile danced across her features as she waited for them to quiet down. She resumed her speech. "It would definitely be the best situation if everyone, no matter who they are or where they come from or what they are like, could have a sense of security while attending school. And almost as important is to have fun while learning and to get to know each other better by having many activities and clubs to bring the kids together to have fun and to learn more about each other. This is the best way to grow closer and to make friends, and that is a very important part of growing up.

"This is what school is all about, a fun and safe educational place for everyone—staff, teachers, and students alike!"

Once more, she was interrupted by loud applause and shouts. The audience was going wild. Flashing a winning smile, she continued, "I'm looking forward to being the vice president and to helping bring the students and teachers and staff together in these ways so that the school can be like a caring community in which everyone has a part to play in making this school a place where we all want to be!

"This is what I'm going to be doing as my life's work. It would help me to be better at it if I can get started now."

Finally, she read the last part. "I have a great sense of humor, I get excellent grades, and I have overcome a terrible handicap, which is a sign of strong character and courage. I would like to serve in this way." She improvised a closing, "please make your decision wisely; vote for me!"

Just as the last word came from her smiling lips, the entire audience of several hundred stood up. Her eyes flew wide. She could not believe what she beheld; she was receiving a standing ovation! The whole audience went wild, and the applause lasted nearly half a minute. She turned around to go back to her place, and noticed that many candidates were not smiling.

With the assembly at its end and after the last candidate had spoken, Shirley went off the stage. On her way to class, she was stopped numerous times by people who had witnessed the speech.

"That was amazing! Congratulations!" One shouted.

"It almost made me cry!" Came another.

Compliment after compliment flew her way until she was overwhelmed. Feeling like a vice president already, Shirley drove into her class. Not only was she happy, but also thrilled and pleased. It was a day that could be engraved in her memory for a lifetime; a moment she would never erase.

The next day, the news had spread like wildfire, and the school talked about her speech and the standing ovation. It came from the lips of teachers who did not know her, and janitors and hall monitors. "It almost made me cry," commented Mr. Martin, shaking his head.

"I wish *I* could get a standing ovation. That was a very powerful speech," Ms. Zanker had stated. But not a single word of the event was mentioned from the lips of all the people in the main office, including the principal.

Before the election, students were allowed to post posters on walls. Campaigning was certainly an enjoyable time for Shirley. She drew pictures on posters of all colors. One picture of animals was drawn on a yellow poster, while one showed a group of children from all ethnic backgrounds holding hands in unity. Even still, there was one that had two friends talking on the telephone, with one recommending that the other vote for Shirley Cheng. But as days passed, Shirley often noticed her posters disappearing from the walls one after another. Someone was taking them down without others approval. *At least*, she thought, *that a few are still left.*

The day that Shirley waited so long for finally arrived; it was the election day. Tables were set during lunch periods for people to cast a ballot. Shirley noticed that she was the only candidate for a student body position with an opponent. She fervently wished she could win; she would enjoy helping the community so much. She had always wanted to be a leader, ever since she could remember.

The voting period ended and the waiting time for the results began. Unfortunately, they had to wait till after Memorial Day weekend to find out the winners. Shirley, for one, was getting quite impatient!

The day school reopened, Shirley quickly moved about in the condo to get everything ready fast. Once they got to the school, the sad news met her; she did not win.

"I will run again next year. I definitely will," she vowed. It did not matter that she had lost the election, she would try and try until she won.

The next day, Shirley arrived at school with good news heading her way; they said that all the freshmen voted for her hands down. Later, she heard rumor after rumor about the election. Some said she had lost the election by less than ten votes, while other said by twenty votes. Knowing she could not rely on the information and mere gossips, Shirley went to find out for herself. She went to seek the two teachers who were the advisors of student government. She asked the first she came to about the votes, "I have the right to know my votes. I only wish to know how many votes I received."

The teacher shook her head. "The vote-count difference is two hundred fifty. If you were close, I would tell you." Shirley persisted some more, but the advisor continued to shake her head. "You can ask Mrs. Shadwell. She has the counts," she told her. So Shirley found Mrs. Shadwell and asked her the same question. A negative answer was given with a shake of her head.

"No, it doesn't matter to you. Why would you want to know your vote count? It can't help you. It won't make a difference to you."

"I have the right to know. Please tell me how many votes I received."

"No, you can talk to the principal about it." And with that, she walked away, leaving Shirley in search of the principal.

"No, Shirley, we are not required to give out the results. It is up to the student government advisors."

Shirley was left in the dust. After a whole day of inquiries, only effort was spent with no result.

When Shirley returned home from school that afternoon, she shared her expedition with her mother.

"This is absolutely not right. Even the vote counts for US presidential elections are told to the public. I smell something fishy. I would have believed the rules if the student government advisors are good people. Why do bad people always end up as leaders?"

Chapter Seventy-Two

After a few false fire drill alarms were pulled by those students who tried to cause commotion, the school year was at last over. This time, Shirley was not greatly disappointed. She looked forward to the next year when she would be a sophomore. She was planning to take SAT II in biology at the beginning of next year. She had to hunt down answers to her queries, but with so much help from Juliet, who received the answers from an informative guidance counselor from another school. Juliet had learned that there was a score choice option available where students were allowed to take the exam more than once then they could choose which score to be sent to the college. Shirley would not be entirely ready for the exam since she had taken only Regents Biology and she knew that the exam covered advanced material. It would be a fun, challenging time for her. She simply wanted to test the waters before making a plunge.

Before she could go home to spend her summer vacation, she needed to take the final and Regents exams for her classes. Shirley inwardly sighed when she took each test, not for the tests themselves, but for Meredith, who was a great disturbance. Meredith came behind Shirley and peered over her shoulders when she was concentrating on the questions. Then when Shirley had taken the Regents alone in one room, Meredith had wheeled around the room upon the office chair, making much noise in the process. All in all, the testing times were never quiet. But Shirley still managed to complete each exam successfully.

Shirley's thoughts of the year both brought a smile and a frown upon her countenance. We need not be reminded of what issues that could have brought distaste in her mouth. All the hardships were behind her now. She knew she would have much more in the upcoming year, but she would handle it well. She hoped to switch Meredith to a different aide. She knew that was going to take some time and great effort. She and Juliet had been writing letters to the school with the issues arising with Meredith, but the principal would not change her. "She's a nice person," he had said.

"Of course she is nice to you. You're the boss. Everyone's nice to you!" said Juliet. Thinking fast using her strategic and witty mind, Juliet had an idea. Only he could make a difference in changing how Meredith treated Shirley. "When you see them, can you ask, 'Shirley, how are you? How's everything going?'"

"But I do ask her that."

"No, ask her that when Meredith is there with her. You don't have to say anything to Shirley when she's alone." Juliet knew that things like this were important. They might seem small, but they worked big.

"I will, Mrs. Cheng." And he did as she had instructed.

As Juliet had predicted, Meredith's attitude toward Shirley changed for the better. Shirley laughed when Juliet told her of her idea. "Mom, you can always devise something like this, you and your devilish mind." Juliet smiled one of her smiles that only Shirley could interpret as triumphant with the battle against the bad.

Thinking of her aides was a waste of her energy, thus Shirley wiped them off her brain cells.

Meantime, it was time to take her awards home and spread the happiness to her family. Her hard work of the year in the academic area was rewarded; her name showed on the principal's list for both the third and fourth quarters. She looked over her last report card and found five averages of one hundred, being mostly for math, other than a score of ninety-nine for first quarter. She had almost an overall math average of one hundred, but had scored a ninety-eight on the Regents exam, bringing the average down one point. And as for English—she never questioned her English teacher about her low grades. She had mentioned it on the final exam essay, where students were asked to write about the year's experience. She had written that her grades had gone "downhill" in his class. After the final exam, he had called her out of the classroom to speak to her.

"Your grades didn't go downhill. Everyone says that they did well in middle school and all that. But this is Honors English, and you did well."

"I did?" asked Shirley, raising a brow. And that was the end of the matter for him—but not for her. She could never stop mulling over it.

She would continue with Honors English, so she picked two titles from the reading list for the Honors Summer Reading Program. Just as with last time, she completed the reading assignment shortly thereafter.

Shirley sighed one day as she sat before her computer, typing a reply to one of her 126 e-mails that she had received overnight. She sighed not because of the great volume of the letters, but because someone had inquired her about Mickey. "Mickey passed away a month ago, on June 4. I had him for two years. I miss him very much, but I know it was time for him to ascend to the animal heaven. Hamsters could live only about two or so years," she typed.

Juliet told her that Mickey was emitting cries before his death. "He must have suffered. He probably knew that his end was up," Juliet stated.

"Yes, that might be. Poor little fellow!" Shirley created a website for Mickey in remembrance. She so very much missed the little one.

***

In July, Juliet bought some digestive enzymes, thinking they could help Shirley, who always constipated. She read the directions carefully, and before giving them to Shirley, she took them first. Several days later, she decided to give them to Shirley since she felt fine on them.

"I have a dietary supplement that may help with your digestion and to ease your constipation and bloating," said Juliet, holding out the bottle to Shirley.

"What is it?"

"It has amylase, lipase, and protease."

"Oh, I know them. I learned about those enzymes in biology class. Lipase breaks down fat, amylase breaks down starch, and protease is the enzyme that breaks down protein." She was somewhat hesitant to take it, but what did she have to lose? She swallowed a capsule with a cup of water. Then she continued with what she was doing on her computer.

She had been creating websites. Before she knew it, she had made eighty-two websites, covering a wide range of topics and delights, including one dedicated to her mother and one on which she listed people's birthdays upon requests monthly.

That afternoon, as she was busy typing away, Shirley suddenly saw black spots floating in front of her. Her heart skipped a beat. It felt like deja vu. She tried to ignore them, but the spots continued to be visible. She was hesitant to tell Juliet, knowing she would be touched with immense worry. But she had to. What if it got worse? Taking a deep breath, she told her, "Mom, I'm seeing black spots."

"What?" gasped Juliet. The gasp nearly made Shirley's heart skip another beat, for it was quite loud.

"Don't worry. It's probably nothing. But it is just the same as what happened in seventh grade."

"Oh, my goodness, it has to be the dietary supplement!" Juliet felt she was falling down a cliff with not a hope of support underneath. Why did she have to buy the enzymes? "Let me find the ingredients of that medicine you took in seventh grade."

Juliet rushed out of Shirley's office and into the bedroom to find her address book, where she had written down the ingredients. With shaking hands, she flipped through her address book and found the page that listed the poison. She gave a few more gasps. It had the same ingredients as the dietary supplement she had just given Shirley this morning!

"I guess writing those ingredients was a waste," commented Shirley, bitterly. "So, this second time really confirmed our suspicion. A coincidence is not likely to happen twice. The same ingredients, the same symptoms!" It could have been so easy to prevent it...

"I am not seeing the black spots anymore," announced Shirley a moment later, holding no trace of happiness in her voice, for she had misgivings that they would reappear.

Juliet decided to take her to the eye doctor. It was too late to make an appointment, so she had to wait for the following morning.

True to Shirley's predictions, the black spots reappeared, and this time they brought along a blurry vision. "I am having problems seeing!"

Juliet's heart pounded wildly. She prayed for a recovery.

***

Juliet drove to the eye doctor. Shirley's blurriness came and went, never lasting for more than an hour. It was a bizarre situation. None of the doctors believed that the enzymes caused the formation of cataract. "The ingredients in this dietary supplement will not cause cataracts," they had stated after reading the ingredients.

Juliet had written down the ingredients of the dietary supplement she had given Shirley a few days ago, along with the symptoms. Shirley had dictated them to her as she wrote. Juliet was going to hand this piece of paper to the doctor, hoping that he would believe them. But he, just as they had expected, did not believe it.

"It's caused by her arthritis," he said.

"No, my eyes had been fine. But just right after taking these enzymes, I began to see the spots," reiterated

Shirley with firmness.

"Her eyes had been fine and her arthritis is fine. She goes to school every day. Her eyesight deteriorated only after she took the enzymes," said Juliet. If the enzymes had not caused cataracts, what else could have?

"Enzymes won't cause that to happen."

Knowing further explanation was futile, Shirley became silent. They had written down the situation. They had done their job. If no doctors believed them, then too bad.

It was up to the doctor to cure Shirley's condition. He prescribed two eyedrops for her.

Shirley received the eyedrops as soon as Juliet got them from the pharmacy. "The blurriness is gone!" exclaimed Shirley after a few drops. "There are still the black spots, but they are fewer now."

"Really? The eyedrops really worked?" Juliet was elated beyond words. "You must rest your eyes now. Don't use the computer for a while and don't read, either. It needs to be completely cured. You can get blind!"

"From now on, we will need to be very careful to avoid any digestive enzymes," said Shirley. "Why will enzymes cause the black spots and cataracts to form in my eyes?"

"I think I know why. Enzymes break down those nutrients and wash them out of your body. Since you don't have many nutrients in your body already because of your pinworm infestation, you will be greatly affected by enzymes, which will drain any nutrients that you do have. Your eyes need all the nutrients, especially fats. So, that's why the enzymes can do so much harm to you. But they shouldn't sell these dietary supplements over the counter, so that they can get to everyone's hands. What if others have the same thing happened to them?"

"But no one has ever complained about such side effects. They think we're crazy. If only they could experience the same thing, then they'll really understand what is happening to me. People are always skeptical when others tell them such and such. They will really believe it if they go through the same thing," sighed Shirley. Why could not others be more open to what others tell them?

"These shouldn't be called dietary supplement; these should be called medicines. In China, you need prescriptions for enzymes. What America really needs to sell over the counter are antibiotics. People can buy antibiotics over the counter in China, consequently saving many lives. Here, we have so many people who die of pneumonia, a disease that people in China can easily prevent. No wonder we have so many pneumonia deaths in America. We have to go see the doctors when we are very ill, and the worst part is that not every time doctors prescribe antibiotics. We need to wait for a fever, and that will be too late."

After the treatment with the eyedrops, Shirley's vision returned to normal. There were no more black spots and blurriness. The eyedrops had been a miracle.

Now she could continue on with her life. But Juliet still insisted that she should not go on the computer that often. Her online friends seldom saw her online anymore. Every time she went online after several days had passed, hundreds of e-mails would fill her mailbox nearly to the maximum limit. She missed her online life. She had stopped updating her websites, but the hit counters kept rising. She was glad that so many people liked her sites so much. She had visitors from Europe, Singapore, and Middle East.

As days became somewhat torpor for Shirley, Juliet went to Dutchess Community College to register Shirley in a class or two to learn something. All the classes for which Shirley asked were full, including chemistry and French. Then without any other choice, she decided to register Shirley in a GED class. At least, it was something to keep her occupied before tenth grade started.

Shirley went to Dutchess Community College for several days, each time not spending more than two hours. The content of the GED class was too easy; they did only simple math calculations and English worksheets on punctuation and capitalizations. But Shirley continued to go, for she thought it was fun to get out of the house and tease her mind with easy work for a change.

But one day, her eyes suddenly felt strange during class, like a foreign object was trapped in her eyes, so she asked to leave. Soon, she was experiencing problems seeing again. Could she ever run away from her horrid situation?

Juliet took her to the eye doctor once more, and he put her on the same eyedrops. Shortly, Shirley's eyes became better and better.

"My vision is even better than before! Wow, I can see everything so clearly. Look, I can see the tiniest print very clearly." Shirley pointed at some small print. "Being on the eyedrops had even made my vision much better than before seeing the black spots." She soon learned how true it was when tenth grade arrived after Labor Day.

When she returned to school, Shirley was able to see the writing on the projector and the green chalkboards. She was unable to see either of them before the incident (after what happened the first time with her eye vision in seventh grade), except only white words on black chalkboards.

Chapter Seventy-Three

In October, a Homecoming football game and dance were scheduled on a weekend. Shirley had been looking forward to the dance and had a dress prepared. She had gone to the dance last year as well. She loved driving around the school gym during dances, but this year, she might encounter difficulties. Her eyesight swiftly deteriorated again. The black spots reappeared, and worse yet, more in number.

In spite of the floaters, she managed to enjoy the dance. She did not go to the games, for she did not like football.

"You should stay home. You should stop going to school and receive home-tutoring," said Juliet.

"No, I'm fine."

"You'll go blind if you continue going to school and working long hours. It is not good for your eyes. You need rest," insisted Juliet.

Still, Shirley would not listen. "I need to go to school and I *want* to go. I love going to school."

Knowing there was no use trying to convince Shirley any further at the moment, though she would always try, Juliet put the black jacket on Shirley.

"So, you're going," stated Juliet with a sigh as she dressed herself. She was bringing Shirley to school every day and going to school to pick her up in the afternoons. Shirley encountered more problems last year while riding home on the bus. They opened the windows, making Shirley shiver with cold. Thus, Juliet had to be Shirley's driver. Not only was she the driver that year, but a part-time aide as well. She went to the school at ten every morning to take Shirley to the bathroom, for Meredith was not performing a gentle job, often hurting Shirley in the process. And so, Juliet went to school three times a day, never failing once, even when she was exhausted, which was often. As a result, Juliet had to be on the road for a total of three hours just going to and from the school every single day. But what made her most concerned and exhausted was Shirley's health.

Shirley struggled on with each day. She was taking honors in three classes: English, global studies, and math. All the work load had been putting a great deal of strain on her eyes. But her eye condition could not be fixed. It fluctuated in accordance to her menstrual cycle. Whenever she had her menstruation, her eyes became cloudy, thick and dry. Then she was able to see like normal after one week had passed into her cycle. It repeated each month.

"This could not be cataracts," Shirley commented several times, "I never heard that cataracts would fluctuate with menstrual cycles. I can't believe that enzymes can cause such a befuddling condition!"

"Pregnant women's lens will thicken because of the hormonal changes. So, maybe it is the same case for you?" one eye doctor guessed.

"Maybe," Shirley agreed.

"I'll see you later," said Juliet, interrupting Shirley's daydream.

"Yes, at ten," confirmed Shirley. "I love you."

"I love you. Here comes Meredith."

***

During October, Shirley was scheduled to take the SAT II in biology at a high school from another school district. It was farther than her own high school, but it was worth the travel since the guidance counselor from that high school was a kind person; he had supplied Juliet with plenty of information. Juliet was allowed to stay with Shirley in the same room while Shirley took the exam. They ordered her test booklet that had enlarged print so she could see better. On the testing day, Shirley took the test in the area of molecular biology. She received 620 on it out of 800. There were several questions that she never learned in biology class. The exam was designed for students who had taken Advanced Placement (AP) Biology class.

During that time, Shirley decided to join the school newspaper club. She asked the receptionist who the newspaper advisor was. Once she received the name, Shirley drove herself to the advisor's room. "Is this Ms. Edwards?"

"Yes."

She decided to go in the room to where the advisor was seated behind a desk, writing. "I'm Shirley and I would like to join the newspaper club."

The advisor nodded and went on writing. "What would you like to do?"

"I'd like to provide artwork for the newspaper."

"What would you like to draw?"

"I can draw anything." Then she hesitated. "But not sports." She was not a big fan of sports, though she liked golf and bowling.

"There will be a meeting after school next Tuesday and you can bring your art samples for the art editor to take a look."

"Sure, I will do that. I will be here then. Thank you, Ms. Edwards." With self-contentment, she drove out of the room. But she did not stop there; she wanted to join more clubs: art club and Everness, a creative writing and art club.

"I'll submit several drawings and poems of mine for your magazine," Shirley told the Everness advisor.

Her next stop was the art club. She met the club advisor, a young teacher with kind eyes, and Shirley liked her immediately. But Shirley decided to join the art and Everness clubs when her eyesight was better since both required good vision, though she had abundant of inner vision.

Tuesday quickly came, and Shirley promptly arrived at the school newspaper room to attend her first meeting. To her delight, the art editor promptly accepted her after seeing some of her drawings, and she received her first art assignment: volleyball. Even though she had specifically told the advisor that she would like to avoid any kind of sports, she did not mind. "It'll be a fun challenge for me to draw something I have never before drawn," she told herself. The next day, she handed in her drawing of a girl hitting a volleyball.

At the end of first quarter, Shirley had to drop English, for her eyes were getting worse. She was highly reluctant to drop it, but it was a Hobson's Choice. She could not read normal print anymore. Meredith had to enlarge every paper for her, including pages from her workbooks and a book they read for English. She continued to work hard in all her other classes, including global studies, where she spent hours taking notes, which the teacher, Mrs. Dolan, required from all of her students.

"Mrs. Dolan, the note taking from the textbook is taking too long for me. It took fourteen pages for last night's note taking. I wanted to make it perfect and don't want to miss any information."

"Fourteen pages! That's a lot. Let me see a couple of pages of your work. Maybe you're putting in too much information." Shirley handed her the notebook.

Mrs. Dolan's eyes grew wide. "Your note taking skill is superb! Everything is nicely written and I like how you abbreviated the words. You are a high achiever, right?"

Shirley nodded, beaming. She felt good that the teacher was pleased with her work.

At the start of November, the CSE had Individualized Education Program (IEP) meetings to discuss how each special education student was doing. When it was the turn to discuss Shirley in the meeting, her English teacher was invited to be in it.

"At the beginning of the year, her eyesight was fine. But later on, her vision deteriorated," said the teacher.

"You can take a few credits each year, but you won't be able to graduate on time. You think you will drop global studies?" asked the IEP chairperson.

"I don't want to drop anything. But if I must because of my vision loss, I will have to," replied Shirley.

"If you drop more classes, you won't be a junior for next year."

"I won't mind."

"How old are you?"

"Sixteen."

"Yes; so you probably won't like it being in sophomore classes."

"I won't mind," repeated Shirley. She did not matter age differences. All she wanted was to complete high school and receive her diploma.

Half an hour later, the meeting ended.

***

Shirley winced a few days later; she had just heard that there would be another meeting for her. She never liked attending the meetings. They rarely had results for anything that were ever discussed and only wasted her precious class time.

She wanted to get it over with as she went inside the meeting room. Juliet sat down beside her. Mrs. Dolan was invited to the meeting this time. They all waited for the teacher to arrive so that the meeting could go underway. Shirley was pleased that Mrs. Dolan, whom she really liked, was going to attend the meeting.

The door swung open and Mrs. Dolan came in. Student and teacher exchanged greetings before the meeting started. Matters such as her eyesight, credits, and bits of other things were discussed. *It is just a waste*, thought Shirley.

Then what suddenly came from Mrs. Dolan's lips startled her.

"Shirley, you are just like me; we are not like those students who are like sponges—they can absorb information just like that," said Mrs. Dolan, squeezing her hand in demonstration. She chuckled, and Mrs. Milton followed suit.

Shirley was speechless. Words were boiling inside, but her mouth was numb as if she had no control over it, just as with her eyes. She could not believe what she was hearing.

"We're slow," Mrs. Dolan emphasized. Shirley had never heard anyone calling her slow; per contra, the comments made by Mrs. Dolan were the exact opposite from the comments made by all others. Shirley had frequently been complimented on how much she was like a sponge and how she could absorb everything that was taught. Moreover, she was getting high eighties in Mrs. Dolan's class. Since it was an honors class, the factored average would be in the high nineties.

Mrs. Dolan's words had the same effects on Juliet, who was also dumbstruck with utmost disbelief. She had never prepared herself to hear such words from the teacher who Shirley had repeatedly reported was good. If she had known that the teacher was like this, Juliet would not have been so stunned.

The meeting eventually ended. Shirley and the fuming Juliet left the room. "How could she say something like that? And you kept saying how nice she was! I am utterly shocked," Juliet rambled. "Wait, I have to talk to the principal about this."

"No, please. Let's go. Forget about it."

"No, I will not stand here and do nothing about the slander. That's exactly what it is—a slander. She *knows* how good you are. Sometimes, once in a while, with things like this, we need to fight back." She did not like to fight at all, but she could not stand injustice, so she had to fight for justice.

Shirley could not drag Juliet away from the main office, thus she had to follow her in.

"I need to speak to Mr. Broderick," said Juliet. They were asked to wait. Shirley paced the floor, hoping to get away from the scene that was going to fire. But she knew that her mother was right. They should not let anyone get away from saying the untruth.

"Yes, Mrs. Cheng?" asked Mr. Broderick once he came out of his office. Without giving him any time to breathe, Juliet repeated Mrs. Dolan's words.

"I'll talk to her about this," he offered.

***

As Shirley was settling down in her French class the day following the meeting, the French teacher told Shirley that she had just received a call from the nurse's office. "They would like you to go down there."

"Why?" asked Shirley.

"I don't know."

Shirley and Meredith went down the elevator, down the halls, and then into the office.

"I'm here. The nurse wishes to see me?"

"Yes, just wait here."

Then the kind nurse went over to Shirley after she was done attending to another student. She pointed at Shirley's chest. "Are you getting that treated?" Shirley always had a few bumps on her skin at the top portion of her chest. But the bumps had been itching lately and was producing pus. Dr. Frank prescribed some medication in case of infection. Just as the woman, who had recommended him to Juliet, had said, he was a wonderful person. Both Shirley and Juliet could easily talk to him. He had always been kind and considerate to Shirley's diseases and needs. Shirley knew that Dr. Frank certainly got on her list of the most genuine and nicest people they had ever had the fortune to meet.

"Yes, who reported this?" Shirley was quite annoyed.

"I can see that it is being treated. I'm sorry, I can't give out that information."

"Well, no one should report such things before asking me about it. It's my privacy."

"I know. I'm sorry. That's all. You can return to

class."

Shirley gave her thanks and left, her blood sizzling. "Who did that? I want to know. They shouldn't do that. That's not right," she kept saying on the entire way back to her French class. She knew it must have been someone from the last meeting. Someone there had reported it. And she had a feeling who it was. "Oh well. Time for class." She hoped that she did not miss much.

Shirley's eyesight was deteriorating more and more as days passed. She struggled with all her classes. She had all her papers enlarged even more. She started bringing two magnifying glasses to school to aid her. One magnifying glass was not enough, so she held two at the same time while reading and writing. She held one piece of magnifying glass on top of the other. She did the same thing while drawing her artwork for the newspaper. She could only listen to teachers in classes, including math and chemistry. Above all, she had to figure out how to complete the work taught in classes. If she could not figure out something on her own, she got after school help from teachers for math and chemistry. But some days were so bad that she was forced to be absent from school, for she could hardly make out where she was going.

"Dear, you can't go on like this! Do you want to be able to see again, or do you want to go blind, instead?" asked Juliet, her voice getting shrill. She was infuriated by her. Shirley was simply too stubborn for her own good. "You work till four in the morning now. You barely get any sleep. How do you expect your eyes to turn out?" Juliet chided. She had been working with Shirley extremely late into the early morning hours. She had to read each math problem to Shirley, who would painstakingly write them down in thick markers. Juliet, in turn, was also affected. She received less sleep than Shirley.

Shirley ignored her mother's warnings and continued attending school, straining her eyes for several hours. But the most frightful thing was that Shirley's vision never returned to normal after her menstruation each month. It would only get better a little and remain the same until her next menstrual cycle when her vision would deteriorate some more. Thus, with each passing cycle, her vision became worse. She had no control over it. Eyedrops did not help any. None of the doctors had any help. The only thing they offered was a cataract surgery. No, she did not want to get the surgery, yet.

Shirley had to drop global studies class, much to her chagrin. Now, she had only three classes to take: French, chemistry, and math. Because of this, she could not graduate on time with her class. But students were allowed to stay in high school until twenty-one to accumulate enough credits to receive the high school diploma. She would go to high school for an extra year or two.

Since she was in school for only three and a half hours now, her bathroom need was omitted; Juliet did not have to go to school to take her to the bathroom anymore.

Chapter Seventy-Four

November was filled with yet another event. Shirley was scheduled to have an ultrasound done for her eyes. Her eye doctor had told her to go have it done at another location. When the day arrived, Juliet brought Shirley to the office. The wait ended and Juliet pushed Shirley to an examining room.

The doctor walked in without greeting either of them; he did not glance in Juliet's way, either.

"Just because we cancelled the appointment a few times does not mean that he should treat us this way," fumed Juliet. Juliet did not like canceling appointments, but she had no choice when they could not keep it for good reasons.

The doctor examined Shirley's eyes, flashing bright light on them. Shirley involuntarily blinked and tears trickled down her cheeks. Her eyes had always been extremely photophobic.

"Keep your eyes opened, or I'll give you anesthesia!" ordered the doctor. He roughly handled her head. Shirley could not keep them open no matter how hard she tried. Then he stood up and went away.

Juliet stood up as well and walked out the door. "We're leaving. How dare he treat you this way. Plus, you are not here to get your eyes examined. We were sent here by your doctor to only get the ultrasound done since your doctor doesn't have the ultrasound machine!"

"Mom, please!"

After seeing that Juliet was about to push Shirley away, he walked in and began the ultrasound. His attitude was milder. "Okay, I'm done."

After the ultrasound, Juliet asked the receptionist to have the doctor write a note to the school, telling them the reason why Shirley had to miss school. Each time a student was either absent or late to school, a note with an explanation was required. They agreed to do so.

After returning home, Juliet read the note that the office had typed. It stated the reason for the absence, along with a recommendation for Shirley to go to Albany Medical Center to see an eye doctor.

***

On the evening on or around November 19, Shirley was doing her math work using a thick black marker on computer paper, while Juliet went about doing her daily household chores. Each problem took Shirley a whole sheet, for she had to write in really large letters in order to see what she was doing. The black ink was running out, so she picked up a blue marker.

Juliet was still outraged by what Mrs. Dolan had said. "Don't think about it anymore. There are just people like her out there. We can't do anything about it," reasoned Shirley. Juliet sighed and went on with her chores.

The sound of a few quick knocks on their door invaded the peaceful moment. Shirley and Juliet stopped what they were doing. They were not expecting any visitors. Shirley grimaced; she did not approve of unannounced arrivers.

"Perhaps the school sent out a tutor for you?" thought Juliet out loud when she saw a woman through the peephole.

"I doubt it," said Shirley.

Juliet opened the door to the woman, flashing her a questioning look.

"Mrs. Cheng? I'm from the Child Protective Services," introduced the woman.

Juliet felt as though Earth had lost its gravitation pull.

"I thought you were a tutor. Please come in. It's a little messy here; I was just cleaning." Juliet led her inside.

Shirley turned around to face the yet-unnamed woman. Her heart was pounding while she forced a wide smile on her face. She did not want the social worker to know she was apprehensive of the sudden visit. Ah, these awful sudden visits! How Shirley loathed them! What was it *this* time? What excuse did the woman have for coming?

She was about to find out.

"You refuse the eye evaluation for Shirley?" the agent asked Juliet.

"No, I have never refused!" exclaimed Juliet. "I agreed to have her school do it for her. I have been waiting and waiting for them to do the eye evaluation for quite a while, but they have never done it; no one has ever showed up. Shirley needs the eye evaluation to receive some help from BOCES. I have been taking Shirley to the eye doctors for all these years." The school had said that they would have a person from BOCES do an eye evaluation for Shirley. That was back when Shirley was in ninth grade. Several months had passed with no further news from them regarding the subject.

The social worker scribbled down what Juliet had said.

"So, you agreed to the eye evaluation?"

"Yes, of course! And I know who must have called you. When you said these words, 'eye evaluation,' I know immediately who called; 'eye evaluation' sounds so familiar. Only the school knows about the eye evaluation—they were the only ones who used those words. So, it has to be someone from the school and that person can only be the guidance counselor, Mrs. Milton. Right?"

"I can't tell you," replied the social worker.

"I know it is her. How could she do this?" steamed Juliet. "I told them to go on with the eye evaluation."

"Are you taking Shirley to the Albany Medical Center to have her eyes checked?"

"I decided to take her to Connecticut instead, because the doctor knows Shirley's eye condition. He had seen her several times and he's a pediatric eye doctor, so he's qualified."

"I'll have to give Shirley's eye doctor a call to see if she can go to Connecticut instead," said the social worker.

What kind of law was this? Did the parents not know what was best for their own children? Did they have to be ordered around by others?

After all was discussed, the two thanked each other. Juliet closed the door behind the woman.

"Look at what Mrs. Milton is doing! We must change her. And this isn't the only time she is doing this. I heard that she had reported to Child Protective Services on another student. How can we have someone like this to be your guidance counselor?"

And thus Juliet tried, but only wasted her energy in doing so. Mr. Broderick would not switch the counselor.

Soon, Juliet received a call from Shirley's eye doctor. "Why would you want to take Shirley to Connecticut instead?" he asked. Juliet told him the same thing she had told the social worker. Thus, he agreed. She asked him if it was he or the doctor—who had performed the ultrasound—who had called the Child Protective Services, and he informed her that neither of them had made the call.

"You need to take Shirley there; this is my advice," informed the social worker when she was the next to call Juliet.

"I will," said Juliet.

***

In Shirley's math classroom, there was a large computer desk exactly to the right of Shirley's seat. Since the large desk, along with the computer on the top, was there, Shirley's space was made narrow. The spot wherein she needed to situate herself was only a few inches wider than her power wheelchair. She always had to turn and back up slowly and carefully to get in a proper position. And thus, she was doing the same thing today.

Suddenly, her joystick caught under the desk and her

power wheelchair went straight toward the desk. Everything happened so fast. Her wheelchair slammed into the desk at a fast speed, pushing the desk against the wall and nearly flipping it over. The edge of the desk jammed into Shirley's chest. She cried out. She could not get the joystick out from under the desk. But, at last, the joystick bounced out.

The entire class fell silent as it was going on. Shirley began to cry. She was so frightened. She had thought that she was going to go under the entire desk.

"Why are you crying?" asked Meredith. Shirley did not answer. "Are you in pain?"

"My chest hurts."

"Do you need to see the nurse?"

Shirley shook her head. She simply wanted to go on with the class.

"Are you okay?" asked her math teacher.

Shirley weakly nodded. Her chest was hurting, but she was alive. It was a frightful experience.

Upon arriving home, Shirley told Juliet about the incident.

Juliet gasped loudly. "Why didn't you ever tell me that you have such a tight spot in the classroom? They should give you enough room for you to maneuver safely! This is outrageous!"

Juliet immediately picked up the telephone and dialed the school's number. She told Mr. Broderick of what had happened in the math class. "It is a matter of life and death," she said.

"I'll check it out," he replied.

Next, she called Mrs. Dalton, the district's Assistant Superintendent for Pupil Personnel Services, to report the matter. She knew that the school district should be aware of such happenings. They needed to make sure the school was a safe environment for all students, especially students like Shirley.

Two days later, Shirley learned that the principal had removed the computer desk, leaving a large space for Shirley to get to her seat safely.

***

In December, Shirley again took the SAT II exam, and it was on a different topic in biology; ecology rather than molecular. This time, she scored ten points higher: 630.

Several days later, Juliet received a letter in the mail from the Child Protective Services Social Worker who visited them a month ago. Juliet read the letter that contained these words: "This letter is to inform you that the Child Protective Services report of 11-17-99 has been unfounded. I have confirmed that you have been addressing Shirley's medical needs." It also advised Juliet to keep the appointment with the doctor at Connecticut on the third of January, which Juliet had scheduled earlier.

"I think this is all so pitiful," said Juliet. "They had to doubt the care of a parent for her own child. I know that there are real abusive cases, but they should clearly see that you're always well-taken care of."

"I know. This is like the fourth time that a CPS had come?" inquired Shirley.

"I think so. Mr. Babbs from the Work Assessment Department had also reported a case. Since I have to care for you the whole day long, I can't go to work, and plus, I have to get up many times during nights to help you change position in your sleep, help you urinate, and get you something to drink whenever you're thirsty. So, I barely get any sleep. They require a note from the doctor, stating that I can't work, with a reason. I gave him the report from Dr. Lehman, and Mr. Babbs had just simply reported that I don't tend to your medical needs, that I refused the surgery, and well…CPS came. Of course, that case was quickly dismissed. Mr. Babbs had picked out only one small portion from the whole evaluation report, ignoring the entire context of the document. He put two and two together and got five. So, using that, he had reported me to CPS. Welfare always asks me to go to work and have a health care aide to look after you at home. With what we have been through with all the aides, the nurses in hospitals, and Agatha, I can't trust anyone to care for you."

"Yes, I remember that case. How pathetic!" exclaimed Shirley. Deciding to change the subject, she said, "I wonder if I'll get an award this year for the National Reflections Program." She had submitted an art entry entitled *Moon Child*. The drawing showed a girl sitting upon a crescent moon surrounded by stars on a black construction paper. It was drawn with gel pens that Juliet bought. Gel pens could be used on dark surfaces, making it much easier for Shirley to see because of the high contrast.

"It's a lovely picture. I think you will. Good thing I bought those pens. When will you ever see well again?" she asked, sighing. Shirley shrugged.

Before school break at the end of the year 1999, Shirley had to stay home for a few more days. She eagerly waited for the day that she could see well enough to return to school. Christmas vacation would give her time to relax her eyes.

But for the time being, she wanted to go to school to catch up with her missed work in math class, so Juliet called her math teacher to schedule a day when Shirley could meet her to learn some material at the end of the school day.

When the day arrived to see the math teacher, Juliet drove Shirley to the school. Shirley had everything prepared in her bag, including black markers with thick heads. "We're here to see her math teacher," Juliet reported to the receptionist, whose job was to make a note of everyone's arrival to the school.

"Okay," she said.

Once inside the classroom, Juliet brought Shirley's desk over to where Shirley was sitting.

The session ended an hour later and another session was scheduled. At least, Shirley was able to get some of her work made up even though she was absent from school.

The next day, Juliet brought Shirley to the school again to get chemistry help. Shirley had missed a lot of chemistry lessons and she was worried about getting too behind in the class.

Upon seeing that Juliet was struggling with Shirley's desk, Mrs. Lalli quickly went to her assistance. She carried Shirley's desk over to Shirley.

"Thank you, Mrs. Lalli," said Juliet, grateful for the help. She noticed that whenever she took Shirley for a make-up lesson, the science teacher always helped her carry the desk.

Mrs. Lalli patiently taught Shirley the missed work, writing down the formulas in markers.

Thanking Mrs. Lalli, they left for the day.

The next session with the math teacher came up. Thus, Juliet drove Shirley to the school again. They reported their visit to the receptionist, who had a queer expression upon her face. When they rode up the elevator and arrived at the math class, the math teacher met them at the doorway.

"I got a call and they told me that you can't come to make up the work when you didn't come to school," said the teacher.

Therefore, they had to leave. "What kind of rule is this?" fumed Juliet. "They should be happy to get a student like you, who wants to learn in spite of the illness! Which student would want to come to learn when they are ill?"

Shirley had dismissed an opportunity to see an otolaryngologist. She had chosen the tutoring session over the appointment. The earwax in her right ear was bothering her to the extent that she felt clogged. Her left ear did not bother her, for she was able to clean it using her left hand, which was able to reach her ear. "Oh well. I will see the doctor the next week," said Shirley.

When the appointment day arrived, Juliet drove Shirley to the doctor's office. The house had a few stairs, so together, the doctor and his secretary lifted Shirley's wheelchair up, with her on it.

The doctor flushed out the earwax using a water squirter.

"Wow! It feels wonderful. I can hear normally again," gushed Shirley, happiness blooming fully from her smile.

"Gosh, it is so big!" exclaimed the astonished Juliet when she saw the earwax.

"It must have been very uncomfortable," commented the otolaryngologist.

"Yes, it had always been a problem, especially on planes," supplied Shirley. She was so relieved that it had been finally taken care of. There was merely a tiny amount of wax in her left ear, so the doctor did not have to wash it out.

Chapter Seventy-Five

Shirley leaned to her right and shifted her position on her wheelchair. She was tired and wished that they could soon arrive at Newington Children's Hospital. It was January 3, the day for Juliet to bring Shirley to Connecticut for the eye examination as advised by the Child Protective Services. They had already been on the road for over two hours. Shirley sighed, "When will we be there?"

Juliet, her eyes bloodshot, answered with a loud sigh of her own, "We should be there maybe in forty minutes." Juliet tried to remember how to get to the hospital. They had not been there for nine years. Shirley dreaded going back to the dungeon, where the last custody case had occurred. But she knew she was only going to see the eye doctor and no one else.

After being on the road for three and a half hours, they arrived at their destination. Juliet pushed Shirley into the building, into the elevator, and then lastly to the waiting room. The appointment was scheduled for eleven in the morning, but it was already thirty minutes past the time. Juliet had stopped a few times on the road to ask for directions. The name of the hospital had been changed, so it took her extra effort in finding the right place.

After a nurse called Shirley's name, they followed the nurse into a room. Moments later, the doctor walked in, and began his examination. He shone bright light on her eyes. As usual, she involuntarily blinked, while several tears trickled down her cheeks. "Keep them open," he ordered, holding her eyelids open with his fingers. With more tears escaping their owners, the examination was over.

With sighs, Juliet could bring Shirley back home. She had fulfilled the Child Protective Services' request. Did they need to force parents to take care of their own children? The eye doctor had recommended an eye doctor in Albany, but Juliet would bring Shirley to the Westchester Medical Center instead.

After arriving home, Juliet lifted Shirley onto the bed, for she was extremely exhausted from sitting the entire day. "So, you're going to the hospital for my grandmother's surgery?" inquired Shirley.

"Yes, on the fifth," replied Juliet.

"I want to go with you," decided Shirley. Kwi Show was going to have a colon surgery and she wished to be a part of the important event. Some of her family members were going as well.

"That's really nice. I think you should go, too."

On the morning of the surgery, where the day was dawning with faint, shimmering blue above the horizon, Shirley was seated beside Juliet, who was following Agatha's car. Shirley wished all the best for her grandmother, who was a highly kindhearted person, a devout Christian who never missed one day of prayer. She always prayed for both Juliet and Shirley's health.

"She is driving so fast. She never drove this fast before," muttered Juliet, trying to keep up with Agatha. "She knows that I have to follow her car and that my van has a lowered floor, therefore I need to be very careful when I drive."

Moments later, the groups arrived at the hospital. After some wait, Kwi Show was taken to a room to prepare for the surgery. Juliet went into the room to make sure her mother was fine.

"My feet are cold," said Kwi Show.

Juliet touched Kwi Show's feet. "Mom, your feet are freezing! Here, I'll warm them up." She began to rub them. "I'll get a pair of socks for you."

"She can't wear socks during surgery," warned Peter.

"Nonsense. I'll ask the doctor," offered Juliet.

"I'll go ask," Peter supplied, going over to a nurse. After he directed his question, he received the answer. "She said that it is fine for her to wear the socks," he told Juliet.

"Where are the socks?" asked Juliet.

"They are in the car," supplied Kwi Show.

"I'll get them," offered Peter. He rushed out of the building and into Kwi Show's car to fetch the thick socks Kwi Show had brought especially for the day. He returned and handed them to Juliet, who put the socks on Kwi Show, who had just received a painful shot to her spine.

"Yi, my, are you *that* fat?!" exclaimed Agatha a moment later when the two of them were alone after Peter had left. It was almost time for the surgery.

"Fat?" Juliet knew she was not fat at all. She was wearing small-sized clothing. She frowned, confused. Agatha had, in fact, said that Juliet was getting thinner just several days ago. Juliet had replied that she had been urinating more on her herbal medicine, so that was the reason. Why the sudden change in comment?

"I have a prescription medicine that you can take," offered Agatha.

"I'm not fat. And I can't take a prescription medicine to lose weight. Since it is prescribed, it will not be for me. It will make me sick," said Juliet. "You know I always need to take diuretics because I always retain water; I have excess fluid, not fat. No, I really don't want it." She did not want to talk about any medicine right now. She needed to focus on Kwi Show's surgery, which she prayed would go smoothly. But Agatha did not leave her in peace and kept on talking about the medicine whenever she had a chance that day.

Later that day, she learned the good news: the operation was performed successfully without any complications. Juliet thanked the Heavenly King wholeheartedly.

That evening, Juliet decided to pay a visit to Kwi Show and Shirley was excited about the idea.

"I'm so glad that the surgery went well." stated Shirley, sitting at the front passenger's seat.

"I'm absolutely glad as well!" gushed Juliet. The two

exchanged several smiles.

They met Agatha after arriving at Kwi Show's room. Being quiet, trying not to make any hint of a noise, Shirley drove to the foot of her sleeping grandmother's bed. Yet, all her efforts were in vain. Agatha immediately turned on the lamp that sat on a nightstand next to Kwi Show; the light fired on Kwi Show's peaceful face, yet she slept on.

"Don't wake her," ordered Juliet in a whisper. "She needs the rest."

Agatha did not say a word, but instead, as Juliet watched in shock, touched Kwi Show's eyelid. "Yi and Shirley are here to see you," Agatha announced. She tried to pry open Kwi Show's eye.

Shirley also watched in shock as the picture played before her eyes. Kwi Show groggily fluttered her eyes open.

"I told you not to wake Mother!" hissed Juliet. Shirley let out a slow and long sigh. Juliet turned to her mother. "I'm so grateful that it went successfully. Now you have a long life ahead of you. You can live happily. Thank God!"

Shirley smiled to herself. Yes, what a divine guidance and support it was!

***

"I really don't want the medicine," protested Juliet on the following day. As much as she wished that the topic could end, Agatha still persisted. "I have only excess water when I don't urinate well. I feel much better now when I'm on the herbal medicine. I have constipation. I simply can't take the medicine!"

"The medicine helps you have bowel movements," Arney, Agatha's eldest son, chimed in.

"Really?" inquired Juliet. She thought of Shirley, who had serious constipation. *But it is a weight-loss medicine and it is a prescription medicine, so it is not for me*, thought Juliet. "No, I don't want it." Annoyed, Juliet turned her head away. When would Agatha stop offering the medicine?

Luck was not on Juliet's side. Agatha, like a stubborn mule, brought up the subject again a couple of days later when they visited Kwi Show in her hospital room.

"Really," sighed Kwi Show, "we really don't want it. Yi will be unable to take it."

"But I already bought you a bottle—it is too late! It can't be returned," insisted Agatha.

"But she doesn't want it," protested Kwi Show, resting—or trying to rest—in her hospital bed.

No amount of refusal could stop Agatha, who brought the bottle to Kwi Show the following day. Kwi Show, not having any other choice, handed Agatha $125 for the medicine. Kwi Show gave the medicine to Juliet when she paid her routine visit.

Upon receiving the medicine, Juliet felt it was a white elephant. She pondered about the situation for a while. That afternoon in her condo, Juliet took the bottle in her hands, clearly mulling over whether to take it. She read the name of the medication: Xenical. On the bottle, it stated that the directions must be read first before taking it. But all she got was a bottle.

"Agatha is so… She had taken the container and instructions away, leaving me only the bottle!" she told Shirley, who was doing her homework. "But Arney said that it helps with bowel movements, so I will try it."

"Mom, without the instructions, you should not take it. You don't even know what the ingredients are!"

"Don't worry, I'll just take one capsule."

"Mom, don't take it!" It was too late; a capsule went down Juliet's esophagus and into her stomach. Shirley shook her head. "I really think you ought not have." Then she turned back to her homework. It was too late for her to do anything about it.

"What is happening to me?" asked Juliet in a state of sheer bewilderment a short while later.

"What's wrong?" inquired Shirley, worried about her mother.

"I suddenly feel strange and I feel so uncomfortable! I feel that my body suddenly lost everything inside. It feels so empty and vacant. What has happened to me?"

"Could it be the medicine you took earlier today?" Shirley ventured a guess.

"The medicine! That must be it!"

"I told you not to take it!"

That night, Juliet gasped when she checked the time on their digital clock. "My eyes! I can't see the time on the clock! The red numbers are all puffed and blurry."

"Sounds like my eye condition after taking the enzymes," thought Shirley out loud. "You really can't see the time?"

"Not only the time but everything. But the time is more noticeable. The numbers are puffed and they mix in with one another, forming a large red blob," sighed Juliet. "This medicine had done much damage. I really want to know what it is."

Next day, Juliet told Agatha of the incident. "Your medicine has really made me sick. I feel absolutely awful after taking it!"

"I *told* you it's a prescription medicine and you shouldn't take it! But you persistently wanted it," retorted Agatha.

Her words stunned Juliet. Every single word she said was a lie. Juliet said nothing else. She had nothing to say to her. She had wholly trusted Agatha and taken the medication. Now she was feeling utterly ill, more ill than she had ever been.

***

On the day of Kwi Show's discharge from the hospital, Agatha called Juliet from the hospital and told her to fetch Kwi Show's coat from Kwi Show's house. It was snowing heavily, so it would be extremely dangerous to drive up the steep hill on which Kwi Show's house was situated, let alone driving Juliet's lowered-floor van, but Juliet was willing to risk it if it meant Kwi Show could be kept warm. As she was thinking about getting the coat, Agatha called again to tell her that she did not need to retrieve the coat. "But bring a wheelchair with you," she said. Agatha made the calls unbeknownst to Kwi Show; if Kwi Show had known about them, she would not have let Agatha call Juliet. First, Kwi Show already had the coat with her. Second, she would not have wanted Juliet to go to the hospital for several reasons: she already had a wheelchair at home and the hospital could provide one if needed; Juliet did not live close by; Shirley would be home alone; and that Juliet had a horrendous health. Moreover, both Agatha and Lloyd were to take her home that early afternoon, and their teamwork would be sufficient without needing Juliet's assistance.

When Juliet arrived at her mother's hospital room, she learned that Kwi Show already had the large coat with her.

"Here, take this." Agatha put a large bundled comforter on the wheelchair Juliet brought. Agatha was about to stack all of Kwi Show's belongings on the wheelchair, when Kwi Show protested loudly.

"No, I don't want her to take them home," said Kwi Show. "I need to use them. She would not be able to return my things to me immediately when I need them."

"No, she will take them," insisted Agatha. She wanted Juliet to take everything, from Kwi Show's luggage containing her clothes to her everyday necessities.

Agatha asked me to come here in such a terrible weather just to take these things home with me? Thought Juliet. Why let Juliet take them to her own condo when Lloyd and Agatha could easily take them with them that day to Kwi Show's home?

Back and forth Kwi Show and Agatha fought as their argument crescendoed. In defiance, Kwi Show lifted a bag to her chest. "You can take them; Lloyd can take them. But if you and Lloyd will not, then *I* can take them myself!"

In the end, because of Kwi Show's persistence, Agatha had Juliet take only the large bundle. Juliet, wheeling the bundle out Kwi Show's room, was surprised to find Agatha walking her out. In the hallway, Agatha said, "This has a plate from the hospital oven." She pointed at the large wrapped bundle.

"A plate?" repeated Juliet in bewilderment. An oven plate? She did not think that the hospital had any ovens.

"Yes." Agatha explained that she could use it to serve food for Kwi Show when she returned home.

Juliet did not like the idea in the least. But what could she do? She did not want Kwi Show to get upset, so she grimly did as Agatha ordered.

Agatha and Lloyd drove Kwi Show home early that afternoon. Only a bit of snow covered the walkway to the front door, for they already had people plow the snow. "You can take the stairs instead," Agatha told Kwi Show. She wanted her to go down the stairs, consisting of about ten steep stone steps, from the garage to the basement, then up another flight of stairs from the basement to get up to the main floor.

"I just had an operation," protested Kwi Show.

"The doctor said that you can take the plane to China," retorted Agatha. Is going on planes the same as walking steep staircases?

"No, I can push her on the wheelchair to the front door," said Lloyd. "It's not good for Mom to take the stairs after such a major operation."

"She can take the stairs," insisted Agatha.

Lloyd shook his head. "I'll push her to the door."

Agatha had to give in to her husband's insistence. He safely pushed Kwi Show to the front door and got her inside.

About a week later, Juliet told Kwi Show about the

oven plate over the telephone. Neither had seen the mysterious plate since Juliet had never unwrapped the bundle. And Kwi Show wondered why Agatha asked Juliet to bring a wheelchair when she did not plan to push her in the first place. Afterward, Kwi Show thought that the reason must be for the purpose of having Juliet bring the large oven plate and everything else to her condo…to get caught by the hospital.

***

As days passed in the frigid month, Juliet soon felt even more uncomfortable as the result of taking the prescription drug. "What's wrong with me? I am having problems breathing." She took a large breath to no avail.

Shirley, being awake from insomnia, could often hear her mother gasping for air. At nights, Juliet was often awakened by suffocation. "Mom, you were gasping in your sleep," Shirley reported to Juliet every time it happened, which was frequent.

"I know. It is so hard to fall asleep. I'm so sleepy, but every time I fall asleep, I can't breathe and it wakes me up," said Juliet.

"I hear you gasping in your sleep," said Shirley, with a sympathetic frown.

Juliet grew more and more ill. She had gained several pounds after the dose. "I am bloating! I no longer can take my herbs that act like water pills ever since I took that capsule. The water is collecting more and more in my body. All the herbs don't work anymore," sighed Juliet. "The medicine has clogged me up. I feel so tight around my stomach—right at my diaphragm; my breathing difficulty is not from my chest area." She felt devastated. Her world, which was already full of problems and hardships, had been utterly turned upside down.

Shirley watched on helplessly as Juliet struggled to breathe each and every day. But the torture would not stop there.

"My body suddenly has bumps! I feel bumps all over my stomach and there is a large one on my back." Juliet felt her body, pressing the skin with her fingers. "They can be easily felt and they are painful."

"Oh no! Could they be enlarged lymph nodes?" asked Shirley, frowning.

"Could be."

***

Music from the 1950s and 1960s filled the condo when Shirley's big day arrived; it was her seventeenth birthday and she was celebrating it loudly with her friends. Shirley had balloons of all colors in several shapes all over the living room. She had blown the balloons until she was blue in the face.

Shirley managed not to run over anything or anyone during the party. She did not inform any of her friends of her poor vision. She thought it was unnecessary. She wanted to focus on the fun and to leave everything else till after the party. She had hoped that none of them would think it odd when she refused to fill out the *Mad Libs* by Roger Price and Leonard Stern each time. She did not want to spoil the merry mood by telling them that she could not see well, and therefore was unable to fill out the activity booklets.

She was grateful that she was able to have the party. She made her famous wish and blew out eighteen candles, an extra candle for good luck. She had made a second wish that year, hoping that her mother could be cured. She wished for new breath for her. Juliet continued to get each precious breath with effort. It was such a misfortune.

As the day's sunshine was replaced by stars and a bright moon, the laughter died away. The fun time was over. It was time to get back to reality.

***

In February, things began to have a turn for the better for Shirley, not Juliet. For one, Shirley had finally switched Meredith to Pat, who was the most diligent aide she had ever known. Shirley felt victorious after she was able to have a different aide. It had taken her and Juliet nearly a year to get Meredith changed, and after all the work and a happy ending, it felt as though they had won a great battle.

Pat did a wonderful job when enlarging Shirley's worksheets and notes. She never complained; she did what she had to do. "I will treat Shirley just like my own child," Pat had told Juliet on the first day. Juliet was immediately comforted. Shirley was already going through so much. She really needed a kindhearted person to watch over her. Not only should Shirley's aide be a helper, but also a good friend on whom Shirley could rely. It was not just about getting books and taking notes. No, it was much more than that. A gentle person was all Shirley needed to achieve the highest level of peace and happiness in school.

It was just the right moment for Shirley festive mood, for the Valentine's Day Dance at her school was scheduled for the following day. She had looked all over for a red dress for the occasion, but could only come to the dance dressed in blue—the same blue dress she wore to the semi-formal in eighth grade. But she felt better when she arrived at the dance, seeing that many students were dressed quite casually; some wore jeans and sweaters.

Her eyesight was poor, but she was able to roam around outside the cafeteria where the dance was held. She went in and out of the room, never staying in there for long, and always made sure she was close to the door. The more she moved further inside the dark room, the more she was unable to see anything.

As she swung to the music, a boy walked in front of her. But she did not know it was she to whom the boy was trying to get the attention, for she could not make much out in the darkness. Then he bent down, "Would you like to dance?" Shirley was a bit startled, but graciously nodded her head. As they danced, small talk started.

"So, what grade are you in?" asked Shirley.

"I'm a senior."

"Oh, I'm a sophomore." Then she asked for his name.

"And I'm Shirley."

By the time Shirley realized it, they were dancing to all the music. They did several spins where Shirley made complete turns in her wheelchair. She was having so much fun and lost herself in her little dreamworld.

Soon, nearly two hours had passed. During one dance toward the end of the evening, a girl walked over and tapped him on the shoulder, apparently asking him to go somewhere for a duty. From the tag on his shirt, which she could not make out clear enough to read it, Shirley guessed he was a volunteer at the event.

"This is my friend," he introduced her to another boy in the senior class before he went away for his responsibility at the dance. Shirley continued the dance with her new partner. But shortly, Shirley had to go home. The dance was drawing to a close. It had been four splendid hours.

***

Another blissful event soon followed the occasion. Shirley had always wished to have a talking parrot for a pet, so it was decided—Juliet was to get one for her. "I would love to have an African Grey parrot! And I'll name him Romeo," said Shirley, hopefully. "I already have a Juliet," she said with giggles, looking at her mother. "And now, I'll have Romeo! You two will make a great pair!"

"Okay, I'll buy one for you," agreed Juliet, her words said with effort as she struggled for a breath.

Shirley had made several calls to local pet shops, asking if they had any African Grey parrots. Eventually, she found a store that could order one that would be newly hatched.

"I would like to have a male African Grey parrot," Shirley told the shop owner.

"Sure, we'll get you one," he promised.

Shirley happily hung up. "I can hardly wait to have a talking parrot," she said to herself. "I will need to work hard to teach him how to talk, but the effort will be worthwhile. I'll have so many delightful times with Romeo."

The last good thing that happened at the end of the month—the most important change for her—was that her eyesight was getting better. Even Pat had noticed the difference with Shirley.

"Am I doing a good job enlarging the paper, or is your vision better? You are not using any magnifying glasses," commented Pat once.

"I don't *need* to use the magnifying glasses anymore—at least, not on the enlarged print!" Shirley squealed happily.

"Oh, I'm so glad, Shirley!"

Shirley felt like celebrating.

In spite of the improvement, her eyesight was still considerably poor. Shirley still struggled on with math and chemistry. She knew and understood what was taught in math class, but on tests, she often misread the numbers and mathematical signs. The numbers that often gave her most trouble were "4," "6," and "8"; she was unable to tell which number was which. And with division signs, she took them as addition signs, thus resulting in mistakes on her tests that were unrelated to her mathematical knowledge. She did well on her math homework, for Juliet had been reading the problems to her, so she did not have to trust her own eyes. She had even gotten the hardest mathematical problem correct one day on a homework assignment. Therefore, it was not the material that was a worry, but her misreading of the questions due to her vision loss was the actual and serious problem. But Shirley felt that they did not understand the situation; they had probably thought Shirley was not very good in math. She had been getting mid eighties for math.

The math course was an honor class, so it would be factored in, making it about ten points higher. Therefore, her resulting math average would be in the mid nineties.

In March, Shirley's vision was better, but she still needed all her school text to be enlarged. Shirley was grateful for finally having a nice aide, who would look out for her with kindness. Pat patiently continued to enlarge each paper, whether it be a graph or a test. She would try it again if the text was not large enough for Shirley.

Shirley was still mostly an A student, except in math. She had been receiving mostly a perfect score on each of her French assignments and tests, and mid nineties for chemistry. She did her utmost in all her classes.

It was also time that the person from the BOCES came to do the eye evaluation for Shirley. "At last, after over a year, the person finally came," said Shirley.

"What a shame! This eye evaluation had caused us so much trouble with the CPS," remarked Juliet.

Darla came with a booklet of questions and exams for Shirley to take. The test included pictures of shapes and dots. The test would indicate how well Shirley was able to see. Shirley was able to get some of them correctly. Then Darla brought Shirley over to a CCTV, where any text could be enlarged to as much as thirty times. "Are you able to see this?" she asked. Shirley nodded. Then Darla shrank the size. Shirley shook her head. "Do you like this?"

"Yes, I do. It's nice."

"I have some supplies I think you might be interested in," said Darla, "I have lined paper with thick lines and graph paper with dark lines."

"That will be very useful for me! I would like to have them, please."

"I'll bring them in next time."

Shirley received the lined paper and graph paper of all sizes shortly afterward. Darla had also brought her some pens with thick heads. Shirley was glad that Darla had come. She needed the special graph paper so badly; every time she needed to make a graph for math class, Juliet would have to go over all the lines on the graph with markers to make them thicker and darker. Now, there was no more need in doing so. It would save much time and effort. Pat photocopied several copies of the graph paper and lined paper, so that Shirley would not quickly run out of them.

"I'm lucky to have such a nice person as my aide during this difficult time," Shirley said to herself. She tapped her fingers on her desk. "I have to make a call to the PTSA today," she reminded herself.

And thus, she called the PTSA chairperson after school that day. She was curious about the result of the National Reflections Program. "We didn't get many entries this year, so there won't be any awards given," the woman told her.

The news disappointed Shirley.

There will be next year, thought Shirley. "I think I can join the art club soon since my eyesight is better!" She spoke to the art advisor twice, and informed her about the situation. "The art teacher seems like such a nice person. I'll have a fantastic time there. I can also attend Everness meetings, too. I just wish I'll have more time. My homework takes too long to do. But I already finished my work today, so…" She thought of something to occupy herself. She had no assignments for the school newspaper club. Her eyes scanned the living room and rested on the television. She was not a television person. The only programs she watched were science and animal shows, along with news. She could no longer use a computer or read books. Ah, how she hungered for them! "I can make crafts!" She had been making all sorts of critters using pom poms, moving eyes, and pipe cleaners.

Chapter Seventy-Six

Before spring break in April, Shirley's eyesight went down without any warning. But she was not surprised, simply horrified. She had expected this to happen. When would the roller coaster ride ever end? Would she be thrown off in the end? Or would she be safely strapped in?

She was back using the magnifying glass. But there were only a few days left till the break. Shirley hoped her vision would get better when they got back to school. At home, she continued to work on her homework. Juliet had bought a blackboard for Shirley so she could see more clearly. She used it to do some of her work. She also had a small white board with a washable surface.

As days passed, Shirley was able to see better. She was really glad; perchance she could see well when school began. But she was greatly concerned about the work she had missed for chemistry. Because no one in the family could ever offer much help, Juliet asked the Mormons if they knew anyone who could come to their condo to teach Shirley the missed work in chemistry. The Mormons had visited them several times since Shirley had asked Juliet to order a video tape on God and Jesus Christ. Juliet thought they were nice people, who were nearly Shirley's age. They agreed to look for such a person.

As they had promised, they brought along a girl, Tina, with them on the following visit. Tina was a junior at the same high school Shirley attended. They got to work forthwith. Shirley showed Tina what needed to be taught. The packet provided by the teacher lay on the table.

Her class was learning the Law of Chemical Equilibrium and they had formulas to write. They were to calculate the kinetic (K) value for chemical reactions. The given general formula was: $aA + bB \longleftrightarrow cC + dD$. And they were to use the expression $([C]c[D]d)/([A]a[B]b)$ for the answers. Mrs. Lalli had told her that it would be impossible to do without seeing it. But Shirley was confident. She would try to do it in her head. She had nothing to lose, only something to gain.

"Are you able to see this?" asked Tina, pointing at the formula she wrote on a piece of paper.

"No, I can't. I can do it in my head."

Tina gave her an example of the problem, explaining each step to her. Shirley closed her eyes and pictured the entire formula in her head, then thought how she should work out the formula. Then Tina gave her a problem to do. "What is the equilibrium constant expression for $N2 + 3H2 \longleftrightarrow 2Nh3$?"

Thinking carefully, Shirley gave her the answer. "$Keq = [NH3]2/[N2][H2]3$."

"Yes, that is correct. How about this: $NH3 + HOAc = NH4+ + OAc$?" Again, Shirley told her the answer. "That is correct."

Shirley was thrilled that she was able to do the problems completely in her head! Tina gave her several more problems, all of which Shirley successfully completed, taking merely half a minute to do each.

"I think that should do it," said Tina. That was all that needed to be done. Shirley had taken less than an hour to learn something and complete several problems that would have taken the class a week of practice.

Afterward, a few days later before the break ended, Juliet took Shirley out to the Danbury Mall to buy the dress for the sophomore semi-formal that was to be at the end of April. Shirley was looking forward to it since she first heard of it when she was a freshman. Since her vision was poor, she held hands with Juliet as they went about in the mall. She had not been out for some time and she liked the feeling of being free again.

A few days before Shirley was to go back, her vision suddenly failed her. She could not believe her fortune. *And this is to have an emperor's fortune?* thought Shirley. She was practically unable to see any text no matter how large it was. She was quite alarmed. How could she go back to school? She even could not make out where she was driving herself.

The truth hit her like a sudden outpour of frozen rain: she could not go back, and would have to stay home and receive home-tutoring. She was extremely devastated. She could not believe that it was happening to her. She was able to see one minute, then she could not see the next. Her vision was a roller coaster, going up and down. But at least the rider knew which way it was going; not Shirley with the vision. It gave no warning; it struck like lightning. How was she able to finish the rest of her work for the year? How could she complete mathematical calculations? She was unable to use Braille because of her arthritic hands and fingers. But someway, somehow, she could manage; she was positive.

She thought of her friends, and how she would miss all of them. But they could visit her at the condo. Samantha, her lab partner in chemistry class, sprang into her mind. *She is such a nice person*, she thought. Samantha never failed to assist her during times of poor vision. Samantha had helped her read small print, copy down information, and she was helpful in many other ways; Shirley was highly grateful for everything she had done for her. Shirley would miss her a great deal.

Juliet informed the school of Shirley's condition, telling them she could not return. Next, she dialed the number she knew so well: the assistant superintendent's office. She had been calling Mrs. Dalton every time a problem arose. Mr. Caufield had been the one who had told her to call her. She was glad she had someone to call. Mrs. Dalton always listened to the problems with patience and tried to resolve each. She was really the only person to whom Juliet felt she could talk and get her message across. She was able to count the times that Mrs. Dalton had helped. With others, she could barely count to her second finger, except, for of course, Mr. Caufield, who was one of the most genuine people she had ever known.

"You need a doctor's note stating that Shirley could not attend school and she requires a tutor," said Mrs. Dalton.

"Okay, I will get it to you. Thank you." Right after hanging up, Juliet called up Dr. Frank.

At the same time, Shirley had found out that the pet shop had found a male African Grey for her, just as she had requested. They were caring for the baby bird until it was old enough for them to bring home. "When is his hatch-day?" inquired Shirley. She wanted to know Romeo's hatch-day, so that she could celebrate it whenever he would be a year older.

She was given some information, not the exact date. She soon calculated his hatch-day. She hung up after saying her courtesy thanks. She asked Juliet to check the calendar. Yes, she had calculated it correctly. She hoped that she could get to be with Romeo soon.

Turning from her thoughts of Romeo to an eye appointment, Shirley inquired, "So, Dr. Foster had scheduled an appointment for me to go to Westchester Medical Center in June?" Dr. Foster was an eye doctor from whom Shirley was seeking treatment. Seeing Dr. Foster was a difficult experience for Shirley each time. Because of her photophobic condition, Shirley would squint, unable to keep her eyes open whenever Dr. Foster examined her, flashing bright light on her eyes. He would not decrease the brightness of the light, unlike Shirley's previous eye doctors, but would instead continue shining the bright light upon her eyes. Whenever Shirley could not keep her tearing eyes open, Mr. Foster would write in his report that she was uncooperative. Was this an act of an uncooperative behavior? Why would Shirley want to be uncooperative? Would they call her that when she was asked to stand up and walk? Shirley's eyes were highly photophobic; she could not go out without wearing both a cap and sunglasses together. The herbal foods from George's store had significantly decreased in quality, so she could not take them anymore to improve her vision. Dr. Foster had referred Shirley to Westchester Medical Center, for he stated that he had never seen anyone with the same eye condition as Shirley. *After the many examinations, he had at last said that*, thought Shirley.

"Yes," answered Juliet, "on June 5."

"But that's the day I need to take a final exam and it's very important," said Shirley, frowning in concern.

"Then maybe you can talk to him about it and ask him to postpone the appointment."

***

"You look stunningly beautiful," remarked Juliet after dressing Shirley in the silver ball gown that they had bought at the Danbury Mall. Shirley was determined to go to the sophomore Semi-Formal regardless of her low vision. "You look like Cinderella. But are you sure that you will be fine?"

"I won't move around. I won't be *able* to move around. I'll just stay in one place. I just want to be there. Besides, there will be others there, like Mr. Martin."

"I am so worried about you."

"Please don't worry. I'll be fine. I'll call you if I need you." Juliet had bought two cellular phones, one for each, in case Shirley ever needed to reach her. "Is it time to go now?"

"Yes," answered Juliet, scrambling around the living room to see if they needed anything else. "I'll put on the earrings for you when we get there, so you don't need to wear them longer than necessary." Shirley had no ear piercing, so she wore clip-on earrings, which often hurt her when she wore them for long hours.

After strapping Shirley's wheelchair in her van, Juliet started the engine. The drive to the school took them twenty or so minutes. Once Juliet parked her van at the curb and got Shirley out, many eyes instantaneously turned upon Shirley. "Everyone's staring at you!" exclaimed Juliet with giggles.

"Really?"

"Yes, because you look too beautiful." Juliet proudly pushed her little princess into the building. Once inside, more eyes turned toward her. Then Juliet pushed her over to greet Mr. Martin.

He gushed at the sight of Shirley. "You look so beautiful! I can't believe it."

"Thank you!" replied Shirley, with a shy smile.

"Can you watch over her?" requested Juliet. "She can't see. She can't even really see you, either."

Mr. Martin sadly shook his head. "Yes, I'm here if she needs me."

"I'm so worried about her."

"She's safe with me."

Juliet made sure Shirley was fine one more time before she left with a worrying mind. Yet the thought of leaving Shirley with the security man comforted her. Both she and Shirley liked him very much. He had once said to Juliet, "You exist for Shirley, who clearly makes you so happy."

Shirley inched her way toward the lighted hall outside the school cafeteria, where the dance was held. She was not planning to go inside the dark room. She knew she would be unable to get back out if she did. She simply sat silently outside the cafeteria. She listened to the voices. She could not recognize them as any of her friends. There were familiar voices, but they were merely acquaintances. She wished that she could join in the dance.

A couple walked in front of her. Were they trying to get her attention? She could not tell. She studied their outlines, but was unable to discern their features to guess whom they might be.

They moved closer to her, and the boy spoke. "Would you like to dance with us?"

"I'd like to, but I don't have good eyesight in the dark, so that's why I'm staying here," answered Shirley, grinning sheepishly.

"Oh, I'll ask them to make the dance floor brighter!"

How considerate of him, thought Shirley. She wanted to know who they were, but held back her question. She did not want to explain what happened to her vision. It was time for enjoyment. Her face flushed with excitement as she anticipated the fun she was going to have. She closely followed them, trying not to appear that she was having problems seeing where she was driving. She was able to make out outlines of the walls. She heard him asking Mr. Martin to turn on some light so that Shirley could go in to dance. "Okay, they have some light on for you," he announced to Shirley. Then the two went inside the cafeteria, with Shirley trailing behind.

Once inside, Shirley did not hesitate a single second. She started to swing in her power wheelchair right away. She would enjoy herself for the night! She wished that she could know who the kind boy was. He had made it possible for her to have a fun time. She did not recognize his voice, though she had a guess whom he could have been. Later, he asked if she wanted anything to drink. She shook her head graciously.

When there was another half an hour left to the dance, Juliet arrived at the school. "How was it?"

"Everything went great. I was dancing for a long time."

"Oh great! I was so worried!"

"Don't worry about me. The time lasted too short."

"You think it is short? You really had fun?"

"Yes, I wished it was longer. I have always thought the dances were too short! How are you feeling?"

"I'm the same, but don't worry about me. I'm glad that you enjoyed the night."

Shirley wistfully gazed at the outline of her mother. She could hear her heavy breathing and knew that Juliet was trying to get a breath. Shirley hated what had happened. She fervently hoped that Juliet would recover and return to the day before she had swallowed the poison. What ingredients did the medicine have? What could have caused such life-threatening, and yet, odd adverse reactions?

***

Shirley, her hands folded before her and her back straight, waited patiently for the tutor to come. It was several days into the month of May, and her first tutoring session was to begin. The tutor, Mrs. Bryson, was coming for chemistry and math work. There was no one to tutor her French. She wondered how much she was able to do. It would be near impossible for most people to do chemistry completely in one's head without seeing anything. When the clock turned to the time of the tutor's arrival, the doorbell rang. Shirley thought with satisfaction and approval that the woman was prompt, therefore she was respectful of others' valuable and precious time.

"Nice to meet you, Mrs. Bryson," greeted Shirley.

The tutor kindly returned the greeting and sat down next to her. "Well, I'm just curious. What are you able to see?"

"I can faintly see colors and movements."

"Can you see me?"

"I can make out a faint outline."

"How about what I'm wearing?"

Studying the faint image before her, Shirley answered, "You're wearing white?"

"Yes, that's good! How about the center of my shirt?"

"No, I can't see that."

"It has a picture of a girl. Well, let's get started. Just tell me when you get tired and we'll stop."

"I will." Shirley nodded.

"I'm not sure how we'll do this. It's all chemistry with formulas. And there's also math work! I am really not sure how you'll do this."

"Don't worry. I can do it. I'll try my best with the chemistry. Please just go slowly and repeat the formulas."

Mrs. Bryson, somewhat concerned about how the

lesson would turn out and how she was going to proceed, began asking Shirley the questions that the teacher had prepared. She started with the chemistry.

"Balance this equation: Zn + HCl ---> ZnCl2 + H2."

"Could you repeat that please?" And Mrs. Bryson did. Shirley, with obvious concentration on her expression, slowly gave her the answer. "1 Zn + 2 HCl ---> 1 ZnCl2 + 1 H2."

"Amazing! That is absolutely correct! This is unbelievable!" She laughed. "Okay, here's more. Balance the following equation: S8 + F2 ---> SF6."

"Well, the first part, which are the reactants are: 1 S8 + 24 F2," calculated Shirley.

"Correct!" Mrs. Bryson exchanged looks with Juliet.

"And the products are 8 SF6."

After Shirley completed several worksheets, it was time to start on the math problems. "I can do Math Course II, but this will be hard to describe to you, with its format and all," said the tutor.

"I'll try it."

"Actually, I'm not sure how to explain the problems." Then Mrs. Bryson told her the chapter's name.

"Oh, that's a new chapter for me, so I don't know what the problems look like."

"Yes, that's right. I think we have to skip over math," said Mrs. Bryson. "You must be tired now. I think you're just *amazing*. You can picture the equations in your head?" She scanned the room, its walls hung with Shirley's colorful drawings. "Being an artist must make it easier for you to picture the formulas in your head!"

"I guess." Shirley laughed.

Calling over Juliet, Mrs. Bryson showed her the chemistry formulas," Look at what she had to do."

"I know," said Juliet, beaming. "I can never do that. She *is* amazing."

"You have a remarkable memory!" repeated the tutor. "Well, when will be a good time for me to come again?"

"Is next Monday in the afternoon good for you?" asked Shirley. The teacher nodded. They scheduled an appointment for the following week.

But before having another tutoring session with Mrs. Bryson, Shirley was scheduled to see Dr. Foster. She would request a change in date for the appointment at Westchester Medical Center.

With her sunglasses and her blue cap on, Shirley was ready to be pushed out of the door on the day of the appointment. Juliet heaved the power wheelchair onto her van, followed by strapping her in.

A few minutes later, they arrived at the doctor's office. "We're here to see Dr. Foster," reported Juliet. Then, Juliet sat herself down on a chair with Shirley next to her.

"I hope he'll change the date," said Shirley. "The final exam is very important. I need to take it. I won't be able to make it up."

"I don't know how you'll be able to take the test without your vision. Who will read the test and write down your answers? I will have to talk to the school about it," sighed Juliet. Then their conversation was interrupted by the nurse, Carma, announcing it was time to bring Shirley to the examining room.

Shirley winced as Juliet pushed her to the room wherein she had been many times. She knew that she would encounter the same problem again once Dr. Foster examined her eyes. That bright light...

Dr. Foster walked in, Shirley's chart in hand, and sat down in front of Shirley while greeting her. As Shirley had expected, her eyes immediately began to produce streaks of tears that trickled down her cheeks. She squinted.

"I can't see your eyes, please keep them open," said Dr. Foster.

"It is very hard to, but I am trying my best," replied Shirley, tasting a teardrop in her mouth. She wiped the tears away and tried to keep her eyes open.

"No, that can't do." Dr. Foster shook his head. He asked a nurse to write down the report of the day. "Shirley is uncooperative; I can't examine her," he dictated.

Shirley inwardly sighed. It was the same as if asking her to stand and when she was unable to, she would be labeled as uncooperative.

"You'll go to see Dr. Chesmore on June 5, right?" the doctor asked.

"Actually, I was wondering, can you change the day. I have a very important final exam that day and I need to take it."

"No, I can't change it; it has to be on that day. He's really busy and it has been hard to make this appointment."

"Then I can't go. I will go next time."

"I strongly advise you to go. But it's up to you."

"Okay, I will go next time. I have to take the final exam."

"Okay." The doctor rose from his seat and walked out.

"Shirley, you should go," said Carma. "You're seventeen, and your mother will get into trouble with the Child Protective Services," she threatened.

Shirley was speechless at what the woman said. Even the doctor did not say such words. How could the nurse threaten her?

"You must go," she warned again.

Juliet and Shirley left the building, disgusted with what Carma had said. "I will talk to the doctor about it when I come next time," promised Shirley.

"Yes, that is a good idea," stated Juliet.

"Let's go home. I'm really tired and I'm yearning to get on the bed now!"

Once back inside the condo, Juliet got Shirley on the bed and tucked her in comfortably. Juliet had recently begun to use the lift, no longer carrying Shirley. The breathing difficulty had made it very hard for her to carry Shirley. She also had a lift installed in the bathroom, so she did not have to carry her to take a shower, either.

***

Mrs. Bryson came six more times, each session lasted an hour. Unfortunately, Shirley was ill for the last session, so the appointment was cancelled. But she had finished the entire year of chemistry successfully. She had made it! No words could replace the happy feeling inside of her. But unfortunately, she could not complete her math and French courses, and she was highly disappointed.

In the meantime, Shirley had received news from her French teacher, who called her, telling her that she had been excused from taking the two French exams, one a state final and the other a school final, which was scheduled for June 5. "I never excuse students from taking the exams, but Shirley had worked so hard and she did so well in class," the teacher had told Juliet over the telephone.

"So, I can keep the appointment after all!" exclaimed Shirley happily. It all worked out perfectly.

At the end of the school year in June, Shirley was scheduled to take the math and chemistry Regents exams. But before the month of June, Mrs. Lalli had excused Shirley from the chemistry Regents. There was no way for Shirley to take an entire exam without her vision. At the same time, Mrs. Lalli and Shirley promised each other that they would keep in touch. Shirley was thrilled that she had made a true friend in a wonderful person. She felt honored to be friends with someone who was once her teacher.

"Then how about math?" questioned Juliet during a telephone conversation with Mrs. Milton.

"I'll talk to the math teacher about it."

Shortly, a couple of days later, she called Juliet back with the math teacher's decision: she had excused Shirley from taking the math Regents.

June 5 quickly arrived. Shirley had everything ready, including a brand-new box of tissue, to bring with her for the scheduled appointment with Dr. Chesmore. Juliet did not know how to get to Westchester Medical Center, so a kind woman, Allie, was going to go with them in Juliet's van to provide the directions. Allie was a woman from a Chinese church that Kwi Show attended, therefore, the acquaintance was made. Juliet was grateful that Allie had offered to go. Not only could she help with the directions, but she could also stay with Shirley if Juliet needed to park her van elsewhere if there was no accessible parking by the entrance of the hospital.

The appointment was at five in the evening, so they started out at three o'clock. Shirley wondered what the eye doctor would be like. Dr. Foster had recommended cataract surgery for her. He had asked her if she wished to receive general or local anesthesia. Shirley was startled that such a surgery would require general anesthesia! She felt more uncomfortable with the surgery. She wished to do more research before making her final decision.

"We're finally here," announced Juliet, searching for a parking space. "I cannot find any spot that is handicapped accessible. I will just have to park at the curb; there's nowhere to park!" She turned to Allie and requested, "Please watch Shirley as I go park my van in a parking lot." Allie stood beside Shirley as Juliet drove toward a parking space. Then she swiftly returned to their side. "Thank you, Allie!"

The party made its way to the waiting room after Juliet announced their arrival with a receptionist. During the wait, everyone received a few rounds of dilating eyedrops required for the proper examination.

"He appears to be very nice," commented Juliet after Shirley was asked to be pushed to the examining room, where Dr. Chesmore had walked in shortly.

"I'm photophobic," Shirley told the doctor. "I can't stand bright light." He nodded in understanding. He began the examination by flashing bright light on her eyes, then dimmed its intensity.

"Is this better?" he asked.

"Yes, thank you." She was able to keep her eyes open. Her mother was correct; the doctor was quite nice and understanding.

"Your pupils are not dilated, so I can't fully see how your eyes are," he said.

Shirley nodded. From what she could remember, all the eye doctors she had been seeing for years had been reporting the same thing—that her pupils were stuck, for she had calcium deposits on her cornea.

After the examination, Shirley had an ultrasound done on her eyes. The test showed that her retinas were fine.

Being that the appointment had ended, Juliet pushed Shirley to the entrance of the hospital, followed by Allie. "So, he would perform the surgery on my eyes," murmured Shirley. "He said to have the operation for one eye first to see how it goes, then we can consider surgery for the other eye."

"Yes, I hope it will go well," said Juliet, taking a deep breath.

"How is your breathing problem?"

"Awful, but I was able to have that breath. Each breath is taking much energy."

"You should go see a doctor. Go to the emergency room." She had been trying to make Juliet go see a doctor.

"What could they do for me? They'll only say I have mental problems. No one would believe me that a weight-loss drug could cause my breathing and eye problems, just like they don't believe that your eye condition is caused by the enzymes. I'm taking cranberry extract and other herbs that act like diuretics to make me lose the water. If I don't, I'll gain more and more weight! And with so much water inside, it is much more difficult to breathe. Thank God for these medicines—or else I could not breathe at all!"

Shirley sighed. A sigh came out of Juliet's pale lips as well.

***

"Hello, Romeo!" Shirley greeted the new member to the family. It was toward the end of June and he was ninety days old. Juliet had just brought him home.

"Hi," came a small voice from the bird.

"Did he really say that?" inquired Shirley, totally taken aback.

"I heard it, too. Maybe they had taught him the word during the time they had been caring for him," guessed Juliet. But when she had called them, she learned that it was not so; Romeo had simply said it on his own.

"What a perfect beginning!" exclaimed Shirley. "Take him out the cage."

Carefully, Juliet put her hands around the bird's feathered body and set him on the round table in front of Shirley. Romeo did not make a single sound when Juliet began patting him.

"He's so tame and sweet," commented Juliet. "Come on, pat him." Shirley stretched out her hand and patted his round head, being careful not to poke his eyes since she could not see him, other than a faint gray form.

"I love you, Romeo. You're so lovely," whispered Shirley.

Juliet placed the wooden toy she had bought next to him. Right away, he chewed on it. Shirley gleefully listened to the chewing and his breathing sounds as he played. Shirley loved this exquisite, precious moment.

Days sped by quite quickly in the presence of Romeo. Shirley spent her entire days with him, talking and stroking his feathers.

But Shirley had something else that occupied her during the summer. Dr. Foster had contacted the Commission for the Blind, explaining that they could help her. "Shirley's legally blind, so they can assist her with things," he told Juliet.

After his contact with the commission, a caseworker, Megan, from the agency came to visit Shirley. She had told her of a library that had books on audio tapes for the blind and physically handicapped people.

"Would you like to register with them so they can send you the tapes?" asked Megan.

"Sure, that will be great. I love to read," replied Shirley, her eyes glistening.

Thus, she received green boxes in the mailbox. Each green container contained a title. Soon, Shirley asked the library to send her classics, mysteries, and thrillers. Along with the audio tapes, they had also sent her a yellow tape player. The tape player was designed for four-track cassettes, which the audio tapes were, and it had changeable speed. When Shirley figured how to use it, she was delighted that she could listen to the books in a fast speed. Each day, the condo was filled with chipmunk-like sounds coming from the tape player.

"Can you really understand what it is saying?" asked the much-incredulous Juliet. "I can't understand a single word! It sounds like baby chipmunks talking." Juliet walked out of the kitchen and sat down beside Shirley.

"Yes, I understand each word perfectly."

"You are truly amazing. I doubt that anyone else can understand it!" Then she rose from the table and walked to the window. "Remus should be here soon. I need to have the kitchen fixed."

"Oh, yes, I almost forgot that the plumber is coming today."

"The kitchen sink has been clogged, and several times, the contents has risen up, making that gurgling noise we have been hearing."

A moment later, Remus rang the doorbell. He walked in, asked what the problem was, and checked the sink. Then he walked out and went down to the basement to check the pipes. Soon, he reappeared.

"It's a problem with the pipes. It's not your problem. It is caused by the upstairs pipes," he told her.

"Oh, I see. That's why it gurgles whenever I hear the

upstairs neighbor uses the kitchen sink."

"Yes, so I will get it fixed."

"And while you're here, I'd like you to check something else," said Juliet, leading him to the bathroom. "Do you see the ceiling there?" She pointed at the sagging area.

Remus walked to the bathtub and raised his head. "Ah, there's leakage! It's a buildup of water. Something is leaking from upstairs."

Accordingly, Juliet composed a letter to the building manager, who was a new one, and she sent it, hoping that it would be effective.

***

"I'm glad that you decided to go," said Dr. Foster after hearing from Shirley that she had kept the appointment. It was on one July afternoon, and Shirley was seated in the examining room.

"Well, I was excused from all the final and Regents exams, so I could go," replied Shirley, then she continued, "Dr. Chesmore had used very dim light to examine my eyes."

Dr. Foster positioned himself in front of Shirley to examine her eyes. He shone light on her eyes. "You are doing very well today," he commented when Shirley did not squint and she was able to keep her eyes open.

"I guess so, I guess my eyes are better."

When Dr. Foster was done, Shirley cleared her throat. "I need to talk to you about something. The last time I was here, after you had left the room, Carma threatened me."

"Oh? How did she threaten you?"

"She told me that if I don't go see Dr. Chesmore, my mother will get into trouble with the Child Protective Services. She should not say those words to anyone." Thinking of what Carma had said made Shirley steam. Carma had not come to greet them, unlike usual. Shirley felt that she was avoiding them. And she knew for what reason, too.

"I'll talk to her about it," Dr. Foster said before getting up.

Juliet opened her mouth to speak after he left the room. "Do you know why you were able to keep your eyes open today?"

"Why? My eyes are probably better."

"No! Not at all! He had used very dim light today! He only did that after you told him that Dr. Chesmore had used dim light."

"Oh, no wonder the light didn't bother me today!"

Chapter Seventy-Seven

Before her third year of high school started, Shirley called up Mrs. Milton to obtain her schedule for the year. "What classes am I able to take?" inquired Shirley. "Can I take Regents Global Studies II?"

"Yes, that's fine."

"Okay. And I'll take English 10 Honors."

"Let me check... Yes, you didn't finish English 10 last year, so you can take that. How about a math class?"

"Math? I can't see," reminded Shirley, "so I can't take math and physics." Shirley was immensely disappointed that she was unable to take the classes she loved. She had been looking forward to physics. And her teacher could have been the same teacher she had for Earth science, for he had been transferred from the middle school to the high school to teach physics instead. Shirley loved math as well, but obviously that was not an option for her.

"I'll take health class for the first semester," said Shirley.

"Any other classes?" asked Mrs. Milton.

"Is there any other class I can take? Can you please read some of the classes?" After the counselor did so, Shirley made her decision to take creative writing class for the first semester. "Can I take any science class?"

"There's an environmental science class," said Mrs. Milton.

"Do they have any labs?"

"No, not really. They'll have labs that don't involve chemicals. You are able to take the labs home and work on them at home without any problems."

"Oh, I'll take that!" Shirley was glad that she was able to take a science class at last.

"You can call Mrs. Larkin to tell her what classes

you'll take."

"I will. Thank you." They exchanged goodbyes before the telephone clicked. Shirley dialed Mrs. Larkin's office number. She was the person to assign tutors for students. There was no one there, so Shirley was obliged to leave a message on the answering machine. Shirley waited till after the short beep before starting her message, "Hi, Mrs. Larkin, how are you? This is Shirley Cheng and I'm calling to let you know which classes I am going to take so you can assign the right tutors for me."

"Let me make a call to your grandmother," said Juliet after Shirley hung up. Juliet never failed to call Kwi Show once nor had she abandoned any of her responsibilities, even when she was suffering so much. She and Kwi Show talked every day. She loved her mother dearly. "Ask Agatha for the instruction sheet for the medicine, as well as the carton," Juliet requested during her conversation with Kwi Show.

"I will. This is so awful," replied Kwi Show with a long sigh.

Accordingly, Agatha dropped off the instruction sheet at Kwi Show's place. Juliet drove to the house to get the information and found herself looking at the bottle's container and instruction sheet. "Look, she gave me only a bottle at first—nothing else!" hissed Juliet. She quickly read the container. "Lipase inhibitor! So, that was the poison! It had caused my own eye problem, with the same symptoms as Shirley's: cloudiness and worse during menstruation! If I knew it has anything to do with lipase, I would not have taken it! I never eat any fat, and I had only a bowl of boiled broccoli the day I took that one capsule. You see? She did not want me to see the directions. She knows that I don't eat fat and I don't have much fat in my body. She knows about my health problems all these years and she's doing this to me!" She felt a surge of sadness sweeping over her. "Good thing I didn't give the capsule to my pearl! I can't imagine what it would be like if I had."

***

One sunny day in August, Shirley and Juliet waited excitedly for a special visitor. Mrs. Lalli was coming over to visit Shirley. Juliet had prepared for the event by cooking Chinese dishes for the teacher.

"Shirley! How are you?" Mrs. Lalli gave Shirley a warm hug. "It's *so* good to see you again."

"So good to have you here, Mrs. Lalli!" Then she pointed in Romeo's direction. "That's my new bird."

"Wow, you have a bird. He's a beautiful bird!" She walked over to the cage and greeted him.

"He's very friendly," said Juliet, sticking a finger inside the cage. Romeo took it in his bill, but his bite was rougher than usual. *He knows there's a stranger in the house, so he's nervous*, thought Juliet. She opened the cage door to let him out. He quickly climbed onto the open door and got out without a tint of hesitancy. He was unafraid of exploring new places and meeting new people. He had been extremely friendly and tame ever since he first arrived to the household, bringing along much love and joy. He was outgoing enough to get on Juliet's hand without having either of them train him. But Juliet was unable to keep him on her hand, for his sharp claws were very painful. But he seldom stayed on her hand for long; he would rather go up her arm and onto her shoulder. When that happened, Juliet's eyes stung with tears from the pain. *I really don't know how other people could stand it*, thought Juliet, gritting her teeth. Once at her shoulder, Romeo would put his bill toward her face, examining her closely.

"I cooked some food for you," said Juliet, turning to Mrs. Lalli.

"You really shouldn't have! Don't trouble yourself with it."

"No, I really want to. You're always so good to Shirley." Juliet brought the dishes and set them on the table.

Romeo walked around the room, and soon, he found

his way to Mrs. Lalli's side.

"He's examining my feet," announced Mrs. Lalli, chuckling. Shirley knew he loved feet, for some odd reason. Whenever he was roaming the floor, he would shoot straight to her or Juliet's feet like a charging goose. He always had a fascination for feet.

Mrs. Lalli and Shirley exchanged news as she enjoyed the food that Juliet had prepared. "You should teach him to talk."

"I am, but I know it will take some time for him to learn how to talk."

"So, you're going to have tutors? How will you learn?"

"Yes. I am going to have two tutors, one for environmental science and health, and the second one for global studies, creative writing, and English. I will also have women's literature class for the second semester after the creative writing class. I will do everything on cassette tapes and a tape recorder."

"You will record your answers on the tapes?"

Shirley nodded. Then they moved on to other topics. Mrs. Lalli had recently retired and she was enjoying her free time. "I do miss teaching. I really enjoyed it."

"I bet. You are an excellent teacher," remarked Shirley. Juliet enthusiastically nodded her head in agreement. Shirley knew it was rare to find good qualities in people, and she felt so lucky to have Mrs. Lalli as her teacher for both biology and chemistry. She had written a letter to Mrs. Milton before tenth grade had begun, requesting Mrs. Lalli as her chemistry teacher. She had happily jumped on her bed when she found out that her wish had been granted.

Some time later, Mrs. Lalli had to get going. Shirley truly enjoyed her visit. She knew it would not be the last time to see her teacher. They bade goodbye as Juliet opened the door to her.

"Where's Romeo?" inquired Shirley when Juliet returned to her side.

"He's under the dining table. He likes his little hideout. Let me bring him to his playground." She walked over to the parrot and took a gentle but firm grasp on him. Juliet tried to lift him from the ground but his claws were digging into the carpet. "He doesn't want to go! He's clinging to the carpet!"

"He is getting wild now."

"He definitely is. He has grown and he wants to roam more."

Shirley planned to devote time to teach him to say a few words. She continued teaching him how to say, "hello." But she seldom had the time to do it continuously, for she wanted to listen to the audio books. Little did she know that she barely needed much effort on her part in teaching him.

In less than a week later, Romeo said, "Hello!" It had taken both of them aback.

"He said it!" exclaimed Shirley excitedly.

"Wow, and we didn't even teach him that long. He is such a fast learner; just like you!"

"I am amazed. I have read that teaching parrots to talk is a lot of work and requires plenty of time and patience. Romeo is amazing. He is so smart!"

That evening, the telephone rang and Juliet found Adam on the other line. "It's for you," said Juliet, handing it over to Shirley, who readily took the cordless telephone.

Shirley had called up some of her friends to whom she had numbers, and began communication with them. She missed all of her friends a great deal. She wished that she could have her vision back, so she could resume schooling. She had been talking with Adam for several days, but she knew they would not get a chance to talk so often when he was to start his senior year in high school.

"Guess what, Adam!" she gushed into the telephone.

"What?"

"Romeo said 'hello' for the very first time today!"

"Are you serious?" he asked, amazement tinting his voice. "That is so cool!"

They conversed for some time until it was time for bed. Shirley knew she would enter into the tutoring world soon in a few days.

***

The tutoring sessions began with Kristen, who would teach Shirley environmental science and health. After introductions were exchanged, she started by reading a few sections in the science textbook. They were learning things that Shirley had already known from biology class. As Kristen read on, Shirley recorded it on her tape recorder that sat in front of her. "These are the questions for chapter review. They are at the end of each chapter," said Kristen. Shirley made a silent note of it.

"I don't have much work for you today. It is the first day, so I'll have work next time I see you. Let's do some reading for health." She read the first chapter in the book. Then she described what each psychologist's theory was. "Shirley, explain to me each level of the psychologist's theories of children's development." Kristen had asked Shirley to practically repeat the entire chart of age groups for over five theories. Shirley was able to describe only a little for the subject. How could Kristen expect Shirley to immediately memorize the whole chart just after hearing it once for the first time?

"That's all for today. I'll see you Thursday," stated Kristen.

"Mom, could you please read the chapter's questions? I'd like to complete them before she comes back. And you can also read the health book," said Shirley soon afterward.

"Sure, I'll be glad to." Shirley pushed the record button and Juliet began. She encountered a hard word for nearly every sentence she had to read, but she tried her best. She had to take a breath several times while reading.

"Mesosphere," Shirley corrected when Juliet got stuck. Shirley fixed her pronunciation each time.

"This is too hard to read! You can understand everything?" Juliet was incredulous.

"Yes, this is easy. I love this kind of stuff."

"I don't know how you can do it."

"It's nothing at all. It's a piece of cake! That's all," said Shirley, stopping the recorder after Juliet had finished the chapter, "you can read me the questions and I'll answer them." Half an hour later, Shirley completed every question at the end of the first chapter. She asked the tapes to be labeled. She would give the tape labeled "Environmental Science Homework" to Kristen next time. "Here's the two tapes that you can put away for now. Don't lose them, please. I need three more tapes for tomorrow. And label one for creative writing, one for Regents Global Studies II, and the last for English 10 H," instructed Shirley. Juliet did as she was asked. Shirley neatly set the tapes alongside the recorder.

Romeo had been silent during the whole recording as if he had known it was not the time to talk. He had been growing more active as days passed. Juliet usually kept him on the play area above his cage. There, he spent hours with his toys, feeding on his seeds, or he simply whistled.

"He's a natural born whistler!" remarked Shirley. "It's actually the first time I have ever heard a bird whistle."

"Really? I thought all birds do that," said Juliet, surprised.

"A lot of birds just tweet or squawk, but he truly whistles." Then her thoughts turned to the tutoring sessions. She hoped that the second tutor would not be like the one she had this morning. Kristen did not give her any time to listen to what she had recorded and review the material taught to her before starting her specific questions. If her questions were general, that would be no problem. But she had asked questions that needed the knowledge of an entire topic.

Shirley's concerns for the second tutor quickly subsided when she met Doris the following day. Doris did what Kristen had done: recording the reading materials into the recorder, but without the barrage of questions.

"So, you'll have homework for today. Do you want me to record the worksheets?"

"Yes, but wait a minute. The homework should be recorded on separate cassettes so I can hand them in," said Shirley, who called out to Juliet, asking for a few more tapes.

"We're running out of tapes," said Juliet, putting labels on the last few tapes left.

"I can have girl scouts donate a box of tapes," suggested Doris. Shirley was somewhat hesitant of the idea. Then she thought there was nothing wrong with it. "I'll have the tapes for you soon," continued Doris. Shirley and Juliet both thanked her graciously.

After Doris recorded all homework assignments, it was time for Doris to leave. "I'll see you soon, Shirley." Juliet opened the door and thanked her.

"How was she?" asked Juliet once the tutor left.

"She's really nice. I like her. I'm going to start on my work now."

"Don't you need to rest now? You are too tired to continue."

Shirley did feel tired, but she wanted to complete her homework. She shook her head and began her assignment. She had to listen to the question and then forward the tape to the end of the questions to record her answers. So, back and forth she went. Her fingers got sore after only a few questions. She decided that she needed two tape players, one to listen to the questions, and the other to record down her answers. The school had bought her a tape recorder, but the recorded tapes were of poor quality, so she would use it to only play tapes.

The next session with Kristen arrived. Shirley had all the tapes ready before her, including the one she had done for homework without being asked.

"I have a worksheet for you this time, and it is on environmental science," the woman announced. "I am not getting any work from the health teacher."

"After you left, I did the chapter review questions for environmental science."

"Oh, you did?"

"Yes," Shirley handed the tape to her, "here it is. You can hand it to the teacher."

"Good, I will." Kristen then promptly started the lesson on abiotic and biotic factors, which Shirley knew well.

"So, tell me, Shirley, would a wooden table be abiotic or biotic?"

"It is biotic, because it is from a once-living thing."

"Actually, it is abiotic, because it is dead."

"I learned that things made from biotic things would still be biotic," said Shirley. "That's what I learned in biology class."

"I'm just going to put down abiotic," decided Kristen. "I'll ask the teacher about it."

"And I'll call the teacher," promised Shirley. And so she did after Kristen left. The teacher confirmed Shirley's answer. She did remember it correctly: a wooden table was biotic.

"What's wrong?" inquired Juliet a moment later when she noticed that Shirley's brows were without smiles.

Shirley told her the experience with Kristen, who had continued asking specific questions after just reading the material once, without even pausing.

"Does she expect everyone to immediately know every answer after only listening to the material for the very first time?" fumed Juliet. "This will not do. Plus, she isn't qualified. She incorrectly taught you the material. We must talk to Mrs. Larkin about this." Juliet called Mrs. Larkin and explained the situation to her.

"We don't change tutors," said Mrs. Larkin, "but you can drop the classes."

"Can't Doris tutor her those subjects?"

"No, those are not in her fields."

"Then I will have to drop the two classes," decided

Shirley. So Kristen came no more, and Shirley would take health the next semester.

What seemed like a bad fortune turned into something good as Shirley soon found out. The environmental science class, Shirley learned from the Student Course Selection Guide, was a factor seven, meaning that it would lower her grade, even if she received one hundred for the class. "Good thing I have dropped the class! If I take that, the highest grade I will receive could not be higher than eighty-eight, which is equivalent to one hundred!"

"Why would they do things like that?" Juliet was flummoxed.

"I really don't know. 'Regular' classes, like Regents classes, have factor eight, thus any grades you receive will not be lowered or raised. If you get a ninety, ninety it will be. With factor 10, the grades will be raised between eighteen and twenty-five points. AP classes have factor ten."

"That's enough, I've heard enough of the nonsense," said Juliet, with a wave of her hand.

"I don't understand why they have such systems. Students should simply get what they earn—not having their grades increased or decreased just because they are taking a harder or an easier class. And plus, I don't think that the honors classes that I have taken are actually any harder than Regents classes. They just have more homework, but I feel that the level is still the same. I haven't had any trouble with honors. They all seem the same to me!"

A telephone ring interrupted their discourse. Juliet answered the telephone to a woman named Leanne. Megan had also recommended the Lighthouse organization, telling Shirley that the organization could provide products that could aid her. Hence, Leanne from the organization was calling Juliet after she was told about Shirley. "When is it a good time to come to see what Shirley might need?" Leanne questioned Juliet. After checking with Shirley on her tutoring schedule, Juliet made an appointment with Leanne.

Therefore, Leanne rang the doorbell several days later when the evaluation day arrived. Leanne checked how Shirley was able to eat and suggested that when she came next time, she would show Juliet how to prepare food for her. She would provide them with dishes with raised edges, so that food could not be easily pushed out. She supplied Shirley with a talking alarm clock and a couple of talking clocks that had key chains, which could be chained onto the bag that Shirley had tied to her wheelchair. "And would this be helpful?" asked Leanne, handing Shirley an orange sheet of cutouts of small circles with adhesive backs. "You can stick one or a few circles on things to identify what the items are."

"Yes, I think that's just what I need. That will be very helpful. I can stick circles on my cassette tapes to tell them apart."

"You can have this for now," said Leanne, referring to the small square sheet. "I'll bring more next time when I come."

Chapter Seventy-Eight

"He *has died?*" gasped Juliet.

"Yes, he has," sighed Kwi Show.

"But he was so healthy and he could have lived for so long. Just because he refused to eat any salt."

Dr. Ling had passed away in November when he was being hospitalized for an imbalance of salt in his body. Thinking that salt was a harmful substance for him, he had refused any intake of it. As a result, his body swelled to the point it became an emergent case.

"I still can't believe it! He was so young-looking and healthy!" repeated Juliet.

"I can't believe it, either."

"We are very grateful to him. If it had not been for him, we would not have been able to come here to America."

"Indeed, we are very thankful," agreed Kwi Show.

"So, you're now all alone. But just like what we planned before, let's move together. But we can't move to your house because it is so inconvenient for Shirley and me. We will disturb you with our poor schedule. Shirley wakes up several times at nights, and when I help her with things, it will wake you. We need to find a suitable house. Your house is on top of a hill, so it is very dangerous for any car to drive there during winter since it is so steep, especially for my van." She could hear that her mother was hesitant.

"You are always so sick. You'll be too tired to take care of both of us."

"No, I can do it. I love to take care of you. I should do it—you're my mother and it is my utmost happiness and wish to care for you. I will even crawl out of my bed during my illness to give you a drink."

"No one else, neither your sister nor your brother, wants to live with me," said Kwi Show.

"I'll look for a house right away. You can't live there by yourself. You need companions. Let's live together as a happy family! I will do my very best to tend to your needs. You won't need Agatha to shop for you anymore. She never buys you good food. How could you possibly get enough to eat when she spends so little each week?" Agatha spent no more than twenty dollars on grocery for three people—Dr. Ling, Kwi Show, and their housekeeper—every week.

As their plans were underway, Shirley called a few of her friends, telling them that she might move away. She was not sure to where they would move. Perhaps it would be to another county. Thinking it might be the last time she would see him, she called Adam and invited him over. In actuality, it had been three years since they had last seen each other. Thus, it was a fine plan. She would see her other friends, too. She called Erin and Anne to renew their communications.

"Hey, Erin, guess who!" Shirley squeaked into the telephone.

"I don't know. Who?"

"Gee, it's Shirley!"

"Shirley? Really?" The surprise was clearly audible in her voice.

"Who did you think I was?"

Then Erin started to giggle. "I thought you were a kid who my friends asked to play a trick on me!"

Shirley burst out laughing. "Ha, I know. I guess my voice still hasn't change. I still sound like a kid."

"Yes, you still sound like a little kid!" reconfirmed Erin.

They grew serious. They asked hundreds of questions about each other's happenings and health for the past year. Shirley told her of her vision loss, which Erin was shocked to hear.

"That's why I can't e-mail you anymore. I haven't been on the computer for a whole year! I really miss it."

After most queries were answered, Shirley had to get off the telephone. "Call me anytime!" It felt wonderful to be talking to her best friend again.

She had to get back to the tutoring world the following day.

The tutoring days sped by with no issues large enough to be labeled as bothersome, though the time was not free of matters that needed to be solved. Once in a while, there was a certain assignment that Shirley was unable to do because of her physical condition, but she were excused from them after explanations from Shirley. Shirley was doing well in all her three classes. She had been receiving mostly A's as usual. She spent hours on her homework, putting her best effort in every piece of work.

The most work load she received was in global studies. Doris had to read chapters and chapters from textbooks, recording every word in her recorder, while Romeo joined in with his songs. Then Shirley listened to them and answered her questions on another cassette. There were many essays to write and questions to answer in detail. Even if only short answers were required, she would voluntarily supply abundant details as if teaching someone the material. She recollected Mrs. Lalli's advice: "Supply answers that are clear and explain everything as if you are teaching the subject to someone who has absolutely no knowledge on the topic." She always remembered that golden rule, though she had always done so, even before meeting the science teacher.

Shirley had to be on her own with all the subjects she took; whenever she questioned Doris for help, Doris could not help. It, to Shirley, did not feel like tutoring sessions, but rather more like a reading class. Doris simply read the materials to her, told her the questions, then left it all to Shirley. Yet Shirley did not mind. In fact, she liked how it went. She was able to do all her assignments on her own. It was the same when she was in school. True, teachers taught in classes, but after getting home, it would be all left to her to do; she had no one to help her with any questions.

Toward the end of the first quarter, the school

supplied Shirley with cassette tapes on which the entire textbooks were recorded, and as a result, it omitted much of the reading Doris had to do.

Whenever Shirley received her report cards, she always notice that at least one class was marked as incomplete. She then would call up the teachers to ask them about it. All the responses were the same: they had received her work late from the district office, where her finished homework were dropped off. And there, the homework would be sent to the teachers at the high school. The process would take up to two weeks in some instances, so it was not her problem. In actuality, she always finished her homework on the same day she received them, except on large projects that would not be due for a few weeks later. But even with those assignments, Shirley would complete them long before the deadline was reached.

Incomplete was not the only issue about which Shirley thought twice. She noticed for every quarter, her English teacher had given her a grade that was lower than the one she earned for the quarter. Seeing this, Shirley often called her up.

"Mrs. Purcell, why did I get a ninety-one for the first quarter?" inquired Shirley. She knew that it should be several points higher. She had received a perfect score on every vocabulary quiz, except on the first, which she had gotten a 90. She received nineties for all of her essays. Something was definitely amiss with the quarter average.

"I didn't get an assignment from you for the quarter when I issued out the report cards, but you'll have it changed when you receive your next report card. You got a ninety-three, instead," answered Mrs. Purcell.

Shirley knew that was still incorrect, but she never questioned her further. She would wait for her second quarter report card.

"Adam's coming over this weekend?" inquired Juliet, cutting through Shirley's thoughts.

"I have invited him over for the Thanksgiving

weekend. I hope he'll come. I have to ask again," replied Shirley, who began dialing his number. After hanging up, she turned back to her mother. "Yes, he's coming on Saturday."

"Okay, great, so I'll get ready," stated Juliet.

Excitement filled Shirley's soul as the scheduled day drew near. But her heart sank when she realized that she would not be able to see him. At least, she thought, she would hear his voice and could manage to see an outline of him.

Shirley and Juliet spent a quiet Thanksgiving together. But as with all the other holidays, it felt just like any other day in the calendar. "Why not enjoy life every day, instead of just celebrating the specific day men had chosen?" they often said. But Shirley did love Christmas decorations in stores and on the houses they passed by on roads. She enjoyed Christmas Day for its music, the trees, and decorations.

Thanksgiving Day quickly passed, followed by the busiest shopping day of the year. "I certainly won't want to go shopping today. It is always too crowded on this day. It is crazy," commented Juliet.

"*I* would like to," gushed Shirley. She liked crowds, especially a packed mall.

"Get a good night's sleep tonight. Tomorrow will be a busy day," reminded Juliet.

Shirley wished that she could sleep well, too. She had not been getting enough rest for several nights. Shirley always experienced difficulty sleeping, but her insomnia had worsened after taking the enzymes, affecting her overall health, including her menstrual cycle, simultaneously with her loss of vision. It seemed that her life had turned topsy turvy all of a sudden. Her insomnia was worse during her menstruation, sometimes leaving her sleepless for weeks. There were days where she could barely get three hours of sleep. But in spite of her exhaustion, she never missed a tutor session or skipped any of her assignments.

***

Adam crossed the living room and reached Shirley's side. He gave her a hug.

"It's great that you can finally come!" remarked Shirley; a happy blanket wrapped around her.

"I can't believe that I'm actually here," he stated. His busy schedule had made it difficult for him to visit her.

"I can't believe it, either."

Soon, small talk began, with Romeo joining in with his chirps. Shirley carefully inched her way to Romeo's cage and opened the door. Swiftly, the parrot climbed out of his cage. As soon as he climbed on top of the cage door, he conveniently used the carpet as his toilet. Shirley giggled and shook her head.

"You naughty bird," laughed Adam. He wiped Romeo's dropping with a tissue.

"He always does that." Shirley giggled, wiggling a finger in Romeo's direction. Whenever Romeo came out of his cage, the first thing he would do was to do his big business.

Juliet served food at Shirley's round table. The two friends' conversation continued. "So, you're moving?" asked Adam.

"Well, I think so. My family is talking about it." In fact, she was not sure herself. She knew that it would take a while for them to make a final decision. She never preferred moving around. She had hoped that she could stay for a long time at the condo. But apparently, it could not be so.

"Well, I think I should get going. I don't want to keep you from other things and I have some homework to do," said Adam after the sun had long hidden itself behind the mountains.

Shirley nodded in understanding. She really had a nice time. She wished that he could visit more often.

He left, adding another happy moment to her

memories. *The first time that he was here and I couldn't even see him*, thought Shirley with a sigh. She had never uttered a complaint about her vision loss. She wondered what all of her friends looked like now. She had thought of what her tutors could have looked like, giving them faces that were perhaps greatly off target.

Juliet thought it was so good of Shirley that she never cried or complained about the tragic happening. Most people would surely go through times of depression if they had to experience what she was going through then, with the sudden loss of her vision. But not Shirley, who never complained about her health. If she had, she would have been complaining a long time ago, and it would not stop, either, for she could complain about so many things in life. Complaining, she knew, was not going to get her anywhere. She simply wished to get on with life, living each day with a cherished feeling.

Although Shirley never complained about her health, she did, however, complain about her grades, and not just blindly, either—she had good reasons to complain when a grade was not issued to her fairly. Sometimes, if Shirley was lucky, she could get a few points back which were rightfully earned by her hard work. So thus, it was the case when she received her second quarter report card. It showed the change in her English average for the first quarter, but it was not just increased to a ninety-three, but rather, a ninety-five. The change in grade for English repeated for the following quarters—from a ninety-three to ninety-five.

"I was hoping that I could get on the principal list. But I can't now. I didn't get my real grades when the report cards were issued out," Shirley said to Juliet. "See? I have a ninety-five for global studies and ninety-five for English for first quarter. The creative writing teacher, Mrs. Carrey, didn't even give me a grade, nor did she give me one for second quarter. I'll make a call to her." She asked for a telephone and dialed the number. Her teacher answered after a few rings.

"Shirley, your writing is beautiful," Mrs. Carrey said on the other line. "You are an A student in the class."

Shirley received immediate comfort. She would simply wait for the third quarter to find out what she received for the creative writing class. She enjoyed writing poems and short stories for that class. Since she was a person who adulated the wonders and beauties of nature, most of her poems were focused on nature. Nature inspired her to write so many delightful pieces. It provided endless topics to write about. It usually took her no more than a few minutes to write a poem. At times, she could write six or seven poems within half an hour. She was thrilled that her teacher liked her writings.

Before the report cards were mailed out, the school had their usual IEP meetings, and Shirley was scheduled for a telephone conversation, instead of an in-person meeting, by Juliet's request, for going to the school was unnecessary, especially when Shirley's blindness had made traveling much more difficult.

Shirley picked up the ringing telephone on the morning of the scheduled meeting. Mrs. Carrey was one of the attendants. They asked how Shirley was doing with home tutoring.

"It's going well."

"You use cassette tapes to do your work." stated Mrs. Costin.

"Yes, and I record my answers using the tape recorder."

"How are you doing in your classes?"

"I'm doing well. I am getting all A's in my classes."

"And she's an A student in my class," reported Mrs. Carrey.

"Oh, that's good. It appears she's just fine there," said Mrs. Costin. "Well, as we talked about before—do you think the adaptive equipment would help you? You can do your work on the computer rather than recording your essays."

"Yes, that will be very helpful." Shirley had been

waiting for them to get the equipment for her. They had mentioned it some time back.

"Okay, we'll get that worked out for you, Shirley. And you will stay in high school for another year or so to get the diploma?"

"I think she can get her GED instead," suggested Mrs. Carrey.

"Actually, I *am* thinking of getting the GED diploma," said Shirley.

"I think that would be a good idea for her," continued Mrs. Carrey.

"Yes, it would be," agreed Mrs. Costin. A few minutes later, the meeting drew to a close, and she asked, "Do you have any questions?"

"Not now, thanks. Thanks for coming to the meeting," Shirley thanked all the attendants.

"You're very welcome. Thank you Shirley, and have a happy birthday!"

"Oh, thank you!" It had taken Shirley by surprise, but she was glad that they knew. Surely, her files were before Mrs. Costin.

Hanging up, Shirley turned to Juliet and told her of what they had discussed. "They'll get the equipment for me so I can use a computer."

"I know; it was discussed before," remarked Juliet. "When will they get it?"

Shirley shrugged. "We'll just have to wait." She had a feeling that there would be some waiting to do.

In the meantime, her eighteenth birthday was coming up at the start of the second semester. She had no plans for any party. All she wanted was to spend it quietly.

"So, Leanne is coming over again, right?" asked Shirley.

"Yes. She said that she will teach me how to prepare food for you. So, I'm going to buy you a hamburger when she comes that day. I want to see how she can teach you how to eat that."

"I think she'll just cut it up into small pieces."

"Yes, but who doesn't know how to do that?"

By and by, Leanne's next visit arrived. Juliet had a hamburger in front of Shirley as they waited for the bell to ring. Shirley was not hungry then and she never liked hamburgers. Ergo, Juliet was to eat it instead.

"Hello, Shirley," greeted Leanne, coming in after Juliet opened the door to her. "So, we're going to have hamburger for lunch today, huh?" Shirley nodded. Leanne began by unwrapping the warm hamburger. She put it inside the dish she brought, and as Shirley had predicted, she cut it up in pieces, bread and all.

"I'm not hungry now," said Shirley, inwardly wincing. The small pieces made it extra unappealing to her.

***

"Shirley, I will have to tutor a full time student. You're only taking one class with me now, and that is just English since you have dropped global studies," said Doris at the start of the third quarter. Shirley had dropped global studies because there was too much work in that class and Shirley was getting exhausted from working for hours each time. She was reluctant to drop it since she liked the teacher and she had received ninety-five for both quarters. She was taking health and women's literature with a new tutor, Mrs. Hannan. "I think Mrs. Hannan can tutor you English as well. Do you like her?"

"That's fine, I understand. You've been really nice to me and I really enjoyed the time. Yes, Mrs. Hannan is really nice."

"I'm glad that you like her. It has been fun. Let me know how everything goes with you."

"Thank you, Doris."

Therefore, Shirley had only one tutor for the second semester. She preferred it this way. Mrs. Hannan had always been highly friendly and nice to Shirley. She felt lucky to be having nice people as her tutors.

Chapter Seventy-Nine

"Happy hatch day to you Romeo!" exclaimed Shirley on the morning of his big day. "You're one year old!"

"Wow, he's really one already?" questioned Juliet, her voice tinting amazement. "Then he's a big boy now."

Shirley sang a different version of the birthday song. "Happy hatch day, dear Romeo. Happy hatch day to you!"

"Then he should eat some long noodles for a long life," offered Juliet. "I'll make some good spaghetti for him." Romeo was an extremely picky eater; it was nearly as hard to get him to eat as it was to get Shirley. "You two are so much alike: the same voice, the same appetite, and the same level of intelligence." Juliet laughed. "He wants spaghetti that is newly cooked only, no leftovers. And he wants some meat sauce on it, too, not just any plain sauce."

"Gosh, *I* don't even want any meat in my spaghetti! He's *a lot* pickier than I am!"

"Yes, and if he doesn't like what I make for him, he'll throw a fit and start dumping the contents of his feeding bowl on the floor."

"He's so cute." Shirley giggled.

"He's so *naughty*!" proclaimed Juliet.

Romeo promptly received a bowl of fine spaghetti with red sauce with small meat, which he truly enjoyed. "I love you! Mama!" squawked Romeo.

"I love you too, Romeo," replied Juliet.

Sadly, their happiness with the parrot would not last long. Taking care of Romeo was becoming too much trouble for Juliet. She had to keep a watch on him at all times to make sure that he would not step on his own droppings. She had to sweep the floor every day. "It is too much for me. It is much more difficult to take care of him than to care for the parakeets. He produces too much dust, which I have to clean off furniture and floors. He is a wonderful bird, but I just cannot keep him." Shirley listened as Juliet continued to mutter, which was growing more often as days passed.

Before Juliet could plan further to whom she could give the bird away, they were expecting a visit from a few doctors. Juliet had read about them in a Chinese newspaper, that Kwi Show was subscribed to, and decided to contact them. They were from Chinatown. She wanted them to prescribe some herbs to help cure Shirley's pinworm infestation. Therefore, they agreed to drive over.

At the same time, Juliet received a package. "This is what I ordered—a bottle of herbs from George's store. I hope this will be a good batch!" said Juliet. She had been ordering the herbs every so often to check on their quality. "Before, the quality was so good. But soon the quality went poor. Sometimes, it can even be harmful! But hopefully it will be good this time. It had helped you so much before. You couldn't even stand the tiniest amount of sunlight, but after taking it, you were able to stand being out in the sun." Juliet got a glass of water and gave Shirley a dose of the herbs.

It was in the early afternoon of the end of March when the doorbell rang. Three doctors walked in, greeting the two. "Thank you so much for traveling this far to come here," said Juliet. "I really don't know how to thank you."

"It's no problem," one doctor supplied. After all introductions were made, they began to examine Shirley. "She has a weak pulse," said one.

"Yes, she always has," informed Juliet. "She has heart disease."

"Yes, it is caused by the arthritis. We'll prescribe some herbs for her and we'll mail them out to you."

After all was said, they left, but not forgetting to shake Juliet and Shirley's hands.

"I want to go inside now," requested Shirley. Juliet pushed her to the bedroom. Shirley was tired from sitting for an entire day. She got Shirley on the bed and sat herself down as well. She, too, was tired.

"Mom," whispered Shirley. Juliet's heart instantly hastened its pace. She could hear that something was wrong with Shirley.

"What?"

"I can't breathe well! Please give me some asthmatic medicine."

"Oh my, again!" Juliet instantaneously scrambled onto her feet and prepared the asthmatic medication.

Frightfully, Shirley still gasped after receiving the treatment. "It didn't work. I still can't breathe!"

"Do you want to see Dr. Frank?"

"Yes."

Juliet dialed the doctor's number to inquire if the doctor was in. She found out that he was not.

"How about Medicus?" the mother suggested.

"Yes," came the same whisper.

Accordingly, Juliet carried Shirley onto the power wheelchair, put her jacket on, and got herself ready. When Juliet pushed Shirley out of the building, the heavens were sending large white flowers to the ground. "It's snowing at this time? At the end of March?" Juliet was dumbfounded. "Just the right time to snow!" she finished sarcastically. Juliet used all her might to push the power wheelchair onto her van.

It was snowing heavily, making the drive to the emergency center unsafe. "It is really dark. The headlights are so dim!" Juliet had been trying to obtain brighter headlights for her van to no avail. She had installed fog lights, which were of no help. She had been told that the design of the headlights was poor, causing the light to scatter rather than concentrating at the front. "I don't like Ford. I always have problems with dim headlights with Ford automobiles. First the Ford Escort and now the Ford Windstar."

Less than fifteen minutes later, her van arrived at the medical center. The blustery wind hollered as Juliet pushed

Shirley toward the entrance. The strong wind nearly took away the only breath Shirley had left.

"Count how many breaths she takes in one minute. Let her take five," instructed the nurse.

Juliet did as she was told. She looked at her watch and counted that Shirley was taking five breaths per minute. Once the nurse returned to her side a few minutes later, Juliet reported the number to her. Following, Shirley was brought to an examining room to wait for the doctor.

"You're hyperventilating. It is because of anxiety," reported the doctor after seeing Shirley for a couple of minutes.

"It is not anxiety. I never really get anxious. But even if I do, this will not happen to me!" said Shirley, gasping.

"You can disagree with me. I would need you to take some tests, like a blood test to determine another cause other than hyperventilating."

"No," said Shirley. It felt so good to be able to disagree or refuse medical advice now that she was finally eighteen. She had no more pressure with doctors. She was free to make her own decision and her mother would never lose her custody ever again.

The doctor left, seeing that there was nothing left to do for her.

"Let's go," said Shirley. "All they can say that it is anxiety. I know that's not my problem. It feels like asthma."

Mustering up all her strength, Juliet pushed Shirley onto her van. "It stopped snowing."

As Juliet drove onto the main road, the entire traffic suddenly stopped. "What's going on?" asked Juliet. "Why isn't anyone moving?" She looked all around her, but her eyes could only meet silence. There were no movement anywhere. "We've been here nearly thirty minutes!"

"What are they doing?" whispered Shirley, still gasping to get a deep breath.

"No one is moving. Everyone is stuck in place. And it is so silent, just like a ghost town! What is going on?" She let down the window as a man walked past her van. "Excuse me, sir, what happened?" Juliet asked the man.

"The road has ice and it is too slippery to move. We're waiting for the truck to come here to throw salt on the ground. The people up there have already been waiting for two hours," he informed her, pointing straight ahead.

"Two hours! This is ridiculous! Thank you," she said, rolling up the window. "We can't stay here for hours just to wait for the truck to come. You can't survive like this." She inched closer to the center of the lanes. Being extremely careful, she slowly drove to the center of the lines of cars. "I'll drive very slowly and I'll get you home!"

"Mom, please be careful. Don't slip."

"I will be very careful. I have already driven past several cars. I saw some of them looking at me helplessly." Juliet giggled. "I'm almost out!" Several minutes later, Juliet's van was free. "We made it. We are off that road. We had been stuck there for about an hour. Here, I can drive at regular speed! You'll be home soon."

"I don't know how you do it," Shirley managed to comment between her gasps.

"We're home," announced Juliet ten minutes later. "But you're still having problems breathing." She sighed, taking Shirley out of her van. "It had to snow tonight!"

Shirley spent that night painfully. Whenever she fell asleep, she was awakened by suffocation. But somehow, she managed to sleep for a bit.

When day dawned upon the valley, Shirley was still gasping.

"I'll take you to see Dr. Frank today," said Juliet.

"But I think he would say the same thing," said Shirley. "Let's go anyway." Then the telephone rang, interrupting their conversation.

"I just wanted to see how you made out," said a nurse from Medicus.

"Thank you for calling. We got home an hour later," answered Juliet.

"Really? Only an hour? We were still stuck on the road at three in the morning!" exclaimed the nurse.

"Wow, you were there so long!" Juliet exclaimed back. Good thing she was brave enough to risk going through the center.

After hanging up, Juliet made an emergency appointment with Dr. Frank.

But as both Juliet and Shirley had known, Dr. Frank gave the same diagnosis. "Oh well, both trips were wasted. I will just have to wait till I get better myself," whispered Shirley. "I don't get anxiety attacks. It's just what all the doctors say."

"You *never* get anxiety attacks; neither do I, even with what we have been through all these years. So, I'll call Mrs. Hannan to tell her of your illness." She found the woman's number and dialed it.

"I hope she'll get well soon," said the tutor. "Call me when she gets better."

Shirley was dizzy and felt tingling sensation on her body. She tried holding in her breath, but it made her feel worse. She tried to ignore it by listening to audio books, but it did not work, either. She stayed in bed during her illness. Nights were spent with numerous suffocations.

One dawn, Juliet was pondering. "Dear, I wonder if it could be your heart problem?"

"Do you have any medicine for heart problems?"

"Your grandmother has really good Chinese medication that is mild. I'll call her and ask her if she has any left. You took it before and it really helped you. It helps your grandmother, too." She dialed her mother's number.

"I do have some left," replied Kwi Show after Juliet told her about the situation.

"Can you ask Agatha to bring it to me? I can't leave here."

"I don't know. I don't want to wake her…" Kwi Show's voice trailed off. It so happened that Agatha was staying with her that time, so it would be convenient for her to drop off the medicine at the condo. "She's sleeping. I don't want to bother her. It will be another hour till she goes to work. It's very difficult…"

"Please, just please let her bring the medicine over. Shirley can't breathe well. This is the only time I have asked help from her."

"Okay, I will let her bring it when she is on the road to work." Kwi Show quietly consented.

After half an hour had passed, Agatha dropped off the medicine at the condo. "I'll call your grandmother and let her know that Agatha had come," decided Juliet, sitting by Shirley's side.

"Agatha told me that next time, call 911—don't call her," sighed Kwi Show.

"This is the only time I have really asked for a favor from her," said Juliet with a sigh of her own.

"Is Shirley's breathing better?"

"Just a little, but she's still having difficulty breathing. I'll give her the medicine to see if it can help her." Juliet soon hung up. She had no time to delay. She prayed as she gave the medicine to Shirley.

"It didn't help," said Shirley moments later. "I will just have to get better on my own."

Juliet was disheartened. "I love you, pearl. Please get well soon."

"I love you very much, Mom. Don't worry."

A couple of days later, Shirley awoke with a weak smile. "Mom, I feel better today," she announced, her voice stronger.

"Really?" Juliet felt the heavy burden lifting off her heart. "Thank God!"

"Yes, it has been five days. I will probably recover in another couple of days. Then I can continue with tutoring!"

"I have given it some thought. I think the herbs had caused you the breathing difficulty. I took it and I felt discomfort. I will not give it to you anymore. It's such a misfortune. All those herbs were so good in the past—all the green drink and herbs. I don't understand why the quality would change. I have asked people about it and they told me that it is caused by the changes in season."

Chapter Eighty

"I'm really glad that you're better. What happened?" questioned Mrs. Hannan when she resumed tutoring sessions with Shirley.

"I couldn't breathe well." Shirley did not supply much information, for there was really not much to tell.

The session quickly ended, for they did not have much work. Before she left, the tutor told Shirley, "Well, it is April now and I'll be going on a vacation during the spring break."

"That's nice. I hope you'll have fun!"

"I will. It's nice to relax out in the sun."

***

During the spring break, Juliet finally gave into Shirley's insistence—Juliet was going to the emergency room to see if the doctor could do anything to lessen her breathing difficulty. After waiting in the emergency room for four hours, Juliet left without seeing any doctors. She had enough of waiting. And soon, she received a bill for over two hundred dollars. "I didn't see the doctor and they want me to pay so much!" exclaimed Juliet. "I don't receive public assistance right now; I have not had it for years already. So, I would have to pay."

"You should go again, or make an appointment to see my grandmother's doctor, Dr. Leng," suggested Shirley.

"Some other time. I simply don't have the time right now. Seeing doctors takes a lot of time."

"Then don't do anything for a day and reserve it for the appointment."

"Then I will have a load of work for the next day. Plus, they won't be able to figure out what is wrong with me."

As the vacation ended, Shirley received bad news: Mrs. Hannan could not continue to be her tutor, because she had broken her wrist during vacation. Yet at first, she still wanted to come. She informed Shirley that she would have someone to drive her to the condo, but she was unable to write. Shirley insisted that she should not come and that she ought to recover from the injury. Shirley had also spoken to Mrs. Larkin, explaining her reasons. If Mrs. Hannan could not write, how could she have her work done? Hence, it was decided that Shirley would receive a new tutor.

"I am really sorry to hear that, Mrs. Hannan. I do hope that you will get well soon," said Shirley into the receiver. She would miss the tutor. Mrs. Hannan was a kind person who always did her work well in reading the information to her.

"I'm sorry about it, Shirley. I hope you'll like your new tutor. But I think you will. And you're only taking two classes now and it is almost the end of the year." Shirley had dropped the women's literature class, for she had found it dull. The current classes were enough to keep her busy. She was experiencing problems with the health class. The health teacher often sent in the work late then gave her an incomplete mark when he did not receive the work back. But it was not her fault; getting the completed work back to the teachers had to take some time.

"Take care," Shirley said before hanging up. She calculated in her head that there would not be many more days left till school closed for the year. It was approaching mid-May. Before she could meet her new tutor, something else occupied her thoughts with a pang of sadness.

Juliet planned to give Romeo away to Jim, a delivery man from a medical equipment company. He had always expressed an interest in the bird every time he came. With this thought in mind, Juliet decided to give Romeo to him. It was better to give the parrot to someone with whom she could keep in contact, so that she could learn how the bird was doing, instead of giving Romeo to a total stranger.

"Jim can take care of him. If we really want to know how Romeo is doing, we can ask him." And so, it was decided. Shirley had no part in the decision. She felt horrible about giving her beloved pet away. But she had no choice. She was not the one who was taking care of him. "If you can walk and take care of yourself, you can buy as many birds as you like. But it is already too much for me to handle to just care for you."

Juliet called Jim on the evening of May 20, asking him to pick up Romeo. Shirley was sleeping then, so she did not get a chance to bid farewell to the bird. When he arrived in his truck, he simply began to wheel the cage outside.

"You can't have him in the cage when you drive the truck. He'll get cold being at the back of the truck!" exclaimed Juliet. She began to feel uneasy. She handed Jim a towel, so he could use it to catch him and bring him into the cat carrier he brought. Juliet's heart gave a few loud thumps when she saw his rough handling of the bird. Then in a matter of a few minutes, Jim drove off, taking Romeo away.

When Shirley awoke the following morning, she was disheartened that Romeo was gone. "We had him for only exactly eleven months. And he was already able to say so many words," said Shirley, sadly. Romeo often said, "I love you" several times in a day, often repeating "you" after the sentence. Thus, it came out as, "I love you, you, you!" She missed him already.

But it was not the time to dwell on her loss. She was to welcome her new tutor the next day.

With much delight, she discovered her new tutor was a person who possessed a fine disposition. She had crossed her fingers that she would not be another Kristen. Before the first session started, Shirley told the tutor, Jane, about the routine for every session. "And then you just record all the homework on the tapes," finished Shirley. Jane had been quiet and attentive during the whole time she laid out the schedule. Shirley was pleased. She liked good listeners.

Jane had only one set of questions for Shirley to answer for English on the book they were reading in class. She left after recording the questions.

Shirley did her homework with thoughts on Romeo. Juliet had called Jim that morning and he had said that Romeo was fine. Shirley learned that Romeo had a new name: PJ.

"He does act like a mischievous PJ," commented Shirley.

"I hope he'll be happy at his new home. I'm going to do some chores," said Juliet. She went to the closet and opened the door, seeing if she needed to discard anything. Then her eyes fell upon the package of herbs that the Chinese doctors from Chinatown had sent. "So, you're not going to take them?"

"No—at least, not yet." Shirley shook her head. She was apprehensive of taking any new medicine now.

***

"I asked about the final exam and the English teacher said that there will not be one for this year. But the class has a research paper assignment. I'll read it to you," said Jane. Shirley pushed the record button and Jane began. It was on a mythology term paper and students should write a report on the topic they chose.

"I don't know how I will get the material in order to do my research. It's not like I can go to the library and that's it. I won't be able to read, and no one can read so many books to me. And plus, that's like they are doing the research, not me. Will you have time to help me to find the books?"

"No, I don't. And we don't have much time left. I just got this assignment and it was sent to me late. School is going to end in just a few days."

"Then I wouldn't be able to do it. I hope the teacher would understand."

"She should. I mean, you *are* unable to do it."

"And there's not much time left. If I had the same amount of time other students have, I could manage. I will need to have all the materials recorded down for me." Shirley knew it would be time-consuming. It was impossible to go forward with the project. She had no choice but to skip the assignment. "Yes, I think the teacher should understand. She had excused me from assignments I was unable to do before. So, she will treat this the same way."

A few weeks after Jane and Shirley bade goodbye to each other, Shirley received her report card. "I have a feeling that the report card will not be problem-free," said Shirley. Juliet tore the envelope open and read the grades to her. "I got an eighty-seven for the English final exam?" asked Shirley, in sheer bewilderment. "Jane had told me that there was no English final exam for my class. What is the eighty-seven doing there? Mom, please give me the telephone. I need to call up my guidance counselor."

"Here you go," said Juliet, handing her the only cordless phone she could use. She was unable to use most telephones; they were either too heavy, large, or small. "I had a feeling that there will be a wrong grade."

Shirley dialed the number to reach Mrs. Milton. "I've been told that there was no final exam for English, but my report card says that I got an eighty-seven on it! Why is that?"

"Well, the English teachers usually pick out a few grades from the writing portfolios that the students had done for the year," answered the counselor.

"But all my essays and writing projects received nineties for the year, except on one."

"Then I don't know why. Talk to the teacher about it."

And so Shirley did. During the conversation, she had learned that the mythology research paper was counted as a major part of the final exam. She explained her reason of why she could not do the assignment, but her English teacher's ears were not open to reasons. Hanging up, Shirley told Juliet about what the teacher had said.

"I was thinking, the teacher should leave the final exam spot on the report card blank since I did not do the research paper. It is only fair," said Shirley. She thought of calling Mrs. Purcell again.

Instead of having Shirley call the teacher, Juliet offered to do it. She was the parent; she had the right to know the happenings of her own child and discuss any problems. Shirley was by her side in case she needed any help with English, which was always a hindrance for Juliet during conversations. Yet she was able to explain things clear enough, thus it did not result in any misunderstanding, though it was the claim of some people who sought excuses for their own mistakes. Shirley hated when people said that something was a misunderstanding, when, in fact, it was something that was simply caused by their own mistakes.

Juliet's eyes glowed with fury after she hung up with the English teacher. Without another word, she called the principal. But all her effort and time were wasted. Both said that an average of eighty-seven was fair. They even asked, "Why is a difference in only a few points such a big deal?"

"It's not just about the points. You should just leave the final exam grade blank on the report card. Why do you have to give any grade to Shirley?" Juliet had demanded. "She should get what she earned. She was unable to do the research paper because of her physical condition and lack of time! She received the assignment at the last minute."

No amount of reasoning could open their eyes and ears. Therefore, Shirley was stuck with an untrue grade, lowering her overall English average from a ninety-five to a ninety-three.

English was not the only class about which Shirley had to call the school. The health teacher had given her a B for her final exam, and Shirley was positive that she had received a grade in the mid nineties. After several calls were made to both her counselor and health teacher, the grade was changed. "He said that there were a few questions in the final exam you could not do, because those questions were taught in class and had not been taught to you," explained Mrs. Milton. "So, you got a ninety-two on it." Shirley had thought the test was the easiest test that she had ever taken. So, why was it only a ninety-two? She knew it was still incorrect, but she did not press further. At least, she had gotten several points back.

***

"I'll have the surgery tomorrow, and Agatha just dropped off a small bag containing a few bottles of eyedrops," Kwi Show told Juliet over the telephone one July evening. "I have no idea what these eyedrops are for and how to use them." She was scheduled for a cataract-extraction surgery with Dr. Foster the next morning, and Agatha was the one who was responsible to make sure that everything would go smoothly. Juliet wanted to be the one to take care of this for Kwi Show, but she and Kwi Show both knew that Juliet was already overwhelmed with the work she had to do for Shirley.

"Ma, then you shouldn't get the surgery when you don't know what they are for," said Juliet. "I can't believe that Agatha didn't tell you, and that she gave them to you at the last minute!" But then, she *could* believe anything with Agatha now. Yet, Agatha never failed to shock her. "I'll cancel the surgery for you."

"Yes, you're right," sighed Kwi Show. She could never depend on Agatha to do anything, only to create problems.

Afterward, Juliet learned that for cataract surgery, patients must be on the eyedrops for three days prior to the operation, using them four times daily, and they would need to use them for a month after the surgery.

Chapter Eighty-One

The fourth year of high school had arrived, and Shirley was in high spirits as she waited for her new tutor to come. The summer months had passed as swiftly and as steadily as a passing thundercloud. She had spent the entire summer listening to audio books from the Talking Book and Braille Library. She knew she had already read hundreds of books. But the library was often slow in sending books to Shirley. They did not have enough staff to do the work. Sometimes, she had to go without any books for a week or more. She loved classics by authors such as Edgar Rice Burroughs, Wilkie Collins, Honore Balzac, Alexander Dumas, William Shakespeare, and Bram Stoker. She hoped that she could complete reading all the classics ever written. The summer, however, did not bring Juliet and Shirley happiness all the time.

Juliet had called Jim to find out how Romeo was doing, but each time, Jim only supplied cursory answers. Then one day, Juliet gave a horrid gasp.

"What's wrong?" Shirley had inquired, getting concerned.

"He had disconnected his line!" exclaimed Juliet in anguish. "He had disconnected especially for me." She did not know whether to laugh or cry. She asked the operator for his new number. Disheartened, but sizzling with fire, Juliet hung up. "His new number is unlisted. "How could he do this? We only wanted to know how the parrot is doing. But he has to come here when I call them to deliver some supplies!" Not so. Someone else came when she called. "He's even avoiding me." Juliet could not believe it. How was Romeo doing? "Did Romeo die or something?" thought Juliet out loud.

"Oh, I hope not!"

"He probably got injured. Jim had treated him roughly when he snatched Romeo by the towel and shoved him into the carrier."

"You said it was a cat carrier. I hope he doesn't have a cat!"

"He never mentioned about having any pets."

The contact with Romeo had completely been cut. The separation between Romeo and Juliet appeared to last forever.

But thoughts of Romeo left Shirley's mind as she was getting somewhat impatient for the wait. Ten minutes had passed and still no sign of her tutor. She thought of the class she was going to take; it was a mixture of science topics. She was thrilled. It was called chemistry/human body, which included health, biology, chemistry, and nutrition, all of which were Shirley's favorite topics. Juliet had called the guidance office and asked the new receptionist, a kind and patient lady, to send the Course Selection Guide to Shirley, so that she could tell Shirley which classes she could be able to take for the year. It was hard to make the selections, for she was unable to take some classes while other classes were reserved for graduating seniors. She was not a senior, even though it was her fourth year. She had only nine credits so far and would need to earn at least several more to be a senior. She had found out from her guidance counselor that she needed about twenty credits to graduate. She feared that she would not earn enough to graduate before her twenty-first birthday, so she was planning to earn a high school equivalency diploma instead. Juliet had been telling her to go for a GED ever since she started high school. "It's just no sense to go to high school and waste your time taking useless classes and color all the time," Juliet had always said. Doris and the creative writing teacher had also recommended that she get a high school equivalency diploma instead. But Shirley wanted to stay in high school to experience life there. She did not want to miss out on anything. Although there were endless problems, she still truly enjoyed the time in the school.

"What time is it?" asked Shirley.

"She's late," Juliet said. Shirley sighed. Most people, who made an appointment with them, were often either late or early by several minutes. Shirley extremely disapproved of tardiness. She thought people should arrive promptly as a sign of respect, especially on the first day. But being late five minutes was fine.

Then the doorbell rang. "That must be the tutor. She's twenty minutes late," said Juliet, rising from the sofa.

"Hi, Sherry!" Shirley welcomed the tutor.

"Hi, Shirley," the tutor greeted. Although she was late, Sherry sounded like a nice person.

As with all her previous tutors, Shirley began telling her of what should be done during tutoring sessions. "And I will hand in my work on the tapes and then you drop them off in the office. Then they send them to the teachers! It's a long process," explained Shirley.

"Yes, I know."

"So, what work do we have?"

"We have some worksheets on the human body. They are for the science class."

"Oh, good!" Shirley could hardly wait to get started on them. Physiology was one of the majors she hoped to receive a degree in from college. Shirley whizzed through the worksheets. "They are so easy!"

"Piece of cake, huh?" giggled Sherry. "Oh, we have one more worksheet, and it is on muscles. There's an assignment where you have to label the muscles. You won't be able to do that, so I'll put it to one side."

"Label muscles? How?"

"Well, you have to draw diagrams of muscles on a body and label their names. You won't be able to do it."

"Yes, you're right. Please tell the teacher that."

"Don't worry about it." Minutes later, all the worksheets were complete. "That was quick. And that's all I had for you today. Hopefully, I'll have more work for you next time."

"Thanks, Sherry, I'll see you then. And please don't forget to let the teacher know about that muscle assignment."

"I won't; don't worry about it."

Sherry came with a unit test in hand several days later. "And there's also an assignment for English, where you have to create a poster about the book the class is reading. But of course, you're not going to be able to do it. I mean, since you can't see." Shirley agreed. "So, how do we do this test?" asked Sherry.

"You can just read each question to me, then read me the choices. And I'll tell you my answers, which you would write down."

The test started and Shirley laughed at each question that was asked. "I find them hilarious."

"Me, too," agreed Sherry.

"They are so easy." Shirley rolled her eyes. Then a question on the subject of muscles made her stop and think. "That wasn't covered on any of the worksheets," noted Shirley. "I never learned that. Could you please circle that? I'll make a guess later." The test took a few minutes to complete. With no other work to do, Sherry left. It was then that Shirley remembered that Sherry forgot to read the circled question to her.

***

"I have some of your work back with the grades," announced Sherry, sitting down to start another session. "Do you want me to tell you the grades now?" Shirley nodded. Sherry took out all the worksheets and read the grades. "A 10/10, 10/10. And you got 5/10 on this worksheet."

"Which worksheet was that?" asked the much-befuddled Shirley.

"It is on the muscles, but I'm not sure what you got wrong."

"Will you call the teacher and ask her about it? I'll

call her, too."

After Sherry left, Shirley asked for the telephone. "I'm calling my chemistry/human body teacher, Mrs. Tighe." She dialed the receptionist, who transferred her to the classroom. The telephone rang on and on until Shirley hung up. "She isn't there. I have to try again tomorrow."

The following day after another tutor session, Shirley called again. She knew that Sherry had left a message for Ms. Tighe.

Shirley greeted Ms. Tighe and told her the reason of her call. "What did I get a 5/10 on?" The teacher told her to hold on the line.

After Ms. Tighe found Shirley's records, she returned on the line. "You did not do the label assignment for the muscles."

"I'm blind, so I am unable to draw the diagrams and label the muscles."

"Then you don't need to draw. Just say which muscle goes where on the body."

"I didn't know I can do it like that. My tutor just said that I can't do it. And that was the end of the matter."

Toward the end of the conversation, Ms. Tighe decided to resend the assignment and let Shirley make it up.

Soon, Shirley encountered another matter. She got the unit test back and found out that she received one point off. Ms. Tighe had taken the point off on the question on which Shirley did not receive any information. She called Ms. Tighe. But the call was made fruitlessly. Ms. Tighe did not excuse her from that question. Shirley had a feeling that it was just the beginning of her problems. She prepared herself for more in the future.

***

"I got a ninety-four for that science class?" asked Shirley in shock as Juliet read her averages on the report card.

"What were you supposed to get?"

"I should have gotten a one hundred. I received one hundred on all the worksheets for that class, other than the 5/10 and that one point on the test, both of which are not my fault. How could I be penalized for something I didn't do?" She was still waiting for the make-up assignment for the muscle diagram from her teacher.

"And you got an eighty for English class," continued Juliet.

"That's preposterous! I'm calling the teacher now." Shirley quickly punched in the school's number. Shirley held the telephone, using her right shoulder for support, and waited for the teacher to come on the line. Since her right elbow could not bend, she needed to hold the telephone receiver using her left hand as the receiver rested on her right ear. Making a call was difficult for her. If she talked too long on the telephone, her left hand and arm would get sore.

"Hello?"

"Hi, how are you? This is Shirley Cheng." The teacher repeated the question and Shirley answered with a, "fine, thanks." She waited for the teacher to speak, but after a moment of silence, it was apparent she was to continue. "I was wondering why I received an eighty for the first quarter?"

"You failed to hand in the poster," supplied the teacher.

"Well, I am totally blind so I am unable to draw."

"Can you color?"

"I can't see, so I can't color. I used to be a fine artist. It's just that I am blind now."

"You don't need to see in order for you to draw. You can just use your imagination. You can ask your tutor to help you."

"My tutor is very busy and she can't stay with me to color and draw." How was the tutor able to help? This was ludicrous. Of course she needed vision to draw and color. Did the teacher really wanted a blob of messy colors? She shook her head in distaste.

She was a student who put her best effort into every school project. She thought of last year: she had struggled with coloring and cutting for her posters for her French projects. She worked for hours with her deteriorating eyesight. Each time, her poster turned out to be the most colorful, containing the most details. But there were times when she could barely see well enough to color. She used magnifying glasses to aid her as she drew. She had spent hours on each project, and coloring caused her hand and arm to get stiff and sore. She glowed every time when she saw her French teacher's pleased countenance. She loved making her teachers happy, and that was the best reward. She took joy in doing her very best. But of course, her French teacher was a wonderful, understanding person, along with many of her other teachers.

"I don't think I can take your class," said Shirley.

"How about you think about it, Shirley, and call me with your decision."

"I will, thank you." Shirley did not need another minute to make up her mind; her decision was already made. She left a message on her guidance counselor's answering machine, telling her that she wished to drop the class. She simply had enough of the nonsense. It was an eleventh grade honors English class, not an art class in middle school. It was not the only class where she was encountering problems. It seemed that this year was full of difficulties with the teachers. She enjoyed all her work, but the teachers had made the experience hard for her. But she would never give in. Now, she had only one class to take.

**

For a long time, Juliet saw that Shirley was happy with her tutor, though Sherry was often late arriving at the condo. She was always nice to Shirley, which was the most important thing in their eyes. They hoped that the happiness would continue, lasting till the year was over. Sadly, it could not be so. Shirley received the unfortunate news toward the end of November.

"This is going to be my last day here. I already called Mrs. Larkin about it and she's finding someone else for you," said Sherry. Shirley was surprised. Sherry did not tell her about leaving before. It was the first time she had received the news. Why was it whenever she had someone nice to be her tutor or aide, they had to leave?

***

One day, Juliet answered a telephone call from a stranger. "Mrs. Cheng?"

"Speaking?"

"Hi, I'm Mabel Murray, the BOCES teacher. I can provide help for Shirley on anything she needs." She went on explaining and asked to come for a visit. Juliet agreed for her to come, and set up an appointment.

When she came, Shirley began telling her all the problems she had with her teachers, especially with Ms. Tighe. Mabel wrote down everything Shirley had said. "You certainly can explain things well!" stated Mabel. "You're very articulate."

"Yes, she really can," confirmed Juliet.

After Mabel finished writing things down, she had nothing else to do, so she decided to leave. "That's all for now. I'll let you know how I do. I'll give you a call."

But Shirley did not hear from her. Juliet thought she would give a call to her instead to ask if there was any progress. "Those issues are not in my scope, so I can't help you," answered Mabel. Disgusted, Juliet thanked her before ending the conversation.

"She only wasted our time. If she can't help you with any issues, then she should've told us when she was here. Instead, she just kept on writing, wasting the whole day for us!" said Juliet.

Mabel came a few more times and nothing was resolved. Each time, an entire day was wasted. She had told Shirley that they could raise pictures on paper so that Shirley could "see" them with her hands. "It might have helped you with that diagram for the muscles."

Shirley agreed for that to be done. But again, no more words were heard from her concerning the topic. *Besides, there are not many, if any, diagrams for classes, and I doubt that it will benefit me much,* thought Shirley.

Chapter Eighty-Two

December was a busy month for Shirley and Juliet, and not because of the holiday season. A lady from Woodstock was to come to evaluate Shirley to see how she could use the adaptive equipment on computers. The school had spoken about the issue with Shirley and Juliet several times since last school year. Shirley had been eagerly waiting for the equipment to use it to do her homework. The equipment was used by visually impaired people, so they could use computers. But it was unclear to Shirley how everything functioned.

She no longer had to wonder as the day for the evaluation arrived. Daphnie, whom Megan had recommended, was the person to teach Shirley how to use everything.

"There are two programs that you can use," explained Daphnie. "One program is called Dragon Naturally Speaking, a voice recognition software, which will type out what you say into a microphone. The other one is JAWS, the program that actually talks to you. It reads the words on the screen, including menus and dialogue boxes."

Shirley was awestruck at how the technological society had advanced through the years. The software sounded like magic.

Daphnie showed Shirley how the programs worked using the laptop she brought. "You can't use your computer because it is not compatible with the software. Would you like to have a laptop or a desktop computer?"

"I would like to have a laptop. It is more convenient for me."

"I will contact Megan, your caseworker. I'll let you know how it goes." When all was done, Daphnie left.

At the same time, Juliet had contacted the GED

department to inquire about the test and to seek a way for Shirley to take it. She reached the GED chairperson, Mrs. Sheehan, who sounded pleasing to the ear, to discuss the matter.

"You have to get a doctor's note stating that Shirley needs special accommodations to take the test, such as using cassette tapes and a tape player, staying home rather than taking the test at the testing location, and having a scribe record down her answers," informed Mrs. Sheehan.

"Okay, I will ask her pediatrician for the note."

"We will be starting a new kind of test after January."

"Oh, what is the difference?"

"The new test will have two math parts rather than just one like the old test. The old test has all multiple-choice questions for math, and the new test will have one part where the answers will be supplied by the test taker, then the other part will have the multiple-choice questions. It also will have more graphs and political cartoons. Shirley can take a practice test first."

"Yes, Shirley wants to take the practice test."

"But we won't have the practice test for the new test for a while, so Shirley will have to take the old practice test instead."

"That's fine."

"But I really don't know how she would be able to do the math section."

"She can do it in her head." Juliet started telling her of Shirley's past successes with all her work. "She was able to do chemistry in her head without seeing anything."

"That is amazing!"

After they ended their conversation, Juliet called Dr. Frank to ask him to write the note and left a message for him to call her back.

***

Juliet opened the door to Shirley's new tutor, but

noticed that she was not the only person she was inviting. Mabel also came—unannounced. The two passed Juliet and went into the living room where Shirley was seated, without greeting Juliet, who felt *she* was the guest instead.

The two sat down at the round table. Juliet, coming around the table, turned to Mabel and said, "Please call me next time before you come." Mabel nodded.

She is very disrespectful, thought Shirley, disapprovingly. Shirley listened on as the two women conversed without minding Shirley. Was this a time to teach or a time to relax and chat? She had been waiting for the new tutor to come to continue what was left off when Sherry was last there, which had been nearly three weeks. She hoped that she did not miss much work during the entire duration of the transaction.

"So, is there any work for today?" asked Shirley, no longer able to stand the women's chattering; over half an hour had passed.

"No, actually not. I didn't receive any work," answered Mrs. Leonard, her new tutor.

"Well, this is what is done," Shirley began to explain the tutor procedures.

"I'll take some notes," said Mabel, taking out a notepad and a pen. "Okay, go ahead."

Shirley felt this was an interview. She continued, "This is the tape recorder that you will use to record any work you have for me, including textbooks, worksheets, and anything you can add. I have cassettes that are labeled." Mabel jotted down everything. "Here's the tape to be handed in for my science class, the chemistry/human body class," Shirley handed a tape over to the tutor. It was the make-up work she had done for the labeling of muscles. "And how can I contact you when I am sick and have to cancel a session?"

"You can call my home," answered Mrs. Leonard.

"Will you be able to get the call since you work at the district office?"

"Yes, but call and let me know soon."

"I'll call you as soon as I know, but sometimes I get sick suddenly, like an asthma attack. I don't want you to waste a trip here."

"I don't want it either. But my husband can give me the message that you called."

"And please let me know as soon as you cannot come or you're late," said Shirley. "And how about snow days when there are delays?"

"Some days with the delays and the snow is still on the ground, I won't be able to come…my arthritis…I don't want to fall."

"I understand." After Shirley explained everything to her, Mrs. Leonard scanned the papers in her hands, seeing which classes Shirley might be taking.

"You're taking honors English?"

"Not anymore." Shirley shook her head to Mrs. Leonard's inquiry. "I dropped it. I had a problem with it. The teacher wanted me to draw and color, which I can't for an obvious reason."

"Why didn't you go to another class?"

"I don't want the same thing happening."

Mrs. Leonard laughed, "Not many other teachers are going to be that crazy. Why were you taking honors English?"

"Excuse me?" asked Shirley, thinking she might not have heard the question correctly.

"Why did you take an honors English," repeated Mrs. Leonard.

"Because I'm eligible for it. My grades are in the nineties."

"Yes, but you don't have to take honors."

"But I *want* to."

"I just thought that you can take a Regents English so you don't have to miss English."

"I have to get going," announced Mabel, rising from her seat. "It was nice meeting you, Mrs. Leonard."

After she left, Mrs. Leonard continued the conversation. "So, are you going back to school?"

"I can't when I can't see. But of course I would like to go back if I can see again."

"I don't think you should go back. Kids can be cruel. I had a student who was sick and had to stay home. But when he came back, kids spread rumors that he had AIDS. And there was another girl who went back and people started saying that she missed school because she got pregnant."

Shirley inwardly frowned; she was stunned that the tutor was actually discouraging her from going back. "But kids won't make fun of me," she stated, unflinching.

"Well…" Mrs. Leonard's voice drifted off.

Mrs. Leonard's mouth kept going and going and going, just like the pink Energizer bunny. Thirty minutes had passed when Mrs. Leonard finally got up from her seat. *She sure can talk*, Shirley thought. And she was not even talking back toward the end.

"It was nice meeting you, Mrs. Leonard. And please don't forget that tape I gave you that has my homework," said Shirley. Juliet walked back into the room and showed the woman out.

"How was it?" asked Juliet.

Shirley rolled her eyes. "She is too talkative! She's been talking nearly the entire time, especially when Mrs. Murray was here. But she is probably just like this on the first day, and that she would not talk and would start to focus on work when we get any work from the school."

Juliet could see that something was bothering Shirley and questioned about it. Shirley was hesitant to tell her, but gave in on her insistence. "She tells me not to go back to school because kids would make fun of me," then she repeated what Mrs. Leonard had told her.

"That is very unprofessional of her to talk to you like that. She should know better than speaking to her student like that."

"I will talk to her about it. She's coming back next

week."

"That's exactly what you should do. Better to fix anything at first before waiting for more problems to mount up in the future."

***

Shirley was ready and prepared for the conversation as she waited for Mrs. Leonard the following week. She had an empty tape inside the recorder. She knew what she was going to say. Then a few knocks sounded. The doorbell, for some reason, did not work for her. The tutor was invited in and Shirley greeted her promptly.

"Mrs. Leonard, before we start on the work, I'd like to discuss something with you."

"Okay," said the tutor.

Juliet pulled out a chair from the dining room and set it beside Shirley at the round table.

"I'll record this," said Shirley, posing her finger above the record button.

"Sure," said Mrs. Leonard. Shirley did not want to go through this, but she had to. She did not want the same thing to repeat itself in the future. She knew if she had a problem, she should say it right away, instead of waiting for time to do its work. It would not work, Shirley had learned. And it was best to record it now in case anyone would deny it in the future, just like what had happened in the past.

Once Shirley started the recording, she began speaking into the recorder. "Okay, here's the conversation with Mrs. Leonard. Today is December 20. Could everybody state their names?"

"Alice Leonard."

"Juliet Cheng."

"Okay, and this is Shirley Cheng. Well, I'm going to discuss something with you in the hopes that you will understand my viewpoint. What I am going to say is that all of these are my beliefs, my feelings, my thoughts, and my personal viewpoints. After Mrs. Murray left and that day was December 13, we continued our conversation."

"Yes," confirmed Mrs. Leonard.

"And during one point of the conversation," continued Shirley, her voice mild and professional, "you began telling me a story. In this story, you told me that you knew two students." Shirley repeated the stories that Mrs. Leonard had told her a week ago. "And during and after your story, you said to me personally that you think I should not go back to school. I think what you said to me and your story were inappropriate for three reasons. First, my personal policy is that other people's personal affairs are really none of my business to know about because I wouldn't want people to spread about my problems if I tell one person. Let's just say that I tell my best friend…tell her such and such of my family problems, and I wouldn't expect her to call up her friends and repeat it to them because it's just not right. I called her up for consultation." Shirley went on without pausing. "Secondly, what you said to me personally that you don't think I should go to school was, I think, discouraging. My reason is that I think that people should encourage others throughout their lives, especially by educators, such as yourself, Mrs. Leonard. A lot of people encourage me to go back to school. And definitely, if I could see right now, I would start school right away tomorrow without a shadow of a doubt. And also thirdly, what you said to me personally really offended me because I know for a fact that if I start school right away, students and teachers would greet me with a warm welcome. But let's just say that what you said is true and that's exactly what's going to happen—that students would ridicule me—even if what you said is true, you still shouldn't have said that to me. For instance, if I go over to an obese person and I tell her 'you're fat'—even though that is a true statement, it's a very hurtful, disrespectful statement, and I shouldn't be making those statements. So, in the future, I really prefer you not to tell me those kind of stories and say those personal things to me. Will you, Mrs. Leonard?"

"I'm sorry. What I told you...it was to let you know that some kids have difficulty going back. Some kids can be cruel, they don't mean to be mean, but they say things that hurt. I wanted you to be prepared when you go back. Some people may say something that can be hurtful," explained Mrs. Leonard.

"I know in my situation that it would not happen. I have missed school many times and every time I went back, I was greeted with a warm welcome. I know what you said are your beliefs and your thoughts, but I really hope in the future that you will keep those remarks to yourself."

"I will, I will. I didn't mean to encourage you to not go back to school. That's not what I meant. I'm sorry that I said something that you took that way or I worded it incorrectly. I'm a great believer in education, and to go as far as you can possibly..."

"Yes, that's my goal," said Shirley, firmly.

"And you have...you have unbelievable abilities, but you know some of this," remarked Mrs. Leonard, "You've been absolutely gifted with..."

"Thank you," said Shirley.

Mrs. Leonard continued, "You have a very logical mind, which...is...you analyze things and...one, two, three..." The three giggled. "I didn't mean to upset you. I'm sorry. That was not my intent. It was more in the way of a warning..."

"Yes, I know that was your personal thought," said Shirley, understandingly.

"I've seen kids hurt."

"I know some kids can be nasty. Well, my first priority here is just to work in harmony. I want both sides to be happy. I mean, if you're not happy, how can I be happy? I want to pursue an education with a one hundred percent happiness. So, you know what I'm saying? I don't want to have any misunderstandings or miscommunications between us. If you have a concern or question, please feel free to talk to me about it; and the same with me. You agree with me on what I'm saying here?"

"Yes, one hundred percent," replied Mrs. Leonard.

"That's great. Thank you very much!" finished Shirley. "That's all I have to say for today. Anything you want to add?" Shirley questioned the group.

They answered, "No." Then the tutoring session began. There was not much work to do for Shirley, but the session was long. Mrs. Leonard talked about anything that had been risen from the topics of the class, so Shirley had to wait for her to end her chatter.

She sure can talk, thought Shirley, getting somewhat to the line of impatience.

At last, Mrs. Leonard ran out of things to say, so she got up from the chair, packed up the materials, and walked out the door after bidding goodbye to Shirley.

"How did it go today?" inquired Juliet. Shirley gestured her hand in a talking motion. "She still talks a lot?"

Shirley nodded. She did not feel like talking for now. She just wanted to lie down and get some rest. Juliet got her into bed.

"I'll massage your legs while you rest," said Juliet. She sat by Shirley's legs after she got her comfortable. Juliet had been massaging Shirley daily for many years. Each massage session lasted at least thirty minutes.

Then the ringing telephone interrupted them. Juliet answered it and recognized the voice of Mabel on the other line. Just as Juliet and Shirley both expected with several winces, Mabel asked to drop by at the condo to check on how things were progressing. Thus, another day was prepared exclusively for her visit. Did she not realize that such visits were causing so much disruption on their part?

Mabel arrived with no lack of questions. She asked how Mrs. Leonard was.

"She is really good. She does things very professionally," replied Shirley. It was the truth. Mrs. Leonard was an organized person who paid attention to what she was doing and one who readily did things as asked by

Shirley.

"Oh, that's great, I'm so glad. So, is there anything else?"

"No," said Juliet and Shirley in unison. They wanted to tell her not to come anymore, but not sure how to word it. Shirley never liked asking someone to leave. She thought about the Chinese proverb: "Welcoming guests in is easy, but inviting them out is hard." How true!

"I really don't want her to come anymore," muttered Shirley after Mabel left.

"I'll call her then. You really don't need her to help you with anything?"

Shirley shook her head. "And the thing is that she has never provided anything she had promised to help me with. I don't want her to come anymore."

After wasting more time with Mabel, Juliet finally had it. She called up Mabel and asked her not to come. No one was at home, so she left a message on the answering machine. Soon, Mabel called back, but Juliet was tending Shirley and could not get to the telephone.

"If you don't want me to come, you would have to call the school," Mabel said on their answering machine.

But she came no more without having Juliet make the unnecessary call to the school.

"Oh, what a relief," breathed Shirley. "All those days were wastes of time."

Chapter Eighty-Three

"Today will be a fun day!" announced Mrs. Leonard, walking in with a large bag in hand.

"Oh, really?" asked Shirley.

"Yes."

"What are we going to do?"

"We have two fun labs to do. You'll have to taste Pepsi and Coca-Cola and tell which is which. And the other one is that you have to smell fifteen items and determine what items you are smelling by their smells," said Mrs. Leonard.

"Oh, I'm allergic to those drinks. Remember I told you last time?"

"Oh, yes, Shirley, I forgot. Then we can't do that one. That's too bad. But we can do the other one, the smelling lab." She called to Juliet, "Could you find several items? I have brought over a few items."

"What kind of things?" inquired Juliet.

"Anything that Shirley can smell. Something that she will be able to identify—things with strong smells."

"I don't know if we have anything here," said Juliet, rummaging in the refrigerator. It was asked of her too sudden. If they had been told about this earlier, Juliet would have prepared the items beforehand.

"How about spices?"

"Spices!" exclaimed Juliet. "I guess I have some." Juliet went to another room but soon reappeared in the living room, with a pair of watery eyes. "No, I just remembered. I smelled some of the spices, and I sneezed. Fortunately I remembered—Shirley has severe allergies, and she just got better recently. She constantly sneezed during the entire day, the whole year round. No, she cannot do this lab."

Shirley had one day discovered a temporary relief for

her allergies by accident. Once, she had been sneezing so painfully that she had thought it was a cold. She asked to take some Chinese cold medicine containing an effective antihistamine. After taking it, her sneezing shortly ceased. At that time, her nose was starting to bleed and it had sore spots from all the sneezing. Ever since that time, she took a capsule to treat her sneezing problem. It worked like a miracle for her allergies. She needed only one capsule and she would spend many days without a single sneeze. Day by day, her condition was better until the frequency of sneezing became low.

"It was so hard to keep her from sneezing. I really don't want to risk it," continued Juliet.

"Oh, that's too bad," repeated Mrs. Leonard.

"Yes, I can't do it." Shirley was glad that her mother had remembered it, or else it could have been too late. "I just got better with my allergies recently. And I don't want them to flare up again. I will have asthma complications when my allergies worsen." Allergies primed the lungs and other parts of the respiratory system so Shirley would be susceptible to asthma attacks. Colds and other viral infections could also trigger asthma attacks for her.

"Shirley can't even be around the kitchen when I cook. She will immediately sneeze. She can't even smell perfume," explained Juliet.

"So, we won't do it," said Mrs. Leonard.

"Would you please let the teacher know about this? Explain to her my situation," said Shirley, beginning to grow concerned. "I hope she'll understand."

"She should," assured the tutor.

"Tell her I have very serious allergies and asthma," repeated Shirley.

"My, you just have everything, don't you, Shirley?" laughed the lady.

Shirley joined in. "Yes, my life is hard. I also have insomnia!" *I have serious constipation, heart disease, and chronic bronchitis as well*, Shirley added silently to herself.

"Well, on to other work. Oh, yes, I forgot to tell you. You received a ninety-eight for your first quarter in the science class."

"Oh, so Ms. Tighe changed it?" Mrs. Leonard was unbeknownst of the incident, so Shirley explained it to her. "But I still need to talk to her about it. I don't know why that it is not increased up to at least a ninety-nine." Shirley yawned as she finished those words. She had not slept well at all last night, and exhausted was an understatement of how she felt. She had been awake for most of the night, listening to the radio and her mother's loud gasps. She felt heartbroken when her mother was awakened each time from suffocation in the middle of the night.

***

The telephone rang once, twice, and then one more time. It was a few weeks later and Shirley was calling her science teacher. "Hello?" a voice answered.

"Ms. Tighe?" asked Shirley. She was calling her for yet another one of her concerns. It seemed that it would not be her last time to call about a problem, though she prayed it would be.

"Hi, Shirley."
"How are you?"
"Good."

Shirley was waiting for the teacher to direct the question back, but she did not, so she stated her reason for calling. "Well, I'm calling in regards to my first quarter average," said Shirley. "Mrs. Leonard told me that you had changed it to a ninety-eight. Is that right?"

"I have to go look at my binder, can you hold on?" Shirley rested the telephone receiver on her shoulder so as to hold on to it better. A minute later, the teacher came back on the line and confirmed the validity of the average.

"How many points did I get for the muscle work?"

"It went from a five out of ten to nine.

"What point did I miss for that?"

"You missed one point because it was late."

"But it wasn't my problem because I never got that make-up work until that time—the time I did it. I completed the assignment on the first day I got it and I handed it in right away on the day of my next tutoring session. So, I don't know why I should have one point taken off for that."

"Because it's my policy—something that is late, I take off 10 percent."

"But I didn't get it till then. I did it the first day I got it, then I handed it in to my new tutor, Mrs. Leonard, right away, but it wasn't till a few weeks later. Then it would take another week to get it to you. So, it's not my problem that you got it late." Shirley should not be responsible for a work that was received late from the office.

"Well, I sent out the work on October 5, and I didn't get the work back till before the Christmas break. So, I think that is more than fair," said Ms. Tighe.

"But my first tutor, Sherry, didn't even read the assignment to me, she just told me that it was something I can't do. And she also didn't read that one question on the test, so that's why I had missed one point on the test." Shirley felt it was useless to go on, but her spirit would not let her give up so easily. All the problems that had been caused by the tutor or the transfer of homework from the office to the school were affecting Shirley's grades adversely. "I shouldn't be held responsible for that test, either. I never got the necessary information for that question. You might have given it to the tutor, but I never got it from anyone."

"Shirley, I grade what I get. That's all I could do."

"I know, but that's not fair to me."

"The work was two months late, so it is more than fair that I only took one point off," reiterated Ms. Tighe.

"But I can't help it that it was two months late. But if I could, of course I would be held responsible for it. I never got a chance to do it. My tutor didn't even read it to me. When I found out that I got five out of ten, I was puzzled.

Sherry was, too. Then we both called you, and you told us that I didn't do the muscle assignment. So, on the last day that Sherry was here, she read the assignment to me, then I handed in my work on the first day that Mrs. Leonard was here." How many times did Shirley need to repeat the story? She felt she was in the song by Bob Dylan, *Blowing in the Wind*.

"I know that's a special circumstance, but it's just my policy. I did make it an exception and send it again, and I let you make it up. And I understand that you are saying that you did it as soon as you got it and all, but from my end that's fair to me."

"But you should understand my situation."

"And I *do* understand your situation."

She sure did not sound like she understands, thought Shirley, bitterly. "If it is my fault, you can take off twenty points and I would think it is fair! I lost my eyesight in tenth grade, and all my teachers excused me from the Regents. All students are required to take them, but I was excused because of my special circumstances."

"I find it hard to argue over one point. Other students come to the class and do the labs and they still get seventies."

"It's not about one point, it's about the principle of the matter. I shouldn't get penalized for something that was not my fault."

"Who should I talk to about this?" asked Ms. Tighe.

"The assistant superintendent, Mrs. Dalton. I forgot to mention that I have an IEP, where it states that I have extended time to do my work and that my work should be done strictly on tapes and tape recorders. So, please talk to her about that. And also, it is the teacher's job to modify any work for me."

"You see, that's the thing. I spoke to Mrs. Larkin about it and she told me that it is not my job, but your tutor's. Sherry is a special education teacher."

"But I was her first student with a vision impairment,

and she had no idea how to modify the work. Please talk to Mrs. Dalton." How would Sherry know how to modify the work? Ms. Tighe was the teacher, and any modification without her approval would not pass.

"I will."

"And what is my second quarter average?"

"It's a ninety-one," answered Ms. Tighe after a pause.

Shirley was puzzled. How could it be so low? All the work that she had done received nineties and one hundred. "How come it's a ninety-one?"

"Because you got a zero out of twenty on the smelling lab. You also got a zero out of ten points on the Coca-Cola lab, but I didn't count you for that because you are allergic to it."

"But I couldn't do the smelling lab for the same reason—because of my medical condition." Shirley was getting irritated. Ms. Tighe should have treated the smelling lab the same as she did with the Coca-Cola lab. "I have severe allergies, and I can't do that lab."

"But your IEP didn't state that you have allergies and that you can't do the smelling lab, right?"

"Does my IEP have to list all the problems I have? I have heart disease and it's not listed. I know my body the best."

"So, why are you taking my class when you can't do the labs?"

"My guidance counselor said that I can take your class. She said that it is fine."

"I'll talk to Mrs. Dalton about it," said Ms. Tighe.

Shirley knew she had no more to say to her and said her usual "thank you" before hanging up. At last, the long, agonizing conversation ended. Shirley's blood was boiling now. She saw no reason and justice in front of her. She needed a way to end this kind of problems from ever happening again. Without hesitating, she picked up the telephone receiver with her sore hand, and dialed the school's number again. She asked for the principal, but he was not there, so she had to leave a message, explaining the problems. "Please let him call me as soon as possible," said Shirley.

"I will, Shirley," a gentleman answered.

Chapter Eighty-Four

Shirley knew it was time to receive her grade point average (GPA) and her class rank. She called up her guidance counselor in January 2002, shortly after the last call she had made to Ms. Tighe. She felt that she had been spending most of her life on the telephone.

"May I know my GPA and my class rank, please?" Shirley knew that she should know how she did in school; everyone else had received the information in junior year.

"Shirley, you don't have a class rank. It would just be a comparison."

"I know, but I just want to know, along with my GPA."

"I will have to calculate it. Could you call back maybe tomorrow?"

"Sure. But how is it calculated?"

"You factor your grades and add them up…"

It was nothing new to Shirley; she already knew the steps. Before calling the counselor again, Shirley had come up with the total points, 772.6. But what could that be? She knew they had charts to list what the numbers would translate to. Thinking hard, Shirley knew the answer. It was a 96.6. She was pleased to have a 97 GPA.

When the time arrived to make the call, Shirley picked up the telephone and dialed the number again.

"Are you available to give me my GPA?"

"Yes, Shirley, hold on." After a minute or two, the guidance counselor came back on the line. "it is based on nine credits. Most of the time, it is based on twenty credits, so this is just an estimate. And it would not be accurate."

" I know."

"Well, you have an approximate average of ninety-six and your class rank is thirty-nine compared to this year's graduating seniors of 575."

Shirley was pleasantly surprised that she had done so well, and had gotten this high on the list. All the students who made it to this level had taken Advanced Placement classes, which meant they had between eighteen to twenty-five points added to each AP grade. Shirley was the only one without any AP classes, and had made it this high among those who had. But Shirley knew her GPA was 0.6 higher.

"Did you get 773?" inquired Shirley.

"772.666..."

"So, it is not accurate?"

"No, it is approximate."

"And my GPA? Is it exact?"

"No, it's an approximate. It is compared to this year's senior class."

"Will this information be on the transcript?" asked Shirley.

"Again, it is approximate."

"Okay, but they can be on the transcripts?" repeated Shirley. Her counselor confirmed it. "So, on your chart, to get a GPA of one hundred, what number do you need?"

"Excuse me?"

"To get one hundred. Maybe it is eight hundred?"

"Let me see...you would need 800.222..."

Shirley was correct once again. "So, let me guess—your chart goes by eight points, and each eight interval means one GPA point. So, if it is 792, it will be a 99 GPA. Is that right?" figured Shirley.

Mrs. Milton hesitated. "Right," she answered. "Okay?"

"So, shouldn't I have a 96.6 GPA?" Shirley was not giving up. She wanted to get the numbers as exact as she could. Why not when they had the chart to help? Why not get the most accurate count? Mrs. Milton confirmed every number that Shirley calculated. Shirley knew she had figured out everything correctly. She no longer had to ask her counselor for her GPA information. She could do it on her own now. She was pleased of her GPA. The 97 GPA was as a result of her "real" grades. Most of her grades did not receive any factors, for they were Regents classes; only three were factored.

The counselor did not answer her question but instead asked one of her own. "So, are you applying for college?"

"Yes, but I'm going to wait for another year."

"To where?"

"I'm hoping to go to very good colleges, like Vassar and Harvard; you know? I have to wait, though."

"You're getting your GED?"

"Yes, at the end of this year."

As they were going to hang up, Shirley remembered another question she had. "Academically, am I eligible for the Honor Key? I know I'm not a senior, and that is for seniors. But I'm just wondering if I am academically eligible."

"The key represents an accumulative index of 680 or higher," Mrs. Milton read the student handouts. "So, you have, because you have 772. But the question is, you're not a senior. You only have nine credits, and that's a junior. That's something you would have to discuss with someone else."

"I will. That's all. Thank you." At length, the conversation ended and Shirley had obtained the information she was looking for. Sadly, she knew that she was not eligible for the National Honors Society for the same reason as with the Honor Key. She was not going to talk to the principal about it, knowing it would not help any. She was touched by disappointment.

The only, and the best, reward Shirley received those years was her self-fulfillment; no paper would bring more happiness and triumphs than a personal inward feeling of satisfaction.

Soon, she called a friend to share the good news.

"Wow, Shirley. That is amazing. You got such a high average without taking those classes." Shirley knew her friend was referring to "those classes" as AP classes.

"Did you get your class rank?" asked Shirley.

"No, I don't like competition."

"I do."

"I'm surprised you do, Shirley. You don't seem like someone who likes competition. You always seem so…"

Shirley knew exactly what her friend meant. She always appeared so quiet and good in classes. But she loved competition and challenges. That was how and why she had enjoyed running for student government in her freshman year.

***

Several days later after Shirley's nineteenth birthday, which was spent quietly with her mother, though she had received several calls from her friends, Shirley made another call to her counselor. She had called for this reason before and had left two messages, but she had never received an answer to her inquiries. "What is my GPA in the 4.0 form?" asked Shirley after greetings were made.

"Why do you want to know?" asked the counselor.

"I have the right to know. I've been told I should know this."

"Who told you?"

"Someone my mom knows." Why was the counselor making it so hard for Shirley to know her own GPA? All the other students could know.

"Who?" persisted the counselor.

"My mom's friend." Shirley was not asking for a top secret information!

"Okay; well, a ninety-six is a 3.89."

"How about a ninety-seven?"

"That's a 3.9." After several minutes of interrogation, Shirley's question was finally answered.

Chapter Eighty-Five

Several more problems arose with Shirley's science class as the days progressed. The readers need not be included in the excruciating incidents. But we should be informed that all Shirley's effort to solve the problems was made in vain.

As Shirley went about, making her calls, Juliet also made some important calls of her own. She called Boston's Floating Hospital for Children and Newington Children's Hospital, asking them to send her Shirley's medical records.

The records arrived in Juliet's hands in February. She scanned the documents and was shocked as she went through the pile.

"No wonder Dr. Robinson grew silent when I told him that you had never seen Dr. Schelling, the doctor he recommended. The records showed that you had been seen by Dr. Schelling all along!" exclaimed Juliet, shaking her head. "And Dr. Schelling had even written a letter to Dr. Robinson, and she had lied many times throughout her letter! I'm not sure how many letters she actually wrote to him. They didn't send me the complete documents."

"That is so odd," stated Shirley, shaking her head as well. "How could a doctor lie about such matters?"

"I'll read you portions of her letter. She even spelled our last name wrong. This letter is dated February 6, 1985." Juliet cleared her throat and began:

"Shirley Chin came to see us in Arthritis Clinic at the floating hospital on February 5, 1985. She seems to be doing better.

"She seems to be taking her aspirin and to have been doing at least some physical and occupational therapy. She is walking some, and is somewhat self-sufficient in activities of daily livings."

"I would suggest the following:

"1. She should clearly continue with an active physical and occupational program. In particular, she needs to walk putting her heels down first. She is capable of dorsalflexing her feet, but she tends to walk on her toes. We would suggest that she spend some time each day walking without her shoes on and learning to have a more normal gait. She should be encouraged to be as self-sufficient as possible.

"2. Concerning her medication, she should continue on aspirin with the level monitored every once in a while to be sure that it is therapeutic (once every month or two would be plenty). I would try to taper her off the steroids at this point. We suggested to Mrs. Chin that she cut the dose to 1½ mg every morning. You might want to reduce it every couple of weeks or so by ½ mg and get her off within a couple of months. The Chins need to be reminded that Shirley is at risk of for hypoadrenalism in times of stress for as long as one to two years. Should she have a serious illness or bad accidents, the physicians taking care of her need to be reminded that perhaps she should receive additional steroids if things look rocky."

Juliet stopped. "This is outrageous. No one saw us when we went to the hospital on that wintry day of February 5! How could she say these lies? And you could never walk then, and Dr. Robinson is the witness. He said that your condition was only getting worse, not any better, when I brought you to see him right before February 5."

"I know, but that's how they were. There are always people like this in the world," said Shirley.

"That's not all," continued Juliet, "I have a bunch of files here. Here's what the developmental consultant from the Boston's Floating Hospital had written on December 20, 1984: 'Shirley has continued to improve in all areas although she still resists walking. She is less depressed and more playful.'

'This hospitalization has been difficult for Shirley and

her family.'

'Mother cannot put the child asleep and keeps picking her up when Shirley protests. She wakes her to eat.'

'Both Shirley and her mother have difficulty in maintaining their relationship but at the same time, allowing themselves to be separate individuals. Mrs. Cheng has difficulty knowing how to be available and supportive and promote Shirley's autonomous striving both physically and emotionally.'

'Shirley did demonstrate behavioral problems during her therapy sessions however, and frequently refused to cooperate with the physical therapist, a problem which was exacerbated by the presence of her mother.'

'On days that her mother remained present during the hospitalization, she still insisted on carrying Shirley, limiting her incentive to achieve mobility on her own. The feeding disturbance that was present at the time of admission rectified itself to a large extent. Shirley would take a sufficient food and caloric intake to satisfy growth requirements by the time of discharge. However, she had demonstrated a pattern of stopping to feed herself when her mother was present, reverting to her prior pattern of refusing to eat and would be pursued and force-fed by her mother.'

'There was considerable difficulty in implementing this therapeutic regimen due to the objections and interference of Shirley's parents. It was felt that the lack of compliance and consistency which had been demonstrated on multiple occasions in the past in dealing with other physicians in other hospitals constituted a serious threat to Shirley's ultimate ability to walk and that it would adversely affect a normally good prognosis of polyarticular juvenile rheumatoid arthritis.'"

Juliet tapped the paper, letting out a whoosh of air between her teeth. "They treat such a loving mother, a most ordinary person, like this with such hostility. How will they treat their real enemy?"

Shirley shook her head with distaste. She could not

believe that the consultant, who was a registered nurse, could say such lies.

"I never woke you to feed you. You never protested when I came to pick you up. On the contrary, you frequently held out your hands for me to carry you," sighed Juliet. "Here's more maddening lies, which are so risible," she cleared her throat again and began to read. "This morning, parents spoke of leaving the hospital, they were found, with Shirley in a warm outfit for out-of-doors, by Dr. Barry in the stairway on the seventh floor, apparently in the process of leaving the hospital. They were asked to return and speak with us about Shirley's treatment. Dr. Persse and Louis Small (hospital's attorney) spoke with the parents at length this morning. Under the threat of going to court to obtain temporary custody of Shirley by the hospital, the parent agreed reluctantly to stay at BFH until Friday 11/9/84. They expect that we will bring Shirley's fever under control by then. It was explained to them at length that Shirley's JRA would not be 'cured' in one week, nor would she walk in that short period of time."

"As of now (11/2/84 evening)

"1. If parents try to leave the hospital, a temporary restraining order should be obtained immediately. Call: security; Boston Juvenile Court; Louis Small; Dr. Barry."

"That's really something," remarked Shirley. "They had it all planned out. Did they actually think that you're crazy? Surely, we would not want to run away and be a fugitive for the rest of our lives. I want to live a normal life, not to be in fear wherever I go!"

"Yes, and that report was written on November 2, 1984 and we couldn't possibly even have *thought* about it so quickly. You were there for only the fifth or sixth day. They can't even *lie* well! They said that JRA can't be 'cured' in a week. Ha, Dr. Chung 'cured' your disease in two days. Your high fever was gone in that short time. They shouldn't think that there is no better treatment than theirs out there!"

Juliet flipped through the files and read another

report. "I'm reading a report that was written on November 5, 1984 and it stated, 'Shirley will not be offered anything to eat or drink at night.' You weren't an ordinary two-year-old who didn't need to drink at night; you didn't eat enough during the day. They wouldn't let me give you milk at two in the morning when they gave you aspirin. You needed to have something in your stomach when you took aspirin. But even if you didn't take aspirin, you would still need to drink at night." She paused. "And here's a report written when you were seven years old, written by a psychologist. As with all the psychological reports, this is not absent of slanders and distortions of your true splendid image."

"Okay, read it. I'm ready." Shirley giggled, finding it all ridiculous.

"Shirley's first admission to Newington Children's Hospital was from May 24, 1990 to June 12, 1990."

"In addition to her JRA, a variety of behavioral issues were noted at the time of that hospitalization. This included significant conflicts related to Shirley's independent feeding of self and typically resulted in mother force-feeding her daughter. Mrs. Cheng often reported that she was greatly fatigued and stressed by the total care she needed to provide for Shirley yet frequently opposed and/or declined a variety of recommended treatments which were aimed at increasing Shirley's adaptive behavior. These treatments included splinting, serial casting, and casting under sedation. Following a variety of these recommendations, a recommendation for surgery was made which mother refused. A decision was made not to pursue the behavioral issues and to attempt to forge a cooperative relationship with Shirley and mother and allow Shirley to be treated on an outpatient bases. If outpatient was not successful over a three-month period in yielding some progress, further recommendation for surgery could be made at that time. However, once discharged, Mrs. Cheng did not follow through on the recommendations and Shirley was readmitted on July 13, 1990 under orders of temporary custody by

DCYS."

Juliet snorted. "We have to endure all that ill treatment and slanders from those hospitals! They *knew* that I was going to take you to China after the first admission. Not following through with their recommendations? What recommendations? Only physical therapy! The only treatments you had received when you stayed in the hospital were physical therapy and naproxen, and even the doctor saw no improvement at all with these two treatments, so that's the reason you got discharged. I didn't see any good results for you either. Why should I 'follow through' what they abandoned? I'd rather go to China to receive much better physical therapy: massage. And they said 'readmission'—it was capture, not readmission. I willingly made an appointment with Dr. Zammit to see him and the eye doctor, but instead, it was a trick. They were all well aware of my plans to bring you to China."

Shirley listened attentively. Juliet continued after taking a large breath, "I have an article that clearly paints the whole picture of this case. It is a foreword written by Dr. Thomas G. Gutheil, M.D., an associate professor of psychiatry from Harvard Medical School."

Excerpted from *Qigong for Arthritis: The Chinese Way of Healing and Prevention: Massage, Cavity Press, and Qigong Exercises,* 2nd Edition, by Dr. Yang, Jwing-Ming. Foreword by Dr. Thomas Gutheil. © 1996 YMAA Publication Center, www.ymaa.com:

"As a woman from two cultures, Mrs. Cheng had had her daughter's illness treated in both America and mainland China. American specialists tended to use standard medications in the treatment of this crippling disease; physicians in China offered a combination of herbal and physical therapies. …the evidence from the child's own history seemed to indicate that a blend of Western and Chinese therapies brought some relief for the child's condition…"

"The child's Connecticut physician recommended surgical repair of the child's knees, hips, and left ankle. The child's mother, by all evidence, presumably competent to make this decision, rejected this recommended operation and expressed her intentions to take the child to China (when that was safe) for less extensive surgery combined with traditional Chinese treatments (recall that Western-Eastern combined therapy had had some success before). However, the mother's refusal of the proposed operation triggered various child-protective actions by Connecticut's Department of Child and Youth Services, following guidelines in the laws designed to cover children thought to be at risk for parental neglect. Thus, the child was taken into custody by the public agency, and a superior court judge authorized the operation. For a physician in my field—forensic psychiatry and medical-legal topics in general—this case has many interesting features in several realms: the question of informed consent to medical treatment; the right of competent individuals to reject treatment (even, theoretically, life saving treatments); problems of cross-cultural issues in individuals who are making complex health-care decisions; racism and sexism in American medical and legal practice (as might relate to the fact that the patient was both a woman and Chinese); and many other clinical, legal and ethnical questions."

"Note that Mrs. Cheng was not planning to give her child no treatment (i.e., to deprive the child of treatment); nor to give the child some idiosyncratic treatment (such as laetrile for cancer); nor to use non-medical religious methods of healing, as in some of the Christian Science Legal cases that have been much in the news lately. Instead, Mrs. Cheng was planning to procure an active treatment regimen for her child, a regimen which drew upon a history of medical research, diagnosis and treatment extending back for literally thousands of years; and which, more importantly, had been empirically demonstrated to have some beneficial effects in this child specifically."

Juliet then got out the report written during Shirley's emergency visit to Vassar Brothers Medical Center on July 29, 1997. "The doctor who called CPS that time told Dr. Madison that he felt there was a 'lack of care' which might have caused your condition," Juliet told Shirley.

"Lack of care—from the aides, not you," said Shirley. "If it had not been for the aides' poor treatment, I would never have gotten asthma."

"And this report says that you were to receive plenty of IV if you did remain in the hospital."

"Fortunately, you got me out of there. We're very grateful to Mary!"

Chapter Eighty-Six

"I'm changing my diet," Shirley said to herself. She had been reading books on nutrition and blood type diets from the audio books she had requested. ALEVE was not working well for her anymore. It was used for acute symptoms, not as a long-term use for relief. She thus decided to change her diet according to her blood type. She read that her blood type should be on a vegetarian diet, so she decided to stop the consumption of red meats. She liked pepperoni. It would be a sacrifice to make, but it would be one that was worth it. She wanted to live a life that would be as free of pain and discomfort as possible. After researching more on the topic, she switched her diet. She was somewhat skeptical, but she thought to give it a try.

In March, merely one month on the new diet, she felt her health had improved on a noticeable level. She was able to sit up in bed on her own. Her joints did not hurt as much. All in all, she felt like a new person. "Don't give me ALEVE anymore, Mom," requested Shirley. "I feel so much better."

As days passed, Shirley was completely off any pain relievers. All she needed to take were vitamins. She still ate tuna and chicken, but completely avoided red meat.

As the year approached April, Shirley soon found herself occupied by thoughts of an upcoming special occasion rather than on the troubles of her science class. In May, a senior prom was scheduled. Shirley had been looking forward to it ever since she could recall. But in order to go, she had to cross another impediment. Since she was not a true senior, her allowance of attending the promenade was questionable.

Taking a deep breath, she called the principal to ask for permission to go to the dance. "You have to call your guidance counselor about that," he answered.

Feeling like someone who was asking for trouble, rather than requesting permission to attend simply a school event, she dialed the guidance office. Mrs. Milton was busy, so she had to leave a message.

Waiting for the answer was the hardest part she had to endure. Would she be allowed to go? It would be her only chance of going. She had the dress ready. It was in the color of bright fuchsia, making the gown appear hot pink if lambent with sunlight. It had puffed sleeves and strands of pearls and pink ribbons at the back. She was planning to invite her best friend, Erin, to the prom.

Ring! The telephone interrupted her reverie. She crossed her fingers, hoped for the best, and answered it.

"Shirley?" asked Mrs. Milton.

"Yes, how are you?"

"You wanted to know if you can go to the prom?"

"Yes."

"You will get your GED this year?"

"Yes."

"Then yes, you can go."

Shirley nearly jumped off her bed with joy. She thanked the counselor. She was going! But that was not the end of the issue. She needed someone to be there for her in case she needed something or anything happened. Juliet was not allowed to stay with Shirley. She was to drive her there and stay in her van for the entire duration of the dance.

"Would you like Meredith to be your aide for the night?" asked Mr. Broderick when Shirley called him to discuss the issue. Meredith still worked at the school, providing miscellaneous help around the building.

"No, I would like to have Pat to be my assistant. She was my last aide. She is really good."

"I'll ask her about it."

The next day, Mr. Broderick called back with the answer. "She said that she will be pleased to be your aide."

"Really? That's wonderful! Thank you so much!"

Juliet also talked to him concerning accessibility

issues. "Can anyone help me push Shirley on and off my van?"

"Yes, there will be someone who can."

All the planning had been completed.

"That's pretty good of him to see that you have an aide for the prom," commented Juliet. Shirley nodded her agreement. "I will have to go find that place. I hope I can find it." Each had called the building for the directions.

"The directions don't seem so hard," remarked Shirley.

"I'll find the place next week," decided Juliet. At the same time, Bob, Shirley's old bus driver, was to go buy two tickets to the prom and reserve a table for her.

"Everything is working out nicely," said Shirley, with a happy expression.

In the meantime, Shirley was going to take the GED practice test that they just received from the mail. "It takes so long to get it," stated Shirley. She listened to each cassette tape for each of the five subjects: writing (essay for part one and grammar for part two), arts and literature, mathematics, Social Studies, and science.

Shirley first started with science. After listening to a question, she recorded down her answer on another tape recorder. After she was done with all the subjects, including the essay, she handed the cassette with her answers to Juliet, who would fill out the answer sheets using Shirley's recorded answers. "And here's the tape to be sent in; it has my essay recorded on it," said Shirley. It had taken her around five hours to complete the practice test.

"I don't know how you are able to do all those completely in your head, especially the essay, math, and graphs!" exclaimed Juliet. "I'll send the answers out as soon as I get the answers down."

***

The day before the senior prom, Shirley received a

call from an assistant principal, telling her that he would provide the help in pushing the wheelchair into the building, which was located in another county. Juliet had spent a day in finding the location of the place. "It is quite far! Took me about forty-five minutes to get there, but it will take us longer when you're in the van since it is dangerous to drive too fast." Juliet normally drove forty miles per hour when Shirley was with her.

All that was left to do was to wait for the big day. Shirley and Erin had exchanged several calls in the meantime, making sure that both parties would go. "I'll call you on the day of the prom to let you know for sure that I'm going. I hope nothing will happen," Shirley told her friend. "Too bad I can have only one date."

"I'm your date." Erin giggled.

"You sure are!" Shirley laughed. "I am so excited about it. What will you wear?"

Erin described her black evening gown. "And how about you?"

"It's a surprise! You'll see when you come."

"Not fair," murmured Erin. Shirley giggled more in reply.

"Well, I have to go. I'll call you after you get back from school," reiterated Shirley.

***

Gods of the heavens decided to cover the sun with gray clouds with the help from the thunder god. Juliet started the engine with a low groan. It had been raining the entire day. "I hope it will stop raining when we get there!"

"It always rained at your prom," recalled Erin.

"I know, it rained last year for my class' junior prom. But I didn't go anyway."

"You still look the same," commented Erin. "That's a very pretty dress. You didn't tell me that you are going to wear hot pink!"

"I do, huh? I haven't seen you for so long, Erin! I wish I could," said Shirley, wistfully. "Oh, it's not hot pink. It is fuchsia."

As Juliet drove on, the outpour of rain became heavier and heavier. "This is a horrible day," sighed Juliet. "I hope nothing will happen."

"Don't worry. Nothing will happen," consoled Shirley. The van drove over the bridge on the glistening Hudson River.

"Oh, the river is so pretty!" gushed Erin. "Right, Shirley?"

"I can't see it," replied Shirley, smiling a small smile.

"You can't even see the river?" asked Erin.

"No, I can't."

"Don't you miss seeing?"

"A lot."

After over an hour on the road, the party of three arrived at the back entrance, where the ramp was located.

Suddenly, as if to shower a welcome on the three, the heavens dumped extra tons of water onto Earth. It was certainly not a fine opening to the event. Juliet quickly put a poncho on Shirley. She asked Erin to put on the other one, but Erin only shook her head.

Pat ran out of the building, followed by one of the volunteers for the dance, who quickly pushed Shirley off the van and into the building. He gasped for air as he struggled with her heavy wheelchair.

"I miss you, Shirley!" greeted Pat. "How have you been? Have you been keeping out of trouble?"

"Yes." Shirley giggled. She nearly forgot to introduce her to Erin. "Pat, this is my best friend, Erin. And Erin, this is Pat, my aide." Shirley pointed, hoping it was in the right direction. It felt strange to be out at a new place without being able to see where she was.

"What table are you assigned to?" asked Pat.

"Table number one. I think it is just by the dance floor."

With Erin following behind, Pat pushed her in the direction of their table. Along the way, several friends of Shirley came to greet her. They had not seen her for over a year already, but she had kept some up-to-date with her vision loss. She was unable to contact everyone, for she did not have their telephone numbers, only their e-mail addresses.

"Shirley, you look beautiful!" gushed Mark, a good friend of Shirley. He was at her seventeenth birthday party. Then Shirley received a hug from another friend, Sarah.

"How's your eyesight?"

"It is not good. I can't see," answered Shirley, shaking her head.

"You look very pretty," came another voice. She recognized that the voice belonged to another good friend, Ayda. How she wished that she could see all of them! Shirley said her thanks a few more times before arriving at her table.

Shortly, food was served. "What is this?" asked Shirley, pointing at her dish.

"I have no idea," replied Erin. The two girls burst out laughing.

"Want to dance?" asked Shirley. "Or I think you should meet some people!"

"Like who?"

"Come on, don't be shy. Just greet some people." Shirley rolled her eyes when Erin simply glued to her seat. Then Shirley started to sway to the music.

"Want me to push you by the dance floor?" asked Pat.

Shirley nodded eagerly. It was time to enjoy herself to the fullest! Erin watched Shirley dance wildly to every song.

"She's the disco queen," remarked Pat, with a few chuckles.

"She's wild," confirmed Erin.

I certainly am! thought Shirley. The night continued

with Shirley never missing a beat. Little did they know that Shirley was feeling unwell that day. Shirley had been up since midnight. But her exhaustion did not show as she danced. It was a night not to be forgotten.

Chapter Eighty-Seven

Soon, Shirley returned to the tutoring days. Mrs. Leonard walked in for another session. The session ended an hour later, for there was only one test to take. Shirley could have finished the session in merely fifteen minutes, but Mrs. Leonard had been talking excessively during the entire time, thus delaying each question. One question from the test would often start up a subject for the tutor to ramble on. Shirley was obliged to listen patiently until Mrs. Leonard continued to the next question. It was not the first time Shirley had to experience the long sessions just because of Mrs. Leonard's chattering. Before, in actuality, it was worse. A session that could have lasted for merely half an hour would end up lasting four times as long—all of the minutes were filled with Mrs. Leonard anecdotes on various subjects, which Shirley never used any brain cells to digest.

"This is ridiculous," stated Juliet, throwing up her hands to the sky. "She talks too much. You should have told her not to talk so much on the first day."

"I didn't know that she would continue to talk endlessly. I thought she was just like that on the first day. But the second time she was here...she did the same thing. I didn't know how to tell her to be quiet!" said Shirley, shrugging her slender shoulders in exaggeration. "She just has that kind of personality. I can't do anything about it. We have only a few more days left. Then I'll be done with high school!"

"What a relief! You are finally out of it. The years have been a living nightmare ever since you started school. It makes me feel that the schools are prisons instead of places of education. They don't allow parents to go to school. They didn't even allow me to take you to the bathroom when you first started school. And plus, everything you need requires a doctor's note! It's too silly. So, without doctors, you can't continue with education? We need doctor notes for this and that, including the GED accommodations. What do they think we are? Not humans? Only doctors are humans," grumbled Juliet.

"Mom, please." Shirley rolled her eyes. Sometimes, she talked more than Mrs. Leonard! Shirley decided to change the subject. "So, you're going to see Dr. Leng next week?"

"Yes, but I'm sure he won't be able to find anything wrong with me."

Just as she had expected, during the medical examination on the appointment day, he could not find anything wrong with her, except he simply commented that she was fat. "It's only after I took the medicine! I gained forty pounds in a very short period of time." She knew that no one could understand such happenings if one did not understand her health problems in the first place. Her situation was different than any other's. The same medicine would not have caused the same adverse reactions for other people. She had no excess fat, only water; the forty pounds she gained was all water, so she still could fit into medium-sized clothing. "I feel that the area around my stomach and diaphragm is extremely tight. I think my lymph nodes are clumped and would not circulate my lymph. Can you not feel the bumps on my stomach?"

The doctor felt her stomach when she lay down on the examining table, but could not feel anything. She had always felt her bumps when standing, thus making the bumps stand out more.

He could not believe that any medicine could cause such side effects, let alone a diet drug. She requested to have a CT scan, to which he finally relented. Thus, a CT scan was done on her soon afterward. When the result was in, she received a call from him, informing her of a nodule by her spleen.

"It's the size of a nickel," he said. Juliet felt her heart

pounding. Could it be cancer? Then she thought it was an enlarged lymph node. He further told her that she could have another CT scan done three months later to see if the nodule would grow bigger.

"Oh! That's awful! I hope it's not..." Shirley did not want to say the awful word.

"Don't worry, love, nothing will happen to me."

"So, you'll get another scan, right?"

"I will. Let me call your grandmother and let her know. I know she will get worried." Ergo, Kwi Show received the news with pain. Then she called Agatha, who in turn called Dr. Leng to get the full story. Minutes later, Kwi Show called Juliet.

"Dr. Leng told Agatha that you have psychological problems," Kwi Show informed Juliet.

"I knew he would think that. He never said that to me," remarked Juliet, both frustrated and disappointed. She knew that whenever a doctor could not diagnose an illness, the doctor would label the victim as mentally ill.

"I really think you ought to see my grandmother's surgeon, Dr. Kohlen, and bring your CT scan film. Let him take a look at it," suggested Shirley. "He might know what's wrong with you. I will go with you and explain your symptoms for you."

"That's a good idea. I'll make an appointment now." Soon, it was scheduled for her to see Dr. Kohlen in July.

***

Shirley's fourth year of high school had ended; the arrival of her last report card confirmed it. "You got one hundred on your final exam for science," read Juliet.

"Finally she had given me a correct grade! I had earned a ninety-nine for the class, but she kept deducting points off my papers, so I received only a ninety-seven."

"You're now done with everything!"

Shirley felt like celebrating, but her cheerful

countenance quickly clouded over. "I wish I could graduate with my class. They are going to the graduation ceremony next Sunday." Shirley had called Mr. Broderick, asking if she could be a part of the ceremony, to have her name called to get her GED diploma. He did not agree to that.

"Don't worry about it. That's really nothing important."

"So, my high school years are really over. I completed ten credits. I wish I had ten more! I think I can take the GED test now since I'm done with everything. I hope I will pass it."

"Pass it? You will do wonderful on it. You did excellent on your practice test. You even got a perfect score on the essay!" Juliet reminded her daughter, a person who asked too much of herself.

"I hope I'll do as good with the new test. That practice test was the old version."

"Should I call Mrs. Sheehan to schedule the testing day? But I think you should wait a bit. You are not sleeping well."

"Yes, I'll wait till I get my sleeping schedule fixed." She then thought of the scheduled appointment with Dr. Kohlen. She knew what she was going to say to him and what questions to ask. She hoped that he would be of some help in easing her mother's misery.

When the appointed day arrived on a muggy July afternoon, Shirley had been up most of the night because of her insomnia. "Dear, you're so tired. I don't think we should go," said Juliet.

"No, we're going! I can hang on. I need to talk to him about your problems."

"But you're so terribly tired."

Shirley obstinately shook her head. She was going and nothing would change her mind.

Accordingly, Juliet drove them to the doctor's office. Shirley talked most of the time during the appointment, asking some questions that were hard to answer by the doctor.

"The nodule is only the size of a pea," said Dr. Kohlen. "It cannot cause any of the problems you are having."

"Only the size of a pea? Dr. Leng said that it is the size of a nickel," reiterated Shirley, a bit puzzled, but greatly relieved. "So, do you think it is cancer?"

"It is very unlikely that there will be a cancer at that location."

"But could it be a part of a cancer that was broken off and transferred to the present location?" inquired Shirley. She wanted to get to every crevice and corner of the entire picture.

"You're asking some very difficult questions. I can't answer that. This film is only of the abdominal area."

"Can she have another CT scan done?"

Dr. Kohlen shook his head. With nothing else to provide, he left the room.

Disheartened, Shirley sighed. "You should have another scan done. What if that nodule gets bigger?"

"Don't worry. I will continue to live. Nothing will happen to me. I'm Wonder Woman." Juliet giggled between short breaths.

***

Shirley's insomnia was making her exhausted. Each day was spent drowsily for her, but she could not fall asleep when she was tired. At two, the doorbell sounded. Juliet opened the door to admit Mrs. Sheehan in. Juliet had scheduled to have the exam started on Shirley's request. Shirley did not know when she would start sleeping better, and did not want to wait any longer. It was already August. She was impatient to get her diploma. "You hurry so much in life," Juliet had always observed. "Do things slowly!"

"Hello, Shirley!" Mrs. Sheehan greeted Shirley at the round table.

"Hello, Mrs. Sheehan, nice to meet you."

"Nice to meet you, too."

"So, it is test time," Shirley excitedly said.

Mrs. Sheehan took out the booklet and the cassette tapes. Shirley already had her cassette recorder ready in front of her.

"So, what subject would you like to start with?" Mrs. Sheehan inquired after she read all the directions.

"Definitely science," chirped Shirley. Science was her favorite subject, and she would complete it in no time. Mrs. Sheehan handed the science cassette to Shirley, who inserted it in the cassette recorder, and hit "Play."

A few seconds of silence passed, then the voice of a man spoke. "This is the science..." Shirley listened to the direction with a sample question. She felt herself getting more excited by the minute as the test went on despite her exhaustion. She had been up since two that morning after only a few hours of sleep.

"Two," Shirley told Mrs. Sheehan the answer to a question.

Mrs. Sheehan recorded it down on the test answer. "It is two, right?" Mrs. Sheehan made sure. Shirley nodded and repeated the number.

Then a chart came up for a question. "Would you like me to describe the chart to you?"

"Yes, please." So Mrs. Sheehan did. After she finished, Shirley listened to the question again. She gave Mrs. Sheehan her answer.

Forty-five minutes later, Shirley completed taking the science test.

"I am too tired to go on," Shirley told Mrs. Sheehan.

"That's fine. Get some rest."

"I can do it next Tuesday," Shirley scheduled the next testing date.

"That's fine. I have time that day." Mrs. Sheehan said after checking her schedule.

"Thank you; I will see you then!" Shirley said

goodbye to her.

"Thank you very much, Mrs. Sheehan," Juliet opened the door for her.

The next session of the test arrived, and Mrs. Sheehan came as scheduled. "So, what will it be this time?"

"I will do math." Shirley loved math, but she would have to do every calculation in her head. She was prepared for it; she had successes with writing and balancing long chemistry formulas and equations in her head. She should be able to do the same with math.

She listened to the math problems carefully. The first few questions were on areas of a building; questions that needed a good deal of calculating and drawing out diagrams on paper. Being thoroughly careful, Shirley calculated the answers and gave them to Mrs. Sheehan. An hour later, she was done.

"How about in the morning this time?" Shirley asked. She had been waiting for the test the entire day till the afternoon. She still had been waking up around midnight. She would have the most energy to take the test at the earliest hour possible.

"What time would you like?" inquired Mrs. Sheehan.

"How about two in the morning?" Joked Shirley. They had a few laughs. "When is the earliest time possible for you?"

"I can do it at eight o'clock."

Shirley nodded. "That's really good. Thank you!" she called after the retrieving figure of the woman.

Shirley meanwhile had two summer get-together's scheduled with her friends from both school districts. She had lost contact with most of her friends from school, so she could only call up the few numbers she had. Six of her friends would come on the upcoming weekend, and her two good friends would come the following weekend. She hoped that these two events would help her get her sleeping schedule back in order, by staying up the entire day and going to bed late. She had struggled to concentrate on the previous two tests, but the third time should be better.

At eight in the morning, the third testing session began. This time, it was the English part one, the grammar section. The questions consisted restructuring a sentence, correcting grammar and mechanics, and many other things that needed the aid of vision. It was a challenge for Shirley. She had to picture the entire sentence in her head, and figure out which was the correct way to write it. She completed the test, taking about the same amount of time as on the previous test. Next test would be on literature, followed by history. Then last but not least, would be English part two, the essay.

There were several graphs with the history test. Mrs. Sheehan had described each. Shirley pictured the graphs in her head, and provided answers after thinking about them. The literature was no problem for Shirley. She always did well with reading comprehension exams, to which the literature was similar.

Finally, on the sixth and last day, it was time for Shirley to write the essay. She would think about the topic and record it on a cassette tape. The essay test topic was to write a special moment of her life. That was quite an easy topic, and she instantly knew what she was going to write.

Some time later, she finished recording her essay. "I'm done, Mrs. Sheehan," she happily announced. She breathed a big sigh of contentment. She was finally done with the entire GED test! Now, she just had to wait for the score.

Juliet was confident that she had passed with no problem. "Not only will you pass, but you'll also receive a very high score," she declared. "I'm going to go see Lydia," she announced.

"The upstairs neighbor?"

"Yes. I called her to let her know that her pipes are leaking. She said that she would do something about it, but never did. It is getting worse. No one is paying attention to me. I called the manager, wrote to him again, and no one is listening to me. I've been told that the leak is the neighbor's responsibility." She went out the door. She came back a minute later. "She didn't open the door," she sighed. "The leak is getting really serious. I can see the water dripping from the new hole. The paint is chipping off. There has to be a way for them to get it fixed! It will become dangerous."

Chapter Eighty-Eight

"I will be there around noon," Daphnie told Shirley over the telephone. She was going to teach Shirley how to use the software.

"So, I'll see you at twelve?"

"Yes, Shirley."

"Okay, that's fine. I'll see you then." In actuality, that was not fine for Shirley at all. She still had not been sleeping well, but the condition was better than the time she had to take the GED test. Daphnie had come a couple of times earlier.

So far, Shirley had only learned some of the basic knowledge of the software. She felt it impossible to really use Dragon Naturally Speaking to do her work. It made numerous mistakes when it typed the words she said. She knew the software required plenty of practice in order to familiarize itself with her voice and the way she talked. Too bad she could not type. How she missed typing!

***

Footsteps sounded behind the door. "I think she's here," said Juliet, going over to the door once it sounded with knocks. Shirley hoped the lesson would go by fast. She did not sleep well last night and did not eat anything, yet; there was no time to eat. She would eat something after Daphnie left.

Daphnie, greeting Shirley, set her bag and the laptop in front of her. "Let's practice more with Dragon. Just say anything into the microphone. It needs more practice. Today, I think I can leave the laptop with you and you can play around it before I come again."

After Shirley finished speaking into the microphone,

she asked Daphnie questions about the usage of the programs. "How do you know if Dragon typed down the right word when the word has homonyms, such as to, too, two?"

"You move to the word to see if it's spelled correctly and highlight it by saying, 'Select word,' then say, 'Spell that.'"

Shirley tried it and it worked. "How do you capitalize a word?"

"Just select the word and say, 'Cap that.'"

"How do I capitalize all the letters?"

"Say, 'All cap that.'"

A knock on the door invaded Shirley's concentration. "Who could that be?" asked Juliet, going to the door. She saw it was Lydia and opened the door.

"I'm moving," said Lydia, "and I wanted to let you know." They shared a hug. Juliet wished her well before closing the door. Now she knew why Lydia did not bother to fix the leak. Now that would be the responsibility of the new tenants, whoever they would be. Juliet hoped that the new neighbors would be nice.

An hour later, it was time to end the session. Daphnie got out her schedule book. "Is Tuesday at eleven okay?"

Shirley asked for Juliet's approbation. "Yes, it is fine," answered Shirley.

"Great. I have it down. See you then." She left, taking the laptop with her; she wanted to scan some of the usage instructions for Dragon Naturally Speaking onto it for Shirley.

Shirley turned her attention to Juliet after Daphnie left. "Mom, three months are up and you should have gotten the second CT scan by now."

"But Dr. Leng won't let me have another scan. He said that I need to see a psychiatrist!"

"I am so ticked off," hissed Shirley, rolling her hands into fists. "But you must get checked again."

"Some other time."

"I hope fervently that you can get well."

***

It was Tuesday, another day reserved for Daphnie. "I have scanned in some of the Dragon's commands onto the computer so you can read it using the Kurzweil 1000," said Daphnie. Kurzweil 1000 could read aloud scanned text, such as books and magazines, so that visually impaired people were able to read most printed text.

Shirley knew it would be useful for worksheets from classes. *Too bad I got it after I finished high school*, thought Shirley.

"Well, we're done for today. I'm leaving the laptop with you and we will continue with the lesson the next time I come," decided Daphnie.

"Wonderful, I'll have fun using it!"

Shirley could hardly wait to try using it herself after Daphnie left, despite her tiredness. She pushed the power button and waited for the laptop to boot.

"JAWS for Windows is ready," announced the computer. She knew the next thing that needed to be done was to enter into Dragon Pad that came with Dragon Naturally Speaking.

"Mom, you have to click on the open button." Daphnie had shown Juliet where the button was and how to use the cursor and the mouse button.

"Just click on 'open'?" asked Juliet. "I just did."

"Nothing's happening! Are you sure you did it right? Is my name highlighted?"

"What does 'highlighted' mean?" asked Juliet. But they finally got into Dragon Pad after another try.

"Wake up," commanded Shirley. It was a command for Dragon Naturally Speaking to start, so that she could dictate into the microphone. Shirley tried again after getting no response.

"Wait, there's a message on the screen," informed

Juliet. She read it to Shirley, who realized it was an error message.

"Is there any button you can click on?"

"It has an OK button."

"Click on it."

Juliet did as she was told. The laptop still remained silent. They rebooted, but the same thing happened—nothing happened. After several more tries, Shirley had to stop.

"Oh, why can't we get it to work? I want to use it so badly. I just have to wait till Daphnie comes next time."

But Daphnie could not keep her next appointment, thus Shirley had to wait longer.

***

"Wow, Mom, look what I'm doing!" exclaimed Shirley, excitement clearly audible in her high voice.

"My! You did all that?" inquired Juliet, beaming with pride. Daphnie had come earlier that day but did not know how to fix the problem that Shirley was experiencing. The only temporary fix to the problem was rebooting; at least, rebooting worked now.

"I figured all this out by myself. But tell me what's on the screen."

"The first line says, 'I'm just trying.'"

"And what does it look like? Is it underlined?"

"Yes! And it is also in red."

"That's great! I did it."

"How did you do that?" Juliet was amazed that her daughter could figure out things so quickly. Daphnie did not teach her how to change the color, style, and size of fonts using the software.

"Oh, I just did it," came the mysterious answer from Shirley. "It's easy."

"Ha, you think *everything* is easy."

"Is the text centered now?"

"Yes, it is. So, you can really use it now?"

"Yes, I can. But it would be quite slow to write long essays. Dragon is still making a lot of mistakes."

"But at least you can use it—you know how to use it."

"Yes, mostly. I know how to change the font and alignment," confirmed Shirley with mirth. "Can you please get me those tapes? I'd like to dictate my stories and poems I wrote for my school assignments." Juliet brought the tapes over, and Shirley began creating file after file of her writings. "It is working pretty good."

***

In October, Juliet's mailbox was full. A few days had passed since she had last checked the mail, for she could never get around to it. She brought the mail inside, set the pile on the dining table, and sat down. Mostly junk mail lay in the pile. She put them aside after scanning through the envelopes.

The second day, as Juliet was cleaning the house, she thought about throwing the junk mail away. An envelope in the pile, however, caught her attention. She looked at it carefully. It was from Albany. A thought of the test rushed into her mind. She carefully slit open the letter.

"Shirley, your diploma has arrived!" Juliet excitedly rushed over to where Shirley sat.

"That's great. I passed!"

"Yes! And you did very good. Your score is 3,280. And the perfect score for the test is four thousand, so you did a fantastic job, especially when you cannot see and had completely done the entire exam in your head! I doubt that not many could do it." Then Juliet read each individual score to Shirley. The average score she had achieved was 650, 730 being the highest, which was in literature.

Shirley felt the diploma in her hands. She was thrilled that she at last had officially graduated from high school.

"Let's celebrate with long noodles," teased Juliet.

Shirley wrinkled her nose, then her eyes immediately lit up again. "I'll call up Mrs. Lalli to tell her the good news!" She dialed her former teacher's number.

"Well, congratulations, Shirley!" The happy voice on the other end of the line said. "I am so happy for you! So, what are your next plans?"

"The eye surgery first, then I'm hoping to go to Vassar then Harvard."

The next call Shirley made was to Mrs. Sheehan, who had asked Shirley to call her when she received any news from Albany.

"I passed the test, and I scored over 3,200," Shirley told Mrs. Sheehan.

"That's great! Congratulations!"

"Thank you!"

"There will be a graduation ceremony in June."

"Oh, I would love to come!"

"You will receive a letter before that time; maybe around April. So, that's a long time from now. Would you be interested in being a student speaker?"

"I would love to."

"So, we'll be in contact when that time comes nearer."

"Great; I can't wait."

The happy feeling was not to last for only one day but for the rest of Shirley's life. She could take her next step in life.

Several days later, Shirley received a card from Mrs. Lalli, with these words: "Sensitivity, intelligence, high moral standards, a marvelous sense of humor, motivation to succeed…"

***

Daphnie came a few more times. Once, the programs were not working well, so she had to reinstall all the software. Then toward the end of October, Daphnie left the laptop for Shirley to use.

"I'm not sure when the school would want it back, but you can use it for now. I talked to them, and Mrs. Costin said that you can use it till the end of this school year." The school had asked for the laptop to be returned at the end of December, but since Shirley had barely had a chance to use it, they had extended the deadline.

"I have AOL now!" Shirley chirped. "I am so excited to be going back online and start e-mailing my friends. I had lost contact with nearly everyone. I have a sinking feeling that many of them had changed their screen names or e-mail addresses, though. I will have to ask around and try to contact all of my long-lost pals."

Daphnie had installed the America Online software on the laptop for Shirley and tried to show how things worked with not much success. "I'm not sure how you get around the buttons on the Buddy List," said Daphnie, thinking hard.

"How about using the Tab key?" asked Shirley.

"Wow, Shirley. You're amazing. It works."

"But how do I get from one individual small window to another window?"

"I don't know."

"How do I close the small windows?"

"I'm not sure. Try saying, 'Close window.'"

"But wouldn't that close the entire AOL program?"

"Maybe, but just try it."

Shirley did so, and as she had thought correctly, America Online announced, "Goodbye!"

"I'll have to find out how to use AOL with JAWS," said Daphnie. "I'll e-mail you the name of the person you can contact concerning issues with JAWS." It was time to leave, so she stood up from her seat, gathered up her belongings, and said, "Have fun, Shirley!"

"I sure will!" Shirley continued using America Online after Daphnie left. But she had no commands that could get her to use the program successfully.

Shirley decided to e-mail a few friends. She dictated the letters on Dragon Pad, hoping that there would not be too many mistakes.

But she could not dictate so long using the microphone, for its headset often hurt her wide head. Daphnie had tried to find it in the largest size, but not a single one of them was large enough for Shirley.

"Your head is too wide for anything," Juliet often remarked.

"Unfortunately, it is. I have problems finding sunglasses and I always have to have the straps of the goggles in the chemistry class to be loosened. Everything is made difficult with my wide head!"

"But your head doesn't look wide. It actually looks very pretty. And it's a good thing! That clearly indicates that you're extremely smart."

Shirley rolled her eyes. She then remembered what the man had said when she was three years old in China. She smiled to herself.

"Please take off the headset. It is hurting me," said Shirley. "If I could only type!" Her soul was famished to use the keyboard. She thought that typing would be impossible for her. Other blind people would be able to type if blindness was their only physical limitation. Since she could use only her index fingers to type, she could not have a fixed position on the keyboard, unlike any typists using all ten fingers. But without trying first, she should not determine that the task was mission impossible. She might be able to manage. "Never say never," she scolded herself. "Dreams build bridges in reality. I'll make this dream into reality."

She started hitting the keys from the top row. The first key from the left, she noticed, was the Esc key. Then she knew there were the function keys. She left them untouched. She was never familiar with those keys. She did not want to cause any problems with something she could not undo. It would be a totally different story if she could see. She explored the entire keyboard.

"Q, W, E, R," whispered Shirley. She repeated each row until all the keys were covered. "I think I will remember them."

After several minutes, she happily called out to Juliet. "Mom, I have memorized the entire keyboard!"

"That's wonderful. You might be able to type!"

"Yes, but it will be slow from counting key by key to get to a certain letter. But at least, I will be typing! I'd rather do it like this instead of correcting every mistake Dragon makes."

***

Shirley received an e-mail from Daphnie the following day. It stated a few keyboard shortcuts that worked for America Online, including Control key +M to open a compose mail window and Control key +F4 to close a small window. Shirley never knew that hitting the Control key in conjunction with another key would execute a function. She started hitting the Control key with every key on the keyboard. She found many more keyboard shortcuts for not only America Online, but for the general use as well. This was not her only discovery she had made.

America Online always conflicted with the Dragon Pad feature, making the laptop freeze often. But one day by accident, Shirley knew how to solve the problem. It had happened with an error message, "This program has performed an illegal operation and will be shut down." After she hit the Enter key, it shut down Dragon Pad. When Shirley went back to continue her use of America Online, she noticed that everything was working extremely well. JAWS was able to read all the menus, when it was not possible before. The laptop did not freeze after an hour of use. Therefore, Shirley knew that Dragon Pad was causing the problems she had been experiencing with America Online.

"I'm not going to use Dragon Pad anymore. It was

why I was having problems before. I will use Word Pad instead. Dragon Naturally Speaking works fine with Word Pad!"

"That's wonderful. So, you're able to use AOL with no more problems?"

"No more problems at all."

As days passed, Shirley completely abandoned the use of the microphone. She was now able to type everything. Although her speed was not fast, it was much more convenient and more fun than using Dragon Naturally Speaking program.

When November arrived, Daphnie came again. "I had the school order the microphone, but they ordered the wrong one!" muttered Daphnie. She had asked them to order a new headset which might be in a larger size.

"Actually, Daphnie, I don't need to use the microphone anymore. I am typing now!"

"*Are you kidding?*"

Shirley gleefully shook her head, her ponytail swinging from side to side. "I am typing quite well, and it's so much better and faster than using Dragon—I won't have to fix so many mistakes."

"Show me how you type."

Shirley started Word Pad and began typing, "How are you, Daphnie?"

Daphnie chuckled. "You're just amazing, Shirley."

Shirley typed some more. She had never had so much fun typing; yes, it was even more fun typing now than it was when she was able to see.

"I think you can use the sticky key feature," said Daphnie after noticing that Shirley was hitting the Cap Lock key to capitalize one letter, then going back to hit it again when she wanted to type in lower case since Shirley was using only her left index finger for typing.

"What's a sticky key?"

"A sticky key allows you to perform the same function as when you hold down two keys at the same time.

For example, when you need to capitalize a letter, you have to press the Shift key and another key together. With the sticky key, you don't have to press the two keys at the same time. Just hit the Shift key once then hit another key. That will capitalize that last key you hit. And the next keys you hit will not be affected by the sticky key. Would you like to use that?"

"Yes, that will help me since I'm using only one finger." Shirley hoped to use two fingers. She had barely started to type just a week ago. Daphnie set up the sticky key function for Shirley from the control panel. Shirley tried it and it worked well for her.

"So, you're really not going to use the microphone?" Shirley shook her head in answer. "Then I'll let the school know that you don't need it anymore!"

Shirley was highly glad that she was finally able to type. She had been typing all of her e-mails. She fully enjoyed her renewed computer experience.

The days sped by much faster, with Shirley spending hours on the laptop while sitting on her soft bed. She soon had found most of her school friends' e-mail addresses and screen names. Her Buddy List quickly contained over one hundred people. "What is the maximum number of buddies that the Buddy List can hold?" Shirley asked herself. It, she knew, used to be one hundred, but it was apparent that the feature had been upgraded. Thinking of no better way to find out quick, she began typing random keys on the keyboard and adding each of her made-up screen names to her Buddy List. It quickly reached the maximum number: two hundred. *Good, I am able to add eighty-two more buddies before I reach the limit*, thought Shirley.

The month of December began with the new tenants moving into the condo to occupy the upstairs rooms. "I saw a woman and several kids, and two of the kids appeared to be twins, and deaf," Juliet told Shirley.

"Oh, then it is a large family. I hope they won't be too loud. But the deaf children must be very quiet, so they won't be so loud then," analyzed Shirley. But they soon learned how wrong her prediction was.

The first week of the new tenants' occupancy was a whole crescendo of jungle animals. Ironically, the deaf twins were the loudest among the pack.

"I can't believe that deaf people can be so loud!" exclaimed Juliet one night when she and Shirley were awakened by the cries. "The twins are making loud noises just outside our window!"

"Gosh, they sound like hollering wolves," commented the sleepy Shirley. "Are they going to be like this every day? They had been like this for the second night. Probably it will only be during the weekends. I really need to get some sleep," yawned Shirley. "Daphnie is coming tomorrow!"

Daphnie came one more time. "I think that this is going to be my last time here for now. There's nothing else left to do."

"Yes, I am doing really well with everything. I am able to use the AOL Instant Messenger™. I pretty much don't have problems anymore, except that the laptop still freezes sometimes."

Shirley bade adieu to Daphnie when their session ended, and quickly turned back to her laptop. She was now typing with two fingers and at the speed of forty-five words per minute. She was thrilled. She felt herself floating on Cloud Nine.

"You were even worried that you couldn't keep up with me on the IM, but you're one of the fastest people I know," Erin had observed earlier when the two friends had chatted online.

Chapter Eighty-Nine

Juliet decided to speak to the new neighbors about the leakage problem. "They need to be aware of it and to fix it right away. They have been here for a week. I wanted them to get settled down before disturbing them with this matter. So, now I think it is the right time. I'm going to knock on their door," Juliet told Shirley, going over to the door. Juliet's footsteps were audible as she ascended the stairs. Then Shirley heard murmurs from the second floor. Soon, the sound of two pairs of footsteps came down the stairs. "Jacinta, here's the leak." Juliet pointed at the ceiling.

"My, that is terrible! I'll call the plumber," Jacinta stated.

"Jacinta had contacted the plumber, and so have I. They should send Remus over soon," Juliet told Shirley on the following afternoon.

The calendar demanded attention for the eighteenth day of the month as Juliet opened the door to Remus, who carried his tools to fix the leak. He opened the wall to get a better access to the cause. Then he changed a valve of the pipes. "That should do it."

"You fixed it?" asked Juliet, to which the plumber nodded. "And the hole? Will you seal it?"

"That's not my job. Someone else can do it."

"How much would it be?"

"Like five hundred dollars. That's all; it's fixed." He walked out, carrying his tools.

But she soon learned that the leakage still existed. That night, as someone was taking a shower from upstairs, the water dripped frenziedly from the ceiling. "He didn't fix it. I had a feeling the problem would still be here." Juliet gritted her teeth. "I have to contact them again. But I will wait for another day or so. I don't want them to say that I should be patient and so on."

She waited for three days and saw that the leaking ceiling was more serious than before. "It is time for me to call the plumber. I've waited long enough. The leakage is getting more serious now with so many people taking showers from up there." She punched in the number to reach the plumber. She told the secretary about the leakage. "Yes, it is still leaking. He has to come to fix it. No, it is still not fixed. Thank you." Juliet waited for the plumber to call her back. Several hours passed. "He didn't return my call today, so I'll have to wait for tomorrow."

Ring!

It was the following afternoon when Juliet answered the telephone to the plumber. "Hello? Hi, Remus, how are you? Yes, the ceiling is still leaking," Juliet informed him. Ergo, he came to the condo the following day. He went to Jacinta's place and turned on the bathtub faucet. He came to Juliet's shower place and saw there was no leak.

"Do you know who's going to pay? Jacinta is," he grumbled. "It is not leaking."

"If it doesn't leak, I wouldn't have called you!" hissed Juliet.

"No, it's not leaking." He was just about to leave when Juliet began to plead.

"Can you please wait for another minute? It is really leaking. If there is no leak today, I'll pay you!" He would not listen and went out the door. As he was about to get into his car, the ceiling began to rain. Juliet immediately scrambled out and called to him, getting quite mad at him. "Come here and look! It is leaking now!" He came back and saw the pour. "You see? It is leaking! You get out of here, you coward! You get out!" Juliet yelled at him, her fury matching that of a thunderous storm.

"What happened?" asked Jacinta, coming down the stairs. "What happened?" Then she saw the leak while Remus was storming off. "You need to fix it," she ordered Remus. He obediently listened to her command like a royal puppy and came back.

"I really didn't want you to go, but I could not stand you!" muttered Juliet by Remus' side.

Moments later, he announced he was done. Without saying another word, he went away. "I really hope it's fixed now," grumbled Juliet.

In no time at all, the rain poured down from the ceiling. Juliet did not even need to turn on her own shower to take a shower; the leak would suffice. She was fuming. Why could he not fix it? She did not waste any time on waiting. She called him, asking him to come, but he refused, saying that it was not his job.

Seeing that the rope had been cut with him, she called the condo manager, who was another new person. "Lucas. The leak is very serious."

"I'll send someone to come to take a look," said Lucas.

By and by, a tall, lanky man went to their condo to check the leakage. "It's dry here," he stated, looking at the ceiling.

"But go up and turn on the water and wait for a while. The leak takes time," said Juliet.

He reluctantly went up and did as he was told. He came down and said the same words. "It is not leaking."

"Elsworth, you need to wait, please."

"No, it is not leaking." With that, he went back up to turn off the water and left the building.

Utterly devastated, Juliet sat down. "It has been nearly a month now since December 18, and the leak is getting worse!" She was surprised such professional plumbers did not understand that some leakage was tricky, so it would take time to leak after the water was turned on. Did they not understand?

"But that's not the only bad thing that is happening," Shirley pointed out. "Jacinta and her kids are making loud noises."

"And they frequently wake us up. I think it would be

horrible over the summer vacation. Can you imagine? Even now over the weekends, they are making loud noises during late night hours. They slam each door, they run up and down the stairs loudly, they stump all over the place, and so on. They are the most inconsiderable and rude people I have ever met. They have no manners at all. And they often have loud guests over and will make loud noises the entire night."

Juliet continued to call Lucas, seeking help. Elsworth came again, but refused to go up, stating that he had seen there was no leakage and there were too many people upstairs. "There's no leakage here." He would not come anymore when Juliet called again. She was not receiving any help. She had witnesses to the leakage, one was her next-door neighbor, Bernice, and another neighbor. They were also aware of the great raucous from upstairs. No one could do anything about either.

But good news finally traveled to Juliet and Shirley's ears to get the current misfortune off from their minds. Kwi Show had decided to move to a new house to live together with them. "That's wonderful. I told you it was a good idea. Now, I'll go find a house right away!" Juliet happily planned away. She contacted a real estate agency and spoke to a woman, Beatrice, who would be her realtor.

And thus, the house hunt had begun. "I hope I can find a good house," said Juliet, concerned that finding the perfect house would take some work. But her worries were fruitless when she had found a beautiful house shortly afterward. Kwi Show made a bid on the house.

"Juliet, Mr. Stanley accepted your offer!" Beatrice called Juliet on the morning of Martin Luther King Jr. Day.

"What!" Juliet shouted into the receiver. She was thrilled. She could not believe that the sound waves could produce such wonderful words in her ears. Juliet thought that the house was a beautiful house in just the perfect size for them to live. The transaction was going smoothly so far. She made several calls and had chosen a lawyer and an inspector for the house.

All that was left to do now was to sit back and wait to sign the contract. "Now we can all live together like a happy family. I can take care of your grandmother." Juliet smiled.

A sound of a bomb suddenly sounded above their heads.

"That really startled me!" breathed Shirley, holding her heart.

"They have no respect. They do everything so noisily and always throw and shovel things around the rooms. And good thing we listen to music every night. They have their alarm clock on every morning for two hours starting from five!"

"I know; and they turn it on whenever it stops ringing."

"They are doing it purposely. But it must be really loud where they are. It is quite annoying. Thank goodness it is winter, or the twins would be outside hollering. But I do feel sorry for them. It must be very inconvenient to be unable to hear and talk." Juliet sighed. "It is so unlucky that they have moved upstairs. But we will be moving out—away from all the noise pollution, including their vacuum cleaner that they turn on in the middle of the night, waking us up!"

"I am so glad that you have found a house and in so little time. We are very lucky. And it is a big present for my twentieth birthday!"

Her twentieth birthday passed with dancing snowflakes and gentle winds whistling blissful tunes outside her window. Again, it was spent quietly with just the two of them. "I can't believe I'm twenty already," gushed Shirley.

"I can't believe it. It has taken me so much to bring you this far. But I thank God that you're able to get this far. Those days had been so harsh and difficult. So much had happened during the old days," reminisced Juliet. "I can't believe we've made it this far. Even though we have been through some very difficult times, we are always so happy. I love and cherish every moment with you. Each and every second is precious."

"Yes, Mom, we love each other so very much! We have so many merry times together. We joke around and always have fun."

"Darling, I love you higher than the sky and deeper than the ocean. I will go up a mountain with swords and go down ocean of fire for you. You are my biggest happiness in life. I love you as much as any mother has ever loved her daughter. My only happiness is in my love for you."

"And you are the very same to me, my loving mom!"

The time for sentimental thoughts was limited, for they were planning to move. Juliet's eyes sparkled, thinking of the house that they would be moving into. "It is such a beautiful house. I really wish you could see it!"

"I will be able to see it after the surgery." Shirley had been doing some research on the Internet on cataract-extraction surgery. She learned about the surgical method known as phacoemulsification, where anesthetic shots and stitches were not needed. She was thrilled upon learning of the facts. She read that the procedure usually lasted fifteen minutes and it was painless during the whole procedure. She had told Juliet of the news. Juliet was glad about it, but not as surprised, for she had heard that China had been using this technique to perform all of the cataract surgeries. Shirley did not want to rush into doing the surgery. She wanted to gather as much information as she could before making her final decision. She did not want to take a reckless risk. She was a practical person who always first sought the facts on which to base her decisions.

"You'll love the den," continued Juliet. "It has two skylights."

"I know that. You already told me that a hundred times," said Shirley, rolling her eyes.

"A hundred times? Maybe just fifteen times." The two burst out laughing.

"When will we move in?"

"The contract will state that. I will sign the contract in a few days."

***

The closing on the house was done in April. At the same time, Shirley received a letter from the GED department, informing her about the coming graduation ceremony.

"When will it be?"

"It will be on June 12 at seven in the evening," read Juliet. "And there's a place to indicate how many guests you will bring."

"Oh, really?"

"So, you can bring anyone you like."

Shirley thought of her close friends. Then both thought of Mrs. Lalli.

"It will be nice to have Mrs. Lalli there," said Shirley.

"Yes, that will be wonderful! But she is so busy! I'm afraid that even if she's too busy, she won't feel comfortable declining the invitation. But it would be so nice if she could come." Juliet thought it was best not to invite her. She knew that the teacher lived quite far, so it would be inconvenient.

Shirley invited only five of her friends. But only Erin said that she would come.

"So, you will come that day?" Shirley asked Erin in an e-mail.

"Yes, I will come," she replied. It was settled.

In May, Juliet had scheduled to see Dr. Leng again, but the outcome was the same as last. "Who is your psychotherapist?" he asked.

"Why would I have to see one? I don't have psychological disorders. I'm really sick. I can't breathe." Juliet simply wasted her breath. Dr. Leng did not believe her.

On the same evening after visiting Dr. Leng, Juliet headed to the emergency room. "I hope I will get to see a doctor this time," she mumbled under her breath.

After an hour of waiting in the waiting room, Juliet was ushered to a bed by a nurse. She had an x-ray taken after the nurse took her pulse. Juliet returned to the bed and lay down. A moment later, a technician walked to her bed and drew the privacy curtain around the bed. "I'll do an arterial blood gas test for you, and it is very painful," the technician warned Juliet before posing the needle above her right wrist. Juliet did not prepare herself for the pain that was plunging into her soul as the needle was stuck in. It was the most painful test she had ever taken.

When it was done, the nurse told Juliet that she could leave. "Everything is fine." Juliet knew that nothing was fine. She was feeling tightness in the area of her diaphragm. How could an arterial blood gas test determine the cause and in turn help to provide a treatment? She could still have enough oxygen count in her blood when a rock was jammed into her chest.

***

"I just checked the mail, and one letter I got said that if you have scored over three thousand on the new GED test, you will get a special recognition award. It also said that you have to call them to let them know this!" said Juliet. "But tomorrow is the graduation ceremony. They should've sent it out earlier. It is too late to call now." She glanced at the clock.

"I'll call tomorrow morning. I hope they'll have enough time to prepare the award."

Shirley made the call on the following morning. "So, you must be excited about it?" asked Mrs. Sheehan.

"Yes, I am very excited. Well, I received a letter saying that people who scored over three thousand on the new test will get a special recognition award and that they should call you. So, I'm calling you to let you know I have scored over 3200."

"Oh, I had thought you didn't score three thousand. I have checked. Well, then, that's good. And you're still planning to make the speech?"

"Yes, I'm all ready."

"Remember, Shirley, a *short* speech! Also, I thought to have you go on the stage first rather than having you go there when all the graduates file in. What do you think?"

"That will be fine."

"And your mom will also be on the stage. She can hold the microphone for you."

"Oh, okay, that will be great! Thank you."

"Do you have any questions?"

"Nope, I'll let you know if I have. I'll see you then!"

"I'm surprised that she allows me to be on the stage with you," commented Juliet after Shirley's telephone conversation ended, "I was never allowed to do anything when you were in school."

"Yes, I'm surprised, too."

"That's really nice of Mrs. Sheehan." Juliet checked the time. "I think you should take a nap. You've been up a long time. If you don't, you'll have no energy for the ceremony." Shirley quickly agreed.

Chapter Ninety

On the evening of June 12, Juliet pushed Shirley onto the stage with much effort. She sat down next to Shirley. It would not be another half an hour till the ceremony began. Juliet described the stage to her. As they were talking, a lady walked onto the stage.

"Hi, I'm from the *Poughkeepsie Journal*," she introduced herself to them. "May I ask you some questions for the paper?" she asked Shirley.

"Sure, I would be glad to!"

"This must be an exciting time for you both."

Shirley nodded. "This is my mother, Juliet. She's here to help me."

"Oh, that's nice. Shirley, how have you come this far?" The reporter asked, glancing at her questions from her notepad.

Shirley began telling her of her background. "I was born in 1983 and I was diagnosed with juvenile rheumatoid arthritis at only eleven months old. So, due to this painful disease, I've been hospitalized for many years between America and China until I was at the age of eleven. I could not get any form of education as a result. But when my health was stabilized at age eleven, I attended special education class. The first day of school, I did not know anything, no English or any other subjects. But amazingly, I stayed in the special education class for only about 180 days and was transferred to a regular mainstream sixth grade class." She continued without a single pause in between. She knew that her time was running out, so she had to hurry. She wanted to get everything said. "But sadly, I lost my eyesight toward the end of my sophomore year in high school."

"Oh," a sympathetic murmur escaped the journalist's lips. "What are your plans for the future? Where would you like to go from here?"

"Well, I'm planning to get an eye surgery. And after and only after a successful eye surgery, I hope to go to Vassar College first then to Harvard University."

"And what will you like to major in?"

Shirley giggled at the thought of her answer. "Well, I love science, so I would like to major in astronomy, microbiology, pathology, physiology, and zoology. I know that's a lot," Shirley giggled some more.

The interview continued for a few more minutes. "I want to live my life to its fullest," Shirley told the journalist as guests were filling up the auditorium. Shirley spoke fast so she could get all the information in.

"Do you have any questions?" asked the reporter. Shirley shook her head. The woman turned to Juliet. "And what would you like to say? How do you feel right now?"

"I'm very proud of her. She is a miracle," stated Juliet, her eyes reflecting the smiles from her soul.

"Well, that's all. Thank you for answering the questions," stated the journalist, rising from her seat by Shirley's right side.

"It's my pleasure," came the bubbly reply before the reporter left the stage.

Shirley's ears enjoyed the sound of the packed auditorium. Then the people clapped when the graduates started to file in. Shirley clapped along, smiling widely. She was glad to be a part of it. Five students got on the stage; they were the student speakers.

The audience grew quiet as the commencement started with speeches from the school and the GED officials. Soon, it was turn for the students to give their speeches. One student, a girl who did not prepare any script, shed a few tears as she told the audience of how she was able to achieve her goals to get this far.

After all the five students had given their talks, it was Shirley's turn. They moved the microphone stand in front of Shirley. Juliet held the microphone to Shirley's smiling lips.

Without taking any deep breath and a second of hesitation, Shirley began her speech.

"Good evening, my fellow graduates. My name is Shirley Cheng. It is certainly an honor speaking to welcome and congratulate every one of you tonight! First, I would like to take this opportunity to thank those people who have made it possible for me to be here tonight: my beloved mom, Juliet, (who is here beside me, holding the microphone), who has been giving me unwavering love, support, and encouragement; Mrs. Sheehan, who had taken the time to personally administer the test to me; and every single teacher who has given me the treasure of knowledge. I have no words to describe how grand I feel right now, so I'm not even going to try. I had encountered numerous barriers in getting an education due to my physical disabilities, but still have striven to prevail, to achieve my hearts desire."

Her bell-like voice floated throughout the auditorium. Several camera lights flashed before her eyes, bathing her in radiance.

"I've been totally blind for three years. So, I took the GED test using strictly cassette tapes and a tape recorder. I did everything in my head without seeing anything, including math calculations and graphs. I also recorded my essay on the tape recorder. And I scored over 3200."

The audience broke out in loud applause. After it died down, Shirley continued. She reached the end of her speech with words of inspiration. "Well, all that's left to say now is that I am thankful to be here, knowing I can take my next step into my journey. And I want to congratulate every one of you for having come this far with your ambitions. Give yourself a pat on the back, and know that whatever you have your heart set on, you shall achieve it, and no matter what hardship you may face, you shall prevail. Be strong, listen hard to the voice calling from your heart. Do what your heart desires, and if anything or anyone gets in your way, turn your head and go in another direction to achieve your goals. Thank you and have a great night all!"

Just as she finished the last word, the entire audience stood up. But of course, Shirley did not know what was happening.

"They are standing up!" Juliet announced to Shirley.

"Really? A standing ovation?" Shirley was amazed. She had not expected to receive another standing ovation for her speech. Cameras flashed brightly before her. It was surely a moment to remember. This was an episode of Shirley's life that would never be forgotten. It was a time of achievement, and yet perhaps, another story adding to the thousands of special memories of many others.

After the speeches, the special recognition awards were handed out to ten students, including Shirley. "Your speech was great," commented the lady, while handing her the award. Then the regular diplomas were handed out. The audience clapped loudly as each of the ninety-four students went up the stage to receive their diploma, reflecting their lifelong achievements.

Shirley held on to a rolled diploma and an award after the ceremony ended.

Several people, mostly parents from the audience, went up to Shirley to congratulate her.

"That's a wonderful speech. It is the best that I have heard for a long time," remarked an official.

"Your speech touched me. It almost made me cry," commented an audience member.

Shirley received more compliments as Juliet pushed her out of the auditorium. A few people came up to shake her hand. "I would like to take your picture," said one gentleman. Shirley gladly posed for the shot. Then she was asked to hold her award for another shot. Thus, another flash came her way.

"Wow, Shirley, you're famous. Everyone likes you," said Erin.

The smile upon Shirley's features was still visible as Juliet wheeled her out of the building.

Early the next morning, Shirley checked the

Poughkeepsie Journal from their website and found the article about last evening's event. Accompanying the article was a large colored photograph capturing the special moment: Juliet, wiping away a tear, held the microphone to Shirley's smiling lips as she talked. Shirley, her eyes flashing, listened on as JAWS read the article, entitled *95 celebrate hard-earned GEDs* by Erikah Haavie. The last portion on the article was especially devoted to her. But she noticed that the journalist had gotten some information incorrect and had missed out on a few important points to make the article clearer. Instead of putting that Shirley had lost her vision in tenth grade, she had written eleventh grade. There was no mention of her first starting in a special education class, nor was her special recognition award mentioned.

Seeing that the article was not clear and accurate enough for the readers to understand it fully, she wrote a letter to the newspaper, stating her reasons for writing and asked that the mistakes be noted. After she completed the letter, she sent it to the newspaper via the form on their website.

The following Monday, another article appeared on the newspaper, with the title, *Three cheers for Shirley Cheng*. Shirley grinned from ear to ear; a whole article wholly on her achievements! But the article contained the same errors since it was based on the first.

A month later, the letter she wrote appeared in the letters to the editor section in the *Poughkeepsie Journal*. Now, she thought, the audience could get the clear story.

Chapter Ninety-One

Toward the end of June, on the twenty-second to be exact, Shirley read about a short story contest called *Talespinners,* put by the *Poughkeepsie Journal.* Once she read it, Shirley decided to enter it.

She thought about the fairy tale she had written for an assignment for the creative writing class at age seventeen, and felt that it would be a good story to submit. She opened the file of *The Magical Gifts,* and performed a word count provided by the word processor, HJ Pad, which came with the screen reader. The story had a bit over one thousand words. The maximum word limit for the contest was three thousand words.

Without a minutes waste, Shirley pounded on the keyboard to expand her story. She read it as she typed along. "The adventure started a long time ago, in a land of green, rolling hills…" the story began. Her goal was to add as much as she could to the story, to make the reader want to read more, without putting in too many unnecessary details. She got bored reading books with excess details.

In two hours, the word count showed Shirley that the story exceeded 2,400 words. She was almost there; she wanted to reach three thousand. But her fingers were getting stiff, so she decided to rest for a while and continue later. It was still early in the morning around nine. Besides, the contest would not end till next month.

At the start of July, Shirley was ready to send out her story. It had exactly three thousand words. She was satisfied; it was perfect.

Yet she sighed, "Now I have to double space this file manually since it is not a feature included in Word Pad."

"I don't understand why you don't have that feature on the laptop," wondered Juliet.

"Because I don't have the fancy word processor, Microsoft Word. They don't have it on this laptop. I don't understand it. All the computers I know of, come with the word processor pre-installed."

"So, why didn't they include it with this laptop?"

"I really don't know. But I can manually double space the story. It is not too long."

"But we are very grateful for having the computer for now. You can do so much now."

"Yes, that's great of them. I am so happy that I can go online and get in touch with many of my friends again and surf the net. And I'm even typing faster then when I had my eyesight! I'm typing fifty-five words or so per minute."

After Shirley finished double spacing the entire document, Juliet mailed the story to the *Poughkeepsie Journal*.

Shirley could not stop thinking of the characters in her story; they seemed to be calling out messages to her.

Two days later, Shirley started HJ Pad, and began another story, which she entitled *Secrecy*. It was the sequel to *The Magical Gifts*. The main character, Princess Sophia would finally marry her good friend, Lord Veldolf. But since he was a lord, he was unable to seek her hand in marriage. Thus, Shirley constructed the story so they would have a way of uniting their love, and not by harm either. Four hours later, she completed the story with three thousand words. But the new story still could not quench her thirst for more. Two days later, she wrote and completed the third story in the series, *Wind of Hope*.

By the time Shirley knew it, she had a total of eight stories from the same series, *The Magical Gifts* being the first. She no longer had a word limit, and her stories passed the five-thousand-word mark.

One day, a sudden idea struck her with full force; why not get the book published? Juliet had also suggested it to her at the same time. She began to search for publishers on the Internet. She found many, but they were traditional publishers, and would not accept a first time author without a literary agency. She e-mailed a few, but received only one reply. It was from a children's publisher who wanted stories only about different ethnic groups. It was not for her then; perhaps, she would submit some stories in the future. Meanwhile, her search continued into many days; Shirley sometimes had to spend the entire day with her research.

Finally, she found a kind of publisher that would accept most manuscripts, known as subsidy publishers that used print-on-demand technology. Shirley knew it was just the publisher she needed. She added one publisher after another to her America Online's favorite place folder. She needed to pick one out of the twenty.

Eventually, after many days into the research, she found the perfect publisher. It was one that would choose which manuscripts they would publish, like traditional publishers, so her book needed to be of fine quality.

"I was just thinking of something last night," Shirley said to her mother. "I am going to write an autobiography."

"Really? That will be great! You know that I always wanted someone to write a biography of our lives. And now you're the one! I am so very happy!"

"It will not be like those ordinary autobiographies. Mine will be in story form and in third person's narration. I'm going to tell it like a story." Who else could do a better job telling her life story than she could?

"Very fine idea."

"But I am worried about some things. I'm always worried that the computer will suddenly crash and that all my writing files will be lost! Above all, I've been told that this laptop has no drive to insert floppy disks, so I can't save any files onto floppy disks."

"Yes, what should we do? I told you to buy a new computer. Your grandma has always insisted on buying you a brand-new one."

"No, I don't want to buy one just because of this. I can manage with this laptop for the time being."

"But this laptop always crashes. We even had to get the modem changed when it broke, and it broke down the second time! And it has Windows 98. You said it's always not compatible with something."

"I wish I have the latest version. But Daphnie said that they had said that Windows 98 Second Edition would be more compatible with the software. But it won't be compatible with the later versions of AOL. I am using AOL 8.0 now, but I don't think the future versions will be compatible with this Windows version. I have downloaded AOL 9.0 and I found out that it is already not very compatible with my screen reader, so I'll just have to use AOL 8.0 instead."

"You also encounter other problems."

"This laptop is pretty much empty. It doesn't have Microsoft Word. Many publishers only accept manuscripts that are created from Microsoft Word, so I can't use those publishers."

"I am very puzzled, Megan from the Commission for the Blind said that many blind people can go to college successfully. I want to know how did those students manage if their computers always crash? You say that JAWS is causing most of the freezing. Daphnie could not help you with any of your problems. So, who can help you? Who helps those blind students in college? They must receive help from others who really know about these software. You were Daphnie's first student who uses both the two programs." Juliet paused. "And you're always on your own doing everything. You have no one to help you with anything with the computer. You had figured out most of the stuff by yourself. I wish there's someone who could guide you." Juliet paused again, clearly thinking of something else. "We will move into the new house on August 20. It is about time." A ramp was constructed for the house, so it would be accessible for Shirley. Kwi Show had already moved into the new house. She was waiting for their turn to move in.

"I'm so glad to be moving out of this condo. Jacinta

and the kids are too loud and the twins are always going in and out of the building late at night," remarked Shirley.

"And the leakage is still not fixed. So, too bad for the new tenants. I spoke to everyone about it, but no one would check the leakage. Jacinta is denying it. But everything will soon be behind us. I know it was He who had sent such a blessed house our way. Plus, Mr. Stanley is such a good person, such a practical and helpful person. He has a great sense of responsibility, unlike so many others. He is also compassionate. He even followed us to the bathroom where I was looking at it to see if it needs any changes to accommodate a shower place for you. But the house doesn't need any changes. It is fine the way it is. You are able to take a shower with no problem. I have seen so many other houses and all needed some extensive changes with the bathrooms."

In the middle of their conversation, the telephone rang. "Hello?" Juliet answered. Kwi Show was on the other side. Shirley could not sign onto the Internet, so she started a new story as Juliet and Kwi Show conversed. "We're finally going to live together!"

"Yes, I have been alone nearly three years," said Kwi Show.

***

Shirley started her autobiography a week after their move on the twenty-eighth. Writing the first few chapters was easy, but she required a great deal of information from Juliet in order to write the main events in details. She was able to complete the first few chapters with no problem. But her writing pace decreased when she needed to gather information from Juliet, who was always busy. Thus, Shirley could not continue with her autobiography for a while until Juliet had some free time to provide Shirley with answers.

Juliet had been extremely busy, attending to both Shirley and Kwi Show and to the house as well. There was much to do in so little time.

Shirley felt like a reporter when she sent out barrages of questions to her mother's way. "So, what year was that in?"

"That was in 1985," supplied Juliet, who was sweeping the wooden floor in their bedroom.

"And where did we go after that?" The interview would continue until she had enough information to complete a portion. Then another interrogation session would follow.

As the manuscript became longer, the screen reader worked slower. Sometimes, the reader would not read the text to her. During this, she had to restart the word processor or the computer. Writing a book with a screen reader was a difficult task. Plus, she could not catch many of the typographical and grammatical errors. If she could see, she knew she would have no problem at all. She could easily notice the errors.

"But I guess it is better than nothing," she told herself.

After writing six pages, she decided to rest. She wanted to read some local and national news. Shirley browsed the *Poughkeepsie Journal* website and learned that she did not win the short story contest; they had already chosen the five finalists and had contacted them. Disappointment fell upon her, but not wholly for herself; the chance of letting others read her work from the newspaper temporarily vanished. She was determined to publish her book more than ever. She wrote these stories not just for herself, but to share them with the world, to let people take a pleasure in reading what she called philosophical fairy tales that gave messages of inspirations.

"I am utterly surprised that you did not win the contest! You have written an extremely beautiful story full of lyrical phrases and great sentiments. I know that is why you did not win. They don't like your kind of writing. It is too wonderful, too beautiful, too lovely, and with characters who are too nice for them to like. What is too puerile, too saccharine, is always despised by some in this society," observed Juliet. "It must be human nature."

Shirley shrugged. "Remember what the judge wrote about my story, *Mary Miller, the Elusive* Lady, for that Halloween scary story contest?" That, she felt, fit in with what Juliet said. "Anyway, I have named the collection of those eight stories *Daring Quests of Mystics*."

"That's a beautiful title. Your stories are like yourself, like delicate flowers." She shook her head as another thought sprang up. "Ha, he had quit his job just for us!" exclaimed Juliet.

Shirley shook her head in pity. "I can't believe that Jim would actually quit his job at the medical equipment company. It takes all kinds in this world."

"Just for one bird; he changed a telephone number and his job for just one bird. What a shame. How does he feel? What good can he get out of this? He must feel uncomfortable now. I don't understand why bad people do the bad things they do. They must live so uncomfortably in life, always in fear. I'd rather live a life that is full of illness rather than living a healthy life full of fears and guilt. And after over three years of suffering with the breathing problem, I finally feel that my problem is a muscle tightness issue. When I am able to urinate more, I will be able to breathe more easily. Thus, my breathing difficulty is exacerbated during my menstruation. I'm glad that it is I who is suffering this condition and not you or your grandmother. You will be unable to live like this. I take herbal medicines to help me urinate to sustain my life and try to eat as much healthy food as I can, so I won't go blind like you. With your poor appetite, you are prone to lose your vision…" Juliet's voice trailed off.

"It is all so sad. I really wish that you will be cured someday!" Shirley hugged her mother.

"Why did I have to take that medicine? Why was I so trusting? I had misgivings about the whole thing and I just took it! Ah, everything is fate. I didn't know that Agatha would do that. She had even said that when I'm good to you, it shows how selfish I am."

"I think that is a very odd comment she had made," remarked Shirley. She still remembered that day when Agatha had said those words. Agatha had repeated the same words twice.

"But I would not have taken it if Arney hadn't said that it improves bowel movements. That's the reason I had decided to go against the odds. And no one believes me. My brother is still saying that it has already been three years and my breathing problem couldn't have been caused by the medicine because it has been three years. Your vision loss is the same situation—caused by medicine more than three years ago!"

Epilogue

With a sigh of contentment, Shirley rested her hands, which were flying about on the keys just a moment ago. The book was complete. It had taken her nearly two months. The autobiography had taken her a much longer time to complete than *Daring Quests of Mystics*, which had merely taken eight days.

Was there anything else to add? Any important information missing? She thought for a while and answered the questions with a little shake of her head. She could not put every single day's happening on paper. Everything in her manuscript was enough to give the readers an understanding of her life, even if not every event could be understood completely. Her life, as with Juliet's, were full of too many events and little issues that could not be easily explained and be understood from the pages of a book. The reader would need to switch places with Shirley for one day to really know and understand their lives, of what they had to endure in the past, what they thought of the treatments they received, and how they felt in knowing that there were no more priceless things in life than love, happiness, and peace. Those were the true valued qualities of life. Nothing else could ever emulate, let alone surpass, those fine and cherished qualities. Neither fame, nor the wealth of the entire world, could ever replace the feelings of true happiness.

"You have done a marvelous job with your autobiography. You write so very well and beautifully. It is truly a success. Perhaps, it will bring you and all others in our situation the recognition we deserve," predicted Juliet with much conviction. "My dear, you are a true magical gift!"

"Let's just see... I hope that more people will be more understanding. The purpose of life is not about money, fame, and successes brought by rank or popularity. Many people can be so materialistic. We see more and more of it as time passes," observed Shirley.

"That's so true. So many people worship fame and money. They readily bow down to those rich and famous. But will they sacrifice for someone who is a pauper? For instance, after my biological father died, no one came to our home, neither relative nor outsiders came, because we became poor. They would not come when we invited them. And when they did come, they treated us with haughtiness. Before, everyone came uninvited to admire him. It's human nature."

"Oh well. It's sad that's how it all is. At least, we are happy the way we are. Maybe what we are going through is a good thing. It's a way for us to find out the true nature of our human race—just all trials and tribulations we have to go through. It is all planned by Him."

"Yes, everything is laid out by God. But we always have something to be happy about. Right now, your success is your new writing career at such an early age."

"I'm very elated about it." *Daring Quests of Mystics* had been accepted for publication and was being published. "I have put a lot of love into that book and truly cherish it. Being blind and using a screen reader is quite hard to catch any typographical and grammatical errors in my writing. If I could only see—it would make everything so much easier. I'll have no problems catching any typographical errors. I hope that the eye surgery that I plan to get will be successful, so I can see this beautiful world again. I miss the world so much."

"We need to find you the perfect eye doctor to perform the surgery. It is hard to, because we should find a doctor who is not only skillful and knowledgeable, but someone who is also caring and compassionate," sighed Juliet. "We'll get many opinions from many doctors. I'll continue to take you to see all of them. But it is so hard on both of us, especially on you. I have to drive for so many hours on the road and you'll have to hold your urine. And there's no comfortable diaper. I can't carry you anymore to those chairs for the doctors to examine you, and they don't have the equipment in the correct height to examine your eyes. They should have ones that accommodate wheelchairs."

Shirley had been seeing specialists for uveitis recently. Each appointment took an entire day. They were no doubt exhausting. It was the beginning of a long search ahead. And what would happen after they did find the perfect eye doctor? Since Shirley's legs and arms were bent, they needed to be supported. How could she lie on the operating table? Plenty of planning and discussion would need to be laid out with the doctor.

"And just as I thought our problems were enough, Agatha copied down my social security number!" grumbled Juliet. Juliet gave her social security number to Kwi Show one day. She told Kwi Show not to let Agatha see it. But when Agatha came that day and asked for the number, Kwi Show handed Agatha the piece of paper with Juliet's social security number written on it. "I had told your grandmother over and over again that not to even let Agatha see it. Not only did she see it, she even copied it down!"

"We can't do anything about it now. Just have to take the good with the bad. We have many thorns to face in the future, and many songs to sing as well. I'll set this autobiography free for the world to see!" declared Shirley. The objective was to let the world open its eyes to the problems that were hiding underneath the gilded land, and to open its ears to the silent cries from people's hearts.

What would the future be like? Would it bring promising health improvements for Shirley? Would she be able to see again, to be filled with an indescribable joy when being surrounded by fulgent colors of nature, and to be able to marvel at the sky gems when they twinkle upon the velvety night skies? All these queries would be answered in time when the right moment arrives. And perhaps, a continuation of the tale of her life would be told in another book.

As she finished these words, the scene slowly faded away until a girl's small, delicate figure was no longer discernible.

Parental Rights in Children's Medical Care Advocacy

What is a more frightening nightmare for parents than their children's illness? It is the fear of losing custody of their children.

In America, parents risk losing custody of their children forever when they disagree with doctors' recommended treatments or even when they want a second opinion.

Just ask the Wernecke family in Agua Dulce, Texas, whose daughter Katie was taken into state custody in 2005 when her parents refused radiation treatment for Katie's Hodgkin's disease. The same thing happened to Corissa Mueller in 2002, Tina Phifer in 1997, and a slew of other parents and children who have been victimized in the past decades.

My mother Juliet Cheng was one such parent whose child was forcefully and wrongly taken away by Child Protective Services over treatment disputes—not only once, but twice.

When I was seven, I had no voice of my own. Now, seventeen years later, I am driven to speak for all the families who risk being torn apart for simply choosing to follow their own hearts and common sense in regards to their children's medical care. Everyone is a potential victim of this injustice when a child falls ill—including your own child or grandchild. I am here to help today's loving parents protect and keep custody of their children.

It is a crime when doctors force unwanted or harmful treatments on children, and it is a violation against humanity when the state tears loving parents and children apart.

The American government needs to deal with each case according to its unique needs, instead of acting upon the same plan for all cases. Just because loving parents who disagree with medically recommended treatment does not mean that they are child abusers or that their child should be torn away from them. In this democratic land of independence, the child-protection laws in the medical system are extremely out of place.

America will be better if it gives freedom to devoted, competent parents. The average parent wants the best for their child. We, the patients in our own bodies and the caregivers who have cared for the patients for years, know what is best for us. Doctors may know what is the best treatment option for us, but even in all their certainty, they cannot force their knowledge and power on us.

So, what is the real issue here? Is it who loves the children the most (parents), or is it who believes they know what's medically best for the children (doctors)? I believe that question can only be answered by God. God created us, so He must know what is best for each and every one of us, but He gives us free will and the right to care for ourselves on our own. He lets every one of us decide for ourselves and choose what to do with our lives, even if it means that we make many mistakes. He does not control us; He simply tells us how to be a good person and informs us of the consequences if we choose to be bad people.

But instead of allowing us the same free will that God gives us, our own people from the medical and legal systems take away our parental rights, snatching children away from parents—their primary source of love and care—in order to do what is "best" for the children. Worse yet, parents are not warned in advance what could happen if they dare disagree with a treatment plan. They are simply reported to Child Protective Services.

Can't we—parents and children—decide what is best for ourselves?

Where is our freedom to say no?

Give Parents the Right to Say No Petition

On the great Martin Luther King Jr.'s Day, January 15, 2007, Shirley Cheng created the Parental Rights in Children's Medical Care: Give Parents the Right to Say No Petition to return rights to the hands of loving parents. Mr. King opened the eyes and hearts of people to accept fellow mankind, now it is Shirley's turn to open the eyes and hearts of people to protect today's parents and the children of our future.

Please sign the petition to support a great cause at: http://www.petitiononline.com/parentr7/petition.html

Should the state send parents to court just because the parent told the hospital that aspirin is worsening their child's condition? Is it okay for the judge to call the parent a child abuser when the parent intercepted unwanted, harmful treatment for their child?

If you want to stop this power abuse, injustice, and nonsense from striking another innocent parent, then sign this petition. The next victim may be your grand child or your best friend's daughter or the woman next door.

Spotlight Raves
Excerpted Reviews

Shirley is an excellent writer and poet with a charm and intelligence that would make anyone envious. Her age and illness has never stood in her way of succeeding and embracing everything that life has to offer.

The Revelation of a Stars Endless Shine is a true story about a Mother and daughters struggle to survive the daughters health problems which consisted of severe juvenile rheumatoid arthritis, blindness not forgetting to mention pure neglect and ignorance of the medical world. This story will take its readers into a world that neither mother nor daughter was prepared for; it was a world of frustration, pain, false accusations, misleading information from medical experts, and possibly the worst experiences of loss that a mother and daughter would ever have to deal with.

The revelation of a Star's Endless Shine is a work of art. Shirley Cheng's writing is absolutely flawless and her ability to bring her reader into the heart of not only herself but also her mother through her words is truly amazing and magical. While reading this book, be prepared to feel every emotion capable to a human being such as: pain, frustration, fear, horror, love, happiness, determination, commitment, passion, and best of all, winning. This book will teach you the meaning of dedication and pure love of a mother for her daughter. It will also teach you about perseverance and strength to never give up in life.

Shirley writes of her struggles that the world has challenged her with from birth. Shirley's story is not only about her challenges and misfortunes, but she also shares with us the love and respect that her mother showed over and over again. It is clear where Shirley has gained most of her positive attributes. Her mother's never-ending energy to keep moving forward reaches out and touches you throughout

Shirley's story.

Recommendation: Womenssselfesteem.com Highly Recommends the book *The Revelation of a Star's Endless Shine* to every person from every walk of life.
—Dorothy Lafrinere
WomensSelfEsteem.com

This is a complex story written in an easy to read, conversational fashion that is disarming, yet sometimes astounding in its micro-details (ie., telephone conversations you get word-for-word); Shirley Cheng seems to have the memory of a titan. Nevertheless, at times you feel some information is missing—must be missing, because why else the poor treatment by one person after another, one agency after another, one doctor after another, one medical aide after another? But then it hits you—these people, these agencies, these medical "professionals" are really, in many cases, THAT awful! The truth is that American medicine, American government schools and American government agencies all too often think they are GOD. But they're not.

In fact, this book poignantly shows how the enormity of the misuse of power, such as trying to take an ill and hurting child away from its primary source of love and security—its mother—in the name of doing what's "best" for that child, is downright horrifying. And rightly so. The medical establishment is one of the biggest offenders in Shirley's life, and we can probably all relate. (No one is saying, incidentally, that there aren't good people to be found in these arenas of public service, and thankfully, Shirley and her mom find some good people, too.)

If nothing else, Shirley's story is triumphant in that her mother rejects what she knows to be wrong for her child, fights the nightmarish resistance of said "establishment" and wins in the end. But the book is also more than that; it is the tale of a sensitive, intelligent, and observant girl who happens to be painfully disabled; she suffers enormously but has the extraordinary gift of a mother who is sold out for her well-being, hook, line and sinker.

Did the mother make mistakes? Of course. She trusted the wrong people, particularly a relative who was no less than criminal, it seems to me, in her actions. But Juliet Cheng's gift of love to her daughter is something that many able-bodied people never get. She is the epitome of the selfless mother/caretaker extraordinaire, shining the light on the lives of quiet, exhausting devotion that mothers like her live daily.

Overall, the author does an amazing job of keeping the reader's interest; I think the book could be shorter, but I honestly cannot say it was ever boring. When you finish the book you will feel an affinity to this Shirley Cheng and her mother, Juliet. You will admire them both, and hopefully, thank the Lord that your "trials and tribulations" have not been as devastating. If you are interested in a story of hardship and happiness, of personal triumph against horrendous disadvantages, of the experience of being female, Chinese, disabled and blind and yet achieving your dreams in an adopted country—then read this book. The level of success that Shirley achieves is remarkable and inspiring— no less than her achievement in writing this book. Her work and courage alone get five stars in my book.

Shirley Cheng is a talented and bright-hearted young woman who is by no means finished achieving. I look forward to her next accomplishments!
—Linore R. Burkard, author

Shirley Cheng has an inspiring story to tell in *The Revelation of a Star's Endless Shine*. How can we not be in awe of her? She suffered through the pain and disability of severe juvenile rheumatoid arthritis and subsequent blindness. She suffered through a senseless custody fight at the hands of meddling social services personnel. She suffered through inconsistent medical care. She remained fearless and positive through it all, going on to maintain a 3.9 grade point average in high school; unable to complete all of

her high school courses, she subsequently passed her GED test with an exceptionally high score. Shirley and her tirelessly compassionate mother Juliet Cheng have been miracle workers, and one cannot help but think that has been their calling.
—Malcolm R. Campbell, Author of The Sun Singer
Campbell Editorial Services

The Revelation of a Star's Endless Shine truly lives up to its title.
—Rebecca Henderson
Allbooks Reviews

Why is it possible in America, the land of the free, that a parent cannot disagree with a doctor's recommendation for treatment? If they do, their child could be taken from them. Social Services can be called in. How could it also be possible for a hospital to take parents to court for intercepting unwanted treatment? Well, in this great nation supposedly run by the people for the people, parental rights aren't what they used to be. We all know people who neglect or abuse their children and intervention is necessary for them. This is not the same. Shirley Cheng's autobiography is about this injustice, about how she, a blind and physically disabled young woman with severe juvenile rheumatoid arthritis, and her mother were treated.

This extraordinary young lady begins her eye-opening autobiography with her birth, taking readers through her life to the age of twenty.

Living with a disease is bad enough. Shirley suffered much pain along with disabilities, difficulties and hardships. She shouldn't have had to justify and battle with doctors, hospitals, social-workers, teachers, aides, guidance counselors, and principals. This is what they dealt with year after year. The professionals that should have been helpful, compassionate, supportive, and understanding, were the very ones who hurt, separated, and lied about them.

Shirley's unique way of writing further provides readers with a window to her intelligence, insight, and nature. Her matter-of-fact, original style and ability to prove a point is powerful.

This book is for those who are suffering, or who have someone close to them who is, from a severe medical problem. It's for those who've battled not only to find a cure for a disease or at least a better situation, and have had to deal with insurance companies, doctors and hospitals, teachers, schools, and social services as well. It will open eyes of readers without these types of problems and of those with compassion and a sense of what is right.

Shirley Cheng offers a look into her world providing disturbing truths about America's medical and school systems. She reveals how some doctors lie on their patient's documents and when cannot offer a solution or diagnosis for a disease often label the victim as mentally ill or depressed. She tells of instances when in a hospital, a staff member turned on her room light in the middle of the night waking her to clean the room, and of when they wouldn't help her sit to relieve her bladder. This book tells of numerous astonishing situations that Shirley and her mother endured. They shouldn't have had to deal with this in America. Unfortunately this great nation has its problems. The state of our medical, insurance, and parental rights needs a severe overhaul. Shirley's Mom, Juliet Cheng, says it best through first-hand experience: "No doctor in China would ever take away a mother's custody when she simply disagreed with medically recommended treatment." Also, "In China, no such things could ever happen. No one would even think of doing it." And about schools: "America's schools feel odd when seeing parents in school." She could not comprehend it. "In China, parents could freely go to the school while classes were in session." Juliet felt that America simply had too many rules and regulations with no exceptions for unique circumstances.

I recommend this book to everyone. America will be

better when it gives power back to parents. Granted, there are times when abusive parents need interception, yet the average parent wants what is paramount for their child and loves them.

A disturbing, and enlightening read. Authentic, honest, and profound. Will change reader's outlook.
—Christina Francine, CFrancine@mail2world.com
Reviewer's BookWatch, Midwest Book Review

This book will capture the heart of the reader and move you to tears as you travel down life's road with Shirley Cheng, a young author with a passion for life. Truly a star with endless shine. Well done, Shirley.
—Wanda Maynard
Sime~Gen - Reviews

Reading of Shirley's physical pain, her increasingly weakening body, the slipshod way she was handled by school aids who were supposed to be helping her, the legal wranglings over her care, would make anyone scream in frustration. Even worse was the way Shirley was treated by an endless list of so-called professionals. Hardly anyone listened to Shirley or her mother regarding her pain, her intelligence or her thirst for education. The indictment of so many people who should have been on Shirley's side, is a sad commentary on our medical, social service and educational systems. In addition, Shirley's father evidently was a manipulator and a cruel man who refused to use his money for the benefit of his daughter. The hardships she and her mother faced feel unendurable. Yet they were endured. And despite poor medical care, despite teachers who seemed uninterested in helping this talented student, despite unfeeling "friends," in two countries, they endured.

Unlike Shirley, few of us seem to have the innate ability to face every day and everyone with a smile regardless of our own painful circumstances. Yet we can read her story with an open heart and choose to integrate her

positive outlook and determination into our own lives in a way that will serve us and those around us. After all, this is the reason Shirley wrote the book. She hoped that her story would inspire others to treat everyone with respect, to stand up for what we believe in and to reach out to those less fortunate.
—*Lynn Colwell, Life and Personal Coach*

This is the story of a mother's dedication and commitment to her child, and it is most of all the story of a strong, brave and determined young woman to live her life to the fullest, even with all its limitations. Cheng dreams big dreams and has the tenacity to make them come true.

This heartwarming story is one you'll want to read.
—*Andrea Sisco*
Armchair Interviews

I read this book in absolute amazement… Shirley, has written her auto-biography in a brilliant way… It's a story of amazing courage and human strengths, for someone to achieve so much, after having being deprived of so much is an awe-inspiring feat.
—*Angela Hooper, Spain, English Teacher and Editor*

The book is written in a lucid, vivid and flowing style and is easy to read. It may take the reader a few days to read through because of the number of pages. But it is certainly not boring and the author holds the reader's attention all through.

The narration is moving at many places and at the same time is also inspiring because of the perseverance of Juliet, Shirley's mother and Shirley herself.
—*Swamy Swarna, India*
Book Pleasures

About the Author

Shirley Cheng, born in 1983, a blind and physically disabled award-winning author, motivational speaker, self-empowerment expert, poet, author of seven books and contributor of twelve, is a miracle survivor with tremendous talents, an exceptional, tenacious spirit, and a colorful personality. She was diagnosed with severe juvenile rheumatoid arthritis at only eleven months old. She spent her early years in constant pain, confined to a wheelchair, and was hospitalized for many years while living between China and America until 1994. Unable to receive any form of education until her health was stabilized, Shirley started attending school at age eleven in a special education class in elementary school. Back then, she knew very little English, and her knowledge on other subjects was non-existent. Miraculously, she mastered grade level in all areas after approximately 180 days of attendance, and she immediately entered a regular sixth grade class in middle school.

Shirley has a voracious appetite for books, reading an average of six hundred pages (three books) daily, and has read over a total of two thousand books. Since sixth grade, she has received 100 on every NYS essay test, and stayed at the top of the class ever since. She was awarded for achieving the highest grade of 97 in Earth science in her eighth grade class. She was the Student of the Year and the Student of the Month, as well as a three-time winner of the National Reflections Program in visual arts. She has a passion for writing both prose and poetry. One of her short stories, *Mary Miller, the Elusive Lady*, received Honorable Mention and was published by the *Poughkeepsie Journal* in 1997, and her poem, *The Colors of the Rainbow*, earned merit status and was published in *Celebrate! New York Young Poets Speak Out* in 1999.

Shirley was a contributor to her high school

newspaper, providing artwork in tenth grade. She received a standing ovation when she delivered a speech as a candidate for student body vice president in ninth grade.

When her eyesight began to deteriorate at the beginning of tenth grade, she had to use two magnifying glasses, holding one on top of the other, on enlarged print to do her work throughout the year, including the artwork she provided for the school newspaper. In classes, she learned only by listening to her teachers, even with chemistry and math, as she was unable to see the blackboard; still she maintained excellent grades.

Unfortunately, Shirley completely lost her vision in April of tenth grade. She then received home-tutoring, and successfully completed all her schoolwork by using cassette tapes and tape recorders. She wrote and balanced long chemistry formulas and equations without vision or Braille (she cannot use Braille because of her severe arthritis). Her high school overall average was 97 (a 3.9 GPA without any advanced placement classes). But Shirley could not accumulate enough credits to receive a high school diploma from her school due to her vision loss. In 2002, she received her high school equivalency diploma. She took the entire GED test, including mathematical calculations, graphs, and an essay, in her head, and received a special recognition award for scoring an exceptionally high 3280. She was a student speaker at the GED graduation ceremony, and received a standing ovation for her speech.

Shirley became an author at age twenty, completing three books within one year. She wrote her books using a screen reader on her computer, typing with her two index fingers at the speed of about sixty words per minute. She successfully completed every self-publishing task, including formatting her manuscripts, on her own.

Shirley wrote her autobiography when she was twenty, and it was first published with the subtitle *A Young Woman's Autobiography of a 20-Year Tale of Trials & Tribulations*, with the ISBN 9781411618602. She inserted, resized, and cropped all the photographs and drawings in this new edition of her autobiography while having her mother Juliet Cheng as her eyes.

In January 2006, Shirley tied for first place in Be the Star You Are! Second Annual Essay Contest founded by New York Times bestselling author, TV/radio personality Cynthia Brian, garnering her a third appearance on Cynthia's live radio show. Shirley's winning entry, titled *The Jewel from Heavenly Father*, is dedicated to her beloved mother. In the following January, Shirley won Honorable Mention in the same contest for her essay, *I Hold the Power*, her personal story of overcoming blindness at the age of seventeen. In January 2008, Shirley was yet again one of the winners in the contest, earning Honorable Mention for her essay, *My Mother: A Fighter, a Victor, a Lover*, which applauds her stellar mother for being a courageous and loving fighter to protect her life at all costs.

Shirley has an immense passion for life and is full of life and vigor. Despite her severe disabilities, Shirley has striven to overcome overwhelming obstacles and she is living the life she loves, while she empowers, inspires, and motivates others to do the same.

Shirley was brought up in a very simple, single-parent, Chinese-speaking family with no influence on education. She pursues her education on her own. She has extraordinary goals with the aspiration of attending college at Harvard University, where she plans to earn doctorates in microbiology, zoology, astronomy, physiology, and pathology, after a successful eye surgery.

Shirley is a true magical gift, a star with endless shine.

Shirley As an Advocate

Shirley is an advocate of parental rights in children's medical care, and aide/caregiver monitoring and screening for students with special needs and disabled people.

As a parental rights advocate, she wants to help today's loving parents protect and keep custody of their children. "When doctors ask yes or no, parents should have the right to say no," says Shirley, a survivor of two custody battles her mother Juliet Cheng had with doctors.

Shirley's last case made international headlines in 1990; Juliet appeared on *CBS This Morning* with Paula Zahn as she fought to save Shirley's life and prevent her from receiving the harmful treatment recommended by her doctor in Connecticut.

To support Shirley in her good cause, please sign her *Parental Rights in Children's Medical Care: Give Parents the Right to Say No* petition at:

http://www.petitiononline.com/parentr7/petition.html

Shirley promotes aide advocacy for the disabled because she was mistreated and abused by one-on-one aides when she attended school. "The trouble with uncaring aides actually lies with the authorities," she says. "If they had listened to my complaints and kept a close watch on the aides, I wouldn't have gone through all the suffering."

Other Books by Shirley

Shirley is also the author of:
• *Do You Love Jehovah? God Almighty's Infinite Love & Wisdom to Propel You to Greatness*
ISBN: 978-0-5870-0079-4
• *Embrace Ultra-Ability! Wisdom, Insight & Motivation from the Blind Who Sees Far and Wide*
ISBN: 978-0-6151-5522-7
• *Dance with Your Heart: Tales and Poems That the Heart Tells*
This book is available in Vietnam, published by the Women Publishing House in 2008 and translated into Vietnamese by Nguyen Bich Lan.
ISBN: 978-1-4116-1858-9
• *Waking Spirit: Prose & Poems the Spirit Sings*
(foreword by New York Times best seller Cynthia Brian)
ISBN: 978-0-6151-3680-6 (trade paperback)
978-0-6151-3893-0 (hardback)
• *Parental Rights in Children's Medical Care: Where Is Our Freedom to Say No? A Look at the Injustice of the American Medical System*
ISBN: 978-0-6151-4994-3
• The Adventures of a Blind and Disabled Award-Winning Author: Inspiration & Motivation to Empower You to Go for Your Own Gold Medals
ISBN: 978-0-6151-7515-7

With highly acclaimed experts, like Dr. Wayne Dyer, Tony Robbins, and Brian Tracy, Shirley co-authored *Wake Up...Live the Life You Love: Finding Life's Passion* (ISBN: 978-1-9330-6305-8) in the bestselling *Wake Up...Live the Life You Love series*; she is also the co-author of *101 Great Ways to Improve Your Life, Volume 2* (ISBN: 978-0-9745-6727-3), along with leading experts, including Jack Canfield, John Gray, Richard Carlson, Alan Cohen, Bob Proctor, et al.

Book Awards

Waking Spirit: Prose & Poems the Spirit Sings is the recipient of:

• The Avatar Award for Spiritual Excellence in Literature (2008)
• Best book in three categories of Reader Views 2007 Annual Literary Awards: First Place in Poetry Nonfiction, and Second Place in both New Age Nonfiction and Spirituality/Inspiration
• Finalist in the national Indie Excellence 2007 Book Awards
• Honorable Mention in the 2007 New York Book Festival Competition in Poetry
• Honorable Mention in the 2007 DIY Book Festival in Poetry

Embrace Ultra-Ability! Wisdom, Insight & Motivation from the Blind Who Sees Far and Wide is a finalist in the 2008 Next Generation Indie Book Awards in the Motivational category.

Shirley on the WWW

Visit Shirley on the Web at http://www.shirleycheng.com to learn more about her, her books, listen to some of her radio show interviews, e-mail her, and subscribe to her monthly newsletter, *Inspiration from a Blind*, to receive words of inspiration, special news and events information, and exclusive offers for members. Her newsletter issues are archived on her blog, http://blog.shirleycheng.com to which people can subscribe via e-mail or RSS.

Personalized autographed copies of all of Shirley's books are available from her website.

Her books are also available through Ingram, from Amazon.com (and their international sites) and BN.com, and also available through brick-and-mortar Waldenbooks and Borders stores.

Shirley is available for interviews, speaking engagements, book signings, and inspirational events.

Photo Album

Shirley Cheng, seven, delighted to be greeted by penguins at Newington Children's Hospital on Halloween of 1990.

Dr. C.Y. Ling in 1965.

Dr. C.Y. Ling and Kwi Show Ling in 1955.

Kwi Show Ling celebrating her eightieth birthday.

Yi Ling (Juliet Cheng) at age sixteen.

Yi Ling at age twenty-eight in both photographs right before coming to America.

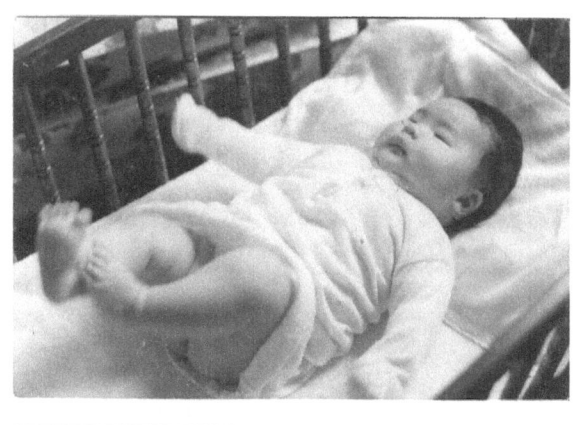

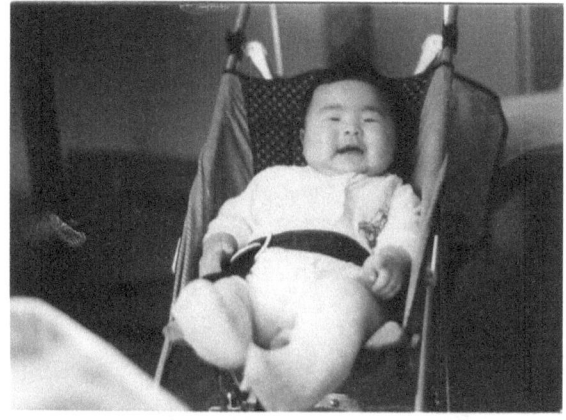

Shirley Cheng was a chubby three-month-old in these pictures.

Juliet And Shirley in Hong Kong during Shirley's first trip to China to seek treatment.

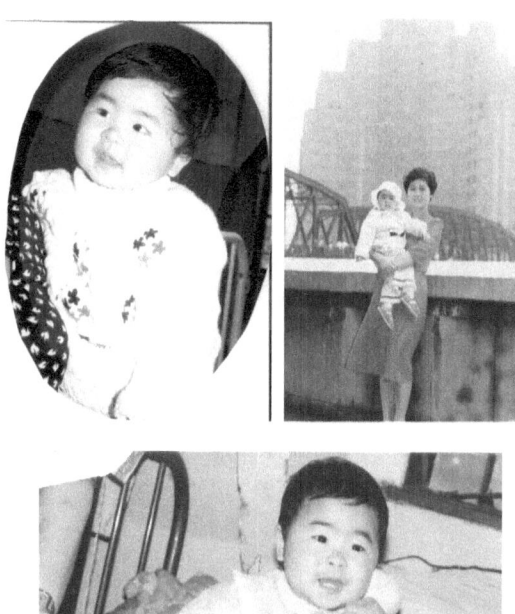
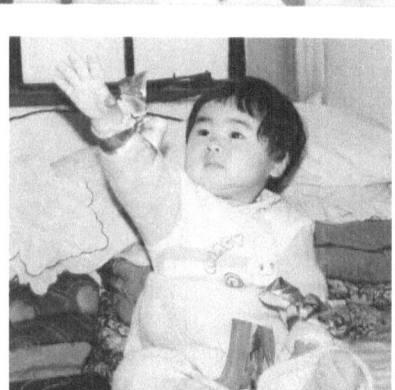

The Happy Baby when she was thirteen months old, seeking treatment in Shanghai, China.

Shirley, two, in North Carolina in these photographs.

Shirley admiring a flower sitting on the front step of her home in North Carolina.

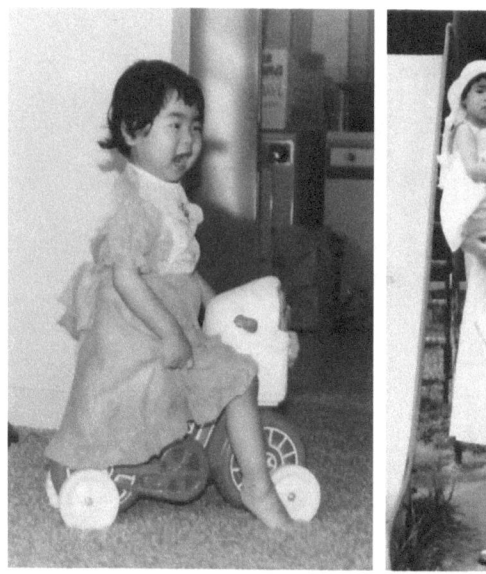 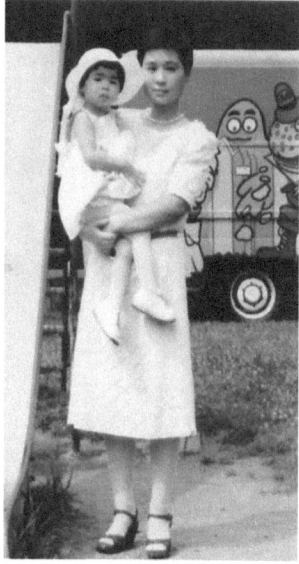

Shirley and Juliet in North Carolina.

More photographs of mother and daughter in North Carolina.
Top left: On the road to the radon mine in Montana.

Left: Shirley, three, managed to stand in Tang Gang Zi. Right: Shirley's first official day of standing while receiving effective shots when she was four in Duen Hua. Bottom left: Grumpy Shirley awakened to take photos.

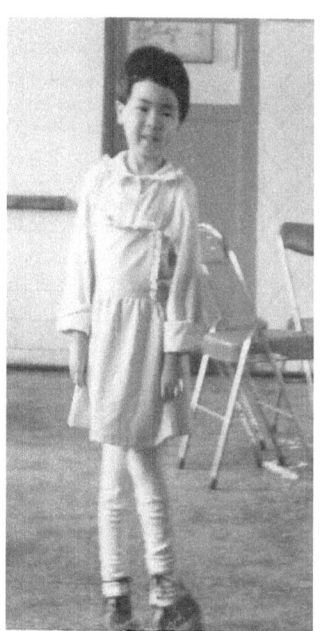
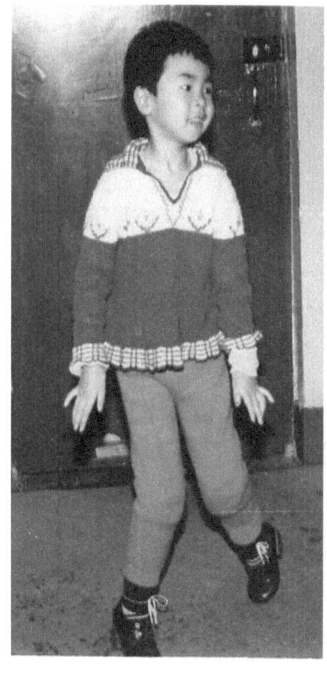
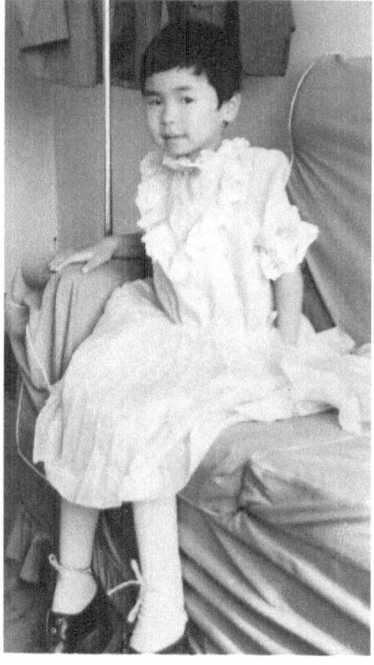

Shirley at age five in China.

Photographs of the smiling Juliet in China.

Juliet And Shirley in Bei Hai Park in Beijing.

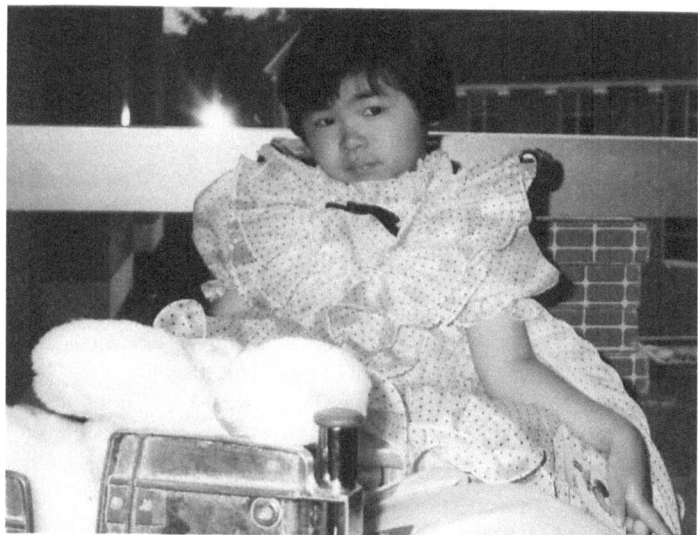

Shirley was seven in both photos; the bottom photo was taken on her first few days in Newington Children's Hospital in May 1990.

Juliet and Shirley on the front page of the September 29, 1990 issue of the *New York Times* regarding Juliet's custody case against the Connecticut doctor over treatment dispute.
Photograph by Joyce Dopkeen, the New York Times

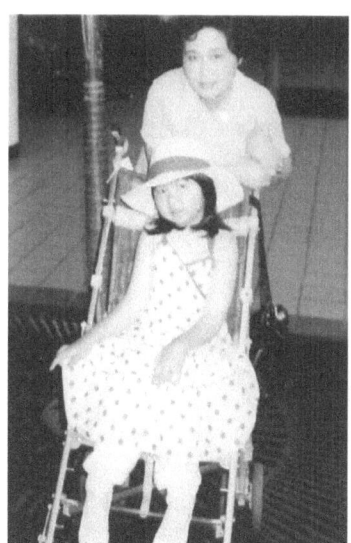

Shirley here was eight. Bottom right: Juliet from prior two years.

Top: Shirley in Blythedale Children's Hospital. Bottom: Juliet and Shirley during the award ceremony for Shirley's winning art entry in sixth grade. *Photograph by Arlene Surprenant, Southern Dutchess News*

Top right: Last day of seventh grade. Bottom left: Dance at eighth grade
bottom right: Shirley's last year as a teenager.

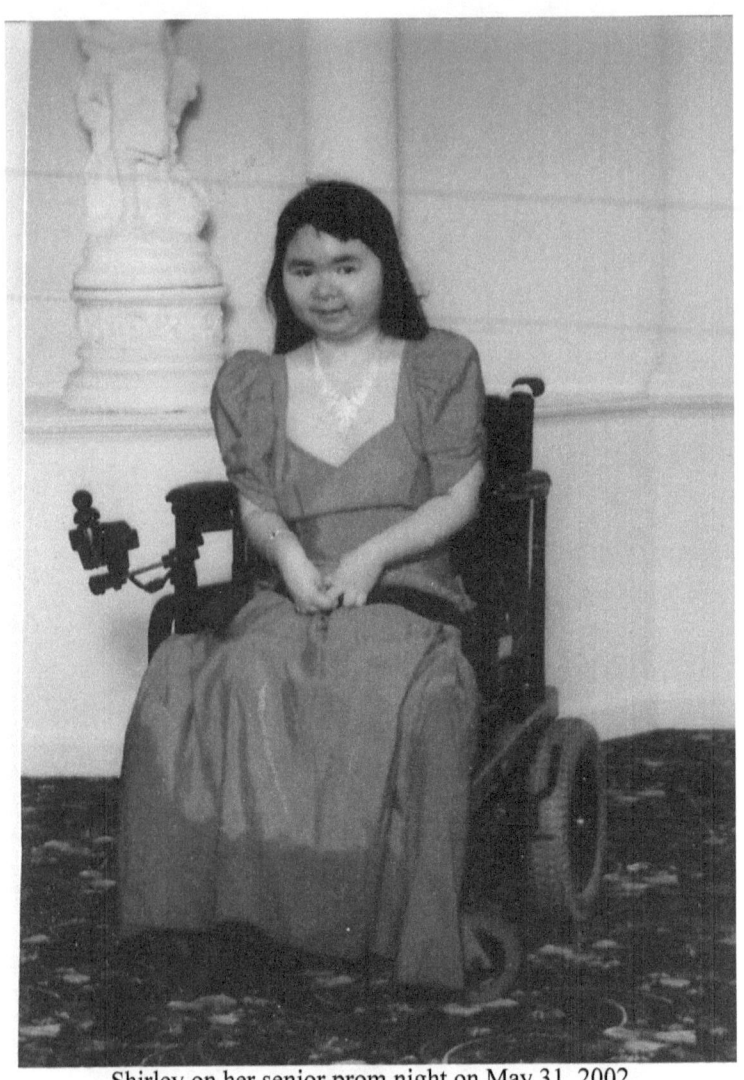
Shirley on her senior prom night on May 31, 2002.

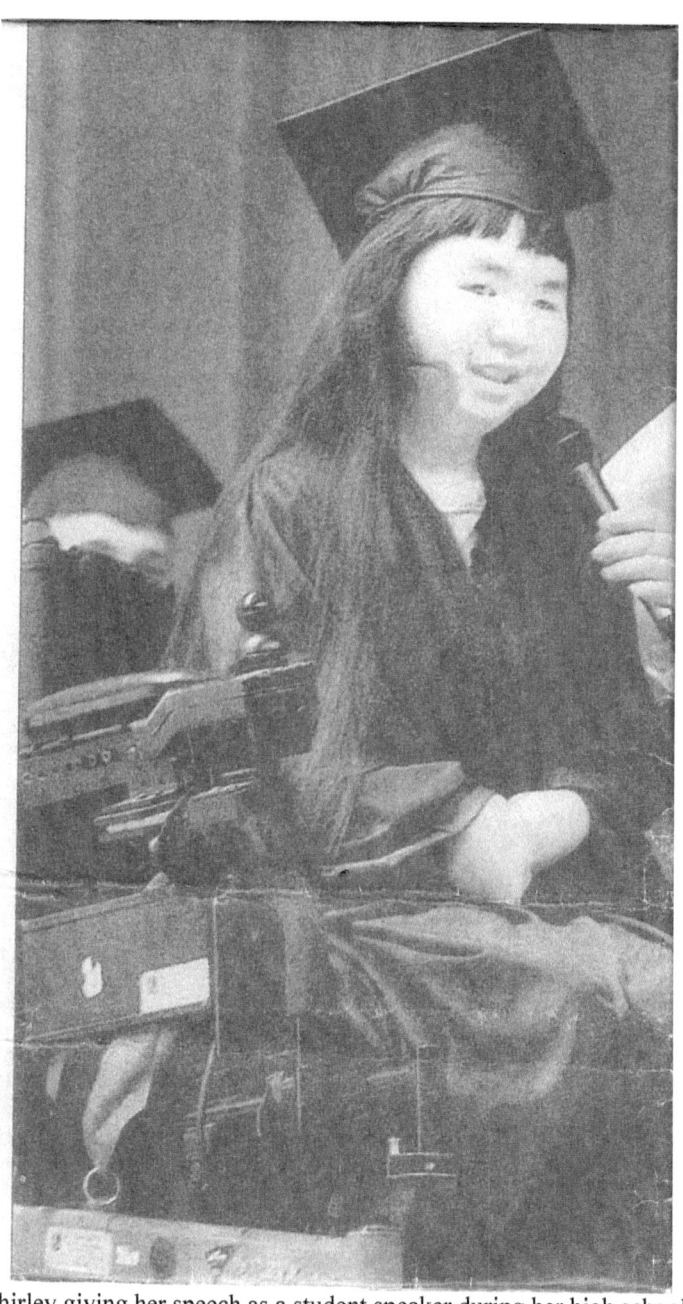

Shirley giving her speech as a student speaker during her high school equivalency diploma graduation ceremony on June 12, 2003.
Photograph by Darryl Bautista, Poughkeepsie Journal

Childhood Drawings
1991 to 1999

Unfortunately, most of Shirley Cheng's drawings from her earlier years are lost, including two sketchbooks filled with cat drawings, with each page telling a different story, when she was eight, as the flood in Kwi Show's basement destroyed them. Many of the drawings found here are simply doodles, and scans of the photographs Juliet took of her drawings in order to preserve them; many of the pictures have faded.

Drawn on Shirley's computer at age fourteen by carefully maneuvering the mouse like a pen.

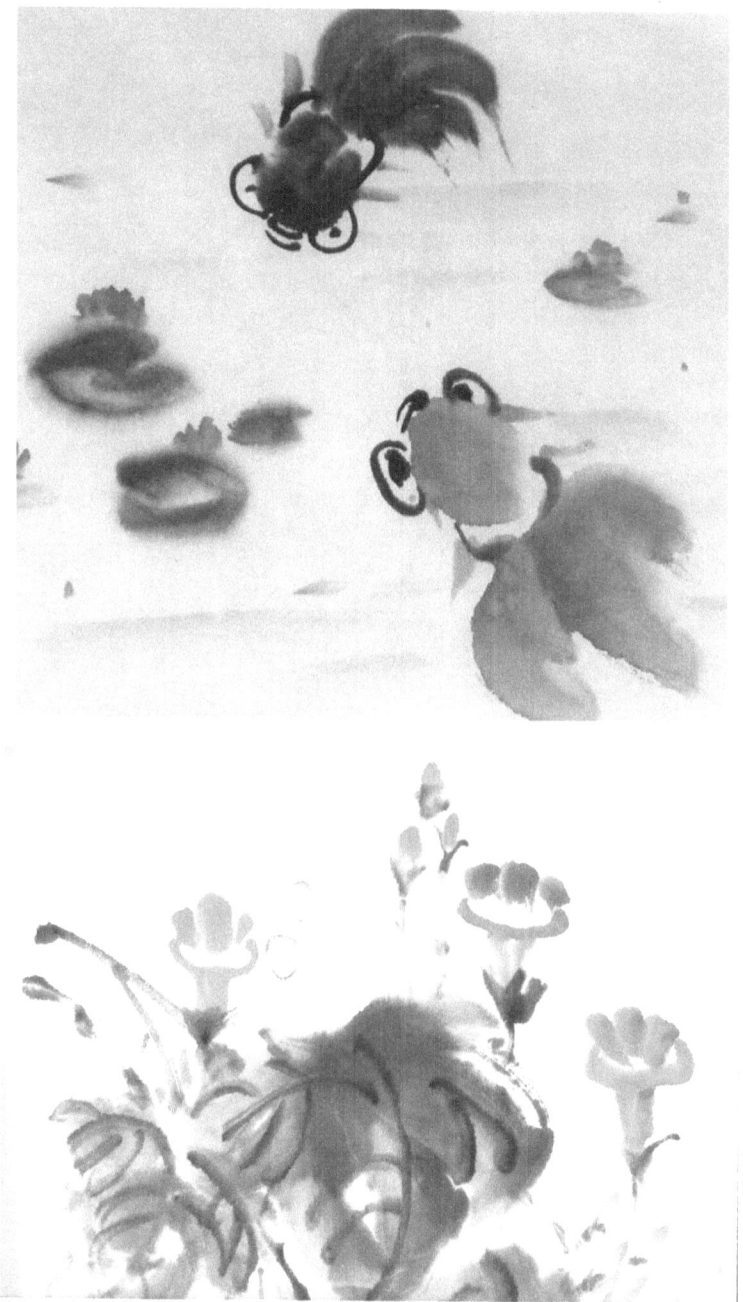
This and the following few pages show the watercolors Shirley learned in China at age eleven.

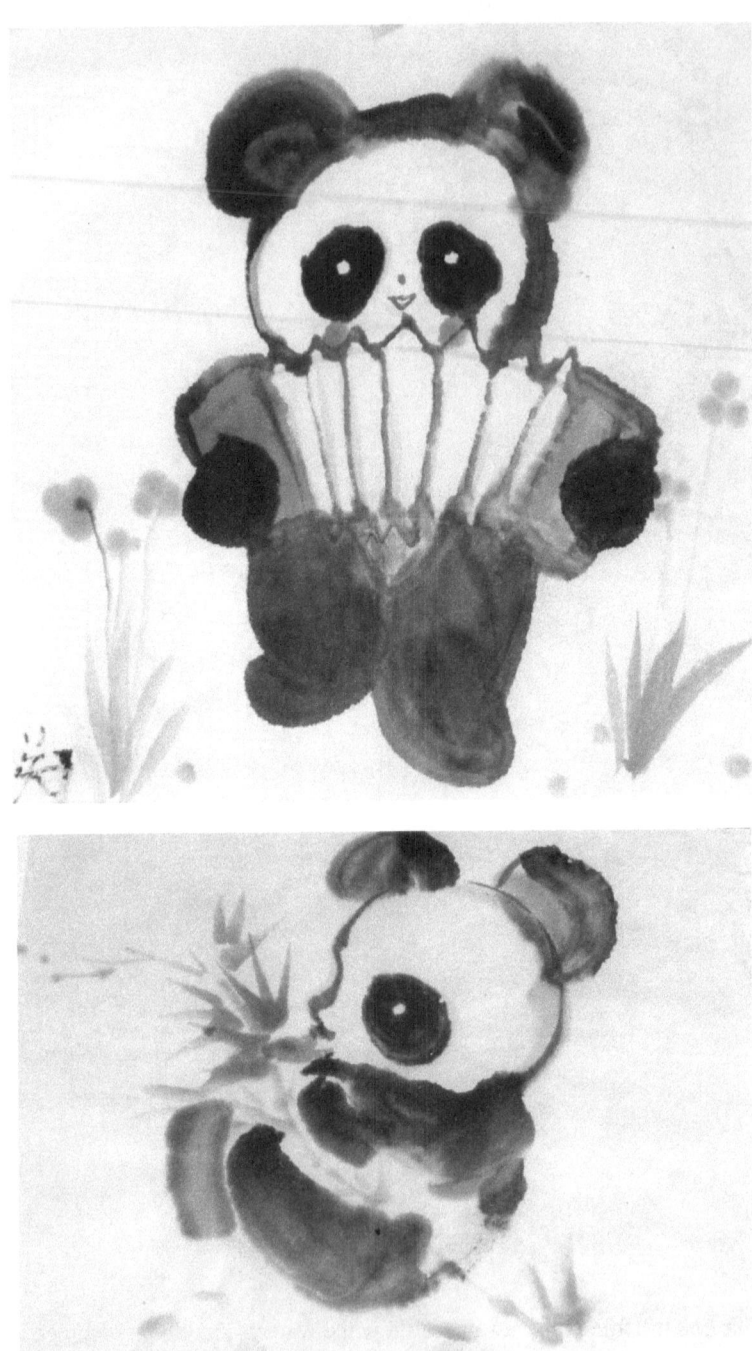

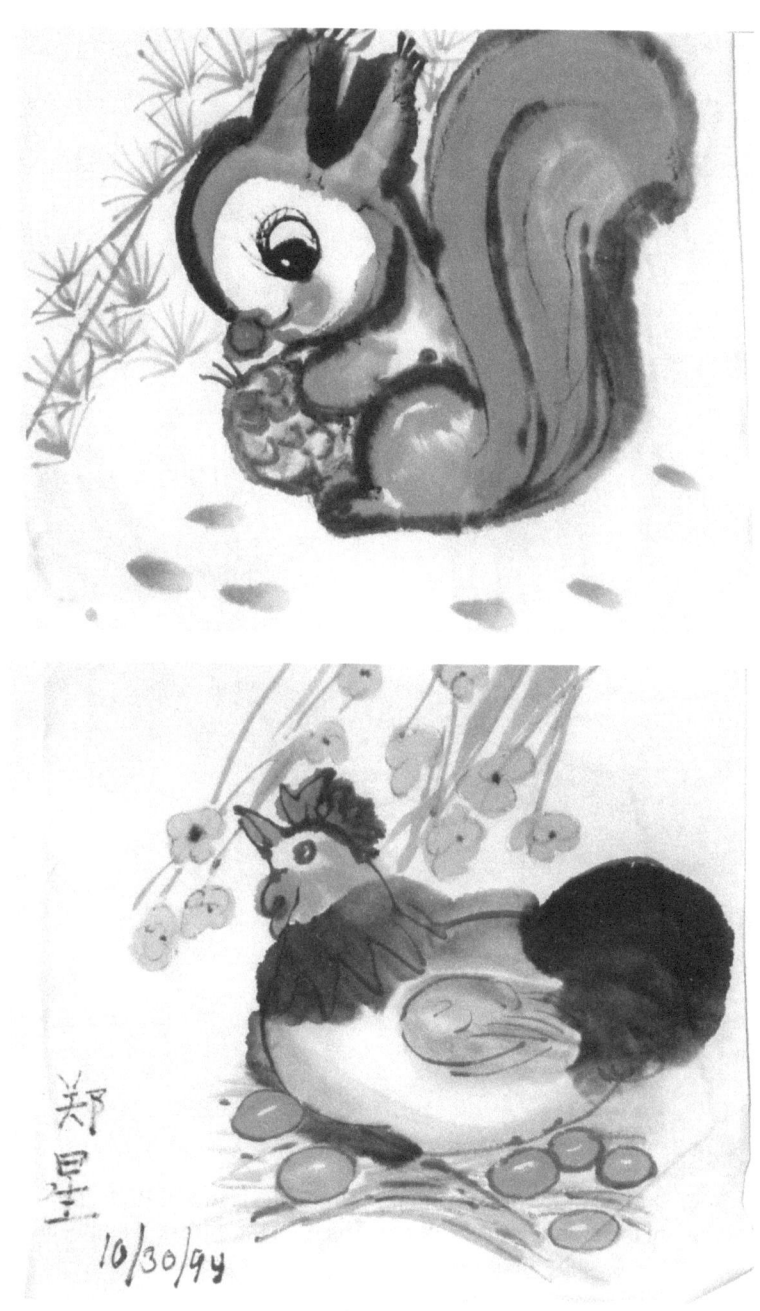

Top: Shirley's first-place winning entry in the National Reflections Program in seventh grade. Bottom: Shirley's third-place winning art entry in the same program in sixth grade.

This page and the following few pages show the pictures Shirley drew on her new computer at age fourteen with the paint program. She drew the pictures from scratch by carefully controlling the mouse like a pen. Each drawing took about half an hour to complete.

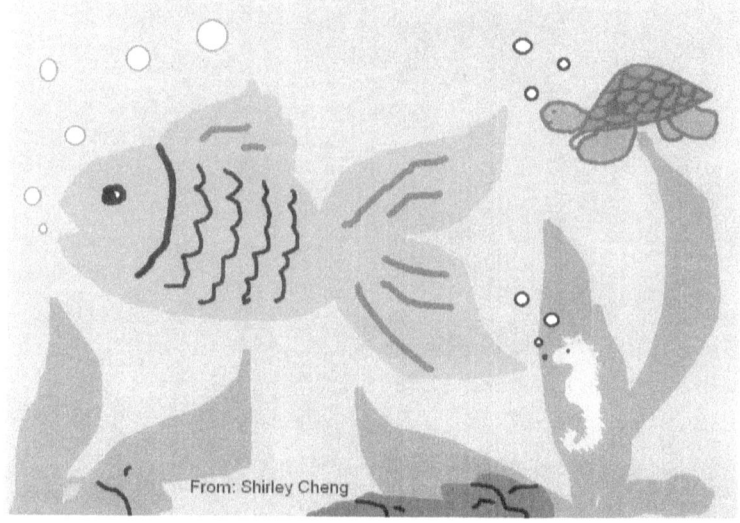

Art by Shirley Cheng

Art by Shirley Cheng

Shirley drew this at age sixteen with airbrush just when her eyesight was deteriorating.

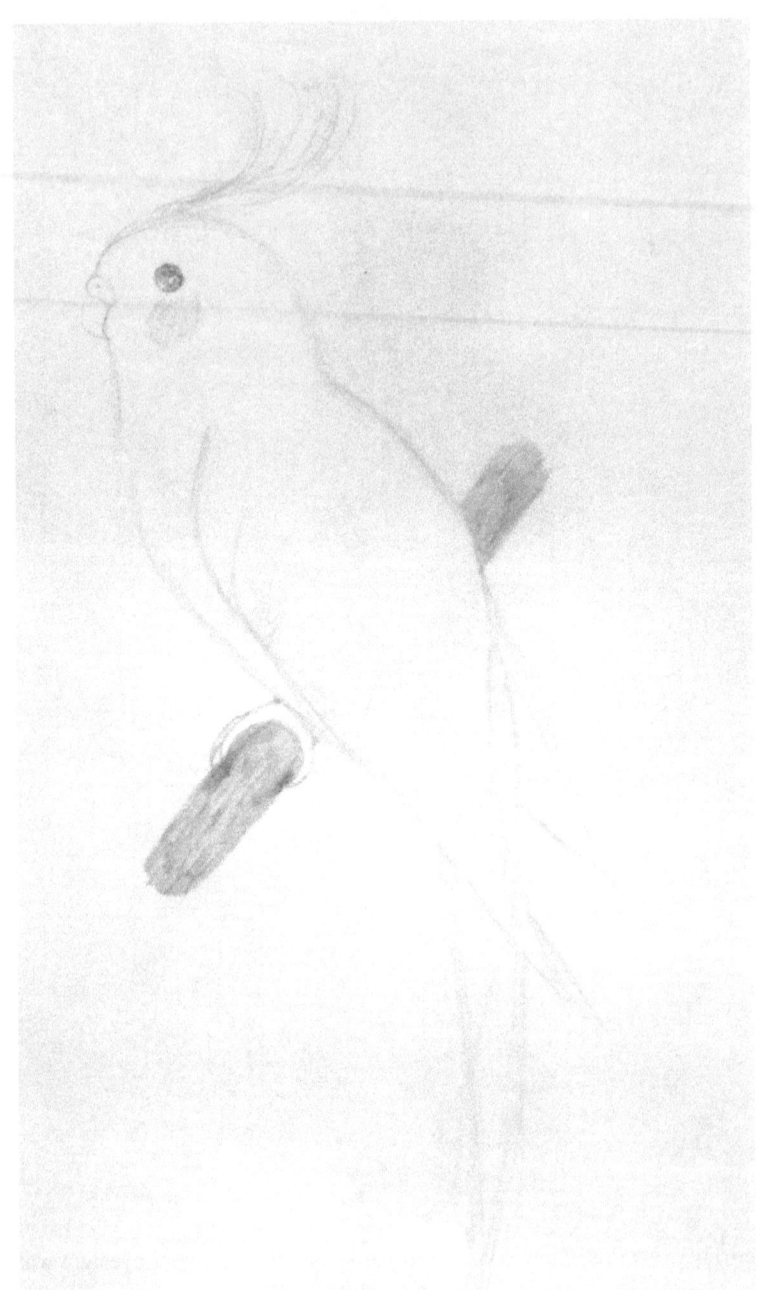

Cockatiels were one of Shirley's favorite animals to draw. This one was drawn at around twelve.

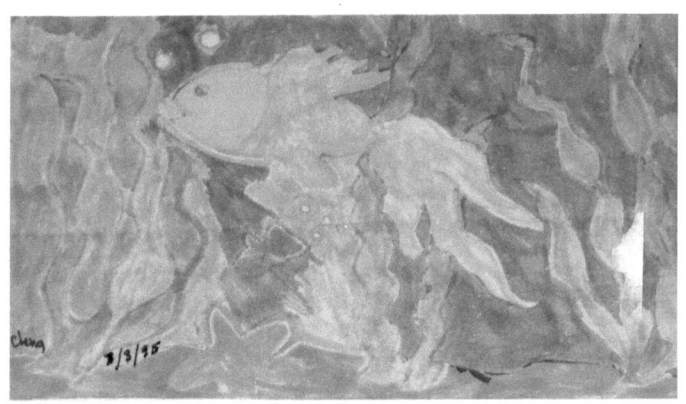

One of the posters Shirley created for her campaign when she ran for student body vice president in ninth grade.